Mastering Writing Essentials

Andrew Macdonald ❧ Gina Macdonald

PRENTICE HALL REGENTS

A VIACOM COMPANY

UPPER SADDLE RIVER, NJ 07458

Vice President/Editorial Director: *Arley Grey*
Editorial Production/Design Manager: *Dominick Mosco*
Production Supervision/Page Composition: *Steve Jorgensen*
    and Noël Vreeland Carter
Art Director: *Merle Krumper*
Electronic Art Production Specialist: *Marita Froimson*
Cover Design: *Bruce Kensaleer*
Interior Design: *Steve Jorgensen*
Manufacturing Manager: *Ray Keating*

Original Art: *Jeanie Duvall, University of Texas at Austin*

© 1996 by Prentice Hall Regents
Prentice-Hall, Inc.
A Simon and Schuster Company
Upper Saddle River, New Jersey 07458

PRENTICE HALL REGENTS
A VIACOM COMPANY

Photo Credits: Photos of Oanh Nguyen, Kunthea Chau Karr, Ellen M. Kocher Plaisance, Kayo Morisaki, Marom
Chau and Sarith and Tan Vichel with their permission; page 297, The United Nations; all others courtesy of the
authors.

Permissions appear on pages xv and xvi which constitute a continuation of the Copyright page.

10   9   8   7   6   5   4   3   2   1

ISBN 0-205-15010-1

Prentice-Hall International (UK) Limited, *London*
Prentice-Hall of Australia Pty. Limited, *Sydney*
Prentice-Hall Canada Inc., *Toronto*
Prentice-Hall Hispanoamericana, S. A., *Mexico*
Prentice-Hall of India Private Limited, *New Delhi*
Prentice-Hall of Japan, Inc., *Tokyo*
Simon & Schuster Asia Pte. Ltd., *Singapore*
Editora Prentice-Hall do Brasil, Ltda., *Rio de Janeiro*

CONTENTS

UNIT ONE: WRITING BASICS

Unit Two: BASIC WRITING PATTERNS AT WORK

Unit Three: WRITING FOR COLLEGE PURPOSES

TO THE TEACHER

Every act of teaching suggests a model of learning. Even the most casual pedagogic impulse—"Here, let me explain this."—presupposes in its acting out how people learn: show, tell, recite back to me. Similarly, no textbook is innocently neutral in its pedagogy, and it behooves us to explain just where we stand and how we think advanced international students learn to read and write in their second language.

Our approach is at once very ancient and yet fairly modern. Just as composition studies rediscovered the rhetorical tradition a generation or two ago, so we believe there is a need to rethink some ancient models of language learning, specifically the role of imitation. Our experience with students who learned their English in a variety of programs abroad suggests that imitation is alive and well as a teaching approach, and that it sometimes provides answers to student questions far more efficiently than more modern methods. However, as children of the process writing movement, we also believe in brainstorming, free-writing, narrowing the topic, revising, and final editing, all in a struggle to create a not-yet-realized final product. Yet a concern persists in the midst of a process writing environment: Do these young writers working step-by-step really understand my mental model of the comparison-contrast essay, my model formed of countless uncritical exposures to countless news features, academic essays, and other cultural exemplars? Or am I asking a blind man to build me an elephant in several easy steps? As recent studies in contrastive rhetoric make clear, the patterns that we as English speakers consider universal in successful writing may well seem alien to writers of other tongues.

We thus try to have it both ways. We begin with model essays, some professional, some student productions, to define rigorously the paradigms dominant in our linguistic culture. But we then try to avoid the shattering oversimplification that leaves students marooned: Just do it! The issue is how to do it, of course, no small question for someone lacking the smaller paradigm of grammatical pattern and the larger ones of the rhetorical movement of ideas.

So our model of learning is something like the following:

Read—understand: absorb the big picture
Practice the nuts and bolts:
    Absorb the details
Practice shaping the larger elements:
    Absorb the pattern
Try it yourself.

We hope this approach helps!

TO THE STUDENT

This book assumes that learning to think in new patterns and learning to write in a new language are inextricably linked. Therefore, it will focus in particular on new patterns of thought and logic, of organization and emphasis. A student who hopes to learn English well enough for success in an English-speaking education system or for success in dealing effectively with native English speakers in a professional capacity must acquire the varied patterns of organization and thought that are the cornerstone of educated writing in English. Using a new language well means learning to think, speak, and write in that language, to change patterns of thought and patterns of writing to fit the language being acquired, and to adapt to a culture, a way of life, a set of values, and a world view which supplement and enlarge a first language.

1. <u>How and what you think about are directly related to the language you use. Learning English, then, means learning to think in a new way.</u>

Language is an outgrowth, a product, of the way we think; study of a language reveals the values and way of life of the culture in which it is used. Language learning is not a one-to-one translation process; it involves learning a new culture, a new history, a new set of values: a new way of perceiving the world. A business letter to be sent to Japan, Turkey, Colombia, Indonesia, Russia, and the United States may need to communicate the same information, but it cannot be effective in exactly the same way because of very different ideas about how business is conducted and what is polite and impolite in language. The courtesy phrases that a Colombian would expect would be different from the courtesy phrases expected by a Turk, a Japanese, or an Indonesian, and all of these might be dismissed as eccentric and a waste of time by an American and a Russian. The way in which the problem is approached, the amount of information and the way in which it is imparted, the format of the presentation, and the introductory and closing remarks would need to be varied to fit the politeness and

thought patterns of each culture addressed. In other words, the idea that you can translate word for word from one language to another and make sense just isn't true.

2. <u>Writing is a vital part of any education, because writing is basic to thinking and education is all about thinking.</u>

Hand-in-hand with learning to think in a language is learning to write in that language, because writing forces you to explore thinking patterns. Someone once said that you don't really have an idea clearly formulated until you write it out, for the process of writing forces you to give order to your idea, to explore its relationship to other ideas, and to discover its significance. The way in which you carry out an argument or try to persuade, convey information, evaluate a product, or compare items follows different patterns in different cultures. Therefore, learning to do these things in English is an important element of communication. In fact, in American colleges, writing is a standard way of demonstrating knowledge and learning no matter the field, so that you can expect to write at length in history classes, science classes, sociology classes, and even engineering and art classes.

Writing in college can be confusing and difficult since writing expectations differ from department to department and from professor to professor. What works well in one situation sometimes fails in another. Consequently, the student must learn to adjust to varied standards and to varied expectations. Some courses involve argumentative or persuasive writing (a common freshman English approach). Others require a lengthy and formal research paper with a survey of authorities in a narrow area and a personal organization and presentation of specialized materials. Some professors want evidence of a "processed" paper, one developed slowly over a period of time, with a number of revisions. Others prefer an in-class essay in which the student is expected to write—rapidly and efficiently—an organized answer to questions about technical materials studied; the most important quality of such an essay is that it communicate a great deal of content information. Still others want evidence of student thought, the application of ideas from the course to specific cases. In other words, the type of writing expected from class to class depends very much on the type of thinking encouraged in the class. Success depends on flexibility!

3. Writing well in English carries over into the professions.

International business dealings, joint ventures, and scientific exchanges all require writing, so much so, in fact, that, when asked by the American Society for Engineering Education, "How important is the writing that you do in your present position?", forty-five percent of a group of distinguished engineers responded that it was "critically important" and fifty-one percent called it "very important." Thirty percent of a group of experienced business people surveyed in the same way by the American Business Communications Association called writing "critically important" and forty-four percent called it "very important."

If engineers and business people, whom we normally do not think of as writing very much, consider writing so important, how much more important must writing be in other fields? For many professionals, writing for publication is a means of moving up in their careers. For others it is a necessary part of day-to-day business. Such writing includes correspondence, memoranda, reports, evaluations, recommendations, projections, and a variety of other writing tasks. Some businesspeople have described the amount of writing they do yearly as the equivalent of two volumes of the New York telephone directory! Such professional writing is highly goal-directed and usually has a clear-cut audience in mind. Therefore, the concepts and approaches of this text will be very helpful in preparing a person to write, not just for the classroom, but professionally.

4. Reading and studying good models are excellent ways to improve writing skills.

Since the beginnings of Western culture, reading has been considered an important way to begin learning how to write well and, in the past, schools taught writing by having students imitate classical writers: their style, their patterns of argument, even their particular way of phrasing ideas. If you enjoy what a writer has to say and how he says it, you can learn much from that writer about how best to say what you want to say. Reading gives you models of tone and voice, word choice and shades of meaning, sentence structure and emphasis, organizational patterns and developmental details. In other words, in addition to building vocabulary, reading helps you learn the important elements of good writing. This is why most chapters in this text will include "Passages for Discussion and Analysis."

A Brief Note About Word Processing

Typed work will be a requirement in many college classes, and the serious student should make every attempt to avoid handwritten papers if possible. It is not simply that typed script looks better and is more professional, that is, more in accord with modern business practice around the world; typing actually improves compositions by allowing the writer to "see" the work better, as distinct paragraphs, sentences, and words without the distractions of eccentric handwriting. Seeing our work in a standard print-face gives it an objectivity that it lacks in the familiar look of our own handwriting, so we gain distance and the ability to evaluate. Spelling checkers are invaluable aids, not only to improving a particular paper, but also to improving spelling skills in general. Grammar checkers work far less well, but some writers find them useful for checking sexist language and other word problems. Some word processing programs have a built in thesaurus (a dictionary of synonyms), which, used with caution, can help the writer recall a useful word. Only the most unambitious writer turns his back on these modern aids to composition.

As the above discussion suggests, "typing" really means "word processing," for even though the line between modern typewriters and computers is blurring, most professional writers recommend the versatility and powerful capabilities of a personal computer. Such a writing tool need not be state of the art and expensive, as long as it offers some choices of format and graphics, and, as noted above, a spelling checker and perhaps a thesaurus. Most colleges and universities provide computer labs for student use.

What about the non-typist, the person who has never had the chance to master a keyboard? Here, the thoughtful student will invest a small amount of time now to gain large advantages later. One need not become a touch typist, a professional who does not need to look at the keys. Even "hunt and peck" two-finger typists, with practice, can type as fast as (or even faster than) they can write by hand. The results speak for themselves, and especially when the time comes for revision: revision on a word processor may take minutes, as opposed to the hours invested in rewriting a whole paper from the beginning. It is difficult for writers accustomed to old-style typewriters to contain their enthusiasm for revising on a computer, for this essential stage in the writing process becomes an intellectual task instead of the manual one of recopying perfectly adequate sentences and paragraphs (and adding new mistakes in the process!). Computers will not magically transform one's writing, of course, but as tools they do allow multiple revision in a very short time with the writer's entire focus on problem-solving. The sense of improvement achieved by such revision gives many writers their greatest pleasure, and is certainly worth the labor invested in learning a computer program.

ACKNOWLEDGMENTS

A large book reflects far more than the efforts of its two authors, and this is a very large book.

Our first thanks goes to this text's initial editor, Joseph Opiela of Allyn and Bacon, whose instinct for what constitutes a textbook, good common sense, and careful instruction and editing helped transform teaching materials into publishable text. We truly appreciate his trust in us and the lessons he taught us.

We also owe an enormous debt of gratitude to Arley Gray of Prentice Hall Regents, whose enthusiasm for and faith in this project allowed its completion. Arley stood firmly by two relative strangers as the pages multiplied. Thanks to his support, this text is more handsome and polished than we could have imagined, and his leadership and good humor sustained our faith through the lengthy production process.

A team of talented professionals also made significant contributions. Kathleen Ossip was a superb copy editor, whose instinct for the right word and phrase was sure and precise. Louisa Hellegers, a uniformly cheerful fount of good sense and sure advice, was a comfort and a reassurance on the telephone; any project, no matter how complicated, would be safe in her careful hands. Steve Jorgensen's layout gave a visual clarity to complex and highly diverse material which Noël Vreeland Carter then saw through the final stages of production. To this Prentice Hall team we offer our heart-felt gratitude.

Jeanie Duvall transformed our prose ideas into the artwork she created for this book; asked to do the impossible, she achieved a quality of vision which speaks for itself. Our thanks also to Sarah Duvall for an excellent and efficient job of proofreading the final version.

Finally, our thanks to our students from abroad over the last twenty years for the brightness and courage they demonstrated in mastering a second language, as the samples of their work in this text attest. Sometimes we taught them; sometimes they taught us. Whichever way instruction flowed, their skills and enthusiasms, questions and needs tested our preconceptions and constantly opened new windows into the mysterious process of writing in a second language.

PERMISSIONS

"The Purpose of a Liberal Education" and subsequent excerpts reprinted from *The University, An Owner's Manual*, by Henry Rosovsky, by permission of W. W. Norton & Company, Inc. Copyright © 1990 by Henry Rosovsky.

Excerpts printed from "The Small Businessman: A Challenging Career Choice," by permission of Kotaro To of Japan.

Reprinted from "The Horror of Essay Rewrites," by Tavel Cowan by permission of the *Tulane Hullabaloo*, Tulane University, October 6, 1989.

Printed from "The Amish Lifestyle: Admirable, but Not for Me!," by permission of Stella Guillen of Peru.

Reprinted from a brochure on "Golden Gate National Recreation Area: Muir Woods," by permission of the National Park Service, U. S. Department of the Interior.

Reprinted from "Blood and the Nation's Health," courtesy of the American National Red Cross, Washington, D. C.

Reprinted from the New Orleans Tourist and Convention brochure by Honey Naylor with the permission of Honey Naylor, Travel and Tourism Journalist.

Printed from "Requirements of an Acceptable Theme," by Raymond Edward McGowan, Composition Specialist, English Department, Loyola University of New Orleans.

Printed from U 2 essays and application letters by Rafael Augusto Serrano of Lima, Peru.

Reprinted from "The Communications Collapse," by Norman Cousins by permission of *Time*, Inc. Copyright © 1990.

Reprinted from *The Heart of Darkness* by Joseph Conrad, published by Bantam/Dell Publishing Group/Doubleday.

Reprinted from Gulf Islands National Seashore brochure, U. S. Government Agency, Department of the Interior.

Excerpts reprinted from "Huge Conservation Effort Aims to Save Vanishing Architect of the Savanna," by William K. Stevens, copyright © 1989, by permission of *The New York Times* Company.

Unit One: Writing Basics

Introduction: THE FOUNDATIONS OF GOOD WRITING: AN OVERVIEW

We think in generalities, but we live in detail.— Alfred North Whitehead

No ideas but in things. — William Carlos Williams

A writer . . . is someone who has found a process that will bring about new things he would not have thought of if he had not started to say them. — William Stafford

---

The Writing Process: Starting With a Helpful Analogy

Drawing a Blueprint: Making Plans

Making a Plan a Reality

Building a Structure vs. Building an Argument: The Nature of Process Writing

Passage for Discussion and Analysis

Writing Assignments

The Writing Process: Starting with a Helpful Analogy

The writing process is a creative act of construction that seems to begin with nothing—a blank page—and ends with a coherent structure that expresses feelings, emotions, attitudes, prejudices, values—the full range of human experience. How a writer moves from a blank page to a final creation is the subject matter of this text. The chapters that follow will explore how writers create from a variety of different viewpoints, some of which may be familiar to you, some of which will be new. Since the writing process is both complex and largely invisible (even professional writers are often uncertain about how they create sentences, paragraphs, and meanings), it may help to try to visualize the process through a comparison with something familiar.

The writing process is often compared to building a physical structure. Both processes have beginnings, middles, and ends; both move from nothing to something; both involve making decisions about different styles, different sizes, and different approaches. Both are creative acts involving imagination, careful planning, and even more careful execution. Both are impossible without extended effort. Just as a builder begins with an empty piece of land and moves toward a completed house or commercial building in a series of stages, so a writer begins with disorganized, random thoughts and moves toward a completed essay or research paper in a series of stages, each with its own requirements and techniques. Thinking about the implications of the analogy, "writing is building," is a good way to start thinking about writing.

Just as a builder must first decide what structure to build, so a writer must decide on a topic.[1] The builder's choice depends on his resources, a contract made with a buyer,

EMPTY LOT + building sequence

or a personal decision about what to place on his own property; in like manner, the writer's choice depends on the resources or information available, the conditions of a teacher's assignment, or personal preferences. Sometimes a builder worries only about pleasing himself; however, most of the time he builds for other people and must worry about pleasing them. The writer too sometimes need please only herself; however, most of the time she writes to communicate with other people and must also worry about pleasing them.

The initial decisions of a builder relate to the property size, the type of building required, and the amount of money to be invested in it. These limit his choices of building size, building materials, and architectural plan. The writer's decisions also relate to purpose, audience, and time deadlines, which limit choices about the length of the paper, the types of material to include in it, and its basic structure.

Within these set limitations, the builder goes about planning his building. Sometimes he might follow a standard blueprint or building plan; at other times he might vary the standard blueprint; occasionally he will create a new plan, but usually within the limits of good architectural engineering

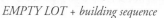

ARCHITECTURALLY DIFFERENT STRUCTURES

[1] "He" will refer to the builder and "she" to the writer throughout this paragraph to avoid pronoun confusion.

predetermined by builders who have gone before him. A writer too has standard patterns she can imitate or can draw on to strengthen her own writing; she might play with variations on these patterns, but even when she attempts to create a new pattern, she does so within limits predetermined by the successes of past writers.

If the builder builds something too unusual, something outside past architectural patterns, he might be labeled a genius or he might be considered an eccentric whose buildings are laughed at. Writers who try to be totally innovative face the same difficulty: They might be labeled geniuses, or they might just be laughed at. Consequently, most experienced builders and writers try to make use of the experience of those who have already proven effective in their field. In other words, imitation of past models works well in both building and writing, although both builders and writers must also express their own personalities in their work.

ECCENTRIC BUILDINGS

Drawing a Blueprint: Making Plans

A blueprint for a house is an architect's plan for the structure. Before the blueprint can be drawn, a lot of decisions must be made. These include which direction the building will face, how many rooms it will have, where the kitchen or living room will be, how many windows and doors there will be, and where they will be placed. In like manner, writing involves decision-making, not just about purpose and audience, but about content. It is easy to come up with a list of details, but it is much harder to think about their relationships, to decide which are general unifying ideas, and which are specific supportive ideas. Thinking out a plan for a paper involves making decisions about what categories your information belongs in, what order of categories to use, and then what details will best support the generalizations that head each category. Making a plan means making decisions about general principles and broad concepts, categories and classification. These key, unifying generalizations or abstractions of a paper are usually planned out in an outline or sketch that provides an overview of the paper: Its basic plan or structure, called a "blueprint" in the construction trade. Only when such a blueprint is completed will the builder be ready to build; only when a set of general categories and their logical relationships and arrangement have been settled will the writer be ready to write.

Moreover, just as the architectural plans of buildings differ greatly from culture to culture (a Spanish-style home is quite different from an American colonial-style home and both are most unlike a traditional Russian or Vietnamese country house), so categories or abstractions for writing are culturally determined, taught by the culture in which we live. They will be at least slightly different in different cultures, and slightly different in different languages. It is the responsibility of honest and effective writers to choose the right details and examples (and enough of them) to make clear the generalizations and abstractions they employ. Furthermore, a writer's blueprint must take into consideration these cultural differences so that the general plan is expressed in terms every reader can relate to. Your first step as a writer, then, is to develop your overall plan or "blueprint," and this will involve identifying general ideas, ideas which can lead to a workable plan.

Making a Plan a Reality

Once the blueprint is made, the builder begins the serious work of making a plan a reality. Similarly, when the general categories have been decided upon and an order established, the writer begins the serious work of turning an outline into a paper. The builder must carefully choose building materials for cost, quality, and availability. The writer, in turn, must carefully select supportive information based on effectiveness and availability. In building, the supportive beams and the framework materials will differ from those of the basic foundation and from those used to fill in the structure, cover the roof, and complete the building. In writing, generalities and abstractions establish the framework of ideas, and concrete specifics transform this framework into a well-developed paper. Just as the frame of a building is not yet a building, so the generalizations of a paper are not yet a paper. In writing, it is specific details that complete the work.

A key question for most writers is how to balance the abstract "frame" and the concrete detail—how much of each kind of writing to use. Unlike building, where the difference between frame and the other building materials is clearcut, in writing the answers are

What is wrong with this structure?

complicated and unsatisfactory, for they depend on the style, type, and purpose of the writing. This problem will be discussed throughout this book; in fact, you should notice that each chapter, in one way or another, adds to the definition of general and specific.

Building a Structure vs. Building an Argument: The Nature of Process Writing

While the notion of writing as building helps us visualize the writing process, as with all analogies, the image is not exactly accurate. Once the blueprint is made, the builder rarely departs from it. He sticks to the plan and builds the structure according to the plan. A writer, in contrast, may change the blueprint or plan repeatedly as she begins to explore her topic and understand it more fully; one plan may be replaced by another and another as work on the essay progresses. It would be very difficult for a builder to change his frame once the structure is up, but a writer can change frames even after the paper has been com-

pleted in rough draft. General unifying categories, specific support, and even the topic focus might change. In other words, while the idea that "writing is building" is a good way to visualize the writing process, it has its limitations. Writing is much more flexible and subject to much more change than building. Writing involves a process of careful thought and planning, building and constructing followed by replanning, reconsidering, additions, subtractions, and sometimes total destruction and demolition before beginning anew. Unit One of this text will describe in detail the nature of this process.

Passage for Discussion and Analysis

The Purposes of Liberal Education

For American students, there are many different reasons for going to college. A common purpose is to acquire the first professional credential, perhaps in engineering, nursing, accounting, or some other field. In other cases, however, the first degree is not intended to provide vocational training. That is especially true in university colleges attached to research universities and in so-called research colleges.[1] Students matriculating at these institutions frequently aspire to membership in the learned or liberal professions, for example, law, medicine, or university teaching. They face years of specialized postgraduate education. A majority of all students in these schools eventually pursue some form of graduate education. The purpose of college then becomes an education in the liberal arts—to study "a curriculum aimed at imparting general knowledge and developing general intellectual capacities in contrast to a professional, vocational, or technical curriculum."[2] Indeed, the attraction and value of the liberal arts is not confined to those aiming for graduate school. This type of curriculum is a perfectly reasonable end in itself.

Liberal arts, liberal education, and sometimes general education, is one way to describe the four years of instruction in some colleges. Ordinarily, the four years are divided into three parts: a year of requirements, focusing on breadth, frequently called distribution, general education (in the narrower sense), or a core curriculum. The equivalent of another year typically consists of electives: allowing students to pursue their own academic interests. Finally, two years—sometimes less—are devoted to a major or concentration in a special subject (English, sociology, mathematics, etc.). The totality of these studies, leading to a B.A. or B.S. degree, is education in the liberal arts…. Some years ago I attempted to formulate a standard for liberal education in our time.

1. An educated person must be able to think and write clearly and effectively. By this I mean that students, when they receive their bachelor's degrees, must be able to communicate with precision, cogency, and force. To put it in yet another way: students should be trained to think critically.

2. An educated person should have a *critical appreciation* of the ways in which we gain knowledge and understanding of the universe, of society, and of ourselves. Thus, he or she should have an *informed acquaintance* with the mathematical and experimental methods of the physical and biological sciences, with the main forms of analysis, and the historical and quantitative techniques needed for investigating the workings and development of modern society; with some of the important scholarly, literary, and artistic achievements of the past; and with the major religious and philosophical conceptions of mankind….

3. An educated American, in the last quarter of this century, cannot be provincial in the sense of being ignorant of other cultures and other times….

4. An educated person is expected to have some understanding of, and experience in thinking about, moral and ethical problems…. The most significant quality in edu-

---

[1] Together, these institutions enroll approximately 15% of all U.S. undergraduates. See Burton R. Clark, *The Academic Life*, p. 18.

[2] *Encyclopaedia Britannica*, 15th ed., vol. 6, p. 195.

cated persons is the informed judgment that enables them to make discriminating moral choices.

5. Finally, an educated individual should have achieved depth in some field of knowledge…. In American college terminology, it is called a "major" or "concentration…." It is expected that in every major, students will gain sufficient control of the data, theory, and methods to define the issues in a given problem, develop the evidence and arguments that may reasonably be advanced on the various sides of each issue, and reach conclusions based on a convincing evaluation of the evidence….

Liberal education is an indispensable prerequisite for professional practice at the highest level. We are entitled to expect superior technical expertise from professionals. A doctor should have superior knowledge of science and disease; a lawyer needs a deep understanding of major cases and legal procedures; a scholar must possess intimate familiarity with the state of the art in a particular subject. All of these attributes, however, while necessary, are far from sufficient. The ideal of a profession should not be a mere flow of competent technocrats. A more appropriate goal is professional authority combined with "humility, humanity, and humor." I want my lawyer and doctor to have a grasp of pain, love, laughter, death, religion, justice, and the limitations of science. That may be far more important than knowing the most modern drug or the latest ruling of an appellate court. Up-to-date information can always be acquired without too much difficulty; human understanding cannot be reduced to asking the computer a few questions.

— **Henry Rosovsky,** *The University: An Owner's Manual*

Questions for Discussion

1. This essay is typical of the type that might be read in a freshman English class. Is it difficult to read? If so, why? Does the difficulty lie in the vocabulary alone? What reading strategies might help you master the language?

2. How does Mr. Rosovsky answer his initial question about why American students go to college?

3. What does the author mean by the term "liberal arts education"?

4. Why does he feel that technical training is insufficient without a liberal arts background?

5. What does he consider the characteristics of an educated person?

6. Which sentence in the final paragraph is the best summary of his key point? Explain.

7. Can you explain his last sentence?

8. Does Rosovsky's definition of "liberal education" correspond to your own personal definition? To the definition you think is most commonly accepted in your country and culture?

9. a. What do you like most about Rosovsky's definition?
   b. What do you like least?

••Writing Assignments

A. Summarize this essay; that is, briefly record its key ideas or arguments in your own words.

B. Briefly explain your educational goals and how they correspond to what Rosovsky says.

Chapter 1: GETTING STARTED

The greatest part of a writer's time is spent in reading, in order to write; a man will turn over half a library to make one book. — Samuel Johnson

Composition is, for the most part, an effort of slow diligence and steady perseverance, to which the mind is dragged by necessity or resolution. — Samuel Johnson

The desire to write grows with writing. — Erasmus

Writing: A Necessary Skill

Good writing is necessary for success in college as well as in many professions. Entrance to medical school, for example, means passing a difficult writing exam requiring an ability to deal effectively with con- troversial medical, social, and political issues. Lawyers spend much of their time doing research and writing briefs or legal arguments based on that research. Although the marketplace is concerned with money, not words, the average businessperson writes the equivalent of several volumes a year: letters, reports, instructions to employees, manuals, and so on. Even scientists cannot escape the need for good writing skills; their experiments, however brilliant, will prove ineffectual unless they can explain them to their colleagues in a written professional paper. Since becoming a good writer takes time, now is the best time to start learning the writing skills vitally necessary for both college and professional success.

Getting Started

Perhaps the first step is to recognize that good writing means clear thinking. In other words, writing and thinking are so inseparable that, if you cannot think clearly about an idea, you cannot write about it. Once the careful thinking has been done, the actual writing will be easier than if you just sat down and tried to write with no preparation at all. Furthermore, the writing itself is often a learning process in which the writer thinks through a subject. Often, despite all your preparation, rewriting many times is the only way to come to terms with an argument or an idea. This is why this book emphasizes writing, not as a single event, but as a process—a progression from thought to draft to rethinking to final copy. Of course, it is not always possible to follow a lengthy process because of limits of time and situation. However, when such a process is possible, it assures a clearer, more logical, more "thoughtful" end product.

Getting started is always the most difficult part of writing. No matter what type of writing assignment you are dealing with, one major difficulty is shared by all writers: filling the first blank page. Do you start with a topic or a purpose, or a series of ideas or information? Do you think first about audience and later about what to communicate to that audience? Is it better to just write down something to begin with, or should you spend some time in thinking and reading first? Writing is a bit like traveling. Just as you might change your mind frequently about your destination or means of travel before you begin your trip, so you might change your mind many times about the purpose, focus, or direction of your paper before you start writing. Once you begin to actually travel, changes of mind become more costly; so too, once you actually write the first draft of the paper, you have committed yourself to a course of action; you have begun a trip in a certain chosen direction, and turning back and starting in another direction will mean lost time and effort. Of course, it might prove necessary to change course, stop at a different port, take an unplanned excursion, but doing so will greatly disrupt your travel schedule; for the writer it will mean a great deal more time and effort. The trick is to plan your general direction as early as possible through prewriting—by narrowing the topic, brainstorming about its possibilities, and thinking carefully about how to handle it. However, then you must be ready to accept the unexpected as new ideas or new information leads you toward more interesting side trips and your final destination.

Sometimes you have no choice about direction. Just as an employer assigns a business trip to a particular place for a particular purpose, so a teacher assigns a paper on a certain topic, with defined limits. In these instances, how to begin may seem more clearly defined. Yet even in such directed situations the actual act of beginning is up to the writer. It is the writer who must do the thinking and the planning that will turn an assignment or a personal idea into an essay or report. However, a series of steps that any writer, amateur or professional can follow will guide the planning and execution of the writing and help one avoid dead ends, pointless wanderings, and disastrous mistakes.

- **EXERCISE 1.1: QUESTIONS FOR DISCUSSION**

    1. What do you usually do when you have to write a paper? Do you just start writing, or do you do other things first? In other words, what steps do you go through?

    2. Would you recommend your approach to others? Why or why not?

    3. If you would like to improve your writing habits, what changes would you make?

The Key Prewriting Steps

STEP I: FINDING A TOPIC

The first step depends on the writing situation: whether you have been assigned a topic or have chosen your own topic. If someone else has chosen the topic, before you can write about it, you must carefully make it your own by identifying what is required and then deciding how you can best deal with that requirement.

Identifying What the Teacher Wants

If you have a paper assignment handout, read it carefully; read it as soon as you get it, and ask questions if you can, even if you know you won't work on it for a while. Write notes on the assignment sheet; be especially careful about definitions of any of the words used (ask about them or look them up and write the meanings down). As you study the assignment, pay special attention to the verbs used; they tell you what is to be done. Underline them. If the verbs are not clear, ask your teacher about them: exactly what is meant by "evaluate" or "analyze"? Next, look at the nouns, especially technical ones; how general or specific are they? If they are general, try to remember if they have been defined a certain way previously. If they are not clear, ask.

Make the assignment a part of your general thinking as soon as you receive it. If you have analyzed it properly, you should have memorized it without trying. Keep thinking about it. Try to explain it to someone else since articulating ideas— putting them into words—is a large part of any writing task. If the general topic comes up in a class discussion, try to relate

---

- ## EXERCISE 1.2: ANALYZING ASSIGNMENTS

Explain what the following assignments ask you to do. How do you know? Underline key words which help you understand the teacher's expectations.

> *Example:* <u>Explain who</u> Fidel Castro is and <u>what effect</u> he has had on Latin American politics. *First you must provide a general identification of Castro and then list his key effects on the politics of Latin America and describe them.*

1. Classify American fast foods in terms of cooking speed, cost, and nutritional value.
2. Define the phrase "a good student."
3. Contrast the quality of papers written with word processors with the quality of ones written by hand.
4. Describe a typical day in the life of a Wall Street stock broker.
5. Some people believe that strict population control will be necessary for the future survival of the human species. Take a stand on this issue and back up your answer with specific support based on recent statistics, trends, or events.
6. Attack the present administration's foreign policy as shortsighted, cynical, and self-serving.
7. Evaluate which of the three products presently used by a certain company best meet company needs.
8. Write a letter complaining about inadequate service and making suggestions for improvements.
9. Decide which word processing program should be used as the Acme company standard.
10. Analyze the case study of companies A and B, and explain which one has the better management and marketing strategies. Use the terminology employed by your textbook.

it to the assignment by asking questions. Review your textbook and notes as soon as possible. If the assignment requires extra reading, begin early. Most of all, think about the topic so it becomes your idea.

Narrowing a Topic

Once you have a clear idea of the assignment or an overall idea of what you want to do, you must find your specific topic. Some college or professional paper assignments will be clearly specified and limited, but even then you will need to decide how you personally will limit or handle the topic and materials. Many college assignments will be very general and undefined; in such a case you will need to think even more carefully about how you will control the topic and materials. You will need to gradually narrow the topic to a point where it is both interesting and manageable, but neither too broad nor too narrow for the assigned paper length.

In other words, you must be sure that your topic is limited enough to be developed and dealt with properly within the available length or time. A topic such as "Hunger in the World Today" or "The Rise of Revolutionary Governments" is far too abstract and general (unless, of course, your teacher wants such a general discussion). You can limit such a topic by asking yourself whether the topic makes you responsible for talking about dozens of countries, in which case you could only do so in very general terms, or whether it will necessitate a focus only on a few representative examples, in which case you could be far more specific. The topics above, for example, could become "Hunger in the Central African States" or "The Rise of Revolutionary Governments in South America." Even these topics would be too general for most college work, even for long research papers. What would each make you responsible for discussing?

- ## EXERCISE 1.3: DECIDING ABOUT TOPICS

    A. If a topic requires a short paper, put "SP" (short paper of 1-3 pages); if a paragraph, "PR" (paragraph length); if less than a paragraph," TN" (too narrow—not enough to write a paragraph on).

    Without actually doing the writing, consider the type and amount of information necessary for each topic; then narrow or expand as necessary. What affects your decision?

    Examples: 1. Second-hand cigarette smoke endangers nonsmokers.
      PR if aimed at persuading a general audience about banning cigarettes in public places, but SP if aimed at an audience of medical experts demanding detailed medical evidence and supportive research and studies.
      2. Cigarette smoke bothers me.
      TN change to "Cigarette smoke makes some people feel uncomfortable and others experience allergenic or asthmatic reactions, both minor and serious."

    1. Three steps in applying for college admission
    2. Efficiency: one important effect of using a daily work plan
    3. Cigarette smoke discolors teeth
    4. Three key benefits of auditing a class
    5. College study hours vs. high school study hours: how long must one study to do well?
    6. Revising your writing on a computer saves time and energy
    7. Employers should not require AIDS testing of future employees
    8. The dangers of jogging
    9. The value of laws requiring motorcycle riders to wear crash helmets
    10. Cafeteria food is greasy

B. The following topics are broad. Most would require a paper of more than five pages. Narrow these broad topics into topics suitable for a shorter paper of 1-3 pages.

Example: Capital punishment= *The effect of the death penalty on deterring murder in Texas in the 1980s.*

1. Why a college education is necessary for modern life
2. The American college system
3. How to choose a college major
4. Language learning
5. Sex education is a good idea.

This limiting process sometimes goes on for a lengthy period of time in any type of paper, because the narrowness of your focus might well depend on what resources are available, how much time you have to do the writing, what you already know about the topic, and how long you want the paper to be. Much more manageable would be "The Reasons the 1992-93 Famine in Somalia was so Devastating" or "The Rise of the Shining Path in Peru." However, even these topics call for lengthy papers. "Three Key Reasons the Shining Path Has Stayed Powerful in Peru" or "Two Negative Effects of Low Rainfall in Somalia in the Fall of 1992" or "How Competing Armed Groups Starved Rural Somalians" would be more within the boundaries of an average length college paper. If your assignment were to write only one paragraph, would "One Key Reason the Shining Path Has Stayed Powerful in Peru" or "One Negative Effect of Low Rainfall in Somalia in the Fall of 1992" be narrow enough? How narrow your topic should be will depend on your purpose and on you.

By the time you finish the above exercises you should have made some important discoveries about narrowing a topic. First of all, how much you can or should write on a particular topic depends very much on your audience and your purpose. For example, "Cigarette smoke discolors teeth" might be sufficient as a single sentence in an argumentative paper warning about the hazards of smoking cigarettes and would clearly be an insignificant minor hazard, unworthy of further development. However, the same idea, in a paper written to train future dentists, might be developed with technical information about the process by which this discoloring occurs or about the best methods for preventing or correcting such discoloration. In like manner, the topic "Three steps in applying for college admission" might make a short paragraph for a typical American student familiar with the college system, but it might take a full paper for the international student who needs an explanation of exactly what to do to fulfill the process step-by-step; for instance, how to prepare for the TOEFL (Test of English as a Foreign Language) and how to apply for it, what regulations to meet for translations of transcripts and for demonstrating the relationship between courses in the U.S. and courses in their country, and so forth. Hundreds of books have been written on "Language Learning," and a discussion of "Three key pronunciation problems Japanese students have and how to correct them" might prove more than enough for a five-page paper.

STEP II: DOING PREPARATORY THINKING

As soon as you receive an assignment, begin thinking informally and casually about the topic and its development. Try not to put off this important step of "preparatory thinking," for it is a relatively painless way of confronting your topic. If you don't have someone you can talk to about your topic, a silent, internal "conversation" might help; try to "explain" the assignment and possible topics.

Imagine yourself talking to the teacher or a small group of classmates about your plans for the paper. Doing so immediately clarifies the problem; you never know exactly what you think until you try to explain it to someone else. Once you put the problem into words rather than thinking about it abstractly, you are forced to define your idea.

It may also help to imagine the "shape" of the essay you intend to write: "The introduction should do this and that, the body should cover at least three main points, I could use such and such as evidence and support...." This visualization, the technique of imagining a solution to a future problem or difficulty, has the great advantage of flexibility and minimal investment of writing time.

Write notes as often as possible, even if "rough" and undeveloped. All your notes will later help you decide on a thesis, organize facts, figures, and other support for your ideas, and even set up an outline. By not forcing yourself to think of your duty (pro-ducing the "perfect" final draft), but rather by think-ing casually, as if you were confronting an interesting problem you read about in the newspaper, your fear of the act of writing will be reduced, and the actual writing will come easily.

The advice of most writing teachers is that your preparatory thinking should involve four major con-cerns: your audience, your persona (projected self-image), your purpose, and your potential materials. These concerns should remain uppermost in your mind from start to finish. This chapter will discuss the first three of these four, while Chapter 2 will dis-cuss potential materials.

STEP III: KNOWING YOUR AUDIENCE

Who you are writing to is very important because it determines the type of language and argu-ments you can use and the assumptions about values and knowledge you can make.

For example, an expert car mechanic can say to another car mechanic, "There's a short in the prima-ry, so the car won't run." To someone who knows less about cars, he would have to explain more by saying something like, "There's a short circuit in the main wiring of the ignition system, so the car won't run." To someone who knows even less about cars, he would have to say, "The rubber or plastic cover-ing on one of the important wires in the car is worn out. Since the rubber covering is worn, the wire is touching metal, so the electricity is not reaching the engine and the car won't run." Notice that even this last statement assumes a knowledge of how electric-ity works. If the car owner knew even less, the car mechanic would have to explain the principles of electricity before he could explain the problem.

In another instance, if you are going to explain how to make your favorite dish to an expert cook who knows about your native food, you can be very brief, use the shorthand language of traditional

---

• EXERCISE 1.4: CONSIDERING AUDIENCE

1. What specific information would you need to know about your intended audience before you wrote a paper explaining how to cook a special dish from your native coun-try?

2. If you were writing a paper explaining how to cook a special dish from your country, what major divisions would you put in your outline? Explain. What would be the best order for this information?

3. What problems would you encounter if you tried to explain a poem from your culture to an American young person? What would you need to explain to the American that you would not need to explain to someone from your country? Find a poem from your culture and prepare to explain it to the class.

4. How does a computer expert's language change when talking to students familiar with computer use compared to new learners? Give specific words and phrases the expert might use with each audience.

5. How do doctors discuss medical problems with patients differently from the way they would discuss the same problem with other doctors? With nurses? Why would there have to be differences?

cookbooks, and just list the ingredients and the order of the steps. However, if you are explaining the same information to an expert cook from another culture, your task is more difficult. You will need to explain not only any special English cooking terms, but also any techniques, cooking utensils, or ingredients unique to the culture. An American, cooking Vietnamese springrolls (a type of eggroll) for the first time, may need information about the use of a wok or cooking pot, the chopping of vegetables, the acquisition and folding of springroll wrappers, and so forth. Explaining to someone who has never cooked at all means that there will be a need for more information, more description, and more details. Such a person might need to be told how to turn on the stove, what type of cooking pots or pans to use, and much, much more. What can be shorthand for the expert must be carefully explained to the beginner.

The age, the educational background, the cultural, ethnic or ideological background (religion, politics, moral values), and the importance of the audience (their position or status) will also affect the type of language, the vocabulary and sentence structure, and even the types of examples and arguments that you will use in your writing. If you are talking to people of the same age and background (your peers), your job is easier because you can use the conversational language most familiar to you. However, if you are trying to impress a potential employer in an interview, you will try to sound more formal, more educated, and more informed, just as you would if you were delivering a speech to an audience seriously considering your proposals. If your audience comes from a different cultural or ideological background, you will need to think carefully about your assumptions and your examples both to assure clarity of communication and to avoid giving offense.

In speech, you automatically adapt and modify your "persona" or self-image and style according to your audience without thinking twice about it. You may sound helpful and kindly to a younger brother or your tone may deliberately remind him that you are indeed older. You speak differently to your best friend than you do to your parents. You change your language according to whether you are talking to your roommate, your professor, your boyfriend or girlfriend, or your employer. The level of vocabulary, the length and difficulty of sentences, the tone you employ, even the content change naturally and inevitably with a change in audience. This does not mean you are a different person at different times, but that you show different people different sides of your multi-faceted self.

STEP IV: FITTING PERSONA TO AUDIENCE

The image of yourself created through your language is called your persona. Whenever you write, your words create a persona, whether consciously or unconsciously. The student who applies to medical school, but makes careless errors in spelling, punctuation, and grammar is projecting a negative image, an unintentional persona of someone who is sloppy, thoughtless, and uncaring (all qualities no one would want in a doctor). The job applicant who focuses on what she wants out of the job, her salary demands and her preferences, without mentioning what she can offer the company, is telling her potential employer that she is self-centered and will not care deeply about company concerns.

Rather than unintentionally projecting such negative self-images, it is best to carefully and consciously control your persona, to change your written language, style, approach, and argument according to your potential audience. The student who writes to persuade her parents to allow her to move to an apartment must consider her father's and mother's values and beliefs, not just her own reasons, before deciding on the exact role to adopt. Obviously, her parents would want proof of studiousness, hard work, maturity, responsibility, and so forth. The student who argues that an apartment of her own will allow her to study harder (away from the noise and the interruptions of dorm life) and will force her to be more responsible (cooking and cleaning and caring for herself) is creating a persona that sounds more mature and more responsible. It is not dishonest to tailor your argument to your audience as long as it remains your argument, one you believe in. Writers who remain unconscious of their persona and never change it to adapt to new circumstances and audiences are usually ineffective.

In other words, dealing with an audience means thinking about how that audience will react to you, the writer, and adjusting the image of yourself to be more compatible with or understandable to the audience. Partly, this means finding ways to get the audience interested in what you have to say. Every writer must find a way of calling attention to herself or himself, and of forcing the reader's attention to the written page. Boredom and the general resistance of any reader to doing serious work are the enemies of every writer.

For a college paper, it is safest to assume an educated audience, one requiring the formality of college-level writing. It is also best to assume that, though your ideal audience will have general information in the field you are discussing and the sort of general knowledge one can expect from people who read the newspaper regularly and watch television, they either do not know the particulars you will focus on or they disagree with your perception or interpretation of those particulars. Expect them to be skeptical, not to share your special interests, to need explanations of specialized terms, and to be easily distracted. Expect too that they will be curious, impressed by logic, and ready to accept a clear, honest approach, but will need signals or guidelines to keep them aware of the progress of your discussion and the relationships of the parts. These assumptions about audience will keep you from making a common writing mistake: failing to explain enough because "the reader will know what I mean."

STEP V: IDENTIFYING PURPOSE AND DIRECTION

Directly related to audience is purpose: the reason you are writing and the effects you wish to achieve. Some types of writing have an automatically built-in goal. The person who writes a complaint letter has a particular audience (the manager, the person in charge who can make a decision) and a particular goal (to get a refund, to get a replacement item, to get an apology). These together affect tone (whether the writer sounds angry and outraged or reasonable but determined), and the type of information he or she includes (proof of complaint, names of those involved, receipts, dates, quotations).

The goal of a job application letter, in turn, is to persuade the reader that the writer is the best person for that job, or at least that he or she is someone who should be in the competition. To persuade the reader of that truth involves considering what the reader values most or needs most for the job, and focusing on those qualities. Can the writer prove a history of hard work? Reliability? Honesty? Good training or a good education? Experience? The sub-goals then are to prove the possession of such qualities. The goal of writing assignments in many college classes is to convey specific knowledge or an understanding of a text or texts.

- ## EXERCISE 1.5: CONSIDERING PERSONA

    1. Imagine you have been stopped by a traffic policeman for a driving violation. Afterwards, you write a letter about this event to
        a. a judge who can lower the fine you have to pay
        b. a friend your age
        c. your father
        d. your car insurance company

    How would each letter be different? Would your persona remain constant? Explain.

    2. If you have been sold a bad car, (a "lemon") you might need to write a letter to
        a. the salesman
        b. his superior or the car manufacturer
        c. your lawyer
        d. your mother.

    Each of these letters would talk about the same problems with your car but the audience of each would differ. Which letter would be the least technical, the most objective, or the most demanding? How would your persona change with purpose and audience? Explain.

Even if a writer's purpose is only to make a good grade in a class, he or she must subdivide that goal into sub–goals that allow precise thinking about what he or she plans to do. What will earn a good grade? Is it writing an error-free paper? Is it length? Is it organization? Is it specific support? Is it proof of research? Is it originality? Is it eloquent language? Or is it some combination? Writers should remember that different audiences create different purposes; there is no single formula for success as a writer.

Cultural differences, of course, create even more complications, so you should not assume that a U.S. audience—whether a teacher, a complaint manager, or a government official—will necessarily react as did the audiences you grew up with. If you have ever tried telling a joke—unsuccessfully—to someone who is not a part of your culture or is just from a different background, you will understand the problem. This unpredictability in audience creates the need for audience analysis to decide what content is appropriate. Clearly then, audience and purpose together directly affect content.

- ## EXERCISE 1.6: IDENTIFYING PURPOSE

    A. Assume the audience for the following exercise is well educated. Label the purpose of each passage as mainly a) to inspire, b) to encourage action, c) to entertain, d) to inform, e) to change someone's mind. There may be more than one purpose; if so, list in order of decreasing importance.

    > *Example:* Pretzels were invented by monks in southern France in 610 A.D. The monks shaped strips of dough to look like the folded arms of a child in prayer. *to inform; to entertain*

    1. At 10:56:20 P.M. Neil Armstrong stepped onto the surface of the moon and stopped to say his now famous words, "That's one small step for a man, one giant leap for mankind."

    2. Dolphins are valuable friends of man: rescuing swimmers who get in trouble in deep water, helping the shipwrecked stay on the surface and move toward land, and serving in peaceful military operations such as retrieving lost weapons or locating missing bombs.

    3. Emma Goldman's irresistible autobiographical memoir, *Living My Life*, is an eloquent, fiery, moving recounting of this famous turn-of-the-century anarchist and feminist's struggle to be free in society and to create a free society.

    4. If we do not receive your late payment within the week, we shall be forced to take legal action and demand compensation.

    5. On April 3, 1860, a mounted rider left St. Joseph, Missouri for Sacramento, California, 2000 miles away. This was the start of the pony express.

    6. Tarzan of the Apes, a favorite childhood hero, was supposedly raised by apes and spent his first nineteen years swinging through the trees until he met and fell in love with "Jane," whom he pursued despite pirates, cannibals, bandits, and a nasty second cousin who stole his inheritance and his girlfriend. According to the story, he eventually settled on his English country estate. Much to Jane's disgust, he occasionally returned to ape-like behavior, for instance, finding and eating earthworms.

    7. This next election is vital to the economy and the well-being of the nation. It is the duty of every citizen, not just to vote, but to inform herself or himself of the issues and of the candidates' positions on them. For a democracy to endure, citizens must participate. Don't take the "demo" out of "democracy" or you will end up with "autocracy."

8. Many of the tombstones of the Old West evoke a very non-modern attitude toward violence. For instance, in Boot Hill cemetery, Tombstone, Arizona, one gravestone epitaph says:

HERE
LIES
LESTER MOORE
FOUR SLUGS
FROM A .44
NO LES
NO MORE

B. Explain why, in terms of purpose, the writers of the following selections have chosen to be <u>mainly</u> abstract or <u>mainly</u> concrete. For example, John F. Kennedy in #1 has a political purpose: to unite the Democratic party behind him in his run for the United States' presidency. How would that goal of unification affect Kennedy's decision to use concrete or abstract diction? How specific can you be when you address a large, diverse group?

1. I stand tonight facing west on what was once the last frontier. From the lands that stretch 3,000 miles behind me, the pioneers of old gave up their safety, their comfort, and sometimes their lives to build a new world here in the West....

   Today some would say that those struggles are all over, that all the horizons have been explored, that all the battles have been won, that there is no longer an American frontier. But the problems are not all solved and the battles are not all won, and we stand today on the edge of a new frontier—the frontier of the 1960s.... Beyond that frontier are uncharted areas of science and space, unsolved problems of peace and war, unconquered pockets of ignorance and prejudice, unanswered questions of poverty and surplus.

   It would be easier to shrink back from that frontier, to look to the safe mediocrity of the past.... But I believe the times demand invention, innovation, imagination, decisions. I am asking each of you to be new pioneers on that new frontier.

   —From John F. Kennedy's acceptance speech to the Democratic convention in California as he began his 1960 campaign for the presidency

2. The $1 bill—people will pray for it, work for it, lie and cheat for it, but few ever take a good look at it.

   It is a piece of paper measuring 2⅝" by 6⅛" with a thickness of .0043". The composition of the paper and ink is a state secret. New notes will stack 233 to an inch, if not compressed, and 490 notes weigh a pound. Every thousand notes cost the Government $8.02 to print. At the same time, over 2 billion bills are in circulation, each with an average life span of 18 months.

   —Stephen L. W. Greene, "The Almighty Dollar" in *The People's Almanac*, ed. by David Wallechinsky and Irving Wallace

3. Two significant incidents early in my life helped steer me toward medicine: my grandfather's death and my uncle's resurrection. When I was six, I watched, helpless, as my grandfather, whom I loved very much, died from high blood pressure; that I could do nothing to help him left me distressed. Then, a year later, my father, acting quickly, efficiently, and effectively, applied life-saving emergency treatment to an uncle who had slipped in the bathroom and sustained a serious blow to the head. When found, my uncle had no pulse and suf-

fered pulmonary arrest; my father's action literally brought my uncle back from the dead. Together, these two events left me determined to be a physician.

—Medical school application letter

---

4. I purchased a new 1996 Claire de Lune sedan on November 18, 1995 from Cowboy Vehicles at 3333 Stone Street, Phoenix, Arizona. During the past five months I have taken the car back for repairs six times and had it towed for repairs three other times. The car repairs totalled $310.20 on November 25, $600.06 on December 20, $420.68 on January 13, $777.43 on February 8 (towed), $223.94 on February 9, $328.34 on February 10 (towed), $252.06 on February 19, $64.74 on February 23, and $450.32 on March 1 (towed). Since purchase, the car repairs have totalled $3427.77. There were 29 different defects, four of which have recurred more than once. The car was returned two times for the clutch (readjustment), three times for the catalytic converter (replacement and readjustment), four times for the rear deck lid (loose), and five times for the air conditioner (fails to cool). The last three defects have yet to be fixed.

—Complaint letter to an automobile dealership

---

5. I would like to apply for the position of Computer Librarian advertised in the May 17th *Times Mirror*. I have experience in word processing, data entry operations, and computer concepts and languages, as well as training in business and finance. Thus, I believe my skills, industry, and educational training might meet the needs of Eagle Mortgage Company.

—Opening to a job application letter

---

6. The Amazon is truly Amazonian in nature. The river and forest system covers 2.7 million sq. mi. (almost 90% of the area of the contiguous U.S.) and stretches into eight countries besides Brazil, including Venezuela to the north, Peru to the west and Bolivia to the south. An adventurous monkey could climb into the jungle canopy in the foothills of the Andes and swing through 2000 miles of continuous 200 ft.–high forest before reaching the Atlantic coast. The river itself, fed by more than 1,000 tributaries, meanders for 4,000 miles, a length second only to the Nile's 4,100 miles. No other river compares in volume; every hour the Amazon delivers an average of 170 billion gallons of water to the Atlantic—60 times the flow of the Nile. Even 1,000 miles upriver, it is often impossible to see from one side of the Amazon to the other... a typical 4–sq.–mile patch of rain forest may contain 750 species of trees, 125 kinds of mammals, 400 types of birds, 100 of reptiles and 60 of amphibians. Each type of tree may support more than 400 insect species. In many cases the plants and animals assume Amazonian proportions: lily pads 3 ft. or more across, butterflies with 8 in. wingspans and a fish called the pirarucu, which can grow to more than 7 ft. long.

—Adapted from Laura Lopez, Johan Maier, and Dick Thompson, "Playing with Fire," *Time*

A Model to Learn From

The following college application letter illustrates one of the most important issues for every writer to understand: the relationship between the level of concreteness and the amount of knowledge you can assume in your reader or audience. The more knowledge your reader has, the more general you can be; the less knowledge your reader has, the more concrete and specific you must be. In other words, a paper varies in length and development according to the knowledge and experience of the audience.

What is the purpose of this letter? Who is the intended audience? Is this letter effective or not? How so? Does its persona fit its audience and purpose? Explain.

COLLEGE APPLICATION LETTER

1600 LaVaca Street
Santa Fe, New Mexico
January 25, 1996

J. A. Smothers
Director of Admissions
Hall of Languages, Room #50
University of Kentucky
Lexington, Kentucky

Dear Mr. Smothers:

I am applying for admission to your program. I have the high school G.P.A., the TOEFL score, and the letters of recommendation that you require, and I meet your financial requirements as well. However, since I am a foreign student, I feel I should give you a brief history of my study of English to demonstrate that my background is adequate for success in your program.

I began studying English when I was fourteen, at the New School of Calcutta, the second largest high school in the city. My first teacher was Jack Bullard, who had an M.A. from Oxford University; I studied under Mr. Bullard for two years, and since he was a very learned grammarian and an excellent teacher, I believe I have a solid foundation in grammar and structure. My next teacher was John Ford, an American Fulbright professor. From him I learned American pronunciation and usage. During this time I used the language laboratory tapes at least three hours a week; I listened to American popular songs whenever I could; and I went to every English language film I could find (I saw *Gone With the Wind* eight times!). In our final year of high school we studied English literature, and I have read *David Copperfield*, *Macbeth*, *The Sun Also Rises*, and *Lady Chatterley's Lover*, as well as much English poetry. Since over sixty-five percent of the students at N.S.C. go on to study in universities in Europe and the United States, I feel my formal language training has prepared me for success in your program.

In addition to my formal training, I have had much informal experience with idiomatic English. During the summer of 1992 I lived in Liverpool, England for three months as a Summer Exchange Student. When I first arrived in the United States, I spent six weeks at the Intensive Language Institute in Washington, D.C., a program in which the students speak conversational English at least four hours a day. Since then I have spent several weekends at the homes of American friends in Westport, Connecticut. I am a subscriber to *Newsweek* magazine and have little trouble following radio and T.V. programs. Thus I feel I can adjust easily to American conversational English, and should have little trouble taking notes or dealing with classmates and classroom responses.

Please let me know if I can provide any further information which might be helpful to you. I enclose the copies of my transcript and TOEFL score, and the proof of financial support. The letters of recommendation should have already been forwarded to you. Thank you for considering my application.

Sincerely,

Raji Krashnapoor

Raji Krashnapoor

- **EXERCISE 1.7: INVESTIGATING THE WRITER'S STRATEGY**

What strategy or plan does this writer have for his application letter?
He clearly has several plans in mind:

1. Raji Krashnapoor is thinking about what his audience does and does not know. Calcutta is far away from the University of Kentucky, and even though English is a common second or even first language in India, Raji knows he must explain very fully about his English background in order to make clear that he is qualified to compete with native speakers. In other words, Raji's general assertion is that his language skill makes him competitive at a college level. To prove this general assertion, he must define the level of study he has reached in very particular terms. Does Raji assume that a simple statement of language skill or TOEFL score is sufficient to prove his ability to compete and to convince university officials that he will not need more English training before beginning course work? How does he make his English abilities unquestionably clear? What concrete details does he supply to support his assertion of language skill? How does such an approach help him better achieve his purpose? Can you suggest other types of concrete detail that might serve his purpose? Mark out all the concrete details in this letter. What would remain? Would what is left be sufficient for Raji's purpose? Why or why not? What could he make more concrete? Specific G.P.A.? Precise TOEFL score?

2. In addition, Raji has tried to anticipate the questions Mr. Smothers might have and answer them before Mr. Smothers can ask them. Raji has focused on the doubts Mr. Smothers might have about Raji's English ability. In other words, he tries to determine the possible responses of his audience. What does Raji think Mr. Smothers might be doubtful about? How do you know? What details has he included to help address those doubts? What type of information helps define Raji's English language abilities? Explain.

3. In order to unify his supportive details and to provide a logical plan for his paper, Raji Krashnapoor has chosen a very natural, basic pattern of development: the time sequence of his studies as they happened. What division does Raji make in his chronological [time order] sequence? How does this organization assist his presentation of information? Does this organizational order help him be more concrete? How?

4. Overall, from reading his letter, what kind of person does Raji seem to be? In other words, what characteristics does he communicate? Careful? Sloppy? Hard–working? Lazy? What in his letter helps create this impression of person and personality? The style? The details? How does the quality of the letter itself aid his cause? Explain. What might have happened if he had failed to proofread and had left in misspellings and grammar mistakes? How would that failure have changed the way his readers view him?

5. What advice would you give Raji to help him make his letter more effective, or do you think it is good enough as it is? Could you suggest other types of general arguments or specific information that might help him convince his readers of his qualifications for university admission? In other words, Raji has built a good solid structure, but he can make it richer and more luxurious by improving the quality of individual sentences and by expanding his letter with more and better details.

Final Checklist

As you write, check the basic prewriting steps as you complete them.

- Identify exactly what your teacher expects.
- Narrow your topic to something manageable within your space and time limits.
- Identify and prepare to write to your particular audience as much as possible.

- Decide on your purposes and plan to stick to them.
- Decide on the best persona for your audience and purpose. What kind of person will you try to sound like? What will your tone be?

- ## EXERCISE 1.8: THINKING ABOUT PURPOSE, AUDIENCE, AND PERSONA

Identify the intended audience of the following paragraphs. Who do they seem to be? What do we know about the audience from the paragraphs themselves—their content, their style, their vocabulary, their examples, their tone? Is their purpose clear? Is the purpose related to the audience?

> *Example:*   Thanks for catsitting while I'm away. The injured cat, Mollie, is in the bathroom. Dr. McSweeny says she should stay there until her medicine runs out. I am leaving it on the bathroom counter, and instructions are on it: one tablet twice a day. She still has a little fever but is on the mend. I am also leaving the hydrogen peroxide on the counter to wash her leg with occasionally just to keep down infection. She should be happy with dry cereal, but a part of a can of kitty tuna should cheer her up a bit. I'm so sorry for the extra trouble. I didn't think you would have so much to do when we talked about this, but I had not counted on this problem. I hope you are not too inconvenienced. See you when I get back.

> Intended Audience: *The cat-sitter, a personal friend who knows about and likes animals and who is familiar with the writer's house and household as well as veterinarian*

> Main Purpose: *To warn of changes in the animal sitting agreement (a sick cat with special needs), to provide new instructions*

> Secondary Purpose: *To apologize for the extra trouble, to thank the friend for helping*

1.   Women as a class have never subjugated another group; we have never marched off to wars of conquest in the name of the fatherland. We have never been involved in a decision to annex the territory of a neighboring country, or to fight for foreign markets on distant shores. Those are the games men play, not us. We see it differently. We want to be neither oppressor nor oppressed. The women's revolution is the final revolution of them all.

—Susan Brownmiller, "Sisterhood is Powerful," *New York Times Magazine*

Intended Audience: _____

Main Purpose: _____

Secondary Purpose: _____

2.   Whether you're considering applying to law school, whether you've been accepted and are anxiously awaiting the first class session, or whether you're a second-year student who hasn't done quite as well as you'd hoped, the impression you may have of the legal profession is that of an intricate, incomprehensible mass that you'd like to be a part of if only it weren't so, well, intricate and incomprehensible. For all of you in those categories, I have some good news. The material taught in law schools today is completely comprehensible to anyone of sufficient intelligence to be accepted for admission in the first place. This is because law, unlike nuclear physics or biochemistry, is the study of human activities on a very visible, familiar level. To be generally aware of society and its many endeavors is to know at least the subject matter with which law deals.

    —Adapted from Jeff Deaver, *The Complete Law School Companion*

Intended Audience: _____

Main Purpose: _____

Secondary Purpose: _____

3.   Why use drama in the ESL classroom? The famous dramatist George Bernard Shaw gave us an answer when he said:

> "There are fifty ways of saying Yes,
> and five hundred of saying No,
> but only one way of writing them down."

That is, drama makes one consider the vast range of interpretations, feelings, and undercurrents possible in language, the way delivery, intonation, gestures, and other body language modifies and changes the meaning of the spoken word. Students learn the need to interpret silences, remarks, reactions. Acting helps students find out the possibilities of written dialogue, and develop awareness of speech features, paralinguistic and extralinguistic features—attitude, gesture, intonation, movement, etc.

    —Adapted from John McRae, *Using Drama in the Classroom*

Intended Audience: _____

Main Purpose: _____

Secondary Purpose: _____

4.   I am a very dynamic, hard-working person, willing to travel, to retrain, and to take on new experiences. The attached resumé indicates my social and organizational skills: I have been very active in a number of student organizations, and have organized social as well as educational activities. For instance, I was highly involved in the Beta Alpha Psi's Southwest Regional Conference, working closely with faculty members, conferees, and students to produce a successful conference. My work experience has been mainly general office work, like word processing, filing, and researching. I began in the Puerto Rican Department of the Treasury as an office clerk and have recently been a clerical assistant in the English Department. This work has improved my writing and social skills. In November, I will take the CPA (Certified Public Accountant) examination as final confirmation of the skills and knowledge acquired majoring in accounting.

Intended Audience: _____

Main Purpose: _____

Secondary Purpose: _____

5. Our organization, College Journalists Associated, has been studying the innovative policies of your paper and has been highly impressed by the significant editorial changes you have made since you took over that difficult and trying position. Consequently, we would like to invite you to be the central speaker at our end-of-the-year banquet. It will be held at 8:00 P.M., on December 6 in the Rice Campus Auditorium. Coat and tie required. We realize you are a busy man and would be happy to compensate you for your time with an honorarium of five hundred dollars. The choice of topics would be up to you, but our schedule calls for a twenty-minute speech. We would be delighted if you would accept. We can promise a large attendance of enthusiastic listeners, anxious to learn more about the ins and outs of editorships. Thank you for considering this possibility. We look forward to hearing from you.

Intended Audience: _____

Main Purpose: _____

Secondary Purpose: _____

6. As to my English ability, I have been working hard, studying English in both Japan and the U.S., in Boston as well as New Orleans. As a result, I feel I have attained a higher level of English skills than my TOEFL score indicates. Particularly, the ESL program has helped me prepare to study successfully at the graduate school level. I have spent this fall semester studying common patterns of development, metaphors, and process writing from sentence to paragraph to complete essay. I have also practiced sentence combining with adverbials, noun and adjective clauses, absolutes, appositives, and so forth. My courses also focused on study skills and library work. My major semester's paper in the Composition/Research course was thirty pages long and included endnotes and bibliography. It dealt with the career of "a small shop owner," and aimed at helping someone consider whether or not to choose this career by discussing the skills and qualities requisite for success, a typical day in the life of a businessman, and the short– and long–term effects of this career choice. I learned to write a balanced combination of my own argument and ideas and authoritative source support. I would be happy to provide a copy of this work on request. It demonstrates my familiarity with business English and my graduate level writing competence.

  —Kotaro To, Japan

Intended Audience: _____

Main Purpose: _____

Secondary Purpose: _____

7. After several months of searching and comparing dresses, I purchased a designer House of Blanche wedding dress from Louder's Bridal Salon on October 2. For a rather high fee, it was specially cut and fitted for me in preparation for my October 30 wedding date. On October 23 the gown was delivered in a plastic dress bag. The following day, October 24, I opened the bag to dress for rehearsal and discovered the following facts. The front satin panel has two large holes in it the size of a quarter. The holes are 11 and 16 inches from the bottom of the satin and lace skirt. Secondly, the entire dress is covered with small green flecks. It appears to have been left uncovered during redecorating. I telephoned your bridal consultant on October 24 at 2:10 P.M. She admitted that the storeroom had indeed been recently painted but claimed that you were the person to settle the problem. I have been trying, unsuccessfully, to contact you ever since. At present it is 6:00 P.M. at the end of your business day, October

25, 1995. I have telephoned your office five times, and spoken to several salespeople and clerks, none of whom will take responsibility or offer to remedy this problem. You have not returned my calls. I must have a wedding dress to wear October 30; you are responsible for providing that dress. I am asking the bank to not honor my check to you until further notice from me, and I am seriously considering my legal options.

Intended Audience: _____

Main Purpose: _____

Secondary Purpose: _____

8.   Before you buy a bicycle, think about what you are going to use it for. If you are going to ride over plowed fields, or on sand flats at low tide, or if you plan to take only short rides to the corner store, get a sturdy coaster-brake model, a balloon-tire bomber—$10–$50. If you plan leisurely shopping trips, weekend excursions up to 30 miles, or commuting for short distances, all on reasonably even terrain, get a three speed. If you like a comfortable ride and maneuverability, you might try one of the newly introduced small-wheeled bikes—$50–$80. If you plan to cover long distances over varied terrain, and if you are willing to adjust to a specialized riding position for the sake of vast improvement in cycling speed and responsiveness, get a ten speed— $80–$300. There are bikes between and outside these three categories, but these give a good sense of the general range.

—Adapted from Tom Cuthbertson, *Anybody's Bike Book*

Intended Audience: _____

Main Purpose: _____

Secondary Purpose: _____

9.   Infectious Mononucleosis (glandular fever) is an acute infectious disease, characterized clinically by the constitutional symptoms of an infection and generalized lymphad-enopathy; pathologically by hyperplasia of lymphatic tissue throughout the body; hematologically by the appearance of abnormal lymphocytes in the circulating blood; and serologically by the presence of a heterophile agglutinin. Although the disease is known to be infectious, the etiologic agent is not definitely established. The condition is more common in its sporadic form, but it also occurs as an epidemic (especially in children and young people—e.g., in schools, colleges, or other institutions), when it behaves like an easily transmitted infection that probably is air-borne. Infection is rare after age 35. For treatment and medication see page 1134.

—Adapted from *The Merck Manual*

Intended Audience: _____

Main Purpose: _____

Secondary Purpose: _____

••Writing Assignments

A. Choose one of the short paragraphs from Exercise 1.8 as a model to imitate. Write to the same audience for the same purpose as the original, but create a paragraph about your own life, problems, interests, or concerns. Imitate the language of the passage: use of personal pronouns, sentence length, complexity, vocabulary, level of abstraction or specificity, etc. You might need to explain more fully than the original, depending on the topic. When you have finished, briefly define your audience and purpose.

For example, #2 focuses on a course of study that most students fear is difficult, and the writer explains why it is not as difficult as it seems. An imitation might argue that most people think science is too difficult for the average person to understand when in fact science builds on the type of common sense observations that one engages in on a daily basis: most people notice that a ball thrown in the air will come back down and can conclude that what goes up must come down; this conclusion is a basic scientific observation. Another imitation of #2 might focus on why students think computer science classes (or math classes or physics classes) are difficult, and explain some simple procedure or approach that will prove them, or make them seem, easier to deal with.

B. Assume that the purpose of the following assignments is to persuade a particular reader or group of readers to a specific point of view through the thoroughness, aptness, and concreteness of your description. Choose one of the topics. Think carefully about your persona.

1. Describe your school from the point of view of a handicapped person.
2. Describe the school registration process from the point of view of one of the following:
   a. of a student going through it
   b. of an administrator describing it to parents
   c. of a faculty member working in it.
3. Describe your school from the point of view of someone from a rival school.
4. Describe those campus activities which would best benefit
   a. a premed student or science major
   b. an art student
   c. a political science major
   d. an international student with an undetermined major

C. Building on what you have learned from the "Model to Learn From" on page 18, write an application letter to a school, a program, or an academic department, or for a job of your choice. Consider your audience and purpose before describing yourself, your credentials, training, skills, and abilities. Provide only material relevant to your purpose and audience, but be as specific as possible to provide a detailed portrait of yourself and of why you should be admitted to that school/get the job.

   Hints for making this letter more concrete:
   1. If applying to a school, look in the college bulletin under the section on admission requirements. Also check the section on special requirements for particular majors.
   2. Ask about admission requirements at the admissions office and take notes on the answers.

3. Ask students who already attend the school what types of standards they had to meet for admission. Keep their experiences in mind as you write.

4. Like Raji, write down specific details about your education— key courses, particular books, test scores, G.P.A. Quote from teacher comments about your work.

5. If applying for a job, consider the job advertisement, the location, the company image.

D. Choose an important historical figure from your country, your state, or your region, and provide your classmates with a short sketch of who she or he was and what she or he did that was so important. Include any famous quotes or any physical characteristics that were notable (for instance, George Washington's white wig or Napoleon's habit of putting his right hand inside his jacket.)

Writing hint: Identifying phrases like the following are useful ways to begin: "Having fought tyranny for forty years…" (a participial phrase), "…who is best known for his work among the city's poor" (an adjective clause), "the father of my country" (an appositive).

Remember, that while people from your country might already know a great deal about the person you are describing, your audience of classmates might know nothing at all. Therefore, you must carefully explain and clarify.

Practice

As preparation, criticize the following opening statements. What could you do to make them better? Change them into one sentence statements that both identify and point the way for the rest of the paper.

Example: Vladimir Vysotsky was a very famous and respected poet, singer and artist. He had a tremendous impact on the development of Russian society. As an author, he dedicated his life to fighting evil and injustice through music and art. He was not an official poet, but his songs touched the hearts of millions of people from all walks of life. They support people in hard times.

First: Decide on your key identifying phrases. Was he really an "artist" in the sense of a "painter" or "sculptor" or was he simply "artistic" in the sense of "poet and singer" or was he involved in some other area of the "arts" like "acting"? Include an indication of nationality and of time period: *Nineteenth-century Russian poet, singer, and actor, Vladimir Vysotsky.*

Second: Decide on the key argument or arguments of your paper: *Nineteenth-century Russian poet, singer, and actor, Vladimir Vysotsky fought evil and injustice through songs, poems and dramatic performances.*

Third: Add some explanation or reasons which make clear this significance: *Nineteenth-century Russian poet, singer, and actor, Vladimir Vysotsky fought evil and injustice through songs, poems and dramatic performances which touched the hearts of millions of people from all walks of life and which still support Russians in hard times.*

1. Alfredo Cristiani was the president of the Republic of El Salvador. He has made several changes in our country. [Which sentence identifies? Which provides the thesis idea? Were the changes good or bad? What kind of changes?]

2. Yoshinabu Tokugawa was the last "shogun" of the Tokugawa Kingdom. He was not a heroic man. But he really saved Japan from becoming a European colony.

3. Luis Muñoz Marín was born in 1898. He died in 1980. He has been the most important political figure in Puerto Rico. He knew and understood the needs of the Puerto Rican poor. He dedicated his life to improving their quality of life.

4. Saô Paulo, Brazil, today has named many public schools and places after José de Anchieta. He was a Jesuit. He was very saintly. He crossed the high, steep mountains to live with the "Tupiniguins" Indians in the inner highlands: to teach them, to help them, and to learn from them.

5. When I was young, I had already known a man who was very important to my country. He is my country's father, Mr. Chiang Kai-Shek. We always remember his great story and thank him so much. Without him, we wouldn't have freedom and prosperity.

6. Juan Carlos of Spain greatly influenced the lives of all Spaniards. He is respected by young and old as well as his wife, Sofia. Franco was a dictator who didn't let Catalans speak their own language, but Juan Carlos let us speak Catalan, which is a part of our whole culture, so we feel comfortable with our country again.

Which kind of information will best communicate the significance of Spain's famous sixteenth-century author Miguel Cervantes to people unfamiliar with him?

1. A summary of his most famous book, *Don Quixote de la Mancha.*

2. A discussion of the Spanish picaresque novel and how Cervantes' books fit the picaresque tradition.

3. A description of Cervantes' satiric social and political targets.

4. A comparison with Shakespeare.

5. A contrast with Shakespeare.

6. An explanation of Cervantes' contribution to the Spanish language.

7. An explanation of how Cervantes' *Don Quixote* captures the essence of the Spanish "soul" and still reflects the basic conflicts of that "soul".

8. Statistics on number of copies of Cervantes' books produced internationally each year and the number of languages into which they have been translated.

9. Information about Cervantes' period as a soldier, the loss of his arm, and his nickname "El manco de Lepanto."

10. Comparison of *Don Quixote* with the Bible in international sales.

Passage for Discussion and Analysis

Horror of Essay Rewrites

I was assigned my first English 101 essay on the first day of class. I was sure I would soon be writing about the same shallow subject that freshmen are expected to write about.

My mouth fell open with surprise when I found the topic was not shallow whatsoever: "Discuss some aspect of the following statement: 'The United States spends 300 billion dollars annually on a cold war we claim to have won but less than 8 billion on the drug war we are clearly losing. In his address to the nation, President Bush emphasized he will not raise taxes to pay for the war on drugs.'"

I was unaware that President Bush had waged a war on anything. So on my way back from class, I snagged some newspapers in order to find out what was going on in the wonderful world of drug wars.

I spent that night looking over the newspapers trying to figure out what topic to concentrate on. I finally picked a topic I thought would be easy to write about.

I was wrong.

By the weekend, I had what I thought was an okay essay, the type that would assure me of at least a B in my senior honors English class in high school. So, I went down to the computer center to type it out.

On Monday, we had small group discussions of our rough drafts. The people in my group could not find anything really wrong with my essay, so I made a few minor corrections and turned the paper in.

The next Monday I received my paper back. When I glanced at my paper, I saw that it was literally covered with pencil marks. I calmly walked outside, sat down, and read the comments.

I had received what I consider one of the worst criticisms I could think of about my writing. The note on the back page began, "Tavel, this paper shows very little content."

I was crushed. I had never been told anything close to that before. My English teachers in high school had praised my writing often, but sometimes they told me that they expected a little more from me. Various newspaper editors I had worked for sometimes edited my work, but no one ever told me that I had "very little content."

I walked around under a storm cloud for the next hour. My roommate refused to leave the room because she was certain I was going to jump out the window.

After I calmed down, I looked over my paper. To my surprise (and dismay), I found out that my professor was right. I really didn't have any content in my paper. I had learned an important lesson: I wasn't in high school any longer. I was actually going to have to work to make good grades.

So that night, I began my rewrite. I had gotten about halfway through my paper when the computer screen all of a sudden went black. I lost my entire essay. I spent the next hour crying and attempting to remember everything I had written. (The law student beside me took his loss better than I did mine; he only cried for a half hour.)

I had put a good five or six more hours into my paper. When I turned it in, I was proud of my work. I was extremely glad to get rid of it.... I knew if I never heard about the war on drugs again, I would be a happy person.

When I received my paper back, I ran outside and flipped to the grade and comments. I made an 80%, the average grade in the class. But, what filled me with joy was the comment, "This is certainly better." I was advised to write one more version to perfect my paper and pull up my grade.

I started another copy that night. Before coming to Tulane, I could not believe the things that a college student would do for an "A". Now I find that I am no exception.

My English professor assigned my second essay today. I get to pick from such topics as drunk driving, eating habits, and violence on television.

I wonder which one will be the easiest to live with. Maybe I will spare myself the trouble and jump from the window.

I just realized that I can't take a dive from Monroe [a Tulane dormitory] after all. I live in a room where the windows open a whole four inches … I have no choice but to write essay number two.

Tavel Cowan, a college freshman,
The Tulane Hullabaloo

• Questions for Discussion

1. Who is Tavel Cowan's intended audience? What mutual problem do they have to face?

2. Is this essay formal or informal? Explain. How do what Cowan says and what she quotes her professor as saying in the second paragraph differ in style? What makes the two styles different? Remember that the more formal style is the one most of you will be aiming for in college writing. How is style related to Ms. Cowan's persona?

3. What is Ms. Cowan worried about? Why? What is her purpose in writing? Is her advice helpful for dealing with the problem?

4. Is this a complaint, a report, or something else? Explain.

5. How long are the paragraphs in the essay? Does the paragraph length create a sense of the author's style? Is the paragraph length related to purpose?

6. What kind of progression or order unifies the details?

7. Summarize Cowan's main idea in one good sentence. What does doing so suggest about her teacher's criticism?

8. What can you learn from Cowan's experience?

Chapter 2: GENERATING CONTENT

Most of the basic material a writer works with is acquired before the age of fifteen.
— Willa Cather

If you would be a writer, first be a reader. Only through the assimilation of ideas, thoughts and philosophies can one begin to focus his own ideas, thoughts and philosophies.
— Allan W. Eckert

Don't think and then write it down. Think on paper. — Harry Kemelman

---

Methods for Generating Content
> Brainstorming
> Freewriting
> Looping
> Clustering
> Mapping
> Listing
> Asking Questions and Seeking Answers
> Observation and Inference
> A Discovery Frame
> Specific External Sources

Final Checklist

Writing Assignments

Application

Methods for Generating Content

Coming up with ideas is perhaps the hardest part of writing, so it helps to have some regular way or ways to get started. The content of a paper may be generated both internally and externally, depending on the topic. Some topics require no other sources than your internal ones: your personal opinions and experiences. Others require external sources to lend authoritative support for perceptions generated from internal sources. Still others require mainly external sources, especially when the topic is outside the realm of personal knowledge and personal experience.

The ability to notice—and to draw connections between what is noticed—is one of the most powerful intellectual gifts humans have. Note that on the chart the two categories of activity—generating and organizing information—reflect the two typical situations writers face when they sit down to write: "I don't know enough and need to collect more material," and "I have enough material (or even too much!) but don't know how to present it."

Generating ideas can be done in a number of ways. It is up to you, the writer, to experiment with these different ways to come up with ideas and then to continue to use those techniques which work best for you. The following are approaches that have worked for other writers.

- Brainstorming ┐
- Freewriting ┤ Generating Internal Information: Ideas, Feelings, Experiences
- Looping ┘
- Clustering ┐
- Mapping ┤ Generating and Organizing Internal Information
- Listing
- Asking Questions
- Observation and Inference ┤ Generating External Information: Facts and Observations
- Discovery Frame
- Specific External Sources ┘

BRAINSTORMING

To *brainstorm* means to think, to meditate, to concentrate, to come up with ideas and information from inside your own mind. The word "brainstorm" creates a picture of a mind engaged in great activity, an image of energy that is almost out of control; of mental force but also mental disorder. Brainstorming builds on discontinuity. The point is to use energy to create something new. Brainstorming begins the creative process with bursts of ideas that at first seem unrelated but which the mind explores, seeking order, relationships, and continuity.

The information you record while brainstorming might be from hearsay (what others have told you),

from past readings, from past classes, or from personal experience. It can be the basis for generalizations and for specific examples. This type of information makes what you write personal and therefore, may make it interesting or vivid or emotionally charged. Description, creative fiction, and light-hearted argumentation may be based mainly on material derived in this way. Nonetheless, it is not always the most effective type of content, because it requires the reader to trust your experience and your personal feelings. In order to brainstorm using more factual and "solid" information, you need to do research that will back up your subjective feelings, and then use brainstorming as a way to synthesize your readings and perceptions without relying on the order or emphasis of your sources.

FREEWRITING

The term *freewriting* does not mean "write on any topic you please," but it does mean write freely and continually on the topic you have chosen or have been assigned as a way of getting started. For a period of anywhere from ten to twenty minutes simply record whatever comes to mind as you consider the topic, and go in whatever different directions your thinking carries

you. Don't worry about grammar, punctuation, logical order, patterns of development, consistency or anything else. In fact, write anything that comes to mind as long as you keep writing.

The idea is that somehow, simply the necessity of writing continuously for a set period of time will break through any writer's block and help you to generate information that you can then use to help you get started on your topic. What you freewrite is by no means a paper, not even a rough draft of a paper, but it is a means of drawing on your internal resources to see what ideas you can come up with on your own. Freewriting means letting your imagination run free, and recording the associations and connections your brain automatically makes. In a way, it is like the free associations encouraged by psychologists to get to the root of a problem: tossing out words so the patient says whatever comes to mind first. In the case of freewriting, you are your own analyst tossing out ideas and free associating about them. The end result is a "stream of consciousness," a seemingly unplanned flow of ideas representing the ungoverned process of the human mind at work.

How does freewriting work? Suppose you have been assigned a paper on Native Americans; you know something about them but really haven't thought carefully about what you know. Your freewriting might begin as a list of what you remember from past experiences, maybe names of tribes and details remembered about them. The key is to record your every thought:

> Let's see Let's see, OK The Navajo, I remember seeing pictures of them herding sheep. Little girl holding a lamb—beautiful turquoise jewelry—rings, bracelets, necklaces, very valuable—still famous for craftsmanship. Pueblos made beautiful pottery, famous for clay, Indian motif rugs, lived in the southwest. In the east I remember the Iroquois from the French-Indian wars. They were tough, long rooms, communal. Didn't they have a legal code of some sort? Mohawk haircuts, running the gauntlet, frightening, Indians in a line clubbing and hitting outsiders who try to reach the end of the line alive. Oh yes, the movie "Last of the Mohicans"—Indians and settlers living together, helping each other;

others working like guerrilla soldiers attacking outposts for European friends. Shawnee, Apache, Comanche—like Geronimo FIERCE They all were fighting the cavalry, battle of the Little Big Horn was important—Indians killed General Custer—yellow hair.

Then the freewriting might move on to contrasting patterns of behavior expressed in disconnected sentences:

> Peaceful Navajo herdsmen, like Pueblo farmers, not at all warlike. It was the Apache and Comanche warriors who took scalps. The plains tribes hunted buffalo and wanted a lot of land. On reservations got guns to fight back, conflict in the Black Hills, 1970's there were still conflicts, armed confrontations with FBI.

However, a distraction might lead you to fix on types of dwellings:

> Fixed hogans, adobe cities in the sides of cliffs, teepees which could be packed up and moved quickly—still a modern sign of traveling efficiently.

This, in turn, might lead to a focus on the differences between tribes.

The more you write, the more you might begin to see patterns of ideas emerging, some of which will need to be discarded, others of which should be pursued. Freewriting assumes that you are dealing with a topic that you know something about; it also presupposes that a great deal of what is generated initially will later prove irrelevant to your final focus. If you have researched and studied a new, previously unfamiliar topic, freewriting is a way to synthesize and make personal what you have learned from reading a number of sources. Its focus is on writing continuity.

LOOPING

Looping simply means looking back at your mass of freewriting every so often, reading it, and trying to come up with a unifying generalization, a summary, or a category that you can use to guide your future freewriting. In other words, after freewriting for a short while, you look for key words or unifying concepts and then free associate again on the basis of these. Stop after a while, and then repeat the process. The idea is to begin to form a direction for your writing so that it becomes less and less "free" and more and more "directed."

For example, looking back at the freewriting on Native Americans, you might focus on any number of ideas:

1. Differences between tribes—aggressive vs. peaceful

2. Indians as friends and enemies during the French–Indian Wars

3. The Image of Indians in *The Last of the Mohicans*

4. Indian contributions to art

5. Modern conflicts with Indians

6. What their form of housing revealed about the values or lifestyle of a tribe.

You might then begin again with any one or two of these summary ideas to get you started thinking more about Native Americans.

- EXERCISE 2.1: FREEWRITING AND LOOPING

   A. Take ten minutes and write down everything you think of when you hear the word *homesick*. When you finish, look for any ideas or groups of ideas you could organize into a composition on homesickness. Write down some categories or summarize the key idea or ideas of your freewriting. What different directions could you explore? Use those categories or ideas to help you freewrite again, this time in more guided directions. Continue this process until you run out of ideas.

   B. The following is a series of details you might come up with when thinking about a topic. Give the paragraph a title which includes a descriptive adjective, and then describe the topic idea in one sentence. There may be more than one possible title and topic.

   Example: Eighteen hours of classes requiring a minimum of three hours study outside class for every hour in class, equals a minimum total of 48 out-of-class study hours per week. However, some classes require more than three hours of work outside class for every hour in class. For example, a three-credit-hour computer class might require 12 to 15 hours out-of-class work per week, and a class requiring library research will add more hours. Meeting with a composition teacher to discuss a returned paper or a future assignment takes more time, beyond the three-for-one rule, and often papers take much longer to write than a student expects.

   Title: "Minimum Study Time" (or "Inadequate Study Time")

   Topic Idea: Studying in college takes longer than people claim (or: The usual minimum estimated study time is inadequate).

   1. The cafeteria food here includes lots of potatoes and large pieces of beef or else macaroni and cheese dishes that seem very oily. Everything has butter in it or takes butter on it. There are no diet drinks available, only very sweet colas and sodas and orange drinks. Even the iced tea choice already has lots of sugar added. I feel like I weigh a ton after eating here, and have already gained five pounds.

      Title: _____

      Topic Idea: _____

      _____

   2. Oprah Winfrey spent part of her childhood in a very poor Milwaukee housing project. She ran away from home and got into trouble but finally straightened up and finished school. At 19 she was anchoring the news in Nashville; she was the first woman to do so; she was the first black to do so. She was a TV street reporter in Baltimore and

worked there seven years as she moved up the ladder of success. Today she is a household word, famous for her own controversial television show.

Title:_____

Topic Idea: _____

_____

3. Agatha Christie's Belgian detective, Hercule Poirot, automatically assumed that the families of murder victims or the police themselves would need and call for his help in difficult cases, and he was offended when they didn't. The harder and the more challenging the case, and the more baffled the police, the greater Poirot's pleasure in finding a solution and a killer. It pleased him most to explain to the Chief of the Detectives where the police logic had gone wrong and why Poirot's logic was right. He accused other people, even his assistants and associates, of not using their grey cells (their brains) or not even possessing them. He claimed that, with a little thought, he could solve even the seemingly impossible cases, and once did so without ever leaving his house.

Title:_____

Topic Idea: _____

_____

4. My dorm room is badly lighted and has dark wall paint; the tile floor is worn and uneven. Some dampness is making the paint peel and blister beneath the window. The view is not very good, since I am on the second floor and there is a parking garage across the way. During the night the plumbing in the walls makes constant noises. I am being charged the equivalent of the cost of a small apartment.

Title:_____

Topic Idea: _____

_____

5. The classroom has 30 student desks crowded together. The air conditioning is non-functioning. There are torn and wrinkled posters tacked on dirty walls. There is no chalk for the blackboards, which have been used many times without cleaning. The teacher drones on and on in a monotone voice. Most of the students are bored; some are sleeping.

Title:_____

Topic Idea: _____

_____

6. You should begin your preparation by attending class regularly, taking careful notes, and then comparing them with those of classmates. As you study, read the text with a pencil in your hand, marking key ideas and summary statements. In class, ask the teacher any questions you might have about lectures or readings that are unclear. Study daily, and think about how the readings and lectures apply to other situations. Discuss the ideas with classmates or friends. The night before a test, review the text and notes. Be sure to get a good night's rest. Get to class early with a couple of sharpened pencils, an eraser, and paper in hand. Be sure to ask the teacher any final problem questions before the test begins.

Title:_____

Topic Idea: _____

_____

CLUSTERING

Cluster means to fit together loosely in a group, as in, "There was a cluster of people waiting outside the movie theater." In prewriting terminology, *clustering* is a type of free-association listing. It begins with a <u>core word</u>, a word that acts as a mental stimulus to make the writer come up with related terms that branch out from the center term. One term leads to another and another to create a complex network of diverse ideas, all related back in some way to the core stimulus word. For example, the term *homesickness* might immediately lead you to branch off in two directions with the words *home* and *sickness*. *Home* might make you think of parents and family, brothers and sisters, your mother's home cooking, your father's earnest lectures, your sister's constant questions, your brother's messy room. *Sickness* might make you think of symptoms like headaches, dull pain in the stomach, and lack of sleep, or it might make you think of cures like rest, vitamins, and cheery phone conversations with loved ones.

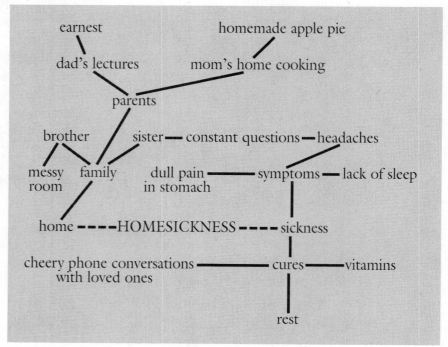

Jotted down as a cluster, these ideas might look like the above chart.

Look back at your freewriting assignment on "homesickness." Does clustering provide ideas for different directions you could go? "What a homesick person misses" could form one organizing category, and how that missing expresses itself could form another that, in turn, could be subdivided into "symptoms" and "cures." In other words, clustering is a good way to generate general unifying categories (abstractions) as well as a way to come up with specific support (details).

MAPPING

Mapping is very similar to clustering, but clustering is more directed, while mapping begins as more free-form association. Basically, mapping means jotting down key words and phrases in any order as they pop into your mind. When your words fill a page, stop and look for clusters or groups that go together, interlocking them with connective lines that <u>map out</u> relationships. The next step in mapping is for you the writer to become your own reader and to ask the sort of questions you would expect your intended audience to ask about the mapped words—questions that will probably lead to more information. Someone who is mapping might come up with the same terms as those which appear in the example on clustering, but the terms might be disordered and random and would have to be mapped out after the listing had stopped. The following is a typical free association list:

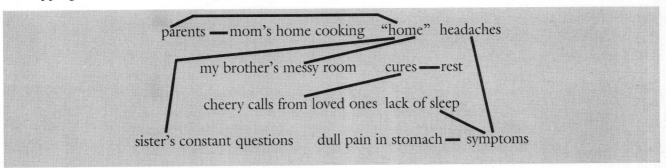

parents   mom's home cooking   "home" headaches

my brother's messy room   cures   rest

cheery calls from loved ones lack of sleep

sister's constant questions   dull pain in stomach   symptoms

Mapping would involve drawing lines to interconnect ideas:

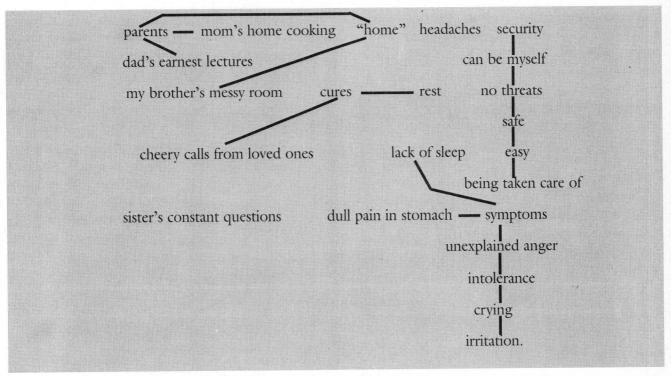

parents —— mom's home cooking   "home" headaches

my brother's messy room   cures —— rest

cheery calls from loved ones lack of sleep

sister's constant questions   dull pain in stomach —— symptoms

The interconnecting lines might lead to lists of more symptoms and more details of what one misses from home:

parents —— mom's home cooking   "home" headaches   security

dad's earnest lectures   can be myself

my brother's messy room   cures —— rest   no threats

safe

cheery calls from loved ones   lack of sleep   easy

being taken care of

sister's constant questions   dull pain in stomach —— symptoms

unexplained anger

intolerance

crying

irritation.

Studying this new map might also lead to more ideas about how to deal with homesickness:

1. Make an effort to make new friends
2. Concentrate on studies
3. Work harder
4. Find out about getting a host family.

In other words, mapping is yet another way to stimulate the mental activity necessary to building a paper and an argument.

• EXERCISE 2.2: CLUSTERING AND MAPPING

• EXERCISE 2.2: CLUSTERING AND MAPPING

Freewrite or list information on one of the following words or phrases. Then cluster and/or map your efforts to stimulate your exploration of your topic.

home cooking	drug abuse	racism
Disneyland	jogging	cheating
urban violence	high school good times	clothing fads
campus activities	how to make new friends	dormitory life

LISTING

Listing is another way to try to generate ideas from inside your own mind, only instead of writing out sentences about whatever comes to mind, you make lists of related ideas. The goal is the same as that of freewriting, but the method is to use fewer words, lists of words rather than sentences, and to begin to create categories by listing things that belong together. For example, thinking about American Indians might lead to lists of tribes, famous battles, contributions to the English language, contributions to American culture, types of homes, levels of civilization, legal codes, various types of art, romantic images, examples of mistreatment, and so forth. At some point, a mental breakthrough should occur, as you realize, for instance, that "legal codes," "art," "romantic images" and "contributions to the English language" might all fit together under the overall heading of "contributions to American culture." At this point your lists will have helped provide a direction for your paper, in this case, a focus on what the Indians have contributed to the U.S.A. Often, you might begin with freewriting as a way of discovering a topic by stimulating the mind and memory. Simply waiting for inspiration about a topic is too passive—a writer *writes* to make something happen!

The next step might be to use lists to generate *linear* information, that is, to form groups of facts, ideas, and perceptions that relate to one another in a logical way. Many writers feel that compiling lists helps them think of more new information. Notice that this technique involves setting up general categories and then enumerating specific details under each category. It is good preparation for making an outline. Listing is also a very effective way to compare or contrast because you can make three columns, one for one side of the comparison, one for the other, and then down the middle a list of what they share or what they have in common. The Unit Two chapter on comparison-contrast (page 296) has a model of this form of listing: Panama vs. Louisiana.

• EXERCISE 2.3: LISTING

Culture shock is a feeling experienced by many who travel abroad and encounter an alien culture or by those who leave home for the first time and experience a lifestyle very different from the one they grew up in. Make a series of lists that will help you think about culture shock. You might consider the signs of culture shock, the effects of culture shock, the types of things that shock, the reasons they shock, and so forth. Compare your lists with those of your classmates. Did you focus on similar ideas or go in different directions? How difficult would it be, once you have completed your list, to write a paper on culture shock? Do your lists provide a good basis for further discussion? Choose the list you feel you have the most experience with and turn it into an effective paragraph. What kinds of information must you add to your list to do so?

ASKING QUESTIONS AND SEEKING ANSWERS

One technique many writers find useful is to write down a series of *questions* and then seek the *answers*. Journalists, in fact, almost always begin with a series of questions as the way to organize their stories: Who? What? When? Where? How? Why? So what? Since journalists are professional writers who must write daily, you might benefit from their strategy. For example, your paper on culture shock might lead you to ask questions like the ones in the box on the right.

Now look back at your assignments on "freewriting" and "listing." Do these questions stimulate more ideas that might be useful on those assignments? What questions could you ask to help you extend your mapped out clusters from the previous assignment?

1. What is "culture shock"?
2. Why "culture"?
3. Why "shock"?
4. When does it occur?
5. What causes it?
6. How can you recognize it?
7. What are its symptoms?
8. Is it physical or psychological or both?
9. Who gets it?
10. Can it be treated? If so, how?

OBSERVATION AND INFERENCE

You can make the information produced by techniques like those above seem more reliable by basing your judgments or arguments on specific observations and on inferences made from those observations. For example, if you are describing a picture, looking closely at it with a pencil in your hand, and writing down precisely what you see—colors, shapes, forms, figures, relationships, style, etc.—as well as what you infer—the painter's artistic purpose, his school of art, meaning, or significance—you are going beyond what is traditionally called "brainstorming" and are responding to external phenomena in order to generate information.

This type of observation and inference is central to most English classes in which you have to read an essay or a piece of literature, observe it closely, make inferences and judgments about it, and then write an analysis based on personal understanding and critical thinking. For example, if you are thinking about writing about the effects of the feminist movement on social manners, you might sit at a busy public entranceway and observe the patterns of door opening, watching carefully to see whether the men open the doors for the ladies or vice versa or whether men and women open the doors for themselves and what rules of politeness are observed. Your observations could form the basis for an interesting and convincing paper, but you could not simply record what you see. Instead you would need to set up some general categories to distinguish between different types of behavior and some generalizations or inferences to make clear what such behavior indicates. Together, the specific observations and the general inferences make for good writing.

A DISCOVERY FRAME

If you turn to the discussion of "Christina's World" in the Unit Two chapter on description (page 169), you will see a typical discovery frame for a description. It is a guide to use in seeking information of a particular type. In effect, you list the key types of information you need to write your paper, and then you go out and find the answers as best you can. A book report form is typical of the discovery frame:

```
                          Book Title: _____
Author              Author's Dates        Author's Place of Origin
Type of book
Dates action occurs
Setting
Key characters
Brief plot summary
Major themes
Evaluation
Recommendation
Other
```

Clearly, the frame provides a list of what information the reader wants or needs. Some discovery frames are "ready made," at least in their general outline: A book report must include most of the information listed above. Other "culturally determined" frames include a film critique, a restaurant review in a newspaper or guidebook, or the evaluation of a consumer product or business machine, such as a personal computer.

While serving the same function as the ready-made models, other discovery frames must be invented by the individual writer to generate questions about a particular topic. In these cases, a writer tries to assure complete coverage of a topic by means of an appropriate frame, particularly if the pattern will be repeated with a series of examples.

SPECIFIC EXTERNAL SOURCES

For college and for business writing it is sometimes best to use the authority of *external sources*, such as statistics, experts, and professional documents. In fact, many college assignments will require external sources; besides, sources beyond your own experiences give your writing greater credibility and greater authority. External sources may include authorities whom you interview, surveys, questionnaires, discussions with other people, government documents, encyclopedias and other reference books, books in general, journals, magazines, films, recordings, maps, professors—wherever information is available outside yourself. Even if teachers don't require such research, it is often useful and lends authority to what would otherwise be personal opinion.

For example, in the case of the paper describing a painting, the student who finds out something about the artist's background and usual style of painting (themes and techniques), something about the artistic school from which this painting derives, something about the historical time period, and critical commentaries by art experts, will be better able to convince readers that his or her judgment and inferences are reliable. In fact, the student will probably make more reliable inferences and judgments and have a better eye for observation because of the extra authority and information found from external sources. However, it is probably best not to start with such external sources until you have discovered your own direction and purpose. Otherwise, the ideas and patterns and logic of your sources might get in the way of generating your own argument. However, once you have your argument clear in your own mind, such sources are a good way to get specific data to back up your generalizations. The Unit Three chapter on summary and documentation (pages 425–448) will provide further advice about using sources.

In conclusion, freewriting, listing, general brainstorming, posing questions, constructing a discovery frame, and drawing on past observations and inferences are good methods for drawing on internal sources to generate ideas and information. Looping, clustering, mapping and drawing new inferences, in turn, help you organize your information and redirect your focus. Reporter's questions and discovery frames focus observation, reading and research. Together, internal and external sources allow you to gather and generate information and ideas to form generalizations that will best communicate with a particular audience. Notice that, while we have listed these methods as ten separate and distinct categories for ease of explanation, in the actual composing process writers will use several methods at the same time, as they do research, brainstorm about what they have learned, compose lists of supporting details, cluster or map their ideas, and so on. A good writer uses all the tools available, juggling them as the nature of the task changes.

- ## EXERCISE 2.4: DISCOVERY FRAMES

   Change the book report frame on page 37 to make it suitable for gathering information about a film. Then set up a frame for the evaluation of a personal computer or automobile. How do the frames differ? Choose one of the topics you have dealt with already in this chapter and create a discovery frame for it. For example, for a paper on campus activities, you might have categories for number of activities, types of activities, number of participants in activities, functions of activities, nature of support (faculty, administration, religious group, business group, etc.), value of activities, and so forth.

Juggling Available Materials

Final Checklist

☐ Have you made good use of your internal sources of information to generate ideas by brainstorming your topic? Freewriting? Listing?

☐ Have you looked for groups of ideas and categories that can help you discover major organizing principles through looping, clustering, and mapping?

☐ Have you made personal observations wherever possible?

☐ Have you developed a discovery frame or asked questions to help you pinpoint what type of information you need to think about or find?

☐ Have you explored external sources of information, including library research (in the card catalog, on the library computer systems, in guides to periodicals, in encyclopedias and almanacs) and interviews with experts or with people who have experienced what you will write about?

☐ Are your books and journals recent? Are they biased in some way or are they reliable?

••Writing Assignments

A. Briefly but clearly summarize the methods of generating information discussed above. Do not simply write one sentence for each method; rather, group together methods which seem to share common approaches. In other words, apply what you have learned about organizing information to organizing this summary.

B. A famous writer, E.B. White, says that a writer is like "a gunner, sometimes waiting in his blind [a place to hide while hunting animals] for something to come in, sometimes roaming the countryside hoping to scare something up." Use what you have learned about the writing process from this chapter to help explain what White means.

C. Use the sample lists on "homesickness" and "culture shock" (pages 35 and 37) as a starting point for generating your own essay on one of these two interrelated topics. Consider audience and purpose in narrowing your focus and selecting your organizing principles.

D. Select an American movie to critique. Whether you view it in a theater or on video, remember that seeing the movie more than once will allow you to be more specific in your description and analysis.

   Create a film discovery frame and use it to brainstorm. You might want to include in it what you liked best/least about the film, what others might value, and your recommendation.

In your paper, explain to a friend why he or she will/will not enjoy this film. Provide three good reasons with explanation. Do not use outside sources. Base your critique only on the information in your discovery frame.

E. You would like to move out of the dormitory or your parent's home and into an apartment so that you can have more freedom. However, you must write a letter persuading your parents to support and finance such a move. Should you focus on your real reason for wanting to move? Brainstorm about your parents' values and concerns. List some reasons for moving that would appeal to those values. Use clustering and mapping to help arrange your ideas into a logical sequence and then write a persuasive personal letter to them on this topic. Exchange your letter with a classmate to brainstorm about what will or won't work with parents.

Application

The "classroom politeness" survey that follows is to assist you in brainstorming about some basic American college classroom values. As you read it, ask yourself which of the following behaviors are polite and correct for a classroom in your country and which are impolite or at least not correct. After each item, briefly write your reaction. Then, since U.S. or college standards may be different from what you are used to, discuss them with your classmates and instructors to get different perspectives and most particularly, a U.S. college classroom perspective. Write a paragraph based on your discoveries.

Classroom Politeness Survey

1. The teacher enters the class at 8:55 for a 9:00 class. The students in the class continue talking to each other. _____
2. The teacher enters the class at 9:01 for a 9:00 class. The students in the class continue talking to each other. _____
3. A student drinks a cup of coffee in class. _____
4. A student eats a bag of potato chips in class. _____
5. A student eats two eggs, bacon, orange juice, and toast in class. _____
6. The teacher sits on the desk, _____
   smokes a cigarette, _____
   drinks a soft drink. _____
7. The teacher calls a student by her first name. _____
8. The student calls the teacher by his first name. _____
9. The student calls the teacher, "Teacher." _____
10. The teacher says a student's wrong answer is stupid. _____
11. The teacher and a student get in a heated argument about politics. _____
12. The teacher and a student get in a heated argument about philosophy. _____
13. A student walks out of the classroom without asking permission or catching the teacher's eye. _____

14. A teacher tells stories about his personal life, stories unrelated to the subject of the class. _____

15. A teacher tells stories about his personal life, stories related to the subject of the class. _____

16. When the bell rings for the end of the class, the students stop listening and walk out on the teacher. _____

17. The bell ending class rang ten minutes ago and the teacher is still talking. Students walk out. _____

18. During a lecture, a student asks a question about his grade on a paper. _____

19. The teacher has begun to lecture and a student walks up to the desk to turn in a paper. _____

20. The teacher has not appeared for class seven minutes after it was supposed to start. The students begin to leave. _____

21. A student arrives seven minutes late and walks in through the door at the front of the class. _____

22. A student makes an appointment with a teacher to meet in the teacher's office. There is a rainstorm and the student cannot make the appointment. What should she do? _____

23. The teacher asks a question and a student cannot answer. Another student joins in to respond. _____

24. No one in the class is responding, so one student tries to answer every question the teacher asks. _____

25. A teacher has given an assignment to be done in class. A student has already done it at home, so he simply reads a magazine. _____

26. A male student wears no shirt to class because the weather is hot. _____

Chapter 3: ORGANIZING YOUR MATERIALS

What [a writer] knows is almost always a matter of the relationships he establishes, between example and generalization, between one part of a narrative and the next, between the idea and the counteridea that the writer sees is also relevant. — Roger Safe

Although, after following all of the instructions in Chapter 1 and 2, you may feel prepared to write, in fact, there are two more key prewriting steps. These steps involve organizing the materials that you have collected from either internal or external sources or both. Listing, clustering, and mapping should have helped you come up with different levels of information that you could use in your paper, some general, some specific. Such processes may even have helped you decide on your key ideas or categories for organizing your paper. However, the *thesis statement* and the *outline* help you come to more definite terms with that organization. This means taking what was simply a list of key points and determining their relationship, their importance, and the arrangement that will best present your ideas to your readers.

Whether you choose to outline first or write your thesis statement first is really a personal decision and will often vary with your familiarity with or involvement in the topic. Both provide a basic plan or direction for the paper.

If you are not very familiar with your topic, do not have a strong opinion about it, or are unsure of exactly what you want to say, it is probably best to begin by developing an outline. Doing so provides a way of experimenting with your argument until you feel confident enough about it to formulate a thesis. It allows you to consider and then reconsider significances and relationships, to rearrange, to discard, to merge, and to change your argument as you develop your outline. Once the outline has been completed to your satisfaction, then it will be easy to write the statement of your main idea, your thesis statement.

On the other hand, if you have the direction, purpose, and argument of your paper clearly in mind, you might prefer to begin with a thesis statement that sums up your key argument. That statement can then form the basic argument and suggest patterns for writing your outline. It will guide the overall topic and the particular divisions that you plan to develop. This chapter will start with thesis sentences and then discuss outlines.

WRITING A THESIS SENTENCE

What a Thesis Sentence Is

The <u>thesis sentence</u> may be the most difficult sentence you write in the whole paper, because it contains your best statement of topic and argument and your plans for developing that argument. A good thesis sentence is a general statement about what your main ideas are, how they are related, and why they are significant; it should be relatively specific and concrete. A good thesis must always be a complete sentence; usually it is in statement, not question, form. Every word should count; no elements unrelated to the central focus of the paper should be included. It sets the limits of your topic, clarifies the direction and purpose of the paper, and provides some indication of your attitude toward your subject. In other words, a good thesis sentence is restricted, unified, and specific, though not, of course, as specific as the body of the paper.

The grammatical techniques of subordination and parallelism are very important in an effective thesis, just as they are in outlining, for they help a thesis sentence fit a great deal of information into a short space. Usually a thesis sentence will list ideas in a sequence (_parallelism_) or will emphasize one idea as major and another as related but less significant (_subordination_). The thesis statement should include key words to suggest these relationships of ideas. The following words are very commonly used in thesis sentences:

- _first... then..., later..._ (to indicate a time sequence)
- _In the beginning..., but finally..._ (also for a time sequence)
- _because of _____, _____, and _____
  or
- _as a result of _____, _____, and _____.
  (to indicate cause/effect relationships).

Subordination (_sub_ means "under," "below," or "lesser"; _ord_ is related to order) means indicating through means of sentence structure that one idea is of less importance than another idea. For example, in the following sentence the punctuation, the semi-colon, indicates that the two pieces of information are of equal significance: _The presidential debates were important; they revealed a great deal about the character of the opponents._ Even if the semi-colon is changed to _for_, the information is still coordinated or equal in significance (_co_ means equal): _The presidential debates were important, for they revealed a great deal about the character of the opponents (and, so, and but are other common coordinators)._ However, if you use a subordinating word or phrase like _because, since, on account of the fact that,_ you are saying that whatever goes with that word or phrase is less important: _The presidential debates were important because they revealed a great deal about the character of the opponents._ If you shorten the clause (with a subject _they_ and a verb _revealed_) to a prepositional phrase by substituting a noun for the verb form, you reduce the significance in the sentence even more: _The presidential debates were important because of their significant character revelations._ In the sentence _The presidential debates were important,_ changing the phrasing to _The important presidential debates changed the minds of many voters_ subordinates the idea of _important._ In other words, any type of grammatical change that reduces the importance of an idea in a sentence is a form of subordination. _Although_ and _because_ are the most common thesis subordinators, with _although_ setting up a contrast and often preparing for an argument, and _because_ setting up a cause/effect argument to be dominated by reasons.

Coordination is also central to good thesis writing because it allows you to make a list of <u>equally important</u> information. Coordination can involve patterns like *either... or..., neither... nor..., not only... but also...* or words in a list which follow the same grammatical pattern and are connected by commas. Parallelism is almost identical to coordination, but does not make the sort of contrast you see in a phrase like, *Not only did he attack his program, but he also attacked his personal integrity.*

Parallelism allows a writer to set up a series of equal and related ideas. If your topic is "presidential debates" and your goal is to explain their significance, your method might be to give several reasons for this significance; such reasons might be expressed in a parallel sequence like the one which follows: *The important presidential debates changed the minds of many voters because of their focus on key campaign issues and their significant revelations of character, motive, intellect, and values.* This thesis indicates two major divisions: *their focus on key campaign issues* and *their significant revelations.* However, the section on *significant revelations* is further subdivided into four concerns: *character, motive, intellect,* and *values.* If your thesis contains a phrase like *as follows,* or a noun which will be developed by a parallel list, the connecting punctuation is usually a colon: *The important presidential debates changed the minds of many voters for several reasons: their personalizing of the candidates, their focus on key campaign issues, and their significant revelations of character, motive, intellect, and values.*

The thesis statement gives a basic plan for the paper. A paper based on the following thesis sentence —*Reading about farm work and doing it are two totally different experiences, because farm work is too close to nature to be romantic; it is dirty, backbreaking, and dehumanizing*—will begin with a paragraph presenting romanticized or idealized pictures of farm work, and then will proceed to discredit or disprove this view by focusing on what is dirty about farm work, exactly what makes it backbreaking, and how it is dehumanizing. In other words, the thesis sentence tells readers that there are four divisions, with the first one minor, introductory, and in contrast to the other three, which are major and which comprise the body of the paper. Readers also know that the writer's attitude is negative and that the plan of development will be descriptive. The thesis, in effect, makes us expect a paper plan like the following:

I. Introduction
    A. Idealistic pictures of farm work
    B. vs. reality

II. Farm work is dirty
    A. Example or evidence
    B. Example or evidence

III. Farm work is backbreaking
    A. Example or evidence
    B. Example or evidence

IV. Farm work is dehumanizing
    A. Example or evidence
    B. Example or evidence

All good thesis sentences are this informative and should suggest a skeleton outline. If they aren't and don't, they need more work.

The thesis sentence does not have to begin the essay; in fact, it may not even appear in your paper (though most college professors probably expect it to). Usually, however, it is the first or last sentence of your introductory paragraph. Wherever it is, it should be used as a guideline, a model to follow as you write your paper. It should be very clear, precise, compact, and well-organized. Even if your thesis sentence does not appear in the paper, writing it is basic to prewriting and usually a near-final step before writing a <u>rough draft</u> (a first version of your paper). A carefully written thesis sentence will help you keep your paper organized by forcing you to put your central idea into words and to set limits on how far it extends. It is an absolutely necessary step for any writer who wants a disciplined and controlled approach to writing. It is a pact with the reader: a commitment to deal with a specific topic in a specific way so that the reader can predict the pattern and plan of the paper. When the body of a paper does not meet the expectations created by the thesis, then the writer must either rewrite the body or rewrite the thesis to make it set up the expectations that the paper does meet.

Thesis Commitments

The following sentences make clear the types of commitments thesis sentences make.

1. Westerners do not understand why meditation has such positive effects, but we do know that, for many people, it is a way to recharge inner batteries and cope with conflict, confusion, pain, and emotional upset.

   Topic: Meditation

   Main Focus: Its positive effects

   Method: Proof it recharges inner batteries and helps one cope

2. An accident victim in a state of shock (cold, clammy skin, irregular breathing, rapid pulse, dilated pupils, weakness, thirst), needs prompt treatment to prevent heart arrest and death.

   Topic: Shock

   Main Focus: Treatment needed

   Minor Focus: Results of lack of treatment

   Method: A process report on steps to follow

3. Norway's giving the American President, "Rough Rider" and enthusiastic hunter and militant, Theodore Roosevelt a Nobel Peace Prize in 1906 for arbitrating the end of the Russo-Japanese War was a purely political act made to win U.S. support for the newly independent country.

   Topic: The 1906 Nobel Peace Prize given to Theodore Roosevelt

   Main Focus: Its political nature

   Method: A study of the behind-the-scenes politics that motivated this act

   Purpose: To prove the decision had nothing to do with peace or merit

4. Famous for claiming that he could single-handedly move the world if he had a lever long enough and a prop strong enough, Archimedes (287 B.C.-212 B.C.) was so far in advance of his age that the principles he enunciated were not accepted or practiced until seventeen centuries after his death.

   Topic: Archimedes

   Main Focus: His innovative mind

   Method: Give examples of his advanced principles and references to when they finally became accepted.

5. Although some students find their first few months of college depressing and lonely, many others discover the excitement and pleasure of challenging new ideas and viewpoints.

   Topic: Student reactions to the first months of college

   Main Focus: The excitement and pleasure of challenging new ideas and viewpoints

   Method: Contrast in introduction between negative reactions and positive; development of body with description and examples of the challenges of college and what makes them exciting and pleasurable.

• EXERCISE 3.1: ANALYZING THESIS STATEMENTS

What information about the topics do the following thesis statements provide? What <u>kind</u> of information do they provide? What expectations do they create about their development? What are the writers' attitudes toward their topics? Which information is parallel? Which is subordinated?

1. To succeed in an American university, an ESL student must adapt to the new language, the new customs, and the new university system.

2. Although homesickness produces both physical and psychological symptoms, this "illness" can be cured by time and by a series of conscious actions aimed at easing adjustment pains.

3. Culture shock results, in part, from changes in the physical details of daily life (food, climate, altitude) but more importantly from changes in the patterns of social behavior, value systems, and philosophies.

4. The Supreme Court of the United States has two key functions: to interpret questionable laws and executive actions and to determine and rule on whether or not they conform to the U.S. Constitution.

5. Although theater in the United States has been strongly influenced by European drama, the musical is truly American in origin and in nature.

6. Famous American architect Frank Lloyd Wright rejected traditional design in favor of simplicity and unity of form and function.

7. Living in Los Angeles has made me understand what Constantinos Doxiadis meant when he said, "Americans may have the best skyscrapers and highways, but they also have the worst cities in the world": L.A. lacks a real center, a sense of community, a likeable personality.

   (What does the colon indicate about the relationship of the last clause to the first part of the sentence?)

8. Gun control laws must be enacted soon: to protect citizens from themselves and each other and to reduce the soaring death rates from both accidental and intentional shootings.

• EXERCISE 3.2: WRITING THESIS SENTENCES

Choose five of the following and write a thesis sentence

1. which contrasts your favorite food with the food served locally.
2. which explains why you think a certain movie is worth seeing or not worth seeing.
3. which advises a friend about what to do or see in some interesting tourist spot.
4. which recommends a good book and explains what makes it good or valuable reading.
5. which warns a friend about what to watch out for when he or she first comes to the United States/to New York/to any crime-ridden city.
6. which warns Americans about which gestures or what body language to be careful about or to avoid in your country or among your ethnic group.[for example, patting someone on the head in Japan or pointing a finger at someone in Indonesia]
7. which explains how to do something.
8. which defines your nationality or the people of the area you are from (e.g., Latin American, Mid-Eastern, Asian).
9. which explains the development of some business or program or system (how it began, what changes it went through, how it is now, what it will be like in the future).
10. which compares some aspect of the educational system of your country with that of the United States or the system used in one region with the system used in another.

What a Thesis Sentence Is Not

A thesis sentence is a sentence, not a title. You cannot write a good paper title and expect it to be sufficient to inform your readers of what lies ahead in your paper. A title such as, "The Rewards of Using Computer Word Processing" gives us a preview of the paper, but it is not a thesis. The difference is not just decorative, but functional. A title identifies and/or announces; a thesis makes a claim that something is true. A thesis for the computer paper would need to be stated as an assertion of belief and purpose: *The rewards of using computer word processing are multiple: efficiency, neatness, and speed, but also better control of logic and organization and a personal sense of achievement unmatched by handwritten work.* What thesis sentences do the following titles suggest?

- My Annoying Apartment
- AIDS Testing in the Workplace
- Hurricanes: Nightmare Winds

A thesis sentence is not a general announcement of topic, and therefore it should not begin, *I am going to talk about…, My thesis sentence is…, Let me tell you…, I want to share some ideas with you about …, My subject is…, This paper will attempt to tell you about…, The topic of my theme is….* Such lead-ins, along with phrases like *I believe, I think,* and *I am pretty sure that,* are unnecessary fillers which distract from your focus on an idea or an argument. You may automatically write this way to get started, but you should cut out such phrases in any revision.

Finally, a thesis is not simply a statement of fact; if it were, there would be no reason to write a paper about it. A definition, a statistic, or a quotation might be interesting, but they do not provide the direction for an argument that is basic to a thesis. Giving readers the height of Mount St. Helens or the number of times it has erupted is not the equivalent of a thesis; instead, a thesis will present an argumentative direction and focus: *The last eruption of Mount St. Helens indicates the need for safety guidelines for local residents.* (*Argumentative* here means "arguing for or against a position.") This thesis leads readers to expect the rest of the paper to enumerate guidelines and the reasons they are needed.e toward the topic, the major divisions of the paper, and an indication of the intended method for organizing or developing the argument.

- ## EXERCISE 3.3: WHAT THESIS SENTENCES TELL US

Which of the following are thesis statements and which are not? Underline the key words of each thesis and explain the projected paper's focus, organization, length, and purpose.

1. Cigarettes are not only costly in terms of purchase price but also in terms of health and social interaction.
2. Alfred Hitchcock's famous movie *Shadow of a Doubt* contrasts the dull but admirable virtues of small town life with the exciting but murderous vices of a big city villain.
3. I really liked the Mel Gibson movie version of *Hamlet*.
4. Students starting college should realize the importance of academic achievement, of not carrying more courses than they can handle well, of attending class regularly, and of pacing their studying.
5. I will discuss the relationship between reading ability and success in life.
6. In recent years, the sex education of school children has become a political concern in my town.
7. Success of the Zero Population movement will insure better living conditions, more food, less pollution—a more comfortable future—but failure might well mean the total destruction of the human race.
8. "To be or not to be" is a famous quote from Shakespeare.
9. Reading a daily newspaper will help prepare one for college classes by expanding vocabulary, by encouraging reading skills, and by providing a cultural background necessary to interpret conflicts and issues, the discussion of which is so important to the American classroom.
10. Why was Abraham Lincoln assassinated?

Judging Thesis Sentences

Notice that the original sentences in the following examples are not really thesis statements whereas the revisions are. How do the originals and the revisions differ? As you read, look for a statement of topic, words which reveal the writer's attitude toward the topic, the major divisions of the paper, and an indication of the intended method for organizing or developing the argument.

What is wrong with the original versions of these openings? What makes the revisions better? What do each of the above thesis sentences tell you about the paper that will be based on them: the general topic or central focus of the paper, the authors' attitudes, the divisions of the paper, the probable length of the paper, the plan for development?

Original: I don't like my apartment house.

Revision: The most annoying features of my apartment house are an overly-efficient air conditioner, malfunctioning showers, and a main lobby packed with leering, staring men.

Original: I sincerely and wholeheartedly believe that AIDS testing doesn't belong in the workplace.

Revision: AIDS testing should not be required for new employees because it is an invasion of privacy and because it leads to discrimination in the workplace, both by fellow employees and by managers and employers.

Original: A hurricane can be a real nightmare.

Revision: Hurricane Andrew's 1992 devastation of southern Florida provides a terrifying image of how unexpectedly destructive a hurricane can be in terms of property, individual lives, and the life of a community.

Original: I am going to discuss Baldwin's discussion of racial hatred that affected his family.

Revision: James Baldwin's main concern, in his essay "Notes of a Native Son," is the injustice which produces hatred, a hatred which destroyed his father, threatened his own life, and would eventually frustrate his new-born sister.

Original: The population of Korea is not growing as fast as it used to.

Revision: The rate of population growth in Korea has changed several times over the past twenty-five years because of the war with the North in the early 1950's, the increasing industrialization of the country, and the various government measures to control growth.

Integrating the Thesis Sentence with Audience and Purpose

A good thesis sentence should take into consideration your audience and purpose. The chart in Exercise 3.4 illustrates this principle.

• EXERCISE 3.4: AUDIENCE AND PURPOSE IN THE THESIS SENTENCE

Fill in the blanks in this chart with appropriate information.

* *

Subject	Audience	Purpose	Thesis
Moving into an apartment	Parents	To persuade parents	Being allowed to move into an apartment would save you money, teach me adult responsibilities, and provide the peace and quiet I need to study well.
Rude treatment	Store manager	To complain about bad treatment	When I tried to return damaged merchandise, your store salesclerk not only refused to recognize my complaint but treated me rudely and insultingly.
Schizophrenia	Psychology students	To inform readers about this psychological phenomenon	Schizophrenia is a puzzling mental disease, with easily identifiable characteristics but less easily identifiable causes or cures.
_____	_____	_____	Hideyoshi Toyotomi was one of the most important political figures of sixteenth–century Japan because he united feuding groups under one government after a turbulent hundred-year civil war.
Cars	_____	_____	_____
_____	Classmates	_____	_____
_____	_____	To give warnings	_____

ORGANIZING THROUGH AN OUTLINE

Once you have limited your topic, you also have limited the number of parts you must organize. Clustering and mapping, in particular, help you find out whether your topic has some natural organization of its own which you can follow. If you are writing a summary, following the original organization of whatever you are summarizing will probably be best. If your topic involves a narrative, a progression of events, a his-tory, a process, or a time sequence, it is easy to follow that original organization. However, in these cases, you must ask yourself whether the time order will allow you to make your key argument as forcefully as you need to or whether some other pattern might ultimately prove more effective. If you are writing a speculation or a per-sonal evaluation, you may find you can organize by cause and effect or reason and result:

Topic: The consequences of population rising at its present rate

By the year 2100, there will not be enough resources

    I. land

    II. air

    III. water

    IV. food

    V. energy

If you are writing an analysis (breaking something into parts to study them) or a synthesis (interrelating information to create connections and an overview), you may have more of a challenge. This is because you must decide what the major parts are and in what order they should be described.

Whatever organizational pattern you work with, it helps to decide what general <u>categories</u> to use before considering specific supportive details. The following are some typical possibilities, possibilities that vary with audience, purpose, and content:

<u>Sample Categories for Organizing an Analysis of Different Brands of Tools:</u>

    Appearance (what each tool looks like)

    Function (the purpose of each tool)

    Importance (most important quality to least important or vice versa)

    Use (how to use each tool)

    Cost (most expensive tool to least expensive or vice versa)

    Frequency (most commonly used, least commonly used)

    Reliability (which lasts longer)

<u>Sample Categories for Organizing a Paper Describing a Friend:</u>

    Physical characteristics

    Style of dress

    Style of behavior/manners

    Education

    Interests

    Family Background

    Personal History

There are probably as many categories as there are things to describe, but thinking about what general category best describes your topic should help.

What an Outline Is

A good outline makes clear the broad, general categories to be developed and the main, specific details to support, explain, prove, or develop those general categories and ideas. It sets up in a clear, skeletal way the essential divisions or arguments of a paper and the evidence intended to support each section. Its basic pattern is from general to specific, from abstract to concrete. In that way, it helps a writer think through and work and rework a plan of action before actually writing out a paper. Once an outline has been prepared, the actual writing should be very easy; this is because the outline reflects the thinking and planning and organizing, all of which comprise the structural <u>bones</u> of the paper.

For example, in the previous chapter the clustering exercise with the term "homesickness" could form a good basis for an outline of a paper meant to define that term. Here is the clustering list:

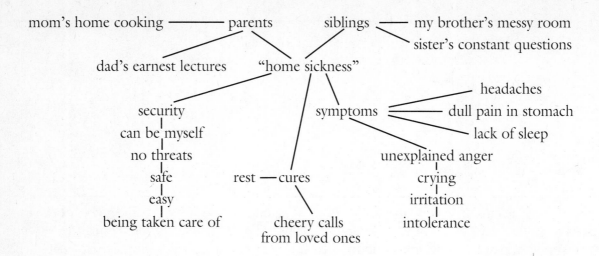

This list is without a spine, a backbone, a skeleton to hold it together; it is like a "blob" of flesh that cannot stand up on its own. However, given this information, it would be easy to give this blob shape and form, to develop a skeleton through outlining. In this case, the two main categories might focus on the two key parts of the core word: 1) How the word home contributes to our understanding of homesickness and 2) How the word sickness contributes to our understanding of homesickness. These categories could in turn be broken down into key elements of family and security and of symptoms and cures with a supportive list. The following outline might grow out of this cluster:

I. How the word "home" contributes to our understanding of "homesickness"
   A. Family
     1. Parents
      a. Mom's home cooking and sympathetic ear
      b. Dad's earnest lectures and desire to help
     2. Siblings
      a. Brother's messy room that makes me feel comfortable and superior
      b. Sister's constant questions that look to me for guidance and wisdom
   B. Security
     1. Can be myself without fear of ridicule
     2. Do not face any real threats
     3. Am taken care of
     4. Feel safe

II. How the word "sickness" contributes to our understanding of "homesickness"
   A. Symptoms
     1. Headaches
     2. Unexplained anger
     3. Intolerance
     4. Crying
     5. Irritation
     6. Dull pain in stomach
     7. Inability to sleep
   B. Cures
     1. Make an effort to make new friends
     2. Concentrate on studies
     3. Work harder
     4. Find out about getting a host family
     5. Rest
     6. Receive cheery calls from loved ones

Since the making of lists is a kind of brainstorming that stimulates old memories and new ideas, the very act of outlining often leads to new ideas and new support. Furthermore, it also leads to more careful consideration of relationships. For instance, whenever you have a list of six or more items, it is best to ask yourself whether or not another subdivision, another set of categories, is possible. In the previous outline, the symptoms could be subdivided into physical symptoms versus psychological symptoms:

   A. Symptoms
     1. Physical
      a. Headaches
      b. Dull pain in stomach
      c. Inability to sleep
     2. Psychological
      a. Unexplained anger
      b. Intolerance
      c. Crying
      d. Irritation

In like manner the cures might be subdivided. There is no one, correct basis for subdivision; instead, you the writer must search for the general categories that would help clarify and unify the particular details. In the case of "cures," this division might be based on "cures that come from outside influences" as opposed to "cures that come from changes within," or "cures that work quickly" as opposed to "cures that take time to work," or "cures that work" as opposed to "attempted cures that don't work." Whatever the basis of division chosen, that division may force you to generate new information to fill out the needs of your categories. In other words, making an outline is a bit like forming a ladder of abstraction and is a process that involves thought about interrelationships, development, and developmental patterns, for such divisions turn simple lists into clarifying ideas.

You may feel that an outline is a waste of time, that it prevents you from getting down to the "real" job of writing. In fact, research by psychologists shows that people have different styles or approaches to solving problems. Some people are "planners," who prefer a very structured and ordered approach to a task, and others are "experiencers," who like to jump right into the middle of the problem. Whether you are a "planner" or an "experiencer" might explain why you are comfortable or uncomfortable using outlines. If you are not a "planner," you might often begin writing sentences and paragraphs before you have developed a formal outline. This approach may work for some students, but most writing experts advise against it since it really only delays the inevitable planning stage.

Sooner or later, you must concern yourself with the order and logic of your presentation. Even a sketchy plan can help to ease an "experiencer" through the necessary steps of organizing materials and help to produce better writing. It is easier to make changes in order and location and content in the outline stage than it is after you have already committed yourself to paper. How much easier it is to move a few fragmentary lines than to transpose whole paragraphs or whole pages! Our best advice, if you are an "experiencer," is to make some minimal plans, even a list of points to cover. You need not necessarily construct long, formal outlines for every paper, but without some "road map" to point out your direction, you leave yourself a lot of work for later stages of the writing, when it may be hard to find just what direction you have taken. Besides, an outline, even a very informal one, helps you brainstorm. It helps you think of ideas that fit together and that will help you expand your paper and make it not only longer but more interesting and more informative. The person who outlines can usually write more and better. Furthermore, if you are doing your work on a computer, with only slight adjustments it is very easy to move from outline to full rough draft by removing the letters and numbers of the skeleton and turning the fragments into complete sentences.

It is particularly important for writers with weak grammar skills to do their planning as a separate stage in which parts of the paper can be easily manipulated. The idea is to settle on the movement of thoughts before focusing on the more specific aspects of language at the sentence level. In other words, an outline saves much time and much worry.

- ## EXERCISE 3.5: QUESTIONS FOR DISCUSSION

  1. Are you a planner or an experiencer? What makes you think so?
  2. When writing in your first language, do you usually begin with some sort of informal plan or sketch of your organization or do you just begin writing?
  3. If you have used an informal plan or sketch of your organization before, how has it helped you? Would you recommend it to others? Why or why not?
  4. Have you ever tried a more formal outline like the one on page 54? What was the result?
  5. Look at the following outlines.
     a. What is their basic structure?
     b. What are their basic characteristics?

c. In the formal outline, what is the relationship of units of information sharing common numbers or letters? What is the relationship of units of information with different numbers or letters?

d. What types of grammatical structures do you notice?

e. How long will the papers based on each outline be?

f. Do the outlines contain sufficient information for writing the paper, or will more details need to be added? In other words, how thorough are the outlines?

INFORMAL OUTLINE: SKILLS NECESSARY FOR COLLEGE

What does a student need to know for college success?
>the expectations: spoken and unspoken
>the grading system
>the classroom system: what is accepted and what is not
>the library system: especially the card catalog and the reference materials

How can a student get this knowledge?
>At home:
>>by talking with Americans or nationals who have studied in the USA
>>by writing to American colleges and universities for information brochures
>Abroad:
>>by talking to ESL teachers and International Student Advisors
>>by talking to regular college students
>>by asking librarians
>>by auditing a class

FORMAL OUTLINE: EFFECTS OF GOING TO A NEW COUNTRY

I. Introduction: Sometimes going to a new country means changing accustomed patterns
II. Adjusting to new customs
  A. Eating habits
    1. Types of food
    2. Table manners
    3. Meal hours
  B. Entertainment patterns
    1. Learning new party patterns
      a. What time to arrive
      b. What to bring
      c. How to dress
      d. What behavior is acceptable
      e. When to leave
    2. Learning new sports
    3. Adapting to new types of humor
III. Changing social patterns
  A. Living without family ties
    1. Trying to become independent
    2. Trying not to set up a substitute family here
  B. Joining new clubs
IV. Changing work habits
  A. Balanced schedule
  B. Regular habits
  C. Focus on individual effort
V. Conclusion: positive results of following this advice

How to Use an Outline

Notice that the formal outline form depends on parallelism [repetition of the same grammatical pattern: noun-noun, prepositional phrase-prepositional phrase, infinitive-infinitive] between letters or numbers of the same type: *trying to become independent/trying not to set up a substitute family here* or *what time to arrive/what to bring/how to dress/what behavior is acceptable/when to leave*. However, it does not require parallelism between different letters and numbers. More importantly, notice that an outline moves from the most general to the most specific as it indents more and more. Each level from *I* to *A* to *1* to *a* becomes more and more specific.

I. One can succeed in developing language skills
   A. By talking in English
      1. To do so, make American friends
         a. In places where Americans get together
            1) In cafeterias
               a) While standing in lines

This pattern of movement from Roman numeral to capital letters to Arabic numbers to small letters to numbers with a half parenthesis to small letters with a half parenthesis represents a standard movement of thought: from generalization to example. The alignment is also important so that a reader can, at a single glance, tell the relationships between the ideas. For every *I* there should be a *II*, for every *a* there should be a *b*, and so forth. (Of course, there can also be more items in the series: *I, II, III*, etc.; *a, b, c*, etc.) It is best to use as few words as possible in each entry. The goal is a skeletal plan; filling up sections of your outline with too many words adds flesh rather than reveals bone.

However, as you make your outline, with each phrase that you add, check to see if you can still ask questions and, if so, add subcategories. For example, in the partial sample outline above, Roman numeral *I.* makes you ask, "How can one succeed?", just as capital *A.* makes you ask, "Where can one make American friends?", *a.*, "Where do Americans get together?" and *1)*, "Where in cafeterias?" However, no question follows naturally from *a)* so you can probably conclude that your queries have gone far enough, at least for the outline.

- **EXERCISE 3.6: OUTLINING**

1. The outlines on pages 52 and 54 are good but could be better. Do they call for a long or a short paper? How would you reduce or expand, develop and improve them? Can you incorporate more materials under some of the subcategories? Can you create more categories? Can you add more details?

2. Develop a sketchy outline (just the Roman numeral and subcategory A./B. levels) for a paper related to your career interest. Make it focus on the type of information a person would need in order to make a final decision about whether or not to pursue this career. Does a reader need to know the requirements for admission to a field, the nature of the work, or anything else?

3. Something is wrong with each of the following outlines. The error may be in the actual format. Not only should the form follow the pattern discussed above, but, as previously noted, for every *I* there should usually be a *II*, for every *a* there should be *b*, and so forth. The problem may be with parallelism. It may be a problem in logic. The problems with logic and content are the most important ones to find. They may include overlapping categories, categories that are not at the same level or of the same type, irrelevant categories, and so forth. Make whatever corrections you think are necessary to improve these outlines. These corrections will probably require changes in form and content.

I. Why I Want to Go to College
  A. To study for my profession
    a. I want to be a dentist
    b. to be able to make lots of money
    c. to gain prestige
    d. not having to worry about the future
  B. because my father wants me to
    a. He didn't go to school so he wants me to
  C. to escape from home
    a. eat what I want
    b. wear what I want
    c. I really want to date as much as I want
    d. Dating whoever I please is important to me
    e. go anywhere I want on a date
    f. being able to drink on dates
    g. to have my own car
  D. It would please my mother
    a. what she thinks is important to me
    b. her pride in me

****

Reasons to Take a Date to Chico's Mexican Restaurant
  I. It's cheap.
    A. You get lots of food for your money.
    B. most expensive dish is $7.50
    C. specials: $3.50
  II. Romantic setting.
    a. exotic Mexican decorations
    b. low lights
    c. not crowded
    d. intimate booths
    e. There are mariachi guitar players
    f. There are mariachi singers
      1. Mexican music is very romantic
  III. The Length of time.
    A. two or more hours to complete a meal—
That's good because it allows time for romance.
  IV. The waitresses are really very cute.

****

How to Make a Spanish Omelet
  A. What to buy
    1) eggs
    2) picante hot sauce
    3) cheese
      a. yellow
    4) mushrooms
      a. fresh
    5) oil

B. Utensils
   1) stove
   2) skillet
   3) fork
      a. and a knife
   4) mixing bowl
      a. mix all the ingredients together in this bowl
C. What to do
   1) break the eggs
   2) chop the mushrooms
   3) I grate the cheese
   4) adding the hot sauce
   5) You should cook the mushrooms in butter
   6) stir them all together in the skillet
   7) don't forget to turn on the burner
     —not too hot
     —not too low
     —medium
   8 the cooking stage
D. The final result should be:
   1) a very tasty dish

•• Writing Assignment

After you have improved the above outlines, choose the topic and outline you know the most about, and base a paper on it. Follow your revised outline carefully for your rough draft (your first version), using only the information from the outline, in the outline order. What does this experience teach you about the value of an outline? Does the outline contain everything you need to say or do you need to add more? If additions are necessary, what sort of additions are they? Explain.

Moving from Outline to Paper

Once you have completed the type of thinking through a topic that writing an outline requires, it is fairly simple to move from outline to paper. In fact, the more thorough and complete an outline is, the easier this movement is.

Look at the following outline. What will your thesis be? Which information belongs in your topic sentences? How do you know?

Outline: How to Develop Language Skills

I. Introduction: the need to develop language skills
II. Talking in English
    A. Talk to non-Americans in English
    B. Make American friends
        1. In the classroom
        2. In the college facilities
        3. In places where Americans get together
            a. In cafeterias
            b. In discos
            c. In parks
    C. Try to live with an American
        1. In the dorm
        2. In a private home
        3. Sharing an apartment
    D. Take a college English course
III. Listening to English
    A. To communications media
        1. Radio
        2. TV
        3. Cinema
        4. Video
    B. To conversations
    C. To lectures
IV. Reading English
    A. Read in class
    B. Do casual reading in the library
        1. Look at a newspaper daily
            a. A local paper
            b. A national paper
                1) *Wall Street Journal*
                2) *New York Times*
                3) *Christian Science Monitor*
        2. Look at a magazine regularly
            a. *Time, Newsweek, U.S. News*
            b. *Reader's Digest*
    C. Keep vocabulary lists of new words from all readings
V. Writing English
    A. Keep a daily journal
    B. Correspond in English
    C. Take a special writing course
VI. Conclusion

The title and introduction make clear the topic (how to develop language skills), and the most abstract headings (the Roman numerals) provide the topic ideas that need mentioning in the thesis:

THESIS: In order to develop language skills, a student needs to speak in English, listen to English as much as possible, read a lot in English, and practice writing in English.

In turn, the main or topic sentences for each section of the paper will build on the Roman numerals and the capital letter subheadings:

TOPIC SENTENCE 1: It is very important to speak as much English as possible by talking to non-Americans in English, by making American friends with whom to converse, by living with an American or Americans if possible, and by taking a college English course.

TOPIC SENTENCE 2: It is also important to listen to English whenever possible, particularly to communications media, but also to conversations and to lectures.

TOPIC SENTENCE 3: Reading English is a must for learning, not just reading for class, but regular use of the library for casual reading, characterized by special attention to vocabulary building.

TOPIC SENTENCE 4: Although most people think writing is unnecessary for learning a language, it is a really effective way to practice vocabulary and communication, so it would be good to keep a daily journal, to correspond in English, and perhaps even to take a special writing course in English.

A natural conclusion would sum up the overall idea:

CONCLUSION: To really learn English effectively, then, it is important, not only to speak and listen to English whenever and wherever possible, but it is also important to read and write in English in order to build vocabulary and to put into regular practice what has been learned.

Once you have progressed this far, you should be able to write with ease. The outline and paper which follow should make clear this relationship between outline and paper, skeleton and body.

MODEL #2

The following outline is based on a student's reaction to the movie, *Witness*, in which Harrison Ford plays a modern detective who encounters the conservative, Pennsylvania Dutch Amish. The movie made the student think about the Amish way of life compared to her own way of life. Therefore, she contrasts the old-fashioned Amish culture with her own through the use of "if" and the hypothetical unreal present tense. The Amish are famous in the U.S. for their conservative lifestyle and their refusal to use automobiles, electricity, and modern machinery. By saying, "If I were Amish," the student implies that all that she says about them is untrue about her own life. First, she wrote the outline; then she built her essay around it. Notice how her outline forms the skeleton for her paper. On the word processor she simply erased, cut and pasted, and added words to "flesh out" her outline into a paper.

The Amish Lifestyle: Admirable, but Not for Me!

I. Introduction: General Qualities of the Amish Lifestyle

   A. Positive qualities
      1. Peaceful, serene
      2. Harmonious
      3. Wholesome
      4. Self-sufficient
      5. Friendly
   B. Negative qualities
      1. Boring
      2. Unfashionable
      3. Nonprogressive

II. Dress and Appearance
   A. True of both sexes
      1. Plain and simple
      2. Dark colors
      3. No jewels
      4. No buttons and zippers
      5. No fancy design
   B. Difference between sexes
      1. Women:
         a. They can wear:
            1) Long and traditional dresses
            2) Dark stockings
            3) Long hair with a cap on the head
         b. They can't wear:
            1) Pants
            2) Makeup
            3) Fashionable dresses
      2. Men:
         a. They wear:
            1) Dark pants
            2) Dark hats
            3) Workshirts
            4) Heavy workshoes
         b. They can't wear:
            1) Jeans
            2) T-shirts
            3) Sneakers

III. Activities
   A. Things they can do
      1. Women:
         a. Get up early and thank God before eating
         b. Cook
         c. Clean the house
         d. Wash the clothes
         e. Sew and embroider
         f. Get the eggs
         g. Milk the cows

      h. Feed the chickens
      i. Make butter
      j. Bake the bread
      k. Take care of the sick
      l. Take care of the children
    2. Men:
      a. Get up early and thank God before eating
      b. Be a farmer
        1) Take the cows out
        2) Plant crops
        3) Dig wells to irrigate the land
      c. Build houses with other people
  B. Things they can't do:
    1. Spend a lot of money
    2. Dance and sing in the house
    3. Drink alcohol
    4. Drive a car
    5. Use machines
    6. Go to a public school or university
    7. Go to the movies
    8. Use electricity

IV. Attitudes

  A. About religion
    1. Believe simplicity is goodness

      a. Plain and simple dresses
      b. Simple way of life
    2. Believe in helping others
    3. Don't believe in violence or fighting
    4. Don't spend a lot of money; barter instead
    5. Don't pay taxes (all money belongs to God)
  B. About sex
    1. Open about sex
    2. Sex in marriage only
    3. Don't marry people of other religions
  C. About progress
    1. Not worried about future (in God's hands)
    2. Don't like changes and progress in their life
    3. Don't make personal decisions

V. Conclusion

  A. What I like about the Amish
    1. Their very peaceful life
    2. Their self-sufficiency
    3. Their friendliness
  B. What I don't like about the Amish
    1. Their reluctance to change and to progress
    2. Their closed ideas

This outline provided the basis for easily writing the paper which follows.

The Amish Life Style: Admirable, but Not for Me!

If I were Amish, the general qualities of my lifestyle would be both positive and negative. I would live a peaceful, serene life, which would be harmonious and wholesome too. It would also be self-sufficient, and I would be friendly with people like myself. However, my life would also be boring and unfashionable, and I would never progress.

If I were Amish, my dress and appearance would be very different from what they are now. No matter what my sex, my clothes would be plain and simple, with dark colors like gray, black, and white. I would not use any jewels or any fancy design. My clothes would not have buttons or zippers. If I were an Amish woman, I would wear long traditional dresses with dark stockings, I would also wear long hair with a cap on the head but I would never wear pants, makeup, or fashionable dresses. If I were an Amish man, I would wear dark pants, a workshirt, heavy workshoes, and a dark hat, but I would not wear jeans, sneakers, nor t-shirts.

If I were Amish my activities would be limited; there would be things that I could do and things that I could not do. If I were an Amish woman, each morning I would get up early and thank God before eating. I would get the eggs, milk the cows and feed the chickens. I would also bake bread and make butter. I would clean the house and cook. I would have to wash, sew, and embroider my clothes by hand. If my Amish friends or my family were to get sick, I would take care of them. I would also take care of the children. If I were an Amish man, I would be a farmer. I would take out the cows early in the morning after thanking God. I would have to know how to dig a well, irrigate the land, and plant crops. I would build houses with other people. If I were Amish, I never would spend a lot of money. I would not dance or sing in the house. I would also not drink alcohol, drive a car or use machines or electricity. I would not go to public school or to the university, only to Amish schools. I would not go to the movies either.

This is because if I were Amish, my attitudes about many things would be different. My attitudes about religion, for example, would be very conservative. I would believe simplicity is goodness. Therefore, I would wear plain and simple dresses, and I would have a simple way of life. I would also believe in helping others, and I would not believe in violence or in fighting. I would not spend a lot of money, but I would get some food by barter. I would not pay taxes because I would believe that all money belongs to God. My attitudes about sex would also be conservative. I would not be able to marry people of other religions, and sex would be permitted only in marriage. My attitudes about progress would not be in agreement with this era. I would not worry about the future because I would believe in God's power, and I would not like change or progress in my life. I would not make personal decisions because my family would make the decisions for me.

On the whole, my life would have things that I would like and things that I would not like. For example, I would like to have a peaceful life. I would also like being self-sufficient and friendly, but I would not like to be reluctant to change and to progress, nor would I like to have closed ideas.

— Stella Guillen, Peru

Ms. Guillen has a clear-cut idea which she supports with specific details. Each paragraph has its own focus but each contributes to the overall thesis idea. Ms. Guillen tells us a lot about the Amish. However, her basic idea is that Amish life is very different from her own life. What could she add to her paper to call more attention to the contrast between her life and that of the Amish? She could use phrases like *Unlike most of my friends, Amish women ...* or *While my friends and I enjoy...*, *most Amish young people never....* Could any of the longer lists in her outline be grouped around unifying categories? What else do you suggest?

WRITING A ROUGH DRAFT

As the above section on moving from outline to paper indicates, together the thesis and the outline are the final steps in the prewriting process. Once they have been completed you are ready to write. In fact, once you have paved the way through prewriting, first with gathering information and later with formulating a thesis and sketching a general outline, the actual writing should progress quickly and easily. You will have already considered your audience and purpose, brainstormed or researched the topic, and made decisions about the direction of your paper and its basic divisions or developmental pattern, so you should be ready to write your rough draft.

A *rough draft* is the opposite of a polished draft. The first just gets down the central ideas and still has ragged edges; the second is smooth, corrected and finished.

When you begin writing on a topic, writing a sentence and then rewriting and rewriting until it is perfect and then going on to the next sentence and repeating the process may make you feel in control of the topic, but in reality this approach is a waste of time and energy. Instead, the best technique for writing your rough draft is to simply sit and write everything down as quickly as you can without paying attention to catching and correcting errors. As in freewriting you should not stop to worry about grammar or sentence structure but instead write continuously through to an end. It is best to try to follow your outline or at least a blocked-out sketch of your idea, but write with the knowledge that you can always go back later and make serious corrections. The best outlines—in fact all plans—should be specific but flexible, so changes can be made with little effort.

As you write, your paper should fall into three basic units: the introduction, the body, and the conclusion. A title is good to have, but is not always necessary; remember that a title is never a substitute for a thesis or an opening idea. The thesis idea must be within the paper itself—in the introduction.

Many college instructors suggest you start with a four or five paragraph essay, with one paragraph for the introduction, two or three paragraphs to develop two or three topic ideas for the body, and one paragraph for the conclusion. The introductory and concluding paragraphs may be brief, but the body paragraphs should be well developed. Later, however, as you perfect your skills, you will want to move on to longer essays, with more body development. As your skill improves, let your purpose be your guide to length and degree of development.

Final Checklist

As you review your writing, make sure you have considered the following.
- ☐ A good thesis sentence is a general statement about what your main ideas are, how they are related, and why they are significant.
- ☐ A good thesis sentence sets the limits of your topic, clarifies the direction and purpose of the paper, and provides some indication of your attitude toward your subject.
- ☐ The elements of a thesis should be clearly stated and interrelated.
- ☐ An outline or sketchy plan is vital to having a well-organized paper.
- ☐ A good outline helps a writer think through and work and rework the plan of action.
- ☐ A good outline sets up in a clear, skeletal way the essential divisions or arguments of a paper and the evidence intended to support each section.
- ☐ Outline numbers, letters, and indentations indicate the basic pattern of an outline from general to specific, from abstract to concrete, with topics of equal generality appearing in parallel headings and sections and subsections reflecting logical relationships.
- ☐ The introduction and conclusion may be left out of an outline, but not of a paper.
- ☐ A rough draft comes only after the prewriting preparation is complete. It builds on the knowledge and plan developed during the prewriting process.

•• Writing Assignments

Choose one of the following topics. Then outline your paper and write a thesis sentence for it before writing your rough draft. Underline the thesis statement in your essay, and turn in your outline when you turn in your essay.

1. Because you are studying English, you will inevitably have to deal with the curiosity of others who wonder why you are doing so. Write a paper explaining to a friend or classmate why you want to learn English well. Is your purpose social, professional, or merely academic? Your explanation might be related to your future goals or to your sense of the value of language study. Back up your general reasons with specific details or examples to illustrate.

2. One of the most difficult factors to control in the writing process is motivation. Even professional writers sometimes suffer from an inability to write because of insufficient motivation. Given your own knowledge of yourself, discuss how you plan to motivate yourself to write enough and to improve enough to pass this composition course. Be specific: don't just say you plan to work hard, to be good, to do the right thing. Rather, explain how you will change your behavior and/or your thinking so that you can and will do the right thing. What specific changes will you make? Think about both exterior motivation (parental pressure; peer pressure; expectations of employer or of profession) and interior motivation (what you do personally to make yourself work harder).

Application 1: Finding Categories

The following information might be used to support a paper about Golden Gate Park in San Francisco. The writer has just randomly listed information about the park, not worrying about order or logic or level of generalization or specificity.

First, categorize all of the information that seems to fit together by supplying a word or words in the blanks beside sentences 1–44, for example, all the information about the gardens. In other words, you are creating general categories to help organize these sentences into groups. Since some categories may overlap, you may have more than one way to categorize a sentence, as in the example, which could belong in a history of the park or, rewritten, could support the idea of beauty.

Second, look at the categories that you create and decide which ones might be pulled together into a broader, more general central idea, a thesis idea for an essay. Insert the categories into the sketchy outline which follows the sentences. Remember that your goal is not to use all of the material but to select which information fits best in your chosen categories.

Finally, write a short paper on Golden Gate Park using the information from the list and organizing it according to your categories. You may need to leave out some information or combine information; you will certainly need to rearrange it.

Categories

<u>history/beauty</u> 1. John McLaren, a Scotsman, began with acres of sand dunes and changed them into a place of beauty.

_____ 2. Swimmers compete year-round in a heated outdoor Olympic pool.

_____ 3. McLaren chose the northern European ice plant to hold back the sand dunes [hills].

_____ 4. At the end of the park is the Pacific Ocean and a lovely beach.

_____ 5. Other choices of activities include horseback riding, softball, bicycling, horseshoes, or jogging.

_____ 6. There is an arboretum [a tree park] with labels in Braille for the blind as well as labels for the sighted explaining the name of the trees and their characteristics.

_____ 7. Youth organizations have picnics on the grounds.

_____ 8. The Academy of Science has a conservatory filled with exotica.

_____ 9. McLaren had a dozen lakes and miles of horse trails and footpaths built, so people could enjoy the scenery he created.

_____ 10. The park was planned and designed in the mid-nineteenth century.

_____ 11. The M.H. De Young Museum was built in 1894.

_____ 12. The Japanese Tea Garden is especially lovely when the cherry trees bloom.

_____ 13. Just north of the park is the Golden Gate National Recreation Area, where one can see daredevil gliders.

_____ 14. Careful planning, love, and care have produced a touch of the country in the heart of an urban area.

_____ 15. City families enjoy the peace and relate to nature.

_____ 16. Seals can sometimes be spotted on the rocks and, farther out, whales blowing spouts of air and water.

_____ 17. McLaren planted a variety of trees, shrubs, and flowers throughout the park.

_____ 18. There are noteworthy pieces by Rubens, Rembrandt, and Van Dyck in the M.H. De Young Museum.

_____ 19. The Academy of Science has a planetarium and aquarium.

_____ 20. There is a small farm with living animals.

_____ 21. Children bicycle through the park.

_____ 22. There are collections from Egypt, Greece, Rome, Africa, Italy, and early America in the M. H. De Young Museum.

_____ 23. There are two windmills with sunken gardens near the Pacific Ocean end of the park.

_____ 24. The Asian Art Museum is near the M.H. De Young Museum.

_____ 25. There is a bandstand for park concerts.

_____ 26. The Japanese Tea Garden includes shrines, paths, pools and a teahouse to enchant visitors.

_____ 27. The park founders dreamed of a place where city residents could relax and find recreation.

_____ 28. The aquarium includes exotic fish from the Pacific coast.

_____ 29. Rodin's Thinker resides at the M.H. De Young Museum.

_____ 30. The Tea Garden was created in 1894, during the San Francisco Exhibition.

_____ 31. There are a number of lovely hiking trails through the park.

_____ 32. A million dollars was put aside at the initial planning stage in the nineteenth century for the development of the park.

_____ 33. In this park one can sometimes see girl and boy scouts identifying exotic plant life for their merit badges.

_____ 34. McLaren used thousands of shrubs to strengthen the land.

_____ 35. Especially on weekends and holidays the sound of concert bands mingles with the calls of birds and the pounding of the surf.

_____ 36. The park is easy to reach by bus or car.

_____ 37. John McLaren spent fifty-nine years planning and improving this park.

_____ 38. The flowers in the sunken gardens include the California poppy, the Indian paintbrush, the seaside daisy, the beach lupine, and the yarrow.

_____ 39. The stated goal of the park's founders was "to provide the best practical means for healthful recreation for people of all classes."

_____ 40. The Asian Art Museum contains thousands of sculptures and objects from throughout the Orient.

_____ 41. McLaren fertilized the park ground with the horse manure swept from the streets and supplied by the city.

_____ 42. The Japanese Tea Garden is in the center of the park.

_____ 43. Just north of the park, in the Golden Gate National Recreation Area, one can enjoy the shoreline walk and the wildflowers.

_____ 44. The fragrance of eucalyptus leaves freshens the air.

Sketchy Outline

First paragraph (Introduction): Identify a general unifying category that could serve as a thesis (pleasures and opportunities offered by Golden Gate Park?). Then name three smaller categories that you will use to develop your broad idea; in other words, "predict" the topics of your body paragraphs.

_____
Unifying category: *prediction* of body paragraphs
#1 #2 #3

Second paragraph (Body Paragraph #1): Name the first smaller category you will focus on. Combine and fit together the sentences from your list that develop, explain, or support the idea of this category.

_____
Body paragraph #1

Third paragraph (Body Paragraph #2): Name the second smaller category you will focus on. Combine and fit together the sentences from your list that develop, explain, or support the idea of this category.

_____
Body paragraph #2

Fourth paragraph (Body Paragraph #3): Name the third smaller category you will focus on. Combine and fit together the sentences from your list that develop, explain, or support the idea of this category.

_____
Body paragraph #3

Conclusion: Repeat in different words from the introduction the broad, general, unifying category and the three smaller categories that you used to develop your broad idea. Then tell your reader something general about Golden Gate Park.

_____
Repeat
Tell significance

_____

In effect, you are deciding on the general ideas that will unify specific details. The first sentence of each paragraph will contain the unifying generalization or main idea for your paragraphs. Your introductory statement will contain the unifying generalization or main idea for your whole paper. Your conclusion will be a reminder of all of these key generalizations. The body of the paper will be the concrete support that fills in the details and completes the construction.

••Application 2: A Tailored Biography

Write a biography of another class member. The biography should contrast or show differences in elements of the personality you describe, or focus on three key reasons the person described is interesting.

My classmate at times is very practical but at other times very idealistic

or *She is a good athlete but also a good musician*

or *His early life was spent in a very rural, conservative place but now he is a liberal urbanite*

or *He is considering entering the priesthood because of his religious devotion but he also enjoys parties, dances, and pretty girls*

or *There are three main reasons Jorge is an interesting person to talk to: his travels, his hobbies, and his enthusiasm for his college studies.*

Think carefully about what verb tenses a biography should use, how you should begin and end, and how many sections or parts you need.

The Process to Follow

1. Before you interview your classmate to gather material, think of a number of questions to ask, questions to help you find a contrast or a center of interest in that person. Get a phone number for "follow-up" questions later.

2. Your classmate will be your external source of information, but you are responsible for how useful that source is! Take careful notes and ask your subject to repeat if you haven't understood. As with any writing plan, your questions should be flexible. As soon as you begin to ask them you will probably begin to discover that some of the questions need changing, expanding, or developing in more depth.

3. Take your notes home with you and brainstorm about them. Then use listing, mapping, or clustering to organize them into a workable plan. Doing so may make you think of more questions to ask to fill in the gaps in your knowledge.

4. Upon completing the interview, you should have a page or so of notes to organize into a coherent essay. Find the one central point that makes your classmate interesting or around which you can center a contrast. Go beyond simply naming the point; explain why you find the particular aspect of the person interesting unless the "why" is virtually self-evident, or state the contrast clearly with words like "on the other hand" or "in contrast." Write a thesis statement and make an outline. As more questions arise, go back to your classmate for more information.

5. Write the answers to your questions in essay form (not in interview form; an interview, when printed, is in alternating question and answer form). Ultimately, your essay should be divided into a four or five paragraph arrangement of introduction or thesis statement, development of the body with the two parts of the contrast or three points of interest, and a conclusion. You should, of course, leave out some of the material you collected in the interview and expand on other parts. Selecting and discarding should probably take place during the outlining stage but may continue during the writing and revising stages. Your expansion may require further questions, or it might simply require more explanation about why the material is interesting.

Your essay should have one central idea (key idea, governing idea, thesis): the person I have interviewed is interesting because.... or the person I have interviewed has two conflicting sides to his/her personality.... Follow the pattern below:

Introduction: Announce the topic; explain; give any other necessary information (a minimum of two–three sentences).

Body: Go into detail about the person, subordinating other information that fits in with the central idea. Leave out any other information that does not fit in (a minimum of five–six sentences per paragraph; two or three paragraphs is necessary).

Conclusion: Comment on what you learned from the person or what the general significance of the topic is (two–three sentence minimum).

6. Remember that there is no topic so interesting that it does not become dull in the hands of an unenthusiastic writer, and the reverse is also true. An imaginative writer can make completely unpromising topics come alive. Dullness is the writer's problem, so ask new questions and seek interesting explanations to make your essay lively.

The Purpose of the Assignment:

Decide on the purpose of your paper and state your goal briefly in the space below:

My paper goal is to show how _____ (name of classmate) has two (or more) contrasting sides to his/her personality: _____ and _____.

Or *My paper goal is to show how _____, _____, and _____ make _____ (name of classmate) interesting.*

Sample Biography Papers

For Analysis

Study the sample essays below, and look for a clear central idea and an interesting topic. What can you learn from their successes and failures?

1. The most interesting thing about Eloy is the tragedy that ended his soccer career. A freshman from Rapid City, majoring in broadcast production, Eloy's soccer career was heading for success, when a tragic accident stopped it forever.

Eloy's youth was one of athletic achievement. Eloy had been playing soccer since he was five. During his sophomore year at Rapid City Academy, Eloy's soccer playing had reached its peak. Eloy was co-captain of the varsity soccer team, and Susquehanna College and West Memphis College offered him scholarships to play soccer for them after high school. Unfortunately, during physical education class the volleyball pole fell off the pole holder and landed on Eloy's big toe. Eloy's toe was shattered, fractured, and thrown off-center. He later underwent four hours of intensive surgery. Sorry to say, Eloy lost both of his scholarships and can never play soccer again.

Eloy's unfortunate tragedy ended his soccer career, so today he can only dream about what kind of future he might have had. One never knows what might happen in one's life. One accident could change a person's goals and life drastically.

Questions for Discussion:

What two ideas does the writer make us expect a discussion of? Does the writer deal with both ideas in the body of the paper? How could this essay be expanded? What parts seem most promising and interesting? Why?

* *

2.   My classmate, Carlos, has two sides to his personality: Carlos the extrovert and Carlos the introvert. On the one hand, Carlos is fun-loving, friendly, out-going, and social. He enjoys parties, going out with friends to concerts and films, and drinking coffee in the cafes downtown while talking to friends about current events. He loves to talk about politics, popular music, and sports. Carlos, in some ways, is a typical extrovert.

However, Carlos also has a quieter side. He is a great reader who spends much time in his university library, in the city's bookstores, and at newsstands. You never see Carlos without a book, a magazine or some other reading material close by him. When you pass him sitting in the lounge before class, he often has his head in a book. He has an expensive stereo music system at home, which he listens to alone, for hours on end. He sometimes attends films and concerts alone when he is in a solitary mood. This contrasting side of Carlos' personality is quiet, introverted, and thoughtful.

Together, the public and the private Carlos provide interesting sides to the character of the same person.

Questions for Discussion

What are the strengths of this essay? What does it focus on? How does it develop that focus? Is it convincing? Why or why not? What changes would improve the introduction and conclusion?

****

Final Checklist for this Application

- ☐ Does your essay clearly answer "Why is this person interesting?" or "What contrast dominates this person's life?"
- ☐ Does your essay have a clear focus on one idea on which every sentence builds?
- ☐ Does it include examples and illustrations to prove your point and clarify your general statements? Three examples is a good minimum.
- ☐ Is your writing as clear, compact, and focused as possible? To test your essay, read it aloud into a tape recorder and play it back to yourself (or have a friend read it aloud to you).

Chapter 4: UNDERSTANDING BASIC PARAGRAPH FORMS

Paragraphing... is the equivalent of long division.... The aim is to divide and discuss. — Winkler and McCuen

The Paragraph Defined

The Importance of Indentation

Paragraph Length

Topic Sentences

Final Checklist

Writing Assignments

The Paragraph Defined

A paragraph is usually defined as a group of sentences, at least two or more, which are about one idea. However, this is not a very specific definition; could you describe a sentence as "a group of words, usually two or more, which are about one idea"? Most paragraphs you will read and write, like most sentences, are more complicated. There may be several ideas in a paragraph, even half a dozen. Furthermore, almost always, if the paragraph is well written, there will be some principle or rule used to organize the sentences so that the combination makes good sense. A better definition, then, is that a paragraph is a group of sentences, usually two or more, which tries to communicate at least one main idea (but perhaps more) through a certain *pattern, order,* or *framework.* Perhaps the best definition is that a paragraph is a composition in miniature. Like a composition, it has a unifying central idea (a topic idea), an organizing pattern that develops that idea with concrete details, connecting words that interrelate ideas, and a final sentence that brings the paragraph to a clear end. However, unlike the composition, the paragraph does this in a single unit which is indented only once. The most common paragraph pattern is a movement from a general organizing concept to more specific developmental details.

The "grammar" of paragraphs in English (the rules or logic which holds sentences together) may be quite different from the "grammar" of paragraphs in your first language. In fact, to some extent, probably every language uses patterns of ideas somewhat differently. In some languages, of course, the paragraph as it is known in English does not even exist, although most languages seem to have some way of indicating a single unit of thought. Sometimes the difference between languages is slight, sometimes great, but the contrast is enough to cause trouble for writers accustomed to thinking in one pattern who now have to write in another. Fortunately, it is fairly easy to bridge these differences by paying attention to the pattern to be mastered in the target language. In papers written in English for English speakers, the key ideas must be developed in well-defined paragraph patterns, so one of the goals of this chapter is to call attention to such forms. What particular kind of paragraphs, in what order, with what degree of development will, of course, depend on topic, purpose, and audience.

EXERCISE 4.1: GENERAL CONCEPTS AND SPECIFIC DETAILS IN A PARAGRAPH

The following sentences show the difference between the level of generalization needed to begin a paragraph and the level of specificity needed to develop that paragraph. Which would be used to introduce a paragraph idea? Which would be used to develop an idea in the body of the paragraph? How do you know? Circle one of the choices.

1. In institution X, it is very common for a professor to dismiss class twenty minutes early or to not attend class as many as three times a month, but in institution Y a professor will take the entire class period and may even go overtime and the Y professor rarely misses a class; if missing class is unavoidable, the Y professor announces the future absence early in the semester, apologizes for the cancellation, and assigns work to be done during the class time.

           Introductory sentence   Body sentence

2. The classroom behavior of professors from institution X differs a little from that of professors from institution Y, particularly in the sense of obligation to students.

           Introductory sentence   Body sentence

3. The American and the Ethiopian concepts of classes beginning and ending on time differ greatly, with the Americans worrying about precision and the Ethiopians being more informal and relaxed.

           Introductory sentence   Body sentence

4. In the American class, students might continue to talk until the precise moment the class is scheduled to begin and the professors usually will not begin, the lecture or the class discussion until that time. In contrast, in France, students will stop talking the moment the professor arrives, and, even if the professor is early, the professor will begin to chat with students about ideas and materials related to class.

           Introductory sentence   Body sentence

The Importance of Indentation

Sentences in English are identified as sentences because they each begin with a capital letter and end with a period, a question mark, or an exclamation point. Paragraphs are identified as paragraphs because the opening sentence of each is indented. It may help to remember that indent means "dent in" or "push in," so an indentation is a space on the left-hand side of the page in front of the first sentence, a space that "pushes the sentences in." Indentations may seem unimportant, but in fact they tell us a great deal. Like the capital letter and the period in the sentence, indentations set off units of thought and guide the movement of our eyes and mind, so that we "stop" and "start" at the ends and beginnings of subtopics in the way the writer wants us to. Indentations are therefore visual devices but also intellectual ones; they are the signals that identify the shifting of ideas in an essay.

• EXERCISE 4.2: RECOGNIZING PARAGRAPHS

The following exercise is to investigate the boundaries or limits of the English paragraph. Given the above definitions, which of the following groups of sentences are acceptable as English paragraphs and which are not? Explain why briefly. How do the rules for paragraphs in English differ from those in your own language?

Example: In summary, then, language remains a mystery about which we know very little. Experts tell us that all human beings have some sort of language, that even the languages of the most primitive people are complex and flexible, and that all languages change and evolve with time. They also tell us that languages reflect the values and the culture of the people who speak them. However, much beyond this limited knowledge remains unknown and perhaps unknowable. Despite numerous theories and lots of guesses, we have no idea how, why, or where language began—and we will probably never know.

Answer: An acceptable English paragraph (a concluding paragraph) characterized by one indentation and unity of subject matter; the first sentence provides the topic idea, and the rest of the paragraph develops it.

1. What causes cancer?
   a. We don't know the basic cause, but we are looking for the answers.
   b. Some conditions that may lead to cancer have been identified:
      — repeated injury to the cells (from overexposure to the sun, excessive radiation, contact with certain chemicals)
      — viruses cause some forms of cancer in animals
      — cigarettes probably cause lung cancer
   c. Nevertheless, because of our limited knowledge of what precisely causes cancer, research to find the basic causes of human cancer is still under way in many fields of science.
   d. Hopefully, the future will provide answers.

   Answer:

2. What causes cancer? Does overexposure to the sun or excessive radiation? Does contact with certain chemicals or even viruses? Does cigarette smoking lead to lung cancer? What about pollution—the fumes, dust, and smog we breathe daily in our air? Does heavy drinking of alcoholic beverages increase the risk of cancer? Can bruises or injuries? Might cancer be hereditary in human beings? Is cancer a disease of some civilizations or does it occur in all civilizations? Despite our limited knowledge of what precisely causes cancer, research to answer such basic questions has been in progress for some time now. We have the answers to some of these questions. Hopefully, the future will provide the answers to the rest.

   Answer:

3. What causes cancer? The basic causes are unknown, although certain conditions that may lead to cancer have been identified. For example, we know that repeated injury to the cells is a factor. Such damage may result from overexposure to the sun, excessive radiation, and contact with certain chemicals. We also know that some forms of cancer

in animals have been caused by viruses. Most physicians and scientists who have studied the problem believe that cigarette smoking is the principal cause of lung cancer. Nevertheless, because of our limited knowledge of what precisely causes cancer, research to find the basic causes of human cancer is still under way in many fields of science. Hopefully, the future will provide answers.

Answer:

4.   What causes cancer? The basic causes are unknown, although certain conditions that may lead to cancer have been identified.

For example, we know that repeated injury to the cells is a factor. Such damage may result from overexposure to the sun, excessive radiation, and contact with certain chemicals.

We also know that some forms of cancer in animals have been caused by viruses. Most physicians and scientists who have studied the problem believe that cigarette smoking is the principal cause of lung cancer.

Nevertheless, because of our limited knowledge of what precisely causes cancer, research to find the basic causes of human cancer is still under way in many fields of science. Hopefully, the future will provide answers.

Answer:

5.   What causes cancer? This is a question that puzzles many scientists. It also puzzles me. My father had cancer and it made my family very sad. He got sicker and sicker and finally died. My family has never been the same since.

Now I know that my family's experience is not unique. Cancer is a plague of modern civilization. Has anyone in your family ever had cancer? Scientists think they know some of the causes. They said my father drank and smoked too much, ate an unhealthy diet, and was out in the sun too much. But my uncle ate and drank as much, was as brown as a berry, and lived on hamburgers and hot dogs, so I don't believe they are right.

Answer:

6.   Now that this text has explored the multiple possible causes of cancer and the continued research into these basic causes, it will now explore the question of detection: how cancer can be diagnosed, what its early warning signals and symptoms are, how it can be distinguished from other diseases, and what immediate steps can be taken to counter it.

Answer:

7.   Great strides have been made in research, diagnosis, treatment, and control of heart disease. Progress has made it possible for thousands of people to survive and recover from heart and blood vessel ailments. Brilliant surgical techniques for correcting heart defects have been developed in recent years. Right now:
—Most people who have heart attacks recover
—High blood pressure (hypertension) can be controlled
—Recurrent attacks of rheumatic fever, which damage the heart, can be prevented
—Many heart defects can be repaired
—Medical science can do a great deal for people with circulatory disorders
As a result of such advances, scientists foresee even greater advances in the near future.

Answer:

Paragraph Length

The next time you look at an English-language newspaper, notice the number of indentations/paragraphs on the front page. Usually, there will be a great number, because the front page of a newspaper is meant to give readers numerous facts about a story, and each fact or group of facts is given its own indentation/paragraph. This arrangement into short paragraphs allows you to "skim"; that is, you can move your eyes quickly down the column and learn the most important facts without reading each complete paragraph. For example, the paragraphing in the following selection is in newspaper style:

The largest land animal remaining on earth, the African elephant, has been the key to that continent's ecology for a long time. However, today it is in serious danger. One of the biggest international efforts ever tried to prevent extinction focuses on the elephant.

The elephant's survival should not be just the worry of environmentalists because the death of the elephant could mean the death of the entire African continent. Unlike other endangered mammals like the tiger and the whale, the African elephant profoundly affects its environment.

As it eats quantities of vegetation, its digestive habits and processes change the forest and the grassland it moves through. The elephant acts as creator and "architect" determining how millions of other animals which share the same environment—zebras, gazelles, giraffes—live and exist.

Because of this, environmentalists believe that the disappearance of the elephant will mean the disappearance of many other species. They fear that whole ecological systems involving forests and grasslands will be greatly changed or even destroyed.

Newspaper articles, in general, are designed to be read quickly and easily, without much concentration. Therefore, you can probably skim the above newspaper-style reading quickly because of the indentation at the introduction of every new idea. The front page, in particular, of an English-language newspaper is usually like this. However, when you turn to the editorial page, where there are columns, features, and regular discussions about politics and social ideas, the indentation pattern changes. Usually, these columns and discussions will use far fewer indentations/paragraphs, because they do not mean to give us a series of facts, but rather to discuss a few ideas at length. These discussions are often much harder to read since we cannot "skim" from one paragraph to the next. This is the effect in the following selection which argues that the United States cannot live up to John F. Kennedy's pledge:

In 1961, a young John Kennedy made his famous inaugural speech pledge: "Let every nation know, whether it wishes us well or ill, we shall pay any price, bear any burden, meet any hardship, support any friend or oppose any foe to assure the survival and the success of liberty." These words have warmed the hearts of Americans and of people around the world ever since. Nevertheless, that pledge was not very realistic. Americans began to learn just how unrealistic during the Vietnam War. Today, even though Americans still like the sound of the idea, acting on it would lead to all sorts of problems. American involvement in Iraq and Somalia surprised many, but the limited involvement in Bosnia did not. This is not only because of the enormous social and economic costs of such commitments, but also because of the slow but steady movement of the American public to distrust and disapprove of the costly role that the U.S. followed for many, many years.

One result of this changing attitude is that more and more Americans firmly believe that certain areas are more important to national interests than others. The U.S. won't totally ignore all other countries, but there are many kinds of relationships between nations that are very different from serious military commitment and there are many degrees of importance and involvement. In general, America has found out the hard way not to view the rest of the world in terms of an automatic causal chain and to understand that there are no simple choices between countries that stand up against dictatorships and countries that don't. Instead, the real world is far more complex, and Americans have begun, or at least should begin, to take notice of and react on the basis of that complexity.

—Adapted from "The U. S. Cannot Live in Isolation," *Time*, (April 8, 1975): 43–44.

One of the reasons textbooks are hard to read is that they are written in long paragraphs like the two above; you look at a page without reading it and say automatically that "it looks difficult." The more advanced the discussion, the longer the paragraphs. The longer the paragraph, the more complex the idea. Discussions about literature, philosophy, or the sciences have particularly long paragraphs since they often examine a single idea in depth.

How long should a paragraph be? As long as it takes to serve its function. An introductory or concluding paragraph may be only a sentence or two long while a body paragraph trying to communicate a complex idea or explore a complicated relationship may take a full page. In other words, degree of development depends on purpose. The amount of development should be enough to cover the expectations created in the topic sentence. For example, the opening of the following paragraph makes readers expect not only a description of what was seen but also an "enthusiastic explanation" of its significance:

> The visitors to the F.B.I. center walked for an hour, from one exhibit to another, the guide giving an <u>enthusiastic explanation</u> of what they were seeing. They learned many things about the name of the F.B.I., its shields, its personnel, its files, and weaponry, and its laboratory capabilities.

This paragraph is undeveloped. It is too short for its purpose (two sentences), and the details following the topic sentence are really insufficient to create a visual image of the tour and to allow the reader to share in the enthusiasm. Margaret Truman, in her exciting mystery novel, *Murder at the F.B.I.*, takes on the same topic, but much more effectively:

> They [visitors to the F.B.I. center] walked for an hour, from one exhibit to another, the guide giving an enthusiastic explanation of what they were seeing. They learned many things—besides meaning Federal Bureau of Investigation, the initials stood for Fidelity, Bravery, and Integrity; authentic shields carried by special agents (*all* agents were called *special* agents) were the size of a half-dollar and had a raised seal covering an eighth of an inch of the agent's photo; there were almost 9,000 special agents, nearly 600 of them female; 176 million fingerprints were on file, and 25,000 were processed each day; blood type could be determined through the examination of a minute trace of saliva, and the lab could tell whether the saliva came from a human being or from a dog or cat; the firearm rooms contained 4,000 types of weapons, including 2,000 handguns and 11,000 different types of bullets; there were 10,000 types of paints used on automobiles, and the lab could differentiate between every one of them….

This paragraph meets reader expectations. It provides vivid descriptive details that help the reader share in the tour, see what the tourists see, and experience the enthusiasm communicated by the tour guide. You should judge your own paragraphs by this standard: Does the paragraph do what it says it will do, as thoroughly and in as much detail as its opening leads us to expect?

- ### EXERCISE 4.3: MAKING DECISIONS ABOUT INDENTATION

  Read the following passage and put an arrow pointing inward at every point you would indent, like this ➔. The first indentation has been made for you. Then compare your arrows with those of your classmates to see where they indented. What clues aid your decision? Is there a single "right" and "wrong" way to paragraph? Be ready to defend your paragraphing decisions.

  ➔Television commercials (especially political ones) differ greatly in the United States and Japan, particularly in the way of expression and the rules about acceptable tactics. These differences result from differences in laws, in consumer taste, and in values and sensibilities. First are the differences in laws. In the United States, it is possible to make political commercials that compare candidates, but in Japan these are prohibited by law. During the elections canvassing for presidential or congressional candidates, numerous advertisements for particular candidates appear on US television. In these ads the candidates appeal to their supporters not only with their election promises but also with their attacks on the weak points of their opponents; they try to create a strong positive image of themselves and a weak negative image of the other candidates. Unlike American candidates, Japanese candidates cannot advertise. If they did, they would lose the election because writers would not support such tactics, but they would also lose financially because they would be fined for breaking the law. Next, US and Japanese commercials differ in the way they are expressed because of differences in consumer tastes. American commercials are usually short and direct. Their creators prefer to show the name and price of products and to include "consumers" using or advocating the product. They focus on how nice the product is, what good quality it is, and how good it will make consumers feel or what good things it will do for them. Japanese commercials, in contrast, are longer and more subtle; they are almost like short movies or plays. Some commercials do not even tell the name of the product; instead they provide vague images about the product to create an atmosphere and to let the audience guess what the product is. Many foreigners can't even tell what products are being sold or what kinds of appeals are being made to consumers, but Japanese have learned by experience to figure out the images and to guess the message. Clearly, the American and the Japanese idea of persuasion is very different. The rules for television commercials also differ between the US and Japan because of different values and sensibilities. Some of the advertising rules in the US are based on the idea of protecting minors from bad habits. For example, cigarette companies cannot advertise their products on American television, and the commercials they can have are carefully regulated by law to prevent them from making a strong appeal to minors. In Japan, advertising agencies worry more about public opinion and are careful not to discriminate against a consumer's sex, race, or occupation. For example, several years ago a food company made a mistake in an instant noodle commercial. In it, as a young couple discussed the noodles, the young husband told his wife, "You're going to make it. I'm just going to eat it." This advertisement was rejected for its discrimination against the "woman" or "wife" as a servant. In sum, differences in cultural values and attitudes between the US and Japan result in differences in laws, traditions, and customs concerning television advertising.

•EXERCISE 4.4: DEGREE OF DEVELOPMENT

Which of the following paragraphs are better? Circle the specific details, and explain what conclusion you can draw from your observations.

1.   English is a mixture of languages, for it has borrowed freely from many languages throughout its history. During the Roman times it added numerous Latin words. Then the Norman conquest brought French words. Later words came from Italian, Spanish, Dutch, Arabic, Persian, and many other languages.

or

English is a mixture of languages, for it has borrowed freely from many languages throughout its history. During the Roman domination of England it added numerous Latin words, including the old English equivalents of *butter, cheese, dish, kettle, kitchen, mile, pound, street,* and *wall.* Then the Norman conquest brought French words related to government, titles of nobility, the military, and cooking, words like *chancellor, court, crime, judge, jury, prince, duke, baron, captain, corporal, lieutenant, beef, pork, veal, mutton, broil, fry,* and *roast.* Italian has provided such words as *bal-*

cony, cavalry, miniature, opera, and *umbrella.* Spanish has given us *mosquito, ranch, cigar,* and *vanilla.* Dutch has added *brandy, golf, measles,* and *wagon.* Arabic has loaned words related to science and mathematics, words like *alcohol, chemistry, magazine, zenith,* and *zero.* Persian, in turn, has given us *chess, checkers, lemon, paradise,* and *spinach.* Clearly then, English has a truly international vocabulary, which includes some words recognizable to speakers of many of the world's languages.

2.   Why do English speakers value concreteness? Americans like machinery and "gadgets" or things; they also seem to like statistics and measurements. It is a constant American tendency to examine their own culture, usually in terms of numbers and empirical data. Advertising often tries to persuade buyers with statistical comparisons: 9 out of 10 doctors agree, 75% of our customers come back, 99 and $^{44}/_{100}$ percent pure. Certainly the English language, with its enormous vocabulary of over 500,000 words, offers a variety of specific ways of saying things. American sports, particularly football and even more particularly football on T.V., may be the most "measured" sports in history. The following might be a typical comment: "This is the longest distance a left-footed kicker has kicked a goal against the wind in this stadium; the last time someone kicked a goal this far was on November 17, 1957, 51 yards." Clearly, it is safe to say that Americans are impressed with concrete details, and that this concern with detail carries over into their writing: American readers like to see details.

or

Why do English speakers value concreteness? Americans like machinery and "gadgets" or things; they also seem to like statistics and measurements. It is a constant American tendency to examine their own culture, usually in terms of numbers and empirical data. Advertising often tries to persuade buyers with statistical comparisons. Certainly the English language offers a variety of specific ways of saying things. American sports may be the most "measured" sports in history. Clearly, it is safe to say that Americans are impressed with concrete details, and that this concern with detail carries over into their writing: American readers like to see details.

3.   Oysters on the half-shell are an inexpensive delicacy thoroughly enjoyed by thousands of Gulf of Mexico residents daily. Oysters, a unique and flavorful bivalve shellfish, native to coastal marshes and the reefs of protected bays, range from a bite-sized inch to a mouthwatering six inches—a royal treat prized by gourmets. When served on the half-shell, the oysters are freshly caught, raw, and absolutely delicious. One hundred percent protein, a medium-sized oyster has only 150 calories. These fabulous little bites of tender juiciness have a delicate taste, best accented by a special hot sauce of ketchup, horseradish, Tabasco sauce, Worcestershire sauce, salt, pepper, and a touch of lemon juice, a blend perfect for dipping. An oyster so prepared and served on a cracker is heavenly.

or

Oysters on the half–shell are cheap and good and popular among Gulf of Mexico residents. Oysters live in the water near shore and come in different sizes. They taste good raw, alone, or with a sauce. They are full of protein and not very fattening.

Topic Sentences

Just as a paper begins with a thesis sentence, a single sentence which describes the ideas of the whole paper, so <u>each</u> paragraph which follows the introductory paragraph should begin with a <u>topic sentence</u>, a single sentence which tells the reader what that paragraph is about, and what the plan or direction of the paragraph will be. Read the following example.

> The electric car can be built with a motor which can generate electricity as well as consume it.

This sentence conveys far less information than a thesis sentence but has just enough to discuss and develop within the limited length of a standard paragraph (about four to ten sentences if kept non-technical). This topic sentence should be followed by sentences which develop and expand its core idea, as in the paragraph which follows:

> <u>The electric car can be built with a motor which can generate electricity as well as consume it</u>. [Topic sentence] When such a car has reached a certain speed, it can be brought to a stop by cutting off the electricity to the motor. The moving wheels then turn the motor, which becomes an electric generator. The resistance produced by the turning motor slows the car, while electricity is also produced to recharge the batteries. [paragraph body]

The topic sentence is often like a miniature thesis sentence. In fact, it frequently, though not always, takes one section of the thesis sentence and repeats its idea to make clear the focus of each paragraph unit. For example, the thesis sentence, *Cigarettes are not only costly in terms of financial outlay but also in terms of health and social interaction*, can be broken down into three paragraphs, each with its own topic sentence:

1. First of all, cigarettes cost a lot to buy and use.
2. In addition, cigarettes can be dangerous to one's health.
3. Finally, cigarettes have recently begun to affect one's ability to interact socially.

Clearly, these topic sentences relate back to the thesis statement and announce the particular direction of each division of this essay of three body paragraphs.

The thesis sentence *Reading a newspaper daily will help prepare you for college classes by expanding vocabulary, by encouraging reading skills, and by providing a cultural background necessary to interpret conflicts and issues, the discussion of which is so important to the American classroom* leads to three main body paragraphs. The topic sentences for these paragraphs might be something like the following:

1. The daily reading of a newspaper will introduce you to new vocabulary important to educated discussion.
2. Regularly reading a newspaper will also help you improve reading skills.
3. Finally, and most importantly, your newspaper reading will provide a cultural base that will help you participate more fully in class discussions.

Consider the following thesis sentence:

> Students starting college should realize the importance of academic achievement, of not carrying more courses than they can handle well, of attending class regularly, and of pacing their studying.

What topic sentences can you predict will appear in the body paragraphs which follow? There should be a section on a new student's need to realize the importance of academic achievement, another on why a new college student should not carry more courses than can be handled well, another on the importance of class attendance, and a final one on students pacing their studying. Sketched out informally, this topic would appear as follows:

Paragraph #1

Thesis sentence (plan for whole paper): Students starting college should realize the importance

    A. of academic achievement

    B. of not carrying more courses than can be handled well

    C. of class attendance

    D. of pacing studying

Paragraph #2

Topic Sentence: Academic achievement is obviously quite important.

    A.

    B.

    C.

Paragraph #3

Topic Sentence: Students should not carry more courses than they can handle well.

    A.

    B.

    C.

Paragraph #4

Topic Sentence: Attending class is vital to college success.

    A.

    B.

    C.

Paragraph #5

Topic Sentence:. Pacing one's studying will prove equally important.

    A.

    B.

    C.

In sum, the topic sentence links each paragraph with the general thesis. It announces the direction and plan of each paragraph. It is vital to developing the body of a paper, for each body paragraph should focus on each key point provided in the thesis statement.

This approach to sentences and paragraphs may seem mechanical and perhaps uncreative compared to the patterns you use in your own language. This is because it is mechanical, although not necessarily lacking in creativity if used properly. American prose values logic, order, and internal coherence over other strengths such as elegance or style. Even patriotic American English speakers might admit that the beauty of their prose compares unfavorably to that of French, Spanish, or other languages, for American culture encourages clarity more than beauty of phrasing or eloquence of delivery. A plain, clear style is considered best. Don't try to fight this cultural preference in your own prose; you will probably never write as elegantly in English as you do in your first language, but you can, with practice, write as clearly as native writers do. So begin with well-organized sentence-paragraph patterns, and worry about elegance later.

- ## EXERCISE 4.6: TOPIC SENTENCES

    A. Narrow your thesis statements written for the exercises on pages 47 and 50 to topic sentences which could be developed in five to ten sentences. Then select two of your topic statements and develop them into paragraphs.

    B. The following sentences were written to introduce paragraphs. These paragraphs were supposed to compare or contrast some aspect of classroom manners in one country versus another, in college versus high school, or in the past versus the present. Most of the opening or topic sentences are at too high a level of abstraction and therefore require much too much evidence to develop properly. Read them carefully and decide:

        a. which are not on the assigned topic at all

        b. which are too general to develop in a paragraph

        c. which would be at the appropriate level of generalization for the assignment.

Be prepared to defend your decisions. Some sentences may be both (a) and (b).

    Example: Vietnamese high school teachers are stricter than American ones and therefore demand more formal manners.

Answer: (b) (involves a contrast in manners with a focus on teacher strictness as a key reason for the contrast but fails to place a limit on types of manners to be focused on; needs a plan, a clear direction, a limit)

Correction: Vietnamese high school teachers are stricter than American ones and therefore demand more formal manners for speaking in class.

This paragraph will investigate the formality versus the informality of various classroom situations involving students speaking to teachers.

1. Classes vary from culture to culture.

2. Some rules of conduct are standard world-wide.

3. If one compares the behavior of students in U.S. and Mexican colleges, one will be astounded at the differences.

4. American students and professors don't discuss politics in class, even shortly before Election Day, whereas in Poland, the election would be the main, if not the only, classroom topic, as it was during the recent Polish presidential election.

5. Classroom etiquette has changed dramatically throughout the years.

6. Twenty years ago a student entering a college classroom with a cup of coffee would have been thrown out, but today this action is an almost daily occurrence. Yesterday's rigid discipline has been replaced by modern informality.

7. What is polite in the Puerto Rican classroom may not be polite in the mainland American classroom.

8. In Spanish colleges, the professor's entrance into the classroom calls for silence and respect because the professor is an authority figure.

9. Panamanian high school classroom behavior differs from American college classroom behavior in acceptable entrances and exits, in patterns for asking questions and giving responses, and in codes about dress, food, drink, and sitting position.

10. Dress codes in private Argentine colleges differ greatly from dress codes in private American colleges.

11. The biggest difference between American and Japanese high school classes is atmosphere.

12. Japanese classes encourage passive acceptance while American classes encourage active argumentation. This difference in classroom philosophy produces differences in classroom participation behavior.

Choose one of the sentences about which you know some details (the focus can be changed to your country), and then rewrite the sentence to make it a good topic sentence; next, write a short sketch or plan for a paragraph. For example, the sample sentence would follow a pattern from general to particular and would use connectives as follows, with the numbers indicating the movement toward greater specificity.

(1) Vietnamese high school teachers are stricter than American ones and therefore demand more formal manners for speaking in class.
    (2) First supportive example:
        (3) In the U.S.,…
        (3) However, in Vietnam…
    (2) Second supportive example:
        (3) On the one hand, in the U.S., …
        (3) On the other hand, in Vietnam, …
    (2) Third supportive example:
        (3) In the U.S.,…
        (3) In contrast, in Vietnam,…

(1A) In other words, American teachers' classroom manners are friendlier and more tolerant of free discussion and open responses than those of their Vietnamese counterparts, who believe students should speak only when called upon and even then with brevity and respect.

C. Explain what paragraphs beginning with the following topic sentences are likely to discuss.

Example: In his film version of *Hamlet*, Mel Gibson uses interesting stage action to make his Shakespearean lines clear.

Focus: Examples of "interesting stage action" Gibson uses to clarify meaning.

1. Montana is a state of many contrasts.
2. The earthquake's destruction of so many buildings and the loss of so many lives in Mexico City was due to faulty construction methods.
3. Given modern time-saving methods, baking a cake can be a quick and easy process.
4. Historically, the swampland surrounding New Orleans has caused that city much trouble.
5. The cowboy movie reflects basic American values and concerns.
6. Television is the modern opiate of the people.
7. Contrary to popular opinion, wolves serve an important function in the ecosystem of the wild.
8. Running and maintaining a car can prove quite costly.
9. Changing people's lifestyles can lower urban pollution.
10. Despite New York's size, its neighborhoods are like those in small towns.

D. Given the following topic sentences, what should the rest of the paragraph do? Select the answer which comes closest to what should be the main focus of the paragraph.

Example:

Topic sentence: Beginning college students sometimes face problems related to their lack of experience with college life.
   a. Name some of the problems you personally have had at college.
   b. Describe some of the typical problems college students initially have with college life, problems which result from inexperience.
   c. Discuss the beginning college students' limited experience.

Answer: (b) Both (b) and (c) focus on "initially/beginning" and on "inexperience/limited experience" while (a) does not. However, "describe" of (b) is more precise than "discuss" of (c). Also, (c) fails to focus on the key concern with "problems".

1. *Topic sentence:* How can we account for the enormous popularity of health clubs, home fitness equipment, fad diets, and our unprecedented reliance on cosmetic surgery?
   a) Discuss a favorite diet.
   b) Compare and contrast home fitness equipment and health club equipment to decide which is best.
   c) Explain why fitness clubs, equipment, diets, etc. are so popular.

2. *Topic sentence:* Public space means something different to everyone.
   a) List some of the different things public space means to different people.
   b) Give a definition of public space.
   c) Talk about human differences.

3. *Topic sentence:* One key word in the debate over free speech on campus is "insensitivity."
   a) Support free speech on campus.
   b) Prove "insensitivity" is a key word, and explain why.
   c) Enumerate the issues involved in the campus debate over free speech.

4. *Topic sentence:* The West's greatest teachers and statesmen have participated most vigorously in a continual process of dissent, discussion, analysis, and redirection.
   a) Provide examples of the types of dissent the West prefers.
   b) Discuss the type of redirection our society needs.
   c) Provide examples of teachers and statesmen who have participated in this process of dissent.

5. *Topic sentence:* The world is full of multicultural, multiethnic, multilingual nations.
   a) Explain why the world needs more such nations.
   b) Define the terms "multicultural", "multiethnic", and "multilingual."
   c) Give examples of modern countries that fit the above description.

6. *Topic sentence:* Success in learning languages means something different to different people.
   a) Enumerate some of the different possible meanings of language learning success.
   b) Describe some of the different ways people try to learn a language well.
   c) Explain what success in learning languages means to you.

Final Checklist

☐ Are your paragraphs clearly recognizable as such? Do they begin with an indentation of five to seven spaces? Are they written in complete sentences? Do they share unity of subject matter?

☐ Does each topic sentence set up the expectations that you want your paragraph to fulfill?

☐ Is the length of each paragraph appropriate for your purpose? While length will vary, in general, a paragraph in the body of a paper will be a minimum of five sentences and may be as many as ten or twelve.

☐ What is important is that each paragraph be adequately developed for its purpose.

••Writing Assignment

A. Combine the following information into two coherent paragraphs with different topic sentences and conclusions. (Hint: In what general topic areas did Boston's firsts occur?)

EVENTS THAT HAPPENED FIRST IN BOSTON

Year	Event
1634	The establishment of America's first public park, the Boston Common
1635	The founding of America's first public school, the Boston Latin School
1636	The founding of the first American college, Harvard
1637	The enacting of the first draft laws
1638	The founding of America's first printing press
1639	The establishment of America's first Post Office
1652	The establishment of America's first municipal water system
1653	The opening of America's first public library
1704	The publication of America's first newspaper (the Boston News-Letter).
1716	The building of America's first lighthouse
1799	The establishment of America's first board of health
1832	The first public singing of "America"
1845	The invention of the first sewing machine (by Elias Howe)
1846	The first demonstration of ether as an anesthetic
1872	The patenting of the first adding machine to print totals
1875	The wearing of the first baseball glove
1875	The publication of the first Christmas cards
1876	The use of the first telephone (by Alexander Graham Bell)
1892	The installation of the first coin-operated vending machine to dispense stamps
1897	The start of America's first annual marathon race
1898	The opening of America's first subway system
1899	The patenting of the first golf tee
1900	The holding of the first Davis Cup Tennis matches
1903	The use of the first automobile police cruiser
1928	The development of the first computer (at M.I.T.)
1944	The development of the first automatic digital computer
1959	The first effective use of oral contraceptives (the pill)

B. Using the information below, write a paragraph on life in Boston.

Mixed population brings international taste: Irish pubs; many Italian, Greek and French restaurants; Kosher delicatessens; a large Chinatown; a sizable Spanish-speaking and Black population

Centers of education and culture: Harvard University and Massachusetts Institute of Technology—good medical and scientific institutions

Many museums and historic centers: Boston Common, Freedom Trail, Site of First Public School, Benjamin Franklin's Birthplace, Faneuil Hall, Paul Revere's House, Old North Church, Bunker Hill, U.S.S. Constitution, Boston Tea Party Ship

Waterfront area with aquarium, seafood restaurants, fishing, lobster dealers

Boston

Sports excitement: Red Sox (baseball), Patriots (football), Celtics (basketball), Bruins (hockey)

Minutes away from summer watering spots and snow-covered ski slopes

A huge population of young adults-so an active night-life

C. Select from the following list of information those details which best support each topic sentence listed below. Use those details to develop a paragraph to support each topic sentence. There may be some overlap or some need for coordination and subordination.

Daniel Boone

Topic Sentences:

a. Daniel Boone opened up Kentucky to American settlers.

b. Daniel Boone was a restless man who could never settle comfortably in any one place. (or the Boones were restless)

c. Daniel Boone was at home in the wilderness.

d. Daniel Boone was no businessman.

e. People respect his contribution to the frontier movement.

1. Daniel Boone was born along the Delaware River only a few miles above Philadelphia on November 2, 1734.

2. He died in September of 1820 (probably on the 6th).

3. He was the most famous of American pioneers and backwoodsmen and is still a man of legend today.

4. He and his family (who were descendants of English immigrants) moved to Reading, Pennsylvania soon after he was born.

5. While still a youth, he drifted southwestward with friends and settled in the North Carolina uplands, along the Yadkin valley.

6. He served as a wagoner and a blacksmith on an early exploratory expedition westward.

7. Then he was a wandering hunter and a trapper.

8. In 1765 he visited Florida and almost settled there.

9. He discovered the territory now called Kentucky.

10. In 1769 Judge Richard Henderson officially engaged Boone to explore the forests and plains of Kentucky to map it out for settlements.

11. Acting on Judge Henderson's orders, Boone negotiated the purchase of that large tract of land (Kentucky) from the Cherokees.

12. Boone also had to open up the Wilderness road in Kentucky and to escort settlers to the new colony of Transylvania.

13. Boone was resourceful, daring, and persevering in his explorations.

14. He established border posts.

15. He fought the Indians and lived off the land.

16. His confidence inspired settlers to stay and fight.

17. He became a frontier legend.

18. Boone was careless about titles and taxes.

19. He lost all the land he had marked out for himself.

20. In his old age he had no place to settle.

21. He had to keep exploring new land for others.

22. In his old age he explored the Spanish territory west of the Mississippi in the present state of Missouri.

23. The Kentucky legislature finally granted him some land because he had "opened the way [westward] to millions of his fellow men."

24. In the 1810's he made long trapping expeditions into Kansas and even as far as Yellowstone.

25. When he died, he was an object of great respect, and people made pilgrimages to honor his memory.

26. A monument was erected to his memory in Frankfort, Kentucky.

27. A biography by John Filson praised Boone's contribution to the frontier movement.

28. Daniel Boone always wore a coonskin cap, Indian moccasins, and deerskin pants and shirt; he carried a long rifle.

29. He was famous for his marksmanship with a long rifle.

30. He was poor when he died.

31. His son was one of the early settlers of Kansas.

32. His grandson was a pioneer in Colorado.

Chapter 5: ORGANIZING PARAGRAPHS

A well-planned sequence of paragraphs, like a well-planned itinerary, makes us feel that we are making progress, with strategically placed rest stops reached when we have accomplished a significant part of the task. — Hans Guth

In harmonious sequence . . . paragraphs must fit on to one another like the automatic couplings of railway carriages. — Winston Churchill

Paragraph Function

Paragraphs have different lengths and different patterns because they have different functions. No list of uses can be complete, but in general, paragraphs fulfill the following functions:

1. Introduce ideas (establish topic and thesis)
2. Develop ideas (make ideas subordinated)
3. List ideas (make ideas coordinated)
4. Relate ideas between paragraphs (provide transitions)
5. Conclude ideas (summarize).

Each of these functions has its own system of organization, although you must remember that there is great flexibility and overlap, so you must expect to see systems used interchangeably or several systems used in one paragraph. If the outline of a paper is its skeleton, then the introduction is the head, the conclusion the tail, and those paragraphs which comprise the central part of any paper the body. The next chapter will discuss introductory, concluding, and transitional paragraphs (1, 4, and 5 above), while this chapter will focus on developmental body paragraphs (2, 3).

Patterns of Paragraph Development

The body of a paper must conform to the patterns established in the thesis sentence or introduction. This means that the body follows an overall logic. However, within each unit of development, that is, within each paragraph, the logic and patterns may vary. A common way to discuss the logic of paragraphs is by method or technique of development. These methods and techniques will be discussed at length in Unit Two, but the following are some typical patterns. Remember that these are only a sampling of possible patterns and that many more are acceptable and likely.

Definition (a statement of the general category to which a term belongs and the unique characteristics or properties that separate it from others in that category)

A class is a group of students which meets with a particular teacher in a particular room at a particular time for a predetermined course of study. The teacher is an expert in the field, such as history, which the students are studying. The room is the place designated by the university where the subject will be taught. The time is also designated by the university as the proper time for this subject. At the end of a set period (a quarter; a semester) the teacher will give students final grades for their work, grades recorded in a university transcript.

—What general category is being described in the above paragraph? What unique characteristics / properties separate it?

Example (specific illustrations, often introduced by phrases like "for example," "for instance," "to illustrate"; the purpose is to describe some particular in order to make a general concept more concrete)

My chemistry class is typical of most of my classes at the university. There are thirty-five students in the class. We meet three times a week at ten in the morning for fifty minutes. The teacher, Professor Jones, lectures to us for part of the time, and then the students work on chemistry problems for the rest of the time. We receive three hours of university credit if we complete this course with a passing score. A midterm and a final exam are scheduled in the syllabus, but there are also occasional pop quizzes and unscheduled exams, mainly on the readings, but sometimes on the class lectures. What happens in this class seems to be pretty much a standard for all my classes.

—What specifics communicate the idea?

Division into Categories or Parts (an analytical method that involves breaking something into parts in order to understand it more clearly; usually characterized by a reference to a number of items: for example, two main parts, five sections, three categories)

My English study involves three key approaches. The first is to attend classes and to benefit from contact with an experienced teacher and with classmates who are trying to learn the same things I am. The second is to listen carefully to pronunciation and listening tapes at home in order to improve those skills. The third is to make myself have as much contact with the real language as possible. This means listening to the radio and television, going to movies, talking to native speakers whenever possible (in the cafeteria, at the laundry room, in the dorm, between classes), and even auditing some regular classes to accustom my ear to accents and teaching styles.

—What parts?

Comparison (a focus on the similarities between two—or more—things: what they share or have in common)

My English class in the United States is very similar to my English class in Japan. In both classes the goal is to learn English. The classes both meet in a small room with movable chairs. In both the teachers make the students study grammar and practice reading. Both have a final goal of being able to speak and understand English. There are quizzes and tests and lots of homework. In both, by the end of the hour, students are exhausted from trying to think in another language.

_____ is like _____

Contrast (a focus on the differences between two or more things: how they are unlike, unshared qualities)

My English class in the United States is very different from my English class in Japan. While my Japanese teacher is very formal and requires the students to sit in neat rows and raise their hands to answer, my American teacher is very informal, puts the chairs in a circle and encourages students to talk a lot. In my Japanese class we never spoke English conversationally; we only read and wrote it. In my American class we converse a lot, ask and answer questions a lot in English, and even give speeches in English. In Japan, when English class is over, so is English use, but in the United

States, when English class is over, students must continue using English to survive such daily activities as eating, catching a bus, and watching television.

_____ is unlike _____ .

Metaphor or Analogy (a comparison of two dissimilar things; a metaphor calls attention to unexpected underlying similarities; it explains an unknown in terms of a known):

    A class is like a prison in which people are kept to be punished or because they are dangerous. Many students feel that school is punishment or that their parents and teachers want to lock them up. The students cannot leave when they want to; they are imprisoned for the fifty minutes that the class meets. Like prisoners, the students are given numbers. Also, like prisoners, the students may be allowed to leave early if they behave well, but if they try to leave without permission, they will be punished and their stay extended.

_____ is like _____ .

Comparison, contrast, and metaphor are similar, but comparison focuses on the similarities between two similar things, contrast focuses on the differences between two similar things, and metaphor focuses on the similarities between two very different things.

Time Sequence (chronological order: the order in which events occur, one after the other as time progresses):

    The western tradition of "classes" began when the Greek philosopher Socrates gathered his students about him. Socrates would sit in a particular place, such as a corner of the market, and would ask students questions about how they knew what was true and what was false. After Socrates came Plato, who described Socrates' method. Next came Aristotle, who set up one of the first schools… Hundreds of years later, schools were run by churches… Now, schools are often set up by national and local governments.

First _____; next _____; finally _____ .

Process (a time order description, step by step, of how to do something or how something works; the focus is on an explanation of events, activities, or actions in the order in which they occur):

    A class begins when the teacher calls the roll. Then the teacher will begin to lecture or to discuss in some way the subject the class is studying. The teacher will often ask questions, give examples, provide demonstrations, and explain problems. Then he will ask the class to work some problems or to write about a topic. The class ends when the bell rings or when the teacher says that class is dismissed.

Beginning _____; middle _____; end_____.

Notice that *Time Sequence/Chronology* and *Process* are similar since both follow a sequence of events. Chronology, however, is concerned only with time relationships, while process deals, in particular, with how something works. Process is commonly used in science and engineering classes, instruction manuals, cookbooks, and so forth.

Cause and Effect (a statement of what happens and/or of why it happens)

    Classes are created and organized either because students want to learn or because learning is required for their future employment or profession. Students who wish to know more about the world around them demand classes to teach them history, philosophy, archeology, architecture and so forth. Students who need to train themselves to be expert in their careers will need courses in mathematics, computer science, biology, and other subjects. As a result, national and local governments have, for a long time, set up groups to meet in particular places at particular times with lecturers who are experts in the field the students wish to study. In other words, education is a matter of supply and demand.

Cause _____; effect _____

Function (a description of the purpose of something, what it is used for, what it does)

    My English class performs a number of important functions, some predictable, some less predictable. Obviously, its major function is to provide an environment in which students can study and learn English. For this purpose it has a teacher and a textbook. However, it also functions to introduce students to the American classroom and the special approaches and techniques that characterize it. Furthermore, it helps ease culture shock by providing a period for adjustment before one has to move into academic classes. In addition, because of the small size and the closeness of the students, it is a place for forming friendships, making alliances, and taking the first steps toward social activities.

—What is its main purpose? What minor purposes does it serve?

Spatial (a description of where things are located; placement in a locale)

My very crowded English class is located on the third floor of Jones Hall on the law school campus. A jumble of student desks fills most of the floor space, with barely room to move between them. In the front of the classroom the teacher's desk is pushed against the blackboard. In the back of the classroom are some low bookshelves crammed against a screen for showing films. On the other three walls are blackboards filled with the teacher's scribbling. The ceiling is low.

—What space is described first? Next?

Sometimes a good paragraph will combine a series of developmental techniques like the ones above to create an interesting whole. In fact, a good writer thinks about a whole series of different organizational techniques, several of which may be used at the same time. One pattern may dominate the paper as a whole, but secondary patterns may differ from paragraph to paragraph to provide internal consistency within these smaller units. It may seem too difficult to think about the thesis idea, the topic idea, the pattern of development, the purpose of the individual paragraph, and the purpose of the overall paper simultaneously, but it is not really different from the photographer who "frames" her picture,

adjusts for the amount of light, and turns the lens for sharper focus. The photographer has developed a series of semi-automatic habits, and so should the writer. The difficulty is keeping your eye on the "big picture" of the general thesis while at the same time making "micro-adjustments" of paragraph level topics. As with picture taking, expertise comes with practice.

The body of a paper is the heart of your writing. It is where the most detailed information is conveyed, where the persuasion, description, or analysis takes place, where you, the writer, make your case. Consequently, it is difficult to limit discussion of the body to this section. The rest of this text will really be about the body of the paper, how to plan it, develop it, and carry it out, how to rework it, revise it, and make it serve your particular purposes.

•EXERCISE 5.1: TOPIC IDEAS AND METHODS OF DEVELOPMENT

Your main task is to identify the basic organizational plan of each paragraph. Does it give examples, make a contrast, comparison, or analogy, define a term or idea, paint a picture to make the idea clearer, follow a time or spatial order? Does it move from general to particular or from particular to general? You may find more than one plan or method at work. For example, a paragraph may be developed by contrast, but that contrast is developed through examples or description. Circle the key word or phrase that identifies the main plan.

> *Example:* The paragraph above that begins *Sometimes a good paragraph...* explains through a brief <u>description</u> of paragraph qualities but mainly through an <u>analogy</u>. Key phrases: *combine techniques* and *not really different from a photographer.*

1. The rain forest of Costa Rica and the coral reef of Hawaii seem worlds apart. They are in different parts of the globe. One is on land and one under the sea. Neither the plants nor the living creatures which inhabit them are the same or even similar. One does not remind viewers of the other. The world of the rain forest is a dense, almost impenetrable one of greens and browns, where sunlight barely filters through, and the air is still. The shrieks of parrots and other multicolored tropical birds pierce the air, monkeys swing from the higher branches, and jaguars and dwarf deer creep silently through the undergrowth. But in air heavy with moisture the sounds are muted and the movement barely visible. In contrast, the world of the coral reef is filled with sunlight, color, and movement. Brilliant shades of fish—greens, blues, even reds and oranges—with stripes

and dots, zig-zags, or alternating slashes of color dart among the chalky white mushroom coral or the bright red coral of a reef rich in nutrients and full of life. Sharks and eels, rays and squid, starfish and sea urchins abound. The dark forest and the sunlit reef, worlds apart and seemingly so different, both provide a rich nutrient base for a multitude of life forms.

2. The Roman Empire in the time of the Antonines extended over much of the known world. It stretched from Scandinavia in the North to Egypt in the South, from Ireland, Spain, and the west coast of Africa in the West to Armenia, Syria, and Arabia in the East. In other words, it covered almost all of the land mass of modern Europe (including Great Britain), the countries of the mid-East (including the Holy Land), and all those African territories bordering on the Mediterranean as well as all the islands in the Mediterranean. By land, one could travel from Cairo to Jerusalem, Antioch, and Nicaea on the Black Sea, then to Thessalonica, Athens, ancient Lugdunum in Gallia (modern France), and Nova Cathago on the Spanish Riviera, and never leave the Empire. By sea, one could sail from Palestine to Cyprus, Crete, Sicily, Sardinia or Corsica, out through the Straits of Gibraltar, north through the English or the Irish Channel to the Bay of Finland and never leave the Roman Empire, so vast were its holdings.

3. Although at first Stratford, England and Ashland, Oregon seem to have little in common, in fact, both are home to live and popular productions of Shakespearean plays and to yearly Shakespearean festivals. One expects to be able to see Shakespeare performed nightly at Stratford, Shakespeare's birthplace, but one does not expect such nightly performances in a rural American state, noted for forestry and fishing more than education. Yet, the Ashland regional theater, founded in 1935, draws more than 370,000 spectators a year to a three-stage jamboree in which, after trumpets and flag raising and madrigal singers, the sounds of *Hamlet* and *As You Like It*, among others, are heard on the night air. Stratford's annual summer festival draws double the number as Ashland for productions performed indoors, not outdoors, and it has less trumpet blowing and flag raising. Nonetheless, both cities pay tribute to that sixteenth-century Englishman who has now become the intellectual property of the whole world. Both strive for clear interpretations, fine acting, interesting sets, and lively action. Both are well worth a visit.

4. The most important function that a leaf performs for a plant is photosynthesis, a unique natural chemical process that uses the energy from light to combine carbon dioxide and water in order to produce sugars and starches to nourish the plant. The parts of this term sum up its action: the Greek words *photos*, meaning "light," and *synthesis*, meaning "putting together" suggest using light to put things together to make something new. Botanists Johannes van Overbeek and Harry K. Wong, authors of *The Love of Living Plants*, suggest an easy experiment to demonstrate this effect. They suggest cutting your name in a piece of aluminum foil and then using the foil to cover one of the two primary leaves of a young plant growing in a pot. After the plant has been allowed to photosynthesize for a few days under the same good conditions it had before the start of the test (water and sunlight), both leaves should be cut off and plunged into boiling alcohol. The result should be that the green pigment dissolves in the alcohol. If the decolored leaves are then placed in a shallow dish containing a dilute solution of iodine in potassium iodide, in a short while, the leaf that remained uncovered will turn blue while on the other leaf only your name will appear in blue. The blue indicates the presence of starch only in the portion of the leaf that received light. In other words, without light, photosynthesis cannot occur, and plants cannot produce sugars and starches on which to live. Too long a time without sunlight means the inevitable death of a plant.

5. A redwood forest, whether in Muir Woods, Yosemite, or the Sequoia National Park is like some aging cathedral. The trees are so huge, so tall that little else can grow on the forest floor. What dominates is a cool, dim light that filters down from above; these soft beams of light penetrate the half darkness of the hushed forest floor like the half light of some cool, dark, ancient European cathedral. Like massive church columns lifting toward God, the massive trunks of forest giants reach upward. Just as visitors stand awed and silent at the wonder and the grandeur of Notre Dame Cathedral, so they stand awed and silent at the wonder and the grandeur of these ancient trees.

6. The clotting of blood is the result of a delicate and complex series of biochemical events, some of which are not fully understood. This mechanism must satisfy two rigorous requirements if life is to be sustained: (1) blood must never clot while it is performing its functions within the intact circulatory system; (2) blood must always clot when any damage occurs that causes a break in the blood vessels. The body must be able to vary this complex response to bleeding ranging from a slight cut to a massive hemorrhage. When tissues are damaged, a chemical is released from the nearby cells and platelets. This initiates a chain of reactions in which calcium plays an important part. The end result is that a soluble protein is converted into a sticky solid that makes a webbed mesh. Platelets, red cells and white cells are trapped in the sticky web and form a jellylike clot. As the platelets disintegrate, they cause the web to shrink. As the web shrinks, it constricts the walls of the torn blood vessel, closes the tear, and stops blood from escaping.

adapted from *Blood and the Nation's Health* (American National Red Cross)

Paragraph Arrangement

The arrangement of sentences after a topic sentence depends on paragraph function. The pattern cannot simply go in any direction the writer wants it to go. Instead, the topic sentence determines the pattern. It sets up the reader's expectations, and those expectations must be met.

SUBORDINATION

Some paragraphs focus on one idea and develop it into more and more specific terms. The following is typical of this form:

Lead acid batteries, which can be used to power electric cars, are simply constructed. [*topic sentence:* the rest of the paragraph must describe the construction] This kind of battery is a box, usually an oblong one of less than one cubic foot in volume, made of plastic or some other synthetic material. Inside the box are "plates" or flat sheets of lead which are surrounded by acid. The number of plates determines the strength of the battery. Each plate is made of lead because of the cheapness and the stability of the metal.

This arrangement goes from a general statement to a more specific statement, to a more specific statement, etc. You can diagram this kind of paragraph as follows:

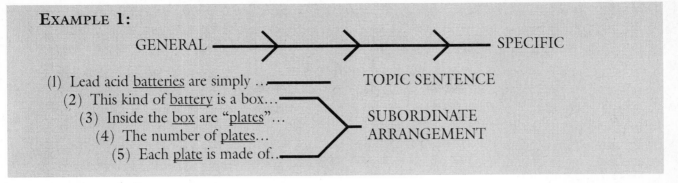

EXAMPLE 1:

GENERAL ⟶ ⟶ ⟶ SPECIFIC

(1) Lead acid <u>batteries</u> are simply ... — TOPIC SENTENCE

(2) This kind of <u>battery</u> is a box...

(3) Inside the <u>box</u> are "<u>plates</u>"... SUBORDINATE ARRANGEMENT

(4) The number of <u>plates</u>...

(5) Each <u>plate</u> is made of...

EXAMPLE 2:

(1) My car has bucket seats.

(2) The seats are covered with leather.

(3) The leather is black.

(4) The black has gold stars on it.

(5) The stars have five points.

The number in front of each sentence represents the level or degree of <u>abstraction</u> of each sentence in relation to the topic sentence. The first sentence is called (1) because it is the most general sentence in the paragraph; the sentences which follow it become more and more specific, so they are in turn called (2), (3), (4), and (5). This kind of increasing specificity is useful when you are narrowing down a subject. You take the reader along step-by-step, making each sentence refer to the one before it. This is called a <u>subordinate</u> arrangement because each sentence is subordinate to or weaker than the one before it, on which it depends. You cannot change the order of these sentences without making nonsense out of the paragraph.

COORDINATION

Obviously, you can't write subordinated paragraphs all the time; sometimes you will write paragraphs which simply list a series of ideas at about the same level of abstraction. The following is typical of this form.

(1) The <u>advantages</u> of the electric car make it the most desirable kind of vehicle for urban transportation in the future.

(2) Since electric motors are quiet by gas engine standards, noise pollution will be reduced.

(2) Electric motors produce no toxic gases which cannot be cleaned up; the ozone they emit can be controlled.

(2) Because of the limitations of battery power, electric cars will be small, allowing more room in narrow city streets.

(2) Finally, the energy shortage will be drastically improved, since electric motors are on the average twice as efficient as internal combustion engines.

Each #2 gives one advantage of the electric car, so, in effect, a coordinated paragraph has a topic sentence followed by a parallel list or series which enumerates. This kind of paragraph is called a coordinated paragraph since it lists sentences of equal levels of abstraction. Each sentence depends only on the topic sentence (in fact, on one phrase of the topic sentence) rather than on the sentence which comes before it. You could put these sentences in any order after the topic sentence, as long as you remember to keep *Finally* for the end of the paragraph, though often you do list them in order of importance or time.

GENERAL ⟶ ⟶ SPECIFIC

IMPLIED TOPIC SENTENCE

The topic sentence in each of the examples of coordinated and subordinated paragraphs is clearly the most general sentence of each paragraph; it is the sentence which controls the others. However, some paragraphs may not even state the thesis or topic, leaving it to the reader to figure out; it may be simply implied without being stated, as in the following example.

(2) Our cities are smoke-filled and polluted.

(2) Our streets are crowded with cars.

(2) We are running short of energy.

(2) Noise drives us to the edge of insanity.

[(1) We are in serious trouble.] Unifying Topic Idea—implied but not stated.

Leaving out the thesis or topic sentence is not always a good idea, for it forces the reader to interpret the meaning of the series of ideas; implied topic paragraphs are difficult to manage. They are sometimes used by experienced writers when the unifying idea seems obvious without being stated but should be avoided by beginning writers.

MIXED PARAGRAPHS

Most of the paragraphs you write will be mixtures of subordination and coordination. They will list series of ideas and develop some of these ideas to levels of specificity three and four, as in the following.

(1) The advantages of the electric car make it the most desirable kind of vehicle for urban transportation in the future.

(2) Since electric motors are quiet by gas engine standards, noise pollution will be reduced.

(3) This advantage may have a temporary negative effect since pedestrians and children might not hear electric cars and thus not notice them.

(4) Pedestrian/auto accidents might thus rise until pedestrians adjust.

(3) However, long term, once such adjustments have been made, workers will produce more in quieter surroundings.

(2) Electric motors produce no toxic gases which cannot be cleaned up; the ozone they emit can be controlled.

(3) Research into ozone control is becoming more common at many universities and research institutes.

(4) Dr. Hans Geltbauer of Rubens College in California has been one of the leaders in this booming field.

(5) Dr. Geltbauer says....

• EXERCISE 5.2 : IMPLIED TOPIC SENTENCES

What unifying idea or argument is implied in each of the following paragraphs? State the implied idea of each as a topic sentence. Would these paragraphs be better if the topic idea were stated directly at their beginning or end?

1. Such activities as making change, buying lunch, asking directions, getting information on how to do the laundry, and finding out bus routes require students learning English to develop and use survival vocabulary. Dealing with fellow customers and sales personnel in a grocery store, a drug store or a discount store results in similar conversational opportunities impossible to duplicate in the student's home country. Whether students are catching a streetcar or a bus, shopping, touring, or working out in the gym, they will hear English spoken all around them. In the evening, going to films, plays, lectures, or church meetings, or just staying home and watching television or talking with roommates or suitemates provide further opportunities to hear and use English.

2. Doctors recommend aspirin to reduce fever, particularly fever caused by a cold. They also recommend it for sore and aching muscles. It helps those suffering from arthritis, and from migraine, pre-menstrual, or just ordinary headaches. Many specialists prescribe it for people who have had heart attacks because it inhibits clotting of the blood and therefore reduces the chance of a repeat attack. Others believe that, taken regularly, it can prevent both strokes and heart attacks.

This kind of mixed paragraph will be much longer than a purely subordinated or a purely coordinated one. Should you list all four advantages of electric cars in one paragraph if you use a mixed organization? Probably not, for if you added (3)s and (4)s to each (2) advantage, the paragraph might go on for pages.

•EXERCISE 5.3: PARAGRAPH ARRANGEMENT

A. The following well-developed body paragraphs are of the length and detail you want to work toward in your writing.

    (1) Using the numbering system shown on page 95, <u>number the sentences</u> in the following paragraphs.

    (2) <u>Identify</u> the paragraphs as coordinated, subordinated, or mixed.

    (3) What does your numbering system reveal about the strengths or weaknesses of these paragraphs? <u>Are these good paragraphs</u>? If not, why not? What could be done to improve them?

1. A Saturday walk along Canal Street in New Orleans will reveal a surprising blend of races and cultures. There is a mixture of blacks, from newly arrived Jamaican or Haitian immigrants, to Nigerian and Ethiopian tourists, to the long-established locals, who have made the city their own. Japanese, Greek, Filipino, Russian, Pakistani, and English sailors move from bar to bar and shop to shop. Cubans, Columbians, Puerto Ricans, and other Latin Americans frequent the discos. The Italian and Sicilian farmers pass, transporting their fresh farm produce to the French Market. Some German businessmen, singing beer songs, try to pick up some French girls who are window shopping. All sorts of people of all shades and all types make up the international mix so characteristic of a port town.

2. U.S. food preferences changed after the 1960's. With Richard Nixon's opening of relationships with China came a new fascination with Chinese food. Whereas in the past American Chinese restaurants served food adjusted for American taste (chow mein, chop suey, fried rice), in the 1970's Chinese restaurants began to hire cooks trained in Taiwan or Hong Kong, cooks who would prepare authentic dishes. These cooks specialized in the special dishes of particular provinces, so Americans became familiar with the differences between Cantonese (the most common style in the past), Hunan, Szechwan, and Mongolian cuisines. Furthermore, diners made this food a regular part of their own diet. As a result of this changed attitude, cooking schools sprang up across the nation, teaching how to stir-fry, how to make eggrolls, how to employ Szechwan spices. Today, most Americans have learned to stir-fry foods on a regular basis and have developed discriminating palates for the cuisines of different regions of China. One no longer says, "Let's eat Chinese"; one says, "Let's try Szechwan tonight," or "How about Mongolian beef?"

3. Self-reliance and independence are very important American values. Children are taught to respect frontier heroes like Daniel Boone or Davy Crockett, who went into the wilderness alone and learned to deal with hostile Indians and hostile land and to make their own way. By the time they are teenagers, young Americans begin to separate themselves from their families and homes. They develop their own set of friends, their own set of activities, and their own time schedule. They begin to think of going away to school or of getting a job so they can get their own car. In fact, the mobility a car provides makes greater independence possible. During their college years, most young Americans already think of themselves as separate from their families, with separate goals and changing values. They prefer going away to college, and living in dormitories or apartments instead of at

home. Usually their first job completes the separation. Many large business firms encourage mobility, transferring a new employee from firm to firm, city to city, and state to state. A typical family might have the parents living in Sioux City, Iowa, a son working in New York, a daughter employed in San Francisco, the grandson studying abroad in Italy, and more distant relatives spread throughout the country. Such physical separation from those closest to one forces the cultivation of self-reliance and independence, the values Americans respect so highly.

4. Many changes have taken place in American life and culture since World War II. At first Americans felt very safe and secure because of their victory, but soon the Cold War and the Soviet advances (like Sputnik) produced a paranoia that led to witch-hunts for Communists and fears of nuclear war. The assassinations of President John F. Kennedy and then of Martin Luther King and Robert Kennedy made Americans distrust each other. The war in Vietnam split the country apart, mainly by generations. The conservative older generation feared Communism would take over Asia and thought the war necessary to world security. The younger generation began to have its doubts. Many did not believe the quarrel was America's quarrel. Some burned their draft cards; others fled to Canada to avoid involvement in the war; many protested on university campuses across the country. Many did not want to die in a foreign country fighting for unclear reasons against an unclear enemy. The conflict between generations culminated in the tragedy at Kent State University when National Guardsmen shot unarmed students—because they were afraid of their ideas and their protest. Vice-president Spiro Agnew claimed to speak for America's "Silent Majority" of conservatives. The conflicts of values and ideals went so deep that not until twenty years later are Americans beginning to come to terms with that past—mainly by rewriting the history of that conflict in their minds.

5. Fast-food restaurants, especially ones with take-out food, have become very popular all over the United States. This is partly because of the rush of the work day. Many offices depend on employees being able to eat on the run or even at work, so take-out pizzas and burgers, salads and sandwiches of all types have become standard lunch fare from New York to San Francisco. This is also because of the increase in working women who simply have no time to work and prepare meals. Instead of coming home at 5 p.m. and then slaving over a hot stove, they prefer to send out for Chinese or Indian take-out, po-boy or submarine sandwiches, boxes of spicy chicken or shrimp, or even gourmet meals specially prepared at local restaurants for those who want good food fast—and don't worry about the cost.

B. Organize the following information on fleas into a single paragraph, unified by a topic statement and connective words. Underline your topic sentence. Identify your organizational pattern.

Fleas: jump 150 times their length (equal to a man jumping over 300 meters); flip every jump; legs land in correct position to hook on to target; Oriental rat flea carried plague—killed more than 50 million people in Middle Ages; accelerate 50 times faster than the space shuttle; can remain frozen up to a year and revive; more than 2200 species; reproduction from egg to adult= three months; survive months without food; two fleas = two trillion descendants in nine months; to fight fleas indoors, use insecticide + vacuuming + shampooing pets

Unit Two will discuss the organization of the whole paper at greater length, but the point here is to be aware of paragraph structure:

Subordinated Paragraphs:
Useful for developing and making specific—one idea developed with concrete detail
> **Weakness:**
> becomes narrower and narrower and therefore makes moving on to another idea more difficult
> **Strength:**
> good for detailed body paragraphs

Coordinated Paragraphs:
Useful for listing a series of ideas
> **Weakness:**
> does not allow much development of specific details
> **Strength:**
> good for introductions and conclusions

Mixed Paragraphs:
The most common paragraph form. Allows listing of a few major ideas and their development into specific detail
> **Weakness:**
> if too many details are included, may be too long and need to be divided
> **Strength:**
> good for briefly exploring several closely related points with examples

If one of your paragraphs, particularly a mixed paragraph, seems to cover too much information, with multiple topic directions, you might be able to turn your topic sentence for the one paragraph into a thesis sentence for the whole paper. If you do this, your (2) level paragraph sentences will become topic sentences for each paragraph of the paper. This is usually called *narrowing your topic* or *narrowing the focus of your topic* to something short enough and specific enough to handle properly. Clearly, you should follow this procedure only if you discover that you have too much information for one long paragraph and that you only need a short paper.

- **EXERCISE 5.4: JUDGING PLANS FOR PARAGRAPHS**

  Which of the following outlines for paragraphs on food have good details and good subordination? Which could be improved? Why? How? Are the paragraphs coordinated, subordinated, or mixed? Explain. What changes in pattern would improve them?

A. 1. Salvadorian food is delicious and not too spicy.
   2. The most typical food is fried.
      3. Examples of fried foods are red beans, which can be mashed; bananas or plantains; and rice, in different flavors.
         4. The beans and bananas can be topped with sour cream or sugar.
      3. The tortilla, made out of corn, is served with all foods.
      3. Tamales are also loved by the Salvadorian people.
         4. Some are made of corn, others of salt or sugar.
(Will all readers understand these food words? What happened to the idea about spices? How can you prove "delicious"? Are tortillas and tamales fried foods?)

B. 1. Curaçaoean food is from many different countries.
   2. Stoba comes from Africa.
   2. Holland brought us its famous potatoes.
   2. The Indians gave us spicy food.
   2. Chinese food came with the Chinese immigrants.
   2. Jambo may be the only food that is truly Curaçaoean.

C. 1. Indian food consists of a variety of tastes.
   2. Vegetable soup has a spicy taste.
   2. Rice pudding is sweet.
   2. Karkarkai has a bitter taste.
   2. Eggplant soup has a mixture of sweet and sour taste.
   2. Squash is the only food which is bland, but it still tastes satisfying.
D. 1. Brazilian food is spicy.
   2. It mostly originated from Portugal and France.
   2. Fish and olive oil is very common.
   2. Cherry is an everyday dessert.
   2. Fancy sauces made out of wines are used frequently.
   2. Other countries have influenced the Brazilian food as well, but the spicy taste is a common taste in all foods.

List problems and suggest solutions.

Unity and Coherence

No matter what the pattern of development, a good paragraph should demonstrate cohesiveness and unity. Each idea must fit together with every other idea in the paragraph. Paragraph unity may be created in a number of ways. A clear topic sentence and conclusion are a good beginning. These, coupled with a recognizable and consistent pattern of development, provide unity of thought and logic.

Repeating a pattern, a phrase, or a key word also calls attention to relationships. Pronoun references and demonstrative pronouns interrelate sentences, and special transition words of time, place, result, and so forth complete the process. In other words, logic of argument combined with connecting words together create unity and coherence. The two models which follow demonstrate how this is done.

Model #1

"Rain forests" and "jungles" are very different worlds. The latter, the jungle, is a place of **nightmares**, threats, and danger with *snakes hanging from trees, leopards crouching on* — life
low-hanging branches, and tigers stalking their prey from behind
impenetrable screens of foliage. The lush vegetation of the — visibility
jungle floor is *a barrier to be fought through,* one that leaves — visibility
even the most daring adventurers dripping sweat in the
steam-bath atmosphere, *bitten and stung by swarms of insects.* — life
The air is alive with *noisy, chattering monkeys, shrieking* — sounds
birds, and humming insects. This green **hell** is worlds apart from the
true rain forest—a natural **cathedral**, untouched, primeval.
Unlike the dense jungle floor, the forest floor is *open,* with
richly colored fallen leaves and flowers forming a plush and — visibility
wondrous carpet of browns, greens, blues, and violets. Because
little light filters through, the forest floor remains *free of*
undergrowth and *one can see a hundred feet or more ahead.* The — visibility
animal life too is more benign: *deer, raccoons, chipmunks* and — life
possums. The rain forest is *hushed, silent,* almost a **dream** of — sounds
paradise regained.

The first sentence, the topic sentence, establishes the topic and the pattern of development: a contrast between rain forest and jungle. The underlined words demonstrate the repetition of these key terms to keep the reader focused on the topic. The word *different* begins the contrast, which is built through a two-part division, with the first half of the paragraph characterizing *the jungle* and the second half characterizing *the rain forest*. The parallel order of the sentences in each section adds to the sense of coherence: dangerous versus cathedral-like, dense and enclosed versus open and free, noisy versus silent, a nightmarish *green hell* versus **a dream of paradise regained**. The words in italics and in bold and the margin categories indicate the contrastive pieces of information. A consistent focus on negatives in the section on *jungle* and positives in the section on rain forest helps carry out the logic of the contrast and distinguishes between the two sets of information that make up the paragraph. Reference words like *latter* for *jungle* and *one* for *barrier* and transitional words of contrast (*unlike*), addition (*too*), and cause (*because*) complete the connections. In sum, this model depends on unity of idea to promote paragraph cohesion.

Model #2

The paragraph below depends on the repetition of key words and linking words indicating a series of experiments to create unity and coherence. Its repetition of *experiments, elephants, local,* and *protect* keep the focus on the topic idea, expressed in the first sentence, refined in the next two, and summed up in the concluding lines. Its series of examples are united, both through connecting words like *one, another, still another, these,* and *such,* as well as through a logic that builds toward greater and greater ingenuity and complexity in working out compromises with locals that will help protect and save elephants.

<u>Experiments</u> to stop the illegal killing of **elephants** and to help **protect** and stabilize **elephant** populations depend on involving **local** residents in African countries like Zambia, Zimbabwe, and Kenya. *These* <u>experiments</u> depend mainly on demonstrating to **local** people that **elephants** can help the **local** economy and improve the well-being of **local** citizens in other ways than through stolen ivory tusks. *In other words, these* <u>programs</u> appeal directly to the economic self-interest of residents by including plans that will show them how to benefit from the **elephant** as a resource to be **protected** rather than plunder to be taken. <u>In one experiment</u>, **locals** acting as trackers, interpreters, and merchants helping tourists observe **elephants** in their natural habitat make enough income to support several local villages. <u>In another</u>, **locals** get first choice of employment in hotels and park services so *they* can earn more money, more steadily, and more safely than they could poaching. <u>In still another anti-poaching experiment</u>, **local** residents actually help rangers maintain the health of the **elephant** herds by selectively removing the sick, the weak, and the injured. The **locals** can *then* use the meat, skin, and tusks of *these animals* as they wish. *The result* has been a thriving leather and meat industry but	**key word** **topic sentence** **other key words** **demonstrative pronoun** **plus key word** **linking phrase** **demonstrative pronoun** **synonym for key word** **begins list of support** **development by** **example** **2nd support: repeats** **form/pronoun** **3rd support: repeats** **form** **time** **demonstrative; synonym** **cause/effect**

also healthy, living **elephant**s which are **protected** from poachers by people who profit from **protecting** them. <u>The Kenya program</u> carefully considers the **local** situation, so that when water is scarce and meat hard to get, **local** hunters are allowed to hunt **elephants** to help the tribe survive the hard times; *in return*, during normal times, *they* agree to **protect** *those* **elephants** as *they* would *their* own cattle, as a private survival source. <u>All three experiments</u> have reduced poaching, and, in <u>at least one, Kenya</u>, the steady decline of the **elephant** has been reversed (with a positive effect on the zebra and other animals as well). <u>Such experiments</u> suggest that, when natives have a direct and personal interest in **protecting** and preserving **elephants** and are allowed to participate actively in decision-making about herd management, *their* own self–interest discourages poaching and stops the all too steady decline of the **elephant** population so tragically visible in other parts of Africa.

synonym for key word

linking phrase
pronouns
key word
comparison

key word

conclusion

pronoun

What do the italicized and boldface words do to create unity in this reading? What words are repeated? Why? How is the conclusion like the topic sentence? What does it add? If you were to summarize this paragraph, which sentences would be most important to examine? Why?

Sometimes a simple misuse of pronouns can reduce unity and coherence. For example, the following paragraph uses pronouns inconsistently.

> <u>Any son or daughter</u> might choose the item in the television ad as a gift for Father's Day. However, the ad gives <u>one</u> the impression that <u>you</u> have to have an extensive education in order to appreciate such an item, when in fact persons without such an education will also be attracted to this item because buying it will make <u>them</u> feel as if other people will recognize <u>one's</u> education. Though this ad gives the impression of persons from the upper-middle class, with fine taste, <u>you</u> can easily see this market consists of persons who want to give <u>one</u> the impression of education and taste, whether or not <u>he</u> really has it.

A few pronoun changes make all the difference between clarity and confusion:

Any son or daughter might choose the item in the television ad as a gift for Father's Day. However, the ad gives the impression that its <u>viewers</u> have to have an extensive education in order to appreciate such an item, when in fact, <u>those</u> without such an education will also be attracted to this item because buying it will make them feel as if other people will recognize their education. Though this ad gives the impression of buyers from the upper-middle class, with fine taste, this market clearly consists of <u>those</u> who want to give the impression of education and taste, whether or not <u>they</u> really have it.

In summary, when you write, set up a topic sentence and meet the expectations it raises; decide on a pattern of development and follow it; use connective words wherever there might be confusion, and always check pronoun references for clarity. If you follow this advice, your paragraphs should be much easier for readers to follow and understand.

- ## EXERCISE 5.5: PARAGRAPH UNITY

  A. Identify every method used to unify ideas in the following paragraphs.

  1. Yellowstone National Park is more than a spectacle of volcanism and erosive forces, more than a parade of wild birds and beasts, more than a scenically splendid landscape. It is a monument to the small band of idealists who had the courage and the conviction to demand that a hustling, growing nation of pioneers and exploiters set aside two million acres of the public domain to be kept intact and natural for the enjoyment of future generations. The new park was to be, according to the enabling legislation, a "pleasuring-ground" for the Nation. Today the meaning of Yellowstone far transcends that original goal. An increasing number of Americans, wearied by the pace of life in the city and beset by its noise, smells, and ugliness, are turning to Yellowstone and other national parks for respite. Here they can slow down, refresh mind and body, and restore the spirit. Here they can reestablish their ties with Mother Earth. Here society can reevaluate its damaged partnership with nature.
     —adapted from "Maps: Yellowstone and Grand Teton National Parks," National Park Service, U.S. Department of Interior

  2. Despite the harshness and severity of the environment, more than 900 kinds of plants live within the [Death Valley National] park. Those on the valley floor have adapted to a desert life by a variety of means. Some have roots that go downward ten times the height of an average person. Others have a root system that lies just below the surface but extends out far in all directions. Still others have skins that allow very little evaporation. Different forms of wildlife too have learned to deal with this heat. The animals that live in the desert are mainly nocturnal, for once the sun sets, the temperature falls quickly because of the dry air. Night, the time of seeming vast emptiness, is the time of innumerable comings and goings by little animals. Larger animals, such as the desert bighorn, live in the cooler, higher elevations. With height, moisture increases too, until on the high peaks there are forests with juniper, mountain-mahogany, pinyon, and other pines. Often, the peaks surrounding the valley are snow-covered. However, it is the little rain that falls on the valley floor that is the life force of the wildflowers and that transforms this desert into a vast garden teeming with small, hardy life. In other words, then, thanks to natural adaptation, Death Valley is an active world of exciting contrasts and wonders—quite the opposite of its name.
     —adapted from "Death Valley," National Park Service, U.S. Department of Interior

  3. In 1717, she [the city of New Orleans] was a mere flicker in the eyes of the French. A year later she was christened [given a name, as with a child] , on the banks of a great river—a Creole princess born in the new Louisiana Territory. She lived among Choctaw and Chickasaw [Native American tribes]; explored dark shadowy bayous [swamp lakes]; lazed on sun-drenched shores; and battled flood and disease. She knew swaggering pirates, and scarifying voodoo secrets. The Spaniards adorned her with architectural splendors, but her proud French Creole origins were apparent everywhere. She warmly welcomed the fun-loving Cajuns who came in 1763, gifting her with incomparable zest. She discovered in herself a natural instinct for soul-stirring music; her cuisine was truly exotic. By the time she became an American citizen in 1803, she was quite famous, as Europeans flocked [came in large groups] to her door. The little waif [small child] on the waterfront was named New Orleans, and she grew up to be the European Queen of the Mississippi.
     —Honey Naylor, Greater New Orleans Tourist and Convention Commission brochure

B. The sentences in the following paragraphs are out of order. Since the original paragraphs were unified and coherent, you should be able to follow the clues of logic and of connective words to restore them to their proper sequence.

1) However, equal protection of the law depends on the courts. 2) This unwillingness may be caused by racial prejudice or by political extremism. 3) All men are equal in the eyes of the law. 4) A particular law court may be unwilling to provide protection. 5) Therefore, when we discuss equality, we must consider race and politics. 6) But doing so is difficult because feelings about race are highly emotional, and political disagreements are hard to resolve.

1) Adults and youngsters alike just mindlessly absorb what they see. 2) The reason is that our whole new generation has spent tens of thousands of hours lying in front of a television set. 3) Television has profoundly affected modern Americans. 4) Their eyes are glued to the screen through programs and commercials alike. 5) As a result, they no longer stop to read or reason or communicate. 6) Instead of building playhouses, forming clubs, making friends, or reading books, they spend their time swallowing the "cut-rate justice" and "superficial problem solving" of television programs. 7) Such a response is dangerous to a democracy.

1) In fact, as far as man was concerned, there were no dinosaurs until about 150 years ago. 2) One could argue that paleontology (the study of fossils) became a science as a result of a change in concepts, a general revolution in thought, and the intellectual climate of the Age of Reason that brought on a period of investigation and a focus on logic. 3) A revolution in thought had taken place both in the scientific community and in the society at large, and the result, Kuhn predicts, was new insights, a "gestalt [perception] switch" so that what had always been there suddenly became apparent. 4) That is, until the early days of the last century, even the most knowledgeable men had looked at dinosaurs with unseeing eyes. 5) But suddenly, in the nineteenth century, people began to "discover" what had been there for centuries. 6) Medieval peoples thought they came from giants or dragons, which fit in with their world view, and dismissed them as irrelevant. 7) And not only to discover, but to look for rational explanations for such natural phenomena, explanations that fit uniform natural laws. 8) They had perhaps seen the bones, but they had not understood what they had seen. 9) The overall intellectual climate encouraged this new vision.

C. The following sentences belong together in a unified paragraph, but the unifying elements are missing. What changes will add order, unity, and purpose?

1) New Orleans has cheap fast food. 2) Sightseers can buy lucky dogs [a special brand of New Orleans hot dog] from street stands, enjoy beignets and coffee at the Cafe du Monde, or grab shrimp or shish kebob on a stick from an Oriental or Middle-Eastern fast-food joint, all for two to five dollars. 3) New Orleans has expensive, high quality restaurants. 4) Traditional French, Creole, Cajun, and Italian restaurants provide samplings of the rich sauces and delicacies that have made the city famous for good food—at anywhere from $25.00 to $150.00 per person. 5) There is plenty of low cost entertainment. 6) Live musicians, alone or in groups, play in Jackson Square for tips. 7) Street performers—jugglers, dancers, mimes, and magicians—do the same. 8) At Preservation Hall one can listen to unforgettable jazz concerts for a $2 admission fee. 9) Entertainment costs can be enormously high. 10) Most nightspots with music or dancing of one type or another have a cover charge of at least fifteen dollars. 11) Inside, prices might run as high as $7.50 for an ordinary drink and even more for some exotic mixture. 12) If one is not careful, he will find himself spending hundreds of dollars in a single night.

Final Checklist

☐ Can your reader easily identify the major ideas of your paper by reading the topic sentences of each body paragraph?

☐ Does each paragraph have a tight focus: a clear idea with carefully selected support?

☐ Does each paragraph have unity of subject matter or are there digressions? Such unity is vital to communication, while digressions are frowned upon in college essays and business letters.

☐ Have you followed a clear-cut pattern of development, used connective words wherever there might be confusion, and checked pronoun references for clarity?

☐ Is each paragraph like a composition in miniature with a clear topic (usually expressed in a topic sentence), development of that topic in a clear-cut, logical pattern, and a conclusion that follows inevitably from the paragraph content?

• •Writing Assignments

A. Write a paragraph on one of the following topics.

1. Give advice to a friend (think carefully about the use of *should*, *could*, and *ought to*).
    a. about traveling to the U.S.
    b. about choosing a university
    c. about an interesting place to visit
    d. about dealing with the immigration authorities
    e. about using public transportation

2. Change the paragraph you wrote for #1 to memories about past mistakes you made, and give advice about how those mistakes could have been avoided. (Use *should have, could have*.)

3. Use *might, may* or *can* to enumerate possible future choices about any one of the topics (a, b, c, d, or e).

B. Write a well-organized paragraph about the English words you have the most trouble with, because of pronunciation, spelling, meaning, or whatever. Be specific. Identify your pattern of development and methods of unification.

C. Rewrite three paragraphs from a previous paper.

1. Make one a subordinated paragraph.

2. Make another one a coordinated paragraph.

3. In the third paragraph use one of the other systems of organization illustrated on pages 90-92.

D. The following paragraphs dully and monotonously repeat the same pattern again and again. Practice what you have learned about coordination, subordination, connectives, and sentence variety to make them structurally more interesting. Then add details to make their content more interesting.

1. There is a bright yellow kitchen in my parent's home. It is a good size kitchen. It is also very convenient. I think it is beautiful too. There is a brass-colored ceiling fan. It keeps the kitchen cool. There is a window. There is a large copper-colored sink under the window. There is an electric stove next to it at the right of the sink. It is also copper-colored. There is a refrigerator to the left of the stove. It is big and spacious. It holds

lots of food. There is a door between the kitchen and the dining area. My mother goes back and forth between the rooms easily.

2.   The rules of human "glancing" are complex. Two people meet. They make eye contact. They find themselves in an immediate state of conflict. They want to look at each other. They also want to look away. The result is a complicated series of eye movements. The eye movements are back and forth. A careful study of this "Gaze Behavior" can reveal a great deal about relationships.

3.   Archaeology is exciting. It is fascinating. It is stimulating. It is interesting. It is absorbing. It is an intellectual pursuit. It is an adventure. Archaeology can enrich our life. Archaeology can enlarge our life. Archaeologists have discovered the modern remains of the ancient city of Troy. They have uncovered clues to ancient Aztec and Mayan cultures. They have uncovered long-buried manuscripts. These manuscripts tell of the daily life of people dead for hundreds and even thousands of years. They have opened up past worlds for us. Archaeology is a good field to study—for pleasure or for a career.

4.   "Social distance" is the amount of space between people when they talk. Northern people tend to like a lot of space between them. They like about two feet. This is about two-thirds of a meter. This makes them feel comfortable. Americans in general like less space. They leave about a foot and a half. This is their "comfort zone." Southern people like the least space. They come from places with a warmer climate. They leave one foot or less between them. This is measured nose to nose. So when southerners meet northerners, the southerners move closer. The northerners move away. What do you suppose is the final result?

E. Correct the order, language, and any other errors in the following paragraphs. Be ready to defend your corrections.

1.   My family is unquestionably middle-class. My two older sisters are already taking university classes. I am on the honor roll. I will graduate from high school this year. I was student body president. I am on the President's list of academic achievers. I really need help financing my college studies. My parents say that my family can't help me to go to college. They think girls need more help than boys. Educating my sisters is straining their budget. My grades and my need deserve some financial assistance. I would like to apply for a scholarship. I have maintained a 3.7 out of 4.0 grade point average throughout high school. I made all "A's" in my math and science classes.

2.   From 1980 to 1989, Florida grew by 30%; it added 2.9 million people for a total of 12.7 million. By the year 2000, the Census Bureau predicts California will have a population of 33.5 million people. There will be less space and less privacy and the need for more psychological and physical adjustments. July 1, 1989 it had 29.1 million people. The bad earthquakes might make people stop moving there. Approximately one in every nine Americans lives there right now. Population trends are very interesting. Such changes in the population mean the lives of future Californians will be very different from those of today.

3.   My first impressions of the city were mixed. A walk along the streets revealed uncollected garbage bags and drunks lying in the street. Soon I came to some beautiful shops filled with expensive modern items from clothes to electrical appliances. The weather was warm in the morning but rainy in the afternoon. Many of the houses were old and uncared for, with peeling paint. The shop windows were bright and attractive. Later I found that I could avoid the bad parts of the city by traveling by bus or car to the nicer sections of town.

4.   "Everything seems so strange, and I don't know what to say to people, and I'm afraid to go out." This is what Maria José said when asked how she was adjusting to life in Boston. Many students find difficulty adjusting. These students are from abroad. Culture shock means a feeling of disorientation. Many people like Maria feel like staying inside all the time to protect themselves from an unfamiliar environment. They don't like the new food, they don't like the new smells, they don't like the new climate, and they certainly don't like the new social relationships. Culture shock may be expressed as homesickness, headaches, or even fear. Time and experience that help one become more familiar with a new place are the only cures.

5.   Today's Americans are transients. One might go to school in Virginia and California, get a first job in Michigan, transfer to New Jersey, and settle in Texas. Today Americans move around a lot. In the past, most Americans lived in close-knit communities where neighbors knew neighbors. Everyone shopped in the same stores, went to the same schools, and worshiped at the same churches. American society has changed a lot in the past forty or fifty years. In many communities neighbors have no time to meet, and, by the time they do meet, one or the other will move away soon. Yesterday's Americans led settled, stable lives. Our world is not our father's world.

F. Add connectives to unify the following paragraphs. These might include: *first of all, secondly, next, then, finally, moreover, furthermore, in contrast, however, although, because, since, this, these, one, such, thus, therefore, in conclusion, in sum, in other words,* and others. There may be more than one possibility for each blank. The key is to make sure your choice indicates a logical relationship.

1.   Culture shock makes one feel disoriented. _____ disorientation may take the form of feeling homesick, feeling frightened, or even feeling physically ill. _____ reactions are normal for anyone experiencing the shock of a new environment. _____, it is not normal to continue feeling this way after you have been in the new country for several months. _____, if you continue experiencing culture shock after this long period of time, perhaps you should reconsider your reasons for being in the new environment and maybe think about professional help or a return home.

2.   Culture shock, a common experience of students studying abroad, results from a number of causes. _____, the differences in food and water immediately affect one's digestion and one's sense of comfort. _____, the differences in languages give one a headache and keep one disoriented. _____, the more subtle differences in styles of behavior, body language, and manners leave one feeling strange and alien. _____, all of the differences in language and culture affect one traumatically.

3.   Going to a strange place can sometimes produce a chain of negative effects. _____ the food looks and smells strange, the new arrival does not eat much. _____ he doesn't eat much, he feels weak and uncomfortable. ____ weakness and discomfort means he won't sleep well. ___ he doesn't sleep well, he is more vulnerable to disease, especially colds and flu. _____, then, travel abroad can sometimes lead to ill-health.

4.   Taxes can be divided into three types. _____ and most noticeable is the federal income tax, due April fifteenth of every year. _____ it is a graduated tax, it will take anywhere from fourteen percent to seventy percent of a person's income, depending on how much the person earns per year and how many deductions he might have. _____ level of taxes are the state taxes. _____ might include a state income tax and/or a sales tax. _____ [the sales tax] is a percentage charged on items purchased in a state. _____ tax may be anywhere from three to seven percent, and is most often placed on luxury

items rather than necessities. _____, there are the city taxes. The city property tax is usually charged home owners, _____ the excise tax is usually levied on vehicles used in the city. _____ so many taxes, Americans are convinced that taxes are too high. _____, they frequently complain that their tax money is wasted on unnecessary, useless, impractical, or even illegal projects, and could be better spent elsewhere, or not be spent at all.

G. Add a topic sentence, decide on a good order, and add connectives to transform the following list of information on heart-related concerns into a unified paragraph.

— Most people who have heart attacks recover.

— High blood pressure (hypertension) can be controlled.

— Medical science can do a great deal for people with circulatory disorders.

— Many heart defects can be repaired.

— Recurrent attacks of rheumatic fever, which damage the heart, can be prevented.

— Heart disease has not been conquered.

— People with heart disease live longer and remain productive longer than in the past.

H. The following paragraphs are potentially good but have key problems discussed in this chapter. Identify the problems and suggest improvements.

1. People's eyes meet before any conversation occurs. This moment varies in different countries. The Americans usually say, "Hi!" or an appropriate greeting. Because eye contact is the sign of acceptance, it is natural for them to say something at eye contact. In contrast, the Japanese tend to avoid eye contact, and consequently, they say nothing. Ignoring another person is not rudeness but a part of politeness for them. It is respect for privacy. For example, passengers on a train try not to meet the eyes of strangers. Eye contact is also different in the city and the country. People are less friendly in a city than in the country. If they do not want to have any relationship with strangers, they simply avoid eye contact. As crime rates are higher in a city, it may be a good idea to avoid unnecessary contacts with strangers. People in the country, however, usually meet the eyes of strangers and talk to them. The difference between people in the city and the country is common both in the U.S. and Japan.

2. In a public occasion such as a party, the different behavior of the American and the Japanese becomes clearer. The Americans wish to talk to each other and become at least acquaintances quickly. Whenever their eyes meet on such an occasion, they will start a conversation, or they may smile at someone in the distance. Why are they so friendly? American history may have an answer for the question. America has not had enough population through her history. Especially in the old West, the population was small and people were exposed to danger from Indians. Therefore, they needed to make friends quickly to survive. Although the threat of Indians no longer exists, it has been important to establish a certain relationship with strangers quickly.

3. The Japanese have different styles of parties from Americans. Usually the people who are invited to a party know each other, and a cocktail party is still unusual. And they sit at a table throughout the party. Therefore, we assume a certain situation that some Japanese people are attending a party, and they do not know each other. They will be quiet for a while. People who are next to each other will start talking first, but it is unlikely that everyone will know each other by the end of the party. This is because they have the same seats throughout the party, and circulation will not occur among strangers except boys who may be eager to be friends with charming girls. The role of

hosts and hostesses is considered differently in Japan. Hosts and hostesses (actually hostesses are unusual) focus on polite hospitality. If it is a houseparty, a wife spends a lot of time in the kitchen to make sure that her guests can have warm and delicious foods. She is not expected to engage in conversation with her guests. In contrast, American hosts and hostesses make sure that all their guests are comfortable and having fun at their party, and they think this is the best hospitality. Significant differences exist at parties in the US and Japan. The Japanese concern about politeness comes from overpopulation throughout Japanese history. Since a huge population has been maintained in a small country, it has been important to keep privacy.

I. Develop an essay about "Hugs" from a list to a final paper.

Step #1: Collect or map related information into lists and clusters. These lists may lead you to add more information of your own about hugs.

Step #2: Identify the overall idea unifying each list, for example, types or kinds of hugs.

Step #3: Divide each list into subcategories, for example, function of the hug.

Step #4: Select any two of your major categories and develop a paragraph on each. You may use the information below as well as any relevant information of your own. Use your subcategories to help you organize and focus your paragraphs.

> Hugging can show you care about a person.
>
> The bear hug is an all-encompassing, sloppy, big hug in which the upper torso is encircled and squeezed.
>
> An international study of couples in restaurants studied the average number of times they touched each other per hour. In Gainesville, Florida it was twice.
>
> The closer to the equator you get, the more hugging people do.
>
> The A-frame hug involves wrapping arms around each other's shoulders and touching faces but not bodies.
>
> People use the A-frame hug as a greeting when meeting.
>
> In many Moslem countries, men are likely to embrace and even hold hands walking down the street.
>
> People have a comfort level for personal space, and if you cross that line, it causes uneasiness.
>
> Hugging makes a person feel wanted.
>
> Parents hug children to show they care.
>
> An international study of couples in restaurants studied the number of times they touched each other per hour. In England, the average was zero.
>
> A cheek hug is a gentle hug when people are seated. It is usually a social greeting.
>
> In some cultures, a hug can come at the end of a business meeting.
>
> In others, hugging is unthinkable and will destroy a business relationship.
>
> The handshake is the proper international business greeting.
>
> A sandwich hug involves three people, so named because one person is in the middle of the embrace.
>
> Hugging makes people feel good.
>
> Hugging can be a social mistake among casual acquaintances.
>
> A group hug involves more than three people.

The group hug often occurs among athletic teams, like soccer players who hug to express unity and to celebrate victory.

Hugs are given as greetings or as farewells.

A side-to-side hug, where people stand shoulder-to-shoulder and put their arms around each other, is common for photo sessions and for couples, walking or standing.

A side-to-side hug might include two people or ten people or, particularly in a photo session, even more.

Sometimes hugs are used to congratulate friends on promotion, acceptance to college, graduation, engagement, marriage, or even a winning lottery ticket.

Italians hug more than Scandinavians.

One should never hug the Queen of England.

A heart-centered hug is a full-body embrace in which the two huggers know each other quite well. It is the common hug of lovers.

In the U.S., Southerners embrace in greeting much more often than do Northerners.

An international study of couples in restaurants studied the number of times they touched each other per hour. In Paris, it was 110 times.

Hugging can be a cultural catastrophe with some foreigners.

A traditional Hawaiian greeting is a flower necklace and a kiss on each cheek with a small hint of an embrace.

Arab women do not touch any man except very close relatives. They do not even shake hands with a man.

An international study of couples in restaurants studied the number of times they touched each other per hour. In Puerto Rico, it was 180 times.

The Japanese bow instead of hugging.

A Mexican *abrazo*, a friendly embrace, is common between friends and acquaintances of both sexes as a greeting much like the handshake.

A just-friend hug = non-sexual; to give support

Jamaicans hug more than Argentinians.

In some places, a smile and a nod replaces the hug.

Young lovers hug to express mutual attraction.

Arabs embrace fellow businessmen.

Russians embrace fellow businessmen with great vigor.

Englishmen do not.

Hug (Webster's definition): "to press tightly, especially in the arms"

Embrace (Webster's definition): "a close encircling with the arms and pressure to the bosom"

People hug to give comfort in time of need.

People hug to give sympathy in time of sorrow.

A too hearty hug from a male to a female can be sexually threatening.

—inspired by Kathleen Keating, *The Hug Therapy Book*

What can you add from your own experience?

Chapter 6: BUILDING PARAGRAPHS INTO PAPERS

If you wish to be a writer, write. — Epictetus

The new writer should observe, listen, look …and then write. Nothing begets better writing than the simple process of writing. — Rod Serling

It takes most of us writers a long time to learn our craft. So keep at it. Don't give up. — Jacqueline Briskin

He that will write well in any tongue must follow this counsel of Aristotle: to speak as the common people do, to think as wise men do. — Roger Ascham

Write to be read by others …choose …words and plot… actions and chart…with the reader in mind. — Robert Cormier

A writer's problem does not change. He himself changes and the world he lives in changes but his problem remains the same. It is always how to write truly and, having found what is true, to project it in such a way that it becomes a part of the experience of the person who reads it. — Ernest Hemingway

---

Writing Introductions
    What an Introduction Is
    What an Introduction Does
    A Final Word about Introductions

Interlocking Paragraphs in Papers
    An Interlocking Frame
    Special Transition Paragraphs

Writing Conclusions
    The Nature of Concluding Paragraphs
    Length, Form, and Function

Final Checklist

Passage for Discussion and Analysis

Writing Assignments

Writing Introductions

An effective essay uses an introduction to establish topic, direction, purpose, and plan; a series of body paragraphs interrelated through thesis statement and topic sentences, through the logic of ideas, through structure, and through transitions; and a conclusion which confirms the thesis statement and brings the paper to a close. Together, these units should create a unified and cohesive whole, bound by structure, logic, idea, and verbal signals so the reader knows exactly what is going on at every stage of the paper and how every part of the paper relates to every other part.

WHAT AN INTRODUCTION IS

There are many different ways to introduce a paper, but there should always be some sort of introduction, even in very short essays. As the word implies, the opening sentence or sentences of a paper of limited length, or the opening paragraph of a longer paper introduces the reader to the topic. <u>Simply announcing a subject area is not an introduction, nor is a mere statement of topic</u>. Your subject area may be "college life," but an announcement that "I am going to talk about college life" is not an introduction, and certainly not a good beginning to a paper. Even if you limit the subject area to a topic idea like "The Difficult Transition from High School to College," you are basically providing a title or preparing for a statement of your thesis or organizing idea instead of introducing a topic. A title might serve to catch the interest of a reader, but it is no substitute for an introduction, and any idea carried in the title should be either stated or prepared for in the introduction.

<u>Unlike a statement of subject area or topic or a title, an introduction includes a number of pieces of information</u>. Some of this information is intended to capture the attention of the reader, some to guide the reader into the paper, and some to provide a sense of purpose and direction. Whether it takes the form of a statement, a quotation, a brief narrative, or a question, the information chosen to capture reader attention is sometimes called the "hook," especially in popular writing. Like a fishhook, the hook "catches" the reader with a "sharp" and interesting idea and will not let him or her go. The hook may or may not be the same as the thesis idea or argument of the paper, but both will usually be found in the introduction. Once the hook has captured reader attention, the introduction should go on to suggest the divisions or sections of the argument or at least its direction. It guides the reader into the body of the paper, and in doing so tries to awaken her or his curiosity or interest so that he or she will read on. In other words, even the statement of direction or thesis becomes a way of keeping the audience "hooked."

For example, a student writing about college life and focusing on the difficult transition period from high school to college might introduce the topic as follows:

> (1) No one wakes you up when you need to get up; instead, they wake you in the middle of the night. (2) Your clothes always seem to be dirty and unironed and it takes a lot of trouble to correct this. (3) Your schedule changes every day, and no one reminds you of where you are supposed to be. (4) You have to constantly deal with problems you have never faced before with no advice or with bad advice from people perhaps as inexperienced as you are. (5) Such are the normal but disturbing adjustments all students must make in their first semester of college. (6) This paper will focus on what types of transition difficulties are normal in the move from high school to college and will give advice about some ways to make coping easier.

In this example, the first three sentences are the hook, to capture your interest and to guide you into the paper. The fourth sentence states the topic idea, and the final sentence of this introductory paragraph provides the thesis plan for the development of the paper which will follow. Together, the fourth and fifth sentence make the thesis statement. As such, they guide the reader's expectations and, in this case, make the reader anticipate a discussion of "normal types of transition difficulties" and some advice about "how to cope."

A title to accompany this paper, with this beginning, might simply state the topic idea, "The Difficulties of Moving from High School to College," or it might try to build on the hook of the introduction, "Out of Place and Out of Sync? Just

Normal College Freshman Blues." However, shorter is better for a title: "Coping with Everyday College Freshman Blues."

Another writer, considering the same topic, might begin with a very different hook:

> Six out of ten college student suicides occur during the first semester of college. Why? The change from the laid-back, easy-going style of most American high schools to the high-speed, cut-throat competition of college, from the protection and security of family and childhood friends to the alienation and insecurity inherent in life among strangers, and from the intellectual womb of accepted values to the challenge of new and perhaps threatening perspectives and values—this transition is emotionally and physically debilitating.

In this introduction the hook is the first sentence. The rest of the paragraph provides the thesis focus: the reason for or explanation of the opening statistic, with a three-part division, focusing on three debilitating changes—in degree of competition, in the security provided by social contacts, and in the security provided by intellectual consensus. A good title would focus on the heart of the thesis idea: "Why So Many Freshman Suicides?"

Still another writer, approaching the same subject matter and the same topic idea, might begin with a question:

> What difficulties are natural to expect in the transition from high school to college? Most young people, leaving home for the first time, face not only more difficult studies but a sudden loss of the comfort, familiarity, and security of home life and a testing of their ability to survive in a new social setting, with more personal responsibilities, and with direct challenges to value systems.

In this case, the question is the hook, and the long second sentence is the thesis idea, preparing readers for a focus, partly on "more difficult studies" but mainly on "sudden loss" and "testing their ability to survive." The latter will, in turn, be subdivided into testing through social setting, testing through increased responsibility, and testing through challenges to value systems. The title might be "Expect the Worst!" to focus on the negative or "The Adjustment Challenges of College Life" to focus on the positive.

Notice that all three of these introductions share the same subject area (college life), all three share the same general topic idea (the normal transitional difficulties inherent in changing from high school to college), but all three differ in narrow focus and particular approach, with their "hook" in part providing clues to the thesis idea, preparing the reader for, or, at the very least, leading the reader into the key idea of the paper.

• EXERCISE 6.1: INTRODUCTIONS AND TITLES

Introduction: What do the following introductions lead readers to expect about the rest of the paper? How do they awaken interest? How long will each paper be? Explain.

Title: What connects the title and the introduction: a summary statement, a key phrase, a hook, or something else?

1. **Title: "Life's Mysterious Clocks"**
   Introduction: One of the greatest riddles of the universe is the uncanny ability of living things to carry out their normal activities with clocklike precision at a particular time of the day, month, and year. Why do oysters plucked from a Connecticut bay and shipped to a Midwest laboratory continue to time their lives to ocean tides 800 miles away? How do potatoes in hermetically sealed containers predict atmospheric pressure trends two days in advance? What effects do the lunar and solar rhythms have on the life habits of man? Living things clearly possess powerful adaptive capacities—but the explanation of whatever strange and permeative forces are concerned continues to challenge science. Let us consider the phenomena more closely.
   —Frank A. Brown, Jr., "Life's Mysterious Clocks," *Saturday Evening Post*

Expectation: _____

Title: _____

2. **Title: "The Eye of the Beholder"**
Introduction: Ask most people to list what makes them like someone on first meeting and they'll tell you personality, intelligence, sense of humor. But they're probably deceiving themselves. The characteristic that impresses people the most, when meeting anyone from a job applicant to a blind date, is appearance. And unfair and unenlightened as it may seem, attractive people are frequently preferred over their less attractive peers. —Thomas F. Cash and Louis H. Janda, *Psychology Today*

Expectation: _____

Title: _____

3. **Title: "The University College: Selectivity and Admission"**
Introduction: Higher education in the United States presents students (and parents) with a bewildering series of choices. Prospective students can select public and private colleges; denominational or non-denominational schools; single-sex and co-educational colleges; large and small institutions; specialized technological institutes; highly selective and prestigious colleges and others that practice open admissions. We have created an entire industry to make these choices more efficient: guides the size of large city telephone directories rate colleges much in the manner of restaurants, awarding stars for quality of teaching, cleanliness of dormitories, climate, food, and general happiness of the student body. School advisers and private consultants (for a sizable fee) will meet with prospective students and parents to refine initial choices into realistic possibilities, suggesting perhaps one famous school where the chances are small but higher than zero; a couple of places where the candidate has a better than even chance; and finally a safety school—if all else fails. A typical applicant may file ten applications.
    —Henry Rosovsky, *The University: An Owner's Manual*

Expectation: _____

Title: _____

4. **Title: "Listening to Music"**
Introduction: We all listen to music according to our separate capacities. But, for the sake of analysis, the whole listening process may become clearer if we break it up into its component parts, so to speak. In a certain sense we all listen to music on three separate planes. For lack of a better terminology, one might name these: (1) the sensuous plane, (2) the expressive plane, (3) the sheerly musical plane. The only advantage to be gained from mechanically splitting up the listening process into these hypothetical planes is the clearer view to be had of the way in which we listen. —Aaron Copeland, *What to Listen For in Music*.

Expectation: _____

Title: _____

WHAT AN INTRODUCTION DOES

An introduction may serve a myriad of purposes. The introduction may provide <u>historical or background information as a basis for understanding or interpreting a present situation</u> as in the following paragraph on the significance of the Berlin Wall. Daniel Benjamin's introduction to a *Time* magazine essay entitled "Wall of Shame" contrasts walls of the past with the Berlin wall:

> The geography of the past is studded with walled cities. Jerusalem and Rome, to name but two from <u>antiquity</u>, fortified themselves against enemies without. Later, <u>in medieval times</u>, the citizens of London and Paris built and rebuilt ramparts to safeguard their liberties, ones that many of their rural contemporaries, burdened with the feudal status of serf, were denied. <u>Only in the 20th century</u> has a city had a wall rammed through its innards, circumscribing the freedom of two-thirds of its people, forcing upon them a serf-like tie to the land. Only in Berlin. [emphasis added]

This progressive discussion of walled cities focuses on what is unique historically about the Berlin Wall: Unlike ancient cities, the wall was built to keep citizens in rather than enemies out.

Sometimes <u>an appropriate quotation by a famous person</u> can be an effective way to begin a paper. An article on modern medicine might begin with a quote by George Bernard Shaw: "I do not know a single thoughtful and well-informed person who does not feel that the tragedy of illness at present is that it delivers you helplessly into the hands of a profession which you deeply mistrust." What does the quotation by Samuel Johnson add to the following introduction?

> "When a man knows he is to be hanged in a fortnight" [two weeks], Samuel Johnson once wrote, "it concentrates his mind wonderfully." The threat of impending ecological doom seems to be having the same effect on public opinion. If historians remember 1989 as the year the Iron Curtain collapsed, it has also been the year that concern for the environment reached a new peak.
>
> —Thomas A. Sancton, "The Fight to Save the Planet"

The essay which follows this introduction focuses on the ecological disasters that have forced Americans to start worrying about what they and their representatives are doing to the environment. Such quotations can be found in one of the many dictionaries of quotations available in most library reference rooms, and

may, if not overused, be an effective way to capture reader interest and focus a topic.

There is an infinite variety of possible openings that provide both a hook and a kind of thesis. The following list cites some of the most common methods an introduction might employ:

1) <u>A startling fact</u>: "Nine out of ten women in a five-block area of this city were raped last year."

2) <u>Statistics</u>: "One out of every four marriages in the U.S. today will end in divorce."

3) <u>A rhetorical question</u>: "Can our earth survive the pollution we are presently inflicting on it?"; "What is Intelligence, anyway?"

4) <u>A definition of a key term</u>: "Real freedom means responsibility."

5) <u>A contrast</u>: "For centuries, a deep appreciation of nature has been central to Japanese art. Now a valuable and timely exhibition at the Museum of Modern Art demonstrates just how completely Japan's postwar artists have broken the old rules."

6) <u>An anecdote</u>: "<u>Bunglers</u> [people who make terrible mistakes] are always with us and always have been. Winston Churchill tells us, in his history of World War II, that in August, 1940, he had to take charge personally of the Armed Forces' Joint Planning Committee because, after almost twelve months of war, the Committee had not originated a single plan."
   —Raymond Hull, "The Peter Principle"

7) A direct statement of its main concern: "The traditional criteria for death are cessation of respiration and heart action, but modern medical technology can keep a patient breathing and his blood circulating long after his brain has died. Technology has necessitated a revised definition."
   —"What is Death?", *Scientific American*

These are only a few of the choices available. Whatever the approach, the introduction should try to capture the reader's attention and to give a preview of what will follow; no matter its length, it must provide focus and direction for a paper.

A Final Word about Introductions

In summary, a good introduction has several goals. First, because it is the first section a reader looks at, it must be interesting enough to capture reader attention, and it must arouse curiosity enough to inspire reading on. Next, it must prepare the reader for what will follow, not just the general topic but also the overall attitude, the thesis idea, and the particular divisions of the paper. In other words, it establishes the plan and direction for the body of the paper. Often, the last sentence of the introduction contains the thesis idea and is the connecting link with the sections which follow. An introduction may employ a number of rhetorical strategies, but as its name implies, its main purpose is to "introduce" the topic to the reader and to encourage the desire to explore that "acquaintance" beyond the first "handshake" so that hopefully the reader will ultimately become "friends" with the topic and perhaps be inspired to expand that "friendship" by reading more on the subject.

• EXERCISE 6.2: IDENTIFYING FUNCTION

Identify the methods used in the following introductions. What do you expect each essay to do? Why? How do these writers capture reader interest? How do the writers invite readers to continue reading?

1. Before coming to St. Augustine, I had never been in any American city and knew about such cities through television. Consequently, I thought that St. Augustine would have numerous skyscrapers like New York and Los Angeles. I expected no space to take walks, many cars, alien people, freezing weather—an unfamiliar world. These preconceptions all proved false.

2. Whether or not there should be a military draft remains a controversial question in this country. However, reinstating the draft could be a good way to send young people back to school, make them consider their futures far earlier than they are presently doing, initiate a military "peace corps" at home for poor inner cities, and make sure that America's young people get the basic training they should have to serve their country in time of need.

3. While much of the world has worried about nuclear proliferation and nuclear holocaust, the real time bomb has been the environment. Unless we reverse present environmental abuse trends, "to be or not to be" may be a question about which the next generation will no longer have a choice.

4. In "The Speech the Graduates Didn't Hear," educator and speaker Jacob Neusner wants to make his student audience aware that they will have difficulty performing in the working world because college life is less demanding and much simpler by comparison. He makes his argument through shock tactics, a cynical and contemptuous persona, and the constant use of irony.

5. In many ways cable cars are an enigma. With no visible form of power, they climb the city's highest hills and, uncomplaining, carry the transit system's largest loads. How do they do it?
   —Lynn Thomas, *San Francisco's Cable Cars*: 6.

6. Baton Rouge—a name which reputedly refers to the red stick which marked the boundary between two Indian tribes—owes more to the French than its unusual name, for it was the French who explored, developed, and settled the region during its significant early years.
   —*The Baton Rouge Visitor's Guide*: 2.

7.   Why are relations between parents and teenagers so frequently marked by squabbling, bickering, nagging, arguing, and—at the other extreme—by stubborn silence? Why do these barriers to family communication seem worse today than ever before? What causes this verbal behavior, and which party is at fault: the adolescent or the adult? Or both? Is the constant bickering or monosyllabic sullenness an inevitable part of adolescent development? Or is it culturally conditioned?

—Laurence Steinberg, "Bound to Bicker," *Psychology Today*.

8.   Scientists at Seragen Inc., a small biotech firm, seem almost embarrassed when they rattle off the list of possible uses for a medicine coming out of their labs. Could a single drug cure cancer? Control AIDS? Relieve rheumatoid arthritis? Stop juvenile diabetes? Ease multiple sclerosis? How about clear up psoriasis? Prevent rejection of transplanted organs? Improve the treatment of heart disease? And do these things with virtually no side effects? If the dreams of people at Seragen come true, all this and more is possible. Their ingenious trick of gene splicing, a substance called IL-2 fusion toxin, is a precisely aimed poison that hunts down renegade cells involved in various diseases, then penetrates and kills them.

—Daniel O. Haney, "School Bets Big on Wonder Drug," *The Times-Picayune*.

9.   The harvest from 311 million U.S. crop acres and many more millions of acres of pasture fed 92 million Americans in 1910. Today, fewer acres provide an even greater supply of food for nearly 200 million. Our abundance of food, more appetizing, nutritious, and convenient today than ever before, can be attributed in large part to progress in the agricultural sciences. The animal, plant, and soil sciences, food science, agricultural engineering, and other biological and physical disciplines have made it possible to produce more and better food. Agricultural economics and other areas of social science have contributed to maximizing return on investment in agriculture, whether the investment has been in production goods or human resources.

—R.E. Geyer, "The Agricultural Sciences," *Bio Science*.

10.   From that time in the distant past when a mosquito first dined on human blood, mankind has been engaged in a guerrilla war against insect pests. In recent years, the conflict has been escalated into all-out and total warfare. Famines caused by insect depredation of crops, and diseases transmitted by arthropod vectors, presently take millions of lives annually. Obviously, we dare not let up in our attack—but dare we continue? According to many conservationists and public health officials, we may win a Pyrrhic victory [a victory in name but not in reality] if we continue poisoning our wildlife and ourselves with the deadly insecticides now employed.

—"Turning Insects Against Themselves," The New York Academy of Sciences, *The Sciences*.

• EXERCISE 6.3: JUDGING AND CREATING INTRODUCTIONS

A. Which of the following are good introductions and which are weak? Explain. How do the good introductions prepare readers for the topic? How could you make the weak ones more effective?

1.   Shakespeare is a very famous English writer. He has been translated into many languages. Most people around the world have read or at least heard about *Hamlet*. *Hamlet* is the story of a son who revenges his father's murder. You will like the story because it is great literature.

2.   Each new dietary study makes eating seem more and more risky. The latest research directly connects colon cancer with the consumption of red meat and animal fat. That leaves fearful consumers wondering whether it is safe to eat any red meat at all.

3.   The authors we've read this semester rely on various techniques for comedy, but they generally seem to favor five particular methods: disguise and role-playing, exaggerated behavior, situation comedy, comic word play, and tag names.

4.   Oil spills from tankers are a serious threat to the environment. They kill birds and marine life, and ruin waters and beaches for years, if not decades. Moreover, the number of spills seems to be increasing. What can be done to protect our environment from such man-made disasters?

5.   The American Civil War caused a lot of problems. Homes were destroyed. A lot of brave men died. Northern politicians passed laws that harmed the South. Many Southerners would like to refight the war. It is a shame that Abraham Lincoln was assassinated because he could have made a difference if he had lived.

6.   The American Civil War, fought from 1861 to 1865 between the northern Union states and the southern Confederate states, was a fight between industry and agriculture, between strong federal control and states' rights, between abolitionists and supporters of slavery. Its effects on the nation were devastating. It caused more deaths than any other war in American history. It cost billions of dollars and ended up destroying the economy of the South so firmly that that part of the nation is only now partially recovering. More importantly, it increased the hatred between northerners and southerners for seventy to eighty years after the last battle was fought, a hatred that still lies beneath the surface of modern north/south relationships. In other words, this war cost America a lot, not simply financial costs but human costs: lives, loyalties, opportunities, and future relationships.

7.   After serving as a Military Police Officer in Burma from 1922-1927, George Orwell returned to England disillusioned with British imperialism. During the decline of the British Empire in the 1930's, Orwell wrote the popular essay, "A Hanging." In it he creates a narrator who suddenly becomes reflective as he witnesses a small Hindu about to be hanged in a jailyard in Burma. Many Englishmen may have been concerned with capital punishment at the time Orwell was writing, but most were still quite detached from what was happening in the rest of the empire; Orwell hoped to break that detachment and to force them to reconsider their views. He relied on a masterful choice of words, striking imagery, and a series of ironic contrasts to argue against capital punishment: "...the unspeakable wrongness of cutting a life short when it is in full tide."

B. Write carefully constructed thesis sentences for five of the short writing assignments listed below. Use parallelism to list the divisions or plan of each proposed paper. Next, add introductory material to two or three of your theses to create short introductory paragraphs for potential papers on the selected topics.

> *Example of a thesis sentence for Topic #1:* Together, Elvis Presley's *concerts, movies* and *rock and roll songs,* deservedly earned him the title, "The King of Rock 'n Roll." [The words in *italics* show the key divisions; this paper will begin with Presley's concerts, then will discuss his movies, and finally will focus on his rock and roll songs; the goal of the paper will be to prove he deserves the title of "King of Rock 'n Roll."]

1. Pick some famous person and give the main reasons he/she is famous. Be precise about the reasons for the fame; provide details, characteristics, and examples.

2. Define a true friend by providing key characteristics and   examples. Your definition might begin by contrasting acquaintances or ordinary friends with very close or very special friends.

3. Describe a hypothetical day without modern forms of communication like the telephone and the FAX. Remember that such a description would require unreal hypothetical forms: "Suppose that ...," "If this were to occur, that would result," "Should this occur, that would follow."

4. Describe what the world would be like if an ice age returned or if everywhere were as warm as the Equator.

5. Contrast the role of women in your country with the role of women in the USA, or contrast views about the role of women in each of two countries.

6. Enumerate or analyze the difficulties of returning to school after many years away, working but not studying.

Interlocking Paragraphs in Papers

AN INTERLOCKING FRAME

As noted in the previous chapter, the thesis sentence determines the topic sentences of a paper, and these together form an interlocking frame that provides logic and unity for a paper. Every writer must make decisions about how long a paper to write and how many ideas to discuss, but once these decisions have been made, they must be expressed through the thesis and topic sentences. For example, the interlocking frame of a paper about electric cars might be broken down as shown below.

Title/General Topic: "Advantages of Electric Cars"
Thesis Idea: Electric cars are desirable: **1st paragraph**
Thesis Sentence: (1) Electric cars would be most desirable for urban use because they could reduce noise pollution and air pollution while also saving valuable space in city streets and even more valuable energy.
1st Topic Idea: Reduce noise pollution: **2nd paragraph**
Topic Sentence: (2) Since electric motors are quiet....
                   (3) This advantage may have a temporary disadvantage...
                        (4) Pedestrian/auto accidents...
2nd Topic Idea: Reduce air pollution: **3rd Paragraph**
Topic Sentence: (2) Electric motors produce no toxic gases...
                   (3) Research into ozone control...
                        (4) Dr. Hans Geltbauer...
                          (5) Dr. Geltbauer says...
3rd Topic Idea: Save space: **4th Paragraph**
Topic Sentence: (2) Because of the limitations of battery power, electric cars will be small...
                   (3)...
                        (4)...
4th Topic Idea: Save energy: **5th Paragraph**
Topic Sentence: (2) Finally, the energy shortage...
                   (3)...
                        (4)...
Conclusion: Thus, for a number of reasons, electric cars really are desirable: **6th Paragraph**

In other words, the structure of a thesis statement has been turned into the structure of a whole paper by changing each key element from the thesis into a corresponding topic sentence. Adding supportive sentences exploring the particular virtue presented in each topic sentence and a concluding paragraph that sums up the virtues of the electric car would produce a paper consisting of one-and-a-half to four typed, double-spaced pages, depending on the amount of concrete detail and the number of examples provided in each body paragraph. To expand the paper with more body paragraphs would involve simply adding more advantages or virtues of the electric car to the thesis statement and then developing paragraphs describing or proving those virtues. Thus, the introductory paragraph system can provide a structure for a whole paper.

The following short essay demonstrates this interlocking system:

Migrant Farm Work: Debilitating and Dehumanizing !

	Title
Americans, remembering the stories of their grade school readers, value the pastoral ideal of the farm as a rosy experience associated with building moral fiber, childhood, and honest labor. The migrant farm experience is a totally different experience, a nightmare, not a pastoral dream, for work in the fields is (1) dirty , (2) backbreaking , and (3) dehumanizing.	hook contrast with hook thesis sentence 3 divisions of thesis
With the heat rising over 100 degrees, the sweat, the dirt, the hard-blowing wind, field worker's clothes get <u>dirty and dusty</u> and stick to their sweaty bodies. Dust and chemicals make the hair heavy and dull. Hands crack and chap from the engrained grime. Clothes become so dirty that no amount of washing can return them to their original colors. When it rains, mud covers shoes and clothes, but the workers can't afford to quit, even if wet all over, for fear of loss of crop or compensation. Under such conditions, shoes and clothes wear out quickly and so do workers.	topic sentence #1 supportive details description connection to next paragraph
Dirt is not the only discomfort. The work is <u>backbreaking</u>. Workers bend back and forth or only forward for many hours along rows half-a-mile long. Their lowered heads ache, their necks get stiff, and their legs are sore from too much walking or from standing too long. Their shoulder blades hurt from moving their arms from side to side or back and forth. Their hands cramp from holding them in one position for too long. When they try to open or stretch them, the pain is almost too much to bear. As if to add to the physical agony, most farmers don't provide toilets; instead, trees, bushes, or drainage ditches must serve that purpose.	transition sentence topic sentence #2 supportive descriptive details focus on pain connection to next paragraph
Such <u>dirty</u>, <u>backbreaking</u> work is <u>dehumanizing</u>. The pay, from $.75 to $1.50 an hour if workers are lucky, is far too low for the work done. At times a person works from fifteen to eighteen hours a day, without overtime, and makes only $15 or less. Such low wages force workers to live from day to day, barely making enough for essentials. These are but a few of the many hardships a farm worker endures. He must suffer filth, extreme temperatures, aching muscles, inhuman hours, and subhuman working conditions, discrimination and depression, but he must go on if he is to survive.	topic sentence #3 (also transition sentence) supportive descriptive details conclusion: 1) summary 2) final point

To expand the paper, you can either add more information to each paragraph or add a new topic idea. The following information could be used to expand an already existing paragraph, and might be added between *The pay, from $.75 to $1.50 an hour if workers are lucky, is far too low for the work done* and *At times a person works from fifteen to eighteen hours a day, without overtime, and makes only $15 or less.*

> They sometimes have to work bringing in the last harvest in temperatures in the mid-thirties; their hands and feet hurt from the cold, but they must keep on. Whether wet from the rain, hot and sunburned from the sun, blown by the wind, or chilled by the cold, a field worker has to keep on working to get paid.

A new topic idea, on the other hand, would be added to the thesis sentence as well as to the body: *The migrant farm experience is a totally different experience, a nightmare, not a pastoral dream, for work in the fields is (1) dirty ,(2) backbreaking, (3) dangerous, and (4) dehumanizing.* Such a thesis change would call for a fourth body paragraph to be inserted between the paragraphs on backbreaking and on dehumanizing, and might necessitate some change in the connecting sentences.

Sometimes the method of development will provide a clear frame to unite paragraphs and ideas. For instance, a comparison or contrast format necessitates a clear movement applying categories to two or more items. That logical movement serves to unite sections into a whole, as in the following example.

A = electric cars

B = gas-powered cars

Thesis idea: (1) A is superior to B.

    (2) Cost of A compared to cost of B

    (2) Speed of A compared to speed of B

    (2) Size of A compared to size of B

An **alternating** pattern of comparison/contrast in the thesis can become a divided pattern in the body:

    Topic Sentence #I: (1) The cost, speed, and size of A are very good.

    (2) Cost of A

    (2) Speed of A

    (2) Size of A

    Topic Sentence #II: (1) The cost, speed, and size of B are not as good.

    (2) Cost of B

    (2) Speed of B

    (2) Size of B

If you write two separate coordinated paragraphs, the topic sentence of the second paragraph usually makes it clear that you are relating the two paragraphs: *On the other hand, gas-powered cars...; In contrast, gas-powered cars....*

SPECIAL TRANSITION PARAGRAPHS

In longer papers, special paragraphs relate ideas between different paragraphs or different sections of a paper. This kind of paragraph is called a transition paragraph because it takes readers from one subject to another (*trans* = across). The following is a typical transition paragraph:

> We have seen that electric cars have several advantages over gas-powered cars, and that the disadvantages of the electric cars are minor. Now we must turn to the question of how long each car lasts, its durability.

Here the change is from a paragraph on advantages to a paragraph on durability, with this short transitional paragraph guiding the reader through that change. Transition paragraphs are usually quite short, like the one above. They are useful when you are changing the subject and are not quite sure how to do it gracefully. Such paragraphs are necessary from time to time, but they should not be over-used, for then you will begin to sound like a magician putting on an act or an announcer in a circus: "Now I will do this!!"; "Next I will do that!!"; "I have done it!!!" Often, instead of transition paragraphs, which are more common in longer papers, a writer will rely on transitional, connecting, or signal words: words or phrases which tell the reader the connection between one paragraph or one section and the next. Such words might indicate contrasts, comparisons, further listings, the introduction of an example, the insertion of a definition, a change of focus, and so forth. Each of the chapters in Unit Two will deal with these specialized signals or transitions and how they function to make particular connections.

Read the following essay. Underline the thesis sentence once and the topic sentences twice. Are the topic sentences in the order the thesis makes you expect? Underline the topic ideas which appear in the conclusion. Are any missing? Circle connective words. Make suggestions for expansion. Add a few more supportive sentences to the body paragraphs. If you could add another topic idea, where would you insert it? How would you develop it?

When I arrived in America for the first time, I discovered that Americans are strange people. They don't pronounce their language the way they spell it; they don't eat their food the way nature grew it; and they are in an awful hurry to get to a place where they have to wait around.

My first problem was with American pronunciation. The Customs Official at the airport asked me, "Weahyafom?" I said, "No, that was not my name." When he said, "I mean, whacontree yafom?" I realized he was asking my place of origin, my country. Another pronunciation which gave me trouble at the beginning was the word "interested," which is often said as "innarested." However, I am learning quickly that English spelling and English pronunciation are like two different languages.

A more serious problem is the American custom of never eating food in its normal state. Rather, it is canned, frozen, dried, or packaged. If you eat at a fast-food restaurant, the food is often fried and kept warm under infrared lights, which means you are served quickly, but there is not much fun involved. To me, eating should be a ceremony, a time to relax and enjoy the food and the company. I will have to learn how to shop at the large groceries, the "supermarkets," to find fresh food I can prepare the way I like.

My last problem is transportation. I do not understand why it is necessary to drive 55 m.p.h. on the freeways, thruways, and expressways in order to sit in traffic (going 0 m.p.h.!) or to drive round and round looking for a parking space. This contrast makes me nervous; I think American transportation must have been less stressful when everyone rode a horse! I have found that driving on side roads and back roads is more comfortable.

In conclusion, my adjustment problems are not that serious. I am learning the spoken language quickly; the other problems, food and transportation, cannot be adjusted to, but they can be avoided.

Writing Conclusions

The Nature of Concluding Paragraphs

Paragraphs which conclude an argument or discussion are often made up of coordinated sentences, that is, sentences of equal significance bound together only by a central unifying idea, not by relationships to each other. This coordinated pattern is common in conclusions because conclusions are general and are not the place for specific detail or for complex, interrelated arguments. Rather, the writer makes a series of statements as reminders of points made earlier.

A concluding paragraph usually refers back to the thesis sentence to bring the reader back to the general claim which was to be proven; there is also a general discussion of the ideas covered in the body of the paper (the topic sentences). However, concluding paragraphs do not repeat the introductory paragraph word for word, even if there is little new information to add. A reader who finds that the conclusion simply repeats the introduction in exactly the same words may feel cheated; he has read all the way through, only to be told exactly the same thing at the end in exactly the same way. For this reason, even a conclusion that restates the thesis idea should do so in new words and phrases and with a greater degree of specificity. In other words, a conclusion is more abstract than the body of a paper, but is usually more concrete than the thesis statement and introduction of a paper.

Concluding paragraphs often begin with a sign to the reader that the end is near: *Thus, we have seen…, In summary, To summarize, In conclusion, Thus, we can conclude.* Other signs might relate to the developmental pattern: *Therefore, Consequently, As a result, Accordingly*, and so forth. Although normally you should not introduce a totally new idea in the conclusion, sometimes you can carry the already discussed ideas one step further or else phrase them in a new way that provides a new perspective to give a sense of closure and accomplishment by showing the importance or significance of what has been said. One good trick is to save a general idea for the concluding paragraph, an idea which is interesting and which shows that your thesis is important, but which does not really fit into your discussion elsewhere. To come up with such a statement of closure it may help to ask, *What has my discussion shown?*; *What important lessons does my conclusion teach?*; *What is the larger significance of this final statement of my essay?*

For example, throughout this chapter and the other chapters on paragraphs there has been a series of paragraphs on electric cars. The following indented paragraph would be a good way to conclude a paper containing these paragraphs about electric cars. The first two sentences sum up the information from the body paragraphs: Electric cars might be able to solve noise and air pollution problems as well as save space and energy; they are clean, silent, and efficient. However, the second sentence and the rest of the conclusion add an interesting image to contrast "the wild animals" of today's road with the manageable machines of the future. While it is not always a good idea to add new information in a conclusion, in this case, the new information is really a summing up of the argument about the change from the internal combustion engine to the electric engine.

> We have seen that electric cars carry the promise of solving our noise and air pollution problems, with the benefit of savings in space and energy. Electric cars do not have the *machismo* of gas-powered machines; they are clean,

silent, and efficient, but they won't be named after mavericks, mustangs, impalas, pintos, or other wild animals. There will not be a lion or a tiger among them. This seems good when we consider the thousands of people killed and maimed by the untamed, four-wheeled beasts of the highway. Let the electric age come in silently, but also smoothly and safely!

Paragraphs which conclude need not conclude entire papers. They can also conclude a section of a paper or the discussion of an idea. When they are used this way, they usually end with a general sentence at a high level of abstraction, as in the next example:

> The contrast in the speed, cost, and size of electric and gas-powered vehicles makes the superiority of the former clear.
>
> However, experiments with steam-powered vehicles suggest yet another viable alternative to gas-powered vehicles... [New Section; New Topic]

The last sentence of a paragraph is often used as a transition to the next paragraph:

> The contrast in the speed, cost, and size of electric and gas-powered vehicles makes the superiority of the former clear; however, the durability of each kind of vehicle must also be considered.
>
> Electric cars are about three times more durable than... [Topic sentence for the next paragraph]

LENGTH, FORM, AND FUNCTION

The conclusions to a paragraph, to a section, to a short paper, and to a longer paper will vary in length according to what is being concluded—perhaps sometimes a single sentence, usually a couple of lines, occasionally a full paragraph, and only rarely a couple of paragraphs—but they will always perform the same function: they will clearly mark the end of the unit.

A conclusion always relates in some way to the beginning of the essay so that, together with the opening, it forms a frame within which the body of the essay is contained. This frame is usually more general than is the body, but the conclusion is less general than the introduction. Some scholars describe this pattern as that of an upside-down funnel, moving from the narrow specifics of the body to the broader generalities of the conclusion. Other commentators prefer a "goblet" as a metaphor.

Introduction

Body

Conclusion

What is wrong with the essays these pictures represent?

The following are mistakes to avoid:

1. Writing no conclusion at all; just stopping.
2. Making conclusion and thesis identical. How boring!
3. Introducing new subject matter not previously discussed in the paper, that is, being digressive.
4. Concluding only about a minor part of the paper, especially the final section, instead of concluding overall.
5. Writing too much; rambling endlessly.
6. Relying on cliché expressions: *Finally, let me say…*, *To make myself perfectly clear, let me conclude that….*

Common ways to conclude a paper effectively include the following:

1. <u>Restate the opening thesis in a new way, usually with more concrete detail that reflects the reader (and writer's) added understanding by the end of the paper.</u>

Opening: The investigations which followed the sinking of the *Titanic* suggested that a small, insufficiently trained crew, insufficient lifesaving equipment and inadequate international radio service were central reasons the ship sank.

Conclusion: Despite the *Titanic's* small, untrained crew and limited lifesaving equipment, if the international radio system had been more nearly adequate, probably most of the 1500 people who died could have been saved.

2. <u>Confirm the writer's goals by summing up the key arguments.</u>

In conclusion, we have three major challenges before us. We have first, to disprove the clichés that persist in discouraging young women from using their intellects; we need second, to focus the coed's attention on her long-run marriage-family-work pattern, rather than allowing her to assume that love conquers all; and finally, for the sake of the nation, if not the women themselves, we have somehow to lift the level of aspirations of our brighter women students, and thereby help to meet today's vast shortage of highly trained personnel.

—Juanita M. Kreps, "Six Clichés in Search of a Woman"

In summary, state public schools have accepted a fair proportion of reservation Indian children on a nondiscriminatory basis—not always without special money inducement from the Federal Government in Federal schools. Some "Federal-Indian" children are admitted by some states only to segregated schools and, in some cases, they are not admitted to local public schools at all. Most nonreservation Indian children in southern states attend separate public schools. It is therefore apparent that, with respect to non-Federal schooling, Indians in some states are denied equal protection of the laws.

—"Status of the American Indian," United States Civil Rights Commission

3. Fix an image in the reader's mind.

Here, then, is the real meaning of the Western: It is a puritan morality tale in which the savior-hero redeems the community from the temptations of the devil. Tall in the saddle, he rides straight from Plymouth Rock to a dusty frontier town, and though he be the fastest gun this side of Laramie, his Colt .45 is on the side of the angels.

—Peter Homans, "The Western:
The Legend and the Cardboard Hero"

4. State the significance of the information, or give an insight that makes the content of the body fall into a clearer pattern.

The old chiefs are gone; the young men are to be found in school rather than in the woods, but the lesson is clear. It is not just the Indian who has to learn from us, there is much to be learned from him—the values inherent in group identity; respect for nature; the right of men to participate in the institutions that affect their lives; and that no policy or program, regardless of how well intended, will succeed without his approval.

—Estelle Fuchs, "Time to Redeem an Old
Promise"

Women's special difficulty is that they are unable to pursue a career on the same terms that men do and yet they are made to feel guilty if they "stay at home" and fail to seek a career. They are allowed to enjoy neither the world of work nor their home. They should be able to choose and find fulfillment in either.

—Edward H. Bloustein, "Man's Work Goes
from Sunup to Sundown but Woman's
Work is Never Done"

5. Give a warning, or leave the reader with a question or questions to think about.

A real honest effort to remove the just grievances of the 22 million Afro-Americans must be made immediately or in a short time it will be too late.

—Malcolm X, "Racism: The Cancer that is
Destroying America"

Henceforth, every nation's foreign policy must be judged at every point by one consideration: Does it lead us to a world of law and order or does it lead us back toward anarchy and death?

—Albert Einstein, "Only Then Shall We Find
Courage"

We have just arrived upon this Earth. How long will we stay?

—James C. Rettie, "But a Watch in the
Night"

6. Provide an apt quotation or employ a humorous or ironic comment or details.

Something said by former Secretary of Labor James P. Mitchell in 1964, the year of his death, underlines the really great need in this country:

The shameful migrant problem will finally be solved when there are enough Americans with wisdom, compassion and good sense to save their final censure [criticism] for those who stand by and seem unable to find within their economy a place for conscience.

—Alice Ogle, "The Plight of Migrant
America"

Breakfast over, he places upon his head a molded piece of felt, invented by the nomads of Eastern Asia, and, if it looks like rain, puts on outer shoes of rubber, discovered by the ancient Mexicans, and takes an umbrella, invented in India. He then sprints for his train—the train, not sprinting, being an English invention. At the station he pauses for a moment to buy a newspaper, paying for it with coins invented in ancient Lydia. Once on board he settles back to inhale the fumes of a cigarette invented in Mexico, or a cigar invented in Brazil. Meanwhile, he reads the news of the day, imprinted in characters invented by the ancient Semites by a process invented in Germany upon a material invented in China. As he scans the latest editorial pointing out the dire results to our institutions of accepting foreign ideas, he will not fail to thank a Hebrew God in an Indo-European language that he is a one hundred percent (decimal system invented by the Greeks) American (from Americus Vespucci, Italian geographer).

—Ralph Linton, "One Hundred Percent
American"

7. End with a final statistic or with final statistics.

Gail's case is unusual but her death was not. The day she died sixty-seven other people in the United States were killed by drunken drivers. In the last twenty-four hours, sixty-eight more people have been killed. In the next twenty-four hours, another sixty-eight will die. Tragedies like these will not be stopped without strict laws, stiff mandatory penalties, better education of both the public and the police, and our own intervention.

—John Lempesis, "Murder in a Bottle"

Building Paragraphs into Papers   125

8. Make a final clarification.

The real value of martial arts study, in other words, has nothing to do with physical feats such as brick-breaking; in fact, it is not even primarily concerned with fighting. In our modern technologized society, it would be easier to buy a gun, or carry a can of mace. Their real value lies in what the martial arts tell us about ourselves: that we can be much more than we are now; that we have no need of fear; and that our capacities for energy, awareness, courage, and compassion are far greater than we have been led to believe. They tell us that all our personal limits—and by extension, our destructive social and historical patterns—can be transcended. Beginning with the next breath, drawn deeply.

—Don Ethan Miller, "How the Bare Hand Passes Through the Bricks"

9. Employ a vivid metaphor.

We are like leaves of the palm tree, each deeply embedded in the tree, a part of the trunk, each opening to the light in a final, separate life. Our world is a human world, organized to implement our highest individuation. There may be ten thousand of us working in one factory. There are several millions of us living in a city like New York. But we are not the masses; we are the public.

—Suzanne K. Langer, "Man and Animal: The City and the Hive"

Whatever it does, your conclusion should give the reader a sense of completion, a sense of closure. It might be satisfying or controversial, challenging or depressing, but it should clearly mark the end of your unit of thought.

• EXERCISE 6.5: EVALUATING CONCLUSIONS

A. Judge the following conclusions. Which are strong? Which are weak? Why? What do they tell you or fail to tell you about the topic, divisions, purpose, and overall idea of the papers they conclude?

1. Together, my neighborhood, the building, the apartment my family shares, and the room where I spend most of my time give my family stability, for we have lived in these surroundings most of my life and hope to continue to do so after I return to Korea.

2. I have many loving, beautiful, unforgettable memories of that home and all I have done and shared with my family and friends there. I often wish to go back and do again what I did in my youth. But one can never really go home again.

3. In conclusion, by looking at two areas very far apart geographically and very different culturally, San Salvador and Miami, we have seen how an economic system determines a similar development of societies and creates similar problems. Comparing these two areas has suggested solutions to mutual problems—the opening up of new economic routes and the diversification of production so that San Salvador and Miami will no longer be single-product cities.

4. In conclusion, what I said in the introduction is clearly true. We need to act now.

5. An intelligent woman, independent, willing to stand on her own two feet, a smartly dressed woman who is willing to voice her views, yet who remains attractive and feminine—that is *Cosmopolitan*'s ideal reader.

6. This paper has discussed the key requirements for being a stockbroker: communication skills and social skills. A person fearful of dealing on a daily basis with large sums of money, of injuring her health from the stress and the pressure, and losing her human nature from focusing on things, not people, had better abandon her hope to be a stockbroker. She simply won't survive in the business. To make a good salary, a broker must learn to temper drive and ambition with ability, service and worth. This career can be a poor one if the broker lets herself be caught up in monetary gain and ignores the human touches, the confidential and trusting relationship between broker and clients.

—Akiko Arai, Japan

7. In conclusion, the decision to become a small shop owner requires hard work, self-reliance, self-control, and a variety of other skills and qualities, but to have a successful shop and to expand or to fail in this business is up to the shop owner himself. The saying, "God helps those who help themselves," sums up the virtues and the vices. Whether he rides a rocket to success or plunges to a business failure is up to the shop owner himself. Success as a shop owner takes daring and courage. The owner must be willing to face the danger of the tiger cage if he is to get the reward of the tiger cubs. Hopefully, by exploring the requisite skills and qualities for success, a typical day in the life of a small store owner, and the short– and long–term effects of this career choice, this paper has helped the would-be shop owner make an informed decision about whether or not this is truly the career for him.

—Kotaro To, Japan

B. Change into concluding paragraphs the introductory paragraphs you wrote in Exercise 6.3B, page 118. What kinds of changes do you need to make?

• EXERCISE 6.6: CONCLUSIONS

The last sentence of your paper should leave your reader with a positive attitude toward your paper and your central idea. Parallelism and other kinds of structural balance, an emphatic word order (reversing normal structures), and compactness of language can add power and force. Read the first paragraph and decide which concluding sentence is best. Explain why.

Then read the remaining paragraphs and write an effective concluding sentence for each one, a sentence that repeats the topic idea in a new way or that clearly brings the idea to a close. The example demonstrates the pattern.

Example: Ancient philosophers, inquiring into the nature of the universe, asked, "How can we know?" or, "How can we be sure any knowledge is valid?" Their concern for validity led naturally to the next important question of philosophy: "How do we know what we know?" or, in other words, "What are the processes of knowledge?" Their answers focused on the difference between knowledge gained by the senses and knowledge achieved by reason. Noting that human knowledge must be inevitably influenced by human ways of knowing, these early thinkers began to question whether any human mode of conceiving the world can have objective validity, that is, whether inquiring into the ultimate nature of reality is not, after all, quite futile. Following this train of reasoning, Socrates concluded that the effort was indeed futile but that one could at least gain knowledge of one's self.

Concluding sentence: Modern man has progressed little beyond these questions and this quest.

1. Although the birthrate in the American family system is much lower than that in underdeveloped nations, the available ecological and demographic evidence now suggests that our population is already too large for our available resources. Effective farming methods and new agricultural technologies assure our ability to grow more with less and thus to feed our population. However, many resources cannot be expanded. These include the water supply, minerals, space, recreation places, and parks, to name only a few. Furthermore, we are still unable to face, much less solve, the problem of pollution and garbage disposal, especially since, as a rich country, we produce more of both than do poorer countries.

Circle concluding sentence:

a. The result of all of these problems is to guarantee that Americans will have a steadily lower quality of life for the future—a reduced quality of life for the future.

b. So, clearly, Americans need to begin a number of steps for controlling population, especially limiting immigration since a lot of new people come in that way.

c. In other words, despite improved technologies, continued population growth guarantees a poorer quality of life for future Americans.

2.   In the 1920's Prohibition laws made it illegal for Americans to make, buy, or sell alcoholic beverages. The result was that more Americans than ever began to drink and that a thriving illegal trade developed. In the 1960's drug laws made it illegal for Americans to grow, use, or buy marijuana. The result was that most young Americans, as an act of rebellion against their elders, at least tried marijuana, and many used it regularly; it is still illegal, yet there are huge crops of marijuana grown nationwide. Even something as common as the 55 mile-per-hour speed laws provoke American drivers of all ages to speed up, so that most drivers in 55 mph speed zones drive 60 mph, many drive 65, and some hit 70 or 80 or even 90.

Concluding sentence:

_____

_____

_____

3.   Morning and late afternoon traffic jams jangle the nerves, while auto exhaust fumes hang over the streets, making the sky seem hazy and causing coughing, wheezing, and choking. The sounds of auto horns, collisions, heavy construction, boom boxes, and barkers assail the ears. Prostitutes ply their trade all hours of the day and night, even at 8:30 in the morning. Street people are an ugly blight on many city sidewalks, begging for spare change, intimidating and threatening passersby. The number of violent crimes in urban areas has soared; muggings are common and drive-by shootings are on the increase. One young lady was horrified to learn that she was the only woman on her block who had not been raped—and that seemed to be only because she worked double shifts and was never home.

Concluding sentence:

_____

_____

_____

4.   Why do we study sociology? Pre–World War II, the American emphasis in sociology was on social reform and social work: trying to meet the problems associated with an immigrant society caught up in rapid industrialization and urban growth. Since World War II, an academic sociological establishment has developed to provide empirical and sophisticated approaches to identifying and solving practical, significant social problems. Today's sociologists study the interaction and relationships among individuals and groups, social organization or disorganization, the evolution and change of social institutions, the changing nature of human attitudes and values. They are interested in the patterns resulting from continued rapid technological expansion: the changing nature of family and institutional life, sexual attitudes, crime and violence, religious values, and interpersonal relationships in politics and government. Sociologists are employed by

government, by business and industry, by hospitals and other agencies concerned with health care, by welfare agencies, by public educational systems, and by many other organizations requiring some systematic knowledge of human behavior.

Concluding sentence:

_____

_____

_____

5.   Since the methods of science have clearly been highly successful, the noted behaviorist, B. F. Skinner, author of *Behavior of Organisms* and inventor of the "Skinner box," believes that the methods of science should be applied to human affairs. He believes that, like rats conditioned by rewards and punishment, our behavior is controlled by our environment. He argues that, under present systems, such controls are created by accident, by tyrants, by parents, or by ourselves. As a scientist, he disapproves of such haphazard conditioning and believes scientists should order a new world in which there is no longer accidental manipulation. Instead, he asserts that a specific plan is needed to promote fully the development of man and society.

Concluding sentence: In other words, _____

_____

_____

_____

Final Checklist

Check the final draft of your essays against this list.

☐ Does your introductory paragraph make clear what you are talking about? If it doesn't make perfect sense to you, you may not be sure yourself about your real topic. Does your introductory paragraph give the reader a good reason to keep on reading?

☐ Is there a clear pattern of organization? Do your connectives both within and between paragraphs make that pattern easy to follow? Try circling concrete words.

☐ Have you used generalizations to establish your basic blueprint or building plan: the principles, categories or overall unifying or structuring ideas? Do these generalizations appear in your text?

☐ Is this organizing structure clearly stated in an introduction, a thesis statement, topic sentences, and a conclusion? In other words, does your essay have a solid foundation which is made clear to the reader?

☐ Do you just have a foundation or frame, or have you actually built a whole structure, with walls and roof, floor and paint, and finished details? In other words, have you, wherever possible, but most particularly in the body of your paper, supported, reinforced, and clarified your generalizations with specific details and specific examples? Have you included descriptive nouns, adverbs and adjectives?

☐ Do you balance the general and the particular? If your reader needs to ask, "What?" or, "Why?" or, "Can you tell me more?" or, "Can you be more precise?", you should be more concrete.

Considering the implications of connective words and the internal logic of the following essay defining a hero, reorder the sentences within each section and then rearrange each section to form a short essay with an introduction, two body paragraphs, and a conclusion. You may simply list letters and numbers rather than writing out full sentences.

What is a Hero?

A. (1) They are ordinary people, but in bad times they do extraordinary things: encourage and teach, or save other people from pain, hurt, hard times or even death. (2) Heroes show human beings' strength, courage, inventiveness, compassion, and sacrifice. (3) Overall, Campbell believes heroes are an important part of culture and mythology because they represent the best in man.

B. (1) Still another example would be the American Founding Fathers like George Washington, Benjamin Franklin, and Thomas Jefferson. (2) Being killed because of his beliefs and his brave practice of them made him an even greater hero. (3) For example, the Greek hero Prometheus taught human beings to make fires so they could cook foods and warm their bodies in cold times. (4) He describes their heroism as coming from the mind or spirit, because these heroes are brave enough to look at the world in a new way. (5) These political heroes helped bring freedom and democracy to this country. (6) Campbell also believes heroes can be teachers, inventors, philosophers, or religious people. (7) Good teachers, they taught a moral code to help people lead better lives. (8) More recently, Martin Luther King was a hero for both blacks and whites, because he fought bravely for civil rights and human rights, and taught brotherhood, equality, and peace. (9) In other words, teaching new ideas and attitudes might prove as dangerous for heroes as battling dragons. (10) Another example would be religious heroes like Buddha, Mohammed, and Jesus, who brought new ideas, new values, and a new way of thinking about God and religion.

C. (1) Modern heroes, like the firemen who risked being caught in the flames of a burning car to free a helpless injured person strapped behind the wheel, continue this tradition of heroically facing danger to save human life. (2) Far from home, family, friends, and a comfortable life, with little food or water, surrounded by dying men, she sent home many young soldiers who would have died without her courageous aid. (3) In Western culture, the hero of myth is like St. George who fights a dragon that breathes fire, for he must bravely fight something bigger, stronger, and more dangerous than himself. (4) First of all, heroes perform acts of physical courage that save people or property. (5) A famous nineteenth-century heroine, the English nurse Florence Nightingale is still respected for her bravery and self-sacrifice while helping those wounded in the Crimean War. (6) But he does it for good reasons: to kill evil and to rescue poor helpless people. (7) These wounded soldiers never forgot her bravery and kindness, and the world still honors her as the world's first great nurse: a heroine who faced physical difficulties but who also taught and inspired others.

D. (1) He says, "Myths inspire the realization of the possibility of your perfection, the fullness of your strength, and the bringing of solar light into the world. Slaying monsters is slaying the dark things. Myths grab you somewhere down inside…. Myths are infinite in their revelation." (2) In general, they do at least one of two main acts: they perform physical acts of bravery that somehow involve saving someone or something, and they bring new ideas or new ways of doing things. (3) They give hope; they inspire, and they teach what is important. (4) In other words, he believes that heroes have an important place in our stories, legends, and myths because they do things people want to do but are afraid of doing. (5) Joseph Campbell, the world's "foremost authority on mythology," "a preeminent scholar, writer and teacher whose work has had a profound influence on millions," discusses the idea of the hero and the hero's importance in world cultures.

Passage for Discussion and Analysis

Dr. Raymond McGowan, a college professor who specializes in English composition, gives the following instructions to his students.

Requirements for an Acceptable Theme

To be acceptable, an essay must have an introduction, a minimum of two or three body paragraphs, and a conclusion. The introductory paragraph must have a thesis (placement is most effective at the very end of the paragraph) that "forecasts" the main points that the writer will develop in each body paragraph. In a fifty minute class, two substantial body paragraphs are about all that you can plan to do, and in a seventy-five minute class, three good body paragraphs should do the job. Too many body paragraphs result in a skipping-across-the-surface approach, sort of like traveling through thirty-one countries in thirty-one days. The writer should choose thoughtfully the two or three points to be developed in those body paragraphs. Each body paragraph, in turn, must have a topic sentence that clearly echoes one of the points forecast in the thesis—and be sure to follow the order used in the thesis. These topic sentences help the writer control the content and direction of the paragraph, and they also help the reader know where the writer is trying to go. Here, the writer serves as a kind of guide for the reader, giving clear signals along the way. The concluding paragraph should do one thing: conclude. Remember that in your thesis you made a promise to develop two or three points, and if you have kept your word, no more is to be expected or needed. Your conclusion should be brief, about half the length of your introductory paragraph.

Essays done in class may contain corrections; just do so legibly (line out the corrected words; don't use parentheses or brackets), either next to what you want deleted, or above the deleted passage. You may wish to bring white-out to class. Essays done out of class should be as neat (and legible) as you can make them; but whether hand written or typed, you must proofread them. One or two corrections per page is acceptable, but much more than that and you really should wonder whether what you are turning in is a final copy or a rough draft.

In many courses, rough draft work must be turned in with the final copy: otherwise no grade.

Write on the front of the page—not the reverse. Why? A teacher has to read your papers, and the "show-through" makes reading such pages a strain on the eyes.

Skip lines if you handwrite; double-space if you type, 1½" margin at left margin, 1" at right, 1" at top, then your title, then two spaces, then begin your text. Indent about ½"—no more, no less. Always use white paper, 8½ inches by 11 inches; college-ruled (about 34 lines per page). Ink must be black, blue-black, or blue. Why? Grey ink, or ink the colors of the rainbow are all hard on the eyes. No broad-tip felt pens either. Word-processed papers should be printed in the highest quality mode available with a good ribbon. Consider eyestrain! Consider your reader!

• Questions for Discussion

1. How are Professor McGowan's expectations different from or similar to what is common practice in your own culture?
2. Why does Professor McGowan emphasize size and type of paper, and color and quality of print?
3. Why does he want papers double-spaced?
4. Why does he limit the number of corrections acceptable on your final copy?
5. Do his comments about paper development confirm or contradict those of your text?

•• Writing Assignments

A. Read the following three paragraphs. Underline the topic sentence in each one once. Underline the concluding sentence twice. Circle connective words emphasizing the relationship of examples. Notice the degree of detail in the examples.

1. Knowing one word can help open the door to knowing related words that serve other functions. For example, if one knows the verb *alternate* (to go from one to another and back again), one can make good guesses about the meanings of related forms. The noun form, *an alternative*, gives the idea of a choice, another possibility, as in the sentence *This won't work; we need an alternative*. The adjective form looks and means the same, as in *I am looking for an alternative solution*. Adding *ly* will make the adverb *alternatively* and dropping the *nate* will change the meaning slightly to *alter*, a verb form meaning *change*. In other words, familiarity with one word form can help one guess about the other forms that word might take.

2. Learning word roots is one way to expand one's vocabulary quickly. For example, the prefix *tele* means *far away* or *distant* whenever it occurs. This root occurs in many familiar words like *telephone* (sound from far away), *telegram* (writing sent from a distance), *television* (vision or visual images sent from afar), and *telephoto* lens (light from a distance). It can also occur in less common words like *telepathy* (feelings shared from a distance) or *telemetry* (measurements taken over a distance). Knowing such roots helps one make good guesses about even more difficult words like *telephotometrograph* (a record of the measurements of distant light—like stars). Learning only a few word roots can mean learning hundreds of new words.

3. Using the dictionary to find the meanings of two- and three-part verbs that start with the same verb form is important for understanding daily conversation. For example, the verb *get* changes meaning with each change in prepositions. *Get over* means "recover from"; *get after* means "punish with words"; *get by* means "do enough to barely *get along* (survive)." However, *get along with* means "have a good relation with," as in the sentence, "I *get along* very well *with* my roommate." A mother might ask her son what he has been *getting up to* in the sense of what he has been doing or in the sense of what he has been *getting into*. The latter suggests she is sure he has been doing something he shouldn't. Have you heard other *get* combinations? *Webster's Seventh New Collegiate Dictionary* lists twenty-one different combinations and there are even more. Being able to distinguish between them is vital to clear communication.

B. Take the topic sentences that you underlined in Writing Assignment A, and develop each one with a different set of examples—your own examples. In other words, learn from the model and then imitate it with your own examples.

C. Now write a thesis sentence or short introduction with a thesis to introduce the three paragraphs developed for Writing Assignment B and write a short final paragraph to conclude the essay.

D. Decide what order to put the paragraphs in. Finally, add transition words to interconnect ideas and to really turn your three paragraphs into a paper.

E. Underline your thesis sentence once. Draw lines to connect each part of it with the corresponding topic sentence. Underline your conclusion to each paragraph twice. Circle your transition words.

All essays should follow this type of pattern with a clear statement of purpose, clear topic statements, and carefully chosen connectives and conclusions.

F. Write a tailored autobiography focused on some particular aspect of your life. *To tailor* means "to shape and fit a project for a particular purpose, as a tailor does with clothes." An autobiography can digress or move away from the subject more easily than other kinds of essays, so you must be very careful to maintain a central focus. You might limit your focus to one of the topics below:

My family
My hometown
My family residence (house, apartment)
My education
My career or work history
My friends or social circle at home
My decision to study in the U.S.
My choice of a place to study
My recent experiences
My present social circle
My present studies
My plans and hopes for the future.

Once you have narrowed your topic, write three topic sentences to control the discussion in your body paragraphs, develop these, and work them into a full composition. Be selective. Do not tell the reader about your whole life, only a significant part of it, with the significance made clear through the three topic sentences.

G. Look back at Model #1 in Chapter 3, the section on "Moving from Outline to Paper," (page 58). That section provides an outline, thesis, and topic sentences for a potential paper—in other words, the skeleton of a paper. After making changes to any part of that skeleton to fit your views on "How to Develop Language Skills," write a paper on this subject. Underline your thesis statement, your topic sentences, and your conclusion. Draw arrows from the topic sentences to their corresponding statement in both thesis and conclusion.

H. The following coordinated paragraph could introduce a paper on adjustments necessary for comfort and success as a student abroad. Take each of its key points and expand them into paragraphs. Then combine the whole into a paper with an introduction and conclusion. You may use the introduction below as the introduction to your paper, or you may rewrite it to fit your particular focus.

Sometimes going to a new country means changing accustomed patterns, especially if the visit is extended, as in the case of a student. First of all, it means adjusting to new customs, for example, about what to eat and when. It also means learning new patterns of socializing because family and friends are far away, and making new friends in a new country depends on local customs for meeting and becoming acquainted with strangers. A lot of times, going to a new country also means changing work habits to fit the new situation and the new expectations. In other words, going abroad to study brings many more adjustment problems than merely language acquisition.

Chapter 7: OVERALL REVISION

True ease in writing comes from art, not chance,
*   As those move easiest who have learned to dance.*—Alexander Pope

Dreaming and hoping won't produce a piece of work; only writing, rewriting and re-
*   rewriting (if necessary)—a devoted translation of thoughts and dreams into words on*
*   paper—will result in an article, story, or novel.* — Roberta Gellis

I might revise a page twenty times. — Prolific British novelist Anthony Burgess

By the time I'm nearing the end of a story, the first part will have been reread and altered
*   and corrected at least 150 times.... Good writing is essentially rewriting. I am positive*
*   of this.* — Popular writer Roald Dahl

A piece of writing is never finished. It is delivered to a deadline, torn out of the typewriter
*   on demand, sent off with a sense of accomplishment and shame and pride and*
*   frustration. If only there were a couple more days, time for just another run at it,*
*   perhaps then....* — Writer, editor and Pulitzer Prize winner Donald M. Murray

---

The Importance of Multiple Drafts

A draft is a version of a paper. A rough draft is the first version: what you write in a hurry initially, just to get all of your ideas down. A final draft is the version that seems complete and ready to submit for criticism and/or a grade. Between the rough draft and the final draft may be two or more other versions as you work to refine and improve your argument. A paper that has been written once, proofread quickly for mechanical errors (spelling, punctuation, sentence structure) and then turned in for a grade does not show adequate effort on the part of the student.

It is good to begin now, at this level, to develop the habits that will bring success in academic courses. One vital writing habit is to write and rewrite and rewrite again. As the quotations at the beginning of the chapter indicate, good writers do. In fact, noted author Donald Murray comments, "When professional writers <u>complete</u> a first draft, they usually feel that they are <u>at the start</u> of the writing process. When a draft is completed, the job of writing can begin."

Revision may be based on teacher comments, particularly in English classes, where the teacher might come around the room and provide feedback (useful responses), as you write: "I can't tell what your thesis is!"; "Can you provide a few more examples?"; "Who will want to know this?"; "What else will your reader need to know?"; "Is this a balanced argument?"; "What is your authority for this statement?" Such comments should be listened to, for they are not made lightly, even though they may sound like casual suggestions. For out-of-class essays, having classmates or dormmates read an essay sometimes provides a basis for revision—if they are honest about what they read. The purpose of writing is communication, and if your readers cannot tell exactly what you mean, you are not communicating. Having someone besides yourself respond to your work provides a sound basis for revision.

When you submit a paper, you will receive professional feedback but also a grade. Consequently, for most college assignments you must learn to criticize your own work and do your own revision first. Composition classes, however, teach you about what teachers expect and how you can meet that level of expectation by providing a chance to respond to professional criticism: rewriting. Learning to criticize and improve your own work is vital to later college success.

Misconceptions about Rewriting

Students and teachers often have very different ideas about what rewriting means. When most students think about rewriting a paper, they think about correcting basic mechanical errors such as word order, spelling, capitalization, punctuation, verb tense and tense agreement, subject-verb agreement, pronoun agreement, in other words, all of the types of errors they practice to eliminate in grammar study. Correcting these problems is certainly important, and no paper is a final draft until such errors have been eliminated. These are often the most visible types of mistakes marked on a returned paper, and teacher comments will often call forceful attention to such errors: *A present tense third-person singular must take an s. You should not be making this type of error with irregular verbs at this stage of your learning process; you had better sit down and memorize those forms. Who is this "you" you refer to in your paper? You have been talking about "the student"; shouldn't you say "he" or "she"? A double negative is okay in Spanish, but never use it in English.* Such errors are the most visible signs that something is wrong with a student paper.

However, it is quite common to receive a grade of *C*, correct all of the mechanical errors marked, and still receive a *C* on the revision. For a grade improvement, the student must also reevaluate the essay, correcting problems with focus, organization, wordiness, tone, development, logic, and so forth. These are the most difficult problems for any student writer to even identify, let alone correct. Such revision is often more easily done if some time has passed between the writing and the rewriting, so that you come to your paper as a stranger would, reading it for the first time. For this reason, science fiction writer Ray Bradbury waits a whole year before rereading and revising a manuscript. He wants to see his own writing with fresh eyes, and, for a revision, you do too. Obviously, waiting a year is impractical for most writers, but even a few days' delay often creates the distance necessary to more effectively evaluate your own writing. Start early, telling yourself you need not finish completely; what counts is to have a commitment in writing that you can read, a few days later, as a stranger would, to judge yourself objectively and honestly. When you are ready to revise, you should ask questions like those in the following checklist.

> ## A Checklist for Effective Revision
>
> **Purpose:**
> ☐ Does the paper meet the requirements of the assignment? Does it fulfill the purpose its introduction or thesis sentence leads readers to expect?
>
> **Audience:**
> ☐ Are the language level, tone, and examples appropriate for the audience? Do any terms need defining or ideas explaining?
>
> **Content:**
> ☐ Do the introduction and conclusion define direction? Are the body paragraphs focused and complete, without wordiness, digression, or imbalance? Is there sufficient detail to make the evidence seem reliable and the logic clear? Could better examples be used? Are all quotations explained and credited?
>
> **Organization:**
> ☐ Is the organization clear, with one idea leading logically to the next, all in support of the thesis?

By now you should have made consideration of audience and purpose part of your standard prewriting procedure. A rewrite should reconsider these two elements. Your language level and examples should be appropriate for the educational level of your anticipated audience. You do not want to insult knowledgeable readers by talking down to them, but you do not want to sound pedantic or too formal by using specialized vocabulary with a less experienced audience.

The details and arguments of the paper should also be appropriate to purpose. As you reread and edit, you must ask, "Does this information help me achieve my goal?", and if it doesn't, "What changes can I make to further that goal?" If you wish to persuade, your approach will be more argumentative than if your goal is simply to communicate factual information. If you want to gain audience consensus or agreement, your approach will be totally different from what it will be if you want to challenge an audience to reevaluate a situation or to take action to change the status quo, the current situation. A good place to begin is with the introduction to make sure it clearly states the direction and aims of the paper.

A good clue that something is wrong is if you have left out paragraph indentations or if paragraphs begin with examples instead of a more general sentence that provides the direction or key idea of the paragraph. Try reading the first and last sentence of each paragraph to see if the controlling idea of the paragraph has been prepared for in the thesis statement. If it hasn't, you are probably digressing.

Language that is all the same level of abstraction is another indication of problems. The language of a paper should be much more specific in the body sections than in the introduction and conclusion. In the same way, the middle sections of paragraphs should include examples and statistics, quotations, and particular details, while opening and closing sentences will be more abstract. Try outlining or using the numbering system discussed earlier. Do any of your sentences begin with *For example* or a synonym? Even a quick glance can identify paragraphs without a "center" made up of proof and evidence. Try writing a <u>minimum</u> of one *For example* sentence after every general statement or claim.

An argument that depends on negative or positive language instead of supportive examples will be weak and unconvincing. Balance is very important in a paper, so, for a rewrite, you should ask which of your ideas are most significant and how much time you have spent on each one. Obviously, if you have more written on your least significant idea and less on your most significant idea, you will need to cut the one section and expand the other. Be on the lookout for wandering discussions: a contrast that compares, a time order that skips around, a definition that strays into argumentation. Other such changes in direction will be further indications of the need to revise. In general, the most common faults among beginning writers are:

1) A failure to settle on a clear, workable thesis and stick to it
2) A lack of supporting evidence.

Both of these problems are fairly easy to identify, though not always by the writer herself or himself!

Applying the Checklist: An Extended Model for Revision

Many times, despite our best efforts, something goes seriously wrong with a paper. Often this is because of a failure to think carefully about audience and purpose and the content necessitated by audience and purpose. Below is a well-written example of what could go wrong. The writer has worked very hard at producing this paper—without success. It is supposed to be an application letter to a university. If writing such a letter were a class assignment, a teacher might refuse to put a grade on it and, if the letter were mailed, most college admission offices would be puzzled by it. Why? What has gone wrong?

Audience: The student is writing to a director of admissions who regularly receives hundreds, perhaps thousands, of student application letters and has little time to waste on nonessential information: does this student meet school requirements? If applying for a special program, does this student meet the requirements of that program? Any other type of information is not only wasted effort, but perhaps detrimental to the writer's purpose. Does the letter address this audience? Is the information about the student's family history, a description of a city, and a discussion of values really relevant? How much of this letter should be

---

Dear sirs:

I am applying for admission to your school and to your business program. I have a good high school GPA and a good TOEFL score. I meet your financial requirements, <u>but</u> because I am a foreign student, I feel I should give you a brief history of myself.

I was born in a small town in Peru, and have German, Spanish, and Indian blood <u>dancing through my veins</u>. The town where I was born is 300 years old <u>with a spanish accent</u> and old-fashioned traditions. <u>As a youth, my family</u> moved to the capital of our country to pursue new opportunities. I went to very good schools.

The capital is cosmopolitan with all the good and bad characteristics of any large city. However, it is also very special because of its age and the fact that the old parts of the city have not really changed much since the seventeenth and eighteenth centuries. The new parts of the city rival those of any industrialized nations, and for me has been the springboard to the United States because of numerous connections. I went to school in Miami too and I wrote well.

I did well in high school and through the years traveling around learned a whole <u>lot I</u> feel international at heart and <u>ready doing</u> well in college. <u>But exposure to these experiences means very little if a person does not assimilate and integrate the experiences which they find meaningful into one's life.</u>

I believe all people share the same basic natural beliefs except they express them differently. I think cooperation, tolerance, maturity, and responsibility are good personality characteristics for anyone, and my younger brother and sisters have taught me them. At your school I want to prepare for my profession but also to be exposed to ideas, culture, tradition, philosophy, and ethnic diversity. I want to be a citizen of the world and am happy to begin my journey at your school with my very small suitcase of experiences that I hope will become a set of luggage when <u>they</u> end.

Thank you for admitting me to your program. I will see you in the fall.

Sincerely,

Rafael Chiapas

Rafael Chiapas

---

eliminated? A good editor would mark out as unnecessary and irrelevant more than half this essay. Here is a writing tip: Perhaps if the student had begun with a list of university requirements in hand and written beside the list exactly how the student met them, the first submitted draft would have had a better focus.

Purpose: The purpose of this paper should be to convince the reader that this student is eligible for admission. Proof of eligibility means providing concrete details. The writer would need to say more than simply "good grades" or "good scores" and instead provide particular grades and scores, perhaps with explanations. The schools attended should be named, the curriculum discussed, the language ability proven. If the purpose also involved admission into a particular program, the writer should find out exactly what the requirements for that program are and aim the body of the letter at demonstrating how exactly the writer's skills, experiences, and level correspond to those required for the program. Saying, "I will see you in the fall," may be looking on the bright side, but it is inappropriate for an application letter to a school which has not yet accepted the applicant.

Content: If indeed, in terms of audience and purpose, most of the content of this letter needs to be eliminated and the remainder needs to be made more concrete, then what type of content should be added? Instead of a general history of the writer's life, or a description of the writer's favorite city or philosophy of life or idealistic commitments, a revision would need to provide specific reasons why this writer wishes to attend this particular school, perhaps the writer's educational goals, certainly the writer's educational history, evidence that the writer is indeed a "good" student, and information about English study and skill.

Organization: Five short paragraphs and a concluding line suggest that there is something wrong with the basic structure of this letter. The movement is from general, introductory statements, to a list of nationalities and childhood history, to description of a city, to an international attitude, to general goals. A better plan for an admissions letter would begin with the purpose in writing and the reason the writer seeks admission to this particular school. The next paragraph should probably enumerate the basic ways in which the writer meets the admission requirements for general education. The third paragraph might focus in particular on English language skills to meet any anticipated objections that further language study might be needed. The final paragraph should cover any other technical details of application not yet discussed and end with some statement of willingness to supply further information.

Style: The basic writing style of this letter is not bad, but the underlined sections indicate problems that need correction. For example, the sentence, *I meet your financial requirements, but because I am a foreign student, I feel I should give you a brief history of myself* needs rethinking for emphasis. Is a contrast really called for, or are these really separate and unrelated pieces of information? Does being a foreign student necessitate a brief history of the writer or is something wrong with this logic? Other problems include a failure to capitalize, dangling modifiers, fused sentences, comma splices, incomplete parallelism, use of a gerund in place of an infinitive, inconsistent pronoun use, problems with pronoun reference, and incorrect connectives. Correcting such "mechanical" writing problems is important in order to learn from mistakes and to avoid them in the future, but such corrections alone are not central to improving this paper. This is mainly because most of the sections with errors need to be completely eliminated from the paper for reasons of purpose and audience. This is true with many papers and is the reason this text advises you to save your worries about stylistic and mechanical corrections for the very end of your revision—a final polishing.

After much rethinking, reorganizing, and rewriting, this writer might produce an improved version like the following (next page). As you read it, apply the "Checklist for Effective Revision" on page 137 to see if indeed it has helped. Does the writer deal effectively with the problems of audience, purpose, organization, and content mentioned above? As a result, do you have a different image of the writer? Does it even sound like the same person? Why or why not? What has produced this change?

Dear Mr. Warsaw:

I would like to apply for admission to the University of South Carolina at Myrtle Beach in order to major in business. My college counselor in high school first suggested USC as a prestigious institution for motivated, independent, and research-oriented students like myself. Its prestigious renowned college of Business would allow me to attain a Bachelor's degree in four years and therefore would provide me with a solid background to enter the competitive business world. After graduating from college, I plan to attend the Stanford School of Law in order to become fully versed in American corporate and international business law. This knowledge would allow me to attain my goal of starting my own trading company that would venture in the Latin American market of non-traditional imports and exports. The purpose of this firm would be to provide low income Latin American families with affordable and alternative materials for the construction of housing. The first step in achieving this goal is to attend the University of South Carolina and take advantage of the many resources and the excellent programs that it has to offer. With this in mind, I ask that the Admissions Department consider me as a candidate for admission to attend USC's college of Business.

Last May I graduated from Advanzar Preparatory School in the top 7% of my class with a cumulative GPA of 3.6. My TOEFL score was extremely high: 700 and my SAT totaled 1100 (550 Math, 550 English). The official scores have been forwarded by the testing institutions. I was awarded first place in the Miami Dade County Youth Fair the year I graduated for an essay entitled "Man's Fall" as well as for a short story called "Muerte de un político." I think they are good, and I would be happy to provide copies on request. In August of this year, I accepted an academic scholarship to attend Dartmouth College. I am currently enrolled as a freshman with good academic standing. I have requested that my official transcript, along with letters of recommendation, be forwarded to you.

As far as my English ability goes, you can see from this letter that it is quite good. I began studying English more than ten years ago. Originally from Peru, I have lived in four different countries, including the United States. As a child, I took a Berlitz English program which got me off to good pronunciation at an early age. When my family moved to the very cosmopolitan city of Caracas, Venezuela, I attended the elite Aguila International School. Classes were taught in English, and the majority of the faculty were American. The student body represented over thirty different countries, including South Africa, Egypt, China, Taiwan, Brazil, the U.S., and others. English served to unite the students, and it allowed us to communicate to each other the experience of travel and living abroad. I benefitted from the contact with such a diverse group of people by learning cooperation, tolerance, maturity, and responsibility. Later, I attended private schools in Miami which taught American culture and language.

At Dartmouth College, I am presently taking "English for International Students," to deal with problems many bilinguals face, particularly thinking in one's native language and translating it back into English. I am practicing generating content in essays, writing concretely, and formulating good summaries. The resultant improved essay writing has helped in my other classes as well. In Sociology 122 I drafted a nine page term paper which contained little or no grammatical errors. My philosophy professor praised me for displaying a high degree of sophistication in language and in understanding Aristotle. In short, I have learned to argue effectively in English and to provide legitimate support.

I am including the official statement of financial responsibility for your records. I look forward to joining the other undergraduates in your class of 2000. I hope the information I have provided will lead you to understand that I have much to offer your school. I am waiting for a reply. I hope to see you in the fall.

Sincerely,

Rafael Chiapas

Rafael Chiapas

This letter now reads like an application letter for admission. It has a strong sense of an audience that needs particular information and tries to provide precise and detailed information to meet that need. The writer knows exactly who the audience is (even the specific name is included). The letter is better organized, and the content is now focused on providing specific information for admissions needs. Even the conclusion focuses on *hope to see you* rather than *will see you*.

However, despite the vast improvement, there are still problems. Notice how many times the writer uses *I* and *me*. Obviously some "I"s are necessary, given the content, but the overall effect is to make the writer sound a bit egotistical. What changes could improve the writer's image? Is all of the information

Mike Warsaw, Director of Admissions
University of South Carolina
240 Conway Dr.
Myrtle Beach, South Carolina 33156

Dear Mr. Warsaw:

I am a transfer student who would like to apply for admission to the University of South Carolina at Myrtle Beach and more particularly for admission to the College of Business. My high school college counselor praised USC as a prestigious institution for motivated, independent, and research-oriented students and suggested that its College of Business would provide me a solid background for entering the competitive business world. After receiving a BBA degree, I hope to attend the Stanford School of Law to study American corporate and international business law, and thereafter to start my own trading company venture in the Latin American market of non-traditional imports and exports. My ultimate goal is to provide low income Latin American families with affordable and alternative materials for the construction of housing. Admission to the University of South Carolina business school will be the first step in achieving this goal. It is with this agenda in mind that I apply as a candidate for admission to USC's College of Business.

First of all, I more than meet your academic requirements. Last May I graduated from Advancar Preparatory School in the top seven percent of my class with a cumulative G.P.A. of 3.6 out of a 4.0. My TOEFL score was quite high (700) and my SAT totalled 1100 (550 Math, 550 English). The official scores should have been forwarded to you by the testing institutions. Furthermore, I was awarded first place in the Miami Dade County Youth Fair the year I graduated for an essay entitled "Man's Fall" as well as for a short story called "Death of a Politician." In August of this year I accepted an academic scholarship to attend Dartmouth College, where I am currently enrolled as a freshman in good academic standing. I have requested that my official transcripts, along with letters of recommendation, be forwarded to you.

As is clear from this letter, my English ability is competitive with native speakers. I have studied English more than ten years, beginning with a Berlitz program in my youth, continued in the elite Aguila International School in Caracas, Venezuela, where classes were taught in English and the majority of the faculty were American, and polished in private schools in Miami which taught American culture and language. I have lived in four different countries, including the United States, attended schools where the student body represented over thirty different countries, and have always relied on English to communicate with diverse people, people who taught me cooperation, tolerance, maturity, and responsibility. My present English class at Dartmouth College. is helping me practice generating content in essays, write concretely, and formulate good summaries. The resultant improved essay writing has helped in my other classes as well: a nine page Sociology term paper with little or no grammatical errors, a philosophy presentation praised for a high degree of sophistication in language and in understanding Aristotle. In short, I have learned to argue effectively in English and to provide legitimate support.

I include an official statement of financial responsibility for your records. If I can provide further information, please let me know. I hope to see you in the fall.

Sincerely,

Rafael Chiapas

Rafael Chiapas

relevant, or could some details be cut? Does the student really need to repeat adjectives describing how wonderful the school applied to is? Why or why not? What would you eliminate?

In addition, the unity of the letter could be improved through general, unifying topic sentences that begin each paragraph and that determine the focus of each. What about the conclusion?

Now look at the third version of this letter. What improvements do you notice? What makes this letter the best of the three versions?

Now audience, tone, purpose, and content all come together in an effective application letter that should produce a positive response from an admissions officer.

An admissions letter calls for a very clear-cut pattern of paragraph development. However, most other types of writing also require careful consideration of how to organize and interrelate materials. A very common, easily remedied, error is not relating body paragraphs directly back to the thesis idea. Examine the following introduction to a paper and the opening sentences to the paragraphs which follow. What needs changing? Why?

The performances of the band, U2, have captivated audiences for nearly a decade with their bold political messages. U2's songs range from ballads of love to songs of rage, from the soothing and inspirational to the fiery and the abusive, but they are always full of passion and vitality. U2 is famous among American youth because their lyrics and their stage performances reflect their upbringing and their political commitment.

Three of the four band members (Adam Clayton, Larry Mullen, Jr. and Paul Hewson, known as Bono) are native Irishmen, and Dave Evans, known as The Edge, is of Welsh descent, but his family moved to Ireland when he was a year old. All of the members of the group went to Mount Temple, a progressive, nonreligious Dublin high school. Three of the group members were Protestants and two were British born. All were outsiders.

U2's first song, "Out of Control," describes Bono's feelings on his eighteenth birthday, two years after the death of his mother and it describes the band members' decision to stay together instead of going to college.

War is U2's most politically outspoken album, for it touches upon the issue of Irish nationalism in Northern Ireland and Solidarity in Poland.

The thesis statement for this essay calls for a discussion of lyrics, stage performance, upbringing, and political commitment. However, how it will do so is not very clear and, in fact, the thesis could be developed with different patterns of organization. The following pattern calls for two sections, one on lyrics and one on performance:

I. Lyrics
  A. How they reflect band members' upbringing
  B. How they reflect band members' political commitment
II. Stage performance
  A. How they reflect band members' upbringing
  B. How they reflect band members' political commitment

The next pattern calls for two sections, one on how their lyrics and stage performance reflect the band members' upbringing and one on how their lyrics and stage performance reflect their political commitment.

I. U2 reflects the upbringing of the band members
  A. Through U2 lyrics
  B. Through U2 stage performance
II. U2 reflects the political commitment of band members
  A. Through U2 lyrics
  B. Through U2 stage performance

An essay which follows the first pattern would change the opening sentences and content of the body paragraphs to fit that organizational plan:

Body Paragraph #1: <u>U2 lyrics reflect both the upbringing and the political commitment of band members</u>. Since three of the four band members (Paul Hewson, Adam Clayton, and Larry Mullen, Jr.) are native Irishmen and the one of Welsh birth (Dave Evans, known as The Edge) was raised in Ireland. *War*, U2's most politically outspoken album, touches on the issue of Irish nationalism in Northern Ireland, while "Stories for Boys" focuses on the difficulties of childhood in a war-torn land. "I Will Follow" and "Out of Control" capture the closeness of family ties as lead singer Bono describes his feelings for his mother and for her early death. "Silver and Gold" attacks apartheid, "Bullet the Blue Sky" captures the horror felt by Nicaraguan civilians during a U.S.-sponsored bombing raid, and "Unforgettable Fire" delineates the effects of nuclear war. In other words, U2 songs reveal their origins, their heritage, and their principles.

Body Paragraph #2: <u>Their stage performance is also indicative of their family and national background as well as of their political views</u>. On stage they wave Irish flags and other symbols of their nationalistic heritage. During a concert in Berlin, Bono stood waving a white flag, symbol of his call for an end to violence.

A stage performance of "Sunday, Bloody Sunday" usually includes mimed violence, while a performance of "Unforgettable Fire" tries to make individual suffering visible as real film clips of Hiroshima play in the background. An audience leaves with dramatic visual impressions that heighten the power of the lyrics.

An essay which follows the second pattern would change the opening sentences and focus of the body paragraphs to fit a different organizational plan:

Body Paragraph #1: <u>U2 reflects the upbringing of the band members through both lyrics and stage performance.</u> Since three of the four band members (Paul Hewson, Adam Clayton, and Larry Mullen, Jr.) are native Irishmen and the one of Welsh birth (Dave Evans, known as The Edge) was raised in Ireland, their early songs sound very Irish and many of their lyrics, like those of "Stories for Boys," focus on the difficulties of childhood in a war-torn land. On stage they wave Irish flags and other symbols of their nationalistic heritage. Both "I Will Follow" and "Out of Control" capture the closeness of family ties as lead singer Hewson describes his feelings for his mother and for her early death and the band members' decision to stay together instead of going to college. The alienation of the lyrics also give a sense of the group's feelings about being outsiders.

Body Paragraph #2: <u>Furthermore, both lyrics and performance reflect the political commitment of band members.</u> The lyrics of *War*, U2's most politically outspoken album, touch on the issue of Irish nationalism in Northern Ireland. "Silver and Gold" attacks apartheid, and "Bullet the Blue Sky" captures the horror felt by Nicaraguan civilians during a U.S.-sponsored bombing raid. Performances emphasize the commitment of such lyrics. During a concert in Berlin, Hewson stood waving a white flag, symbol of his call for an end to violence. A stage performance of "Sunday, Bloody Sunday," a song whose powerful, angry lyrics describe war, hate, and inner conflict, usually includes mimed violence, while a performance of "Unforgettable Fire," which delineates the effects of nuclear war, tries to make individual suffering visible, as real film clips of Hiroshima play in the background. Together, sight and sound make for powerful political statements.

Why would either of these two approaches be better than the original? It is very easy to forget that your audience may not be familiar with your topic and may need guidelines for understanding, and signposts to lead from section to section and idea to idea. In other words, a good revision considers the expectations created by the thesis statement and reworks organization to fit the pattern indicated in the thesis. Part of this reworking involves checking to make sure that topic sentences refer back to and reflect the essential ideas of the thesis divisions to be developed in each paragraph.

• EXERCISE 7.1: REVISING FOR AUDIENCE

First define how the following passages fail to consider audience. Then rewrite to aim them more directly at the level, knowledge, and values of their audiences.

1. *Intended Audience:* Expert cooks

In order to make hot and spicy ranch–style Mexican beans quickly, get a large skillet, turn a top–of–the–stove burner on medium, put the skillet on top of the burner, and add to it 6 strips of bacon which have been cut in half to make 12 short strips. Don't overlap the bacon; make sure each piece has space to cook in the skillet. When the bacon is sizzling (little bubbles form in the oil that cooks out of the bacon) and the bacon has begun to turn a little crispy and light brown, turn it over. Warning: don't let the bacon burn; you want it brown but not black. In the meantime, chop two medium onions into small (about a quarter inch) pieces. Do the same to half a green bell pepper and half a red bell pepper. When you remove the bacon from the skillet, toss in the chopped onion and pepper and cook it (turning it regularly) until the onion has become clear. Then add two 1–pound cans of tomatoes with chili peppers. (Rotel makes these). Stir and mix. Cook on medium for 15 minutes to cook down the liquid. Then drain the liquid from 2 cans of dark red kidney beans and add the beans to the tomato mix. Stir. Cook for 15 to 30 minutes or until the liquid is almost gone. Then serve hot with Spanish rice and fajitas (beef skirts grilled).

Problem? _____

---

2. *Intended Audience:* A group of elderly, retired senior citizens

The term "senior citizen" to describe old people, 65 years and higher, has tried to change the way people look at the elderly. Instead of a burden to society or a "problem" to be dealt with or a "non-functioning" social unit, they are transformed, by this term, into long-term achievers from whose wisdom and experience others can benefit. The term emphasizes that retirement does not end a person's usefulness to society. Many senior citizens devote their energies to social programs such as the Foster Grandparents, and work with the underprivileged and handicapped, visit the hospitalized and children's homes, tutor youngsters, teach vocational classes, and conduct adult workshops in order to share ideas and pass along knowledge. Many live independent lives in retirement communities where age is considered a benefit and younger people are excluded.

Problem? _____

_____

3. *Intended Audience:* The university administration

Registration is a long, tedious process that takes students a lot of time and energy and that should be made easier for them. I personally have had to wait in lines of thirty to fifty people, only to be told that I had the wrong form or needed another signature and would need to repeat the process. Often times a student cannot even complete registration in a single day, but must return the next day to more long lines. Good courses and good times fill up quickly, and then students whose names come later in the alphabet have to revise their entire schedules, juggle times, and repeat the waits in long lines to get new class cards, only to be told another class is closed and more juggling is necessary. Wouldn't it be better to have preregistration by phone for returning students? My friends tell me it works well at other schools, reduces lines and waiting, and makes for fairer opportunities for getting desirable classes.

Problem? _____

_____

4. *Intended Audience:* A group of highly conservative, highly religious people

Despite speculation about test tube babies being "dehumanized" and the process itself being "unnatural," the possibility of test tube babies could have far reaching benefits for future generations. First of all, it will make possible some controls on genetic quality. For example, as is already possible in a New York sperm bank, it will enable selection of superior egg and sperm taken from intelligent, successful people who have not reproduced on their own and whose genetic material would be otherwise lost to the gene pool. Furthermore, it will allow geneticists to select out genes carrying congenital problems and insufficiencies. It will provide the personal satisfaction of reproduction to those who can not or will not reproduce under present conditions. That is, people who are highly motivated to have children but are unable to do so will be able to become parents. In turn, career women, who cannot afford time out for childbirth, will be able to reproduce vicariously. At the same time it will reduce dangers to mothers from overworked kidneys and from changes in body chemistry. Ultimately, test tube reproduction may be necessary to human survival if the environment becomes so polluted that natural reproduction becomes too difficult.

Problem? _____

_____

- ## EXERCISE 7.2: REWRITING FOR PURPOSE

Look first at the stated purpose. Then read the paragraph which follows to determine whether it sticks to its purpose. If it does not, where does it go wrong? Once you have defined the problem, rewrite to focus on achieving the stated goal.

1. *Purpose:* To warn of the dangers of tampering with genetics

Amazing new modern techniques now permit scientists to transplant genes from one organism to another: from plant to animal and vice versa. Recombinant DNA researchers have successfully transplanted foreign genes into the loops of DNA in bacteria. Such transplanted genes are readily accepted by the bacteria and can even reproduce themselves in succeeding generations. In other words, scientists, following carefully set up National Institute of Health guidelines, are now able, in effect, to create new life forms. Although the safeguards aren't required of, or followed by, commercial companies, most scientists are naturally careful. The guidelines, of course, ban transplantation of cancer viruses and require that scientists use only weakened E. coli bacteria that can't survive for long periods away from the lab. We don't really know very much about such newly created organisms, but, as far as we know, no accident has occurred. Of course, no one knows how such new life forms would react to an environment outside the laboratory, and some people are afraid these experimental forms could eat up chemicals, change the soil, injure the environment, or even spread cancer or infection or create new diseases for which there is no cure. However, since no one really knows what could happen, and since scientists have kept life forms created by genetic transplants confined in laboratories, we just don't know.

Problem? _____

_____

2. *Purpose:* To explain the difference between punk rock and rock and roll music

The dictionary definition of punk rock is, "a primitive form of rock and roll often featuring sociopathic lyrics and sometimes delivered with defiant vulgarity." This definition is not fair because punk rockers are not psychopaths; they are not mentally unstable though they may sound antisocial. Besides, the definition makes it sound as if this music is like the type of rock and roll that Elvis Presley did in his early days. Punk rock music is music with a loud, unsteady, hard beat, played very fast, with simple, repeated chords. The lyrics are about society and its problems, and there is nothing too rude for punk. A few examples of well-known lyrics are the following: "It's not what you can do for your country, but what your country can do for you...," "It's a holiday in Cambodia," "I was born in the blank generation, and I can take it or leave it each time," and "I'm so bored with the U.S.A." Punk rock is sung very loud. The band members (three, sometimes four) dress in tight, old, dark clothes. There is no comparison with rock and roll. Rock and roll has a fast, hard, steady beat, but many songs may be slow. The lyrics are mainly about love or making love, and there are long musical intervals. Songs might be called "Peggy Sue," "Michelle," "Love Me Tender," or "In the Still of the Night." Punk songs are short but not sweet. Some may be only a minute or so long. An album might have twenty songs on each album. New Wave focuses more on music and less on rudeness.

Problem? _____

_____

3. *Purpose:* To defend the death penalty for murder

Because taking human life is a serious matter, especially for the innocent victim and his family, I firmly support the return of the death penalty. Let's take a look at both sides of the issue. People who oppose capital punishment argue on religious grounds that it is wrong to take a human life and that two wrongs don't make a right, but execution is the only punishment to fit the crime and the only one strong enough to offer hope for deterring future homicides. When New York got rid of the death penalty, the murder rate increased 60 percent. At the same time, the type of murders changed from 80 percent crimes of passion in which killer and victim knew each other to only 50 percent crimes of passion and all the rest crimes against strangers. Nevertheless, opponents of capital punishment point out that it is possible that the police have made a mistake and that sometimes the wrong person would be executed for the crime. Under anti–capital–punishment laws murderers only suffer a minor inconvenience—given probation, at most a few years in prison. We really need to change our laws to make it harder for criminals to get probation. This lack of risk is the main reason for our soaring homicide rate. We need to once again make the punishment fit the crime by reinstating the death penalty.

Problem? _____

_____

4. *Purpose:* To explain which marketing method is best for our very small company's present goal of winning a large share of a small local market

Undifferentiated marketing, which focuses on common consumer needs, goes after the whole market through mass distribution and mass advertising. It is economical, but intensely competitive and hence, perhaps less profitable. Differentiated marketing, which operates in several market segments with separate offers to each, aims for higher sales, a stronger position in each segment, and repeat purchasing, while concentrated marketing, which goes after a large share of one or a few submarkets, is best for limited company resources. It requires specialized knowledge and specialized approaches, and may therefore involve higher risks.

Problem? _____

_____

• EXERCISE 7.3: CONTENT PROBLEMS

Which information is relevant and belongs in the paragraph? Which information serves no function and should be eliminated? Mark out the unnecessary or irrelevant sections.

1. *Audience:* Medical school admissions officer

   Purpose: Admission application, explanation of the reason for having taken so many business courses

In my early youth I never really wanted to be a doctor and resisted even considering medical school for a long time, because I come from a family of doctors and have been pushed in that direction since childhood. My family has always assumed I would follow the family tradition as my sisters have. Part of my rebellion against my family was to study business, even though it is an area of study that I was attracted to, interested in, and good at. My junior and senior year I did very well in my business classes, and put most of my effort into what I expected to be my future career. I put just enough effort into math courses to pass acceptably, although even then I did a respectable job in my true science courses. In fact, I got much better in science and made higher grades the more science I took. I also did pretty well in some computer science classes. I did best in English, where I made an *A* in literature.

However, near the end of my business program, when I began to consider what my studies meant in terms of practical job application, I realized there was very little I wanted to do in business as a lifetime career. All my business choices seemed ordinary and unexciting. Instead, despite my resistance to it, I kept finding myself drawn toward medicine, first taking science courses with the idea in mind of combining business and science, and finally taking full–time science courses because of the fascination they held for me. This is why my senior year has lasted so long.

2. *Audience:* Anyone considering a career as a jazz pianist

   Purpose: To describe a typical day in the life of a jazz pianist with a focus on the physical and mental concentration and exertion required

A jazz pianist might start practicing in the morning and spend all day at the piano, except for occasional, short breaks. After breakfast, for example, she will practice basic exercises to warm up her fingers and to fix patterns in her mind: scales and chords. Anyone watching might laugh because the exercises look so strange but they serve a good function. When her fingers are tired, she might listen to music for inspiration and then imitate the sounds. Such imitation might sound silly but it is necessary to learn and grow musically. Listening to the recordings of good musicians helps her develop her musical imagination, improvise better, and have a better sense of what is successful. It helps her develop a deeper feeling for rhythm. While listening, she might not look as if she is working, but she is. In the mornings she might also spend her time making her fingers and body strong so she can stand hard practices and long performance hours; to do so, she does regular body exercises, stretching and bending and jogging. Jogging or swimming, for example, help build stamina, improve muscle tone, and aid breathing. Swimming also is good for getting rid of shoulder tension. Besides, swimming can be just a fun escape too because it is always good to get away from work. These routines will be the most unpleasant work of the pianist; yet they dominate her day.

3. *Audience:* General

   Purpose: To prove Madame Walker exemplifies the American dream

The life of Madame C. J. Walker exemplifies the American dream of rags-to-riches success. Her parents died when she was six years old, and she was left a helpless orphan. Orphans in this country, as in most countries, have a very rough life; they get pushed around by adults, abused, and mistreated. She married at 14, but was left a poor, widow lady at 20—with a small child to support. Early marriages are not a good thing. They lead to headaches and troubles and conflicts. In this case, an early marriage left her with a daughter to support. She took in washing to support her daughter and herself. Then, one day, while she was thinking about how cosmetics manufactured for white women didn't really do anything for the looks of black women, she got the idea of manufacturing cosmetics for black women. Today, of course, a look at *Ebony* or one of the other black audience magazines demonstrates beauty products produced especially for blacks. It took her time and trouble to start a small business, but, once it got going, her fortunes changed. Her company grew and grew until she had 300 employees. By the time she died in 1919, she had built herself a mansion and had started several philanthropic efforts. Ms. Walker, a poor widow, uneducated and black, was one of the first American women to become a millionaire by her own efforts.

4. *Audience:* General

   Purpose: To explain what bionics is

The six–million–dollar man sounds like science fiction, but today biomedical technology is making fiction a reality. Have you ever watched that television program? Did it seem unreal to you? There is a lot of action, but it is hard to believe some of the things the six-million-dollar man is supposed to do. Nevertheless, some of the biomedical technology in the story is real. For example, it is now possible to repair many injuries. Metal bones replace real ones. Artificial arms and legs are powered by electric energy and some by nuclear energy. Glass eyes can have a sub-miniature television camera. New ears can be painted to look real and a very sensitive, super-small microphone can be put in the opening to create hearing. This is what bionics does or tries to do: replace body parts! Biomedical technicians design and build machines and devices to help people move and work. They help the handicapped live more normal lives.

- ## Exercise 7.4: Rewriting to Correct Problems with Content and Organization

First identify the problem or problems. Then correct them.

1.   For example, people who are polite to others may be described as "insincere" if they are pleasant and not pushy. If they don't let themselves be drawn into fights with strangers, if they politely wait their turn in the grocery line, if they fail to use their car aggressively in heavy traffic, they might be criticized as "unassertive." People who are nice to employers or teachers or any one else who outranks them might be attacked as "apple-polishers," while people who believe their personal lives and those of others should be private might be called "inhibited" or accused of being "ashamed" of their past or perhaps even overly "secretive." In her syndicated newspaper column, Miss Manners has a whole list of such reversed–meaning words.

Problem? _____

_____

2.   The car purchase itself means you will end up paying about $6000, for a lower priced car. However, buying the car is just the beginning of your expenses. You have to buy collision insurance, and, if you are an unmarried male under 21, that means payments of as much as $100 a month. If you don't have the full cash amount for the purchase, you will have to get a loan with high interest rates and pay a monthly note of around $200 to $300. Next, you have to buy gasoline at well over a dollar a gallon and in some areas almost $2. Then there are the expenses for maintenance (tune-ups, lubrications, oil changes if you don't do them yourself) for another $30 to $50 per month—if you are lucky. Urban parking fees, traffic tickets, damages for fender benders, and the costs involved when your car is vandalized or stolen add up to a big chunk of anyone's paycheck. Driving an average of 100 miles a week at 25 miles per gallon will end up costing you $5 to $7 a week for gas. Owning a new car can be highly expensive for a student, particularly in a high crime urban area.

Problem? _____

_____

3.   In the current debate over capital punishment, the liberals all cry about the poor little condemned criminals and forget all about the innocent victims and their grief-stricken families who have seen the bloodied, mangled bodies of their loved ones. I firmly support the return of the death penalty, but all those liberals pull out a bunch of unreliable statistics that ignore the facts. It is sad and ironic that those people who say they value life want to let the mean, ugly, hardened criminals, who rape and kill without compassion, go free. They want to let murderous villains back on the streets after only a few years in prison. This makes the liberal opposers of capital punishment as guilty as the murderers and lunatics they defend.

Problem? _____

_____

4.   Born in Brookline, Massachusetts in 1917, the second-oldest child in a family of nine children, John F. Kennedy became one of the most respected United States presidents.

First of all, his father, Joseph P. Kennedy, was a very successful businessman, who increased the family fortune and invested wisely. He very carefully made sure that young John had a safe, protected, happy childhood. Joseph Kennedy hired the best assistants, nannies, and tutors money could buy to take care of and supervise the children and to provide lively activities to entertain them. Of course, some said he was closely connected with organized crime and made a lot of his money through tactics in stock market trading that were later made illegal. Later, Joseph Kennedy became Ambassador to England and took his family with him to London. There he made sure the teenaged Kennedy had a chance to experience the excitement and culture of Europe by participating in the social activities of the British aristocracy and by traveling through many countries. He hoped that his son's European experiences and high–level connections would make him interested in international affairs—as it effectively did.

After John Kennedy graduated from Harvard University, he enlisted in the Navy and, during the Second World War, commanded a PT–Boat in the Pacific. His father had always wanted a son in politics, so when John's eldest brother, Joseph P. Kennedy, Jr., was killed in the war in 1944, John Kennedy was guided by his father to enter politics in his place. Joseph was blown to pieces while carrying explosives on a secret mission over Germany. John left the military in 1945 and started working on a new and possibly unwanted career.

Kennedy was the Congressman from Massachusetts from 1946 to 1953, the Senator from Massachusetts from 1953 to 1960, and the President of the United States from 1960 to 1963, the youngest president ever elected and the first Roman Catholic president. His father's money and behind–the–scenes influence helped him get all of these positions. He paid Ted Sorensen to write books for him. However, he did good things in office. His inaugural address pledged to help the people of the world help themselves through his "New Frontier" programs of federal aid to education, medical care for the aged, a Peace Corps, an Alliance for Progress, and major civil rights legislation for black Americans. Many idealistic Americans still respect the useful programs he started. His Peace Corps is still a model of America at its best, and his civil rights legislation began major social changes that have made for greater equality under the law.

Kennedy died in Dallas, Texas on November 22, 1963, the fourth American president to be assassinated. His death was a terrible loss to the country and the world, for he had grown with his position, and his youth, his vigor, his idealism, and his world view had captured the hearts and minds of people everywhere.

Problem? _____

_____

_____

Final Considerations For Revision

Before typing or printing out your final version, slowly read your draft out loud, preferably to a friend, but if not, alone; doing so will help you catch errors that slip past a "sight" reading. Some writers even read a draft into a tape recorder and play it back to hear the words and structure "performed" before they are read by the teacher and are "heard" by her inner voice. Finally, before you turn in any paper for a grade, you should <u>proofread</u> carefully to be sure that there are no errors, and that one idea leads logically to the next. Then put the <u>final</u> or <u>clean copy</u> into good form, making sure it is typed neatly on good quality paper and double–spaced. You now have a final draft!

Passage for Discussion and Analysis

The Communication Collapse

A neighbor's daughter showed me a question from a state bar examination she took recently. It called for a 500–word essay having to do with an aspect of interstate commerce. My concern here is not with the question; I assume it pertained to a conventional legal issue. My concern, rather, is with the time allotted for the essay: 30 minutes. This absurd limitation for a serious piece of writing is not unusual. Essay–type questions in high school and college examinations routinely allow half an hour or less for expository answers. In the very act of testing writing skills, the schools foster poor writing habits.

Clean, precise writing or speaking requires systematic, sequential thought. Words have to be crafted, not sprayed. They need to be fitted together with infinite care. William Faulkner would isolate himself in a small cell–like room and labor over his words like a jeweler arranging tiny jewels in a watch. Thomas Mann would consider himself lucky if, after a full day at his desk, he was able to put down on paper 500 words that he was willing to share with the world. Much of the trouble we get into (as individuals of organizations or as governments) is connected to sloppy communication. Our words too often lead us away from where we want to go; they unwittingly antagonize friends or business associates. We are infuriated when our position is not understood and then becomes the collapsing factor in an important business deal. Or we are terrified when the leaders of government miscommunicate and put their countries on a collision course. The school can have no more important function than to teach students how to make themselves clear. But by putting speed ahead of substance, the school creates false values. Racing against the clock is not an ideal way to organize one's thoughts or arrange one's words. The same hazards apply to speed–reading. Yes, we are bedeviled each day by a mound of papers, and we need to have some way of getting swiftly at the vitals of letters or articles or presentations. But the habit of skimming is too easily carried over to creative writing. Few things are more rewarding than the way the mind can hover over a luminous paragraph or even a phrase, allowing it to light up the imagination. The way the mind transforms little markings on paper into images is one of the highest manifestations of human uniqueness.

The teacher in high school who made the greatest impression on me would often devote the full classroom period to a single passage from a literary work, helping us get inside the author's mind and effect a junction between purpose and artistry. I still have a vivid memory, for example, of the way she slowly read the passage from Swift in which

Gulliver was tied down by the Lilliputians. Each word became part of a picture in the mind. I don't know how long it took for Swift to write this particular description, but it helped open young minds to the kind of imagery that belongs to creative expression. We had the same sense of literary splendor when our teacher read—so carefully and lovingly—from Thomas Hardy or the Brontës, or when she asked one of us to read Flaubert's word portrait of Emma Bovary. On the opposite extreme, one need not strain for specimens of poor communication in everyday life. Like polluted air, it surrounds and encases us. I see it in the wording of informed–consent papers that patients are asked to sign before undergoing medical procedures. I see it in the small print of insurance policies or on the backs of airline tickets. I struggle over it in tax forms or information from government agencies. I agonize over it in the instructions that come with do–it–yourself kits. I strain to comprehend it when I stop to ask directions, or when I hear a sports announcer explain why an outfielder played a single into a triple or why a wide receiver ran the wrong route.

Much of the stumbling and incoherence that gets in the way of effective communication these days has its origin in our failure early on to develop respect for thought processes. The way thoughts are converted into language calls for no less attention in formal schooling than geography or mathematics or biology or any of the other systematic subjects. Squeezing essential meaning into arbitrary and unworkable time limits leads to glibness on one end and exasperation on the other. We need not put up with either.

—Norman Cousins in *Time*

• Questions for Discussion

1. Summarize Norman Cousins' main argument. What does he consider necessary for good writing? Why?

2. What does he oppose? Why?

3. Do you find his argument convincing? Why?

•• Writing Assignments

A. Revise any of your recently written major compositions. Consider changes to improve your control of audience and purpose, persona and content. What new kinds of information do you need? What changes in structure or kind and degree of detail will you make?

B. Rewriting to Change Perspective

In the following examples, two writers describe exactly the same room with exactly the same furnishings, but because of their different perspectives and different points of view, each sees it differently. Write your own description of the same hotel bedroom using the same information but changing the focus.

To do this well, you should study the two original paragraphs carefully. Find the topic sentence that controls the point of view of each paragraph. Then look at the details and vocabulary. How are they selected and arranged to give the best support to the topic idea? What does one paragraph leave out that another includes? Why? Then limit your own paragraph focus to one of the following:

1. The old-fashioned hotel room was a perfect honeymoon spot: clean, comfortable, and anonymous, yet somehow romantic and homey.
2. This hotel bedroom was a health and safety inspector's model of cleanliness and safety.
3. The hotel room was a charming combination of modern convenience and old–fashioned elegance.
4. The hotel room, clean, comfortable, and orderly, was an inviting retreat for the worn and weary traveler.
5. The hotel bedroom, with its impeccably immaculate appearance, will surely give the weary, exhausted traveler the uneasy impression of staying in a hospital ward room.
6. The bedroom, so clean and bright and old–fashioned, offered too many temptations for a precocious and energetic child.
7. The Victorian elegance of the hotel room instantly transported its guest back in time to a gentler, more graceful age.

A Hotel Bedroom

The walls were whitewashed and bare of picture or ornaments, and the floor was covered with a dull turkey-red carpet. The furniture was a set, all the pieces having a family resemblance to each other. The bed stood against the right-hand wall, a huge double bed with the name of the hotel on the corners of its spread and pillowcases. In the exact middle of the room underneath the gas fixtures was the center table and on it a pitcher of ice water and a porcelain match safe, with ribbed sides, in the form of a truncated cone [a fancy matchholder with matches for lighting the gas lights]. Precisely opposite the bed stood the bureau, near to the bureau was the door of the closet, and next to this in the corner was the washstand with its new cake of soap and its three clean, glossy towels. To the left of the door was the electric bell and the directions for using it; and on the door itself a card as to the hours for meals, the rules of the hotel, and the extract from the code regulating the liabilities of the inn-keepers. The room was clean, aggressively, defiantly clean, and there was a smell of soap in the air. It was bare of any personality; of the hundreds who had lived and suffered and perhaps died there, not a trace or suggestion remained. Their different characters had not left the least impress upon its air and appearance. Only a few hairpins were scattered on the bottom of one of the drawers and two forgotten medicine bottles still remained on the top shelf of the closet.

—Mark Twain

The efficiency of the hotel room with its defiant cleanliness, precise arrangement, and numerous rules and regulations was sure to immediately make any visitor ill at ease. A visitor could not help but feel himself dirty in contrast to the gleaming whitewashed walls, the newly waxed furniture that was without a trace of dirt or dust, the conspicuous washstand with its fresh bar of soap and three newly laundered towels, and the almost overpowering smell of soap that permeated the air. The precise arrangement of the room—for example, the bed placed squarely in the exact center of the room under the single light, like a bull's eye, and the bureau standing straight across from the table with two identical chairs set equidistant from the bureau's sides—further added to the visitor's sense of being an intruder. The hotel's overwhelming number of restrictions and regulations covering almost every perceivable action were stifling, as were the limited times meals were served, and the ominous extract from the code that regulated the liabilities of the innkeeper. All together, the hotel room's efficiency and precision would inevitably create a sense of discomfort and would intensify a guest's self-consciousness so he could never totally relax.

Chapter 8: REVISION AT THE SENTENCE LEVEL

Blot out, correct, insert, refine,
Enlarge, diminish, intertwine;
Be mindful, when invention fails,
To scratch your head, and bite your nails.
—Jonathan Swift

Writing is hard work. A clear sentence is no accident. Very few sentences come out right the first time, or the third. Keep thinking and rewriting until you say what you want to say.
—William Zinsser

The writer must survey his work critically, cooly, as though he were a stranger to it. He must be willing to prune, expertly and hard-heartedly. At the end of each revision, a manuscript may look…worked over, torn apart, pinned together, added to, deleted from, words changed and words changed back. Yet… maintain… freshness and spontaneity. — Children's book author Eleanor Estes

Nothing is more satisfying than to write a good sentence…. This does not just happen. It requires skill, hard work, a good ear, and continued practice. — Barbara Tuchman

Improving Writing at the Sentence Level

When you first begin to study a language, you learn to use short simple sentences, ones that have a single subject and a single verb and are not complicated by many modifiers. However, as your understanding of a language improves, your sentences become longer and more complicated to express more complicated ideas and more complicated relationships. Sometimes you might find yourself translating from your own language rather than "thinking in English." Therefore, build any complicated sentences on basic, simple patterns for clarity. A sentence should never be so long that the reader loses his way in it.

The Importance of Revising Sentences

Writing good sentences is a skill vital to success in a university, in business, and in communication of many types, but it is not a skill that comes easily and automatically. Instead, it must develop slowly, over time, through practice. One measure of the progression of a student from high school–level writing to university-level writing is an increase in average number of words per sentence, an increase in sentence complexity, and an increase in the variety of sentence patterns used. Where the high school student might have a sentence length average in the teens, a university student will have a sentence length average in the twenties. A long sentence in English might run forty to fifty words or so. If you find yourself regularly writing long sentences, you might want to divide them into two sentences or edit them, for such sentences put strains on organizational grammar and syntax. However, if you are regularly writing short sentences, you will need to practice sentence combining for clarity of relationships and smoothness of sentence flow. Some languages, such as Spanish, permit sentences of sixty, eighty, even a hundred or more words, and if such a language is your native tongue, you will have to work hard to keep your English sentences short and direct, as English style dictates. Count words; read sentences aloud; have a friend read them to you. A sentence that cannot be read aloud properly cannot be read silently either.

Since readers, including graders in college courses, perceive complex sentences as a measure of sophisticated thinking and writing, it is most important that the serious writer improve sentence style. Revision is a good place to begin working on sentence improvement.

Confronting Dullness

Beside expecting sophisticated thinking and writing, readers want to read something that is interesting. They don't want dull, tedious, repetitive patterns that put them to sleep. For this reason, in addition to questions of purpose, content, and development, as you revise your papers, ask yourself what you can do to make your writing more interesting. Sentence variety is a good way to enliven dull paragraphs and to keep readers reading. As you rewrite, try to change patterns, using some short sentences, then some long sentences, subordinating sometimes, using parallelism other times, trying various sentence forms like participles, noun clauses, adjective clauses, absolutes, appositives, and so forth. For emphasis, put in a short sentence like this one after a long one. Readers notice this. The following discussion should help you move toward a more sophisticated style.

Movement Toward a More Sophisticated Style

In your movement toward a more complex sentence style, you must consider your options for word order and arrangement. Read the following set of sentences.

> An accident happened last night.
> It happened on July 2 at 10 P.M.
> It was raining.
> A diesel truck smashed into a crowded city bus.
> Six people were killed.
> Ten people were injured.
> The truck driver was drunk.
> A stoplight was faulty.

As written, they sound immature and unformed because they are short, simple sentences, and yet the ideas they express are clearly closely related. A mature style requires that these sentences be joined into two or three sentences at the most, and a single sentence for the best effect. Take time to combine these into one sentence. Don't worry if you are pulled in different directions by the interpretation of what happened. This is only natural when you just have facts and not indicators of meaning, importance, and relationships. Write out some of the different versions, and consider their virtues and their problems. Then study the following discussion.

Rules for Effective Sentence Combining

Study the following rules for sentence combining.

1. <u>When you have general and specific information, use the specific.</u> In this case, *an accident happened* is general while *a diesel truck smashed into a crowded city bus* is a much more specific expression of the same idea; *July 2 at 10 P.M.* is more precise than *last night.* In English composition, the fewer words used to express the same information, the better. Once your idea has been compacted, you can then proceed to add new details, new information, new relationships to make your sentence cover more territory.

2. <u>Look for relationships.</u> *Six people were killed* and *Ten people were injured* express the same type of information and could be combined with parallelism: *Six people were killed and ten injured.* The information about the rain, the truck driver, and the stoplight might also belong together as reasons for the accident: *A diesel truck smashed into a crowded city bus because it was raining, the truck driver was drunk, and a stoplight was faulty.* In this case the idea could be expressed more compactly by using *because of* followed by a noun series. Since there are adjectives for two of the nouns, adding an adjective to the third noun would make for better parallelism: *because of heavy rain, a drunk truck driver, and a faulty stoplight.* However, before going further, you will need to decide which ideas to subordinate and which ideas to emphasize. The following combinations are all possible.

    a. <u>At 10 P.M. on July 2 because of heavy rain, a drunk truck driver, and a faulty stoplight, a diesel truck smashed into a crowded city bus, killing six people and injuring ten.</u>

This sentence emphasizes the fact of the accident and subordinates the reasons and the effects on people.

    b. <u>At 10 P.M. on July 2 because of heavy rain, a drunk truck driver, and a faulty stoplight, six people were killed and ten injured when a diesel truck smashed into a crowded city bus.</u>

This sentence emphasizes what happened to the people and subordinates the specifics of the accident and the reasons for it.

    c. <u>Heavy rain, a drunk truck driver, and a faulty stoplight caused a diesel truck to smash into a crowded city bus, at 10 P.M. on July 2, killing six people and injuring ten.</u>

This sentence emphasizes why the accident happened and subordinates the specifics and the people.

    d. <u>Heavy rain, a drunk truck driver, and a faulty stoplight killed six people and injured ten when a diesel truck smashed into a crowded city bus at 10 P.M. on July 2.</u>

This sentence emphasizes why the accident happened and what its effects were on the human beings, but subordinates the details of the accident.

Clearly, in each case the decision to coordinate or subordinate reveals the writer's values and concerns, what is important to him or her and what is not. Obviously, the structural arrangement in these sentences has great legal and moral consequences, and could be manipulated by anyone—a prosecutor, a defense lawyer, a newspaper editorialist—wishing to lay blame on one party or to protect another. As a famous commentator said, "Facts are stupid things"—it is structure and arrangement that creates most meaning.

3. <u>Be aware of the implication of sentence structure and control it rather than letting it control you.</u>

Sentence Variety Illustrated

Joseph Conrad, a Polish immigrant who did not learn English until he was in his twenties, taught himself the language while working as a sailor, and began writing literature at age thirty-two, going on to become one of the great novelists writing in England. His novel, *Heart of Darkness,* demonstrates the way good writers vary their sentences and try to directly relate sentence choice and meaning. Read the following and see if you can understand how:

> <u>Going up that river</u> [**a gerund**] <u>was</u> like traveling back to the earliest beginnings of the world [**a gerund with prepositional modifiers**], when <u>vegetation rioted</u> on the earth and the big <u>trees were</u> kings [**parallel clauses—a complex sentence**]. An empty stream, a great silence, an impenetrable forest [**fragment**]. The <u>air was</u> warm, thick, heavy, sluggish [**simple with parallel adjectives**]. There <u>was no joy</u> in the brilliance of sunshine [**simple, expletive**]. The

long stretches of the waterway ran on, deserted, into the gloom of overshadowed distances [**simple with prepositional phrases**]. On silvery sandbanks hippos and alligators sunned themselves side by side [**simple with initial prepositional phrase and alliteration of "s" sounds**]. The broadening waters flowed through a mob of wooded islands; you lost your way on that river as you would in a desert, and butted all day long against shoals, trying to find the channel, till you thought yourself bewitched and cut off forever from everything you had known once—somewhere—in another existence perhaps [**loose, compound-complex, with participial phrases and parallelism**]. There were moments when one's past came back to one, as it will sometimes when you have not a moment to spare to yourself; but it came in the shape of an unrestful and noisy dream, remembered with wonder amongst the overwhelming realities of this strange world of plants, and water, and silence [**compound-complex with participial and prepositional phrases, parallelism, alliteration**]. And this stillness of life did not in the least resemble a peace [**simple**]. It was the stillness of an implacable force brooding over an inscrutable intention [**simple**]. It looked at you with a vengeful aspect [**simple**]. I got used to it afterwards; I did not see it any more; I had no time [**compound**]. I had to keep guessing at the channel; I had to discern, mostly by inspiration, the signs of hidden banks; I watched for sunken stones [**compound**].

Which clauses are dependent (subordinated)? Which are independent (main)? What is really interesting about the passage is the progression of sentences and ideas. At first, Conrad records impressions with a complex sentence to set up his overview and then with a fragment and simple sentences to give a quick look at all the new exciting scenes. Then, as his narrator travels deeper into the strange land, he becomes confused and lost and unsure of realities, expressed in the tangle of compound-complex sentences. However, once the narrator regains his self-control and begins to return to business, the writer relies on compound sentences made up of short, interrelated, simple sentences to give a sense of speed and efficiency.

Developing an awareness of the close relationship between what you say and how you say it will inevitably make you a better writer, one with a high-level command of English (remember, Conrad learned English in his twenties!). Studying this relation between sentence structure and meaning is only one of the many concerns of the student who is revising a paper.

- ## EXERCISE 8.1: IMPROVING SENTENCES

    A. From each of the following single sentences, make a series of independent sentences; i.e., write as many simple sentences as you can in order to determine how much information has been fit into this short space.

    1. Because he had been studying all night, his head ached and his eyes burned, but he had to stay awake in order to take the math exam at 1 o'clock, the biology one at 3, and the English one at 6.

    2. Since Fred was run over by a truck, he is less friendly than he used to be, for now he jumps in the air when someone talks loudly, turning his head quickly in their direction, thinking they will run him over.

    B. Using parallelism or subordination, combine into one sentence the information contained in each group of sentences which follow. You will probably need a compound or compound-complex sentence for #6.

    1. Ship Island is protected by the National Park Service.
       Ship Island is unspoiled.
       Ship Island is home to a large variety of water birds.
       Some of these birds include the laughing gull.
       They include the sandwich tern.
       They include the royal tern and the least tern.

They include the black skimmer.
They include many types of marsh birds.
One marsh bird is the red-winged blackbird.

2. Warm tidal pools wind along the shore.
The shore is secluded.
Sparkling sand dunes wind along the secluded shore.
There, sea oats help the island retain its natural beauty.
The sea oats are graceful.

3. The trip to the island takes seventy minutes.
It crosses the Mississippi Sound.
The Sound was used by European explorers.
Those explorers first arrived on these shores in the early 1600s.
However, today, one only sees shrimp boats.
Also one sees intercoastal tugboats.
Sometimes one sees ocean-going freighters.

4. At the beach one can swim.
One can surf.
One can fish.
There are many beautiful shells that a visitor can collect.
Some of these have sea creatures in them.
One can explore the dunes.
One can just relax.
A picnic area is available.
One can see dolphins leaping and playing not too far out.
One can feed the gulls.
Sometimes one can see pelicans dining on small fish.

5. Ship Island was cut in two.
There is now an East and a West Ship Island.
A hurricane did this.
Its name was Camille.
It had 200 mile-per-hour winds.
It brought 30 foot tides.
This happened in 1969.

6. Fort Massachusetts is part of the Gulf Islands National Seashore.
It is located at the west end of Ship Island.
Ship Island was important to the defense of New Orleans.
It was important to the defense of the Gulf Coast.
This is because it has a deep water harbor.
This is also because it was located along a shipping route.
The fort was once a vital part of the nation's coastal defense.
It was one of the last masonry coastal fortifications built in the U.S.

7. Barrier islands are special places.
They appear permanent.
They appear static.
In fact, they are continually changing.
They are moving parallel to the mainland.
They are moving toward it.
Or they are moving away from it.

8. Barrier islands protect the mainland from storms.
   However, storms may cause an island to disappear.
   Storms may cause an island to split in two.
   Storms may push a dune line completely across an island.
   Hurricane Frederic did this on parts of Santa Rosa Island.
   This happened in 1979.

9. Barrier islands give shelter to plant communities on the islands.
   They give shelter to animal communities on the islands.
   These communities are rich.
   They protect such communities in the sound. [shallow inland water]
   They protect such communities in the bayou. [slow-moving, coastal river]
   They protect such communities on the mainland itself.
   Protection is the key word.

C. Combine the sentences in the following paragraph to make only half the present number of sentences. Be careful to make decisions about emphasis, order, and importance.

There is nothing tastier than an American cheeseburger. There is nothing more nutritious than an American cheeseburger. Its meat patty is cooked over a fire. The meat patty is thick. The fire is mesquite. The style of cooking is grilled. A slice of cheese is melted into its top layer. Then it is served on a bun. The bun is freshly baked. The bun is smeared with mayonnaise. It is smeared with mustard. It is topped with lettuce. The lettuce is crisp. The lettuce is cool. It is topped with tomatoes. The tomatoes are juicy. The tomatoes are red. It is sprinkled with dill pickle slices. It is sprinkled with jalapeño slices. It is served with potatoes. The potatoes are hot. The potatoes are fried. The frying is the French style. The potatoes are cooked twice with their skins on. The cheeseburger is served with a Dr. Pepper. The drink is large. The drink is icy. The cheeseburger is a meal that cannot be beaten.

D. Combine sentences using parallelism to focus on goals.

John F. Kennedy was a man who had been in war as a hero. He had been a bestselling historian. He had also been a popular senator. He was elected president in 1961. His inaugural address was formal and determined. He delivered his inaugural address with the purpose in mind of letting his countrymen know his commitment to their and the world's needs. He also wanted to calm the fears of his opponents. Furthermore, he wanted to reassure America's allies that he would stand by past agreements. He warned opponent nations that he would be willing to negotiate. He also made clear that he would be willing to be tough.

Moving from General to Particular

Concrete details and specifics figure importantly in English prose because, in general, Americans value concrete data such as numbers, statistics, and, in general, precise examples—what is often called "quantifiable" information. Even British English may be a little less "concrete-oriented" than American English, so your first language may well differ from American prose in this regard, and you may have trouble adjusting to the seemingly inexhaustible hunger for "concrete data" in the U.S. One of the most frequent comments writing teachers make is, "Where is your specific [or concrete] support?"

One way to overcome this communication problem in your own writing is to always support your general ideas with examples, description, or details, and this usually means including adjectives and adverbs. Develop the habit of following general sentences with a new sentence that begins *For example*. Perhaps more than any other writing habit, the *For example* sentence can improve your explanations and your prose by making them concrete and clear. For example, a general sentence about how demanding a teacher is could be followed by an example of what the teacher actually does that makes students think she is hard:

> For example, she includes extra materials on tests, materials based not simply on the readings, but on inferences students should make from the readings, so that twenty percent of her students regularly flunk her tests. In addition, she gives extra-long assignments during the vacation breaks, some requiring as many as ten pages of grammar exercises, some library research, and readings of from twenty to thirty pages.

Such details make clear exactly what you mean by a *demanding* teacher.

An example, of course, is a kind of concrete "fact"; it usually refers more closely to the real world you live in, rather than the abstract world of language and ideas which exists only in your mind. The list below is what is sometimes called a <u>ladder of abstraction</u> :

ABSTRACT	
transportation	food
vehicle	vegetable
gas-propelled vehicle	potato
automobile	Idaho potato
Volkswagen	fried Idaho potato
a Volkswagen Beetle	Belgian-style fried Idaho potato
the classic yellow 1965 VW owned by Fred	Belgian-style fried Idaho potato served at Fred's restaurant on Dec. 4, 1995 at 7 p.m.
CONCRETE	

All the words except those at the bottom of the list are abstractions; they move closer and closer to the concrete as you move from top to bottom, but basically they are <u>categories</u> which might include millions of "real" examples. Of course, it is absolutely necessary to use categories when we think, speak, and write. If we didn't have categories, we would be like small children, pointing at things with our fingers rather than manipulating word symbols in our minds the way adults do. However, it is worth remembering that abstract categories exist <u>only</u> in the mind, so they will naturally be slightly different for each person, creating constant, if slight, misunderstandings. Most beginning writers write at a level somewhere in the middle of the ladder of abstraction but should try to move toward the bottom of the ladder: in other words, to meet the expectations of U.S. readers by writing as concretely as possible!

In the following example, there are a number of ways to make a dull, abstract sentence concrete:

<u>Initial sentence</u>: *A person entered the room.*

<u>Questions you might ask</u>: Which person? What kind of person? How did the person enter? Which room? What is the room like? Why did this person enter the room?

<u>Identify more precisely through more informative nouns</u>: *a person=my classmate ; room=classroom, office, bookstore*

<u>Add modifiers to specify more precisely</u>: *The tall, good-looking, Peruvian guy in my English class; the messy office of the international director*

<u>Add a name</u>: *Juan Carlos, the tall, good-looking, Peruvian guy in my English class*

<u>Strengthen the verb</u>: *entered=jogged, strolled, ran, danced, crept*

<u>Add a descriptive adverb</u>: *danced merrily, crept quietly, rushed angrily*

<u>Add an explanatory reason</u>: *to report his 560 TOEFL score, to purchase his textbooks for the semester, to complain about the unexplained reduction in computer lab hours*

<u>One possible result</u>: *Juan Carlos, the tall, good-looking, Peruvian guy in my English class, rushed angrily into the messy office of the international director to complain about the unexplained reduction in computer lab hours.*

You can transform a dull, general sentence into a more interesting and more informative, concrete one if you practice the following:

- Replace vague words with more precise ones
- Substitute names for absolute nouns where possible
- Change dull verbs to lively ones
- Give measurements
- Specify times
- Supply dates
- Add adjectives, adverbs, and other modifiers.

The secret is to <u>show</u> through words, not just <u>tell</u>.

- **EXERCISE 8.2: GENERAL VS. SPECIFIC**

  A. Place the following lists of words in order from most abstract to most concrete. In other words, construct a ladder of abstraction for each set.

  Example: four-bedroom ranch-style home, house, structure
  changed to
  structure, house, four-bedroom ranch-style home

  1. dog, sheepdog, canine, mammal, Belgian Sheepdog, animal, my beautiful black and gray Belgian Sheepdog, quadruped

  2. school, university, University of California, institution, institute of higher learning, The University of California at Berkeley

  3. the Slash Pine growing in my backyard, Slash Pine, plant, tree, life, evergreen tree pine tree

  4. North American, Susan Jones, human being, Georgian, U.S. citizen, Atlantan

  5. sweet potato pie, food, organic matter, potato, vegetable, sweet potato

  6. Vladimir Horowitz, musician, pianist, artist, concert pianist

  7. two ten-dollar bills, money, funds, possessions, twenty dollars, the two ten-dollar bills in his wife's wallet

  B. The words below are general or abstract. Find two or three concrete equivalents (either single words or phrases).

  Example: foreign student = the Chinese student from Taiwan in my Math 101 class; my classmate Tsai Wong from Taiwan.

  GENERAL TERM   SPECIFIC EQUIVALENTS
  government =
  book =
  house =
  university =
  flower =
  plant =
  bird =
  food =
  boat =
  dessert =

  C. 1. Identify which of the following words are general and which are specific. Could the specific ones be made even more specific? Explain how. What types of problems do you encounter as you try to distinguish between general and specific?

Romeo and Juliet	responsibility	mankind
house	ten pennies	huge
dormitory	items	14 feet by 16 feet
beauty	my daughter-in-law	deep-blue eyes
purple	trust	a poem

  my family's two-story brick home in Dayton, Ohio
  two 1909 Indianhead pennies in mint condition

  2. Make the abstractions from the above list more concrete. What is gained? What is lost? Can you make the concrete items even more concrete? For example, can *Romeo and Juliet* be more concrete? How?

D. Add concrete descriptive details that will show, not merely tell.

Example: The house is old-fashioned.

Built in the 1850's, the three-story, wooden, frame house with Victorian dormer windows, cupola, balconies, and a widow's walk, as well as unusual scrolls and woodwork, is typical of the old-fashioned gingerbread style.

1. My dog is lovely.
2. His girlfriend is a troublemaker.
3. My room is dull.
4. Her roommate is messy.
5. That food is awful.

There are a number of simple ways writers can make their writing less general and more detailed,. The following are a few of these ways.

Using Nouns to be Concrete

A very simple way to make your writing more concrete is to use descriptive nouns. For example, *the man* is a very vague term. It could refer to hundreds and thousands of very different people. You have learned to modify such a term by adding phrases like *the man whom you know* or *the man in the car*. Nonetheless, in many cases, a substitution of one noun or noun grouping for another is best: *the mailman, the police officer, my English professor, the madman, the trash collector, the football player, the taxicab driver, the Catholic priest, the Baptist preacher, the film star, the corporate executive*. These are all men, but they are very different men.

Using Modifiers to be Concrete

Another way to make your writing more concrete is to add modifiers to clarify. Modifiers might provide information about physical qualities (size, shape, color, age, material, temperature), about nationality, race, or religion, about location or time and so forth. For example, the noun *man* could be modified or replaced as follows: *The short, well-built, young, Thailandese student speaking to the class* or *The bald and wrinkled old Vietnamese Buddhist priest in the saffron-yellow robes* or *The tall, slender, fiery-tempered, red-headed, excursion director*.

Using Sensory Adjectives to be Concrete

Your words should create vivid visual images, so that the phrase, *the girl* might become *The tall, thin girl with the long, blonde hair and large, blue eyes* or *the dog* might become *the hairy, gray-and-white sheepdog with the dark, expressive eyes*. Words might add <u>tactile</u> details, so that *the basement* becomes *the cold, damp basement in my grandmother's old house* or *the nose* becomes *the soft, wet, velvet nose of my tiny kitten*. They might add <u>olfactory</u> details of smell, so that the *bad odor* becomes *the sickening stink of rotting, day-old shrimp*. They might add auditory details of sound, with *the noise* becoming *the ear-shattering boom of screaming jets breaking the sound barrier*. They might even add gustatory details of taste, making *the chili* into *the fiery hot chili* or identifying it as *strong and peppery, but delicious*.

Using Adverbs to be Concrete

Adverbs help clarify too, particularly about degree, intensity, and manner: *mildly interested, thoroughly exhausted, spoke slowly and carefully, wrote painstakingly*. Notice that the more concrete you

---

• **EXERCISE 8.3: PRECISION**

To practice being more precise, list nouns that could be substituted for the words in the following list. Are these substitutes exact equivalents of the originals? How much do they differ?

woman, animal, building, car

Use your dictionary and thesaurus to add sensory adjectives to the following nouns; what very different meanings do they create? What other types of adjectives can you add?

Example: earrings = glittering, golden earrings
dark, flashy earrings
soft, velvety, azure earrings
tinkling earrings
crinkled, silvery earrings
large, jangling earrings

wind   voice   pie   evening   river   dog   fish

---

become, the more specific vocabulary you need, and the more frequently you will need to consult the dictionary and thesaurus to find the exact way to create the picture in your mind through words.

Using Numbers to be Concrete

Saying that your friend has some cats is very different from saying that your friend has twenty-six cats, three of which are pregnant. Saying that you had to wait for your friend is different from saying that your friend made you wait one hour and fifty-three minutes. Numbers carry meaning!

Using Verbs to be Concrete

Many beginning students tend to overuse the verb *to be*, especially with expressions such as *there was* and *there were*. Such expressions should be removed for greater compactness of language. Usually, removing them allows the writer to turn the verb into an adjective clause or a participial phrase into the main verb. Looking for an important noun and changing it to a verb is another step forward in the move toward concreteness. Take, for example, the following two sentences: *There was some grass which was covering the lawn. It looked like a blue-green carpet.* Removing *There was* and other fillers results in:

> *Some grass was covering the lawn. It looked like a blue-green carpet.*
>
> ↓
>
> *Some grass was covering the lawn like a blue-green carpet.*
>
> ↓
>
> *The grass covered the lawn like a blue-green carpet.*
>
> ↓
>
> *The blue-green grass carpeted the lawn.* [noun to verb]

This final sentence is more compact, more precise, and more visual. This is the process of change your sentences should go through as they move from the wordy, inexact, and general to the compact, precise, and specific.

Add numbers to make the following more concrete.

1. The test was long.
2. He is tall.
3. She writes her boyfriend regularly.
4. That room is big.
5. My roommate eats a lot when nervous.

- **EXERCISE 8.6: SPECIFIC VERBS**

    A. Change each italicized noun to make a more specific verb.

    Example: His brother was a professional *driver*. = His brother drove professionally.

    1. That beautiful ship traveled by *sail* around the world.
    2. Alexander Graham Bell was the *inventor* of the telephone.
    3. My teacher was a *speaker* at the international conference.
    4. He does the *work* of a waiter.
    5. He does the work of a *waiter* on tables.
    6. She put her money in stock *investments*.
    7. Her friend is responsible for the *management* of the company.
    8. The workers made their *complaints* to the labor organizer.
    9. Her Japanese friend made *arrangements* of flowers.
    10. That man was the *assassinator* of the president.

    B. Choose a more concrete verb to replace the present one.

    Example: The teachers *said* he had done good work. = The teachers praised his work as good.

    1. He *went* to New York by plane.
    2. She *sat* in the easy chair.
    3. The dog *made* a loud doggie noise.
    4. The accountant *took* money from the bank illegally.
    5. *Put* the picture on the wall.

    C. Rewrite the following sentences to make them more concrete.

    Example: The child is sick. = My six-year-old niece has a severe case of spinal meningitis. [Specific illness + intensity]
    The classroom is ugly. = My Intensive English classroom has dirty green paint, cracked walls, and worn-out desks. [Visual details]

    Ask questions to help you think of details. For example, for sentence # 9 you might ask: What kind of plants? Whose yard? Which part of the yard?

    1. He lives in America.
    2. She loves to travel abroad.
    3. His grades were really bad.
    4. Her health is poor.
    5. She is nice.
    6. His party was just great.
    7. She is so beautiful.
    8. My new car is nice.
    9. There were many plants in her yard.
    10. The weather in this country is hard to object to.

Final Checklist

☐ Are the sentences compact, focused, and varied in length, type, and pattern, with relationships clear?

☐ Is the level of abstraction and the type of pronoun reference appropriate for purpose and audience?

☐ Have you used strong verbs, effective vocabulary, and persuasive details?

•• Writing Assignments

A. Correct and revise the following writing samples. Correct mechanical errors, but also think in terms of purpose, audience, focus, organization, and content. Rephrase, rewrite, add, delete as seems appropriate.

1. Pennsylvania is famous for its covered bridges. We have bridges in my country too, but they are all open, not covered. Pennsylvania's early bridge builders understood that a roof would protect a bridge's timbers from the environment. The environment they worried about was the alternating problems of too much sun and too much rain or snow. Snow is never a problem for bridge builders back home. The early Pennsylvania bridges were built from wood. Without the overhead protection, a wooden bridge may last only 25 to 30 years. I don't really understand why they didn't just use metal or something like that. However, many of those covered Pennsylvania bridges have stood up to the elements for 100 years or more and are still standing.

2. The typical eighteenth-century Pennsylvania German house was simple. It has been called frugal. It looked medieval. The roof was steep. In the center of the roof was a chimney. Small windows. Thick walls. Very often, the door was Dutch style, with the top part of the door and the bottom part of the door opening separately. The Hans Herr House is a superb example of Germanic architecture. It is located in the village of Willow Street. Willow Street is near Lancaster. Lancaster is, of course, in Pennsylvania. The Pennsylvania Dutch are really Germans, but the name comes from the German word for German: "Deutsch." Like the Deutsches Houses in San Antonio and Fredericksburg where German descendants meet.

3. At the beach the days are always beautiful, the sun bright and the skies clear. The sand is soft and white, the water warm and clear, and, most of the time, the waves high and good for surfing. Most of the time the sun beats down strongly, and the palms sway in the gentle breezes. One can walk along the shore and watch the waves beating against the face of the cliff and the wind blowing on the water and sand, or one can go tubing in the water, riding the waves to the beach. There are also big rocks along the shore with small caves, inside which are strange plants and all kinds of fish swimming in small holes. On the difficult road there, between the bounces and the curves, one can see beautiful beach scenes, cows grazing contentedly in pastures, high hills sloping down to the shore, and many kinds of brightly-colored tropical flowers and palm trees—all green and bright in the summer sun. All these make Shalpa Beach a lovely place to visit—a place to relax and to admire the beauties of nature.

4. Dear sirs:

    I would like to apply for a job with your company because everyone says you are so good to your employees and because I would like to live in Miami where your company is. I got good grades at the university with a major in computer science, so I should be an asset to your company. I really like working with computers, and I think

I'm good at troubleshooting. My school was very good in this field, and my teachers have all said that they would recommend me. Enclosed is my resume. It tells you everything you need to know. I would like a starting salary of at least $30,000 with some good benefits. I will be going to the beach in Miami in two weeks and will come by for an interview then. I really look forward to talking to you. See you in two weeks!

    a. What is the purpose of this letter? What has this writer done that will defeat that purpose?

    b. What kind of information should be left out? What kind of information has been left out that should be included?

    c. Does the tone of this letter fit the purpose? How could the tone be improved?

    d. What is the effect of the repetition of "I"? How can this writer reduce this effect?

B. Study the following paragraphs, and rewrite them to change the focus in one of the ways suggested below.

1.   The Oregon ranch is far from the nearest city. High, snow-covered mountains are visible in the distance. A white fence encircles the ranch. Horses graze in the fields. A small stream from the mountains runs through the flat valley. The barn has a huge peaked roof for shedding snow. The small, wooden, ranch house sits near the barn. A worn pickup truck is pulled up in front of the house. A red dirt road leads up to the ranch. There is no one visible.

    a. Add details to emphasize the beauty of the scene.

    b. Add details to emphasize the loneliness and isolation of the scene.

    c. Add details to emphasize the rancher's worries about his ranch. What could go wrong?

2.   Many people complain about going to the dentist's office, but going to my dentist is something I am always glad to do. My dentist is very professional, a neat, careful man who worries about causing too much pain and does all he can to reduce it. Usually, when I go, I am already in pain and his professional calm is reassuring. His reception room is cool and clean, a pale green with quiet lighting. His receptionist is friendly and sympathetic. Once in the dental office itself the only bad part is the initial shot to numb all feeling. After that I only feel relief that my problem is being taken care of competently and efficiently.

    Does this paragraph reflect your personal experience in a dental office? Write a paragraph about your experiences. Decide whether the details would be negative or positive. Provide descriptive details that will make the emotional nature of that experience clear.

3.   The Lonely Trail dude ranch in the Colorado Rockies near the Continental Divide is designed for people who really want to get away from the troubles and worries of urban life. Set 25 miles up a dusty mountain road amid the solitude of mountain beauty and quiet streams, the ranch is nearly 10,000 feet above sea level, in a high valley near a national forest. It is spread over 150 acres, whose only buildings are a ranch house, a barn and a handful of aspen-shaded guest cabins. Horses and llamas graze peacefully in the shadow of tall mountain peaks, and large trout swim in the pure, clear waters of the nearby Rio Grande. There are no telephones, no computers, not even a typewriter. The only entertainment is the scenery, the fishing, the hiking, the horseback or llama riding, and the elk herds which roam across avalanche slopes. Hummingbirds are a major source of entertainment at the ranch, sipping nectar from flowers and feeders. Fall and winter guests can count on the joy of skiing to their destinations.

    a. Describe this ranch from the point of view of a bored teenager.

    b. Describe this ranch from the point of view of a real, working cowboy.

Revision at the Sentence Level 165

Unit Two: Basic Writing Patterns at Work

Chapter 9: DESCRIBING

Often while reading a book one feels that the author would have preferred to paint rather than write; one can sense the pleasure he derives from describing a landscape or a person, as if he were painting what he is saying, because deep in his heart he would have preferred to use brushes and colors. — Pablo Picasso

---

The Key Steps in the Descriptive Process

    Gathering Details/Looking Closely

    Deciding on a Focus

    Making Assertions/Thinking about Underlying Assumptions

    Grouping Details in Categories: The Thesis and Outline

    Moving from Thesis and Outline to Rough Draft

    Inserting Transitions for Unity and Clarity

    Combining Sentences for Clarity and Focus

A Model to Learn From

Final Checklist

Passages for Discussion and Analysis

Writing Assignments

Applications

Description occurs in every type of writing. Novelists and short story writers describe characters, places, scenes, and action. Many college freshman essays begin with descriptions, trying to create vivid, memorable pictures of people and places. Travelogues, character sketches, reports of various sorts, movie reviews, and letters to newspapers—even to some advice columnists—depend on description for their effectiveness. Although technical, the writing of engineers, archaeologists, historians, and scientists (from biologists and chemists to etymologists, who study word histories, and ichthyologists, who study fish) may be mainly descriptive, sometimes coupled with analysis: They describe machines and how they work, processes, experiments, natural cycles. Such description may be highly technical, involving the formal vocabulary of a specialized field, but it is similar to the simple descriptive letter written to a friend in that it must create a visual picture in the mind.

Good descriptive writing is always concrete, with plentiful details and examples; it always involves giving close attention to the special meanings of words and any extra meanings they may carry with them; and sometimes it uses metaphors and similes to make the description more powerful and more vivid.

Good description begins with good observations: looking closely at someone, something, or some place. It also involves classification: dividing up the details according to a pattern, often one based on "space" or "location". A classic story about academic analysis illustrates the need for both close observation and the establishment of general categories or patterns.

Samuel Scudder, an American biologist from Harvard University, wrote a famous essay entitled "Take This Fish and Look at It." In it he talked about a lesson his zoology professor (Professor Agassiz) once taught him. Professor Agassiz, a fish specialist, assigned him a dead fish to observe. The young Scudder, after hours staring at the fish, attempted to draw it, an attempt that forced him to look more closely and that helped him discover new features in the fish. However, his detailed description of the structure of the fish and its various parts won only the comment: "You have not looked very carefully…. look again, look again!"

Embarrassed, Scudder looked again without success, until his professor advised him to sleep on it and suggested he might then have a better answer in the morning. Scudder describes the painful process of study that followed, "For three long days he placed that fish before my eyes, forbidding me to look at anything else, or to use any artificial aid. 'Look, look, look,' was his repeated injunction." The result was that Scudder, by his own report, had "the best" science lesson he ever had; he was forced, not only to observe the

"Take this fish and look at it!"

particular details, but to give them meaning by relating them to the patterns of the species and by determining in what ways they differed from the standard. Scudder learned, in his professor's words, that "facts are stupid things… until brought into connection with some general law" that gives them meaning and substance.

This is the lesson all writers must learn before they can describe effectively.

Learning to look analytically is essential in many professions: the dentist sees minor irregularities in your teeth that suggest a problem with closing your jaw, the mechanic looks at the spark plugs in your car and can make guesses about the state of your engine, the professional cook can tell the age and condition of the vegetables at a glance. Professionals learn to look by describing what they see very precisely and then evaluating their description. With an expert, as with Agassiz and Scudder, the process involves having determination and mental toughness, resisting boredom, and not quitting easily.

The Key Steps in the Descriptive Process

Gathering Details/Looking Closely

A common freshman English class assignment is to describe a picture presented to the class. The lesson the professor hopes to teach is the same as the one that Professor Agassiz taught young Scudder: to look closely and to classify and categorize observations to give them meaning. The prewriting preparation for this type of assignment involves collecting information, facts, and details. Setting up categories from the very beginning helps improve observation and organization. The following prewriting discovery frame for a picture description is typical of the type of preparation the careful writer should do whenever his or her task is to describe.

PREWRITING DISCOVERY FRAME

TITLE

FRAME
>   size
>   shape
>   details

MAIN SETTING
>   human figure(s)
>   sex
>   age
>   race
>   weight
>   height
>   shape
>   position
>   condition
>   clothing
>   style
>   color
>   condition
>   appearance
>   color of skin
>   hair
>   eyes
>   distinguishing characteristics
>   details

BACKGROUND
>   buildings
>   number
>   style
>   type
>   shape
>   color(s)
>   condition
>   details
>   other background

GENERAL COLORS, SHAPES

VISUAL PERSPECTIVE

TONE, "FEELING," "IDEA," MOOD

GENERALIZATIONS

ARTIST

- ### EXERCISE 9.1: PREWRITING ASSIGNMENT

    Follow Professor Agassiz's advice in the following assignment. Look very closely at the picture entitled *Christina's World*, painted by the American artist Andrew Wyeth. First observe the picture carefully. Think about it and take notes on it. Use the prewriting fact sheet to help you observe more closely. Then brainstorm about the mood or the feelings or ideas the picture communicates. Discuss the picture with your fellow students, and add to your fact sheet.

    At first it might seem as if there is nothing to say, but look closely; then find a general statement or central focus around which to organize your ideas. You should take at least an hour, maybe more, for this prewriting procedure. Remember the student observing the fish!

Deciding on a Focus

With the permission of the Museum of Modern Art, New York

The following introduction to a description of *Christina's World* illustrates a common writing problem: lack of a clear focus. The writing is detailed and includes a list of the main items visible in the painting, but it lacks a direction, a focus, a unifying idea. Basically it is just a list:

> Andrew Wyeth's *Christina's World* depicts a girl, a lot of land, a big house, a farm, a store room, an outhouse, and gray sky in the background. The painting is 14 centimeters wide and 8 centimeters high. The big, old farm house at the top has a double floor, six front windows, two attic windows, six right-side windows, a big door, and a tall ladder at the front....

The revision which follows is better because the writer provides an organizing idea: *The picture transmits a mix of feelings, but most especially solitude and desperation.* The opening still contains a list of key items from the picture, but now the list illustrates a general concept. The paragraph still needs work, particularly on connecting ideas, but providing a general organizing concept has been the first step in improving the original.

> Christina's World, a famous picture by Andrew Wyeth, transmits a mix of feelings, but most especially solitude and desperation. The solitude is clear from the absence of persons, animals, or flowers, and the gray sky, dry grass, and pale colors are depressing. The picture contains four princi-

pal elements: a reclining girl (presumably Christina), fields of dry grass, grey sky, and old, wooden, farm buildings.

> First of all, the girl stretches out on the grass, alone, with her left hand in front of her right, her body twisted to the right as if she is trying to get up. Her body position makes her seem helpless or in need of help. Her messy hair and faded dress....

The final section of the discovery frame (Perspective, Tone, Feeling, Idea, Mood, Generalizations) asks you to look for patterns, to classify, to categorize, to generalize. This is because generalizations provide the focus and the organizational pattern of a good description. Different viewers might focus on any one of the following themes: Isolation, Poverty, A Dilapidated Farm, An Old-fashioned Way of Life, Illness or Deformity, The Mysteries of the Painting, the Artistic Perspective, the Time Period, or even speculation about "What is Christina's World?". An essay might argue that the farm, despite its appearance to the contrary, is indeed inhabited, or it might argue that the girl in the painting, Christina, is the central focus. Whatever the focus, that focus limits and defines what the writer must do. Each detail must fit the focus and contribute to proving and supporting the general idea expressed at the beginning or end of the description.

• EXERCISE 9.2: PREWRITING ASSIGNMENTS

1. Since the the key focus of many of the potential themes in "Christina's World" is negative, words that start with *un, in, non,* or *dis*—all signs of the negative—might be effective. You might use words like *uninhabited, unhappy, undistinguished, unable, inability, inhospitable, incapable, ineffective, nonexistent, nondescript, disorderly, disheveled, in disarray, in disrepair, disjointed, disconcerted, disenchanted* to help make your focus clear. List other negative terms or details you might use for the figure of Christina, the buildings, and the farmland.

2. Decide on a central focus for your description of "Christina's World" and choose details from your prewriting list that could help you develop that focus. If there are not enough details on your original list, look again to find what else you could say.

Making Assertions/Thinking About Underlying Assumptions

You must be careful to make clear the basis of your *assertions* [the ideas that you state as true] and *assumptions* [the ideas that you believe are true—usually without examination or evidence]. You usually assert an idea in your thesis and then provide evidence for that assertion in the body of your paper. Assumptions are sometimes hard to recognize because people automatically believe some "obvious" things to be true without questioning them. For example, writers describing *Christina's World* might easily make assumptions about the figure for which they have little or no evidence: she is sad; she is in pain; she wants to escape to the city. Is it truly possible to know about the feelings of a figure in a picture or the history or background of such a figure? Why or why not? Always build into your description some evidence or support for your assumptions and assertions. A second problem in descriptive writing comes about when writers write subjectively and draw conclusions that few other observers would share, conclusions which are personal and eccentric. For example, a student who decides Christina, the girl in the picture, comes from a broken home and has been beaten by her father may be projecting personal concerns into the picture but is not really dealing with facts.

• EXERCISE 9.3: MAKING ASSERTIONS AND RECOGNIZING ASSUMPTIONS

A. Are the following statements about *Christina's World* facts or assumptions? Which assumptions are supportable and which are not? Why? What type of concrete details or other types of information could be used to help prove the supportable assumptions?

1. Christina is about 23 years old.
2. Her face is very wind–burnt, and looks distressed.
3. The scene is the 1920s.
4. It is the American midwest, probably the state of Kansas.
5. She is worried about getting home.
6. Her legs are injured.
7. She is lonely and depressed.
8. Andrew Wyeth was lonely and depressed when he painted this picture.
9. Andrew Wyeth tries to communicate the loneliness and isolation of Christina's World.
10. The two–story house has two chimneys and attic windows.

11. Christina looks young and helpless.

12. Andrew Wyeth wanted his viewers to understand the limitations of Christina's world.

13. The painting is depressing and sad.

14. Part of the field is cut; part is uncut.

15. No telephone or electricity lines are visible.

16. The farmhouse has no modern methods of communication with the outside world.

17. The farmhouse is being renovated.

18. A ladder stands against the front of the house.

B. The following sentences also have problems with logic, idea, or form, for the writers have not thought carefully about what they are saying. What is wrong with the following? How could you change them to make them more accurate and more precise?

1. She has long hair.

2. She is looking at the house.

3. The picture is 90% grass and 10% sky.

4. The way that she sits and the way that she grasps the grass tells us a lot about her.

5. She is thinking about her world.

6. She is hopeful about her life.

7. She is unhappy because anyone in such a situation would be.

C. What does the following description of the room make you think about the people who live there? List the assumptions you make about them. Explain your reasons for those assumptions.

> *Example:* Assumption: The residents are wealthy.

> *Reasons:* the large room, the expensive furnishings and equipment, the tiled swimming pool

At Home at Falling Water

The main entrance to the 12 foot by 16 foot family room is a doorway in the north wall. As you enter through the doorway, on the left, against the wood paneled east wall, is a large tan couch with oak and gold trim, at each end of which is a small stand with a lamp. A coffee table made from a single piece of wood stands in front of the couch; on it are some up-to-date copies of *National Geographic Magazine* and *Anthropological Review*, a book about the American west and about nature photography, and on top of the magazines, a beautiful granite and crystal paperweight. To the left of the doorway against the north wall is another, smaller couch, which matches the first one. A large floor lamp stands beside it, and in front of it lies a large Navajo style rug in different shades of brown and cream. On the rug sleep two large dogs, one a very woolly sheepdog whose hair hides its eyes, the second a young German Shepherd with very large ears which stick up straight.

To the right of the second couch is a bookcase, which extends to the ceiling the full length of the western wall. In the bookcase is an expensive modern stereo system, a television, and hundreds of books. In the southwest corner near the bookcase is a large, comfortable, reclining chair. A curved lamp shines over the chair for easy reading and swivels to facilitate reading of the book titles on the shelves. Right in the middle of the western wall to the right of the second couch is a doorway leading to the kitchen and dining area. Opposite the first doorway and the large couch are large picture-window patio doors, through which one can see a patio with lounging chairs, a rectangular swimming pool, and a backyard full of trees and flowers. The swimming pool is decorated with colorful Mexican tile and a statue of St. Francis of Assisi stands at one end. A bird feeder, surrounded by colorful birds of many different kinds, hangs from the patio cover. A large mirror on the wall above the largest couch reflects the scene from outside. There are African, Mexican, and American Indian masks on the other walls.

The patio is on the south side of the room. Inside, in the southeast corner, stands a large potted plant, tall and beautiful. Above it, a fancy Mexican style birdcage containing a talkative green parrot hangs from the ceiling. On the arm of the couch nearest the parrot sits a large, orange cat, which stares intently at the parrot, its tail and eyes moving as the parrot moves.

Grouping Details in Categories: The Thesis and Outline

It is best to decide on a unifying thesis and to plan a general outline or at least sketch out a plan for your list of details before actually writing a rough draft. Even a casual thesis and outline helps you figure out a plan for giving your information an order and a progression. A thesis focused on what is old-fashioned in the picture *Christina's World* might ask what is old-fashioned about the girl and then what is old-fashioned about the farm. The outline would reflect this division:

An Old-fashioned Girl on an Old-fashioned Farm

Thesis: Both the girl and the farm in the Andrew Wyeth painting *Christina's World* look old-fashioned.
I. The Girl
    A. Hair in loose arrangement—1920s–40s style
    B. Clothes in 1930s to 40s styles
        1. Pale pink
        2. Short sleeves with a wavy edge
        3. Black chain belt
        4. A-line dress
            a. Long skirt (mid-lower leg)
            b. Close-fitting
        5. Men's work shoes with no socks
    C. Activities old-fashioned—like Depression days
        1. Rough hands look as if she has worked hard physically
        2. Messy hair looks as if she works outside
II. The Farm
    A. Buildings in style popular from 1920 to 1940
        1. Large plain wood house with windows in roof
        2. Many rooms for many children
        3. Chimneys, so fireplaces instead of central air/heat
        4. No electric wires to house
        5. No telephone lines to house
        6. No porch
        7. Storehouses attached to side
        8. Outhouse or chicken house near main house
    B. Farming methods old-fashioned
        1. No modern farm equipment visible, not even a tractor
        2. Only visible farm machine for use with horse or ox

---

- ### EXERCISE 9.4: CASUAL THESIS AND OUTLINE

    A. Reread Exercise 9.3C on page 172, "At Home at Falling Water." Then quickly write a thesis and outline supporting the assumption "Wealthy Residents" or one of the other assumptions you made.
    B. In Exercise 9.2 on page 171, you should have decided on a focus for your description of *Christina's World* and begun to select details to fit it. However, if you have not yet decided on a focus different from the one above, do so. Then write a thesis statement and an outline to reflect that focus.

Moving from Thesis and Outline to Rough Draft

A thesis and an outline allow the writer to think carefully about the description before committing ideas to paper. The writer of the "old-fashioned" thesis might decide that he or she isn't really sure about the dates for particular styles nor about periods of architecture and therefore probably should change the focus to something more manageable. The writer might recognize that many of these same details would also help to prove poverty, and that a few changes in the thesis and outline could make possible the paragraph printed below. In order to clarify in your mind the relationship between writing and outlining, the comments in brackets and the outline alongside help reveal the underlying pattern of this paragraph printed below. How close is this pattern to the original outline plan with its focus on "old-fashioned?"

The painting "Christina's World" focuses on a poor girl on a poor farm. [thesis idea: two parts of outline] The girl wears an old dress, faded and discolored from use. Its ruffles, long skirt, and tight lines are out-of-date. Her shoes look as if she has worn them for many years; they are heavy like men's shoes. She looks skinny and under-nourished; her hands look red and rough as if from hard work. She is turned toward the distant farm buildings [transition to II.], which also show signs of age and wear [repeats topic focus]. Their wood is gray and weatherbeaten; the house needs paint and repairs (new roof, new wood). The homemade wood and wire fence is about to fall down. There are no animals, except maybe chickens, no tractors or trucks or farm machinery: just one old plow to be used with a horse. There is no electricity, no telephone lines; the house has only chimneys, so there are only fireplaces for heat. The toilet is an outhouse, and the farm is so poor there is not even a dog!

I. The Girl
  A. Poor Clothing
    1. Old dress
      a. Faded/used/discolored
      b. Out-of-date
        1) Ruffles
        2) Long skirt
        3) Tight lines
    2. Shoes
      a. Old/worn
      b. Men's shoes
  B. Body Worn
    1. Skinny/underfed
    2. Hands red/rough
II. Poor Farm
  A. Buildings old/worn
    1. Gray/worn
    2. Needs paint
    3. Needs work
  B. Fence falling
  C. Missing items
    1. No animals
    2. No machinery
    3. No electricity
    4. No telephones
    5. No modern heat
  D. Ancient plow
  E. Outhouse

This is only a paragraph, and clearly there is a lot more to say about the painting. What suggestions can you make for expanding and developing the idea? It is important in descriptive writing to select words and specific details to create a clear picture so the reader can see what you see. The following description of British author Frederick Forsyth selects very specific details to help create a word picture of clothing and style:

Forsyth is an <u>old-fashioned</u> chap, both by nature and appearance. Smooth and quiet-spoken, he seems deliberately to project a <u>dull</u>... [manner] as self-protection. His trousers have razor-edge[s]..., his shoes are <u>mirror-polished</u>, and he smokes through an elegant cigarette holder.— "Britain's Shy Spymaster at Work," *London Sunday Times*

Notice that it is the adjectives that most effectively create the picture of someone who is well-dressed and seemingly very much a part of the British aristocratic establishment: trousers with <u>razor</u> edges, shoes <u>polished</u> like <u>mirrors</u>, and <u>elegant</u> cigarette holder. A few precise words make a big difference.

• EXERCISE 9.5: WRITING WITH VISUAL DETAILS

Write your own paper describing *Christina's World*. Use your thesis idea and your outline to help you maintain your focus. As you write, add specific descriptive details, descriptive nouns and adjectives wherever possible. In other words, make your description as concrete and visual as possible.

Inserting Transitions for Unity and Clarity

A paper without transitions lacks the logical connectives that help guide a reader from idea to idea. Without them, the reader has to guess about the logical relationships. With them, the reader has, in effect, a map, with the important spots clearly marked so it is difficult to get lost. Although there are a number of different types of transitions possible, the most common transitions for descriptions of pictures and places are <u>spatial</u>; they call attention to <u>locations</u>. The following are typical of the words and phrases you might need to use to make clear location and placement:

on the left	on the right	in the foreground
in the background	in the middle	in the center
in-between	in the distance	in/at the bottom right
in front of	behind	in the top left-hand corner
in the rear	to the side	before
against	on top of	there
opposite	across from	beyond
nearby	next to	adjacent
attached to	close by	close to
north	south	east
west	under	through
above	below	beneath
between	in front of	in back of
inside	outside	on top of
on	in	over
on either side of	surrounded by	surrounding

- **EXERCISE 9.6: SPATIAL TRANSITIONS**

   A. Apply as many of the words on page 175 as you can to the figures. When writing, use them in a carefully chosen order: clockwise (the direction a clock's hands move), counterclockwise (the reverse direction of a clock's hands), from front to back, etc.

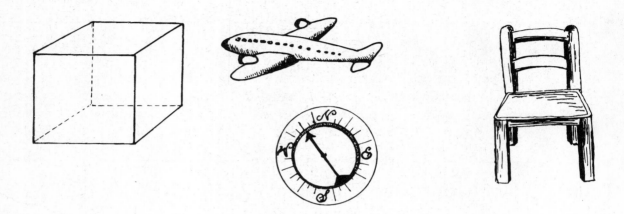

   B. Briefly describe the igloo and its inhabitants, focusing on spatial relationships.

   C. Underline the words that indicate the spatial relationships in the following description of the Gulf Coast barrier islands. What other type of relationship unifies the information in this description? Then compare the picture created in your mind by the paragraph and the reality it describes. What differences do you notice?

Life flourishes on and around the barrier islands, but salt determines the kind and abundance of plant life. Near the Gulf, plants such as the sea oats, which are tolerant of high salt levels grow well. Behind the primary sand dune, small bushes and some trees can be found, but they never grow much higher than the dunes that protect them from the salt spray. Farther back, freshwater collects in marshes among old dunes and supplies trees with water. Animal life on these barrier islands, too, is limited by the plant life, which provides food and protection. This is a special little world extraordinarily affected by the whims of nature. Behind barrier islands the waters of the sound [inland branch of the sea] and bayou are less salty. Here, nutrients washed down from the mainland support a rich marine life. Here too, shrimp and fish valuable to commercial fishermen move through many of their life cycles. On the protected mainland itself an abundance of life can thrive in the coastal marshes and more in the island pine forests.

—Adapted from National Park Service brochure on the
Gulf Islands National Seashore, Mississippi/Florida

D. Look back at the description of "At Home at Falling Water" in Exercise 9.3, page 172. Then, carefully considering the transition words the writer provides, sketch the scene. What makes it easy or hard to visualize this scene?

E. Review your paper on *Christina's World*. Are the connections between ideas clear and easy to follow? Wherever needed, add transitions to help better connect your descriptive details.

Combining Sentences for Clarity and Focus

As discussed earlier, descriptions should always be as compact and as visual as possible. In fact, a good revision will involve sentence combining and use of parallelism to express the same information in less space; at the same time it might involve adding more descriptive details, details about color and "texture." A sentence that says *From the color of her arms and the way she acts, it seems she has difficulty walking to those unpainted houses* needs more information. The reader will invariably ask what color her arms are and how she acts. A revision might say *Her thin, yellow arms and twisted body suggest the diffi-*

culty she has crawling toward those run-down and weathered, gray frame buildings on the hilltop. Why is this version better than the original? How do the changes improve the next set of sentences? Remember that, especially in descriptive writing, specific is usually better than general!

Christina is the first <u>thing</u> one can see in this picture. She is skinny; her hair is <u>puffy</u>; her dress is old, which suggests the <u>period in which she lives.</u> She is resting on her hips and supporting her chest with her arms. Her hands are swollen and red, showing the everyday use she applies them to. From all these characteristics one can develop [<u>does the viewer or the artist develop</u>?] the idea of tiredness [<u>too general</u>].

CHANGED TO

Wearing a <u>well-worn, old-fashioned</u> dress, Christina, whose <u>lonely</u> figure dominates our view of <u>the 1930s</u> farm, lifts her twisted body toward the distant horizon. Her swollen, red hands, her skinny, yellow arms, and sweaty, messy hair suggest a weak physical state or else hard work.

[<u>Note use of adjectives and parallelism to focus the description</u>.]

The first <u>thing</u> you see in the picture is a girl lying on the grass. She seems to be the central figure in the picture. She has short, dark hair. She is wearing a long dress. The color of her dress has faded. She is a slim, young girl. She must be a farmer's daughter. She is wearing leather shoes. She has her back toward you. The young girl seems to be looking at the farm house in the background of the picture [<u>short, repetitive sentences</u>].

CHANGED TO

The central figure in the picture is a slim, dark-haired young girl, possibly a farmer's daughter, wearing a long, faded, pink dress, heavy leather shoes, and a practical bun. Stretched out amid fields of yellow-brown grass, her body turns toward a weatherbeaten farm on the distant horizon. [<u>What problems has the revision corrected? What grammatical changes have been made</u>?]

- **EXERCISE 9.7: SENTENCE COMBINING FOR REVISION**

  A. Adding specific details makes writing more descriptive, while using adjective sequences compacts information. Combine the following sentences to form better, more complex ones. Where possible, use adjective lists to reduce wordiness.

  Example: She married. She was happy. She was attractive. She was 20. She had a rounded figure. It was pleasant. She had a tiny waist.

  CHANGED TO

  When she married, she had been a happy and attractive girl of twenty, with a pleasant rounded figure and a tiny waist.

  Example: Now she was fat. Now she was shapeless. This was the result of the postwar years. The postwar years were characterized by hardship. They involved worry. There was a lot of hard work.

  CHANGED TO

  Now she was fat and shapeless, the result of all the postwar years of hardship, worry, and hard work.

  1. The house made of wood looks very old. The authentic farm house has two floors and an attic. The roof is peaked with two dormer windows in the front of the attic.
  2. She is looking at the big house which is far from her. The big house has a second floor which is made of wood and it looks very old.
  3. A ladder is set up against the front of the big house. There is a chicken coop in front of the big house. The big house has a chicken coop which is surrounded by a wire fence. It is half-fallen. It has wooden posts.
  4. She was thirty. She looked younger. She looked vulnerable.

5. He was an aristocrat. He was smart. He was spoiled. He was a prominent social figure. The society was Parisian.

6. Her expression was hard. It was hostile. It hid her inward fear. Her fear was of facing the unknown.

7. The woman walked into the room. She was tall. She was beautiful. She wore a brown dress. It was elegant. She had a scarf around her throat. It was silk. Pearls were knotted through it.

8. He was a fair-haired man. He was in his early thirties. He had irregular features. He had blue eyes. He carried a small suitcase. He also carried an attaché case. It was leather. It was smart. It had initials in gold.

9. He wore a sweater. It was made in France. It had a roll-neck. He wore trousers. They were casual. They were dark. His shoes were suede. They were two-tone. He looked like a well-off professional on holiday in the country.

10. He was handsome. He was an old man. His skin was white. It was transparent. It stretched over his bones. His bones were fine. His eyes were black. They looked into a past of his own. His hair was as fine as down. His smile was the smile of the old who are content.

B. Write a series of simple sentences giving your impression of the school or college you are attending, of the section of the city in which you live, or of a picture that interests you (it must be available for viewing). Then combine these sentences into longer ones that are more carefully interconnected.

> *Example:* 1. When I first arrived at Stanford, I was impressed by the size of the campus. 2. It was like a huge park. 3. It had many giant eucalyptus trees. 4. They were very beautiful. 5. The buildings were also beautiful. 6. They were in a Spanish style. 7. Some of them had colorful murals decorating them. 8. The buildings extended in all directions. 9. There were too many to count.
>
> CHANGED TO
>
> When I first arrived at Stanford, I was impressed by the size of the campus, for it was like a huge park with many beautiful, giant eucalyptus trees. The beautiful Spanish-style buildings, too numerous to count, extended in all directions, some decorated with colorful murals.

• EXERCISE 9.8: RECOGNIZING FOCUS

A. Identify the focus of each of the following paragraphs. Each writer is looking at the same picture, but is selecting very different details to support an individual focus. The italicized words in each paragraph are clues to focus. Look for the topic sentence of each paragraph, the connective words, and the plan or order. What gives the paragraphs internal unity? Explain.

1. The farm house is run-down, but *lived in*, for the windows of the house are open, a ladder stands against the front, and a shirt hangs on the clothes line. The grass near the house and barn has recently been cut, and a well-worn dirt road winds up to the house. Birds circle an opening in the roof of the barn, a sign of crops stored there and therefore of *habitation*. The most obvious proof that the farm is *occupied* is, of course, the presence of Christina.

   FOCUS?_____

2. The girl in the painting, apparently Christina, is *the main focus of the painting*, for, standing two centimeters high and being four centimeters long, she is the *largest* visible object, larger than even the farmhouse or barn. Furthermore, she adds a splash of *color* to a composition dominated by dull grays and tans; her dress is pale pink, her narrow belt black, and her hair, pulled in a loose bun and lightly blowing in a slight breeze, black with touches of lighter browns. Her pale skin contrasts with her dark hair, and her pinkish hands look rough. *But not only do her color and size make her the center of attention; so too does her position and perspective.* She half-sits, half-lies, with her body twisted toward the horizon; her weight rests on her right arm and hand, which are placed near her hips, while her left arm reaches forward and upward. Her head is turned away from the viewer so her face is not visible. Her neck pushes it forward and upward as if she is straining toward the distant farm.

   FOCUS? _____

3. The *dull* colors, the *absence* of many signs of life, the run-down condition of the farm buildings, and the *sick* appearance of the girl make this picture look *very depressing*. First of all, four-fifths of the picture is gray-brown grass: no trees, no flowers, just *dead* grass! The other colors are those of weatherbeaten wood (a worn gray) and the faded colors of Christina's clothing (pale pink, black, gray). Next, there are *no* people except Christina; there are *no* cars, *no* phone lines, *no* animals (except some lone birds in the distance). Even the gray cloudy sky is *empty*. Then there are the run-down buildings, with no paint, worn roofs, and half-fallen fencing. Finally, the girl herself adds to the sense of *depression*. Her face is not visible, but her body is twisted in a strange and awkward position. Her arms are yellow and skinny; her hands are swollen and red. Her hips are large and her shoulders narrow. The result of this combination is a <u>sad</u> picture that makes the viewer want to turn away.

   FOCUS? _____

4. The painting, *Christina's World*, offers many *mysteries*. The first *mystery* is the girl herself. *Why* is she reclining on the grass, alone, holding herself up with both hands like a person who cannot stand? *Why* does she look so thin and sick? *Why* is her skin so pale and unhealthy looking? *Why* do her hands look red or even bloody as if she has used them for some hard task? *Why* is her hair flying? Is it from the wind or from work? *Why* is she so far from the farmhouse? *Why* does she twist her body toward it in so strange a position? Does she want to get there and can't? Or does it hold a *secret meaning* for her? These are just a few of the many *mysteries Christina's World* brings up.

   FOCUS? _____

5. The *perspective* of the painting emphasizes Christina's *isolation*. The *largeness* of Christina (2 cent. x 4 cent.) in the left front contrasts sharply with the *tiny* images of farm buildings in the right background (1/2 cent. x 1 cent.), and suggests the great *distance separating* girl and farm. The cut grass surrounding the farm area makes the uncut section where Christina sits seem even *farther away*. The large field of dead and yellowed grass, covering well over three-fourths of the area, seems to *cut Christina off from the rest of civilization.* There are *no* trees visible, *no* telephone poles, *no* vehicles except an abandoned plow. Even the worn track up the hill toward the farm disappears into the grass as it comes near Christina's section of the picture. Two or three birds on the distant horizon are the *only other life visible* besides Christina.

   FOCUS? _____

B. Look back at your own first or second draft and rewrite it for focus. Use the sentence combining technique discussed above to help you revise and improve your own paper. Also, add interlocking words that tighten the focus.

A Model to Learn From

Read the following description of Austin, Texas. It focuses on what kind of town Austin is for a student to live in and describes the city's general features.

Austin is a nice town for a student because of its mild climate, its varied geography, and its many recreation facilities.

Austin's climate ranges from lows in the 20s to 30s in the winter to highs of over 100 in the summer, but the mean temperature is probably in the 70s or 80s, so one can be comfortable most of the year. It doesn't rain much, only a few inches a year; it snows perhaps once a year, and the sun shines about 80 percent of the days of the year. This climate is perfect for outdoor activities like swimming, hiking, jogging, and having outdoor parties.

Austin geography is varied. It has low hills of a few hundred feet in the west, flat land to the east, rolling country to the north, and desert about 100 miles south. The Colorado River, one of the great rivers of Texas, flows west to east just to the south of downtown Austin, and Lake Austin, Lake Travis, and Lake L.B.J. lie within driving distance to the west. You can swim, sail, waterski, ride in a power boat, paddle a canoe, and scuba dive in these lakes; if you feel lazy, you can just picnic or watch others enjoy themselves.

The University of Texas, which has 45,000 students, also provides many recreation facilities. The large number of students means there are films, theater, sports (including football, basketball, baseball, track, tennis, golf, swimming, soccer, and ping pong), political groups, and religious organizations (Catholic, most of the Protestant churches, Jewish, Moslem and most of the other major religious groups as well). Student clubs provide many services for special-interest groups, such as the Martial Arts Group, the Longhorn Club, and the Future Geologists Fraternity.

On the basis of the above evidence, it is easy to see that Austin is a good town for students, since it provides a temperate climate, a varied geography, and enough activities for any interest.

What is good about this description? First of all, it has five paragraphs: a short introduction and conclusion and three well-developed body paragraphs. While long is not necessarily better, several body paragraphs are often necessary for the ideas to be developed as thoroughly as they deserve. Improvements in length

should always reflect more detailed development rather than "padding" or repetition. Another strength of the description is its framework of general categories and the specific details that develop that frame.

However, the description uses the general word *nice* to describe the city, a word that could refer to the physical beauty of the environment, the friendliness of the people, the good quality shops, the college town ambience, the western style of the area, and so forth. It does provide some evidence of *niceness*. What does this writer assume most students look for in a university town? Is this writer's idea of a "nice" student town the same as your idea? The thesis would be stronger if the writer had used a more specific phrase instead of *nice. A physically comfortable town with varied activity choices* would be more exact. How would you express the idea more accurately and precisely? Could the conclusion be reworked and used to provide a better opening?

Clearly, although this description is a good beginning, it can be improved; it is a typical rough draft. Its central idea could be made clearer and better focused, and its description could be enhanced with more adjectives, more descriptive nouns, more details overall. Moreover, the description could be more carefully tailored to the needs of a particular audience. For example, if written to a music enthusiast, the description might focus on the musical opportunities the city offers, from jazz and blues to country western to classical music, while a letter to a more scholarly person might focus on the number and quality of the libraries and bookstores.

A good description goes beyond initial surface impressions. Learning to write well means learning to look closely, learning what to look for, how to see it, and how to categorize it. This type of "vision" is a skill vital for success in any profession, for learning a career means learning to see with the eyes of a professional. This chapter begins with the lesson biologist Dr. Agassiz finally taught young Scudder, as he forced him to "look, look, look" at his assigned fish. A doctor, a lawyer, a computer analyst, a politician, an artist, and a steelworker can all read the same description and see the same words, but they will understand it in different ways because of the way their careers have taught them to "see" things. Taking a writing course is one way of learning to look and of forcing yourself to see more deeply and with more understanding. Therefore, it is an important form of preparation for the thinking skills necessary in any profession: "to see into the heart of things."

- **EXERCISE 9.9: QUESTIONS FOR DISCUSSION**

  If you were to write a letter to a friend back home, explaining what a city you are familiar with has to offer, what type of categories would you use? What kind of details would you include? Explain.

Final Checklist

☐ Have you observed closely and with detail? Do specific details dominate your paper? Do you use adjectives and adverbs, subordinate clauses and phrases? Remember that the more specific and the more detailed a description, the more visual and the more effective.

☐ Do your words paint a clear and vivid mental picture? Do they produce the effect you intend?

☐ Do you have a unifying pattern of organization? Is it clear and easy to follow? Does it unify the details? Have you carefully selected your details to support your focus or your unifying idea?

Passages For Discussion and Analysis

The San Juan Mission

The San Juan Mission in present day San Antonio, Texas was a self-sustaining community. Within the compound, Indian artisans produced iron, wood, cloth, and leather goods from the workshops. Orchards and gardens outside the walls provided melons, pumpkins, grapes, and peppers. Beyond the mission complex, Indian farmers cultivated corn, beans, squash, sweet potatoes, and even sugar cane in irrigated fields. A few miles southeast of Mission San Juan was Rancho Pataguilla, which in 1762 reported 3,500 sheep and nearly as many goats. These products helped support not only the San Antonio missions, but also the local settlements and presidial garrisons in the area. With its surplus, San Juan established a trade network stretching east to Louisiana and south to Coahuila, Mexico. This thriving economy helped the mission to survive....

The... days [of the new Indian converts] were highly structured. At sunrise, bells called them to morning Mass, singing prayers, and religious instruction, after which they returned to their quarters for the morning meal, usually a corn dish. [Then] some men headed for the fields, orchards, gardens, or quarries. Others stayed behind to tan cattle leather and to forge iron in the workshops. A few spent long stretches [of the day] tending livestock at the distant ranches. The women learned to cook, sew, spin, weave, garden, fashion candles, and make pottery. Fishing and arrow making were the specialities of the older residents, while children over five practiced their catechism, usually in the Spanish language.... The ringing of the noon Angelus [church bells] called everyone to the midday meal, typically consisting of a basic corn dish with a daily ration of beef, garden vegetables, and fresh fruit. After a brief rest, work resumed until the bells summoned everyone home at sunset. The Indians were led in a mass recitation of the rosary, accompanied by chanting and singing. After the evening meal of fish, beans, and corn, curfew ended the day.

—From "San Antonio Missions,"
National Park Service

• Questions for Discussion

1. For what kind of audience is this selection written? How do you know?

2. Does this selection try to convince about an idea, entertain, inform, or do a mixture of these? Explain.

3. Where do you find the main idea or ideas? Does the writer maintain a clear focus on that idea? What kind of evidence does the writer provide to prove that idea?

4. Underline the descriptive nouns used in this passage. Then circle the descriptive adjectives. What does doing so reveal about how specific or general this passage is?

5. How does the writer connect or unify ideas? That is, how does the passage fit together as a unit?

6. Point out examples of parallelism in the passage. How does parallelism help the writer save space?

7. What does "highly structured" mean in the context of a school? What does it mean here? How long did the Indians work each day? Were they paid for their work? In other words, what was the mission concept of good Indian behavior? Would those who oppose Columbus Day agree with this view?

8. Give the selection an appropriate and informative title.

Modernity

Modern man often feels that his private life is a series of traps. He feels limited economically by his education, and dreams of the challenges and achievements that might have been his if he had only studied harder and longer. He feels trapped by a marriage and by children that make demands on his time and energy and that offer little in return. He finds the pressures of relatives, neighbors, job, and family forcing him into patterns and routines that he dislikes or feels uncomfortable with. He must watch what he says around in-laws and employers, set a good example for the children, remember his wife's birthday, socialize with people he despises, and day-by-day in a hundred trivial ways do things he would rather not do. In fact, the more ambitious he is, the more he looks ahead to future possibilities, the more trapped he feels by the present—like a wild animal longing to run free and to live out its natural instincts, but bound by four walls and a steel lock.

—V. L. Macdonald

• Questions for Discussion

1. Where do you find the main idea? What kind of evidence does the writer provide to prove that idea?

2. Underline the descriptive nouns used in this passage. Then circle the descriptive adjectives. What does doing so reveal about how specific or general this passage is? Is it more specific or more general than the preceding passage? Explain.

3. What does the writer do to connect or unify ideas? That is, how does the passage fit together as a unit?

4. How does parallelism help the writer save space? Point out examples of parallelism in the passage.

5. Explain the significance or function of the last line.
6. Give the selection a more appropriate, more informative title.

Paris

I am standing on the Pont des Arts in Paris. On one side of the Seine is the harmonious, reasonable façade of the Institute of France, built as a college in about 1670. On the other bank is the Louvre, built continuously from the Middle Ages to the nineteenth century: classical architecture at its most splendid and assured. Just visible upstream is the Cathedral of Notre Dame—not perhaps the most lovable of cathedrals, but the most rigorously intellectual façade in the whole of Gothic art. The houses that line the banks of the river are also a humane and reasonable solution of what town architecture should be, and in front of them, under the trees, are the open bookstalls where generations of students have found intellectual nourishment and generations of amateurs have indulged in the civilised pastime of book collecting. Across this bridge, for the last 150 years, students from the art schools of Paris have hurried to the Louvre to study the works of art that it contains, and then back to their studios to talk and dream of doing something worthy of the great tradition. And on this bridge how many pilgrims from America, from Henry James downward, have paused and breathed in the aroma of a long-established culture, and felt themselves to be at the very center of civilization.

—Kenneth Clark, *Civilization* New York: Harper & Row, 1969: 1.

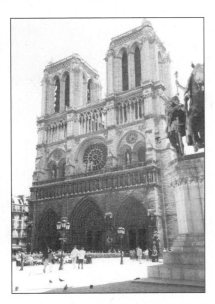

• Questions for Discussion

1. Where do you find the main idea? Does Clark provide a topic sentence? What kind of evidence does Clark provide to prove that idea?

2. Underline the descriptive nouns used in this passage. Then circle the descriptive adjectives. What do they have in common? How do they contribute to the central idea? Explain.

3. How does Clark connect or unify ideas? That is, how does the passage fit together as a unit?

4. What kind of people does Clark connect with the area described? Why?

5. What is "civilization" to Kenneth Clark?

6. Give the selection a more informative title.

The Curse of Memory

From the surrounding hills, walled Jerusalem looks like a peaceful bit of heaven in gilded pinks and grays. Appearance was never further from reality. "A golden basin filled with scorpions" is the way an Arab geographer described the town ten centuries ago. In the 1920s the novelist and polymath Arthur Koestler found the residents still "poisoned by religion." Some 50 years later, Nobel laureate Saul Bellow paid a visit and attempted to identify the city's venomous complexity. "Instead of coming to clarity one is infected with disorder," Bellow concluded after his Jerusalem experience.

The prominent Israeli author and Jerusalem resident Amos Elon offers reasons why. The most basic: "Moslems ridiculed Christians for pretending that God could have a son by a mortal woman. Christians considered it preposterous that the archangels had dictated the whole truth about God to an illiterate tribesman from an obscure town in Arabia. Jews scorned both for their implausible legends, unmindful that it might seem just as implausible that God had made a special covenant with them only, leaving the rest of mankind in darkness. Christians believed in the Eucharist but regarded as absurd the refusal of Moslems and Jews to eat pork."

[As a result] Jerusalem, where one can read 4,000 years of trouble in the stones, is extremism's natural habitat, an unavoidable reminder of past glories and humiliations,… a paradox where centuries of hatred and violence have occurred in the name of love and peace.

—R.Z. Sheppard, "The Curse of Memory," *Time* (September 18, 1989): 95

•Questions for Discussion

1. Where do you find the main idea? What kind of evidence does the writer provide to prove that idea?

2. Notice the number of quotations used in this passage. What kind of quotations are they? How do they help the author develop his idea? Why does the author rely on quotes?

3. What does the writer do to connect or unify ideas? That is, how does the passage fit together as a unit?

4. What does the author mean by "paradox"?

5. What do the metaphors add to the description?

6. The original title of this piece is "The Curse of Memory." Give the selection a new title of your own, being careful to make it appropriate and informative.

Everything began shaking in Candlestick

SAN FRANCISCO—I am writing this column in the most frightening position I have ever been in, 200 feet above the ground in Candlestick Park, which just moments ago was shaking as if the entire stadium were on a wagon being wheeled over cobblestone. An earthquake, they call it out here. It occurs with some regularity, and even as I type these words, the stadium occasionally rolls—aftershocks—with the concrete, the steel supports, everything shaking as if suddenly there is no such thing as sturdy, not anymore.

There are people running across the field, players heading for the exits, grabbing their wives and their families, the festive atmosphere of this World Series Game 3 suddenly ripped apart. And yet, such is the nature of sports that when the initial quake hit, at 5:05 p.m. Tuesday, rumbling the stadium and swaying the field, some fans roared, they raised their fists, they made jokes. "It's God. He's a Giants fan!"

What do you do when the very ground beneath you begins to tremble when you are in the upper bowl of a mammoth stadium and there are reports of cracks in the concrete? I was on the phone with an editor in my office, discussing the night's work, when the roller coaster feeling hit.

"Tom," I said, "the stadium is… moving."

"What?"

Suddenly the TV screens went out. The phones were gone. The rumbling continued for 15 seconds, and in an instant, every little tidbit of earthquake advice came splashing back. Find an open space. Get away from anything overhead. Avoid doorways.

Stay alive.

Bret Butler was running sprints on the outfield when the earth began to quiver. "I felt like I was drunk or something," he says now, holding onto a member of his family. "Then I looked up in the stands for my wife. My mother. I was screaming for them, to get out on the field. I still don't have everybody."

Suddenly there are no players here, no fans, no reporters; there are just people, and many of them are streaming down the ramps, leaping over the walls. Some are bare-chested, raising their beer cups and screaming "WOOH!"

I have a little television plugged in my ear and the first pictures are coming across. They are, for someone who does not live with the daily threat of earthquakes, terrifying. The Bay Bridge is missing a chunk; it is dangling in the water. The Nimitz Highway that runs along the Oakland side of the bay is split in crooked lines, with cars stacked up. There are fires blazing and reports of buildings collapsing, and they are now saying it is the worst earthquake since the big one of 1906.

It is the kind of thing you hear about, but never envision yourself involved in. It happens elsewhere, right? You have a cousin or an aunt who told you about "the time I was in an earthquake." But it was usually a rumble of the bed, a little shake. Not a stadium rocking. Buildings don't fall down, do they?

Out on the field now, the players are collecting their loved ones, counting heads, streaming for exits.

I can only describe the feeling as the noise of a jet plane, combined with the shaking of a bumpy bus ride. That is the outside feeling. What you feel inside depends, I suppose, on your level of courage.

"LADIES AND GENTLEMEN, THOSE IN THE UPPER LEVEL ARE BEING ASKED TO EVACUATE THE PREMISES IMMEDIATELY.'"

And that is where I am now. The game has been postponed. The World Series will wait. Suddenly the story that was the only story on the front pages this week will have to move over. This is far more important. There are cars hanging from bridges and walls collapsed and there may be lives lost, and baseball just doesn't seem that important anymore.

"What are they saying?" people yell. "How big?" "How bad?"

"Did you feel that, man?"

"I am never coming back here. Jesus. Get out of here. This whole thing could collapse."

Years from now, I am sure, people will talk about where they were during this earthquake. It will become a war story, a badge of courage in the sports world, a yarn that may grow larger and more horrible with each retelling. It is hard to imagine that now. The realization is that something harsh and terrible has just happened here, smack in the center of the nation's biggest game. I am sitting in an upper deck that is moving, and we may never look at the World Series the same way. God, how can we?

—Mitch Albion, *Detroit Free Press*

• Questions for Discussion

1. What does this writer do to give readers a sense of really being there and of experiencing the earthquake first hand?

2. Can you find any visual or auditory details?

3. What is the effect of his using quotations?

4. Have you ever been in an earthquake? Does this writer make you feel as though you have been? How does he do so?

5. The original title of this piece is "Everything Began Shaking in Candlestick." Give the selection a new title of your own, being careful to make it appropriate and informative.

Writing Assignments

Describing the familiar

1. Write a paragraph describing an area that you are very familiar with, perhaps a section of your school or of your hometown. Decide what single over-all idea you wish to communicate about it; then list adjectives and nouns that will help support or create that idea. Finally, put them together in a descriptive paragraph. Exchange paragraphs with your classmates to find out if they understand the key point you are trying to emphasize. If they don't, make changes (including additions) to communicate your idea more clearly.

2. Select a single room that you know well to describe in detail. Use spatial transitions to help you organize your description but also look for an overall unifying idea. Prepare for your description by drawing a sketch of the room and filling it in with details of what is located where. What idea or ideas could unify your description?

3. Write an "Insider's Guide" for visitors to your hometown or to a city you know well. Tell them what they should see and do. It should be a guide to your city's most interesting tourist spots, historical or cultural centers, shopping areas, or other major points of interest. If you think that your hometown has no such places, think of some familiar city which does. You might want to make suggestions about how to spend a day or how to spend an evening or how to spend a week: where to go, what to see, what to do, what not to do, where to eat, what to eat, what not to eat, how to get around comfortably and inexpensively, what to buy, how much to pay—whatever a visitor should know about.

4. Describe one of the following:
    your favorite food
    the most interesting place you have visited
    the dullest place you have ever visited
    your best friend
    someone you don't like very much
    a bad restaurant you know about
    a good restaurant you would recommend
    an exciting movie
    an exciting series of events
    a funny/frightening/embarrassing/or meaningful incident.

5. Describe your initial impressions of a city/a university/a region. Compare or contrast that first impression with your later views.

Describing from a new perspective

1. Visit some place in the city you haven't been to before or some part of the university campus you haven't been to before, and describe as concretely as possible how this new experience changes your overall sense of the city or university. What new insights does your visit to a new place give to the old and familiar?

2. Describe the setting/clothing styles/behavior at a typical night entertainment spot you are familiar with from any negative perspective.
    OR
Describe an entertainment section of your city from the view of someone who disapproves and wishes to change it.

3. Describe some aspect of American life as a stranger/foreigner/extraterrestrial from outer space would see it if his only contact with it were through television: for example, family life, police work, romance.

4. Describe a parade, street party, or some large public event from the point of view of the following:
    a. a police officer working a sixteen hour work shift
    b. the National Safety Council responsible for reducing accidents
    c. a social activist who thinks the money could be better spent elsewhere.

5. Describe a cultural event (an opera, a ballet, a symphony) from the point of view of:
    a. an enthusiast who really enjoys such events
    b. someone who has never seen or heard such a thing.

6. Describe a friend or acquaintance from three different points of view, perhaps that of a teacher, a classmate, and a rival or of a younger brother, a parent, and a girlfriend. The key is to identify the different points of view and to provide a sense that the person you describe is different things to different people.

C. Describing the unfamiliar

1. Look closely at the following pictures. Choose the one you feel most comfortable with or most interested in and, drawing on the approaches and techniques you have learned from the discussion of Wyeth's *Christina's World*, write an essay describing it. Don't try to discuss everything. Begin by brainstorming; use the fact sheet at the beginning of this section to help you do so. Then decide on a central unifying focus. Next, select those details which fit your focus and organize them into a brief outline. Next, write your paper as compactly and as specifically as you can. Afterwards, check for transitions and focus. Try sentence combining to help you revise more effectively.

With the permission of The Art Institute of Chicago

Frank Lloyd Wright's Falling Water

2. Famous, innovative architect Frank Lloyd Wright said, "A house is more a home by being a work of art." Use the picture and the information provided below to develop a short description of Frank Lloyd Wright's architecture. Decide on a clear thesis idea to unify your details.

Wright's goal: organic domestic architecture; gracious, practical, affordable, livable residences for the average American family in suburban and rural communities.

Wright's contributions: the first carport; first use of radiant heating and walls fully covered by curtains or drapes ("curtain walls") and a multi-level, cantilevered roof; all natural materials; outside access to every room; elevations that follow the natural contours of the site; walls, windows, doors, furnishings, light fixtures, hardware all integral parts of structure; unity of architecture and nature; surrounding landscape integrated into the design of the house.

> *Examples:* Robie (1909) and Dana-Thomas (1902) in Illinois, The Imperial Hotel in Tokyo, Japan (1915), Falling Water in western Pennsylvania (1938), and the Rosenbaum House in Alabama (1940).

3. Sometimes a description can be made more interesting by relating the shape or form to something familiar. For example, Victor Hugo describes the battlefield of Waterloo in terms of a huge letter A laid out on a map and indicating the key roads crossing the area. What would you expect an A-frame house to look like? Sixteenth-century English manor houses were often built in the shape of a letter E in honor of Queen Elizabeth the First. The main frame and front of the building would be the backbone of the E (looking down from the sky), and three "wings" would extend from that main structure. Any description of such a structure would need to begin with the letter E.

In like manner, some modern rooms are L-shaped and long halls form natural Ts when they meet other halls or crossrooms.

A description of New Orleans (often called the Crescent City) might begin with the C-shape or crescent moon shape created by a bend in the Mississippi River.

Describe something that can be made clearer or more visual in terms of a letter of the alphabet or a familiar shape, such as a city, a neighborhood, an area, a building. Doing so should make it easier to capture the essential form of the place.

•• Application

A. Description of a City in a Letter Tailored to a Friend's Interests
Write a letter to a friend describing the city where you are studying or a city you have recently visited and would like to share with your friend. Be specific about what you think your friend would like or not like. Before you begin your letter, list your friend's interests, for example, " Marisol likes dances, restaurants, and amusement parks" or, "Kwak likes to visit historical places, museums, and famous battlegrounds." Then tailor your letter to those interests. In other words, don't try to describe everything about the city. Instead, select only that information which you think will appeal to and interest your friend. You might focus just on what the city has to offer the art student, the lover of music, the night owl, the fun lover, the student of architecture, the animal lover, and so forth.

Draft of a Tailored Letter:

My friend Susan loves to eat different food and learn about different cuisines.

Dear Susan,

I would like to give you some information about the city in which I live, lovely Lafayette. The city of Lafayette has excellent food and lots of different kinds of nice restaurants. I know you would like to learn about different cuisines so I am going to give you some more information.

Food in Lafayette is an art because they like to present their food nicely and tastily just like painting a picture. Cajun cooking is one of the special Lafayette styles. I love Cajun cooking myself. You will like it too. Cajun means a mix of the French and Canadian people. Cajuns live in the state of Louisiana. Cajun food is very famous in Lafayette. Their famous dishes are seafood platter, catfish Jean Lafitte, jambalaya, gumbo, red beans and rice, etc. When you come to visit me I will take you to one of the Cajun restaurants. They have Cajun music too. It is a very different atmosphere. I know you will love Lafayette and the food in Lafayette.

I hope I will see you soon. Then you can taste and see the art of Lafayette food yourself.

Your friend,

Saya

This letter is a good start, but it needs more work to make the description come alive. Hints on how to give your letter more concrete descriptive details:

1. Look in the yellow pages of the telephone book. If your focus is what food a city has to offer, count the number of restaurants; list the different types of restaurants—Italian, Chinese, Spanish, seafood, etc.; give some examples of the range in price, quality, style, and so forth; recommend a favorite restaurant and explain what you like about it that you think your friend will like. The phone book often has introductory sections on a city's attractions.

2. Go to a tourist center and pick up brochures to quote from.

3. Visit places you plan to recommend, and observe them closely with your friend's likes and dislikes in mind.

4. Interview classmates and acquaintances about the city; get their recommendations, and ask the reasons for them.
Exchange letters with your classmates. Have them write questions in the margins of your paper about what your friend might ask, and you do the same for them. Then, considering their questions, rewrite your letter in its final form.

B. Description of Culture in a Letter to a Friend
Write a short description of a classmate's country and culture. It should be in the form of a letter to a friend, with a focus on what you have learned about the culture that is interesting/ important/ valuable or necessary to know.

Prewriting:

1. Before you ask questions about your classmate's culture, make some notes about your own: what other people should know about your country/ your culture/ your people, what is valuable about it, what other people can learn from it, what it has contributed to the world community or what it could potentially contribute. Consider its values, concepts, or attitudes, and its ideas about scholarship, science or beauty. What is memorable about its history, its public personalities, its food, its lifestyle? Jot down some notes as you brainstorm.

2. Prepare some questions to elicit information about your classmate's culture.

3. Interview each other, taking notes on what you learn.

Sample section of a draft:

When most people think of Mexico, they think of bullfights and guitar players, of ethnic dancing and Mexican rodeos, of men in big hats and women in colorful Indian costumes. However, this is not what my classmate's life is like, for he lives in the capital city, takes the metro or a bus to school, and wears blue jeans and a plain shirt. What he thinks of when he remembers his culture is food, the tamales and coffee he eats on cold mornings, the wonderful mid-day meals he eats in snack bars and taco stands near the university, and his family's varied and spicy cooking in the evening . . . .

Conclusion: Mexican culture is summed up by the rich, spicy, and flavorful Mexican cuisine, ...

Chapter 10: Using Process Analysis

First things first — Anonymous

The Key Steps in Process Analysis
    Considering Purpose and Audience
    Determining the Sequence of Events
    Dividing Information into Manageable Units
    Unifying through Transitions
    Defining Specialized Terms
    Avoiding Common Pitfalls
    Making Sure the Process is Complete

Models to Learn From

Final Checklist

Passages for Discussion and Analysis

Writing Assignments

Applications

A process analysis is probably the simplest pattern of essay writing to learn because the logic is so clear: It follows the sequence of events as they occur in time. Your earliest English lessons may have asked you to describe your daily schedule following a time order: time of rising, steps in getting ready for school (taking a shower, brushing teeth, getting dressed, eating breakfast, rebrushing teeth, making bed, gathering school materials), your class schedule (first grammar class, then reading class, next conversation class, finally composition class), afternoon plans (eat lunch, take a nap, play tennis, do homework), and evening plans (eat supper, watch television, prepare for the next day's classes). In a similar way, a "process analysis" is organized by time, with each step in a series of actions described as they would occur step-by-step to ultimately produce some final product or to make very clear how to perform a particular task. As a survey of book titles will indicate, this is a favorite pattern in American English. Check in your school library and see how many books begin with the words "How to...." You will find books on *How to Win Friends and Influence People*, *How to Be Your Own Best Friend*, and so forth. The majority of such works are process analyses.

Engineers frequently use this form of writing to explain how to use tools and machinery, while scientists use it to explain how natural cycles and natural processes work. Every mechanic has a "how to fix it" car manual to help him "troubleshoot" when he can't figure out what is wrong with the car he is working on, and every biology book involves descriptions of natural processes. In bookstores and on newsstands you will find an assortment of "how to" books on everything from how to lose weight fast to how to pick a husband or wife to how to write for publication. Even in the newspaper there are special columns on how to take stains out of carpets, how to cook special dishes, and how to behave properly in a formal social situation. Personal applications of this approach are frequent. In fact, students must consider "How to Write an A Paper," "How to Pass my History Class," "How to Ask for a Date in a New Culture," "How to Succeed in an American University." In other words, organization by time order, particularly process order, is one of the most common thinking and writing patterns in English. Do you think this is true in your language as well?

The Key Steps in Process Analysis

Considering Purpose and Audience

A process analysis usually involves one of two goals: 1) to explain a process clearly enough so that someone can understand it, or 2) to explain a process clearly enough so that someone can perform that process. Writing so that your reader is able to perform the process described may require more detail or a different type of detail, explanation, and warnings than is necessary if ability to understand, not do, is the goal. The writer of a physics textbook, for example, may want readers to understand how light moves or energy is transferred; however, the writer of a biology lab manual will want readers to actually perform the process of experimentation, dissection, and so forth. How detailed and practical instructions are and whether they are indeed instructions or simply explanations depend totally on the writer's purpose.

In process papers the instructions to the reader or the explanation of the process must be tailored to fit the knowledge and needs of the instructed. The discussion about audience in Unit One applies most strongly to this form. Simply imagining the differences in the instructions you would write to different audiences about how to boil an egg makes the point. What would you have to say to someone who had never cooked before? To a native of the most primitive jungle in Brazil or Borneo, a person who had never seen a stove or modern kitchen? To an extraterrestrial from the planet Mars, or someone like E.T. in the movie of the same name?

Obviously, what you would need to explain in each case would depend on how much your audience knew. A professional cook would need no more instructions than, "Boil an egg." The less the audience knows, however, the more you need to say, and in extreme cases—the native from the jungle, the extraterrestrial—you might have to explain "boil" and maybe even "egg." This is a formula: *The less the audience knows the more you have to explain; the more the audience knows the less you have to explain*. This simple idea may seem obvious when stated this way, but many serious failures of communication occur because the writer fails to imagine how much his or her audience knows. As a reader, you know that some instructions fail to instruct because they assume you know more than you do (think about hard-to-read textbooks or technical manuals!). However, failures can also occur in the other direction: Telling an expert audience far more than they need to know is a waste of time and may even be rude.

The following example tries to explain how international students studying English can find good books at their level to read. However, the writer assumes too much knowledge on the reader's part and fails to explain sufficiently. The underlined words in brackets call attention to what the reader's questions might be.

If you are studying English and you've never read any books in that language except for your textbooks, you should follow four suggestions. First, because it is very difficult to read most books all the way to the end because of vocabulary and sentence structure, it is best to look for a book at your level. [How can you tell what your level is?] To judge the level, find out the vocabulary level of the book. [How?] Use this criteria to judge the book. Some books show you this. [What kind? Where can we find them?] If you don't know how wide your vocabulary is, just guess.

[Don't we need a standard for guessing? Beginners: 700 to 1500 words in English, Intermediates: 2000 to 5000, Advanced: 5000 +?] You can guess by reading a few pages. [Looking for what?] Next, after selecting some books, you should think about what kind of story you like. [Shouldn't you decide what kind of book before selecting some books?] Being interested in a topic will help you finish the book. You should guess what kind of story the books are [How?] and also use the student grapevine. [What? How?] Finally, the most important point is to enjoy reading. Even if you know the outline of the story, it's not easy to read in English. Try to finish reading the book you have chosen. After that, you must be satisfied about it, and you will want to read another book. [Why?]

A clear-cut explanation of how to determine your own reading level and the reading level of possible books to be read is essential to this explanation; specific examples of books that would fit each category from near beginner level to advanced or college level would clarify even more. The problem here is a failure to consider audience.

When writing a process description, your choice of audience and purpose also affects your choice of form. Should you rely on command forms or give advice with an informal "you" pronoun? Or should you follow the model of many engineers and scientists and rely on the passive voice to add greater distance and formality?

A process analysis may be written in command forms: *Do this, do that, then do the other.* This form has an implied subject (you) and takes the simple, infinitive form of the verb, but without *to.* Your process analysis may be made more personal by speaking directly to the reader: *you should do this; then you should do that; next you should do the other.* You might write *You need to do this, you might do this,* or *you must do this.* You might share in the activity with your reader, *let's do this.* Or you may make your process analysis more formal by using *one : one should do this, one should do that, next one should do the other.* A compromise between informality and formality is to use a noun to identify who is most likely to perform the action:

A good electrician knows the importance of carefully keeping the connecting wires separate.

A gardener can use these seed holders to start plants growing early indoors.

Sometimes writers focus on a machine in action or describe the process through the passive voice so that the human element is left out:

The long back rod is then attached to the motor with a solid nut and bolt.

After the line has been marked in chalk, the initial cut is made.

The passive voice most frequently occurs in technical writing to describe the actions of processes, especially mechanical and automatic ones, but it is overused in that field. In engineering classes you may be required to use only the passive for describing processes, but most good writers recommend that you use the active wherever possible. Your particular choice of form may depend on purpose, with the command patterns sounding more personal and direct and the passive patterns sounding more "scientific" or objective. However, no matter your choice of form, you must be consistent. If you start with *you,* use *you* all the way through. It is confusing to start with *one,* switch to *you,* then try commands, and finally return to a particular title like *the student.*

• EXERCISE 10.1: COMMAND AND ADVICE FORMS

A. The following paragraphs on "Regulating Study Time" rely on command forms. Underline the commands and change them to an advice form (*You should/ought to/need to*). Which approach is better for the goals of these paragraphs? Why?

Learn to regulate and control your environment when you study and practice. Choose a quiet time, and find a place where distractions are few. Train your family and friends to be considerate of your right to study effectively. Shut yourself off from others; close the door, turn off the TV and radio, take your phone off the hook, or hang a "do not disturb" sign on the door. For example, Ginger chose her two-year-old son's nap time as her study time. She closed her door to neighbors and took the telephone off the hook. This was her time to study, and she used it wisely.

When you study, monitor yourself. Are you really using your new language, or are you daydreaming, doodling, and studying in unproductive ways? As you begin to work, make a list of what you intend to accomplish. Give yourself an amount of time for each item. With your eye on the clock, see whether your time schedule is realistic. Check each item off your list as it is completed. This will help you set small objectives and give you a sense of accomplishment when each portion of your study time is finished.

—Marjory Brown-Azarowicz, Charlotte Stannard, and Mark
Goldin, *Yes! You Can Learn a Foreign Language*

B. Change the following sentences to command form.

> *Example:* You should study these forms carefully.
> Single command: Study these forms carefully.
> Shared group activity: Let's study these forms carefully.

1. You should ask for the overseas operator.
2. You need to check with your advisor before signing up for a course.
3. You must take English 101 before English 102.
4. It is best to take some Intensive English classes before entering university classes full time.
5. You should be prepared for culture shock.
6. When you are not sure about something, you ought to ask.
7. One should think first; then one should speak.
8. A student must bring proof of his academic record.
9. You shouldn't believe everything you hear.
10. You must not walk the streets alone at night; it is not safe.

C. Now change the following command forms to sentences of advice or necessity; these forms use *should*, *must*, or *have to* to give advice. Then turn this list into a paragraph giving advice on steps to take in case of a hurricane.

1. When a hurricane threatens, be sure to listen for the official weather reports, both on radio and television.
2. Note the address of the nearest emergency shelter.
3. Fill tubs and containers with water, in case the water systems stop functioning or get polluted.
4. Make sure your car's gas tank is full.
5. Board up or tape windows and glassed areas and remove furniture that is close to them.

6. Stock up on supplies like flashlights, batteries, candles, canned heat, canned goods, charcoal, can openers, etc.

7. If the hurricane strikes, stay indoors and away from glassed areas.

8. Keep a window or door open on the side of the house opposite the storm winds.

9. If you detect gas, shut off the gas supply to the meter and do not light a match.

10. Eat and drink nothing that has been touched by flood waters.

11. Use the telephone only in an emergency.

12. Beware of the "eye of the hurricane," a sudden quiet period, because the winds may resume again suddenly in the opposite direction. If the wind direction changes, change the door or window that is open too.

13. Most important of all, use your common sense and be careful.

14. Never try to drive while the hurricane is hitting.

D. Where possible, change the passive forms to active ones.

1. The blood test should be made immediately, before any other tests.

2. Whether the spacecraft should circle the moon and return to earth or whether it should fire the Service Propulsion System engine and go into orbit should be decided by the top level NASA officials.

3. A dull saw blade should be attended to by being sharpened or by being replaced.

4. The wheel is turned by a series of gears that are connected to the main body of the engine.

5. After the initial adjustment has been made, the process should be repeated to insure accuracy.

6. Two screws are needed to support the main frame.

7. These should be inserted before the final product is used.

8. The Edison storage battery, which was developed by Thomas A. Edison and put on the market in 1908, can be modified for many uses.

E. Considering Audience and Purpose

1. Rewrite the inadequate sample paragraph on finding good books from page 453. Follow the suggestions in brackets for expanding and improving the paragraph to consider more carefully the needs of its intended audience and the ultimate goal to be achieved.

2. Analyze the following paragraph in terms of audience and purpose. For whom is it written? What problems does it anticipate? Make a list of potential problems these special travelers might have.

If you plan to travel the Yukon-Charley Rivers, you must not only plan carefully and exhibit caution, but also possess good back country skills for wilderness survival. Know and test your gear before you arrive because equipment failures in remote places are more common than you might think. Bring emergency food stocks—more than your scheduled time requires. Prepare for being weathered in. Wear quality clothing (plenty of wool) that can be layered for changing conditions. Sturdy camping and rain gear and good insect repellent are also essentials. Tents should be designed to keep out insects and withstand strong winds. Remember that self-sufficiency in all respects must be your guiding rule along these rivers. In fact, winter travel is recommended only to those experienced in cold weather camping and survival techniques and even in summer harsh weather, high winds, and rain can produce hypothermia. River water temperatures are cold and mid-channel spills can be lethal. Furthermore, once you leave the well-traveled Yukon River corridor in this vast country, you are completely on your own. Boil drinking water at least one minute to prevent Giardia problems, and keep your food supplies separate from your campsite to protect yourself from bear attack. Leave your itinerary with someone, and notify that person when you complete your trip.

—Adapted from "Yukon-Charley Rivers," U.S. Department of Interior brochure, National Park Service

---

Determining the Sequence of Events

A process paper relies on a basic forward movement in time to organize its information; however, it has its own special pattern for its own special purposes. A process paper usually begins by telling the reader:

1. What process will be described and why
2. What materials are needed
3. Where the needed materials can be obtained
4. What key steps comprise the process.

If there are a number of steps, a process description divides them into groups of steps that belong together and then deals with the substeps in each unit. For example, a description of how to cut off a dead or an unwanted branch from a tree might be divided into the following key groups:

1. How to make the undercut on the bottom side of the branch

2. How to make the major cut on the top side of the branch

3. How to take care of the "wound" after the branch has fallen.

As you describe the process, it is appropriate to anticipate reader problems, to think of what could go wrong, and to give warnings. It also helps to describe what will happen if the steps are followed correctly. The conclusion may do the following:

1. Remind readers about the most difficult or most dangerous steps in the process
2. Tell what the end product will be
3. Explain why it is important to follow the process guidelines step-by-step.

PROCESS DEVELOPMENTAL FRAME

Name of Process _____
Who needs to perform this process _____
Why _____
(Goal) _____
Tools/materials/ingredients needed _____
_____
Where they can be purchased _____
_____
Key Steps _____
_____
_____
_____
Explanation of Steps: _____
Step 1 _____
_____
Step 2 _____
_____
Step 3 _____
_____
Step 4 _____
_____
What could go wrong/ Warnings _____
_____
End result of process if done incorrectly _____
_____
End result of process if done correctly _____
_____

Keeping the time order in sequence is one important key to success in this pattern; as long as the time order is in sequence, the pattern is probably going to be acceptable. However, if your description of a process begins with the end results, then describes the hardest steps, then switches to the initial steps, and ends with the materials and tools needed for the process, your reader will be very confused, and your paper will seem illogical and disorganized. Oddly

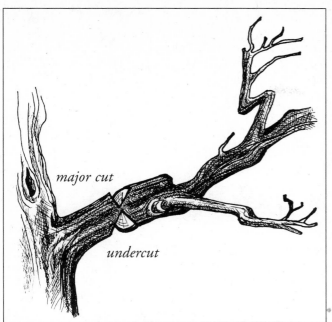

major cut

undercut

remember earlier points they forgot to put in, moving forward in time again, then returning to an earlier step, discussing a future step, and then returning to the present step. Another difficulty is deciding which of several simultaneous actions should come first. Simple though the rule may seem, <u>a process analysis should follow a time order.</u>

Another key to successful process analysis is careful selection of details. Even though your paper moves forward in time, it does not cover every event in that movement; to do so would be tedious and boring and nonproductive. In real life, every single minute, no matter how boring or painful or embarrassing, must be lived through; in a process paper, the boring, the irrelevant, the embarrassing can be selected out and never reported, unless necessary to the idea that unifies the essay in which a time sequence is used. In other words, time provides a sequence for arranging information, but what information appears in that sequence depends on topic and purpose.

enough, putting events or actions in the order in which they occur naturally in time, from past to present to future, sometimes proves most difficult, with writers starting in a direction, backtracking as they

---

• EXERCISE 10.2: THINKING ABOUT ORGANIZATION

Put the following sentences into proper order. Underline the words that indicate the relationships between ideas and help you determine the correct order.

1. When the test begins, move quickly through it, skimming questions and answering those questions which you readily know. When you take a standardized test, find out early whether or not points will be deducted from your score if you give a wrong answer. Taking standardized tests requires special skills and special approaches. For example, if two of three answers have a similar focus or pattern, probably the answer is one of those two, so you have narrowed the possibilities a little bit. This will tell you whether you should answer only those items you are sure of or whether you should arbitrarily choose a response to answer all items quickly before the test is collected. To make a good guess, look for internal clues. Later, begin again more slowly, focusing on the harder questions. Hopefully, if you follow this advice, your test scores will be greatly improved. Making good guesses is very important. As you work, try to keep pace with the time limits of the exam so you don't get caught short.

2. This means reviewing difficult vocabulary, skimming class notes for content, memorizing key ideas you underlined or marked during your daily study, and trying to both anticipate possible questions and prepare answers for them. Then, review the course objectives, recent assignments, recent class activities, and your teacher's style of communication in the light of this information. If you follow this advice, you should be intellectually and psychologically prepared for successful test-taking. In order to take tests successfully, it is best to first spend some time preparing. Also, ask your teacher how the test will be graded and whether or not you can examine previous tests in order to note style and content. Studying your classnotes for clues to what your teacher values most can be most helpful. In other words, use your time wisely in the day or days before

the test. Finally, be sure to get a good night's sleep the night before the exam. That is, find out the content, format, time, length, and location of the test. If you have followed a daily study plan, you will be better able to cope with test anxiety and test preparation, but if you try to cram the night before you will just panic. First, make sure you know what the test involves.

3. When passengers finish boarding, the grip [connection which grips the cable] takes hold, and the cable car is ready to begin the trip up San Francisco's main tourist street, Powell Street. Once the platform crew turns the cable car, they push it off the rotating turntable into a slight depression. Because they are single-ended, San Francisco's Powell Street cable cars require turntables at each end of the cable line to reverse direction. This depression places the grip low enough to reach the cable. After passengers get off, the cable car drops its connecting rope and coasts onto the turntable, a massive steel and wooden disk that the crew move in a circle by hard physical effort. In other words, the cable cars cannot make a loop; instead, they must be turned around at each end of the line.

   —Adapted from Lynn Thomas,
   San Francisco's Cable Cars

4. Be sure that you hold the pencil steadily before and while you insert the pencil into the hole of the pencil sharpener; otherwise, the pencil will shake, and the lead part of the pencil will then be broken. The lead part should be exposed and sharp; if it easily penetrates a piece of paper, you know you have a sharp pencil. In order to sharpen a pencil with an electric pencil sharpener, you need a pencil and an electric pencil sharpener. Then hold the pencil on the eraser end, using your thumb and index finger to grip the pencil firmly. After you have a firm grip on the pencil, insert the pencil end without the rubber material into the hole of the pencil sharpener for about 1.5 seconds; then the pencil sharpener will start to work automatically. When it does, pull out the pencil. Hold the electric pencil sharpener on the desk steadily, and then plug in the pencil sharpener. After a little while the sharpener will stop automatically.

Dividing Information into Manageable Units

A common process analysis pattern is to first define the purpose of a process and who will use it, then give directions about materials needed and where to acquire them, next, to divide the process into key steps and substeps and to develop each of these steps in a time order with built-in warnings and advice, and then to end with a description of the hoped-for final result. Such categories of information help provide a deeper sense of unity and structure and help transform a list of directions into a true process essay.

The writer who tries to explain how to call long distance needs to decide who needs to know this information and why, how much explanation is necessary, and what sort of warnings will help. The explanation might need to be divided into four possible types of long distance calls: direct dialing, collect, use of a credit card, or use of coins. Each is more complicated than the one before it and therefore demands more and more explanation. The ending should explain what should happen if the reader follows the directions carefully. Writers who don't make such divisions into categories will find themselves with a lengthy and confusing list of steps that will be harder to follow than three to five clear-cut steps that are then subdivided with explanations and discussion. Process descriptions aimed at understanding a procedure rather than doing it may simply identify the process, describe events in a time sequence, and end up with a discussion of the implications or significance of such a pattern or of the negative consequences of not following this pattern precisely.

Unifying through Transitions

A process analysis calls for transition words of time both between sentences and within sentences: Obviously, the reader requires a series of "signals" to indicate the points in time throughout the process and the movement of the description through these points. Time words used within sentences to begin adverbial clauses include *when, while, as, whenever* for actions occurring at the same time and *before, after, since, until, by the time that, once, now that, as soon as* for action occurring at different times. In prepositional phrases you might use *from... to* or *until, during, at, at the same time as, by, while, when, since,*

• **EXERCISE 10.3: THESIS SENTENCES**

Explain what divisions the following thesis statements or introductions anticipate. In other words, what will the essays which follow the opening statements tell us about and in what order?

1. The language of childhood is not the language of adolescence; nor is it the language of maturity, for as we change, our language changes.

2. When I first started school, I adored my teachers, but as I moved into junior high and high school I began to feel resentment, hostility, and even contempt for them; now that I am in college I have learned to both fear and respect them.

3. The more one learns, the more there is to learn. The college sophomore has learned a little and thinks he understands all, but by the time he is a junior or a senior, he understands that he doesn't have all the answers, and by the time he has finished graduate school he is not even sure he knows all the questions, much less the answers. This is a normal pattern of maturation.

4. Geologists tell us that the Cape Cod peninsula of today is the product of 11,000 years of molding: by glaciers during the Ice Age and by wind and waves, tides and currents for centuries thereafter.

5. Writing an effective process analysis involves three major steps: prewriting/planning, writing a rough draft, revising for clarity.

---

from then on. Between sentences you might use the following: *first, second, third, then, next, a little later, before that, after that, in the meantime, meanwhile, afterwards, soon thereafter, two weeks later*. The connective words used in adverbial clauses of time are very important in clarifying time relationships.

In addition, there are the common overall connective time phrases. These are most regularly used for the following purposes:

- *To introduce items in a series*: first, second, third; in the first/second/third place; the first/second/third step; first of all, secondly

- *To indicate a particular time*: in 1995; in the past/present/future; yesterday/today/tomorrow; in the fifteenth century/twentieth century; at present; right now; at that time; in those days; last Sunday; next Easter; at the beginning of the month; at six A.M.; the first thing in the morning; two weeks ago

- *To indicate frequency*: occasionally; sometimes; often, frequently; infrequently; not very often; now and then; day after day; year after year; again and again; once in a while; regularly, irregularly

- *To indicate duration*: during; briefly; for a long time; minute by minute; for years/months/days; momentarily; within seconds; moments later

- *To indicate the beginning*: at first; initially; in the beginning; since; before then

- *To indicate a midpoint*: while; then; next; soon thereafter; a little later; much later; sometime later; with time; after a while

- *To indicate the end and beyond:* finally; lastly; last; in the end; eventually; subsequently; later; afterwards; ultimately; at the end of

- *To indicate action at the same time:* in the meantime; meanwhile; as it was happening; at that moment; at the same time; simultaneously; as; while; when; during

You will probably not need to use all of the above, but you should learn to identify the "signals" in the writing of others and incorporate some of them into your own prose.

• EXERCISE 10.4: RECOGNIZING TRANSITION WORDS

A. Circle the connecting words that make clear the steps in the process.

1. The 1980 volcanic eruption of Mount St. Helen followed a process typical of most eruptions. Most accounts suggest that the first indication of anything unusual was an earthquake. This earthquake was followed by, and probably caused, the collapse of one side of the volcano dome. The initial landslide followed the quake by mere seconds and consisted of the collapse of at least two large sections of the mountain's north flank. Moments later, eruptive activity was sighted near the middle of the north flank, above the lower landslide area and near the summit. As it occurred, there was a loud rumbling accompanied by a pressure change. Shortly thereafter, the upper slide area was blown apart as the eruption area expanded. Climbers on nearby Mount Adams reported a shock wave similar to that associated with a nuclear explosion within thirty seconds or less after the start of the eruption. Several distinct lava flows began moments later. Within minutes, a large dark eruption cloud shot upward and outward and blackened the sky. The vertical eruption blast was followed by a horizontal blast, and the top of the mountain blew. The whole initial process occurred in a few short minutes that left viewers stunned and awed. This pattern recurs with most volcanic eruptions: earthquake; landslide; simultaneous vertical eruption, rumbling, and pressure change; lava flow; dark cloud; major horizontal eruption.

2. A successful stockbroker follows a careful pattern of client contact. Each day when she goes to her office, as soon as she obtains the market price on a ticker, she calls those clients affected by market changes. When a stock which her client is holding rises suddenly, she may recommend her client sell at once; on the other hand, when a stock which she has an eye on buying falls, she may recommend her client buy it. However, she will probably contact a security analyst in all these cases. *Career Choices: Economics* tells us more about this contact. It argues that an analyst relies on microcomputers to "analyze balance sheets and cash flow" and to get "fast answers to client's questions" so that she can be more confident about the advice she gives and the decisions she helps make. (134) "A broker receiving a call from a client wishing to buy a particular stock directs the purchase order to the floor of the appropriate exchange, via computer," says *Career Choices*, which goes on to explain the rest of the process: the buyer and the seller seek a price agreement and effect the trade, record the transaction immediately and send the price of the stock back to the broker's office by computer; the broker then relays the information to her client. (134) In this way, the broker earns her stock commission. The success of the relationship between the broker and her clients depends on this process working smoothly and efficiently; its end result is profit for both parties involved. However, a failure by broker or client to interact in this way could mean loss for both. —Akiko Arai, Japan

B. Complete the paragraphs with appropriate time words or expressions.

1. _____ you study, you should mark your book carefully. _____, underline the major points, the most significant ideas or information. _____, _____ you reread make vertical lines in the margin to reemphasize the points you feel worth memorizing for class. _____ , make comments in the margin to summarize, emphasize, or simply remind you of essential ideas. _____ you have finished reading a second time and marking a second time, you can set aside your readings _____ just before a test. _____ you wait outside your class, _____ you go in, quickly review the marked and underlined sections as well as your notations. The result should be a much higher grade on your next examination.

2. If you hope to write a good resume for job applications, you must carefully follow a series of steps. _____, make a list of all of the information you think will be important to include, from personal data, educational background, and key courses to job experience and special skills. _____, arrange these in abbreviated order according to a standard resume form: usually with name, address and telephone number at the top, followed by brief personal data, education, special skills, job experience, and list of references. The education and job experience list should move backwards in time from most recent to most distant. Your _____ step should be to consider your audience and the particular job for which you are applying and note any special requirements or emphases that might help, for instance, value of knowledge of another language, experience traveling or dealing with other cultures, typing speed, familiarity with computers, and so forth. _____ review your resume, and add details related to such special considerations. _____, before you mail it off, check for typographical errors, spelling mistakes, and use of complete sentences instead of phrases. The _____ step is to correct such errors. Hopefully, this process will help you look better on paper and get a better job.

Defining Specialized Terms

Before a process analysis is complete, it is important to read it carefully with your audience in mind, looking for terminology special to the process and building in short, simple, clear definitions. These definitions may use an appositive (a noun used as an adjective to describe a noun) with commas, dashes, or parentheses to provide synonyms, key characteristics, function, or other identifying information:

> Airbrush, *a precision paint sprayer,*
>
> Airbrush—*a precision paint sprayer*—
>
> Airbrush *(a precision paint sprayer).*

Definitions may use a participial phrase or a relative clause:

> Airbrush, *otherwise known as a precision paint sprayer*
>
> Airbrush, *which is a precision paint sprayer.*

Or they may be significant enough to require a more detailed explanation:

> Airbrush, *a precision paint sprayer used to apply color and shading to photographs, prints, or drawings as well as to highlight film background.*

The key is to provide sufficient information at the right time for the reader to understand the term, but not so much information that a digression results.

Avoiding Common Pitfalls

A process analysis intended to be a plan for action should build in guidelines to help the reader avoid common mistakes. For example, a process involving contact with electricity should provide careful warnings about keeping positive and negative terminals separate and perhaps even describe what will happen if this advice is not taken. The warning might be quite strong if the electricity involves explosives: *Make sure that the black wire and the red wire never touch, for if they do, the electrical charge will pass between them so rapidly that you will have no time to escape the explo-*

- ## EXERCISE 10.5: PROVIDING DEFINITIONS

   Integrate the information on "Tools and Parts" below into the description of the processes described below in (1) and (2) using appositives, participial phrases, and relative clauses. In other words, include the information on "Tools and Parts" to define and describe the tools needed to change a tire on an automobile or to make a word processor work and the parts of the car involved or of the word processor involved.

   1. <u>Process</u>: Remove <u>wheel cover</u> or <u>hubcap</u> with the <u>wheel-cover key</u>.
      Slightly loosen the <u>nuts</u> or "<u>lugs</u>" which hold the wheel on.
      Use the <u>jack</u> to lift the wheel into the air.
      Remove the lugs and the wheel.
      Replace with the <u>spare tire</u>.
      Reverse the opening steps of the process, replacing the wheel and the lugs, tightening the lugs, lowering the wheel with the jack, and replacing the hubcap.

      <u>Tools & Parts</u>:

      The <u>wheel cover</u> looks like a large metal plate which covers the outside of the wheel; hubcaps cover the wheel also but are sometimes smaller.
      The <u>wheel-cover key</u> is shaped like a "T," with a round body with a shaped hole at the end and a smaller crosspiece.
      The <u>nuts</u> or <u>lugs</u> are fat and thick, and often have six flat sides and a cone-shaped inner side.
      The <u>jack</u> is either a square metal device, with a body made up of two scissors-like parts or a long metal pipe or rod with a corkscrew-like thread on the outside. Both kinds of jacks have handles which can be "cranked" or turned quickly.
      Nowadays, the <u>spare tire</u> often looks like a plastic toy tire, about half the width of the regular tires.

2. <u>Process</u>: Begin using a computer.
   Turn on the <u>on-off switch</u>.
   Take hold of the <u>mouse</u>.
   Locate the <u>cursor</u> on the screen.
   Move the cursor with the mouse to the <u>icon</u> or <u>window</u> you want to open.
   Double-click on the <u>button</u> located on the mouse.

   <u>Tools & Parts</u>:
   The <u>on-off switch</u> is about the size of a man's fingernail.
   The <u>mouse</u> has a "tail" formed by an electrical cord and is about the size of a deck of cards.
   The <u>cursor</u> is a small blinking line of light or an arrow visible on the screen.
   An <u>icon</u> is a small symbolic picture; <u>a window</u> is a rectangular box with a name printed on it.
   The <u>button</u> is a plastic lever which can be depressed a couple of centimeters.

---

sion which will follow, and there will be no remedy for this mistake because you will have been blown to pieces.

Most processes will not have such a high danger potential, but they will all involve some potential for error that may result in unpleasantness. A process involving the use of a ladder, for example, might caution readers to make sure the ladder is placed firmly on solid ground and braced to avoid slippage. If the ladder is made of metal, however, and is to be used around high-current electrical lines, the cautions should be loud and clear: *Watch for overhead power lines!* If the potential for injury is great, you might even need to include advice about medical care or refer the reader to experts who should be called in at some stage to assist with the process: *In case of accidental swallowing, call the Poison Control Center at....*

If the potential error can be remedied, then you should build in advice about how to rectify mistakes. For example, a tree-surgery manual might advise readers that, when cutting an unwanted branch from a tree, failure to make an undercut might result in the branch breaking off unevenly leaving a jagged edge. Readers might also be advised that leaving this edge is not only unsightly, but it could also be injurious to the tree because it could collect water or attract insects that could cause rot and maybe eventually hollow out or kill the tree. The remedy would be to care-

fully even off the edges and apply a sticky substance to shut out the air, possibly tar or a special tree guard. Another variation on the built-in warning is to describe at the end what will result if the process is not followed carefully; for example, a recipe might point out that a special dish should be light and airy and several inches high, but that, if done improperly, will be heavy, solid, and a quarter-inch high.

Making Sure the Process is Complete

A final revision check should make sure that the reader has been provided all information necessary to perform the process and all steps in the procedure. A reader who is following the process step-by-step should not find, in the middle of the process, that a necessary tool has never been mentioned or that a vital step has been forgotten. How irritating for the reader! Just as missing one digit in a telephone number can prevent making contact, so missing one detail in a process could mean the difference between success or failure in performing it. However, especially when you are describing a process you know well, it is easy to forget that your reader needs careful instructions about what you know how to do automatically. Take care to be thorough and to make sure your process analysis is complete.

Models to Learn From

Model #1: In the following two examples the writers address fellow students worried about test-taking. Each paragraph gives advice about how to prepare, but the first lacks connectives and the second includes them. The words in italics in the second version are connectives; they focus on the chronology of the process: what to do first, what next, and then what. The second paragraph is clearly better than the first simply because of these connectives. Remember that an essay which fails to connect ideas is likely to confuse the audience and to leave readers wondering about the relationship between pieces of information.

    1) If you have an exam on a textbook, read all of the assigned materials in the book. Underline and write out every word you don't understand. Look up the underlined words in your dictionary and write a short definition in your own words. Reread the text so you make sure you understand everything. Consult your word list . Underline the important phrases and sentences. Read the text one more time to fix the ideas in your mind. Quickly skim the text, looking most particularly at the underlined sentences, the titles and subtitles, the words in bold print and italics, and the final summaries.

    2) If you have an exam on a textbook in one week, it is best to read all of the assigned materials in the text first. As you read, underline and later write out every word you don't understand. When you finish reading, look up the underlined words in your dictionary and write a short definition in your own words. Then reread the text so you make sure you understand everything. Consult your word list as you do so. During this reading, underline the important phrases and sentences. The day before the exam, read the text one more time to fix the ideas in your mind. Finally, on the exam day, quickly skim the text, looking most particularly at the sentences which you have already underlined, the titles and subtitles, the words in bold print and italics, and the final summaries.

The second paragraph above is a good start, but the writer might find it useful to discuss even more steps. Reviewing an expert's advice about studying might provide more ideas. For example, you could discuss the SQ3R (Survey, Question, Read, Repeat, Review) method of study and its suggestion that you turn titles and subtitles into questions and then search for the answers to those questions as you read. Most books on study techniques suggest trying to put the ideas from the textbook into your own words, reading a section and then summarizing its key points and restating its most important information from memory. In fact, isn't memorizing key points often vital to most study plans? Does trying to explain what you remember to a friend or merely aloud to yourself help you remember? In other words, even without experts, if you think carefully about the above paragraph, you can come up with more ways to describe, enumerate, or explain more fully the key ideas and argument of the paragraph.

In addition to such extra information, the second sample paragraph needs a final statement to clearly bring it to a close. A workable ending might emphasize the results of following the procedure: *If you follow this procedure, you should be able to do well on whatever type of exam your professor gives you.* Always check to make sure you close your process analysis.

Model #2: The following section of a long essay describes part of the daily procedure of a criminologist doing scientific study of crime scenes. The overall essay plan is a straightforward movement in time from the pre-work morning to morning tasks, lunch, afternoon activities, and post-work evening. The selection which follows provides only a section of the morning activities. Its goal is to provide a sense of the process one criminologist follows in pursuing his career. As you read, observe the connectives that keep the time progression clear.

    A criminologist's work is varied and complex, requiring a number of very different skills and abilities. [Thesis] His assignment, based on police department crime reports, is arbitrary. He is often designated head of a three-man team, including a photographer and a detective. Once assignments are clear, the team meets to decide their plan of action.

    Usually, the first step is for the group to visit the scene of the crime; their slogan is, "You may be too cunning for one, but not for all." At the scene of the crime, the initial procedure is to photograph the place and the small details. Usually, the police have already cordoned off the area and have hopefully kept all but essential personnel out of the area. The criminologist heading the team tells the photographer which objects or places to photograph and from what distance or angle. Care must be taken to avoid contaminating the site: no smoking, no discards, no walking in key areas except following designated procedure. The second step is for the detective and criminologist, together, to write or record a physical description of the location. This is very important because later a good description might help the criminologist solve many problems. The description must be detailed, precise, and accurate. The third action is the collection of evidence in plastic bags with labels for identification. All three team members participate in this step. This initial collection focuses on obvious items like weapons, buttons, cigarette butts, but the next on the collection of minutiae, the nearly invisible clues. As Alexandre Lacassagne wrote in his *Manual of Criminology*, the difference between two hairs could say everything, so the collection procedure must be careful and meticulous, with no hair, no fingerprint missed. Consequently, a criminologist needs to control the movement of evidence, and finally the routine tests of fingerprints, ash, cartridges, liquids, tablets, poisons, blood, semen, hair, fibers, ink, paper, paint, skin, and so forth. These tests are done on the spot. This is methodical work which requires care by all of the team. A mistake <u>at this point</u> could mean a criminal is never caught or goes free later on.

—Angel Ricardo Guevara, Mexico

The above selection demonstrates the key qualities of a process analysis, no matter what the topic: a clear-cut time sequence to organize, direct, and clarify, a series of steps followed, some explanation of the significance of the steps, and some cautioning about potential problems. Clearly readers are not meant to be able to duplicate this process because not enough technical detail is provided, but they are meant to understand the complexity of the process and the care for detail it involves.

Model #3: The next example also uses a time order to present a clear topic idea. Here, the goal is to give advice about a process the reader might wish to follow: choosing the best teacher for specific needs. The intended audience is students, and the pattern follows the process of choice step by step. Are the steps clear? Are they helpful? What type of information does the conclusion add?

Here in the United States finding the best teacher for the personal needs of each student is very important and sometimes requires a carefully considered process.

<u>Your first act</u>, if you are going to take classes in a North American school or college, is to determine your goals and course expectations. <u>The second step</u> consists of collecting all the information available about possible teachers. To do so, you can ask your advisor about whether particular classes will fit your goals. However, it will be even more helpful to collect details about courses through the "grapevine," information gained from students who have already taken a course. <u>At this point</u> you must be careful about the quality of your sources: a person looking for an easy course might not be as helpful as someone who appreciates a challenge. In other words, you must also compare what your source values in a teacher and a class and what you value in a teacher and a class and judge the source's comments accordingly. <u>The third step</u> is to analyze yourself and think about whether you have enough background to deal with the class. By this I mean considering whether you will be able to understand the teacher and be able to do what he or she will expect from you, or whether it will be so hard for you that you won't have enough time for your other classes. <u>The fourth step</u> is to attend the class the first two weeks and find out for yourself what the class is really like. <u>The fifth and final step</u> is deciding whether you really want to stay in that class with that teacher or whether you would prefer to move to another section, or also whether you want to drop that course and add another one. However, <u>this final step</u> must not be delayed too long or you will have trouble changing courses and catching up in a new class. Furthermore, make sure your school permits this kind of course change!

Finding a good teacher is really important for your development as a future professional, so remember that you have to be honest with yourself and think about whether you really want to learn or whether you just want to pass the course in the easiest way. Let your goal be your guide to teacher selection.

—Sonia Lainfiesta, Guatemala

Is the above process easy to follow? Is the time sequence accurate? Are problem areas explained? What more could or should be discussed?

Final Checklist

☐ Have you considered your purpose and audience? Does your introduction establish who will need to know about or use the process and why, what tools or materials are necessary and where they can be obtained?

☐ Have you divided your process into key steps and substeps that are both clearly recognizable and manageable?

☐ Have you included connective words to unify your discussion and to provide your readers with clues as to your basic organizational plan?

☐ Have you consistently followed a time sequence?

☐ Have you described, enumerated, or explained fully? Have you included advice and warnings? Can someone who reads this process understand how it works or actually perform the process?

☐ Is your conclusion clear? Does it suggest the end product or end effects of a proper process?

Passages for Discussion and Analysis

How to Overcome Your Nightmare: The TOEFL

The idea of taking the TOEFL (Test of English as a Foreign Language) causes insomnia to people whose native language is not English, especially to students who have been studying in an Intensive English Program for several months and need to pass this requirement to start regular classes in a college or a university in the United States. If you are in this position, you must learn certain important and successful tips in order to obtain your dream score. This paper provides such important tips, especially about preparation in formal classes, studying outside your classes, and practicing on your own.

You have to be prepared to fail your first TOEFL because it is unknown territory. Nevertheless, taking the TOEFL is necessary to learn your level and to see your difficulties and weaknesses in each one of the three sections: (section 1) Listening Comprehension, which measures your ability to understand American people speaking, (section 2) Structure and Written Expression, which measures your ability to recognize appropriate written English, and (section 3) Vocabulary and Reading Comprehension, which measures your ability to understand non-technical reading.

The first step, studying TOEFL in classes, requires that you pay 100-percent attention in your English classes, where teachers always give advice about possible tricks in the TOEFL. For instance, in your grammar course you will hear about (1) parallelism, the balance or repetition of grammatical structures and patterns (The girl wears black shoes, a blue shirt and white jeans [pattern between adjectives and nouns]), (2) agreement among nouns, verbs, and adjectives (The old man was very happy because his friend told him the good news about social security), (3) countable and noncountable nouns, and nouns not used in the plural (foods: sugar, coffee, milk; metals, mineral, gases: gold, iron, coal, oxygen; abstractions: democracy, beauty, ugly, old; fields of study: philosophy, chemistry, architecture), while others are either countable (referring to individuals in a group) or noncountable (referring to an undivided item or food). You will hear many other examples like these; therefore, it is a good idea to buy a small notebook, in which to write TOEFL-related rules and tips.

Your reading courses will teach you other, different, clues and habits, for example, (1) skimming, reading quickly to get a general idea of the entire paragraph, (2) looking for punctuation marks, subordinate elements, and important symbols such as periods, quotation marks, colons, semicolons, question marks; and words like *when, because, after, however*, and so forth, (3) restatement, often the repetition of the thesis in the conclusion, (4) inference, drawing your own conclusion from facts presented in the paragraph.

In your TOEFL class you will practice each section on different days, so your teacher will explain to you what your mistakes were and how to avoid them. You will learn about the SQ3R system, which means Survey (read the first and last sentence in the paragraph), Question (ask questions about the paragraph such as *who, what, when, where, why*), Read (refer to the paragraph and look quickly for the answers to your questions), Review and Recall (remind yourself of the most important ideas in the paragraph).

The second step, studying TOEFL out of the classroom, is performed on your own initiative. You have to review the tips jotted down during classes and to find others through practice. Looking for material to study is not hard; an intensive English program library will usually have useful specific sources on each section. You can ask for a tape recording of the first section which has the same pattern as the official TOEFL, and along with your tape you will receive two books, one containing the questions and the possible answers for section 1, as well as short practices of the other two sections. Another contains the correct answers and an explanation of the reason for those answers. In this way, studying questions and answers, one can become an expert in the listening comprehension part. In addition, listening to the T.V. and the radio are also good methods to begin to understand American speech. Your ear should become able to distinguish the sounds as words, not just babble. For the second and third sections you can use the previously mentioned books and another on *Reading for TOEFL* which has five complete practice tests. There is also a *TOEFL Prepbook*, which you should buy, because it provides not only practice exercises, but also techniques for taking the test.

The third step depends on your desire to score well on the test. Once the source materials are on hand, don't put them away in a drawer; on the contrary, practice seriously on and on and on; doing so is the KEY to overcoming your limitations, slowness, and nervousness, and to using your best ally, TIME. Continuous practice has made students into TOEFL masters, so dedicating about twenty minutes daily to studying TOEFL should prove beneficial and rewarding. Two weeks before the official TOEFL will be given, you must focus on reviewing your notes and on spending a great deal of time practicing. Your goal is to achieve in the practices the level you hope for on the real test, obeying the same rules and the official time limits. Use an alarm clock to precisely time each section; this measure helps you to work more accurately, and more confidently. Keep in mind that the more you practice, the better you will do.

Finally, the day before the official TOEFL reread your notebook a bit and then relax: watch T.V., listen to the radio, or enjoy a book. Be sure to get a good night's sleep; if you have trouble sleeping, do some physical exercise or take a small glass of an alcoholic beverage (but no more than a small glass). Avoid sleeping pills because they might leave you groggy the next day. The next day wake up early, take a refreshing bath, have your favorite breakfast, arrive about 15 minutes before the test, and choose the most comfortable chair because you are to be there approximately two and one-half hours. The last tips are important and easy to memorize: 1) darken and fill the circles totally; 2) trust your first answer, and don't change it unless you have a strong basis for doing so, because nine times out of ten it is better than your second choice; 3) if you don't have enough time to do the questions well, guess the answers rather than leave blank circles (within the four possible answers one is obviously wrong, another is the opposite, and one of the two remaining similar ones is the correct one; therefore, you have a 50-percent possibility of being correct).

If you carefully follow the steps and the suggestions mentioned here, you should finish the TOEFL with flying colors and achieve the wonderful result of your long, hard work: your DREAM SCORE.

—Hedelim Fabrega, Panama

• Questions for Discussion

1. Who is Ms. Fabrega's intended audience? How do you know?
2. What is the purpose of her paper? Does she aim simply for understanding a process, or does she want her readers to be able to perform it?
3. Circle her connective words. What do they reveal about her organizational plan?
4. Does she provide clear advice? warnings? helpful suggestions? a clear result?

Choosing The Best College For You

When we are children, our parents usually choose our schools for us. Even when we have input into the decision, we don't usually get much experience with the process of choice itself. So when we reach adulthood and are faced with choosing a college or university, or even a graduate program or professional school in law or medicine, we often have little basis in experience for doing so. The phenomenon that developed in the 1970's, that of large numbers of undergraduates changing majors three or more times and transferring from one institution to another, provides an additional reason for investigating the choice process: no one who has made a bad choice needs to remain stuck with it, for transferring is easy, but you want to avoid making the same mistake twice.

The first step in the process of choosing your institution is to develop an understanding of how educational institutions acquire their reputations. Shakespeare's famous character Iago, speaking of "reputation" says, "Who steals my purse steals trash…/But he that filches [steals] from me my good name/Robs me of that which not enriches him, /And makes me poor indeed." Educational institutions also guard their reputations jealously, for their "names" are hard to come by and even harder to regain when lost. What does it mean for a school to have a "name"? Curiously, there is no accepted system or definition of quality where colleges and universities are concerned, although many ratings systems are available from a variety of sources, from the ultra-serious to the completely frivolous. The main thing to remember, however, is that our reputations come from what others think and say about us, not from what we think and say about ourselves. So by all means take the second step, and send off for your prospective colleges' glossy brochures and catalogs, their twenty minute video, and their list of tame alumni living in your hometown—just don't believe everything you hear. Rather, concentrate on what others say about your future home for four years.

The third step of the process, after studying and internalizing all the self-promotional documents you get through the mail, is to do some reading. Start at a bookstore, whether a college store or one in your friendly neighborhood mall. Find the college prep shelf, and look over publications such as *The Insider's Guide to Colleges, The Fiske Guide to Colleges, The*

Best Buys in College Education, and *The Right College*, all of which give good advice for under $15.00. There are too many such guides to list here, so skim through them while standing at the bookstore shelf; you certainly don't need to own more than one or two guides unless you just want to help support their authors. Keep looking: there are guides to everything from the best party schools to the best "value." For an example of the latter, check out *U.S. News and World Report* magazine's yearly ranking of the best return for your educational dollar, listed by geographical region and other useful categories. Check your library for back issues, and while you're there, check their shelf of college catalogs and other informative materials (ask the reference librarian).

The fourth step is to round up some of the "others" who create reputations and whom we talked about above so you can interrogate them energetically. This quizzing has two preparatory substeps: (a) narrowing down your list of possible schools to keep the process manageable (four or five are nice numbers, large enough to provide some options, small enough to avoid bankruptcy of time and money) ; (b) preparing a list of questions to ask. This latter may seem unnecessary, but it helps to brainstorm as long a list as possible. For instance, you might prepare to ask about student-teacher ratio, financial aid, work-study programs, academic requirements, available housing, graduate school acceptance rates, quality of computer and other laboratory facilities, number of Ph.D.s in your specialty, and so on. Remember that you don't have to ask everyone every question.

When you're ready, short list and questions in hand, start finding your victims. If you are already attending a college, look in its catalog or bulletin for a list of local faculty and where they got their degrees to see if there are any alumni of your prospective new school close at hand and available. If there are, call their departments and make an appointment for a short interview; even busy people are flattered to be asked about their alma maters. Go in with your list of questions and fire away. This is a good time to ask if there is a local alumni organization for your prospective school; if there is one in town, they will be happy to find someone for you to talk to. Remember to ask when your interviewee graduated: conditions can change drastically in a few years, though some things, such as climate, stay the same.

Suppose you can't find anyone to interview. The alternative is the telephone, which could be expensive, depending on the distance from your prospective school. However, a fat phone bill is still a lot less than an airline ticket, and at this point in the process you're not ready for that large an investment in what may be a dead-end inquiry. Whom should you call? The admissions office is a good place to start; ask their advice about people to talk to. Of course, they will point you toward people with favorable opinions, so try to think of ways to find balanced judgments. Ask about students from your home town: could you talk to one or two? Offer to have them call you collect. Ask to talk to students and faculty in a department you might be interested in as a major. Ask to talk to the president of any club or campus organization you might possibly join. If you are an international student, call the international office and see if you can talk to a student from your home country. The idea is to find some human and personal connection which will allow you to talk familiarly and honestly with someone truly informed about the realities of life at the institution.

After your telephoning, your next step is to sit back and evaluate your information. Do what you do whenever you make a decision: make lists of pros and cons, talk it over with friends, think it through. Don't be afraid of intuition and "feel": try to imagine your life at the school on the basis of what you have found out so far. After all, you will have to live there twenty-four hours a day, so make some room in your decision for intangibles.

Your next-to-last step, if you can afford it, is a visit to the institution. There is no substitute for a visit, particularly if you can stay overnight (cheap accommodations are available at many schools), for this is your chance to see if all the advertising—all the "hype"— lives up to its promises. Set up your visit as far in advance as possible, and try to go when classes are in session (an empty campus doesn't tell you much). To prepare, repeat the phone process, beginning with the admissions office and asking for a referral to another person or telephone number whenever someone says they can't help. When you make your visit, be sure to leave at least an afternoon for wandering around, hanging out, nosing about. Visit the department you might major in and notice the activity or the lack of it: Are students lining up to see professors? Are all office doors closed? Check out labs, and any other facilities where you might spend a lot of time. Eat in the cafeteria, strike up some conversations, and in exchange for a cup of coffee, solicit information: Are introductory classes taught by professors or by teaching assistants? How large are classes? How concerned is the administration about student welfare? Find out the gossip about strong and weak programs: Are any in decline? Is published information about the school's programs accurate? Is it up-to-date? Are any superstar professors leaving? Don't feel guilty about such talk; this is the "grapevine" on which reputations hang.

Now it is time for the final step in the process, the decision itself. Try to imagine your typical day at each school, activity by activity. Remember the point we began with, that reputations are fragile things made up of the opinions of many people about myriads of programs, professors, departments, functionaries, and so on. What matters to you is not just some abstract notion of an academic reputation, but rather how the institution can help you in some specific ways, how it can move you toward your potential in a fairly narrow field of interest or set of behavior. What matters is how the college will serve you, not how it serves others; the best programs in the world will do you no good if you are not interested in them.

Does this seem to be a difficult process? That's because choosing a school is a difficult decision for many people, as are most life and career decisions. There are usually too many variables and too little clarity, with resulting feelings of uncertainty: Will I make the right decision? Will I be unhappy? Will I fail? Make your choice and relax, knowing you've done all you can to prepare, and that most people end up satisfied with their choice even after much less preparation.

• Questions for Discussion

1. Summarize the advice from this essay as a couple of clear-cut steps you could tell to a friend.

2. Does this writer give any warnings?

3. Do students in your country shop around for schools? Why or why not?

4. Why do you think American students shop around for schools? What do they gain by doing so? What do they lose?

5. If you were going to give a friend from home advice about choosing a college, what would you tell them? Provide a brief process they can follow for making a successful choice.

•• Writing Assignments

A. Frequently you must explain to a friend how to do something simple but unfamiliar. A common pattern is to name the process and perhaps why you would want to do it. Then divide the process into steps and explain each step with details. Look at the following pattern.

> *Example:* If you want to find the most popular places students eat, to save money and to eat better yourself, it is best to tackle the problem scientifically. [process, reason for it, approach] First, interview as many students as you can. [first step] This means asking close associates, first roommates, suitemates, and apartmentmates, then classmates. [explanation of first step] Start up conversations in the cafeteria about the quality of the food, and say, "Isn't there some place better?" [more explanation of first step] Next, keep a list of responses either on paper or mentally. [second step] After you have a good list, select those few that are named most often. [third step] Then check out these recommendations by eating there yourself. [fourth step] The result should be better food than that in the cafeteria and fun too. As a side effect, you will probably make many new friends as well. [conclusion/results of process]

Now imitate this pattern to write a long paragraph or a short essay telling new students "how to do" something they have not had previous experience doing. First write in command forms; then rewrite using advice forms.

1. How to get a credit card.
2. How to apply for a scholarship.
3. How to find a doctor.
4. How to catch a bus downtown.
5. How to make a long distance call out of the country.
6. How to exchange your money.
7. How to renew your visa.
8. How to memorize information.
9. How to figure percentages in mathematics.
10. How to use a simple calculator.

B. The next paper topics involve more complex processes and therefore require more detailed explanations. Use the process developmental frame from earlier in this chapter to help you generate ideas. Choose one of the following topics to write about.

1. How to fill up a car with gas at a self-service station.
2. How to change sections of a course.
3. How to report a burglary.
4. What to do if a policeman stops your car.
5. How to get out of receiving a traffic ticket.
6. How to improve listening skills.
7. How to cook a simple dish from your country or region.
8. How to open a checking account at an American bank.
9. How to meet Americans or how to make new friends at college.
10. How to register for classes.

C. The above topics all require a description of a process that readers will put into actual practice. Write the other kind of process description, one to be understood but not necessarily carried out, for example, how snow forms. Choose your own topic. Again, use the process development frame from earlier in this chapter to brainstorm.

Applications

A. Write an essay giving advice about effective language study to anyone planning to study or do business in the U.S. How should one begin? What steps should one follow? Where, what, and how should one study? Use your own experience as a starting point for this advice. Draw on your own study of English, both past and present, to support your recommendations and to lend strength to your warnings. Tell readers what has worked well for you that others might imitate and what has not worked well for you that others might avoid. The following examples integrating advice and personal background should help you start thinking about your own approach:

1. My study of English, which began in Hong Kong in 1978 and has continued to the present in Atlanta, makes me a good person to give advice about what works and does not work when studying a language.

2. It takes a long time to have command of a language. Hopefully, my nine-years learning experience will provide readers some insights into what to avoid and what to seek in language learning.

3. The study of English is like a journey to new places, where one learns new things in an exciting and fun way, but it is also tiring and frustrating because of the distance to be covered before the journey nears its hoped for destination: bi-lingual competency. My experience suggests that the language learning process is one of slow and diligent dedication.

4. The popular saying, "No pain; no gain," is true of language study. In my case, my past and present pains with English will hopefully bring me gains in the future: in my career and in my personal life. By following the painful steps I followed, others too can achieve such gains.

5. One must move from a naive view of language as a matter of grammar and one-to-one translation, to a more mature view of language as a reflection of a people and a culture that will take a life-time of rewarding study and personal contact to feel at home in. My advice to others is to study a language by getting to know the people who speak it and the culture it reflects.

B. Write a letter to a friend or to a group of friends back home who are considering studying abroad. Your letter should be a guide on how to deal with problems resulting from conflicting cultural assumptions, stressing not the etiquette questions involved but rather the adjustment of one point of view to another. Your guide should explain how to adjust to a different way of thinking about education, about business, about friendship, or how to deal politely with strangers. It must use as its evidence or supporting examples incidents and situations from your experience or that of your friends. Divide your guide into categories, for example, different ideas about social distance, touching, degree of familiarity and friendship formation, misunderstandings resulting from differences in politeness formulas, classroom differences, racial attitudes, and so forth.

CHAPTER 11: CLASSIFYING

Classification… helps us chart our way. — Hans Guth

Classification, the major way human beings process information, is basic to organized and logical thought. It involves making divisions based on categories, dividing into groups and subgroups according to carefully designated standards. No matter the field or the purpose, division into parts and classification into categories are key analytical processes for establishing clear relationships. When faced with a confusing array of data, classification allows us to sort out the material and to define meaningful patterns from chaos. By sorting and labeling, we are searching for a system that will give meaning and order where none previously existed. The process is the same as the one scientists use to make sense of the plant and animal kingdoms, dividing them into classes, families, genuses, and so forth.

Classification is among the most natural and intuitive of behaviors. Political and business surveys seek categories that will make sense of voters or customers:

single, married, divorced
lower-class, middle-class, upper-class
no-car family, single-car family, two-car family multi-car family
Republican, Democrat, Independent, cross-party voter
high-school dropout, high-school graduate, junior college graduate, college graduate, master's degree, Ph.D.
retarded, average, gifted

unemployed, employed part-time, employed full-time
blue-collar worker, white-collar worker, professional
temporary visitors, illegal aliens, resident aliens, natu-
ralized U.S. citizens, native-born U.S. citizens
unskilled, semi-skilled, skilled
child, adolescent, adult
rural, suburban, urban

Eastern, Western, Southern, Northern, Midwestern
tropical, subtropical, temperate, polar.

All of us classify without even thinking about it. In this chapter, you should begin to consciously use the technique as a useful and necessary tool with which to organize your thinking and writing.

The Key Steps in Classification

Deciding on Purpose

Because the particular way in which you classify depends entirely on your purpose, you must decide purpose before taking any other steps toward classification. For example, if you want to discuss transportation and have no clear goal in mind, there are simply too many directions to explore. Not only are there far too many types of transportation to be dealt with easily (jumbo jet, single-engine airplane, steamboat, outrigger canoe, horse, mule-drawn wagon, speedboat, streetcar, 18-wheeler, limousine, etc.), but these types can be categorized or grouped in dozens of different ways. Categories of transportation might be based on location—by air, by land, by water— and these categories might be further subdivided with, for instance, water craft designated as sea-going, river-going, or lake-going. However,

depending on the reason for subdividing in the first place, the divisions of transportation could just as easily be based on size (tanker, freighter, cruise ship, ocean-going yacht, sailboat, rowboat) or type of fuel (gasoline, coal, steam, electricity, animal, or human power) or cost or efficiency or public versus private, and so forth.

If, however, your goal is to explore the transportation possibilities for tourists within a city, then your bases of classification might be cost, convenience, and efficiency, and your paper will classify city transportation according to these standards: Which forms are the cheapest? Which are close to tourist areas or cover tourist territory and are convenient to use? Which of those meeting the first two standards are the most efficient for the purposes of tourists? In other words, why you classify and how you classify are inseparable concerns.

- EXERCISE 11.1: RECOGNIZING ACCEPTABLE GROUPINGS

  In the following classification groups, circle the category that does not belong, and briefly explain your choice.

  Examples: herding dogs, <u>working dogs,</u> guard dogs, drug-sniffing dogs, guide dogs

Working dogs does not fit because it is too general. All of the dogs in the list are categories of working dogs.

  1. boats with diesel engines, sailboats, steamboats, luxury liners
  2. efficiency apartments, dormitories, a brick home, condominiums
  3. low-fat, low-nutrition, low-calorie, low-cholesterol, low-salt
  4. rainy season, 4 seasons, 2 seasons, unchanging season
  5. qualified nurse, pediatrician, gynecologist, obstetrician

- ## EXERCISE 11.2: DECIDING PURPOSE

Underline the categories in each of the following. Then state the purpose of the classification.

Example: People can be divided into three categories based on their body shape and orientation. Although the average human being may be a mixture of these three, some humans are mainly "<u>digestion-oriented</u>", some "<u>muscle-oriented</u>" and some "<u>brain-oriented</u>." The physical correspondence is a thick body for the digestion-oriented, a wide body for the muscle-oriented, and a long body for the brain-oriented. These terms, "thick", "wide", and "long" do not refer to particular weight or circumference or height, but to the overall dominant appearance of the body: Does it seem wider or longer or thicker? Basically, these patterns relate to the Greek medical words of body classification: endomorph—thick (grown more from the inside layer of the egg), mesomorph—wide (the middle egg layer), and the ectomorph—long (the outside egg layer). There is a direct connection between such physical categories and psychological behavior, connections this text will explore further.

—Categorization from psychology text

Purpose: To provide readers a clear, simple way of discussing body types and to suggest that there is a relationship between body type and human psychology. This classification makes us expect more discussion of that relationship.

1. International students who make below a 400 on the TOEFL test will be placed at the beginner level, those who make between 400 and 450 at the intermediate level, and those who make over 450 at the advanced level. However, if there are enough advanced students to make up two sections, those students will be further divided according to whether their goal is pre-college preparation or English learning for other purposes.

—Pattern of division for an Intensive English Program

Purpose _____

_____

2. The weaker papers submitted for the midterm exam can be divided into three types based on the types of errors committed. The first and most disturbing mistake was a failure to answer or deal with the question asked. Instead, students answered some other question that went in a different direction than the exam called for. Such responses resulted in automatic "Fs". The next type of mistake was to assume that the teacher/reader would understand, and therefore the writing remained at a high level of abstraction instead of providing specific support. Such responses, in general, received "Ds". The third type of mistake was the reverse of the second, a wealth of specific details but no general, organizing abstraction to provide unity and direction. Papers in this category tended to receive "Cs".

Purpose _____

_____

3. The organizational structure of business firms depends on the function of the firm, the lines of authority or command chain, the departmentalization of the firm and the relationships between those departments, the various positions and standing committees in the firm and the titles of such positions and committees. However, despite the complex-

ity of such structures, in general there are three major types of organizational structures: the line organization, the line and staff organization, and the committee organization.

—Categorization from a typical introduction-to-business text

Purpose _____

_____

4. Famous eighteenth-century Englishman of letters Samuel Johnson divided critics and opponents into three categories based on their method of criticism: roarers (they depend on the loudness and strength of their voice to be heard over others), whisperers (they project an air of secrecy and importance as if whispering trusted information to a carefully selected audience), and moderators (they claim to be impartial seekers of truth, but undercut their opponents through faint praise and through calls to justly consider the other side). All of these, Johnson calls "envious," "idle," "peevish," and "thoughtless."

Purpose _____

_____

5. Bertrand Russell divides useful devices (what he calls "machines") into three categories based on their degree of resistance to human beings and their success in that resistance: those that break down (furnaces, lawn mowers, electrical fuses, tape recorders), those that get lost (pliers, keys, women's purses), and those that don't work at all or work only momentarily and then never work again (barometers, car lighters, flashlights, car clocks). He argues that those objects which get lost never break down and vice versa so that these are not overlapping categories, though he ignores the rare exceptions—like the car which will invariably break down in the middle of a heat wave and congested traffic when it is full of people but which might also get lost late at night in a parking lot when its owner is tired and drunk and fearful of a mugging. He concludes that those machines which never work at all have "attained the highest state possible for inanimate objects" because they have conditioned man "never to expect anything of them."

Purpose _____

_____

Determining Bases for Classification

Once you have decided on purpose, you have, in effect, already limited your basis or bases of classification, but you should think carefully about exactly what is involved. Sometimes one basis will suffice for the distinctions you need to make; sometimes two or more bases are needed. For example, if your goal is to encourage overweight readers to participate in sports activities that will assist weight loss, you might classify those activities according to their difficulty or ease, the time required to engage in them, and the efficiency of weight loss involved. If your goal is to recommend the best family dog, then you must decide on the qualities needed in family situations ("good with children" but also "a good watchdog," "comfortable in a home situation," "companionable," "responsive to more than one person," etc.). Once you have decided on such qualities, you can then apply them to a series of particular breeds to determine the type that comes closest to the standards you have created.

One of the safest ways to approach a writing task is to keep your topic flexible. Suppose your writing task is to discuss "fad" or fashionable diets, with the general topic, *Americans are obsessed by diets and especially by "fad" or fashionable diets.* However, your time is limited, and you can't explore your topic in more detail. If you have ten sources—five diet books and five articles—the simplest approach might seem to be to discuss the major books or articles in order of importance: view of diet book #1, view of diet book #2, view of diet article #3, and so on.

However, this approach would let the individual diet books guide your argument and would end up as a summary of what other people said rather than your own argument. Besides, this approach would be inefficient, boring, and ineffective. Your thesis idea would get lost in a list. A better approach might be to classify fad diets according to the kinds of dangers they involve, especially if your purpose is to warn your audience. For example, you might set up the following categories:

I. Diets that produce malnutrition (example: Drinking Man's Diet)

II. Diets that cause deficiencies of necessary vitamins, minerals, or trace chemicals (example: macrobiotic diet)

III. Diets that introduce poisons or harmful amounts of substances into the system (examples: pre-digested protein diets; banana diet)

However, the problem with this approach might be the potential for overlapping categories: the banana diet introduces too much potassium, but it also produces malnutrition and deficiency of vitamins. This difficulty with overlapping categories would need to be resolved before this approach to classification could be used effectively. Perhaps there could be a fourth section on diets that produce all three problems. Can you suggest other solutions? A possible thesis might be: *Health-conscious dieters should be very cautious and investigate fad diets before relying on them, because such diets could produce malnutrition, cause deficiencies of necessary vitamins, minerals or trace chemicals, and even introduce poisons or harmful amounts of substances into one's system.*

Still another possible approach would be according to daily average nutrition requirements, as in the following essay plan:

I. Discuss the balanced food intake for an average, healthy person, based on age, sex, weight, and height

II. Attack fad diets that fail to meet this balance according to degree and type of danger, most dangerous to least dangerous

III. Advise about diets that do meet the balance requisite for health, naming good diet plans and listing their good qualities

A possible thesis in this case would follow a pattern like this:

Because such fad diets as _____, _____, and _____ fail to provide the balanced food intake requisite for good health, one should carefully choose a diet plan like _____, _____, or _____. These recommended diet plans all involve _____, _____, and _____ to reduce weight, but also provide _____, _____, and _____ to assure health.

Still another approach might be to classify according to psychological appeals of fad diets:

- Appeals to convenience (painless; require minimal change in life style)

- Appeals to fashion ("bandwagon" appeal of everyone is doing it)

- Appeals to getting back-to-nature (an "organic" food diet)

- Appeals to mystic togetherness (macrobiotic diet).

A more conventional classification might be by type, followed by an evaluation of relative advantages and disadvantages:

I. Liquid diets (examples: predigested protein diet; Drinking Man's Diet; Grapefruit Juice Diet)

II. Solid Diets (examples: diets focused on one type of food—vegetable, fruit, meat; diets which limit caloric intake; diets which limit weight or size of portions)

The above category possibilities suggest that a writer's task is really that of making choices. The choices are between alternative ways of organizing materials, and the choices can multiply if the writer applies intelligence and imagination to the topic. While all these choices may seem confusing, multiple possibilities should be welcomed by any writer. Problems usually arise when the writer can see only one way of approaching the topic; then any breakdown in the approach will lead to failure of the paper.

• EXERCISE 11.3: DECIDING BASES FOR CLASSIFICATION

List potential bases for classification for the following topics.

Example: diets: by liquid/solid; by appeals in advertising; by degree of danger (most to least); by efficiency of weight loss; by cost; etc.

1. Campus sports
2. Cars
3. A good date
4. Colleges
5. Fast-food

Subdividing the Category into Clearly Distinguished Units

Once you have decided on the basis or bases of classification, you are ready to break those groupings into subgroups. Often, this is a key step of outlining since outlining, in effect, involves the creation of subdivisions within broader categories. For example, subdivisions about diets might focus on examples and their general characteristics, benefits and limitations, or degrees of danger. If your general topic is "blue jeans", and your goal is to persuade readers that *Blue jeans in modern American life combine both the democratic and the anti-democratic qualities of American culture,* your contrasting categories for classifying jeans would be those with egalitarian appeal versus those with snob or status appeal. Your "snob appeal" category could be subdivided based on place of origin (European is classier), based on designer labels like Calvin Klein, Jordache, or Oscar de la Renta, based on price (import $50–200+; designer label $50–100), and based on changes from past patterns (more fashionable colors, up-to-date material, new designs and emblems).

A discussion of endangered species might classify these species as plant or animal, subdivided by family or genus, or it might classify them by the types of measures needed to preserve them: passive measures versus active measures. These broad categories might, in turn, be subdivided into such subcategories as protection or preservation of present habitats, habitat restoration, species reestablishment from one area to another, and captive breeding zoos; then, further development with discussion, explanation, and examples can be added.

Defining and Illustrating the Subdivisions

As in most good writing, a paper based on classification, ultimately, should depend on concrete detail to develop its categories. For example, a paper on endangered species will eventually need to name some of those species and, if the classification focuses on measures to preserve them, describe in detail some of those measures. Take as an illustration the subdivision on captive breeding zoos mentioned

• EXERCISE 11.4: SUBCATEGORIES

Select one of your topics from Exercise 11.3 and subdivide your categories. For example, if your topic was "diets" and your categories "liquid" versus "solid", your subdivisions under "liquid" might be predigested protein diets, diets limited to fruit juices and vitamins, and diets involving large quantities of water intake, while your subdivisions under "solid" might include diets focused on one type of food, diets which limit caloric intake, and diets which limit weight or size of portions.

above. The red wolf might be a good supporting example:

> On the endangered list, the red wolf is presently being bred by the National Park Service on Horn Island, eight miles off the Mississippi Gulf coast. Captive-born pups are released on the island (along with their parents) as soon as possible to develop survival skills. Once the young are mature enough, they are recaptured and released on the mainland for life in the wild, while the adults are taken back to the breeding pens to continue propagation of healthy young wolves. Such captive propagation is typical of the National Park Service efforts to actively preserve endangered species.

An essay classifying luxury cars might develop the thesis that prestige depends on avoiding economy and on showing that the owner has money to spare:

> Overall, the Cadillac Seville represents the best luxury car buy. It is the top offering from a company that sells three of the top seven luxury cars. It lists for $48,662 (the highest priced car sold by an American company) and, with options, regularly sells in the mid-$50,000 price range. The Seville is not the largest car sold in the United States, but it is the second heaviest; this massive weight gives the car the least miles per gallon rating of any of the luxury cars. Fuel costs for the Seville should run about $1200 a year (by comparison a Plymouth Champ's estimated yearly fuel cost is about $400). It not only has the basic requirements of luxury cars, but also has leather seats, climate control air conditioning, advanced cruise control, mahogany inserts, plush carpet, and many other extras that make driving like having "a tea party in the sitting room." Thus, the Seville is an automobile for those who can afford the best luxury car sold in America—the luxury of waste.

Concrete detail brings abstractions to life and creates new opportunities for the writer. In other words, classification is only the first step that creates empty "boxes" or "containers" (*captive breeding zoos, best luxury car*) which can then be "filled" with facts, concrete details, and descriptions.

Avoiding Common Pitfalls

Too Many Categories to Handle: If your initial topic is "television programs", in addition to the topic being too broad, you might find the number of possible categories far too much to handle. If you classified by genre, where would your categories stop? Would you include soap operas, cartoons, westerns, romances, mysteries, game shows, news programs, wildlife programs, drama, adventure, and science fiction? What other categories belong in this list? Clearly, too many categories to handle and too broad a topic go hand in hand. This means the writer's job is to narrow the topic until it can be easily divided into no more than four categories and preferably two or three. For example, "television programs" could become "television detectives," subdivided into three categories: the violent detective who relies on karate chops and guns; the peaceful and "intellectual" detective who reasons his way to a conclusion; and the more balanced detective who is neither "overly physical" nor "overly cerebral," just "human." This division would allow you to limit your discussion just to detective programs and just to the portrayal of detectives in those films, and would give you the basis for a workable thesis about extreme depictions of detectives compared to more balanced television detectives.

Overlapping Categories: Let us suppose you decided to divide your topic on television shows into two categories, those which entertain and those which educate. Unfortunately, you would run into another problem: overlapping categories. While there well may be some shows which only entertain and some which only educate, in practice many programs both educate and entertain. In fact, good educational films should be entertaining, and good entertainment often involves some learning process as well. Food should be both tasty and nutritious; mothers should be sources of both love and discipline. The problem with such categories is that they are not clear-cut enough in their differences to provide the writer with a useful topic. In other words, these are not distinctive categories, and therefore some other type of division is needed.

Incomplete Divisions: Another common problem is with incomplete divisions, two categories where there should be three, three where there should be four: an insufficient number of categories to provide the full range of possibilities. The either-or fallacy illustrates this problem: either you are for us or you are against us. The reality is that you may not be for or against; you may instead be neutral. In other words, three categories are needed, not two: those who are for us, those who are neutral about us, and those who are against us. For example, in the case of gun control, it might be possible to support banning some categories of weapons while permitting others or permitting weapons for some people but rigidly excluding other groups from possessing guns (like those with police records). The medieval division of personalities into four types today seems far too limited a way of categorizing human personality possibilities. The accepted categories of that period were the choleric personality (bad-tempered, proud, ambitious, risktaking), the sanguine personality (friendly, outgoing, artistic, active, funloving), the melancholic personality (contemplative, scholarly, easily depressed), and the phlegmatic personality (lazy, unhurried, content, diplomatic, unruffled). Do you think all human beings fit neatly into these four categories? Western medicine thought they did for hundreds of years.

Dividing sports into two categories, those involving competition against others and those involving competition against yourself, suffers from the same problem of incomplete division, because some sports also involve man competing against animals as in hunting competitions, fishing competitions, rodeos, and bullfights, or they involve man competing against the forces of nature: the wind (sailing), the mountains (climbing), the cave (spelunking). Would it be better to divide sports into those involving competition between groups, between individuals, between the individual and himself, and between the individual and nature? What problems do you anticipate with these categories?

- ### EXERCISE 11.5: IDENTIFYING CLASSIFICATION ERRORS

    What common errors have been committed in the following? Identify the error and, where possible, explain how you would correct it.

    1. Restaurants can be divided into three categories, those that are always bright and clean, those that are sometimes dirty, and those that are always dirty.

    2. As far as I'm concerned, there are only two main types of television programs: those that put me to sleep and those that keep me awake.

    3. Television stereotypes women as housewives, sex-objects, know-it-alls, or career types.

    4. Most sports can be classified as either skill sports like tennis and basketball or contact sports like football and soccer.

    5. Immigrants can be divided into two key groups: the assimilated and the unassimilated.

    6. Machines work for man, against man, or with man.

    7. Dogs can be classified by weight (toy, normal, heavy) and height (6 inches, 21 inches, 30 inches and larger), by hair length (short hair, long hair), by behavior (friendly, unfriendly), and by function (sheepdogs, guard dogs, working dogs, family dogs).

    8. Students can be divided up according to where they sit in the classroom, with those in the very front being eager to work hard and learn, those in the middle being average students who want to blend in with the crowd, and those in the very back being anxious to avoid work and participation.

    9. Mall shoppers can be classified as window shoppers, comparison shoppers, penny-pinchers, serious buyers, and those in a hurry.

    10. There are two kinds of people in the world: the organized and the disorganized.

Unifying through Transitions

The common organizational pattern for classification is to set up a list and then to follow that list with ordered number references: first, second, third. For example, a discussion of redwood trees might begin, *Although redwood trees once covered much of the Northern Hemisphere 140 million years ago, climatic changes have left only three species of redwood today, each with a limited range: the coast redwood (Sequoia sempervirens), which grows along the Pacific coast, the giant sequoia (Sequoiadendron giganteum), which is restricted to the Sierra Nevada's western slopes, and the dawn redwood (Metasequoia glyptostroboides), found in a remote area of China. In like* manner, you might say: *There are three important types of tests a student must know about: _____, _____, and _____ The first, _____, is characterized by... The second... The third and final....* This pattern is the most common used to unify papers developed by classification:

1. There are ____ types of dates: _____, _____, _____

2. My school provides facilities for _____ major types of sports: _____, _____, _____

3. Teachers can be classified into _____ types according to _____, _____, _____

• **EXERCISE 11.6: UNIFICATION**

Complete sentences 1–3 above with your own classifications. Then set up a pattern like the one demonstrated above and fill it in with details for a discussion of the following:

1. Types of computers
2. Types of Saturday night activities
3. Types of roommates
4. Types of _____ (invent one).

A Model to Learn From

The following is typical of a paper for a technical writing or business class or for giving advice about purchases. It is not complete, but the sections included give a good sense of the organizational plan, the attention to detail, and the developmental form that make this writing effective.

Introduction:

For the serious engineering student [audience], few tools make problem solving easier and less time consuming than a programmable scientific calculator which can perform long, repetitive calculations with just the push of a few buttons.[importance of topic] Unfortunately, buying a good one can be very expensive (up to about $700.00) and confusing [problems] because they all offer different features at different prices, a balance between which can be achieved. [some categories] To aid students, the calculators chosen for this report, the TI57, TI58C, HP34C, HP33C, and the Sharp PC1201 [items to be compared], are all priced at or under $150.00 and are flexible enough to easily handle both the student's programming and arithmetic needs. [basis for their selection] In an attempt to find the balance between feature and price, and to determine which of the five is the best buy for the normal engineering student, six standards of judgment—price, flexibility and extras, number of memory locations, number of program steps, continuous memory, and logic used—will be evaluated. [criteria for evaluation of items] Although the calculators differ in more than these six areas, these six are the most important characteristics for comparing basic programmable calculators.

Body:

There is no significant difference in the size and weight of each calculator. They are small enough for the student to carry by hand or in a bag, and yet large enough for easy operation. Each unit is of solid construction with a hard plastic case that can usually survive a fall from a desk. They are each equipped with rechargeable power packs that operate for three continuous hours, enabling the student to use the calculator for a complete final exam even if he doesn't turn it off between uses. They each incorporate a click-touch feature to minimize entry errors. The two TI models use algebraic notations, allowing the operator to enter problems as they are normally written. The HP models use reverse polish notation, a machine language new to most students, but easily learned with a possible advantage of fewer keystrokes for large problems. Due to the simplicity of both methods, no one machine has a particular advantage. All four models contain a full range of mathematical, trigonometric, and statistical functions. [comparison of common features]

The significant differences, then, lie in the special features, the storage capacity, and the price. [transition and topic sentence focused on contrast] The HP-34 goes a step beyond the other units by incorporating a feature to find real roots of a function and to solve definite integrals of functions that can be keyed into memory. In addition to the features mentioned above, the TI-58 has a preprogrammed chip that provides over 5000 steps of the most useful problem solving techniques. Also, other chips are available for about $20, each providing 5000 additional steps for use in different fields, making it by far the most versatile and powerful mathematical aid of the group....

Conclusion:

Clearly, the TI calculators offer much more for the money. If the student is really short of cash, the TX-57 is probably the best buy, for it will get a student through college adequately. However, because of its versatility and greater capacity, the TI-57 is by far the best calculator of the group, for it will not only be the greatest aid during college years, but will serve equally well later in the field, thus eliminating the need to buy another calculator.

- **EXERCISE 11.7: QUESTIONS FOR DISCUSSION**

    1. How many different calculators will this student evaluate and compare/contrast?
    2. How many different evaluative divisions will be covered?
    3. How long do you predict this paper will be? two pages? six pages? ten pages? twenty pages? Why? Clearly, limiting the number of choices and the number of categories for evaluation is vital to limiting the length of your paper.
    4. Why is a comparison-contrast pattern which alternates between calculators necessary? How would a pattern which talks all about one calculator and then all about another change the nature of the information and the overall effect of the argument?
    5. What does the conclusion do that is the same as the introduction?
    6. What does the conclusion do that is different from the introduction?

Final Checklist

☐ Have you used the same principle or basis of selection for all of your divisions?

☐ Do items grouped within a class share characteristics essential to the basis of classification?

☐ Does each class have an identifying label?

☐ Have you included at least two items for every subdivision?

☐ Have you limited the categories to a manageable number?

☐ Do your categories overlap? Do they include all possibilities?

☐ Have you taken advantage of familiar, existing categories?

☐ Do your categories explore the full range of possibilities?

Passages for Discussion and Analysis

A. The following passage is aimed at helping college students choose the best sport for staying in shape, with limited cost and limited players. The numbers signify the criteria applied.

Choosing the Right One-On-One Sport

In these days of health consciousness, the sports craze is thriving as never before. Almost all activities, from individual sports like distance running to team games like soccer, have experienced a huge increase in participants. However, some people who would like to stay in shape find solitary jogging monotonous and team sports like soccer or softball too hard to arrange for two full teams. [the reader's problem] The perfect median between these two extremes is one-on-one sports such as racquetball, handball, squash, and tennis. [a possible solution] This paper will examine the merits of each of these sports and recommend one of them for beginners. [paper plan and goal] These four sports, as opposed to slower one-on-one games like table tennis or badminton, are fast, competitive games that require coordination, concentration, and stamina. The object of each of these games is to hit the ball so your opponent cannot return it after only one bounce on the floor or ground. The basics of these sports are easily mastered, so a beginner can start playing almost immediately. [shared positive attributes]

Although a beginner's personal preferences must finally decide between racquetball, handball, squash, and tennis [sports to be compared], he can base his decision on a few factors that involve all four of these sports. These factors are: 1) expense of equipment required, 2) availability of playing courts, 3) difficulty of play, and 4) amount of exercise involved. [Key criteria to be applied] By evaluating each sport in each of these areas, a beginner's choice can be made much clearer. As an employee of the University Division of Recreational Sports, I am continually exposed to all of these sports and can accurately provide the information needed about each of them. [proof of writer's authority]

The first, racquetball, has enjoyed a boom in popularity over the past few years. This game is played on an indoor rectangular court with a short racquet with a teardrop-shaped head and a bouncy two-inch diameter ball. The balls can be purchased at two for $4, so the biggest equipment expense is the racquet. Depending on quality, it can range anywhere from $8 to $100, but a good quality metal racquet will cost about $25. (1) The main drawback to racquetball is the unavailability of courts due to the increased popular demand. There are no public courts, so private clubs, the YMCA, or university facilities are the only alternatives. If a player is not a student, he may have to pay a steep annual membership fee or up to $9 per person, per hour to play at a private club.(2) If a player can get a court, then he can immediately understand why the sport is so popular. Racquetball is a very simple game to learn: there is no stroking form to follow, so a player just hits the ball with the racquet any way he can so that it hits the front wall once. Good eye-hand coordination is needed to hit balls that take some unusual bounces off back and side walls, but once this aspect of the game is mastered, the game can be enjoyed by anyone.(3) Racquetball is a very fast game: each point requires the players to be on their toes and ready to sprint to the ball. The game is never delayed by chasing after balls since they are confined inside four walls.(4)

Handball is played in the same size indoor court as racquetball, but players use their hands instead of a racquet to hit the smaller, denser handball. Equipment includes the balls, at two for $3, and handball gloves, which range from $15 to $20.(1) Since handball is played on the same courts as racquetball, it is hard to get a court unless they are reserved specifically for handball. Usually, authorities set aside some courts for handball to protect handball players from being overwhelmed by the number of racquetball players.**(2)** Although handball is played in the same way as racquetball, it takes more time and effort to learn to hit the ball correctly. A handball player must also be able to use both his left and right hands to hit.**(3)** Once these skills are acquired, the game is just as fast and exciting as racquetball and provides just as much exercise.**(4)**

Squash is another indoor game played on a smaller court with a long, thin, badminton-like racquet and golfball-size balls. This equipment is somewhat less expensive than that of the others, because of the smaller mallet of this less popular sport. **(1)** There are not as many squash courts as there are courts for the other two types, but since they are less in demand, it is easier to find one open.**(2)** Squash is played similarly to racquetball, but the ball dies very quickly since it is very soft. It must be hit harder and with more arm force than a racquetball. For beginners, the game is slower, but with experience it can become just as fast as racquetball. The extra reach of the longer racquets and the smaller courts compensate for deadness of the balls.**(4)**

Finally, tennis is another sport that pits two players against each other, but they must hit the ball with a long, sturdy racquet over a net on a large, outdoor court instead of against a wall indoors. Good equipment is a little more expensive than that of the other games. Three balls cost about $3 and a solid racquet is about $40.**(1)** Nevertheless, the great number of public courts make it possible to play almost any time the weather permits, for a minimal fee, if any at all.**(2)** Tennis is also more difficult to play than the other games; form plays an important part in this game and learning the basic strokes is essential to success. The fact that it is more complicated than the other three games we have discussed allows for an advanced player to develop more strategies and techniques.**(3)** Tennis is a slower game than racquetball, handball, or squash since the distances are greater and the ball is free to bounce off the court. As a result, the exercise comes with longer, sustained rallies. **(4)**

Any of these sports will fill the needs of a beginner looking for a fast, competitive game, but racquetball is the best choice since it is easily learned, requires no special skills, and is the most exciting of the four.**(3)** [evaluating conclusion] This sport will whip anybody into shape with its fast, intense play.**(4)** Both handball and squash are good alternatives, but require a little more experience to get the same amount of exercise as racquetball. Tennis provides the least relative activity per hour of play, but should be recommended for a player who wants a sport that involves more skill and intelligence. [summary contrast] In the long run, all of these sports involve intricate strategies and skills when a player becomes advanced enough, but for pure activity and enjoyment, racquetball is the best bet. [evaluative conclusion]

Complete the chart to sum up the key information presented in the above paper. Following the numbers will help.

	racquetball	handball	squash	tennis
(1) expense of equipment				
(2) availability of courts				
(3) difficulty of play				
(4) amount of exercise				

Does making this chart help you find any problems with the essay? Has the writer left anything out or has she covered all of the essentials? What kind of information does the conclusion provide? Why?

B. The following paper builds on a division into parts. It takes the abstract concept "friendship" and subdivides it into categories that help students understand the difficulties involved in forming cross-cultural friendships.

Making Friends Across Cultures

Making friends with host nationals is an excellent way for foreign students to learn the language, become familiar with the culture, and make their stay an overall satisfying experience. However, making friends across cultures seems easier for some people than for others due to a number of factors that either help or hinder intercultural friendship formation. Application of these categories to friendship possibilities should make it possible to achieve a higher rate of success in making new friends abroad.

The first set of factors relate to cross-cultural understanding. Clearly, cultural similarity facilitates the growth of friendship since people from similar cultures will usually understand each other better and become friends more easily than do people from dissimilar cultures. Related are commonalities since friends usually have much in common: race, religion, education, age, attitudes, interests, and so forth. Although foreign students might not share racial, religious, or educational backgrounds with host nationals, they might share more universal commonalities, such as age, attitudes, and interests. Furthermore, different cultures have different expectations about the nature of a friendly relationship. For example, people from individualistic cultures like that of the United States expect more independence from friends than do people from group-oriented cultures like those of China or Japan. Sharing expectations facilitates friendship formation.

The search for friends is also facilitated if the sojourner has had previous experience abroad, preferably not just tourist trips but longer stays that required some adjustment. This is because culture shock interferes with friendship formation. Sojourners [traveler] who know the host culture well, including its patterns of daily life, social structure, perceptions of time and space, customs, behaviors, beliefs and values, will find it easier to make friends than sojourners suffering from the crisis of adjustment to a new environment that seems negative and even threatening. People from any culture are more approachable if someone knows and accepts their ways. The same is true for language-related skills. Sojourners who can communicate well in the foreign language will have fewer problems making contact and pursuing friendships than those who can not. Moreover, communicative competence means not only linguistic skills but also knowledge of nonverbal language and the rules of conversation and the formulas for politeness.

A whole set of personality characteristics also influences friendship formation. Basically, those who are outgoing, tolerant, and good-humored have a better chance of initiating friendships than those who are shyer, less tolerant, and less good-natured about differences. Related is self-esteem. Because self-confident people are not afraid to start conversations and do not give up quickly in the pursuit of friendship, people with self-confidence often make friends more easily than those who lack such self-esteem. In addition, "personal identifiers" have an advantage over "cultural identifiers"; that is, people whose identity is personal and individualistic usually have more intercultural friends than those who define themselves mainly as proud members of their home culture.

Other key influences on friendship formation are time and proximity. Free–time is a definite necessity since developing close interpersonal relationships takes time. Thus, an unmarried student can expect to have more time for friendship than a student in the company of a spouse or family. Similarly, a "cross-cultural seeker," who desires contact with host nationals and wants to learn about their culture, usually acquires more intercultural friends than a "task-oriented" student, whose sole purpose is to study hard and get a degree. Proximity, too, is a natural requirement for friendship formation since physical closeness and frequent contact increase the chances of finding and cultivating friendships. Thus, people who share housing with host nationals and regularly participate in community events usually have more intercultural friends than people who spend most of their time by themselves or with other foreign students.

Friendship, of course, is not only dependent on the sojourner's characteristics, but also on elements in the host culture. Consequently, some host nationals might be prejudiced and uninterested in foreigners. This status quo is unfortunate but difficult to change. The host culture might also favor friendship styles that are not to the sojourner's liking. A lot of foreign students in the United States, for example, are confused by the fact that first names, hugs, and invitations are often used in casual contact. In many other cultures, these are reserved for close relationships, and, in fact, many sojourners dislike their casual use and find it strange.

Finally, the last and most significant influence on friendship formation is "chemistry," a special term which refers to the intangible bond that attracts people to each other. Even if all other factors are present, people might still not become friends if there is no "chemistry" between them.

To conclude, of the approximately twelve factors that influence the development of intercultural friendship, some are not easily controlled during the sojourn because they are pre-existing (cultural similarity, commonalities, expectations, sojourn experiences, personality, and self-esteem) or because they depend on the host environment, or intangible bonds (host culture elements and chemistry). Many of the qualities, however, can be changed by the sojourner during the stay by building communicative competence, acquiring cultural knowledge, making cultural and social adjustments, assuring proximity, and taking time. No matter whether the other factors are present, foreign students in search of a friend can always focus on these changeable ones and thus do their best to have a satisfying social life and a successful stay.

—Adapted from Elisabeth Gareis, *Intercultural Friendship: A Qualitative Study*

• Questions for Discussion

1. List Ms. Gareis' key factors affecting intercultural friendship formation and their related subcategories; your list should move from factors which cannot be controlled to factors which can be shaped or modified.

2. Of those factors which can be controlled, which have you personally seen at work? Explain.

3. Does your personal experience confirm or call into question this analysis? Explain.

4. List conversational skills (or "rules of conversation") that you think help friendship formation.

5. Ms. Gareis is focusing on friendship between cultures. Would her categories work equally well for people within the same culture? Explain.

6. The above categories give us one view of friendship. What are some other ways of classifying friendship?

•• Writing Assignments

A. Classify local restaurants based on criteria important to a student who wants to take a date there. Cost? Romantic decor? Accessibility? Then, write an essay making clear that criteria and bringing in local examples to develop it.

B. Write an essay which classifies student housing in order to advise new students about how to spend their housing funds wisely.

C. Write an essay classifying available local recreational activities. Your goal is to advise new students about the best ways to spend their free time.

D. Write an essay which classifies available student transportation. Your goal is to decide the most efficient transport system for students who live on or near campus, or for those who live at some distance from campus.

E. Define scholastic honesty, as if for a college catalog or publication describing the rights and obligations of college students. Use the following exercise to brainstorm about the subject.

Decide the degree to which the following are appropriate or inappropriate in terms of academic honesty.

Never OK/Rarely OK/Sometimes OK/OK/Perfectly acceptable/should be done

a. Copying someone's homework

b. Allowing someone else to copy your homework

c. Using words from a book in a paper which has a bibliography at the end but not quotations or footnotes

d. Turning in a paper actually written by your roommate or a friend for last semester's class

e. Paying someone to write a paper for you

f. Working on a paper with a lab tutor who does half the work for you

g. Working on a paper with a friend who makes major changes in your work

h. Copying from a student who leaves her paper uncovered during an exam

i. Overhearing students calling out correct answers on an exam and writing down these answers yourself

j. Bringing prohibited notes on a "cheat sheet" into an exam

k. Reading a summary of an assigned book (like the various "Notes" for sale in college bookstores) instead of the book itself

l. Borrowing the notes for a class when you have missed half the lectures.

Applications

A. **Making Choices by Evaluating Possibilities:** Select an item which involves choices and which requires classification for intelligent purchase or use. Examples are consumer items or tools, such as a car, a bicycle, an electronic calculator, a television set, the choice of which college best meets your needs, which diet will be the best suited to your personal needs, which sport will best fit your busy schedule and yet provide what you need in the way of relaxation and exercise, and so forth. In other words, this essay should help you choose the better of two or best of three possible selections. Your criteria for choosing a topic are:

1. Complexity makes classification necessary (economy cars come in dozens of brands and models, each different from the others; wooden pencils do not)

2. An interpretative judgment is necessary (toilet paper comes in dozens of brands but not much interpretation as to value is necessary in making a choice).

Once you have chosen a topic, classify the items according to whatever bases are relevant (for example, sportscars come in two- and four-seater models, closed and convertible styles, and so forth); make clear what these bases consist of. Then make an interpretative judgment: Decide which item is best and which worst for a particular use or purpose. The cost of the item is of course a factor; for example, deciding which automobile model would be the best buy for a particular person would involve

1. Classification of various models according to, for example, price, comfort, reliability, and endurance

2. Interpretation of the meaning of the classification.

The classification, in effect, organizes a series of facts into parallel categories, but does not in itself lead to a decision about best or worst unless only one basis is being used (for example, which car is cheapest). Most real-life decisions involve interactions between various bases or categories (for example, price versus comfort versus reliability versus endurance), and this is where interpretation comes in. Make your standards of judgment clear.

ITEMS FOR EVALUATION

	1	2	3	4
first basis				
second basis				
third basis				
fourth basis				

Prewriting Developmental Frame

Complete the above frame to help you plan your paper. Across the top (horizontal line) list the items to be evaluated. Down the side (vertical line) list the bases of evaluation. Fill in the middle part with appropriate information to fit each category.

B. **Job Classification**: The purpose of this exercise is to help you set up a series of values and qualities for your "ideal" job and to apply these standards to a number of possible choices. An ideal job is not necessarily a job you expect to hold someday soon, but rather a goal you are aiming at. When you work on this classification, you should spend as much time thinking about yourself—your own goals, values, and abilities—as about the job itself. Note that even in the ideal world, trade–offs are necessary: You must give up something in order to get something.

Prewriting:

Complete the following prewriting exercise. Think carefully and make notes before filling in the blanks so your answers will be considered and accurate.

1. *Function:* Put in rank order (#1 the most important, #2 the next most important, etc.) salary, prestige, satisfaction with fellow workers, contribution to society, future personal advancement, satisfaction with the work itself. Then, explain in a couple of sentences the reasons for your rank-order.

2. *Description:* In a couple of sentences, describe the worst job you can imagine. Be specific about its characteristics.

3. *Personal Definition: My main goal in finding a job is ultimately to provide happiness. Happiness, in terms of what a job can provide, means....* (complete this definition in a couple of sentences).

4. *Example:* List three examples of jobs that come close to your ideal job, explaining each kind of job in detail.

5. *Characteristics:* Decide which of the following fit your ideal job and which do not. Check the appropriate items. Then, sum up the results in a couple of sentences. Note that parallel structures allow a great deal of material to be organized into a few short sentences.

_____indoor work   _____high stress conditions

_____outdoor work   _____low stress conditions

_____strict deadlines   _____strict working hours

_____flexible deadlines   _____flexible working hours

_____work alone   _____work in brief, intense periods

_____work in teams   _____work spread over regular periods

_____manual labor   _____work is problem solving

_____non-manual labor   (responding to situations)

_____work is initiating action   _____work with people

_____work under clear authority   _____work with things

_____work self-directed, little authority   (numbers, words, physical things)

_____work has concrete, immediate results

_____work has long-term, ill-defined results

As you work on these sections, try expanding them with details such as the following:

Characteristics: Would involve a variety of activities; would not require that I live in a large city; would make a contribution to society; would be reasonably lucrative ($20,000-$25,000 a year) and offer chances for advancement; would not require eight hours a day in an office; would involve taking responsibility and making decisions.

Analysis: A job that allows me to make use of my talents in mathematics and physical sciences; one in which I could make use of my natural mechanical abilities; one that does not require study of a foreign language or literature, subjects in which I do poorly.

Examples: Some jobs that might fit my specifications are civil engineer, veterinarian, airline pilot, rancher, or ecology consultant. Ones that certainly would not fit my standards are law, advertising, accounting, or writing.

Function: Provide a comfortable living, a sense of accomplishment and self-respect, and a satisfying outlet for my energies and talents.

In working out these categories, you will be spelling out what, in your opinion, a job for you should be.

Writing: After completing all of the above, write an essay setting up the criteria of your ideal job. You may repeat the information you generated above, but be selective and organize it into essay form. Your introductory paragraph should set up your key categories; the body paragraphs should apply the categories in detail to specific job possibilities; the concluding paragraph should sum up.

Example: My decision about a future career is based on a number of personal and social factors. I don't care about prestige or high salary or even personal advancement. Nor do I mind long hours and emotionally trying tasks. What is important to me is contributing something to society by helping others; yet at the same time I would like to be able to enjoy the hours I would spend working. I would enjoy working directly with people on a daily basis. I enjoy problem-solving situations, self-direction, and flexible hours and flexible deadlines. I need a job that would provide a feeling of self-worth rather than one with a mindless routine aimed at personal advancement. Consequently, my ideal job would be people-oriented. Among my possible options are working as a psychologist, as a social worker, or as a therapist.

All three would give me the sense of accomplishment that comes from helping others, but they can also be both demanding and stressful. Although a psychologist has the advantage of receiving the largest salary of the three, it is also probably the most demanding and the most stressful, because it requires more involvement with individual pressure to produce positive results than do the other positions. Working as a social worker can also be very stressful because of the large amount of paperwork it involves. In addition, it is often dangerous because it is frequently necessary for the social worker to travel to impoverished places to find those in need of help. A therapist might also encounter stress and demands, but much less so than the other two. A psychiatrist potentially can bring home a very high salary, and can live more than comfortably, but therapists and social workers make much less. The salaries of therapists and social workers are basically the same, though they may vary according to the amount of experience and the place of work....

Chapter 12: USING EXAMPLES

Example is the school of mankind. — Edmund Burke

Key Concerns in Development by Examples

Development by examples may seem too obvious to need discussion, for the use of these concrete "samples" of how and why we think comes naturally to us, even as children. Nevertheless, one of the most common criticisms college instructors make on student papers is, "Where is your evidence? You lack sufficient proof! Provide examples!" We often forget that we must give specific details and illustrations to make a general point clearer or to provide evidence for generalizations. Examples lend strength and force to an argument. They help readers understand the reasons for a writer's personal opinions and make any essay more interesting.

No matter what field you plan to study or what subjects you write about, using examples will be necessary. The student who writes only a paragraph in class after fifty minutes may only need examples to expand and support a discussion. It is no exaggeration to say that one good idea followed by a series of examples often produces an excellent essay. This is because, whether in mathematics, science, sociology, history, or English, examples clarify, expand, and explain. The following example from a popular physics textbook is typical:

Speed is simply the ratio of distance traveled per time. That is,

$$Speed = \frac{distance}{time}$$

<u>For example</u>, if we drive a distance of 60 miles in a time of 1 hour, we say our speed is 60 miles per hour. More precisely, we would call this our *average* speed, for the speed of our car during the trip usually undergoes some variation. If there is no variation we can refer to our motion as *constant* speed, where *equal distances* are covered in *equal intervals* of time.

<u>We are all familiar with acceleration in an automobile.</u> In driving we call it "pick-up" or "get-away"; we experience it when we tend to lurch toward the rear of the car. Suppose we are driving and in one second we steadily increase our velocity from 30 miles per hour to 35 miles per hour, and then to 40 miles per hour in the next second, to 45 in the next second, and so on. We increase our velocity by 5 miles per hour each second. This change in velocity is what we mean by acceleration. . . . Notice that acceleration is not the total change in velocity; it is the *rate of change*, or *change per second*.

—Paul Hewitt, *Conceptual Physics*

In this case Paul Hewitt uses something everyone is familiar with, car acceleration, to demonstrate a general principle of physics. His simple example makes an abstract idea concrete and develops it, leading to further discussion.

Examples can serve multiple functions. They might be examples of effects produced by a particular cause; they might be part of a comparison, or add

Whiskery cat

information for a contrast. In other words, examples may be used to expand any of the other organization patterns. In the following example, the writer proves the importance of cats' whiskers by listing their functions. This list of functions is, in effect, a series of examples of how cats rely on whiskers.

Cat Whiskers: Sensitive Multi-functional Instruments

The whiskers of cats are highly sensitive instruments that cats rely heavily on for a number of functions. It is because whiskers are so vital to preserving a cat's nine lives that cats get really bothered when people accidentally touch their whiskers. At night or in the dark, <u>for example</u>, whiskers help cats determine whether they can fit into cramped spaces— such as a hole in a tree, the inside back of a favorite chair, the opening in the back fence, or under a sleeping person's chin. Whiskers also help cats detect the direction of wind and thus, in combination with a feline's acute sense of smell, help cats determine the source of an alluring odor— whether a whiff of tuna, the smell of a mouse, or the signs left by roaming tomcats. <u>In addition</u>, whiskers protect the eyes of cats on the move, whether through the undergrowth of a tangled backyard or the more dangerous protrusions of an urban jungle. Whenever anything touches the cat's whiskers, the cat automatically and rapidly shuts its eyes. Because a cat would be really lost without its whiskers and new ones take months to grow back, you should never cut them.

What thesis does this writer try to prove? Where do you find it? How many examples support this thesis? Does the conclusion add any new information? What is lost when you summarize this selection in one good sentence? What does this loss tell you about the importance of examples?

Deciding on General Categories

As you have learned from previous chapters, good prewriting involves setting up general categories around which to gather supportive details. In the case of examples, there must be some idea or concept or point for the examples to illustrate. Obviously, an essay can never begin with <u>for example</u> because the reader would immediately ask, "What is this an example of?" A student explaining influences on career decisions might divide the topic into three categories: the influence of past studies, the influence of personal experience, and the influence of family and friends. In a short paper this might be far too much to cover. A decision to focus just on the influence of family and friends will require a new set of categories or divisions: perhaps the strong influence of a father or a mother, of a successful sibling, or of a close personal friend in making such a decision. Another approach to the same topic might be to set up two categories: positive family influences on career decisions and negative family influences on career decisions. In such a case, the writer would need to further decide whether to begin or end with the positive influence and what particular examples to include. Depending on purpose, the writer might choose instead one extended example to illustrate the influence of family or friends on career decisions. In other words, the same topic might be developed with examples in a number of ways, and you will need to decide about the pattern of development before you can choose examples that support the topic.

- ## EXERCISE 12.1: DECIDING ON CATEGORIES

    A. Decide how the following series of topics might be subdivided into categories to be supported with examples. Then choose one category for each topic and give an example that would effectively support or illustrate the idea.

    > *Example:* Types of short-answer exam questions—Categories: 1) those requiring no words to answer, 2) those requiring a single word answer, 3) those requiring multi-word answers. Examples of category 1): matching, numbering, true/false items

    1. Types of teachers
    2. The main tourist attractions in _____
    3. A good party
    4. The functions of work
    5. The importance of recreational activities

    B. Write a well-organized paragraph which analyzes or categorizes the cuisine of your country. Choose one category, such as by region, by type, by cooking method, by season, by number of calories, by food groups, by degree of cooking or non-cooking, or others.

    C. Find some significant categories or divisions to help you organize the following information about British Columbian culture. Write a topic sentence to reflect all of your categories. Then use this information to write a well-organized paragraph about British Columbian culture.

    1. British Colombia = a vital part of the Pacific Rim
    2. In the late 19th century, large groups of Chinese laborers came to work constructing the trans-Continental Canadian Pacific Railway
    3. Immigrants from India, Pakistan, Malaysia, and the Philippines (post World War II)
    4. Early setters almost entirely British (from England, Scotland, Ireland, Wales) or British descendants from central Canada

5. Immigrants from Hong Kong, Vietnam, Thailand, mainland China, Formosa, and Japan (1970s to 1990s)

6. In 1871 all but 9,000 of the 56,247 inhabitants were Native Americans

7. Large Chinatowns in Vancouver and Victoria

8. Railway (completed 1885) = influx of new people

9. After World War II = new wave of immigrants

10. Buddhist bazaars

11. Scottish tea dances

12. Jewish art shows

13. Danish bingos

14. Fijian dances

15. Slovenian wine festival

16. Native Indian art—wooden carvings, paintings

British Columbian Totem Pole

Making a List of Examples

Sometimes you start a paper with a general topic idea, decide on subtopics or supportive categories, and then brainstorm to generate a list of supportive examples for each category or subtopic. Sometimes, however, the brainstorming begins with the formulation of a series of examples on a central topic, examples around which a paper will be built. These approaches are usually called <u>deductive</u> (beginning with a generalization) and <u>inductive</u> (beginning with evidence). The type of approach you choose depends on you, your purpose, and the particular writing situation, but whether you begin with ideas and then a list of examples or begin with a list of examples and search for categories or groupings, you must end up dealing with both and their mutual interaction: a set of categories and a series of examples to illustrate the ideas or concepts of each category. Remember that a list can be interesting, but it is prewriting, not an essay. Only when a list is expanded and explained does it become a topic. The following began as a good list and has not yet been transformed into a good topic.

The Japanese use several proverbs to explain some ideas. For example they say:

Even a monkey falls down from a tree. (Even a professional sometimes makes a mistake.)

If you love your child, let her travel. (Don't try to control your child too much.)

Choose the long way when you are in a hurry. (Calm yourself down when you are in a hurry so you don't waste time.)

A prayer to Buddha for a horse's ears. (There is no value in foolish wishes. Even if you teach something to foolish people, they never understand, so don't waste your time.)

Prepare a walking stick before falling down. (Provide ahead of time for possible mistakes.)

It's only a rumor which has neither roots nor leaves. (It's completely untrue.)

There is usually not smoke without fire. (There is something true in a rumor.)

Change your bad habits in order to see others' bad habits. (Don't criticize others without considering your own faults.)

I think these sayings translate only with great difficulty.

This list is a good beginning for an essay, but it is not yet an essay. It already has an overall topic idea: Japanese proverbs or sayings "translate only with great difficulty." What could be done to provide focus and direction?

Even if each example is followed by a brief discussion, all the writer will end up with is a list with added commentary like the following:

Their saying, "A walking dog can be hit by an electric-light pole," means that anybody can make a mistake, even a person who is good at everything. This proverb also means one should not be too proud of himself, for nobody can be perfect.

Another saying, "A drowning person will even try to catch hold of a straw to be saved," means that a person in an emergency situation will try to do anything to save himself, even if he knows it can't help him. In other words, even if we know that the trouble can't be overcome, we will still make a futile, desperate effort. It is human nature to try.

Developing with examples should mean interrelating examples to make a coherent and logical whole. The relationships between the parts should be clearly recognizable.

You might be able to make an expanded list more interesting, and less like a list, by looking for a pattern or for categories to give a sense of order and progression. In fact, finding categories that divide up the overall topic is a good way to begin developing a list into an essay. Furthermore, as we have seen in the preceding section, making divisions and categories is always a good way to organize and expand materials. For example, some of these Japanese proverbs sound very much like American ones and could be easily translated, while others are not at all like American ones and would be much harder to explain. As any native English speaker could quickly tell the writer of the list, "There is usually no smoke without fire," "Prepare a stick before falling down," and "Change your bad habits in order to see others' bad habits"

sound very much like the following English sayings: "Where there is smoke, there's fire," "Be prepared," and "People in glass houses should not throw stones." However, some of the other proverbs like "a prayer to Buddha for a horse's ears" would not make much sense to Americans without explanation.

In other words, the proverbs could be tested on some native speakers to discover the degree of difficulty in understanding, and then divided into categories based on degree of difficulty: easily translated, difficult to translate, impossible to translate. Setting up such categories might allow the writer to discover that she has examples to fit two categories but needs to generate more for the third category. Only when this has been accomplished should the writer go on to explain more fully, generalize more, and thereby change her list into a real paper. A good thesis statement around which to organize the list of information might be as follows: *Although some Japanese proverbs translate very easily into English, the majority (the most interesting ones) are so closely related to Japanese religion, society, and culture that they are more difficult to translate.* This thesis with divisions provides a sounder intellectual basis for discussion than does a simple list of examples.

• EXERCISE 12.2: GENERATING LISTS OF EXAMPLES

List examples you might use to support one of the following topics.

Example: The United States National Parks Yosemite and Yellowstone allow urban man to experience the contact with wild life that his ancestors once knew: the beauty and the potential danger. a) see wild animals in their natural habitat, b) see natural forests, not forests planted by humans, c) breathe clean air, d) drink untreated and unpolluted water, e) climb natural trails over hills and mountains.

1. Going to a new school can be very exciting but also a little frightening.
2. Knowing how to use a word processor can save the student a great deal of time and effort.
3. Watching television in English is a good way to develop conversational skills, build vocabulary, and find out about the culture.
4. Regular exercise, if done correctly, can be highly beneficial to your health.
5. Regular exercise, if done incorrectly, can be injurious to your health.

Deciding on a Logical Order

Whenever you sit down to write, once you have completed the brainstorming part of your process, you should begin to look for a plan, an order, a set of unifying concepts. For example, a student assigned to describe her room might discover that her list of details includes some items which are traditionally Asian and some which are very Western. She might then take as her thesis the idea that her room reflects the Western styles which have modified her basic, underlying Eastern spirit. She would then divide her paper into two parts: examples of those items which reflect Western taste and Western interests, followed by examples of those which reflect her underlying Eastern spirit and values.

At other times examples might fall naturally into a time order. The thesis *Going away to college produces numerous changes in the way one thinks and in the way one acts* should be followed by two sections: changes in the way one thinks and changes in the way one acts. However, within these sections you might focus on the chronological order of changes: what kind of changes occur first, what kind of changes occur later.

Another good pattern for organizing examples is to go from least important to most important or from most important to least important. For instance, a student writing about how going to college will change her life for the better might begin with examples of the minor changes and lead up to the most important major changes. A student trying to persuade his parents to let him move into an apartment might, in turn, begin with his most persuasive reasons (with examples of how they would work) and end up with his less persuasive reasons (with examples of how they would work) added at the end as a bonus after the main persuasion has been completed. In other words, providing a logical order or plan of discussion for a series of examples makes your writing easier to follow and more persuasive.

• EXERCISE 12.3: LOGICAL ORDER

The following details are all related to the study of archaeology and in particular to the implications of the latest archaeological studies. Write a thesis statement that will interrelate these varied examples. In other words, despite their seeming differences, you must look for what they have in common. Then put them together in an organized paragraph with a topic sentence and conclusion.

1. Recent studies suggest that Jews and Christians may have lived in harmony over several centuries of Roman rule, worshipping side by side.

2. A shop beneath the stairway of the Temple of Castor and Pollux yields evidence the Romans practiced sophisticated dentistry, including orthodontics.

3. Excavations at Herscherkeller in Lower Bavaria indicate a very early, flourishing agricultural economy based on fertilizing crops and rotating them.

4. The discovery of "special burial deposits" in Britain suggests the Druids had a very complex religious system involving the disposal of the dead.

5. New archaeological finds in the Southeastern U.S. show it is possible Hernando deSoto and his conquistadors acted far more savagely against Native American Indians than was previously thought.

Evaluating Support

Overall, the two major problems with many student papers are that they provide an exhausting list of examples and details with no divisions or categories to give them meaning or they discuss their topic in general without the specific examples that would illustrate it and make it come alive for the audience. Carefully selected examples that are relevant, focused, and unbiased provide interest and promote understanding. Divisions and categories provide logical order and give meaning to examples. The two must go hand in hand for effective writing.

Adequacy

A student who goes to one college party and on the basis of it argues that all American college parties share the characteristics of that one party simply does not have adequate support for his or her statement. Even three examples may not be enough to prove a broad generalization. For example, a generalization about American colleges would need examples from different parts of the country so that the different regions are considered; it would also need examples from different sized colleges (1000 students? 5000 students? 50,000 students?) and from different kinds of colleges: urban vs. suburban vs. rural, private vs. public, religious vs. state, liberal arts, technological, and community colleges vs. major universities, and so forth. In other words, the evidence must be sufficiently representative to prove your case.

How many examples are enough? As with so many questions about writing, it depends. In this case, it depends on the nature of your examples. How many apples do you need to bite into to conclude the whole bag is rotten? Two? Three? Certainly not five or six, for apples are very similar, and we know from common experience that a fairly small sample is usually adequate. How many people would you need to meet before you concluded that everyone in a certain town is cold and unfriendly? Probably a good number, since human beings are famously variable, and surprises keep happening. Of course, some human behavior, such as accent or pronunciation might require a smaller sample: *All five people I talked to had a slow, Southern drawl when they spoke....* A wise teacher once said, "Three trees make a row," and that's a good general rule for many examples (four or five don't hurt, either). The most useful rule of thumb is to let your purpose be your guide, but, if you use several examples, find a way to order or arrange them to best support your thesis and make clear the logical relationship between them.

- ## EXERCISE 12.4: ADEQUATE SUPPORT

  Which of the following paragraphs has adequate support? Which do not? What could be added to make the weaker paragraph stronger? List the types of examples needed to strengthen the weaker paragraph.

  1. *Technology* denotatively means development of machinery and science for man's use. However, the connotative meaning differs between countries and cultures. What does the equivalent word for *technology* connote in your country? In Peru, Indonesia, Ethiopia, and other developing countries, *technology* is a positive word meaning progress, while in a developed, industrialized country like the U.S., technology may, in turn, have negative connotations as well—for very different reasons. That is, it might make hearers think of developments to improve man's life, but it might also make them think of the negative consequences that accompany progress.

  2. We often assume that all people fear failure, pain, and death, and that the feelings these words convey are universal, though we might note cultural differences even with these basic terms. For example, the connotations of the word *suicide* will vary widely, depending on the attitude a culture has toward self-killing. In Japan suicide is sometimes an honorable form of death; in a predominantly Christian society it is usually considered a sin. What we are saying is that almost no word, apart from very simple concrete nouns (*chair, cup, table*) and grammatical connectives (*and, but, however*), can be separated

from its cultural background. To learn connotations we must learn cultural attitudes: how a culture feels about the things the word describes. For example, while *rice* in most countries denotatively means a kind of grain for cooking, *rice* in Japan has had the special connotation of *wealth* or *money* ever since the feudal days when the government collected *rice* instead of *money* for taxes. Just as *rice* is the "staple of life" in Japan, so bread, is the "staple of life" in this country. Thus, Americans use *dough* and *bread* as slang terms for *money*. In another case, when Latin Americans say, "he is drunk," they mean he has had a few drinks and is feeling good. When an American says, "Let's get drunk," he might mean, "Let's have a good time," "Let's do something daring," or "Let's do something serious or sinful," depending on the speaker's religious and philosophical attitude toward alcohol. However, in many Moslem countries, if a person says, "Let's get drunk," he may be breaking his faith, suggesting a sinful act, and exposing the fact that he has serious social problems. As is obvious from these few examples, very few important words can be divorced from the culture in which they are used.

3. The case of Joe Barnes and Dorothy Harper is a vivid example of why the death penalty must be applied in order for justice to be achieved. In this horrid episode, Joe Barnes was sentenced to five years in prison after he raped Dorothy Harper. After thirteen months, he was <u>paroled</u> [set free conditionally] for good behavior. Nevertheless, he found Harper a second time and brutally raped and killed her and her 13-year-old daughter, as well as Harper's neighbor, who was visiting. The prosecution asked for the death penalty while the defense asked for life imprisonment. It is true that killing Barnes would not bring Harper and her daughter back but it would grant justice. Life imprisonment without parole would certainly not be enough punishment because of the degree of this terrible crime. This man, without provocation, brutally killed three innocent people. He did not simply injure their lives; he destroyed them. A sentence of life imprisonment would be very disproportionate to the crime committed. Barnes knew perfectly well what he was doing. There was no question of insanity as a justification. He simply chose, deliberately and intentionally, to rape and then murder three innocent and defenseless women. Barnes' motive was clearly revenge since he spent months tracking Harper down. Motive, intent, and act, together prove culpability. Therefore, it is only justice that he and others like him face the consequences of their choices and deeds.

—Elsie Toro, Puerto Rico

•• **EXERCISE 12.5: WRITING ADEQUATELY DEVELOPED PARAGRAPHS**

The sample paragraph which follows demonstrates development by examples. Study it, and then write your own paragraph about one of the topics listed below; develop it with examples. Do so by first listing possible examples; then expand that list with explanations.

1. Names in my language can be very confusing for Americans.
2. Going to college can be very expensive.
3. English grammar rules have many exceptions.
4. The pronunciation of English words can be very difficult.
5. A positive attitude improves language learning.
6. A negative attitude limits language learning.
7. The students in my class differ in interests and background.
8. American greetings vary with age and situation.

Example: American names are often confusing because there are different names for different relationships. [topic idea] For example, a baby might be named Suzanne Lee Smith on her birth certificate, but no one ever calls a baby a name like that, so as a small child she might be called "Suzy" or "Sue." As she gets older the "Sue" might remain, but some might call her "Sue Lee" or "Susan." Close high school friends might teasingly call her "Oh Suzanna" after the popular song or a "black-eyed Susan" after the flower. When her parents are angry, they might call her Suzanne Lee, and her teachers will probably call her by her full name initially. When she becomes an adult and marries, she will probably change her last name, so she becomes Suzanne Jones (nickname Sue). If she becomes a professional, she will take the title of that profession: Officer Jones, Professor Jones—although she might also keep her original last name as a professional name. Sometimes she might simply be called by her married last name: Jones. Other times she might be called by her initials: SJ. However, no matter how old she becomes, her family might still call her by her childhood names—even on her hundredth birthday. In fact, the name used in adulthood will probably indicate the degree of formality or informality in the relationship.

Relevance

As we have seen, examples improve the quality of a paper, but you must be careful about the selection of your examples. First of all, they must really be examples of the point they are meant to prove. Including statistics on marijuana use will not prove anything about cocaine use, nor will information about what happens in one country prove anything about another country. If your thesis is that the Olympic Games promote international goodwill, examples of nationalism will not really be relevant. If your focus is on Mexico's Indian heritage, examples of the cosmopolitan nature of that country's capital will be irrelevant. If your topic is American and Russian cooperation, your examples should clearly establish such cooperation.

What examples could you use to prove that English is important in international relationships? It would help to name world organizations that use English for their conferences, to discuss the fact that international treaties are written in English and to provide information about the use of English in trade negotiations or in international currency exchanges. What type of examples would not fit? Would the fact that most international airports use English to give pilots instructions really prove the importance of English in international relationships? Using examples well is not simply a matter of listing; it means making decisions about what is logical support and what is not.

• EXERCISE 12.6: RELEVANCE

Underline the sentences which do not belong in the following selections. Explain why they are irrelevant.

Example: Successful analysis involves considering audience, purpose, persona, and method of argument. One must consider to what group or groups the essay is written and how you know. Are they educated or uneducated, conservatives or liberals, optimists or pessimists, opinionated or flexible? Do they have expertise in the field discussed or is it new to them? One must also ask about purpose. Sometimes the purpose will be clearly stated, perhaps in the introduction or conclusion; other times it must be guessed from context. Does the writer seek to amuse, enlighten, warn, criticize, or convert readers? There may be a number of different purposes, some major, some minor. Next to consider is persona. Persona is always hard to deal with because it means analyzing whether the image the writer projects is credible and trustworthy or unreliable and incautious. <u>The word "persona" comes from Latin and is related to the English word "person." In Latin it means a "mask," but whenever words are borrowed the meanings or connotations often change</u>. Finally, argument includes a consideration of structure or organizational plan, methods of development such as comparison or analogy, strategy and so on. Studying these four is called rhetorical analysis. *Digression on word origin moves away from analysis.*

1. All good writing is a fight for clarity, a fight that can never be entirely won because of the varying possible meanings of words and sentences. Clauses that seem crystal clear to a writer focusing on what seems a straightforward statement of facts may seem cloudy and ambiguous to a reader trying to understand them in terms of a particular and even unique situation. Getting rid of such linguistic confusions and ambiguities is like plugging up the holes in a disintegrating dam, with each repair sometimes only producing new confusions, new ambiguities, new leaks. Just think of the problems the Dutch have with their dikes. Always the sea is trying to break in. Dikes are especially vulnerable during storms. The North Atlantic can be a fierce attacker and floods are always possible.

2. This year, National Children's Book Week will be celebrated with a Children's Literary Festival, which will take as its theme, "Read Missouri." This festival offers a series of activities, including authors reading their works, workshops on literary themes, storytelling, and reading competitions. One author/illustrator, Thatcher Hurd, will talk about his bright, witty, picture books for children. He remembers standing at his hotel window and looking down at the mighty Mississippi River. He thought it would be a lazy river, but it is really immense and powerful. The Mississippi is very important, as a source of water, as a means of transportation, and as a link between different sections of the country, though sometimes it can get dangerously out of control as it did in the floods of 1993.

3. Because Americans come from so many different parts of the world, they are very interested in untangling the roots of their family trees. They want to know where their ancestors came from, how they came, and when they came. They want to know what kind of work they did and some are curious about whether their lineage links them to slaves or to royalty, to famous historical figures or to famous historical events. In response to this curiosity, the Utah Genealogical Society has collected at its main library in Salt Lake City 170,000 volumes and more than a million rolls of microfilm. The library is open on Tuesdays and Thursdays from 9 A.M. to noon and 6 P.M. to 9 P.M.; Wednesdays, 1 P.M. to 5 P.M.; and Saturdays, 9 A.M. to noon. Moreover, there are now 1,100 Family History Centers in 43 countries. A computer program developed in 1987 allows access to more than 118 million surnames of people from ninety countries who lived from 1600 to the late 1800s. More and more Americans are turning to such centers and programs to learn more about their personal genealogy.

4. The advent of the videocassette has revolutionized movie viewing in America. More and more Americans watch more and more movies in the privacy and comfort of their homes. In fact, millions of Americans rent a cassette or two for the weekend, and millions of others buy their favorite cassettes to play and replay. Parents can monitor what their children see, and young couples can watch a movie with greater privacy. As a result, numerous video emporiums have sprung up throughout the metropolitan areas. The stores come in different sizes according to the business demand of the local area. Some stores are local outlets of giant nationwide chains, others are medium-size stores, and a few are mom-and-pop shops. Their size tells us a great deal about the nature of the area

in which they have sprung up. All cater to a wide range of interests. Video movie-buffs look for old films, releases from the '30s, '40s, and '50s as well as foreign films, current favorites, and ones that showed briefly in town at the local theater and then disappeared from the screen.

5. Japanese students have trouble understanding English pronunciation because of the differences in sounds and the variations in native speaker dialects. First of all, they have great trouble distinguishing between "l" and "r" and sometimes pronounce *light* as *right* or hear *light* when the speaker means *right*. My family is from Japan, so we all get confused about English. People from Boston add an "r" to vowels, calling *idea, idear* or leave off the "r", calling *car, cah*. Japanese has different pronunciation in different parts of the country too. This is why I have scored badly on the TOEFL.

Function

Examples are used in two key ways: 1) as evidence to provide concrete proof of an idea or assertion; and 2) as a method of expanding and "fleshing out" a discussion, to provide interest, to illustrate. For example, if we claim that the weather in a certain city is uniformly terrible, examples provide proof: snowstorms, ice storms, heat waves, tornados. This pattern is so common instructors often speak of "the example paper" as a type of essay. In contrast, examples less integral to an argument may serve to "bring light to" an idea as extra support. For instance, a writer who assumes his audience agrees with his analysis of the weather of a city, might use an illustration simply to reinforce and enliven: *Consider the great snowstorm of 1993....*

Quality and Reliability

Statistics can provide good supportive information and are an important type of example to use to develop an idea authoritatively. However, as is true of all examples, statistics should be selected carefully: they should be accurate and <u>they should be objectively presented</u>. Which of the following statements is more impressive? Why?

1) According to a study of almost 22,000 children, conducted by Dietz and Gortmaker (a sociologist at the Harvard University School of Public Health) and published in the *American Journal of Diseases of Children* (May 1987), since the 1960s <u>obesity</u> [being fat] has increased by 54 percent among American children age 6 to 11 years old and by 39 percent among children age 12 to 17.

2) American children are getting fatter every year.

3) Unlike Asian children who tend to have healthy diets of vegetables and seafood and avoid heavy beef, American children, according to a survey conducted by The Vegetarian Society of America, are damaging their hearts, clogging their arteries and moving toward early deaths because of their parents' love of animal flesh and animal fat.

Clearly, statistics add power to a statement. However, it is very important to make clear the source of those statistics. Don't say *reports show* or *statistics prove*; instead, provide specific documentation for your statistics: where they came from and who put them together. An almanac, a national poll, a well-known research organization, government bureaus and surveys, encyclopedias, and research funded by nonprofit foundations should be reliable; however, information about a company from that company or from individuals or groups with economic interests or a political or social agenda should not be trusted. Always ask yourself whether your source is reliable or whether it has a bias or prejudice that affects its statistics.

•Exercise 12.7: Function

Look back at Exercise 12.6 on page 248. Do the examples in the exercise paragraphs provide concrete evidence of the central idea or do they simply expand for the sake of interest? Explain.

- EXERCISE 12.8: JUDGING STATISTICS AND GENERATING SUPPORT

    A. Circle the statistics in the following paragraphs. Where the information is available, underline where the statistics come from. What overall effect do the statistics produce? Which paragraphs seem more trustworthy? Why?

    1. According to the Independent Insurance Agents of America, the 1906 San Francisco earthquake and fire cost $5.8 billion in current dollars. Now California state officials estimate that the 1989 San Francisco earthquake, when the totals are finally in, will prove to have been the most expensive natural disaster in U.S. history. As of New Year's 1990 it had already cost over 5.5 billion dollars in damage claims. The American Red Cross says that, along 75 miles of the San Andreas Fault, at least 729 homes and apartment buildings were destroyed and 4,950 others damaged. The State Office of Emergency Services (OES) reported 6,568 people displaced as of October 22, 1989, 4,500 in Santa Cruz County. Officials confirm well over sixty deaths where I-88 collapsed, and at least 21 people killed elsewhere in Northern California. The state OES reports that 3,011 people were injured in eight counties of Northern California.

    2. Reports indicate that more and more students are choosing smaller, easier, more intimate junior colleges as places to start their college educations, rather than larger, harder, more anonymous state universities. These very useful reports make it clear that the impersonal nature of the oversized state schools are going to make them non-competitive in the future.

    3. By 2020, the number of U.S. residents who are Hispanic or nonwhite will have more than doubled, to nearly 115 million, while the white population will not have increased at all, reports William A. Henry, author of *Beyond the Melting Pot*. Henry notes that one American in every four already identifies himself or herself as Hispanic or nonwhite. Henry, building on Census statistics, asserts that by 2056 the "average" U.S. resident will trace his or her descent to Africa, Asia, the Hispanic world, the Pacific Islands, Arabia— "almost anywhere but white Europe." The continuation of current immigration trends and current birth rates will mean that, by the year 2100, the Hispanic population will have further increased an estimated 21%, the Asian population about 22%, blacks almost 12%, and whites a little more than 2%.

    4. It has been estimated that the human population of 6000 B.C was about five million people, taking perhaps one million years to get there from two and a half million…. The doubling time at present, however, seems to be about 37 years. If growth continued at this rate for about 900 years, there would be some 60,000,000,000,000,000 people on the face of the earth. Sixty million billion people! This is about 100 persons for each square yard of the Earth's surface, land and sea….

        —Paul Ehrlich's essay "Too Many People," from *Population Bomb*

    5. Last year the world's population passed 4 billion. Barring a holocaust brought on by man or nature, the world's population right now is the smallest it will ever be again. How did it reach 4 billion? For the first 99% of man's existence, surprisingly slowly. For the last 1% of history, in a great rush. By 1750 the total had reached only about 800 million. Then, as the Industrial Revolution gathered momentum, population growth began rapidly to accelerate. By 1900 it had doubled to 1.6 billion; by 1964 it had doubled again to 3.2 billion; and by the end of the century it is projected to double again to about 6.3 billion. Given today's level of complacency in some quarters and discouragement in others, the likely scenario is for a world stabilized at about 11 billion.

        —Robert McNamara's essay "How to Defuse the Population Bomb" from *Time* Magazine

B. List the kind of examples or statistics (not the actual numbers or examples) that could be used to support five of the following assertions. Then, write a paragraph based on one of your lists.

> *Example:* Assertion: *Cars are necessary for life in urban America*: a) the number of communities not served by public transportation, b) samples of limited routes and schedules of various forms of public transportation, c) average number of miles workers must travel to work.

1. A university recreation center is important for student health.
2. Cars are harmful to the individual and to society.
3. Television teaches us a lot about a culture.
4. Television provides an unreal view of a culture.
5. Technology makes our daily life better.
6. Technology threatens our future.
7. Being cooperative makes for good business.
8. Being competitive makes for good business.
9. The library is an important part of any university.
10. Intensive English programs are a bargain for the language student in a hurry.

Unifying through Transitions

Some key expressions for introducing an example are *for example, for instance, to illustrate, to clarify*, or *Take the case of*. However, words for adding information also introduce examples: *moreover, furthermore, also, in addition, too, another*. You might list examples: *first, second, next, then, the third, further, finally*. You might also use such internal constructions as *such as* or *like*. If the examples are of results or are contrasted or compared with each other, then transitions of cause/effect or comparison/contrast might also be appropriate. If they are hypothetical examples, they might begin with *If, Suppose*, or *Let us suppose*.

- **EXERCISE 12.9: TRANSITIONS AND CONNECTIVES**

  The following sentences are out of order. Look for the transition words for clues about how to rearrange them to make a coherent paragraph. What logical pattern does each writer use to organize the information? Notice the importance of statistics and specific details in the narrations.

  > *Example:* 1) Still another function is as a quiet place to study and think, like a study hall. 2) First of all, their main function is to provide resource materials for students: books, journals, magazines, encyclopedias, and other reference guides, bibliographies, and indices. 3) Finally, it is also a place where students can read recent newspapers and magazines to pass their leisure time enjoyably and profitably and to practice reading a foreign language. 4) Libraries serve a number of functions. 5) However, they also provide professional librarians who stimulate student thought about topics and research possibilities, guide their research, and suggest possible sources beyond what the student has considered. <u>Answer</u>: 4, 2, 5, 1, 3 = a list of functions from most important to least important.

A. 1) Over this rich two-way road traveled the city's first public transit, a horse-drawn omnibus known as the Yellow Line. 2) The winter of 1849, which saw 50 inches of rain, found mules, miners, and respectable citizens struggling up to their necks in mud, and drunks drowning in it. 3) It followed a 3-1/2 mile path from the Post Office at Clay and Kearny Streets, along Kearny to Mission, ending at Mission Dolores. 4) Within six months of the discovery of gold at Sutter's Mill in 1848, San Francisco's population had grown from 2,500 to 25,000, and going back and forth between town and Mill had become a problem. 5) Others were quick to follow this lead, and by 1857, four omnibus lines traveled the city's plank roads and competition had forced the fare down to a dime. 6) The fare was fifty cents on weekdays, and a whole dollar on Sundays. 7) Barrels, parts of ships, and wooden crates were used to make roadways passable. 8) Then some clever person employed the redwood plank, and the first official plank road was born.

B. 1) The underwear is very lacy, very sexy, and very expensive. 2) "Farouche," an exotic fragrance by Nina Ricci of Paris, is even more expensive. 3) About forty percent of the ads are for liquors. 4) *Cosmopolitan* takes it for granted that its readers have money and are willing to use it to make themselves more attractive and sensual; it also assumes that they are impressed by the exotic and the European. 5) The remaining ads feature cigarettes or underwear. 6) The cosmetics are American-made by Revlon, Coty, or Max Factor, but the perfumes are European, most of them made and bottled in Paris. 7) As a consequence, *Cosmopolitan*s ads feature expensive items designed to make their readers stylish, beautiful, and cultured. 8) Dana Perfumes advertise Tabu and 20 Carats with a note saying, "only $35 for each sensuous ounce." 9) These drinks are imported—Cheri Suisse from Switzerland, Canadian Club Whisky, Kijafa from Denmark—and the persons advertising them are beautiful blondes and big handsome men—images of what the readers would like to be or would like to possess. 10) For example, over fifty percent of all the ads in the magazine deal with cosmetics and perfumes. 11) The cigarette ads are either very "macho" (Winston, Marlboro) or very feminine (Eve, Virginia Slims). 12) In sum, the quality and expense of the products advertised in *Cosmopolitan* suggest the values and the dreams of that magazine's audience.

Models to Learn From

Model #1: In their essay on "Teaching Language to an Ape" from *Scientific American*, Ann and David Premack use a series of supportive examples to argue that man's prejudice in favor of his own species makes him exaggerate the human child's understanding of language and causes him to be extremely skeptical of the experimentally demonstrated language abilities of the chimpanzee. They hope that their findings will make readers rethink such prejudices and come to understand that members of other species have similar abilities, particularly language abilities; the Premacks' ultimate goal is to encourage new attempts to teach suitable languages to animals other than man.

Obviously, most readers would not share this goal and would perhaps feel threatened with the idea of animals as their linguistic equals, so the researchers face the problem of convincing their audience that language is not what sets man apart from lower animals. In order to argue their case the Premacks give specific examples of chimpanzees who have demonstrated language abilities. Their first paragraph begins with a series of successful experiments over a forty-year period. This list of examples is organized chronologically, but its strength comes from its citation of four examples of chimpanzees successfully adapting to some type of language use.

Chimpanzee learning alphabet

Over the past 40 years several efforts have been made to teach a chimpanzee human language. In the early 1930s Winthrop and Luella Kellogg raised a female chimpanzee named Gua along with their infant son; at the age of 16 months Gua could understand about 100 words but she never did try to speak them. In the 1940s Keith and Cathy Hayes raised a chimpanzee named Vicki in their home; she learned a large number of words and with some difficulty could mouth the words "mama", "papa" and "cup." More recently Allen and Beatrice Gardner have taught their chimpanzee Washoe to communicate in the American Sign Language with her fingers and hands. Since 1966 in our laboratory at the University of California at Santa Barbara we have been teaching Sarah to read and write with variously shaped colored pieces of plastic, each representing a word; Sarah has a vocabulary of about 130 terms that she uses with a reliability of between 75 and 80 percent…

Topic Sentence

first example

second example

third example

fourth and most important example

Although their main method of development is by example, the Premacks organize their examples in a time sequence: from early experiments to more recent ones. Furthermore, the first three examples are based on the experiences of others while the fourth example draws directly on the writers' own personal experience. This is an effective pattern of evidence: authoritative support from others to make more believable the support based on personal experience. The two together make for an effective discussion. Notice too that there is a progression of success as well, with each experiment going a step further than the one before it. At the same time there is an attempt to be very precise: *a vocabulary of about 130 terms, a reliability of between 75 and 80 percent.*

Having first demonstrated their ideas about chimpanzee language capacities through studies done by others, the Premacks focus their attention on their personal study of Sarah. They describe in detail the natural chimpanzee communication system and the experiment they are most familiar with: teaching the chimpanzee Sarah to communicate with a language system constructed by human beings. They write that:

…The hint that she [Sarah] was able to understand words in the absence of their external referents came early in her language training. When she was given "name of" to learn new nouns, she was able to use "color of" to learn the names of new colors. Eventually she was taught to correctly follow complicated written instructions: "Sarah insert the apple (in the) pail (and the) banana (in the) dish." To correctly interpret the compound sentence Sarah had to understand the notion of constituent structure: the hierarchical organization of a sentence, that "apple" and "pail" go together but not "pail" and "banana," even though the terms appear side by side. Moreover, she must understand that the verb "insert" is at a higher level of organization and refers to both "apple" and "banana." Finally, Sarah must understand that she, as the head or the noun, must carry out all the actions. If Sarah were capable of only linking words in a simple chain, she would never be able to interpret the compound sentence with its deletions. The fact is that she interprets them correctly. If a child were to carry out the instructions in the same way, we would not hesitate to say that he recognized the various levels of sentence organization....

The Premack's description of Sarah's learning process is their key example, the evidence that justifies their conclusions (the underlined hypothetical statements).

The approach used by the Premacks illustrates good use of examples. An effective essay built by examples consists of generalizations that establish the key points of an argument and then specific examples to prove each generalization.

Model #2: Sometimes an argument will depend on one main, extended example to make its case. While an earlier essay in this chapter took a series of proverbs and categorized them for discussion, the next takes only one proverb and explains it in detail with examples. In this essay, the proverb is not the example. Instead, the example of a friend's mistake and the danger that mistake brought helps explain the proverb.

> "A little knowledge is a dangerous thing" is a common saying that affects the daily lives of most people. It warns people that thinking they know a lot more than they do can prove dangerous, as it did to a friend of mine.

This friend of mine used to be very fond of reading medical books and thought he knew more than real doctors themselves. He always believed that if he were sick, he could look his illness up in some medical book, prescribe some medicine, and treat himself. One time when ill and feverish, he ignored friends who advised him to send for a doctor, replying, "Nonsense, doctors are of no use; I know as much as they do, and I can treat my problem by myself." After two days of taking his self-prescribed medicines, his condition worsened and he nearly died. Only a friend carrying him to the nearby hospital where doctors operated immediately saved his life. After the operation, he felt better and gradually recuperated. That experience made him realize that a little knowledge was not enough to judge and treat his own medical problems. He became "a sadder, wiser man." His experience and his hard-learned lesson is what this proverb means.

A little knowledge is a dangerous thing, because it always causes us to be conceited. When we begin to study a certain subject, we always think that it's easier to learn than it is, and as we begin to know a little more about it than others who know nothing at all about it, we become too self-satisfied and think we know more than we do. Thus, we may stop studying, thinking we are already prepared to practice our field. However, a really learned person is humble about his knowledge, because he realizes that the more he knows, the more he has to learn.

Notice that the first body paragraph clearly explains the incident/example that helps illustrate the proverb and that the second body paragraph discusses that incident to make sure the reader understands exactly what it reveals about the proverb.

Final Checklist

☐ Time and space determine the number of main points possible to develop with examples. Have you limited your topic? Is it of manageable scope?

☐ Have you done more than simply list examples? Have you integrated them into your argument or discussion by providing unifying categories?

☐ Are your examples relevant? Do they clearly support your main points?

☐ Have you eliminated digressions but included all essentials?

☐ Have you provided sufficient examples to prove your point? Are these examples representative and the best for your purpose?

Passages for Discussion and Analysis

When in Rome Do as the Romans Do

1. GOOD TIME MANNERS

Attitudes toward time differ from country to country and culture to culture. Latin Americans, for example, are customarily later than the times announced or scheduled for appointments and parties, though how late varies with the occasion and the particular country. In contrast, Germans and Swedes and Americans from the northern states expect people to arrive precisely on time and will sometimes stand outside a door staring at their watch until the exact moment to knock or ring the bell. Consequently, anyone who hopes to do business abroad or simply demonstrate good manners while traveling around the globe needs to learn new codes of etiquette to fit in with local protocol. What is polite in Rome is rude in Helsinki and what is looked on with favor in Miami, Florida will be unsatisfactory in Boise, Idaho. Learning local time protocol will not only flatter your hosts and make your visits more pleasant, but will also make you a good ambassador abroad; instead of causing embarrassment, misunderstanding, and offense, you will instead demonstrate your respect for your host culture and your own international aptitude.

Although you yourself must learn what is polite in terms of time in any given place, it helps to have some general guidelines for wide areas. In the main, northern areas are more precise about time and southern areas less. A dinner invitation for seven o'clock in Chicago, which has a strong northern European influence, means that you must arrive at or before that time, while a dinner invitation for seven in New Orleans, which has a strong Italian, Spanish, and French influence, means you should come sometime between 7:15 P.M. and 8 o'clock. In Sweden, a 7 P.M. invitation means a 7 P.M. arrival time, while in Mexico a 7 P.M. invitation means not before 7:30 P.M. or 8 P.M. and a 7 P.M. party invitation might mean "Come around 10 or 11 P.M." Americans who are invited to a Mexican party scheduled for 7 P.M. and who arrive at 8 P.M., might find themselves the first guests of the evening. Standard Bombay expected arrival time is also 15 or 30 minutes later than the time given, but rarely as late as the Mexican expected arrival time. In Arab countries, in contrast, a dinner invitation might be incredibly flexible; in fact, in some rural areas it might mean, "show up sometime on the invited day" if it is for a celebration. In other words, you should find out what the local custom of time and invitation involves before you set out for dinner or a party.

2. To Tip or Not to Tip

All too often when traveling abroad we mistakenly assume that the patterns of our culture are acceptable in other cultures. For example, the question of a tip seems minor, but attitudes toward tipping differ greatly from country to country and sometimes from region to region. The Japanese, for example, disapprove of tips and of any overt passing of money from hand to hand. Japanese porters and taxi-drivers charge for their services, but do not expect and are not given an additional tip. Restaurants build an automatic ten percent service charge into the bill and waiters and waitresses expect no more; nor do chambermaids or hotel service personnel unless they are asked to perform services above and beyond their normal duties. In such a case, the tip is wrapped up in paper or cloth and passed unobtrusively. In Egypt and Morocco, in contrast, every minor service requires a tip because tips are the main or even the only source of income for many. In Latin America most urban areas require restaurant and service tips but many rural areas do not. In the United States, a 5 percent tip might be given for normal service in a small town Texas restaurant and a 10 percent tip for good service, but such a tip would be insulting in San Francisco or New York, where 15 percent is the norm and 20 percent or more the reward for good service.

3. Customary Greetings

Customary greetings differ from country to country. In Japan, the main greeting is a bow, though sometimes a handshake is acceptable these days, particularly between businessmen. In Germany and Sweden, in turn, a handshake says hello or goodbye (before, not after, you put on your coat) and the best type of dinner gifts are flowers—with the wrapping removed—or a box of chocolates. Greetings in the United States differ by region, with a handshake common between business people, friends and family in the north, but a hug between relatives and friends in the south.

In Mexico, the handshake is reserved for business associates and for distant acquaintances but an *abrazo* or light hug is the greeting of choice with friends and relatives, while a hug and a kiss is reserved for longstanding friends. In India, most greeters bring the palms of their hands together in front of them; men may shake hands but kiss or hug only very close friends of the same sex. The Cambodian greeting is also the palms of the hands brought together in front, with a slight bow or nod. Men might shake hands, but they might also hold hands, and kiss and hug family and friends of both sexes. In other words, it is best to watch what others do before blundering with a greeting customary in your culture but not in the culture you are visiting.

•• Questions for Discussion

1. What is the attitude toward time in your culture? What is considered polite, what rude, for attending a business conference? a dinner? a party?

2. How do you greet people in your culture? Strangers? Business partners? Acquaintances? Close friends? Family?

3. What is the attitude toward dress in your culture? What kind of clothing is proper for a dinner invitation? for a party? for attendance in a public place: a cafe? a restaurant? a museum? the classroom? a place of worship?

4. What about gifts? Does one take a gift? Under what circumstances? What kind of a gift? If someone admires something in your culture, what is a polite response?

5. When are meals served? How large are they? How frequent?

6. What is the attitude toward money? Who pays at a restaurant? How is money for extra expenses paid? Tips? How paid? How much?

7. What about talking in public? How loud? To whom?

8. What about smoking in restaurants and public places? On the street?

9. Is drinking allowed in public? Where is it allowed/prohibited?

•• Writing Assignment

Choose one of the topics raised in the above questions to develop into an essay using examples and illustrative details.

Trends in Transportation

Americans are traveling more than ever. From 1969 to 1990, the U.S. resident non-institutionalized population grew by 23 percent. During this same period, the number of *person trips*[1] grew by 74 percent and *person miles of travel,*[2] by 65 percent.

Traveling in private vehicles is the preferred mode of travel. In 1990, 86 percent of person trips and 88 percent of person miles traveled were in private vehicles....

[As one result of this trend] motor vehicle crashes are the leading cause of death among Americans under 35 years old. More crashes occur in urban than rural areas, but more motor vehicle deaths occur on rural than on urban roads. In 1990, the death rate was highest among males 16 to 24 years old and 80 years and older. Over half (54 percent) of deaths involved occupants of passenger cars, 19 percent involved pickups, vans, and utility vehicles, 15 percent were pedestrians, and 7 percent were motorcyclists.

Since 1980, vehicular deaths have trended downward except for those involving occupants of pickups, vans, and utility vehicles. Also, between 1975 and 1988, the fatality rate (number of automobile occupants killed per 100,000 automobiles registered) decreased from about 28 to about 21; the occupant death rate was higher (30 deaths per 100,000 registered vehicles 1 to 3 years old in 1990) in small pickup trucks and small utility vehicles than in other types of passenger vehicles. Improvements in automobile and roadway design, the reduction in the proportion of young drivers on the road (due to changing age distribution of the population), increased use of safety belts, and a focus on the issue of drunk driving, all contributed to this decrease.

Motor vehicle deaths, 1980 and 1990		
Victim	1980	1990
Occupants		
Passenger cars	27,390	24,243
Pickups, vans, utility vehicles	7,578	8,452
Tractor trailers	884	506
Other heavy trucks	354	180
Motorcyclists	4,961	3,120
Bicyclists	965	850
Pedestrians	8,070	6,468
Other	889	710

Source: Insurance Institute for Highway Safety, 1991, Facts, 1991 Edition

[1] A person trip is a trip by one or more persons in any mode of transportation. Each person makes one person trip; four persons traveling together in one auto make four person trips.

[2] Each time one person travels 1 mile, one person mile of travel results. Four persons traveling 5 miles in one vehicle account for 20 person miles of travel.

Sixty-seven percent of passenger vehicle (cars, pickups, vans, utility vehicles) fatalities in 1990 were drivers. More than half (55 percent) of passenger vehicle occupant deaths occurred on Friday, Saturday, or Sunday, and 54 percent occurred in crashes between 6 P.M. and 6 A.M.

In 1990, the death rate in the smallest passenger cars (wheelbase less than 95 inches) was more than 4 times that in the largest cars (wheelbase greater than 114 inches). Efforts to increase fuel economy standards have renewed the debate concerning the relationship between auto size and safety.

Although downsizing [making smaller] could refer to reductions in length and width as well as weight, fuel efficiency is most closely related to weight, according to a study conducted by the General Accounting Office. Crashworthiness [safety level in an accident] is more directly related to exterior size—wheelbase and crush space—and safety features than it is to weight.

Heavier cars are more "aggressive"; that is, they hit a fixed object or another vehicle with more force than would a lighter one. Median weight of passenger cars in the United States decreased by about 28 percent (1,100 pounds) between 1975 and 1988. During this period, the range of automobile weights decreased significantly: the difference in weights of cars in the 95th and 5th percentiles was over 3,000 pounds in 1975 and under 2,000 pounds in 1988. Thus, the "aggressivity" factor has declined since 1975.

A comparison of 1- and 2-year-old cars on the road in 1976–78 and 1986–88 shows that 66 percent of all cars weighed 3,000 pounds or less in 1986–88, compared with only 28 percent in 1976–78. For cars weighing 3,000 pounds or less, the fatality rate decreased from about 35 to about 24.

The General Accounting Office study concluded that automobile downsizing has two offsetting effects: crashworthiness is reduced, but so is "aggressivity." An increase in the proportion of lighter cars would lead to a decrease in occupant fatalities in two-car accidents; in collisions involving automobiles with trucks and heavier vehicles, however, occupant fatalities would increase. Between 1976–78 and 1986–88, the death rate for two-car collisions declined 22 percent, whereas the death rate for all other multivehicle accidents increased about 11 percent....

Sources: American Automobile Association, Environmental Protection Agency, Insurance Institute for Highway Safety, 1990 Nationwide Personal Transportation Study, U.S. Department of Transportation, Office of Technology Assessment, U.S. Department of Energy, 1990 Highway Statistics, National Highway Traffic Safety Administration.

—Joan C. Courtless (Family Economist), *Family Economics Review,* 1992, Vol. 5 No. 2, U.S. Government publication

• Questions to Consider

1. What is the effect of using so many statistics?
2. How reliable are the statistics? How do you know?
3. What conclusions can you draw from this data?
4. Are statistics important for arguing persuasively? Why?
5. What safety advice could you give on the basis of these statistics?
6. How do the examples in this essay differ from the examples in the first Passage for Discussion?

•• Writing Assignment

As a government document, the above selection reports statistics but draws few conclusions on the basis of them. In the main, readers are expected to interpret such information for themselves. However, such documents (available in the government documents section of most college libraries) are good sources of information for developing an argument. On the basis of the above reading, write a well-developed paragraph which explains the relationship between automobile safety and automobile size/weight. What choices face the buyer of a car who is weighing safety concerns and size/weight? Use statistics from Joan Courtless' report to give your paragraph strength and credibility. Be sure to credit your source with internal citations. See Chapter 19 for how to do so.

•• Writing Assignments

A. Expand the following lists into paragraphs by adding explanations that clarify the examples. Add your own examples to the lists if you wish.

1. <u>Topic Sentence</u>: One confusing phenomenon in English is that the language includes a lot of two-word paradoxes, words that seem to contradict each other when put together.

   Examples: pretty ugly
   working vacation
   loose tights
   tight slacks
   freezer burn
   original copy

   Pattern for body development: name term, explain seeming contradiction, give real meaning (you may need a native speaker "source" to explain the exact connotation) as in the following:

   Example of body development: For instance, the expression "old boy" seems like a contradictory statement because "old" is associated with many years and "boy" with few years. However, when used together, "old" changes meaning and implies respect or affection, so that the term "old boy" really means "someone the speaker feels affection for." A similar term, "old lady," might literally mean a woman who is old, or, in slang, it might mean someone's girlfriend or wife, that is, a lady he has affection for.

2. <u>Topic Sentence</u>: American car manufacturers name their cars after animals in order to associate them with animal characteristics like speed or strength or agility.

   Examples of animal/car names:
   Mustang
   Pinto
   Maverick
   Cougar
   Bobcat

   Look up these animal/car names in a good English dictionary! Is this true of car-naming practices in other cultures?

B. Here are some examples of how people answer the telephone in different languages and cultures. Examine the list, then develop a topic idea and write a paragraph, using the following as examples.

Examples of telephone greetings:
Greece: "Come in"
Russia: "I am listening"
Spain/ Costa Rica: "Tell me"
Cuba: "Speak"
Mexico: "Well?" or "Command!"
Argentina: "Hello!" or "yes"
India: "Greetings"
Iran: "Yes"
Germany: "Hello, who is speaking?"
Italy: "Ready, with whom am I speaking?"
Japan: "Excuse, excuse"

You can add to this information by asking Americans and people of other nationalities how they answer the phone.

C. Combine the following information into an effective paragraph.

Focus: multimessage gestures, which have totally distinct meanings depending on time and place.

Gesture: raised hand with thumb and forefinger forming a circle.

In U.S. and England = always "OK" (from idea of perfect, exactly right, precise)

In Europe= sometimes imitates U.S. OK

but

In France, with downturned mouth = worthless (from circle=zero=nothing)

In Malta = male homosexual

In Sardinia and Greece = obscene comment or insult to male or female, usually a sexual proposition

In Japan = money (circle imitates shape of coins): usually hand is sideways instead of up

D. People in different cultures use different cultural signals (signs or cues) to communicate without words. For example, there are set signals for use in romance, ways to let members of the opposite sex know you are interested or not interested in them. These signals may be through eye contact, facial expressions, gestures, movements, distancing, tone, and so forth. Discuss such cultural signals with your teacher and classmates. Look at the examples in the Passages for Discussion and Analysis on cultural attitudes about time to see how effective specific examples can be. Think about the examples in the exercise above. Then write your own essay about cultural signals.

Step #1: List examples of signals used in your culture. They could be about movement/gestures, distance/space, timing, eye contact, touching—any form of cultural communication signal. Find at least one example for each category, since you will need a minimum of three examples to write about and a few extra makes writing easier.

Step #2: Once you have a list, explain each example completely.

Step #3: Then, write an introduction and conclusion. The introduction might be only a few sentences introducing which kinds of signals you will talk about. It should provide categories or divisions for organization. The conclusion should decide whether the signals you talk about would be understood by people outside your culture (you can ask class members to find out).

•• Applications

Choose one:

A. You have been asked by a university in your home country to report on the <u>campus atmosphere</u> at the school you are presently attending. Your report will be published in a campus periodical, so it should be formal. Choose a likely area (the cafeteria, the library, the student center, the athletic center, the computer lab) and describe it: the people, their activities, anything else significant that you see. Be specific. You will need to set up content categories (clothing, greetings, good-byes, etc; see below), and then cite specific examples and details within each category.

Categories and classification (# 1)

Sex _____ Age _____(estimated)   General appearance
Race/Ethnic Background _____   Height _____
                                                 Weight _____
Clothing: Body type _____
    Male   Female   Complexion _____

_____   _____   Articles carried:
_____   _____
_____   _____
_____   _____

Hair Styles: Jewelry/ornaments
    Male   Female

_____   _____
_____   _____
_____   _____

General Behavior: _____

Noise Levels: _____

Social Contacts: _____

B. You have been hired as a buyer for a chain of clothing stores, one that specializes in students' clothes. They want a report on what students are <u>wearing this year</u>. Report to them, being as specific as possible. Again, you will need to set up content categories (see below) and then cite specific examples and details within each category.

Clothing categories and classifications (# 2)

	Male	Female
Type (pants, dresses etc.)		
Style		
Color		
Quality		
Price Range		
Accessories		
Material		
Formal/ Informal		

Method: In both A and B your method should be scientific and objective; describe from observation, not from memory. Your report should make clear what methodology you used. For example, *I have based the following description on observations made while stationed in front of the student center on Sept. 24, for a period of thirty minutes.* Or *Students who catch the shuttle bus in front of the Law School on a typical late Monday afternoon in September....* Note that samples should be <u>representative</u> (a typical group which corresponds to the general population) or <u>random</u> (every tenth person who passes). If the basketball team walked by, for example, they would not be representative of the student population in height.

Chapter 13: DEFINING

A definition is the enclosing of a wilderness of ideas within a wall of words. —
Samuel Butler

Key Steps in Defining
>   Deciding Purpose and Scope
>   Distinguishing between Denotation and Connotation
>   Exploring Multiple Approaches to Definitions
>   Avoiding Common Pitfalls

Models to Learn From

Final Checklist

Passages for Discussion and Analysis

Writing Assignments

Application

Key Steps in Defining

As any language learner knows, definitions are vital to survival in a new language, and most newcomers to a language are lost without their language-to-language dictionary close by. Although these books usually only provide synonyms in the native language, not true definitions, they help learners understand and communicate at the initial stage of language learning. However, even after learning a language well, students find that definitions must remain an important part of their thinking and of their writing.

As you become more fluent in a language, you learn how inadequate a simple "definition-by-synonym" approach can be, for there are words and concepts that simply don't translate very well (or at all!) from one language to another. Besides, there are few exact synonyms even within a given language, for human nature resists unnecessary duplication, and people give slightly different meanings to words that the beginning student might think are exact equivalents. English is particularly rich in apparent synonyms because of its Latin, French, and Old English vocabulary.

Many U.S. college examinations depend on the student providing thorough definitions to selected vocabulary from the readings, vocabulary crucial to understanding the subject matter, with an exam grade depending on the thoroughness and accuracy of the definition. For example, an examination in biology might involve definitions of microscopic life forms to distinguish between "flora" and "fauna".

Definitions are also an important part of developing an idea or an argument and will prove necessary, not only in freshman English, but in essays and papers written in all areas of college studies. How you define a word or idea determines what you will discuss or argue about, whether it is "life" in an abortion debate or "human rights" in a political discussion.

Before writers can discuss ideas, they must first establish what words will mean and what specialized definitions they will employ. Otherwise, readers unfamiliar with the terminology used throughout an essay will be confused and lost. The major reason for using definitions in most papers is to make sure your readers understand your terminology. A definition clarifies meaning. However, definition can also be an important form of argumentation. That is, you can use different forms of definition to develop an argument and to persuade your audience. This argumentative form of definition can use all the other methods of development: examples, description, process, comparison, contrast, causes, effects, and so forth.

Deciding Purpose and Scope

A definition can be as long or short as necessary. In some cases, a single synonym or example will suffice to define. In other cases, a full sentence may be necessary. In still other situations, a controversial definition may require a full-length essay to clarify, describe, and clearly define. Argumentative definitions, by their very nature, require greater scope than definitions written simply to make meanings clear.

Distinguishing between Denotation and Connotation

A good definition distinguishes between the denotation of words, the literal, obvious, and explic-

it meaning, and their connotations, their emotional associations. The denotation could be called the simple or factual or dictionary meaning of a word. The denotation of the word *home*, for example, is *the place where someone lives, his residence, his house*. Foreign language dictionaries and inexpensive English-to-English dictionaries often give only denotation; that is, a synonym or brief explanation (*casa* = home; house; domicile; the place where someone lives). However, the larger English-to-English dictionaries will add some reference to connotation, defining home not only as *a family's place of residence (domicile or house or habitat)* or *one's place of origin* but also as *the social unit formed by a family living together, a place of rest and refuge, the abiding place of one's affections,* or *the location of our deepest feelings and emotions.*

A larger dictionary provides a more complete definition of the word, with both the denotative or factual meaning and the connotative or emotional meaning. A word like *home*, then, means much more than *the place where someone lives,* it implies *the place where a person feels most comfortable and safe, where beloved friends and relatives are, where he or she can relax, let down his or her hair, and be himself or herself.* In fact, when you look carefully at the word *home,* you begin to realize the idea of a literal, geographical place, a particular location, a "house", is not even necessary for the full meaning—what someone really means by "home" would take a long time to describe properly. The implications and associations are clearer in the compound word *homesick*: missing family, siblings, friends, lovers, mother's home cooking, a native language, a climate, a certain way of life, a certain way of doing things—all of the characteristics which make a country, a city, and a neighborhood uniquely *home.*

- ## EXERCISE 13.1: DENOTATION VS. CONNOTATION

    A. Find the denotations and connotations of the following words in a large English language dictionary. How do they differ?

    Example:

    home —

    denotation: <u>a dwelling, a house, a building in which to live</u>

    connotation: <u>wherever a person's family is, the center of emotional family ties (a person, a building, a region, a way of life, a style of food or music, a life style), safety, security, acceptance</u>

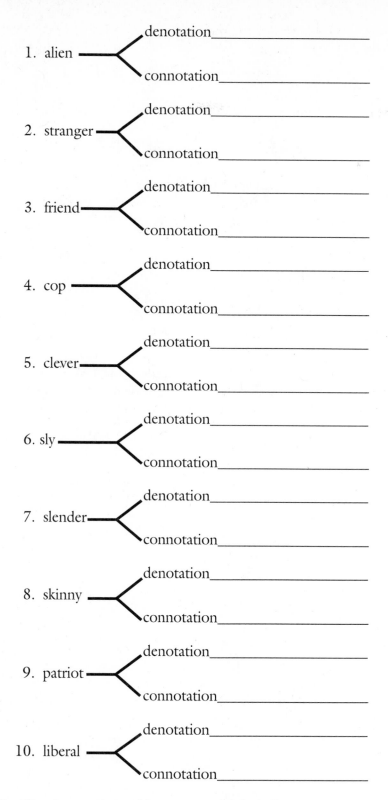

1. alien — denotation_____
   connotation_____

2. stranger — denotation_____
   connotation_____

3. friend — denotation_____
   connotation_____

4. cop — denotation_____
   connotation_____

5. clever — denotation_____
   connotation_____

6. sly — denotation_____
   connotation_____

7. slender — denotation_____
   connotation_____

8. skinny — denotation_____
   connotation_____

9. patriot — denotation_____
   connotation_____

10. liberal — denotation_____
    connotation_____

B. Use the word *scorching* as a participle/adjective in a sentence about the weather (the sentence should make clear what the word means). Then write another sentence using some form of the word *scorch* in a non-weather meaning (it is often used as a verb in connection with food, ironing clothes, and even language). What would you mean if you said *Her words were scorching?*

C. Write down nouns or adjectives for the movement of air, in order, from very great movement to very little or no movement.

hurricane
cyclone
tornado

/_____/_____/_____/_____/_____/_____/

very little   very great

D. In English, changing the preposition adjoining a verb or changing the context can change denotation and connotation. For example, the verb *to make* can mean *to create, construct, form or shape,* as in the sentences, *I made a birdhouse,* or *I made a bomb.* It can mean *to give a new form or use to,* as in *I made a doghouse out of that old applebox.* It can mean *to earn,* as in "to make money": *How much did you make last week?* Sometimes it means *to prepare or start,* as in "to make a fire" or "to make plans."; other times it means *to force or compel,* as in *The teacher made us redo the homework exercise* or *I made the mechanic lower his bill.* It might mean *to cause to become,* as in *He claims his mother made him what he is today* or *The Olympic champion says that a good diet and hard work are what have made her so successful.* In a crime film, a criminal will *mak*e (or recognize) an undercover policeman. In other words, one verb might have multiple possible meanings that change with preposition and context.

Choose another common verb whose usage has puzzled you (*look, check, get, put*) and write a paragraph explaining the multiple possibilities. (You will need a large dictionary!) What will your topic statement be? Use the above explanation as a model to imitate.

E. Explain the difference between the following expressions. You might have to ask a native English speaker for help.
1. old man/senior citizen/golden ager/dinosaur
2. lawyer/shyster/ambulance chaser/hired gun
3. conscientious objector/draft-dodger
4. cried/wept/bawled/sobbed/wailed
5. slim/slender/thin/lean/skinny/emaciated
6. mist/fog/rain
7. raw/damp/humid
8. statesman/politician/political hack
9. He's a pig/rat/dog/chicken/wolf/beast [said about people]

F. Provide a concrete description or example to illustrate the following abstract ideas.

Example: freedom = To a college student leaving home for the first time, freedom means the chance to make personal choices: to choose one's own friends, to stay up as late as one pleases, to wear clothes parents might disapprove of, to drink beer, and to listen to loud music half the night.

Notice that this definition of *freedom* limits the term to a particular perspective, gives it a more specific meaning, and then makes that meaning more specific with a series of examples.
1. alienation
2. friendship
3. trust
4. rejection
5. success
6. culture shock

Synonyms or Word Roots

Good dictionary definitions follow certain rules and procedures in order to make the definitions useful and clear. A definition may be useless if the synonym is rare or difficult, for example, defining *geoponic* as *pertaining to tillage or husbandry* is not as helpful as saying *related to farming or agriculture*. Never use synonyms or definitions which repeat the word to be defined or some form of that word. For example, saying that the word *differ* is a verb which means *are different* doesn't really explain, nor does saying a hammer is used to hammer other things or a frying pan is used *to fry* foods. These are <u>circular definitions</u>. Nonetheless, providing <u>synonyms</u> is a good way to define. In fact, it is often the easiest way to explain: "*an automobile is a car*"; "*a domestic engineer* is really just a homemaker or a housewife"; "*the heat* may be a slang word for cop or policeman". Such definitions by synonym may be very helpful, especially if the synonym is simpler or more common than the original word. Consider the following:

> auto = *car*, <u>but</u> <u>not</u> *automobile*
>
> translate = *taking words from one language and changing them into words in another language*, <u>but</u> <u>not</u> *taking words from one language and translating them into another*
>
> amateur = *a player who does not take money to play*, <u>but</u> <u>not</u> *a player with amateur status*
>
> optometrist = *an eye doctor*, <u>but</u> <u>not</u> *a doctor who practices optometry*

Do you understand why the first definition is superior to the second in each case?

Word roots may help somewhat as well. For example, the word *automobile* comes from the Latin *auto* or "self" and *mobile* or "capable of movement." In other words, the root distinguishes the automobile from vehicles like wagons, sleighs, and rickshaws which require an outside source of power: horses, oxen, human beings.

In longer definitions, a number of synonyms can be used to convey the target idea: "The <u>best college</u> for any given student is not just an <u>educational institution</u>, but also a true <u>group of teachers and learners</u>. A college (from the Latin *collegium* or "society") is <u>a school</u> of <u>shared interests</u>, a <u>community</u> with <u>common values</u> . . .".

Antonyms or Negatives

Another method of definition is through antonyms or negatives: saying what something is not. Technically, this method does not fully define because it doesn't tell us what something <u>is</u>, only what it isn't. Defining an *amateur* as *a non-professional* helps clarify the meaning, but defining a *car* as *neither a truck nor a bus* doesn't help very much. However, in a longer definition, saying what something is not might be an effective way of developing your idea. For instance, when dealing with a difficult definition like that of *good parent* (for example, at an adoption hearing), the court might begin by defining with negatives: a good parent <u>does not</u> abuse his or her children, he or she <u>does not</u> expose the youngsters to bad influences, and so on. In turn, a young person defending a less-than-perfect grade report might argue that, "A good student is not just one who makes all As; nor is it one who always gives the answer the teacher wants to hear." Gwynne Dyer in *War* introduces his topic with an enumeration of negatives:

> Wars are not an interminable series of historical accidents, nor the product of the machinations of evil men, nor yet the result of some simple, single cause like capitalism or overpopulation. Neither is warfare merely the heritage of our evolutionary past, an outlet for our "natural aggressiveness." War is a central institution in human civilization, and it has a history precisely as long as civilization.

The final sentence after Dyer's negative catalogue is a positive affirmation of what war is. This is a useful writing pattern for introductory paragraphs.

Examples

Another simple method of definition is by example. Saying *A car is a four-wheeled vehicle like a Ford Escort* might make the word clear enough for your audience. This is only useful, however, if the example is familiar enough to be recognized. When you say, "A <u>celebration</u> is a period of time during which normal life is suspended and people find means of amusing and enjoying themselves; for example, the New Orleans celebration of Mardi Gras is typical," the example of Mardi Gras as a celebration will make sense only to those who have heard about the Mardi

Gras celebration. You might go farther and say "Mardi Gras or the Brazilian Carnival in Rio de Janeiro," a second example, but again your reader might know nothing about either celebration. The problem with defining by example is that it presumes the reader shares your cultural experience and thus is familiar with the example, which must also be a true representative of the term to be defined. A further limitation of definition by example is that it is not analytical; that is, it simply shows but does not explain. As with a negative catalogue (see the war example on page 267), a series of examples is an excellent way to begin an essay.

Analysis: <u>Genus differentiation</u>

The most accurate form of definition, used by scientists, legal experts, scholars, and others concerned with the exact meanings of words, is definition by analysis. This system involves placing the word to be defined in a general category (a <u>genus</u>; the word is commonly used in biology to mean "family" or "class" or "group") and then <u>differentiating</u> it from all the other members of the general category, that is, saying what makes it special or unique. The pattern is from general to specific. To illustrate, an *auto* can be defined as belonging to the general category or <u>genus</u> of *passenger vehicle* and the differentiation can be expressed as a relative clause or a participle: *which is usually propelled by an internal combustion engine and which normally accommodates two to six passengers* or *usually propelled by an internal combustion engine and normally accommodating two to six passengers*. The second part of the definition differentiates *auto* from *bus, train, horsecart,* and so on, all also passenger vehicles. Now look back at the definition of *celebration* on page 267. Even without the example, readers should understand what the word means because of the genus and differentiation section of the definition. Can you identify which is which? The following definitions rely on a similar pattern:

> freshman = a college student (<u>genus</u>) in his first year of undergraduate study (<u>differentiation from second year, third year, etc.</u>)

> a watch = a timepiece (<u>genus</u>) designed to be worn or carried on the person (<u>differentiation from clocks</u>)

> a cannibal = a person (<u>genus</u>) who eats human flesh (<u>differentiation from all other people</u>)

wine = fermented or alcoholic (<u>differentiation</u>) grape juice (<u>genus</u>)

Note how leaving out one part can make the definition inaccurate. If you say a freshman is a college student (the genus) but leave out the <u>differentiation</u> (*in his first year of undergraduate study*), the statement is misleading because sophomores, juniors, seniors, and graduate students are also college students, but they are not freshmen. Leaving out the differentiation is like simply giving a synonym, only one more general than the term defined. Leaving out the genus, in turn, makes the "family" relationship unclear. For instance, saying a freshman is in his first year of undergraduate study and leaving it to the reader to guess *college student* makes for a weak definition.

In longer works, the genus-differentiation method often takes the form of an extended differentiation. For example, a definition of <u>physician's assistant</u> might begin with the genus, a <u>medical practitioner</u>, but then focus on differentiating the physician's assistant from nurses, on the one hand, and doctors, on the other: *Unlike nurses, physician's assistants can sometimes write prescriptions.... The assistant, however, must have her work reviewed by a doctor...* This differentiation takes the form of a <u>negative catalogue</u>, which suggests how several approaches to definition can be used at once.

Analogy

Sometimes an analogy helps clarify an argument. In debating the abortion issue, analogy might be used to support the famous Supreme Court decision that abortion is legal only up to a certain stage of fetal development. For example, the growth of a fetus might be compared with the development of other living things. A plant, for example, has a fertilized seed which grows to produce a fruit or vegetable, and at some point in the process the seed becomes recognizably different from its earlier state: it becomes a tomato, an apple, or so forth. Yet most people would not call even a growing seed a fruit or a vegetable—not until it becomes recognizably a plant with roots, stem, and leaves. In like manner, the argument might be that a fetus does not become an infant until it attains infant form, with clearly distinguishable features. Opponents would attack the analogy by pointing out differences between human

- ## EXERCISE 13.2: DIFFERENTIATION

  Complete the following definitions, adding the differentiation to the genus.

  <u>*genus*</u>   <u>*differentiation*</u>

  Example: Science is "the art of systematic oversimplification " (a remark by Karl Popper).

  1. A celebrity is a person who
  2. A penniless person is one who
  3. Cop is a slang word
  4. An employer is a person,   while an employee is one
  5. An avocado is a tropical fruit
  6. A pacifist is a person
  7. A terrorist is a person
  8. A quotation mark is a type of punctuation
  9. Capitalism is a system
  10. Socialism is a system

beings and vegetables—as a form of comparison, any analogy can be criticized for its lack of correspondence between parts.

An argumentative definition might use analogy to make a more powerful statement. Calling pornography "a disease that eats away the soul" is a much more vivid statement than calling it "any scatological or sexual reference that goes beyond the legal bounds of decency." This is because an analogy creates a picture in the mind of the reader. In this case the image makes you think of the negative effects of pornography; it suggests a moral or religious condemnation; and it carries a series of implications. A disease is contagious. A sick person must be given medicine to counter a disease, and a doctor is justified in taking drastic, even painful, action for the patient's own good. By implication then, pornography must be controlled for the good of the community, and "medicine" administered (a moral lesson, a fine, imprisonment) for the good of the "sick" user of pornography. How does the following definition use analogy to provide a counterview? *Pornography is a soothing, beneficent antidote to psychological problems caused by repressive early sexual training.*

In longer essays, analogy often serves as the "skeleton" on which a definition is built, with the writer reminding the reader of his comparison at difficult points in the discussion.

- ## EXERCISE 13.3: ANALOGY TO DEFINE

  Create an analogy to help you define a word.

  Examples: Science is the great <u>antidote</u> to the <u>poison</u> of ignorance.
  Religion is the <u>opiate</u> of the people. (Karl Marx)
  Television is <u>chewing gum</u> for the mind.

Analysis by Division into Parts or by Classification

Analysis breaks a general term up into its components; it takes things apart, naming each part in turn and carefully explaining their relationship:

A ceiling fan has three different parts, each of which has an entirely different function. The shaft allows the fan to be hung from the ceiling and serves as an axle for the fan to turn on. The motor hangs from the bottom of the shaft, and its weight serves to stabilize the entire apparatus even as it turns the blades. The blades themselves push the air either downward or upward, depending on the direction of the motor.

Notice that analysis can often overlap with function, as will be discussed on pages 271. The following definition of *physics* is based on making clear the broader categories into which this science fits.

Science first branches into the study of living things and non-living things: the life sciences and the physical sciences. Life science branches into such areas as biology, zoology, and botany. Physical science diverges into such areas as astronomy, chemistry, and physics. But physics is more than a part of the physical sciences. Physics is the most fundamental and all-inclusive of the sciences, both life and physical. Physics, essentially the study of matter and energy, is at the root of every field of science, and underlies all phenomena. Physics is the present-day equivalent of what used to be called *natural philosophy*, from which most of present-day science arose.

—Paul Hewett, *Conceptual Physics*

Analysis by parts is often found, as in the above example, in technical and scientific writing.

The most common form of conversational definition is to say what something looks like or what its key qualities are:

A true sports car is built low to the ground, with a resultant low center of gravity. It has smooth lines which lessen wind resistance or "drag," and it often is given the look, as well as the name, of a fierce bird of prey or other predatory animal.

Citing characteristics or describing appearance in this way assists classification.

Comparison–Contrast

Comparison–contrast defines by showing similarities between the term or idea defined and another term or idea, but mainly it shows what the term is not:

Wine, like grape juice, takes on the color of the grapes from which it is made and has a fruity taste which ranges from the sweet to the tart; unlike grape juice, however, wine is alcoholic, with a potency measured by the percentage of alcohol created during fermentation. Wine is, as a result, usually considered an adult drink, while grape juice is often given to very small children.

A more sophisticated example is a contrast of science and technology in order to make their differences very evident:

The distinction between science and technology is not clear to most people, who are easily convinced that all implementations of science constitute "progress." The purveyors of technology are often able to prevent or stop debate on issues having to do with encroaching technology with the statement, "You can't stop progress." But progress in science and progress in technology are entirely different.

Progress in science excludes the human factor. And this is justly so. The scientist, who seeks to comprehend the universe and know the truth with the highest degree of accuracy and certainty, cannot pay heed to his own or other people's likes or dislikes, or to popular ideas about the fitness of things. What scientists discover may shock or anger people—as did Darwin's theory of evolution. But even an unpleasant truth is more than likely to be useful; besides, we have the option of refusing to believe it! But hardly so with technology; we do not have the option of refusing to hear the sonic boom produced by a supersonic aircraft flying overhead; we do not have the option of refusing to breathe polluted air; and we do not have the option of living in a nonatomic age. Unlike science, progress in technology must be measured in terms of the human factor. Technology can have no legitimate purpose but to serve man—man in general, not merely some men; and future generations, not merely those who presently wish to gain advantage for themselves. Technology must be humanistic if it is to lead to a better world.

—Paul G. Hewitt, *Conceptual Physics*

Create a chart that shows the key contrasts presented above.

Function

One of the most natural ways to define is to explain function: *A word processor is a personal computer which operates as an "intelligent" typewriter. A word processor receives input from its operator, usually by means of a typewriter-like keyboard, displays the input in the form of words and sentences on a monitor, and then prints the results on paper automatically.* The following example defines *gestures* through function.

> A gesture is any action that sends a visual signal to an onlooker. To become a gesture, an act has to be seen by someone else and has to communicate some piece of information to them. It can do this either because the gesturer deliberately sets out to send a signal—as when he waves his hand—or it can do it only incidentally—as when he sneezes. The hand-wave is a Primary Gesture, because it has no other existence or function. It is a piece of communication from start to finish. The sneeze, by contrast, is a secondary, or Incidental Gesture. Its primary function is mechanical and is concerned with the sneezer's personal breathing problem. In its secondary role, however, it cannot help but transmit a message to his companions, warning them that he may have caught a cold.

> —Desmond Morris, *Manwatching: A Field Guide to Human Behavior*

Process

A definition might explain the steps that produce a phenomenon. Defining "well-educated," for example, might mean enumerating the steps in an education, steps that result in being "well-educated." A definition of a racist might focus on a similar process in order to suggest how racism might be combatted:

> A racist is not born, but produced. His attitudes are a product of early parental training, either overt or implied, a product of his school system, his church, and his neighborhood. From his earliest years he grows up hearing one group of citizens spoken of in negative terms; he sees racist acts; he is invited to share in name-calling and aggression. If the same child were placed in a different environment at an early enough age, all his so-called "inherited prejudices" could be totally reversed, for changing the people, organizations, and systems that produce his racism could change his attitudes and perceptions.

The pattern is to trace, step–by–step, what happens when, in order to clarify meaning.

Questions

Questions are not a common form of definition, but they may be used to make the reader think about the complications of a term, and its multiple possible interpretations. *The Intimate Environment, Exploring Marriage & the Family* relies on questions to make its student readers think about the very different ways in which we use the word *family*. What do you learn from its questions?

> Does "the family" mean the nuclear family—the married couple and their offspring? Is the husband-wife relationship the core of the family, or is it the mother-child pair? Does "family" include the family tree—the aunts, uncles, cousins, grandparents? Does it include the dead, whose influence some researchers have detected two generations beyond the grave? If "the family" means the nuclear family, is the whole family as a unit "the unity of interacting personalities," as Burgess put it? Or is the family a separate reality for each member?—the child's view of the family may not be the parental view; the wife's view may not be that of the husband.

> What is the irreducible basis of the concept of family: blood ties, marriage, living together, a sense of identification, a sense of obligation? Some combination of these? How does the quality of experience in groups called families differ from that in nonfamily groups? Will any definition apply across all cultures and historical periods?

> —Arlene Skolnick, *The Intimate Environment*

•EXERCISE 13.4: GENERATING DEFINITIONS

Complete the following sentences.

> *Example:* Medieval universities taught <u>only three key professions—law, medicine, and theology</u>—whereas today universities teach <u>a varied curriculum ranging from arts and sciences to physical education, business, and even "marriage and family</u>."

1. A university is a place where…
2. Three functions of a university are…
3. Universities are divided into colleges; for example,…
4. A university differs from a college in that…
5. When we say "university" in my country, we mean…
6. A university degree is necessary…
7. Failure to receive a university degree results in…
8. The university years are a time when young people…
9. Most universities award degrees in….; these degrees mean…
10. A university is like…
11. Universities were formed because of the need to…
12. Parents think of a university as…while students think of a university as…
13. Universities differ in cost,…
14. All universities have in common…

Now combine this information into a good working definition of a university. Is it complete? Is there anything else you can add? What different methods of definition have you used?

• EXERCISE 13.5: IDENTIFICATION OF METHOD

Identify in the margin the different methods of definition used in the following selections.

	Method
1. Schizophrenia. The word means "split mind," but it's a misnomer [bad name]. What schizophrenia really represents is the disintegration of the mind. It's a malignant disorder, cancer of the thought processes, the scrambling and erosion of mental activity. Schizophrenic symptoms—delusions, hallucinations, illogical thinking, loss of touch with reality, bizarre speech and behavior—embody the layman's notion of *crazy.* They occur in one percent of the population in virtually every society, and no one knows why. Everything from a birth trauma to brain damage to body type to poor mothering has been suggested as a cause. Nothing has been proved, although much has been disproved, and…the evidence suggests a genetic predisposition to madness. The course of the disease is as unpredictable as that of a	<u>word root</u> —————— <u>synonym</u> —————— —————— —————— ——————

flash fire in a windstorm. Some patients experience a single
psychotic episode that never recurs. Others recover after a
series of attacks. In many instances the disorder is chronic
but static, while in the most severe cases deterioration
progresses to the point of total breakdown.

    Despite all this ambiguity, the relationship between
madness and murder is clear: The vast majority of schizophrenics
are harmless, less violent than the rest of us. But a few are
stunningly dangerous. Paranoid, they lash out in sudden bursts
of rage, often maiming or killing the very people working
hardest to help them—parents, spouses, therapists.

    —Jonathan Kellerman, *Over the Edge*

2.   *Are Black Holes Real?* A black hole is the leftover remnant
of a very large star that has exploded and collapsed. Much of the
material of the very large star is squeezed down into a ball
smaller than the planet Earth. This ball of matter is so tightly
packed that it produces more gravity than any other object its
size in the universe. Although the ball is still hot, and still
glows like any hot star, the light it produces is trapped by its
own gravity. Because the light cannot reach our eyes, the
remnant of the burned-out star disappears from the universe.
It becomes a "black hole."…

    … A black hole at the center of a galaxy could swallow
nearby stars and grow larger and larger, like a hungry monster,
swallowing more and more stars as it grew. The cloud of matter
around such a black hole would be extremely hot and bright.…

    —Christopher Lampton, *The Space Telescope*

AVOIDING COMMON PITFALLS

Confusing Connotations

The problem with connotation is obvious. No
dictionary can give us the full connotations of a word,
and most smaller dictionaries don't even try because
connotations change with time, and depend on context and situation and regional associations. For
example, a perfectly ordinary expression, overused by
a politician or a commercial, might come to be used
ironically or tongue in cheek in response.
Furthermore, synonyms often have very different
connotations and can only be used as substitutes in
very special cases. For instance, someone who is cautious about money might be called *prudent* or *thrifty*
but their equivalents, *tightfisted* and *miserly* carry far
too many negative connotations to be truly equal.
The same difficulty occurs with antonyms with opposite denotative meanings, but not necessarily opposite
connotative ones. For example, *generous* is the opposite of *tightfisted* but not of *prudent* because of differences in connotations between *prudent* and *tightfisted*. In order to make completely sure that you are
using a synonym or antonym correctly, compare its
dictionary meaning with that of the word you wish to
substitute it for. If there are major differences, you
need to find a different synonym or simply use the
original word. Such potential confusions confirm the
importance of considering connotations in order to
use words correctly.

Confusing False Friends

The connotations of a word translated from one
language to another may change radically, even
though its dictionary denotation may remain the

same and even though it may seem to be the same word. The verb *molestar* in Spanish sounds very much like *molest* in English and may even be translated as *molest* or *bother* in a small dictionary. However, *molest* is an inappropriate translation because in English it is associated not simply with "bothering a person" but with "sexually attacking a person." Such words, which look similar in two languages but have very different connotations, are called *false friends*. Such a mistake can be avoided by paying attention to the context in which a word is used. Sometimes, however, the difficulties of translating are more complex, especially where a word has associations in one culture that it does not have in another. For instance, in Japan the word for "teacher" suggests "predecessor", one who goes before and shows the way; "teacher" in English has no such connotations.

Confusing Cross-Cultural Connotations

Truly mastering a language, then, really means learning the connotations of its words, and this in turn means learning about the associations made by the culture and the values on which the associations are based. Luckily, many connotations remain basically the same when we translate from one language to another, especially if the cultures are similar. This fact allows us to communicate effectively in a new language. There are large sets of words whose connotations we can assume remain much the same in all cultures and languages; obvious examples are *home*, *homesickness*, *parents*, *husband*, *wife*, *child* , etc.

Note, however, that even basic words like these may have different connotations in different cultures. Foreign observers often remark that Americans have much less respect and feeling for family ties and relatives than people in more "family-oriented" cultures; that the husband-wife relationship is looser and more variable than in more traditional societies; that, because of concerns about population size, overcrowding, and personal freedom, many young, urban Americans disapprove of having large families with many children, a practice that is considered a virtue in many parts of the world; that old people in the U.S. get less respect than old people abroad. Do the words in italics above mean more or less the same in your language as they do in English? If there are differences, do differences in culture and values explain the differences in connotations?

Sometimes the problem is that English has several words with gradations of meaning for what is only one word in another language or, in reverse, a language has several words for what is only one word in English. For example, Greek has more possible variations of meaning for *love*, than English. Eskimo languages, in turn, have far more words for different types and qualities of snow than English.

When you choose a word, you often reveal your personal and cultural attitudes toward the thing you name. If you refer to a 35-year-old woman as an *old maid*, *spinster*, or *unmarried older woman*, you show that you expect women to marry early; if you refer to

---

• EXERCISE 13.6: FALSE FRIENDS

Write a paragraph about one or two "false friends" from your language, explaining the difference between their meaning and use in your language and in English.

If you cannot think of any false friends from your language, think of words in your language that would be false friends for English speakers, that is, words borrowed from English that have been modified or have changed meaning in your language. Explain.

Example: The French word *procureur* means "a person who has the right to represent people in legal matters" or, more commonly, "a public prosecutor," as in the phrase *procureur de la République*. In English, however, this word, *procurer*, has no legal associations at all. Instead, it commonly means a *pimp* or *a man who obtains prostitutes on request*, though sometimes it is simply an old-fashioned or formal way of saying, *someone who obtains something*. Because of this big difference in the meaning of the similar sounding words, a speaker should be very careful not to translate by sound but by meaning.

the same woman as a *career woman*, you are not identifying her by her marital status.

In addition to your attitudes toward the <u>things</u> you name, when you choose a word you may also show how you feel about the <u>person</u> of whom you are writing, that is, whether you feel they are equals, superiors, or inferiors. Notice the differences between saying *sanitation engineer* and *garbage collector* or between *statesman* and *politician*.

Models to Learn From

Definitions serve a number of functions. They may introduce a topic, help clarify, warn, instruct, set standards, or even call for standards where there are none.

Model #1 The following definition of the Spanish word *simpatico*, a word which is now sometimes used in American English, avoids synonym definitions because the writer believes there is no precise English equivalent. Therefore, the differences between the English word *sympathetic* and the Spanish word must be clarified, and that clarification necessitates examples of the word in use.

Simpatico is a linguistic false-friend [**general category**], which sounds very similar to the English word *sympathetic* [**comparison**] but which does not mean exactly the same as *sympathetic* in its most common usage [**contrast**]. It does not mean *having pity or compassion for someone else, capable of sympathizing with another*, nor *showing favor, approval,* or *agreement*. [**negative definition**] Instead, it gives the sense of the English slang phrase "on the same wavelength," or might be associated with "good feelings" or with being "attractive " or "likable." [**synonyms**] Its meaning is related to the word "congenial" but it is more encompassing. The phenomenon is well-recognized in English: some actors are *simpatico* (heroines, heroes), and some aren't (villains or heavies). [**contrasting examples**] Soap-opera actors must be simpatico, or they will be replaced. Lyndon Johnson couldn't make himself *simpatico* no matter how hard he tried, nor could Richard Nixon; John F. Kennedy, on the other hand, oozed *simpatico*. [**contrasting examples**] We say he had "charisma" but that's only partly right. [**syn-**

- **EXERCISE 13.7: CULTURAL CONNOTATIONS**

List words from your language that are difficult to translate into English because of differences in cultural attitudes or cultural assumptions. Be prepared to explain the differences and the difficulties involved, either in class discussion or in a paper. Note that explaining the differences in words means explaining about your culture, the way people think and why.

Example: Many times a direct translation from one language to another does not make clear subtle distinctions. This is true of American Indian languages. *The World of the American Indian* explains some of the distinctions Native Americans make.

Some Indian languages…express subtleties which English glosses over. When I say, "He is chopping wood," the words give no hint about how I came to know this. In the Wintu language of northern California, I would say, *"pi k'upabe"* if I had seen the woodsman at work. If I had heard but not seen him, I would say, *"pi k'upanthe."* If someone told me about it, the form would be *"pi k'upake*—I understand he is chopping wood." Or if I guess the act is going on because that is what the person usually does at this time, I would make it, *"pi k'upa'el*—I assume he is chopping wood." Distinctions like these are hard to reconcile with the notion that Wintu is "primitive." —National Geographic Society

Consider the above explanation when choosing a word from your own language and culture to clarify. A good choice of a word to explain would be one which has very strong emotional connotations which would not be clear to a native English speaker.

1. Select one or two words in English that reflect attitudes or values your culture does not share and explain those values.
2. Draw on personal experience to discuss two or three English words whose connotations have given you difficulty.
3. Colors often carry special associations. Determine the color associations from the contexts which follow. Do these colors carry the same associations in your culture? Briefly compare or contrast color associations in your culture with those in English.

> *Example: White* for purity at weddings in the U.S.; *red* for good luck at weddings in Vietnam and China.

1. White: He told a little white lie. They tried to whitewash the political situation.
2. Black: He knew the man's secrets and used them to blackmail him. The sharp-tongued critic blackened the actor's reputation. You don't want to get a black mark on your record. The union will blackball that proposal. He was the black sheep of his family. The Black Death killed thousands of people during the Dark Ages.
3. Yellow: The soldier ran away from the battle; he was just plain yellow. In other words, he was yellow-bellied. Yellow journalism gives the rest of news reporting a bad name.
4. Blue: She felt quite blue because her boyfriend was so far away. "It's been a blue, blue Monday; I feel like running away from the blues." A common African-American music sung in the South about the difficulty of life is called the blues.
5. Green: He is new at his job; he is still green; he is a greenhorn (a cowboy term).

---

onym] When Spanish-speakers say, "Mary's three-year-old has sympathy," it sounds peculiar to native English speakers, but you can find her child very *simpatico* . [differentiation]

Such a definition explains language differences that do not translate easily, especially not in oversimplified language-to-language dictionaries.

Model #2 Correct definitions are vital when giving instructions. The following advice on precautions needed for the hurricane season defines the two phrases used most frequently in radio and television reports, so readers will be able to understand the warnings and take the precautions needed.

The hurricane season begins in late summer and runs through November 30. During that time, if you live in the Gulf south or along the Atlantic seaboard, you might frequently hear two key phrases repeated on radio and television and in daily conversations: *hurricane watch* and *hurricane warning*. Basically the term *hurricane watch* means that a hurricane is close enough to affect you personally so you should listen carefully for advisories. By "close," weath-

er forecasters mean that a hurricane may threaten an area within 24 hours though their predictions may prove totally wrong and the hurricane may move on to some other area instead.

A *hurricane warning* in turn, means that a specific area is expected to receive the full force of a hurricane and all of the effects that accompany it. Hurricane warnings usually name particular coastal areas where winds are expected to reach 74 mph or higher.

If you reside in an area in which a warning is issued, you should begin to take immediate precautions. Such precautions include covering windows with shutters or boards or at the very least putting tape on them so the glass, if broken, will not fly at you. Residents should be sure to buy or have on hand several important items. These include flashlights with batteries or candles with matches or lighters to use when the electricity goes off, a battery-operated radio to keep up with news reports, canned foods that do not need cooking or heating, bottled water, a first-aid kit, extra medications, and candies for quick energy. When the electricity goes off, the water is contaminated, the stove doesn't work,

- ## EXERCISE 13.9: TRANSLATION DIFFICULTIES

  Choose a word in your language for which there is no English equivalent. Define and explain it, clarifying meaning. Briefly explain why it is so difficult to translate into English. Use the *simpatico* paragraph pattern as a model to imitate.

and there is no way of getting the news, people begin to wish they had understood the weather forecast definitions and had taken their warnings seriously.

This type of instructional definition is also important in textbooks and "how to" manuals.

Definitions, whether of a few phrases, a few sentences, or several pages, are a regular part of good writing. They enable you to introduce new terminology and to explain specialized vocabulary and in-group diction; they sometimes determine the basis of the discussion or the rules of the argument. Short definitions are common examination questions (*Define the following terms and give an example of each*) and are frequently necessary in legal, technical, or scientific writing. They provide a foundation for discussion and communication. In other words, this is a form you will use again and again throughout your academic and professional life. However, you must be careful to note differences in connotations and differences in meaning due to personal and cultural variations.

- ## EXERCISE 13.10: DEFINING TO INSTRUCT

  Write a definition to instruct or explain. As is always true for writing projects, choose a topic you know <u>well</u>!

Final Checklist

- ☐ Are your definitions clear, complete and nonreversible, i.e., not repeating the term to be defined?

- ☐ Have you considered both denotations and connotations?

- ☐ Have you been careful not to let personal or cultural differences obscure your meaning?

- ☐ Have you relied on an adequate dictionary, a collegiate dictionary with 200,000 words or more?

- ☐ Have you carefully provided both the class or category (genus) and the unique or distinguishing characteristics?

- ☐ Have you chosen those patterns or forms which will best define your term or idea?

Passages for Discussion and Analysis

Where The Heroes Are

My own idea of heroism is so much more than just doing our jobs, getting along, simply surviving our daily challenges and adversities, even tragedies. It is going beyond survival, building on life's challenges to emerge tougher and more capable because of them…. More than anything, a true hero sparks our recognition of the hero within ourselves.

Who are the heroes today?

The fact is, we frequently confuse fame and celebrity with heroism. There are, of course, entertainers and sports stars, duly celebrated for their high levels of talent and achievement, who go beyond their professional endeavors to inspire and motivate us, sometimes in truly heroic proportions. But celebrity, by itself, isn't heroism.

To find today's heroes, you need to look no further than the people around you—family members, friends, neighbors, community associates—people whose heroic qualities we tend to miss. Let me tell you about…my heroes….

Recently, my father, Len Coffee, lay weak and delirious in a hospital bed. Fearing his death, I thought back upon his life—and mine with him.

As an infant, Dad had contracted polio—then it was called "infantile paralysis." He survived but was left with a withered [weak, dried up] right arm, which he carried with the elbow canted [bent] out, and a shortened left leg. He always walked with a rolling limp. Over the years, he worked hard at half-dozen supervisory jobs in the building industry, lost a business and ended up with little more than his Social Security pension. There had been hard drinking on the isolated construction sites during the war, and alcoholism had ensued. But I can never remember him being unemployed, not even during the earlier years of the Depression. There was always food and a roof for Mom, my sister and me.

Only in reviewing all this during his crisis did I realize that, in spite of his physical circumstances, I had never looked upon my dad as crippled or handicapped—probably because he himself never used those terms. I never heard him blame his problems on his physical disabilities.

What is more, he went beyond just surviving his circumstances. He taught me all the things a father was supposed to in those days—to play ball, to fish and hunt. He had been a Boy Scout master, and he included me—when I was a first- and second-grader—in all the activities with the older boys. He always pursued his love of cooking, and more intensely so when my sister got older and Mom started working as a school secretary. All through our schooling, Dad and Mom supported Sis and me in all our endeavors. They never missed a ball game or a swim meet or a school play, even though they had to make up the time at their jobs. While I was a POW [Prisoner of War], they counseled and consoled many a POW wife and family as well as my own. To this day, Dad is active in the Navy League, the local chamber of commerce, and in the church functions—usually behind the scenes in the kitchen.

Had he not recovered from his illness, our family would have lost the most loving father, grandfather, and great-grandfather we could ever have had.

Why did my dad have to become 78 years old and near death for me to realize for the first time that he had been "crippled" all his life?

Because he didn't live it that way. In spite of his handicap, problems, and probably pain, he reached beyond a troubled existence to help his fellow humans and to be a loving dad. That's why my Dad's my hero….

Indeed, there are heroes around us every day in our families, schools, neighborhoods, and workplaces.

—Gerald Coffee, Captain, U.S. Navy (ret.), *Parade Magazine*

• Questions for Discussion

1. Captain Coffee rejects a stereotypical definition of heroes that he thinks his audience probably agrees with. What is this rejected definition? Why does he reject it?

2. What definition does he offer in its place? That is, what is the thesis idea of this essay? What major point does Captain Coffee make about real heroes?

3. List characteristics Captain Coffee associates with heroism. Beside them, list examples or incidents that illustrate each characteristic. How does Coffee illustrate his definition?

4. Do you agree with Captain Coffee's definition? Why or why not?

5. Notice that Captain Coffee mentions being a prisoner of war only once and then only to focus on the loving support of family and friends, both their support of him and of his fellow POWs. What kind of image do you get of the writer from his writing? You would probably never guess that he is one of America's real heroes, a man who spent years as a prisoner of war in North Vietnam, a man who helped, supported, and encouraged his fellow POWs and assured the survival of men who would have given up without his example. How does this knowledge affect your reaction to his definition?

6. Media-defined "heroes" tend to be few and larger-than-life, a special kind of superior person, or sometimes someone who is simply very well-known. How is Coffee's definition more democratic than these?

The following introductory definition from Richard Restak's *The Brain*, seeks to interest readers in a scientific topic and to provide a general overview of what will be dealt with in more detail later:

Definition of the Brain

Weighing less than sixteen hundred grams (three pounds), the human brain in its natural state resembles nothing so much as a soft, wrinkled walnut. Yet despite this inauspicious appearance, the human brain can store more information than all the libraries in the world. It is also responsible for our most primitive urges, our loftiest ideals, the way we think, even the reason why, on occasion, we sometimes don't think, but act instead. The workings of an organ capable of creating *Hamlet*, the Bill of Rights, and Hiroshima remain deeply mysterious. How is it constructed? How did it develop? If we learn more about the brain, can we learn more about ourselves? Indeed, are we anything *other* than our brain?

Some of these questions remain unanswered, others ("Is the brain the mind?") may remain forever unanswerable. But...on the basis of what is now known, neuroscientists have begun to suspect that our very humanity may someday be defined by the chemical and electrical activities within our brains....our hopes, our dreams, our lusts, and our ambitions may someday be defined in terms familiar only to the neurochemist and the neurophysiologist....

physical description

functions

cause/effect

Having briefly described the brain and its general function, and having established the basic questions one must ask about the brain, Restak moves on to establish definitions of the "brain" already in use and to formulate the simpler definition he will rely on in his text.

Prior to any meaningful discussion of specifics, we need to get some rough grasp on what we mean by the word *brain*. Basically, what is a brain? Surprisingly enough, a straight-forward definition of a brain is difficult to come by. Textbooks devoted to the brain rarely provide a useful definition. One of them begins: "The brain is made up of individual units—the nerve cells and the glial cells." But this is only a <u>circular</u> definition. The brain is a collection of nerve cells. Nerve cells compose the brain

A <u>more precise and encompassing definition</u> of the brain can be found in the dictionary: "The portion of the vertebrate central nervous system that constitutes the organ of thought and neural coordination, including all the higher nervous centers, receiving stimuli from the sense organs, and interpreting and correlating these with stored impressions to formulate the motor impulses that ultimately control all vital activities, that is made up of neurons and their processes organized into layers and nuclei of gray matter and tracts, decussations, and fasciculi of white matter together with various supporting and nutritive structures, that is enclosed within the skull, being continuous with the spinal cord through the foramen magnum and with the cranial nerves through various other openings."

Although this definition is encompassing, it is also overwhelming. For our purposes, the brain can be defined simply as the part of the central nervous system that is contained within the skull. The rest of the central nervous system can be found in the spinal cord....

textbook definition

division into parts

dictionary definition:

function

function

division into parts

location

location

Note the rejection of the overly complex, technical—"encompassing"—definition in favor of the author's own working definition. Setting up faulty definitions in order to show the superiority of one's own is a common pattern of argumentation.

This essay defines further by dividing the brain into its parts and discussing the physical makeup of each, then by discussing function as related to each part and to the brain as a single unit, by providing pictures and charts, by discussing historical definitions and understandings of the brain, by suggesting what brain disorders teach about its function, by detailing the process of the brain's evolution and its particular development from fetus to adult, and so forth. It also explains what the brain is not:

Our brain isn't simply the sum total of our cerebral hemispheres. Cats in heat, raging bulls, murderous jungle foragers—these creatures have brains, too... however... poorly developed.... Would we be totally at the mercy of our instincts if we didn't possess cerebral hemispheres?

The analogy with animals keeps the focus on the mysterious uniqueness of the human brain. Obviously then, given the projected plan of the book, a basic definition of the brain was a necessary starting place.

The next definition, from an article on "Science and the Citizen" in the *Scientific American.*, was written at a time when new discoveries about life and death had made old definitions obsolete. Scientists had learned that the human heart could keep beating after the human brain had stopped all but basic functions, and that one could therefore be dead as a unique living being but, by old definitions, still be technically alive. At the same time the new technique of transplanting from the legally dead to the living had opened up new scientific possibilities that required keeping the dead functioning until a transplant could be made, but it had also opened up the negative possibility of someone who had donated his body to science being worth more dead than alive. In order to meet both the positive and negative possibilities, this short essay records a reasoned attempt to establish new criteria for defining death. How is the definition developed? What authorities does it cite to give its criteria weight? What different patterns of definition do you observe?

What Is Death?

The traditional criteria for death are cessation of respiration and heart action, but modern medical technology can keep a patient breathing and his blood circulating long after his brain has died. Now a special Harvard University committee has recommended that brain death, or irreversible coma, be considered a definition of death and has drawn up a set of guidelines for determining when there is no discernible activity of the central nervous system. The 13-man committee, drawn from the faculties of medicine, public health, law, arts and sciences, and divinity, was headed by Henry K. Beecher of the Harvard Medical School. Its report was published in the *Journal of the American Medical Association.*

the old definition

the reason a new definition is necessary

authoritative sources for a new definition

According to the committee, a permanently nonfunctioning brain is characterized by certain clinical signs. One is unreceptiveness and unresponsiveness of the patient to any external stimuli or inner needs. Another is lack of any spontaneous muscular movement or any unassisted breathing—or effort to breathe—over a period of at least an hour. Finally, there are no reflexes: the pupil of the eye is fixed and dilated even in the presence of a bright light, there is no swallowing or yawning and usually no stretch reflex. These clinical signs constitute primary evidence of brain death; electroencephalograms should be considered secondary because they may show spurious [false] waves. A "flat" brain-wave pattern, according to the report, constitutes confirmation of brain death.

enumeration of primary characteristics of brain death

secondary characteristics

most important characteristic

The final determination of death through irreversible coma should be made only when the clinical and encephalographic tests have been repeated at least 24 hours after the initial tests. The determination should be made by the physician in charge; it is "unsound and undesirable" to have the family make the decision.

process for declaring brain death

Then the family should be informed. "At this point, death, is to be declared and *then* the respirator turned off." The decision, the committee noted, "should be made by physicians not involved in any later effort to transplant organs or tissue from the deceased individual."

• Questions for Discussion

1. We all know something about traditional definitions of death as depicted in film and literature. How does the above definition differ from the traditional ones?

2. How authoritative is this writer's source for the new definition of death? Explain.

3. What do the quotation marks indicate? Why are they important?

4. What tone does the writer take in presenting this definition? Why? What personal qualities must he communicate to his audience if his ideas are to be listened to?

5. Why is it important to establish the procedure to be followed in declaring brain death? What are the possible legal repercussions or results?

6. Why do you think the writer feels he must include the last sentence? What possible abuses does he fear? Explain.

7. The above is clearly a scientific definition written for very practical reasons. Would all writers agree with this definition? For example, when poets or novelists define death, is their definition so scientific? How would a religious specialist such as a priest, a minister, or a theologian define death? Would an insurance representative view death in the same way?

•• Writing Assignments

A. Expand the following information to make good short definitions.

1. Altruism=a pattern of behavior=the performance of an unselfish act; two properties: 1) benefits someone else, 2) disadvantageous to benefactor (helpfulness at a personal cost)

   Examples: 1) donating time, money, energy, goods to help the poor, the homeless, those injured in natural disasters; 2) diving into flood waters to save a drowning child when one could drown too or entering a burning building to rescue those who cannot get out alone.

2. Religious displays=submissive acts of reverence performed towards supreme beings.

   Examples: kneeling, bowing, kowtowing, salaaming, prostrating (lowering body); chanting; sacrifice; offering gifts to gods; making symbolic gestures of allegiance. Why? to show respect, to appease gods, to obtain favors, to avoid punishment.

3. Displacement activities=small, seemingly irrelevant movements made during moments of inner conflict or frustration.

   Example 1: nervous girl repeatedly opening and closing bracelet clasp, crossing and uncrossing legs, chewing on lip, fiddling with hair, other forms of fidgeting.

   Example 2: tense airline passenger repeatedly checking ticket, taking out passport, putting them away again, rearranging hand-baggage, checking for wallet, also head-scratching, earlobe-tugging, face-pulling.

B. Look up five words from your reading in a good dictionary. Then define them in your own words. Note whether you use an appositive, an adjective clause, a participle, or some other form to develop your definition.

C. Define the type of government of your home country, or the type of food eaten there, using three different types of definition. In the margin, name the types of definition used.

D. Define your name or that of a classmate by its word roots or history or historical associations. Did someone famous have the same name? Does that affect what people think of when they hear your name? A good dictionary may help.

E. Write a definition to introduce an aspect of your culture you are very familiar with. Your definition could be of a typical food, a national clothing style, a cultural practice or celebration, such as a festival or, in fact, any aspect of the culture unique and complex enough to require definition.

F. Define an important theoretical term from one of your textbooks by providing particular examples to make the theory clear. For example, for a sociology class, a definition of "cultural conflict theory" might focus on examples from your local community of differences in cultural attitudes leading to a breaking of the law, for example, immigrants consistently not paying sales tax or breaking legal regulations because of a different attitude toward such taxes and regulations in their home country.

G. Sometimes a definition needs to be longer and more complicated. Choose one of the following examples or a word that you have heard in conversations but that is new enough not to be in most dictionaries yet. Define it using some of the strategies talked about in this chapter.

Base your definition on questions asked of at least two native speakers of English.

1. yuppie
2. nerd
3. politically correct
4. techie or techy
5. rapper
6. Generation X
7. grunge
8. _____

> *Example:* A *hacker* is an expert in computers who uses technical expertise for enjoyment as well as professional advancement. The word comes from the verb *to hack*, meaning in slang "to have sufficient ability": *She can hack it in chemistry, because she has a good background in sciences.* Where computers are concerned, *hacker* takes on the sense of a very computer-capable person who may or may not be an amateur but who definitely spends long hours with computers "hacking through" difficult problems and developing a sophisticated and unusual technical expertise.

Application

Write an essay defining a complex word or phrase, one that necessitates an extended, argumentative definition. This term might come from your major field or from some controversial social or political issue. It should require broad enough treatment to allow you to write several full paragraphs. The word *freedom*, for example, would be too broad, but the word *privacy* might be manageable. Your purpose is to control and manage your readers' perception of your term and of the ideas or values associated with it.   .

Sample terms to define:

a good student	a foolish parent
a bad student	a bad environment for a child
a fair test	a good language program
an unfair test	an efficient secretary
a good teacher	a reactionary government
a bad teacher	

Prewriting: List facts or specific information to support your definition, considering possible patterns like distinctive characteristics, typical parts, comparison/ contrast, examples, function, and analogy.

Writing: Break up your definition into manageable units. Your introduction should discuss the controversy associated with the term and take a stand on that controversy. Your body section should support your stand, using a number of different methods of development.

The following is an example of the type of prewriting discovery frame you might use to help you develop your extended definition.

Discovery Frame for a Definition of EUTHANASIA

Purpose: to provide a balanced view of euthanasia

Origin: Greek for "a good or peaceful death" from *eu* for "good" and *thanatos* for "death"

Dictionary definition: "the painless putting to death of persons suffering from incurable diseases."

Cause/Effect: 1) improvements in medical technology have made possible a much wider range of choices between life and death—artificial life-supporting mechanisms, new drugs, artificial transplantation of organs to prolong life—but have raised the question of quality of life; 2) demands of the individual patient to exercise rights over own health and to make own decision about life and death—a moral issue

Function: Positive: to allow individuals to make personal decisions about their own life, to give the terminally ill a chance to end their lives early if the pain is too much, to counter a technology that can keep a body functioning when the mind is gone or recovery is impossible; Negative: to provide an escape from life and its pains, to provide a person a chance to give up.

Division into Types: Indirect/Passive (remove hospital machinery and allow a natural death); Direct/Active (administer or allow patient to administer a poison to end life).

Examples: Indirect: Kathleen Quinlin, who was in a coma for years, curled up in a fetal position, unable to eat, drink, communicate, technically alive, but non-functioning, probably suffering irreparable brain damage, kept alive by hospital machinery at great expense to family and friends who suffered from seeing her in that condition; finally taken off the machines by a court order; <u>Direct</u>: Dr. Kevorkian administers or assists the administering of a drug to end their lives when the pain is too much for them to want to endure any longer.

Comparison-Contrast: <u>Opponents</u> call euthanasia "murder" and fear it might lead to "genocide," the killing of the handicapped, the old, the weak; they argue that no one has the right to take a life or to assist the taking of a life—even one's own life. They fear a "slippery slope" down which we will "slide" from permitting the terminally ill to die naturally to putting to death unwanted people, the very old, the handicapped, the different. <u>Proponents</u> call euthanasia a "blessing" or a "right" and talk about the importance of "quality of life" as opposed to simple existence; they argue that an individual's life is his own and that a "living will" (a document expressing a person's wishes about how to die) should be legally sufficient to allow euthanasia in case of a terminal illness or terminal accident, and that suicide should be a matter of conscience based on personal values, not a legal concern.

Chapter 14: COMPARING AND CONTRASTING

Comparison and contrast are so much a part of daily life that people are often not aware of using them — Paul Eschholz and Alfred Rosa

Key Concerns in Comparison-Contrasts

The comparison-contrast structure is used in government, history, literature, business, the arts, the sciences. College assignments ask you to compare or contrast one system with another (capitalist vs. socialist, Republican vs. Democrat), a leading figure or an age with another (Lincoln vs. Kennedy; the Medieval period with the Renaissance), one type of architecture with another (Greek neo-classical with Frank Lloyd Wright's modern American), cost and benefit choices between companies and products, and so forth. You can use the comparison-contrast pattern to write about almost any kind of topic, as long as it involves two or more ideas or concepts. It can even be a comparison of different parts of the same whole. What is important for the pattern is a sense of tension or opposition for contrasts, or a similarity or shared characteristics for comparison. Because it is probably among the most common essay question forms on both in-class and out-of-class assignments and later a very common form in writing in the professions, it will be your key to effective communication in business, college, and life.

1. Is comparison-contrast a major writing pattern in your culture? Think back to your major examinations in school: What did the questions ask you to do?

2. Think of recent occasions when you have used comparison-contrast either in a writing assignment or in a practical situation. If a writing assignment, what was compared and/or contrasted? If a practical situation, what things—two apartments, schools, vehicles—did you compare or contrast?

Distinguishing between Approaches

1. <u>Comparisons</u> focus on the similarities between two or more people, places, or things, while <u>contrasts</u> focus on their differences. Teachers sometimes use the word "comparison" to mean a paper that both compares and contrasts.

2. Trying to compare or contrast more than three things usually becomes difficult. A one-to-one comparison is easier, though a comparison of three or more items is common in business writing (particularly evaluations of products).

3. The most common pattern for comparison-contrast alternates between the two things: first one, then the other; then the first again, followed by the second. This form, called an alternating style, is often best for a single paragraph or a short paper dealing with direct opposites.

4. The hardest form to do correctly, a block style, looks first at one thing completely, then at the other completely, and finally concludes about the two. It depends heavily on connective words to draw attention to parallel or antithetical relationships. It is often the best form to choose when the alternating form will result in too much repetition or will result in no parallel points to compare. The block pattern should follow the same order in both its parts. Often the discussion of the most important or most complex of the two topics of comparison comes last in the block sequence.

5. Many writers of longer essays use both alternating and block forms together in the same essay, depending on the nature of their information.

6. Setting up general categories of information to be covered prevents comparison-contrast papers from degenerating into simple lists.

Discovering Categories

One of the most important skills for writing good comparison-contrast essays is the ability to find unifying categories, units of information that fit together around a central idea or concept. These categories then form the basis for topic or thesis sentences and keep an essay from being merely a list.

For example, the following lists of information emphasize the difference between restaurant diners surveyed in New York and in Los Angeles, but to write an essay based on these lists you would need to organize using the categories. The following may not represent the real New York or Los Angeles style of dining (it may be out of date or simply wrong); however, it provides a good example of unifying categories.

The first type of information, Category 1, relates to types of food preferred and attitudes toward nutrition. The contrast between what is eaten for main courses and for dessert and what beverages accompany the meal would belong together here, perhaps given greater unity by a sequence which follows the order of the meal from main course to accompanying drinks to dessert. The next category, Category 2, might be the nature of the restaurant preferred and the reasons for that preference, while Category 3 examines attitudes toward service.

• EXERCISE 14.2: GENERATING INFORMATION

List the key points of similarity or difference for four of the following sets of topics.

travel by bus/travel by plane	classical music/rock music
a friend/an acquaintance	high school/university
food in my country/food in the USA	dogs/cats
climate in my country/ climate in the USA	my mother/my father
what I do at home/what I do while traveling	
clothing styles in my country/clothing styles in the USA	

Example: Amish/Hindu

Hindu

One of biggest religions in the world
Millions of Hindus worldwide,
   mainly in India
"God helps those who help others."
Pray to a God with many different
   names and forms
Go to temples whenever they want
Eat vegetables as a part of their
   religious belief

Amish

Small part of a small religious group
Thousands of Amish,
   mainly in Pennsylvania
"God helps those who help themselves."
Pray to a God with three parts
   (Father, Son, and Holy Ghost)
Go at set times for particular services
Have no food regulations except fasting
   for purification

Topic A   Topic B

1. _____   _____

2. _____   _____

3. _____   _____

4. _____   _____

NEW YORK	LOS ANGELES
Category 1	
Diners favor classic cuisine	Diners prefer salads and pastas
Like meat (beef and pork)	More vegetarian oriented
Like substantial meals	Like roughage (salads with fibrous vegetables)
Barbecue popular	Rice and noodles popular
Enjoy cocktails/heavy liquor	Prefer carefully selected wine with known origin
Large percent chose dessert (35% more than in L.A.)	Only small percent chose dessert —usually fruit
Aware of nutrition but not obsessed by it	Obsessed by nutrition; insistent on healthy food and healthy appearance
Don't mind high calories	Watch calories carefully

NEW YORK	LOS ANGELES
Category 2	
Go to restaurant straight from office; eat, then run to show, suburbs, or office again	Go home, change clothes; spend evening dining out
Dining related to power—making contacts, making deals, confirming deals	Dining related to status—who is who
Diners prefer privacy—choose private booths, small rooms, low visibility	Diners stare openly at each other—choose large open rooms with high visibility, sometimes broken up by tiers
Value their eating companions	Value the broader social experience

NEW YORK	LOS ANGELES
Category 3	
Prefer waiters to be professional—quiet, stern, serious, attentive, distant, non-interfering	Want waiters to be friendly, personal and chatty; enjoy waiters praising food and making personal recommendations

—adapted in part from Martha Duffy, *The Whims of Bicoastal Dining*

Once categories have been generated, it becomes much easier to think about argument and plan. For example, a discussion of the nature of the restaurant preferred might come logically before the discussion of types of food served, and a discussion of the reasons for eating out or for eating in a particular type of restaurant might be of greater significance and therefore come closer to the end of the discussion. Whatever you decide, setting up categories is the first step in generating a thesis idea and constructing a plan of organization.

Choosing Standard Forms: Block and Alternating

The block form described on page 288 works best when the information in topics A and B are of a different nature (oceans compared to rivers; boats compared to aircraft), or require different lengths (little to say about one, much about the other) or different directions of discussion (requiring divergent subdivisions). The block form is also more often used for writing to informed readers who share your overall views and can be trusted to recognize connections and relationships themselves; the alternating form is best for arguing a relationship that the reader doesn't know about or doesn't agree with, so the relationships of comparison and contrast are very clearly spelled out one by one in small units.

The Block Pattern

The virtue of the block style is that it allows you to describe one unit very thoroughly before beginning a second one. However, the problem is that in a weakly written block pattern the reader must do much more of the work, drawing the parallels and contrasts, and sometimes looking back at the first unit to see its relationship to the second. To help the reader avoid this problem, a good writer will build in reminders of details and will make the second unit follow exactly the same pattern as the first unit. Nevertheless, the reader of a block pattern essay must participate more actively in the comparing and contrasting than the reader of an alternating pattern.

• EXERCISE 14.3: EXPLORING CATEGORIES

A. Write a thesis sentence for a paper on <u>five</u> of the topics from Exercise 14.2 on page 289. To do well, you must decide on unifying categories.

Example: Topic=learning Spanish/learning English

Thesis: Learning Spanish is easier than learning English, because of its easier pronunciation, regular spelling, and less extensive vocabulary.

B. The following contrast discusses measuring the quality of campus life, in part, by the degree to which a school provides a sense of concern and community for students. In the margin, list the categories or types of information used to organize the paper.

Categories

Choosing a college is a very important step that determines the type of education you will receive. Some colleges, as Ernest Boyer, Carnegie Foundation President, points out, can be "factories" set up to mass produce hundreds, even thousands of graduates, while others may be "caring institutions" designed to meet the special needs of individuals.

<u>The first</u> type of college is basically what Boyer calls "a credentialing center," a place   goals of institute
that mechanically provides services "the way a fast-food chain dishes up hamburgers."
<u>Such schools</u> are more committed to serving their own interests than truly educating _____
students in effective, well-rounded ways that consider their personal, social, and intellectual needs. In other words, such schools have minimal commitments to education.
<u>They</u> may have introductory classes of hundreds of students, with teaching assistant _____
graders rather than professors, to meet with students about their work. <u>Their</u> freshman _____
English classes are also large and impersonal, and only final grades matter, not the development of the individual as a human being.

<u>The second type</u> of college offers a more humanistic, humane, and civil approach _____
to education. It assumes that students really matter and provides special services that demonstrate that view to students. Classes at <u>such schools</u> are smaller and more intimate and teacher-student ratios are low so the student has contact with a professor and that professor deals on a personal level with the student's education. A writing class, at
<u>such a school</u>, averages twenty students and will never have more than twenty-five students; furthermore, the teachers guide the students through the writing process to help them develop skills. <u>Such schools</u> inspire far more loyalty <u>than the first type</u> because students can genuinely feel that their school is doing its best for them. Students feel a greater sense of belonging at schools that have a vision of the future that includes the individual student, rather than merely the institution for its own sake.

In other words, different colleges create different senses of community, and <u>the ones that aim at true community, interaction, and responsibility</u> will be quite different from <u>those that aim at mass-producing a final product</u>.

C. Use the list of information about dining out in New York and Los Angeles on pages 287-288 as the basis for an effective description of the differences. If possible, add other contrasts based on your own experience or knowledge. Decide which categories of information to focus on in what order. What kind of information should come first, second, third, last? Why? Should this information form a single paragraph or a short paper?

Example of the Block Pattern

The following student paper describing a classmate contrasts contradictory qualities or characteristics of that classmate: his realistic side versus his "dreamy" side. As you read, consider whether this information could be put in alternating form and, if not, why not.

Larry S. is a sophomore student majoring in print journalism. He wants to be a fiction writer, a good one. However, he has two different conflicting facets—he is both a "realist" and a " dreamer." [thesis idea: contrast between A and B]

Although he has wanted to be a fiction writer since he was little, his "realist side" told him, "Don't be a writer because there is no future and no money in writing!" [topic idea A: one side of Larry] As soon as he graduated from high school, he went to college in Colorado. He majored in biology in order to enter medical school. It seemed to him that becoming a doctor would ensure a successful future for him. However, he soon got bored because that was not what he really wanted to do. Thus, he decided to leave school. After a couple of months, he began to study business at the university. He believed that a business degree would provide him with more opportunities and greater success. He said that he was a very indecisive person at that time. His "reason" dominated his "passion." He forced himself to study biology and business rather than print journalism in order to make sure his future would be prosperous.

Eventually, he could not control his passion for writing. After studying business for one year, his "dreamy" personality told him: "Be a writer because this is what you really want to be!" [topic B idea: Larry's other side] This strong desire made him change his major to "print journalism." However, no matter what kind of degree he has, there is no guarantee for writers. Although there are many talented writers in this world, only a few have an opportunity to be successful. Writers must not only be talented but also lucky. Now Larry hopes that he can publish his first book while he is in college. In order to accomplish this "first step" of becoming a writer, he has been writing a comic book. He plans on sending it to D.C. Comics, Inc., which is one of the largest conglomerate comic book companies in the world. In this case, Larry's future depends on the editor's taste. If the editor does not like Larry's comic book, Larry might have to change his writing style or send it to another company. If, on the other hand, the editor believes that Larry has talent, his comic book will be published. Thus, Larry will obtain instant fame, or so he hopes. He knows how difficult it is.

However, the more difficult it is, the more determined he is to be a writer. Like being a gambler, being a writer is thrilling, but risky. Yet this is what he really wants to do!

In other words, Larry is finally moving toward his real dream. His "dreamy" side seems a little stronger than his "realistic" side. A degree in print journalism will be a type of "realistic insurance" for a more successful future, but his dream is that the day when we can all see his name in print as author of a book will not be too far away. [conclusion: both sides of Larry's personality, A and B]

—Sayako Saito, Japan

Sayako is writing a form of biography, but instead of simply providing a chronological history, she has made her topic more interesting and more meaningful by providing a contrast that reveals the underlying nature of her subject, Larry. Notice that one piece of information in one section does not correspond directly to another piece of information in the next. In other words, the block form often works best when the two parts to be compared or contrasted cannot be talked about in exactly the same way.

The Alternating Pattern

The following paragraph comparing the Amish (a conservative Protestant sect) and the Hindu religions is typical of the alternating pattern. In this case there are very direct parallels, with information about one corresponding directly to information about the other. When you have this type of similar information, the alternating pattern is often best. Notice how the writer goes back and forth between the two parts of the comparison-contrast, either within a single sentence or in separate sentences. Always, a statement about one part of the comparison (A) is followed by a statement about the other part of the comparison (B). Watch too for the repetition necessary to make this formula work.

Example of the Alternating Pattern

The following essay was written by someone who had just seen the movie *Witness* and had become interested in parallels between the Amish and the Hindus of India.

The *Amish and Hindus* are *both very different* religious groups that normally would not even be considered together. *However*, *the two* religions share *some similarities and more differences*, **related to size, belief, and form of worship.** *The Hindu* religion is one of the biggest religions in the world with millions of Hindus worldwide, though most are in India. *In contrast, the Amish* religion is a small fragment of a small religious group with thousands of people, many in Pennsylvania. *Both* groups believe in God *but* they believe in different ideas of God. *Both* believe in "Service to Humanity and Service to God," *but the Amish* also believe that "God helps those who help themselves," while the *Hindus* believe that "God helps those who help others." *Hindus* worship statues of gods with flowers, *but the Amish* don't. In fact, they disapprove of statues. Both groups pray to their God in their homes and in special holy places (a temple for the *Hindus*, a meeting place for the *Amish*). *Both* believe in one God, but the *Hindus* pray to a God with many different names and forms, *while the Amish* pray to a God with three parts (Father, Son, and Holy Ghost). The *Hindus* go to temples whenever they want to go, *but the* Amish go at set times for particular services. *Hindus* eat vegetables as a part of their religious belief, but the *Amish* have no food regulations, except sometimes fasting for purification. Despite all of these *differences*, the Amish and the Hindus *share* a common bond: They are *both* very religious people and *both* believe strongly in their God and in pleasing him. *This bond* should make the *differences not seem important* when they meet.

In the above passage, for each statement about Hindus there is a direct and parallel statement about the Amish; the words that interlock ideas are italicized and the categories of information providing logical unity in this paragraph are in boldface. Circle the words which emphasize similarities. Draw a box like this around the ones which emphasize differences.

- ### EXERCISE 14.4: BLOCK AND ALTERNATING PATTERNS

  A. Look back at Exercise 14.3 B on page 291 and analyze the method of development used in the paragraph on the contrasting goals of American colleges.

  Method of Analysis: List the key contrasts made in the essay. Put all negative nouns and adjectives on one side, all positive ones on the other side. What central contrast do they create? Is the contrast balanced or is one section longer than the other? Which form is used, block or alternating? Why? How would changing the form of organization change the effect? What metaphor carries the key idea? How does it strengthen the contrast?

  B. For each set of information given below, first find the unifying categories, and then choose or write a concluding statement which contains your key argument or topic idea. Next, write a long, well-developed comparison-contrast paragraph using two or three of your categories.

  Use an alternating pattern. Then try to change it to block pattern. What problems do you encounter in making the change? Why?

1. **Women who work outside the home**	VERSUS	**Full-time mothers and housewives**	Category
Paying jobs		No pay	income
Set hours		Night and day	hours
Spend work time: doing career-oriented labor		Spend time: cooking, cleaning shopping, washing dishes and clothes	type of work
Send children to day-care			
May hire a maid and give her directions		Having and taking care of children: training them, entertaining them, feeding, cleaning clothing them	

Outside the home	In the home	
Meet people/socially active	Solitary except for brief social contacts	_____
Change necessary for professional advancement	Change necessary as children grow	_____

The above prewriting lists could support very different conclusions based on the same information. Sketch out a paragraph that concludes:

    a. that women who work outside the home work harder than full-time mothers and housewives

    b. that full-time mothers and housewives work harder than women who work outside the home.

    c. Invent your own conclusion!

2. **Amazon River**   **VERSUS**   **Nile River**   **Category**

Amazon River	Nile River	Category
In South America	In Africa	location
4000 miles long	4100 miles long	length
170 billion gallons of water per hr.	2.8 billion gallons of water per hr.	
Dense jungle on each side	Arid land on each side	
2,000 miles of continuous 200-ft.-high forest	No forests	_____
Stretches into eight countries besides Brazil, including Venezuela to the north, Peru to the west and Bolivia to the south	Stretches from East African lake plateau to Mediterranean, to include Egypt in the north, the Sudan, Ethiopia and Kenya in the South	_____ _____ _____
2.7 million sq. mi. of drained land	1.1 million sq. mi. of land drained	
Both have rich deltas		_____
Land known to Europeans in the 16th century; Spanish and Portuguese explorers	Known to Europeans since the earliest times; Roman, British explorers	_____
Famous for flora & fauna	Famous for ancient Egyptian ruins, Assawan, Gebel Aulia, and Makwar Dams	

After deciding on categories of information, develop a unifying topic idea to include two or three of the categories, for example:

    a. The Amazon and the Nile have long been the "lifeblood" of their areas.

    b. Although the Amazon and the Nile differ in location and terrain, they are similar in size and influence.

    c. Invent your own conclusion!

3. **Cultural Contrasts in Business Letter Forms**   Category

USA   *Japan*

Gets directly to business   Begins with small talk   _____

Initially impersonal   Personal: friendly greetings;   _____
                                         good wishes; discussion
                                         of weather

Short and to the point   Longer and more indirect   _____

Business and technical   Emotive words dominate   _____
  words dominate

A "no-nonsense" tone   Eventually gets down to business
  called "business-like"   with a "by the way"   _____

Tendency to say every-   Seldom reveal true feelings
  thing bluntly, with no   clearly because conflict   _____
  frills, to communicate   would endanger values:
  idea of honesty instead   group culture harmony
  of elegance

Openness and directness   Courtesy, politeness important   _____
  important American values   Japanese values

If you can, add to this list of characteristics. Then set up a third, parallel list for information about business letters in your country. If you are from Japan or the United States, interview a classmate from some other country about business letters in his or her country so that you will have three countries to compare and contrast. Look for categories of information such as "style" and "content". Consider these possible conclusions:

a. U.S. business letters reflect the American belief that "time is money" while Japanese business letters reflect the Japanese feeling that unity and harmony are very important values.

b. Differences in attitudes about courtesy affect the nature of business letters in different cultures.

c. Invent your own conclusion!

Ultimately, write a unified paper with two or three categories of information to compare and contrast.

_____

Developing Content

By Asking Questions

The process of comparing and contrasting should begin with questions. For example, if investigating different cultural attitudes toward time, you might test your own values with such questions as:

> Do I rush to arrive early for appointments? Do I feel uncomfortable when I am late for an appointment? Do I like to be early? How early? How late do I consider so late that I must excuse myself? What about dinner engagements? Parties? How late do I believe one can be and still be polite? Am I a clockwatcher? Do I feel disoriented without my watch or does not knowing the particular time not bother me? Can I let time go by without doing anything "constructive" or do I believe that every moment counts? Do I get irritated when kept waiting? Am I uncomfortable when waiting in lines? Do I make lists of things to do? Do I have a low sense of time urgency or a high sense of time urgency? Are these attitudes unique to me or do they reflect attitudes basic to my culture?

Such questions should start you thinking about the differences between your attitudes and those of a culture you must deal with. If, for example, you survey classmates, roommates, or friends and find attitudes that differ greatly from your own, such differences could be the beginning of a good paper. In other words, asking questions is an effective way to brainstorm and to move from self-generated information to supplementation by external sources.

By Listing

As Exercises 14.3 and 14.4 make clear, another effective brainstorming technique for comparison-contrast papers is to list. However, a comparison-contrast list takes a different form from the usual brainstorming list; usually you need three columns instead of one: the first for item A, the second for contrasting information about item B, and the third in the middle for shared qualities, as you saw with the Amazon and Nile comparison on page 294. For example, someone comparing and/or contrasting Panama and Louisiana might begin with a list such as the following.

Panama	Louisiana
country in Central America	state in USA
Similar in size	
_____ sq. miles	_____ sq. miles
Shaped like a snake	Shaped like an L
Swamp and jungle	Just swamp; no jungle
Lake near Panama City	Lake near New Orleans
Problems with corruption in government	
Economy depends on canal	Economy depends on river
Panama City an international port	New Orleans a national and an international port
Water is very important to both	
Speak Spanish	Speak English
Borders Atlantic and Pacific	Borders Gulf of Mexico
Center for goods from east and west	Center for goods from north and south
Historically dominated by other governments	
By Spanish, by U.S.	By Spanish, French, Northern U.S.

As you continue to consider Panama and Louisiana, asking questions will confirm the need for research: Exactly how large is each place? Specific square miles? Population? Particular dates for the historical events? Precise import and export goods? Clearly a good encyclopedia or almanac could help. The reference room of your college library is a good place to begin filling in information gaps.

By Narrowing the Focus

Even if you collect more specific information, a paper that merely incorporates or includes the information from this list in a series of comparison-contrast sentences would not be very good because this information is still too general, too scattered, too diverse. However, this list will help you decide on a focus, perhaps on Panama and Louisiana's mutual history of outside domination, on reputed problems in the government, or on both places as crossroads and trade centers. In other words, you must narrow the topic to something more manageable. The list suggests that two cities in the two areas have much in common and that what is in common is related to water, so per-haps "water is very important to both cities" could be the starting point for a new, more focused list. (Other topics are also possible.)

Panama City	New Orleans
Capital of a country Panama	Most important city of a state, Louisiana
Due to location on water	
Both important port cities due to location	
Both trade centers for national and international goods	
Central trade focus for East/West axis due to canal	Central trade focus in US for North/South axis due to river
Panama Canal connecting Atlantic and Pacific	Mississippi River connecting heart-land of America with international waters
Both set on lakes which provide city water and city entertainment	
Both surrounded by swamps which limit usable land space and produce problems with mosquitoes and sickness	

This new list has uncovered and focused on a very interesting connection between the two cities: the important influence of water on their history, on their economy, and on their welfare. It has also intro-duced the possibility of a division into the negative versus the positive effects of water. At this point, the list has helped provide the groundwork for a possible paper and a set of categories for further exploration.

By Outlining

Once you have a suitably narrow comparison-contrast topic, the next step is to set up a general outline and to collect details to fill it in. The follow-ing outline might be a starting point. Key words tell the reader that this will be mainly a comparison paper (both), built on a cause/effect relationship (affected); it will be divided into three main sections (history, economy, welfare) and will explore these in each city (Panama City and New Orleans) in terms of the positive and the negative (both negatively and positively). Such key words should be repeated in a different form in the conclusion.

Initial Outline

I. Thesis: The water that surrounds both Panama City and New Orleans has greatly affect-ed the two cities both negatively and positively, in terms of their history, their economy, and their welfare.

II. Body of paper
  A. How water affected history
    1. Of Panama City
      a. Negatively
        1) Swamp made travel difficult
        2) Produced mosquitoes
          a) Malaria and yellow fever
          b) Thousands died
      b. Positively
        1) Isthmus between two oceans attracted travelers, tradesmen, business
        2) Led to building of famous Panama Canal
    2. Of New Orleans
      a. Negatively
        1) Swamp made travel difficult
        2) Produced mosquitoes
          a) Malaria and yellow fever
          b) Thousands died
      b. Positively
        1) River between north and south attracted travelers, tradesmen, business
        2) Led to building of port
  B. How water affects economy
    1. Of Panama City
      a. Negatively
        1)
        2)
      b. Positively
        1)
        2)
    2. Of New Orleans
      a. Negatively
        1)
        2)
      b. Positively
        1)
        2)
  C. How water affects welfare
    1. Of Panama City
      a. Negatively
        1)
        2)
      b. Positively
        1)
        2)
    1. Of New Orleans
      a. Negatively
        1)
        2)
      b. Positively
        1)
        2)

III. Conclusion: Thus it is the water that surrounds these two cities, the swamp, the lake, but most importantly the canal and the river respectively, that have made these cities what they are after many histori-cal problems: important port cities that are international trade centers.

Comparing and Contrasting 295

- EXERCISE 14.5 NARROWING THE TOPIC

A. Which of the following topics are acceptable for a four-page paper? Which would need to be narrowed down? Offer suggestions for limiting topics to cover less material. What topics do you anticipate writers will have problems finding enough information to write about? Are any of these topics too difficult to research? Will interviews with knowledgeable "informants" help?

> *Example:* A Contrast between Asian Families and American Families
> Problem? too broad
>
> Add limiting adjectives: A Contrast between Modern Indonesian Urban Families and Modern Californian Urban Families
>
> Add limiting phrases: A Contrast in Attitudes toward Children Between Modern Indonesian Urban Families and Modern Californian Urban Families
>
> Add limiting nouns: A Contrast in Attitudes toward Children Between Modern Indonesian and Modern CalifornianUrban Parents
>
> Reduce for clarity of focus: Disciplining Children: the Different Attitudes of Indonesian and Californian Urban Parents
>
> Reducing further: Physical versus Verbal Discipline: Contrasting Attitudes between Indonesian and Californian Urban Parents *What makes this last topic more manageable?*

1. Eating at a Fast-Food Restaurant versus Eating at an Old-fashioned Restaurant
2. Religion in Ecuador versus Religion in the United States
3. The American Idea of a University versus the Colombian Idea of a University
4. A Contrast between the Japanese Karaoke Bar and the American Karaoke Bar
5. Violence and Crime in the United States versus Japan
6. Vietnamese Eggrolls and Chinese Eggrolls: Similarities and Differences
7. Mexican Attitudes towards Pets versus American Attitudes towards Pets
8. Jazz versus Blues
9. Traditional Chinese Music versus Traditional American Music
10. My Hometown compared to My College Town

B. Select one of the topics mentioned in A. Narrow it to a manageable focus for a three- or four-page comparison-contrast paper. Explain what you must do to meet the expectations established by your essay title. Then write the paper.

This outline, an experimental sketch of a writing plan, commits the writer to three body sections, and within each section, a part about Panama City and then a part about New Orleans. This is called a <u>modified block form</u>. That is, the information about one unit (Panama City) is presented together as a block of information, before readers are given similar information about the second unit (New Orleans).

The above outline calls for a very long paper. If the writer is not prepared to commit to a paper of over ten pages, he or she should probably change the outline, perhaps to focus only on the negative or only on the positive effects of water on the history of the two cities. Such a change would eliminate the need for an *a* and *a b* division like those presented above. Instead only positive (or negative depending on the choice) details about the particular city would be presented.

Notice too that the details in section II. A. of the outline are repetitious. The section on New Orleans merely repeats the section on Panama City. When this happens, it is perhaps best to change to an alternating form such as the following, which allows you to discuss the two together rather than as separate units. Some teachers prefer the alternating style in student papers because it forces the writer to draw more careful parallels between parts of their topic.

TOPIC: How water affected the <u>history of the two cities</u>

I. Negatively

  A. Swamp made travel difficult in both

    1. Slow and difficult

    2. Easy to get lost

    3. Danger from quicksand, alligators, snakes, and so forth

  B. Swamp produced mosquitoes in both

    1. Malaria & yellow fever

    2. Thousands died

II. Positively

  A. Isthmus between two oceans in Panama City attracted travelers, tradesmen, business, as did the river between north and south in New Orleans

    1. Became international trade centers

    2. Became local trade centers

  B. Isthmus and river led to building of famous Canal in Panama City and of ports in both cities

Water in Panama (above) and in New Orleans (center and right).

• Exercise 14.6: Outlining for comparison-contrast

1. A paper contrasting fast-food restaurants with old-fashioned ones might consider type of food, quality of food, quantity of food, price, speed of service, type of service, music, atmosphere, decor, table setting, reasons for the choice of one over the other. What else might be considered? Make a brief outline for a paper on this topic. Be prepared to defend the logic of your plan.

2. Choose one of the other topics from the list in the Exercise 14.2 on page 289 (after they have been limited). Brainstorm about the type of information necessary to develop the topic. Then write an outline that will provide a logical plan for that information.

3. Which of the two potential paper topics you have selected is easier to outline? Why? Which do you personally know the most about? Which will require outside sources of information? What kinds of information will you need to gather?

Employing Self-Criticism

Learning to write well means learning to criticize your own efforts. One way this book will help you learn self-criticism is to provide a sample of the type of analysis teachers make of student efforts so you can learn to analyze your own work, see what is missing, and make corrections on your own. Writing is thinking and thinking must involve analysis.

Model #1: Cuzco and Chiclayo

Although both Cuzco and Chiclayo are cities in Peru, Cuzco is in the mountain region and Chiclayo is on the coast. Therefore Cuzco is higher than Chiclayo. These cities differ not only in the elevation at which they are located but also in their language use, architecture, weather, and nightlife. [thesis sentence; unifying categories]

The language in these cities is very different. The people in both cities speak Spanish, but most people in Cuzco also speak Quechua, the Inca language, because the Incans had more influence on Cuzco than on the people from Chiclayo and because the Cuzcans want to keep the original language. Also in some parts of Cuzco they speak English because there is much tourism, while Chiclayo does not have much tourism. The Cuzcans keep some Incan customs like language, dress, meals, and different events while Chiclayo maintains more of a Spanish-oriented culture.

The structures of Cuzco are completely different from those of Chiclayo. In Cuzco the houses are little and most of them were built with large stones by the Incas, whereas those in Chiclayo reflect the Spanish influence, with big houses made of brick and adobe. Cuzco also has several churches which were built by Incas but with Spanish influ-

ence. Cuzco has beautiful, ancient architecture while Chiclayo has more modern architecture. The Cuzcan houses also have peaked roofs because in this city it rains a lot whereas Chiclayan houses have flat roofs because there it does not rain much.

In Chiclayo, the weather is hot, windy, and dry because the city is on the edge of the desert and there is no vegetation around it. Also, it is very close to sea level, 20 meters above sea level. The nearness of the Pacific Ocean influences the weather. In Cuzco the weather is cold, and it is rarely windy because Cuzco is located 1500 meters above sea level and surrounded by mountains. Therefore, when people who live on the coast go to Cuzco, sometimes they have difficulty breathing. The principal activities in both cities are agriculture and commerce but Chiclayo is more business-oriented than Cuzco.

On the weekend the life in these cities is very different because the weather affects the attitudes. In Chiclayo families go to the beach or to several clubs to swim or play games and sometimes they go to Piura, a city located next to Chiclayo, to eat or to go to other beaches because it only takes two hours by car. In contrast, in Cuzco families usually go to the public square where they talk with their friends. They also have traditional parties that are very interesting for those who want to know about Incan traditions because the people show off traditional dresses, typical music, instruments, dances, and meals.

Both Cuzco and Chiclayo are very interesting cities, Cuzco because of its closeness to Inca history and traditions and Chiclayo because of its beautiful beaches and its friendly people.

—Stella Guillen, Peru

Model #2: Japanese Baths Versus American Baths

One of the biggest <u>differences</u> between Japanese and American lifestyles is the bath. Most Americans do not know about the Japanese bath.

<u>Unlike</u> the American bathroom system, the Japanese bath is in a separate room from the toilet. In the Japanese room for a bath, there is a bathtub, a bath-tank (which is used to boil water), a shower, and washing space. <u>Compared to</u> the long rectangular American bathtub, the Japanese one is square and bigger. Usually the shower is at the wall in the American bathroom, <u>whereas</u> the Japanese shower is connected to a bath-tank by a long hose.

<u>Unlike</u> the American who takes a shower in the morning to start a new day comfortably, the Japanese takes a bath before going to bed because the Japanese bathe to lose their tiredness and to wash off the day's sweat. Before taking a bath , the Japanese pour hot water into a bathtub, or pour water in and boil it. Then the Japanese wash dirt off their body at a washing place and soap themselves completely there. Then they soak their body in the hot water. Thus, the Japanese take a lot of time to take a bath. <u>Unlike</u> the Japanese, Americans wash their bodies in bath-tubs and very rarely pour hot water on their body.

Taking a shower in the morning was one of the most difficult things to get used to when I came to the U.S.A., for I could not understand why the American takes a shower in the morning. But now that I am used to doing it I am not able to start a day if I do not take a shower. In fact, now, I sometimes take a shower twice a day. [<u>Would a less personal conclusion about the reasons for the differences or the effects of the differences be better? Why or why not?</u>]

---

1. What do these papers do well?
2. Do they use the alternating, block or modified block form?
3. Which of the two is easier to outline? Why?
4. Which of the two is better developed? Explain.
5. Do they need more information? Why or why not?
6. What types of information could be added?

The Cuzco–Chiclayo paper is a good model to imitate. However, the second essay on baths is not. The discussion of Japanese baths is an example of a potentially good paper that fails to live up to its promise because the writer has not thought enough about the difference between what she knows and what her audience knows. She knows about Japanese baths but her audience doesn't, so she needs to describe and explain more fully. She also needs to think about her topic and purpose. Should she merely discuss the physical differences between baths and bathrooms? Are physical differences by themselves significant or interesting? Should she instead think more carefully about the reasons for the physical differences and try to connect these reasons with cultural ideas about bathing, attitudes that produce the physical differences?

In other words, her revision should probably deal with such questions as the following: Do most Japanese know about the American bath? Does the bath serve a practical function? A recreational one? A psychological one? What is the significance of these differences? Why do they exist? Are these the major differences? Do they reflect different ideas about bathing? What do these details reveal about the difference in purpose and in attitude toward baths in the two cultures? How does this writer's personal experience relate to the contrast between the two cultures? The contrast in purpose between Japanese and American baths? The paper should really be about differing definitions of the word *bathe*: in the U.S., a simple, utilitarian action to clean the body and start the day; in Japan, a ritual loaded with meaning which has more to do with relieving stress and ending the day in sensuous pleasure than with simply washing the body for practical purposes of hygiene.

Unifying through Transitions

The comparison-contrast form should always be immediately recognizable from the transition words used. For comparisons, the most common connectives are the following:

alike	in a similar way	similarly	equally important
both	in like manner	accordingly	the same
like	in common	in accord	neither.

You say *They look alike* but *He looks like his father.* *Both* and *neither* emphasize shared qualities or activities, ones that are held *in common* or *the same*. Words related to addition of information also frequently appear in comparisons (*in fact, furthermore, too, moreover, in addition, also*). Comparisons also tend to use adjective patterns with *as... as*, as in *she works as hard as her sister, so... as*, as in *she doesn't think so quickly as her sister*, or *-er* or *more* words of comparison with *than*, as in *he thinks faster on his feet than his friend does*. The superlative form with the article *the*, as in *the best player, the worst job, the most important goal, the least common method, the tallest building* might also be used in comparison papers.

For contrasts, the most common connectives are:

although	in contrast	the opposite
but	in spite of	though
despite	instead of	unlike
differ from	in turn	where
different from	nevertheless	whereas
dissimilar	nonetheless	while
even though	on the one hand	yet
however	on the other hand	

These words are used in different situations, with *although/even though/despite* setting up expectations that are not fulfilled and with *while/whereas/in contrast* making direct contrasts. *Nevertheless/however/on the one hand* connect between separate sentences, *in spite of/despite/instead* of introduce nouns, and *although/while/whereas* introduce subordinate clauses.

- ### EXERCISE:14.7: WRITING ASSIGNMENTS

  A. 1. First identify the categories of information provided in the following lists. **Categories**

   1. Abraham Lincoln   John F. Kennedy   _____

   Both 7 letters in last name

Born in Kentucky in 19th Century	Born in Massachusetts in 20th Century	
Born in modest log cabin	Born into wealth, power, prestige	family position
Father a dirt-poor farmer	Father a rich businessman/ American ambassador to England	
One year in frontier school/ self-educated	Educated at the best schools like Harvard	_____

   Both avid readers

Spoke with country accent ("git," "thar")	Spoke with urban Boston accent	_____
Narrow-chested/stoop-shouldered	Well-built, but bad back	_____
Wrestler/weight-lifter/log splitter	Football player at Harvard	_____
Successful lawyer/a noted storyteller and speaker	A Navy Commander/ a popular Senator, a noted speaker	_____

Sixteenth president of the USA	Thirty-fifth president of the USA	_____
Elected president 1860	Elected president in 1960	_____
A wartime president (Civil War)	A cold-war president (Cuban Missile Crisis)	_____

   Both concerned with civil rights   _____

Much respected as antislavery/ pro-human rights/peacemaker/ a man of conscience	Much respected for Peace Corps/ human rights legislation/ Alliance for Progress	_____

Famous for Gettysburg Address	Famous for Inaugural Address	_____
Helped African-Americans gain freedom	Helped African-Americans win Civil Rights	_____
Nicknamed "Honest Abe"	Called affectionately "JFK"	_____
Assassinated while in office on April 14, 1865	Assassinated while in office on November 22, 1963	_____

Both killed on a Friday in the presence of their wives _____

shot from behind _____

shot in the head _____

Both succeeded by a Senator Johnson— _____

Southern Democrats with 13 letters in their names: _____

Andrew Johnson (born 1808)　　　　Lyndon Johnson (born 1908) _____

Both killed by Southerners who favored unpopular ideas and _____

had 15 letters in their names _____

John Wilkes Booth (born 1839)　　　Lee Harvey Oswald (born 1939) _____

Both assassins killed before brought to trial _____

Both warned by secretaries: _____

| Lincoln's secretary (named Kennedy) advised him not to go to theater | Kennedy's secretary (named Lincoln) advised him not to go to Dallas | _____ |
| John Wilkes Booth shot Lincoln in a theater and ran to a warehouse | Lee Harvey Oswald shot Kennedy from a warehouse and then ran to a theater | _____ |

2. Select three or more of your categories as the basis for your essay.

3. Use the categories to help you construct a thesis and topic sentences.

4. Use a modified block form to develop an effective comparison-contrast.

5. Include transition words to connect ideas.

B. Compare a famous American with a famous person from your country, region, or cultural heritage. What made these people famous? What do/did they have in common? How are/were they different? What difficulties did they have to face? What has each contributed to his/her culture or country? Begin with a chart like the one for Lincoln and Kennedy, citing information about one on one side and the other on the other side.

Chart

A Famous Person from your Country, Cultural Heritage or Region	A Famous American
Name _____	_____
Origin _____	_____
Dates _____	_____
Background _____	_____
Education _____	_____
Position _____	_____
Activities _____	_____
Famous Quotes _____	_____
Significant Acts _____	_____
Importance _____	_____

Avoiding Common Pitfalls

1. If you use the block form, make sure that the organization of one paragraph or section of your comparison-contrast is repeated in the next paragraph or section of your paper: A 1, 2, 3, 4; B 1, 2, 3, 4.

2. In the alternating form, make sure that every (A) has a corresponding (B) and that the information in (A) and (B) shows parallel similarities or differences.

3. In a modified block pattern be sure that alternating topic sentences and alternating paragraph conclusions keep the reader focused on the essential categories.

4. Use enough transition words to allow readers to follow your ideas. Don't take for granted that the reader can see the same connections that you do. Spell out those connections clearly, or you might find they never occur in your readers' minds. In particular, pay attention to transitions in the block form to assure that readers see the parallels you intend.

5. Keep your paper from degenerating into a disconnected list by employing unifying, clarifying categories.

• EXERCISE 14.8: TRANSITIONS

A. Underline the topic sentence of each of the following paragraphs. Then underline the transitions that help create the comparison-contrast argument. Do they use an alternating or a block form?

1. Puerto Rico already has a population problem, and it is bound to get worse. A comparison between Puerto Rico and the states of Mississippi and Colorado makes clear the extent of the problem. First, the state of Mississippi has 47,233 square miles of land and a population of 2,573,216, while Puerto Rico has 3,459 square miles of land with a population of 3,552,037. In other words, Mississippi is thirteen times larger than Puerto Rico but has a million fewer inhabitants. Secondly, the state of Colorado has 103,595 square miles of land and a population of 3,214,394. That means Colorado is thirty times bigger than Puerto Rico but with three hundred thousand fewer people. In Puerto Rico a square mile area holds 1,027 people. Such statistics explain Puerto Rico's present problems with poverty and crime, and suggest future dangers unless steps are taken soon to stabilize Puerto Rico's population situation.
    —Efrain Gonzalez, Puerto Rico

    Form: _____

2. American and Japanese classes differ in schedules, manners, and content. American classes begin in September and end in May. In contrast, Japanese classes begin in April and end in March. Furthermore, Americans don't have classes on Saturday, whereas Japanese do. Once in school, the patterns of behavior differ. Japanese students change their outdoor shoes to a kind of soft tennis shoe when they enter school buildings, but American students do not. When American classes start, students don't greet the teacher in a formal way. However, when Japanese classes start, students stand up and bow to their teacher and after classes are finished, they do the same again. In American classes, students should not call their teacher, "Teacher," but instead should call them "Dr. last name" or "Mr. or Ms. last name." However, Japanese students usually call their teachers merely, "Teacher" and never use a teacher's first name. American teach-

ers seem to be informal with students, whereas Japanese teachers and students have a more distant and formal relationship. While American students might speak out in class to answer a question enthusiastically, a Japanese student will quietly raise a low hand and will answer only if called on. Furthermore, Japanese teachers are stricter than American teachers. What students study is harder too. Japanese students are required to learn English from junior high school on, but Americans don't have to learn another language. Japanese math classes are more rigorous, and there is less time for the fun and games that are a part of most American high schools. Overall then, Japanese and American classes differ in when they start, what students are expected to do, how classes are conducted, and what is taught.

Form _____

3.   On June 17, 1775, British regulars faced an assemblage of independently minded colonial militia at the Battle of Bunker Hill. Both armies fought courageously and learned much. The colonials, many shaken by their first taste of war, proved to themselves that in direct confrontation they could stop the British army, a force superior in training, equipment, and organization. The British, in turn, learned a new respect for the determination and resourcefulness of colonial forces. Both lessons were painful. The Americans had indeed shown they could stand up to the British in traditional open field combat, but they paid for this knowledge with 400 to 600 casualties. The British, in turn, captured Bunker Hill, but, out of the 2,200 soldiers engaged, 1,304 became casualties. As a result, the British, now aware of previously unsuspected dangers, attempted no further actions outside Boston for the next nine months. During that time the Americans also used their new knowledge of their strengths and weaknesses to search for and find the stronger leadership that would be critical to success in further battles. The next military action found the British more cautious in their attack and more respectful of the fighting ability of the colonials, but it also found the Americans more determined and better organized under the leadership of George Washington, the newly chosen Commander-in-Chief of the newly organized Continental Army.

Form _____

B. Complete the paragraphs with appropriate connecting words.

1.   _____ fossil energy, the energy of the sun is almost inexhaustible. Solar energy will exist as long as our sun exists; _____, fossil energy is being steadily depleted. Fossil fuel must be burned and therefore pollutes, _____ solar energy is clean and non-polluting. _____, solar energy is available worldwide; _____ , fossil fuel is available only in limited areas.

2.   Dogs, _____ human beings, respond well to love and affection. In fact, dog owners frequently discuss how much they have _____ with their dogs, while dog watchers note that frequently dogs and owners seem to _____ characteristics. A thin owner might have a thin dog, _____ an energetic person might have a very active dog. _____ dog and owner begin to act in _____ patterns: rising at the same hour, feeling excited or depressed on the same days, responding to people in a similar way.

The following paragraphs fail to follow a standard comparison–contrast pattern or commit errors of logic or form. Study them carefully. Be prepared to discuss what expectations and pattern the writer establishes, and when and where the writer breaks that pattern. Offer suggestions for improvements.

1. Early Spanish gold seekers went up the Paraguayan river system to find the riches of the Incan Empire, which lay on Paraguay's western edge. However, Paraguay itself didn't have mineral wealth, so it was settled mainly by farmers instead of treasure hunters. It was generally ignored by the Spanish government. Independence came in 1811. Peru was originally the center of the Incan Empire, which stretched along the coast from Colombia to southern Chile. Then it became the seat of Spanish power in colonial South America. Peru achieved independence in 1824.

   Errors _____

2. My friend Francisco is really very much like my friend Gopal. They are shy, and don't talk easily with people. They are athletic: Francisco lifts weights and plays soccer; Gopal studies karate. One is from Panama and the other is from India. They both enjoy science. Francisco studied biology and enjoyed the lab. Gopal is a pre-medical student and hopes to be a doctor someday. Francisco is a good artist. He draws quick sketches of his teachers and classmates on the computer and makes everyone laugh because they are satiric and funny and true to life. Gopal is not an artist, but he is good with machinery of every sort and spends a lot of his time with it. So you see that my two friends are very much alike despite their differences.

   Errors _____

3. Modern scientists have made many, very different predictions about the future. Robert Preholda, an expert in biological technology, predicts that anti–aging pills will one day be available. He also believes that people will be able to be cloned (to reproduce an identical twin through asexual reproduction). Jean Rostand, a world-renowned biologist, and author of dozens of science books, doesn't believe brain transplants will ever be possible. He does think some animals can be "humanized" by putting human hormones into them to increase their intelligence. He thinks chemicals will be able to get rid of exhaustion. Internationally respected biologist, Dr. E.S.E. Hafew, from Washington State University, predicts that very soon a woman will be able to walk into an embryo store and select a baby with specific physical, mental, and emotional attributes, have the embryo implanted in her uterus, and in nine months give birth to a genetically guaranteed infant. They all see these changes as good. None of them talk about the dangers or negative side of such changes.

   Errors _____

4. Both artists chose a print form which could be reproduced again. Utamaro's medium was the wood print, which was produced entirely by hand. The paper used with it was thin and transparent, and the wood block was usually cherry wood in order to produce very clear lines. In contrast, Cassatt relied on three media: dry point, soft ground etching, and aquatint. Although she had previously done sketches, oil paintings, and pastels, she was and still is treated as if she were originally a printmaker. Utamaro started out in different media too but became most famous for woodprints. Nancy Mathew remarks on Cassatt's involvement in the late nineteenth-century "etching revivals" and on the prestige "increasingly attached to printmaking."

   Errors _____

Final Checklist

- ☐ Have you observed the overall patterns of good writing with a clear thesis idea and concrete support? Does your thesis make clear that a comparison or contrast will follow? Does it establish the key relationships to be covered in your paper?
- ☐ Is your structural pattern (block, alternating or modified block) clear, consistent, and balanced? Do you provide equivalent information for both sides of your equation?
- ☐ Do you provide unifying categories? Are your categories included in your thesis and topic sentences?
- ☐ Do your connective words guide the reader through the relationships established in your paper?

Passages for Discussion and Analysis

The Mountains of Mexico and Iceland

Although both Mexico and Iceland have mountainous regions, the Mexican region reaches much higher above sea level (18,855 feet) than the Icelandic one (6952 feet). However, these regions differ not only in height but also in vegetation and population. From sea level to 3000 feet, Mexico has palms and tropical vegetation and 15 persons per square mile, while from 3000 to 11,000 feet these change to hardwoods, grain fields, and some desert. This latter area is very densely populated, with 25 persons per square mile up to 7000 feet and 140 persons per square mile from 7000 to 10,000 feet. Not until the 11,000 to 12,000 foot level does the terrain become comparable to that of Iceland. This Mexican region is like the Icelandic sea-level-to-2000-foot area, though it has evergreen trees where Iceland has birch trees. However, this area in Mexico is unpopulated, while in Iceland it has 10 persons per square mile. From 12,000 to 15,000 feet in Mexico and from 2000 to 3000 in Iceland there is little vegetation; however, in Iceland this area supports 10 persons per square mile, while in Mexico the comparable area is unpopulated. About 15,000 feet above sea level in Mexico and about 3000 feet in Iceland the region is barren and uninhabited. Mexican mountains are snow-covered in the cold months, while Icelandic mountains are snow-covered year-round. The Icelandic volcanoes provide geothermal heat that could eventually take care of the needs of the entire population; the Mexican volcanoes do not. Clearly, the Mexican mountain region is more amenable to human and plant life than the Icelandic region; the Icelandic area supports at least 14 times fewer people, but more for its vegetation than the Mexican region does for the same vegetation.

major similarity
obvious difference
key divisions for discussion
spatial arrangement
contrast between Mexican levels
comparison with Iceland begins
difference
similarity
difference
similarity
conclusion: summary of major differences

•Questions for Discussion

1. Underline the specific details in the above paper. What is the effect of the details?

2. Is the form block, alternating, or modified block? Explain.

3. How does the type of information affect the form used?

4. Put this information into a chart form. Is it easy to do so? Why or why not? What would be the two main divisions? What subdivisions should there be on each side?

British Columbian Indians: Patterns of the Past in Patterns of the Present

The waste disposal habits of the Indians of British Columbia seem very strange to outsiders, but they are only applying <u>ancient</u> practices to <u>modern</u> times. <u>For centuries</u>, exploiting the abundance of natural products and the cleansing effects of nature, the Indians have regularly moved from place to place. <u>Traditionally</u> they lived in one place only long enough to use up the natural resources; they would pile high

their oyster and clam shells and their leftover bones, leather, wood, etc., all around their longhouses (communal dwellings), and then they would move on to build other homes , leaving the waste behind. They do the same <u>today</u>, only their trash is modern. They build a house at the bottom of a hill, and around it build up a pile of tin cans, discarded refrigerators and stoves, burned out cars. Then, when the discards get to be too much and too high, they move further up the hill and build another house and start another pile of trash. The phenomenon seems very strange to outsiders, not at all one's romantic image of natives in a primeval [natural] forest. Nonetheless, it was the custom of <u>generations before</u> the <u>modern</u> development of non-natural trash, which lasts, for all purposes, forever.

•• Writing Exercise

Decide on a very narrow contrast topic, manageable in a paragraph (how people in your country greet each other as opposed to how Americans greet each other, the main features of an American neighborhood versus the main features of a neighborhood from your city, use of cosmetics or jewelry in different countries, typical ways to spend leisure time after class here and in your country or city, etc.). Brainstorm; make two lists of possible supportive details, one list for each side of the contrast. Then write your description.

William K. Stevens, in a *New York Times* article on the "Vanishing Architect of the Savanna," captures the importance of elephants to the African environment and their vital effect on other creatures in the area. Stevens argues that the extinction of the African elephant would change the landscape and would endanger other species. The key underlying contrast is between a land with elephants and a land without elephants. You might find it difficult to read, but use your techniques for guessing, and focus on the key ideas, the key argument, rather than on understanding every word.

Vanishing Architect of the Savanna

It is the elephant's metabolism [rate of energy use] and appetite that make it a disturber of the environment and therefore an important creator of habitat. In a constant search for the 300 pounds of vegetation it must have every day, it kills small trees and underbrush and pulls branches off big trees as high as its trunk will reach. This creates innumerable open spaces in both deep tropical forests and in the woodlands that cover part of the African savannas [grasslands]. The resulting patchwork, a mosaic [mixture] of vegetation in various stages of regeneration, in turn, creates a greater variety of forage [food] that attracts a greater variety of other vegetation-eaters than would otherwise be the case.

In studies over the past 20 years in southern Kenya near Mount Kilimanjaro, animal researcher [Mr.] Western, has found that when elephants are allowed to roam [go where they want to] the savannas naturally and normally, they spread out at "intermediate densities." Their foraging [search for food] creates a mixture of savanna woodlands (what the Africans call bush) and grassland. The result is a highly diverse array of other plant-eating species: those such as the zebra, wildebeest, and gazelle, that graze [eat grass]; those such as the giraffe, bushbuck, and lesser kudu, that browse on tender shoots, buds, twigs, and leaves; and plant-eating primates such as the baboon and verbet monkey. These herbivores [plant-eaters] attract carnivores [meat-eaters] such as the lion and cheetah.

"When the elephant population thins out," Western said, "the woodlands become denser and the grazers are squeezed out." When pressure from poachers [illegal hunters] forces elephants to crowd more densely onto reservations, the woodlands there are knocked out and the browsers and primates disappear.

Something similar appears to happen in dense [thick] tropical rain forests. In their natural state, because the overhead forest canopy [cover of leaves] shuts out sunlight and prevents growth on the forest floor, rain forests provide slim pickings [little food] for large, hoofed plant-eaters. By pulling down trees and eating new growth, elephants enlarge natural openings in the canopy, allowing plants to regenerate on the forest floor and bringing down vegetation from the canopy so that smaller species can get at it. In such situations, the rain forest becomes hospitable to large, plant-eating mammals such as bongos, bush pigs, dulkers, forest hogs, swamp antelopes, forest buffaloes, okapis, sometimes gorillas, and always a host [large group] of smaller animals that thrive [live well] on secondary growth. When elephants disappear and the forest reverts [goes back to an earlier state], the larger mammals give way to smaller, nimbler [quicker] animals such as monkeys, squirrels, and rodents; "As the forest becomes more mature," Western said, "one loses the abundance [large number] of large animals in the forest, and it's quite possible that in some places they would disappear as the elephant disappears."

"On the savanna," he said, zebras, wildebeests, and gazelles, "would disappear in some very important areas that are now grassland."

•• Writing Assignment

Summarize the above argument in five or six sentences. Look for the idea behind the descriptive details, the idea the details prove or support or help readers visualize and understand. Compare your summary with those of classmates. Include Stevens' contrast and his cause-effect argument.

•• Writing Assignments

A. Use the following information to help you develop a paragraph or paragraphs on ways humans signal agreement/acceptance (*yes*) or denial/refusal (*no*). Develop some possible topic sentences. What different patterns of organization do they call for?

1. Head Nod: several vertical up and down head movements with the "down" elements stronger than the "up" elements

2. Function: to acknowledge listening, to encourage continued speech, to signal understanding, to signal agreement, to confirm facts

3. Meaning:
   a. *Yes* for most peoples of the world, including Australian Aborigines, Amazonian Indians, Eskimos, Samoans, Russians, Japanese, Chinese, many African tribes, Americans, New Zealanders, and a majority of Europeans
   b. In Ceylon, movement depends on type of question, the type of *yes* involved

4. Origin: the beginning of a bowing action—submission.

VERSUS

1. Head Shake: head turns horizontally from side to side, with equal emphasis to left and right

2. Function: to signify disapproval, to signal not understanding, to signal disagreement, to say "I can't," to say "I won't," to say "I don't know."

3. Meaning:
   a. *No* or some equivalent negative response: nearly global range
   b. Similar to head sway (rhythmic head tilt from side to side), which means "yes" in Bulgaria, Yugoslavia, Turkey, Iran, Bengal, and Greece. Origin: "I'm all ears," emphasizing listening carefully

4. Origin: infant rejection of breast (babies do this when they don't want their mothers' milk).

B. Choose <u>one</u> of the following topics. First, informally outline your ideas. Then, write a well-developed paragraph based on your outline. Underline your topic sentence and circle your transition words. Although the main pattern of development will be contrast, you might need to classify, divide into parts, use process, give examples, or describe to develop your idea. When you have completed your paragraph, reread it carefully and correct any errors.

1. Contrast the writing problems you have now with the writing problems you had at the beginning of this course.

2. Contrast good study habits with bad study habits.

3. Contrast the informality of spoken English with the formality of written English, providing examples to illustrate your points.

4. Contrast ideas about good writing in your culture with ideas about good writing in this culture.

5. Contrast attitudes toward the role of women in your culture with attitudes toward the role of women in the USA.

C. To contrast the teaching style in your country with the teaching style in the U.S., draw a chart with your country on one side and the U.S. on the other. Then list categories to be compared or contrasted. (Alternate topic: Contrast teaching style in high school versus teaching style in college.) In either case, your categories might include the following:

Teacher's dress: casual/informal/rarely wear suits/sometimes jeans
Teacher's stance: sit on table/cross and uncross legs/move around a lot
Type of presentation: lecture? discussion? question/answer?
Manner of presentation:
Teacher's relationship to students
Dominant type of tests

You might think of other categories like *eye contact*, *rules*, *method of correction*, and so forth.

If you don't know much about the teaching style in the U.S., observe your teachers carefully; ask permission to sit in on a regular American university class to observe interaction; interview American students.

1. Once you have made a complete list of everything that you can think of related to teaching style, decide on logical groupings for your information. For instance, do dress and stance go together? Is "manner of presentation" related to "relationship to students"? Then, develop a topic sentence for each grouping.

2. Develop each of your topic sentences into a paragraph, expanding the information from your list to help you develop your ideas.

3. Decide on a logical order for those paragraphs and write a thesis sentence that will express that order.

4 Finally, combine your thesis and paragraphs into a single paper, with a conclusion to sum up the key differences.

D. Compare and contrast modern American and ancient Roman baths in terms of size, appearance, and function or

Compare and contrast a modern bath in your own country with that of the ancient Romans, again in terms of size, appearance, and function—or whatever else seems significant.

Roman Bath

Japanese Bath

Western Bath

E. Compare and contrast the native clothing of two or three countries. You may base your description on what you see in the pictures or on your own personal knowledge.

Japan

Turkey

Greece

El Salvador

Japan

Thailand

F. Compare or contrast any one of the following sets of two or three. Your paper may be based on personal knowledge, on what you observe in the pictures below, on what you find out from interviewing others, or from library research:
1. Gauchos, Cowboys, Samurai
2. American Kitchen, Indian Kitchen, Vietnamese Kitchen, Russian Kitchen, Ethiopian Kitchen, Mexican Poblano Kitchen, That of Your Country   (Choose two or three)
3. Wedding Dresses: Vietnamese, Russian, American, Cambodian, That of Your Country

Cowboys

Samurai

Gaucho

Rural Mexican

Rural African

Russian

Wedding Dress

Vietnamese

Western

Russian

Cambodian

Japanese

G. Write a well-organized paper about the problems foreign students encounter in the U.S. and problems at home. Develop it using comparison-contrast.

H. Generating Information: INTERVIEW PAPER

1. Pair off with someone from a country (or city) and, if possible, a language group other than your own. One person will be the interviewer for about ten to fifteen minutes. Then the interviewer will become the interviewee for another ten to fifteen minutes.

2. Think of <u>two contrasting ideas</u> about the other person that would be interesting to write about. For example, the person had an easy life in the past/the person had a hard life recently; the person is quiet and religious/the person likes to go to parties and have a good time; the person is interested in sports/the person is interested in academic studies like history; the person was shy as a child/the person has an active social life as an adult.

3. Ask questions that call for very specific answers. Then ask follow-up questions. Your questions should produce "for example" sentences to support your two general ideas. If you ask about your partner's future goals, ask why he or she has these goals, what motivated the choice of goals, how your partner plans to achieve them, what steps he/she has already taken toward them, what steps he/she is presently taking, what difficulties he/she anticipates, what difficulties he/she has already had.

I. Write a comparison/contrast paper on attitudes toward time in your culture and in another culture.

1. Brainstorm about attitudes toward time in your culture in the manner suggested in Chapter 2.

2. To help yourself start thinking about this topic, read the following brief discussion.

A survey of nations on the subject of time perception and personality suggests major differences, with Japan having the fastest pace of life on earth and Indonesia the most relaxed. A clue to national attitudes toward time is the accuracy of a nation's public clocks, with the Japanese and the Americans getting the highest rating for time accuracy and with the Swiss next in line. However, Italian clocks are noted for their slowness, and in many nations public clocks don't even exist since no one worries about the time at all.

Westerners worry a great deal about the future, as our obsession with savings banks and insurance companies confirms, while many Arab nations follow the philosophy that, since the will of Allah determines all, man need not worry. In the West, businessmen and students worry about mismanagement of time, and both suffer stress from time pressures. Businessmen in Russia are far more casual about time and students in Germany find themselves pressured only at the end of the semester.

Think of at least three "clues" to how the U.S. and your own culture think of time such as the accuracy of public clocks and the promptness with which classes start, stores open, buses or other public transport run, parties begin, and so on. The discussion of cultural customs on page 255-256 might also act as a springboard to more ideas.

Application: Contrast Analysis

Compare and contrast the two essays on Patzcuaro and Guanajuato, Mexico, and judge which of the two is more effective and why. Use the guidelines for revision on page 137 to help you evaluate what these essays do well and what they need to do better.

1. Patzcuaro and Guanajuato

Patzcuaro and Guanajuato may seem very much alike to Americans. They are both Mexican cities so they both are alike in some ways. Spanish is the main language (though many people in Patzcuaro prefer Indian languages). The people in both cities eat spicy food and dress differently from Americans. However, Patzcuaro and Guanajuato, though both very interesting, seem very different to Mexicans.

Guanajuato is a more northern, Spanish colonial city. It is more modern than Patzcuaro. There is a famous university with a law school, many kinds of businesses, many hotels and restaurants—and a focus on tourism because of a famous silver mine, colonial style architecture, and the mummies [preserved bodies from colonial times]. Peoples from Guanajuato feel like part of the Mexican center, not like in Patzcuaro where everything is Indian and the people don't even like the central government. Patzcuaro and Guanajuato are both surrounded by mountains, but Guanajuato is in a dry area while Patzcuaro is in a wet area. Also, many people visit Guanajuato from the United States and from other parts of Mexico because it is a famous tourist city. They particularly like the stone streets and the little bridges and the fireworks celebration and costumes on the Day of the Dead.

I go back to Patzcuaro for my vacation because it is quiet and peaceful and has beautiful nature. Guanajuato is very vivid and active, but it is also very noisy and the smoke from cars pollutes the air.

It takes two hours or more to get to Patzcuaro from Guanajuato by car. Even though Patzcuaro and Guanajuato are very different, they are both very close to my heart. I love Patzcuaro and I also love Guanajuato. So I spend some of my time in each city.

2. Patzcuaro and Guanajuato

Although Patzcuaro and Guanajuato are both cities of Mexico, both in beautiful mountainous regions and both good places to go to on vacations, they are really very different. These cities differ in their language use, their architecture, their weather, and their lifestyle.

The language in these cities is very different. The people in both cities speak Spanish, but most people in Patzcuaro are Indian and therefore also speak Tarascan, the local Indian language, because the Tarascans were never conquered by the Spanish and still don't consider themselves a part of Mexico under the federal government rule. In contrast, the people from Guanajuato are mainly of Spanish, not Indian, descent and so they use the standard language of Mexico. Also, in some parts of Guanajuato they speak English because there is much tourism, while Patzcuaro does not have much tourism and an English speaker is very rare. The Patzcuaro citizens keep some Tarascan customs like language, dress, meals, and different events, while Guanajuato maintains more of a Spanish-oriented culture.

The architecture of Patzcuaro is completely different from that of Guanajuato. In Patzcuaro the houses are little, with small rooms, and most of them were built in a traditional Tarascan style with local materials and red clay roofs. In contrast, those in Guanajuato reflect the Spanish influence with big houses made of brick, adobe, and stone. The churches of Patzcuaro are few in number and strongly reflect Indian influence, Indian ideas about religion, and Indian Gods, while churches in Guanajuato have only the Spanish influence, with Spanish-style architecture and a Spanish idea about God. Patzcuaro has beautiful ancient Indian-style structures while Guanajuato has colonial Spanish architecture. The houses in Patzcuaro also have steep, red-tile roofs because in this city it rains a lot, whereas houses in Guanajuato have flat roofs because there it does not rain very much.

In fact, in Guanajuato, the weather is hot, windy, and dry because the city is on the edge of the northern desert areas and the vegetation around it is scrub brush, cactus, and mesquite. Even though it is in the mountains, it rains less than in Patzcuaro. In Patzcuaro the weather is almost always wet and usually chilly, particularly at night, because of the altitude; the city is high above sea level and surrounded by mountains. The principal activities <u>in both cities</u> are agriculture and commerce, <u>but</u> <u>Guanajuato</u> is more traditionally business-oriented <u>than</u> Patzcuaro. <u>Guanajuato</u> has little stores and shops, artisan centers, and a huge, indoor, central market, whereas the main business in Patzcuaro is conducted by trade in the Indian markets.

On the weekend the <u>life</u> in these cities is very <u>different</u> because the <u>weather</u> and the <u>racial influence</u> affects attitudes. <u>In Patzcuaro</u>, the families go to the markets or fish for "pescado blanco"—tasty white fish—in the local lake; sometimes they have special Indian ceremonies, or they may go to the central hotel and watch television in the hotel lobby. <u>In contrast, in Guanajuato</u> the families usually go to the public square where they talk with their friends. They also have large parties with food and drink and Spanish music. Much of what people in Patzcuaro like to do is Indian in nature; much of what people in Guanajuato like to do is what people like to do in big cities in Mexico and in the United States: date, dance, and drink with friends.

<u>Both Patzcuaro and Guanajuato</u> are very interesting cities, Patzcuaro because of its closeness to Tarascan Indian history and traditions, and <u>Guanajuato</u> because of its Spanish-colonial style and its friendly, modern people.

Patzcuaro

Guanajuato

Chapter 15: USING CAUSE-EFFECT ARGUMENTS

Every why has a wherefore. —*William Shakespeare*

Key Concerns in Cause–Effect Arguments

Deciding When to Use Cause-Effect Arguments

The patterns of cause-effect arguments are almost as important to learn as the comparison-contrast patterns, both for successful college writing and for mastery of a chosen career. This is because arguing from cause-effect is basic to logic, to thinking, to progress.

Scientists ask what causes a rainbow to form or why sometimes frozen rain is produced instead of snow. They ask what keeps life attached to a round ball that is in constant motion and why what goes up usually comes down. In fact, most scientific concerns begin with the investigation of patterns, looking back at those actions, events, occurrences which produce a verifiable result. The experimental method is by its very nature an investigation of observable causes and effects. Scientists seeking a cure for cancer or for AIDS try to isolate exactly what produces those diseases in order to determine what is necessary to treat them; at the same time they experiment with different possible treatments to find out what works—what produces the desired effects.

An accountant, trying to understand why a bank is failing, will look back at the account books, the financial records, to seek an explanation in bank finances. A pilot with engine failure will rapidly "troubleshoot" or test out a number of possible caus- es in the hope of regaining control of his aircraft. A student of history will be asked to explain the events that led up to a moment or phenomenon of great his- torical importance: why Rome fell, what produced World War I, why Brazil, alone among the Latin American countries, is Portuguese-speaking. A social scientist might wonder why only man and the ant practice the art of war and whether the tendency toward war is biological or environmental, a product of instinct or of will.

You too will use cause-effect arguments; in fact, you have been using them most of your life, intu- itively and instinctively, with little or no conscious awareness of their format. How many times have you had a car not start and puzzled why? You probably asked yourself, "Is the gas tank empty? Did I leave the headlights on and run down the battery? Is there a mechanical or electrical problem in the engine?" In other words, you were investigating causes. If you speculated about what would happen if you couldn't find the cause and get the car running—no way to get to school or work easily, high mechanic's bills, irritat- ed people who depended on you for transportation— you were considering effects.

No matter what your field of study, at some time or another you must deal with cause-effect concerns. Here are some examples of how you will meet cause–effect in college courses:

For a history course: What chain of causes pro- duced the American Civil War? What were the effects of Reconstruction on the South? If the Spanish, rather than the English, had colonized the coast of North America, how would today's world be differ- ent?

For a political science course: What characteristics of seventeenth-century Puritan thought laid the foundation for capitalism? Examine the causes that led to the crumbling of the Soviet Union. Why has- n't the same pattern occurred in mainland China?

For a literature course: What motivated Hamlet's action? What social or human changes did he hope to produce?

For a sociology course: What effect is the AIDS epidemic having on the social habits of modern youth? What effect has the increase in the number of women working outside the home had on the family economy?

For a biology course: What are some of the ben- efits of genetically altering vegetables? What negative effects might human genetic alteration produce?

For an education course: What has caused the increasing interest in computer science courses nationwide? Why has the number of geography and foreign language majors in U.S. colleges and univer- sities declined? How has the feminist movement affected elementary education?

For a psychology course: What causes depression? How can it be treated?

The cause-effect pattern can be very versatile. It can be used in formal and informal situations: a sci- ence paper, a business letter, a conversation with friends. It can be expressed in a narrative (for exam- ple, a case study of a business failure); it can be hypo- thetical (*if one should observe the following, it might mean that... .*); it can occur within any of the other developmental patterns discussed in this unit.

The search for causes and effects is a constant human concern, but few think much about just how that search should be conducted. The purpose of this chapter is to make you conscious of cause-effect analysis as a writing pattern, a formal way of present- ing and organizing your thoughts and of demon- strating the findings of your personal search.

Considering Goals, Categories, and Relationships

Whether the goal of your cause-effect argument is to evaluate or to understand past events or to warn of future events, to seek a solution or to advocate change, to institute policies or to criticize past poli- cies, state that goal clearly but cautiously. Your read- er will respect you more if you admit that there may be other possibilities worth considering. Stating that poverty is the only cause of crime, for example, does not explain white-collar crime, nor all the poor peo- ple who don't commit crimes. Saying oppression causes revolution oversimplifies. Saying a bad self- image causes drug abuse or violence focuses on one cause but ignores others. A good argument requires clear thinking about cause and effect, and such think- ing often involves admitting you don't know all of the causes of a phenomenon. However, once you have settled on your goals and your basic argument, the next step is to divide your causes or effects into categories to facilitate discussion. Typical categories may be long-term causes versus short-term causes,

• EXERCISE 15.1: EXPLORING CAUSES AND EFFECTS

A. Thinking about personal goals

1. What made you decide to study English? Classify your reasons and briefly explain them.

2. How will studying English change your work potential and assure a different future?

3. If you have traveled abroad, how has travel to a foreign land affected your views? your values? your attitudes? your sense of self? Explain with examples.

4. Discuss your short-term goals (what you plan to learn over the next semester, what you think you need to improve, what you hope to achieve from your courses).

5. Discuss your long-term goals (how you plan to use English in the future, how it will help you with your career, how studying English will change your life).

B. What do the following opening lines suggest will be discussed in the paper they introduce?

1. Why is the sky blue?

2. What would happen if an atomic bomb were dropped on Washington, D.C.?

3. Suppose I am offered that job in Boston. How would my life be changed?

4. There are a number of definite "no-no's" to car maintenance. For instance, running a car engine without oil will do immediate and irreparable damage.

5. The United States would be a very different place if the French, not the English, had won the French and Indian Wars.

6. By the year 2100, the world population will have reached unmanageable proportions.

---

physical causes versus social or psychological causes, short-term effects versus long-term effects, possible effects versus definite effects. Such categories will help you plan and outline your argument. To express clearly whatever relationships you finally determine exist, you must also decide on a logical sequence. This may be a time order: first causes, then effects in the order in which they occur, or an interlocking chain of events, sequenced as the chain builds. This may be an order based on significance: major causes before minor or contributing causes, main effects before minor effects or a reversal of movement from minor to major.

Cause–effect arguments provide a sense of a logical pattern which interrelates what might otherwise seem like unrelated information. For example, *It is raining heavily* and *There have been a number of car accidents downtown* might seem to go in very different directions—the weather and the traffic—but the statement *Today's heavy rain has caused a number of car accidents downtown* provides a logical unity to those elements. A cause–effect argument can focus primarily on causes or primarily on effects, but both

cause and effect must be mentioned for the argument to be complete.

Deciding on a Logical Approach: Two Case Studies

Deciding on a logical approach can prove more complicated than it may at first seem. Should you focus on effects or causes? Which effects or which causes and in what order? The answer grows out of the purpose and the information available. Consequently, a good writer must be ready to revise and reevaluate an argument in the light of new information or simple logic.

Case Study #1: Not long ago, a popular magazine published a short article on longevity in the United States. The article noted that people in North and South Dakota in the far north of the U.S., on the average, live longer than people in any other part of this country. In speculating as to what cause produces this recorded effect, the article concluded that people respond well to extreme temperature changes, that the Dakotas have extreme temperature changes (very hot summers, very cold winters), and that therefore changing weather must be responsible for long lives. What possibilities has the article not considered?

The following list is to help you brainstorm about why human beings talk. Drawing on your personal knowledge of why you and your friends talk, expand the list with details and examples of your own. What personal or social reasons do you have for talking? Why do so many radio and television listeners respond well to talk shows? How long do you and your friends talk on the telephone? How often do you call family or friends? How do you feel when you have no one to talk to? Then decide on a focus and a goal and write a cause–effect paragraph based on some part of the list and your generated information. Begin with a question which the rest of your paragraph will answer.

1. The average talker uses about 9000 words an hour.
2. The average talker uses around 30,000 words a day.
3. Human beings talk to express feelings and emotions.
4. They talk so as not to feel alone.
5. They talk to work out ideas.
6. They talk to persuade.
7. They have personal reasons for talking.
8. They have social reasons for talking.

Careful thought might suggest a number of other possibilities the writer should have considered. For one thing, the Dakotas are sparsely populated; there are almost no urban centers, and the ones that do exist are small compared to cities in places like California or East Coast states. How could a sparse population relate to longevity? To disease transmission, for example? The Dakotas are also highly rural; people grow their own food and don't rely as much on products imported from distant places, products perhaps once sprayed with insecticides to insure beauty or with chemical additives to add color or to preserve them. Could diet then contribute to longevity? Have the authors perhaps mistaken a minor, contributory cause for a central cause?

For genetic reasons, some people live much longer than others. For example, people from the Republic of Georgia, formerly in the U.S.S.R., are famous for record longevity rates. It would be interesting to find out how many immigrants from high longevity areas originally settled in the Dakotas.

Think of other possibilities for Dakotan longevity. Are you familiar with a famously long-lived population elsewhere? What causal factors would be involved in a scientifically controlled longevity study? Clearly, unlike this popular magazine, you must be cautious about making definitive statements about causes unless you are sure the cause is simple and clear. Otherwise, you must merely suggest possibilities: This or that factor could produce or contribute to this effect.

It would be a mistake to name one cause when there are, in reality, many. In fact, oversimplifying is the main mistake that writers using cause–effect arguments make.

Case Study #2: The psychiatrist in the famous book Sybil examined a young patient who was suffering from multiple personality disorder. The psychiatrist, in the course of a series of client-patient interviews discovered that the young girl had been severely tortured as a child (beaten and physically abused) and that each time the torture became intolerable she would shut out the pain by escaping into another personality.

The psychiatric writer concluded that Sybil had as many as ten or even fifteen different personalities. This conclusion led to a hit book and film. While this explanation is certainly interesting, if indeed childhood abuse were the only cause of multiple personality disorder, then you would expect all abused children to suffer from it. Yet they don't. Since they don't, you must conclude that there is some other, perhaps interlocking cause or causes. Today psychiatrists are still debating the cause of multiple personality disorder. Some attribute the disease to genetics. In the case of Sybil, her mother might have been mentally disturbed since she treated her daughter so badly. For a father to know about such abuse and do nothing to aid his daughter suggests there was something very wrong with him as well, so perhaps a disturbed family relationship could be a partial cause. Perhaps an inherited disposition toward mental illness contributes to the effect of multiple personality disorder.

People with multiple personality disorder may lack a chemical that normal people possess, but this possibility leads to more questions about causes. Is the lack of the chemical caused genetically or is it the result of environmental factors? Or do both these possible causes interact?

As with many other diseases, the search for the cause of multiple personality disorder is a study of multiple causes. The difficulties of highly trained experts in isolating causes should teach us all to be careful when we construct cause–effect arguments.

Sometimes it is best to use a <u>causal chain</u> to make clear causal relationships and to organize your own paper. A causal chain conveys the idea of, not a single cause, but a whole series of causes, some major, some minor, all interrelated. Sometimes, the focus of such an argument is on a political or environmental chain reaction, a series of events which "snowball" or combine to add force with growing effect. The pattern is usually as follows:

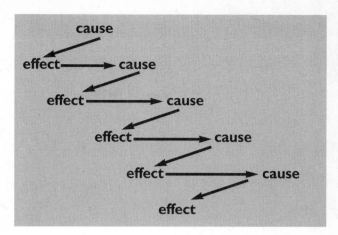

An example of this type of chain in action can be found in the third of the Models to Learn From on page 333.

Overall then, the nature of your topic determines the logical approaches possible for your argument. Your job is to determine that inherent logic and use it to organize and lend authority to your paper.

• **EXERCISE 15.3: BUILDING CAUSE–EFFECT ARGUMENTS**

Use the following information to develop two cause–effect paragraphs, one on the physical difficulties humans will face in space and one on the psychological difficulties. Don't try to be all-inclusive. Limit your focus and set up organizing subcategories to avoid paragraphs that merely list.

Example: Limit your paragraph on the physical difficulties to just difficulties with the atmosphere, and subdivide that topic into three categories: air content, air pressure, humidity.

What Humans Face in Space

Humans face the necessity of creating, in space, an environment which will reasonably duplicate the one we are accustomed to on earth.

Physical difficulties:

must have stable air supply (two pounds of oxygen per day; otherwise, brain damage from lack of oxygen)
must have controlled temperature (protection from extreme heat and cold)
must have controlled humidity
must have protection from weightlessness (body consumes its own calcium; bones begin to disintegrate)
must have protection from radiation (cosmic rays; solar radiation)
must have protection from changes in pressure
must have protection from meteoroids
must adjust to weightlessness: difficulty walking about and shifting position, flexing arms, legs, and neck (physical clumsiness)
must cope with physical fatigue
must maintain personal hygiene (washing body, waste disposal)
must maintain body strength in weightless environment
must deal with the motion sickness/nausea experienced by many astronauts and cosmonauts
must endure inner ear problems (balance)
may face death.

Psychological problems:

people accustomed to day-and-night cycle perform best when they work, eat, and sleep in usual manner—
but no natural cycle in space
accustomed to free movement and earth gravity
accustomed to the earth's horizon and visual orientation
psychological need to make minor adjustments to environment to relieve monotony
must cope with mental fatigue
from confinement in small compartment (claustrophobia)
from long commitment to one task
from boredom
difficulty working with others in close quarters
must cope with fear of the unknown and obsession with what could go wrong
separation from family
depression from food served in toothpaste-like tubes
disorientation
decline in power of perception
impaired judgment
decline in alertness
irritability
indecision
low morale
insanity.

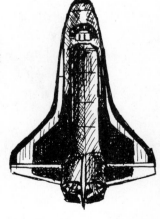

•• Writing Assignments

Choose one of the following topics to write a short paper on. Decide whether you need an interlocking series, a list of causes or effects with examples, or a focus on a couple of main causes or a couple of main effects with detailed support.

1. Explain what key writing problems you have and why you think you still have them.
2. Explain how improving your writing skills will influence your future—your education? your career? your sense of accomplishment?
3. What made you decide to go to college? Was there one key reason or a series of interlocking causes?
4. What do you hope to learn from your college courses? What will be the effect of getting a college education?
5. How will your choice of a career immediately affect your life? Decide on a single focus: academically? financially? socially? personally?
6. How will your choice of a career affect your long-term lifestyle?
7. If you have recently been successful at something (written an A paper, performed well in athletics or music or so forth), explain what produced that success.
8. If you have recently failed at some effort (written a weak paper, failed a test, were unable to persuade someone to go on a date with you, lost a race, and so forth), place blame or responsibility for that failure. What caused it?
9. What caused you to choose the school or institution you are now attending? What effects have resulted from this choice?

Deciding Correct Verb Tense Relationships

Usually, seeking causes involves past-tense forms: an event has already occurred, and you ask what produced it. However, the goal of such an investigation or study may also be to allow you to predict similar results in the future. A doctor wants to know the symptoms whereby she can recognize a disease and she also wants to know what produced that disease. In that way, she can both warn her patients about what to avoid and recognize the signs of the disease so she can begin treatment before it is too late. A historian studies the causes of past wars and crises in order to better understand the nature of and the solution to present and future ones.

When you focus on potential effects, use future tenses (*will, shall, are going to*), or modals of advice (*should, ought to*), probability (*may, might, could*), or warning (*must, have to, need to*): *Computers <u>will change</u> communications as humans presently understand it; we <u>should be</u> very careful never to start a* *nuclear war, for, once started, it <u>would be</u> impossible to stop; allowing oil companies to continue to spill thousands of tons of oil off our coastlines without penalty <u>could well mean</u> the end of our shoreline sea life.* Often the hypothetical future forms are used: *If the world population continues to grow at its present rate, our children's world will be a nightmare land of overcrowding and pollution, with a lack of such basic necessities as nourishing food, pure water, and clean air.*

Overall then, unless totally historical, cause–effect arguments usually connect the past and the present or the past or present and the future; also they explore the whys and predict future possibilities in logical ways. A composition which employs a cause or an effect argument must inevitably be based on logic. Its goal is to convince readers that the causes or effects which it presents are plausible and worthy of serious consideration. In other words, such an argument must be connected together in ways that readers will accept as sound, authoritative, and knowledgeable.

- **EXERCISE 15.4: CAUSE–EFFECT FORMS**

    A. Explain why some of the paragraphs use past tense, some present, and some future. Which of the following arguments focus on cause? Which on effects? Which are hypothetical and which real? Are any not really cause–effect arguments?

    1. In the past terrified observers of eclipses of the moon and the sun found explanations in myth. The Chinese believed that a great dragon trying to swallow the sun produced a solar eclipse, while the old Norsemen believed that two huge wolves forever chased both sun and moon and that eclipses occurred when the wolves almost captured and devoured them. Modern man, however, realizes that eclipses occur when the earth moves between the moon and the sun so that sunlight cannot reflect off the moon, or when the moon moves between the sun and the earth and blocks earth's view of the sun.

        Tense: _____ Reason for it: _____
        _____ Nature of the argument (cause, effect,
        neither cause nor effect, real, hypothetical): _____
        _____

    2. The earth's soil, the thin surface film upon which life depends, is formed by powerful forces, some large, some minute, some occurring with dramatic speed, others taking centuries to complete their effect. Daily, surface rock is acted upon by external forces—water, ice, heat, cold, wind, oxygen, plants, and animals—some of which tear down stone into tiny rock particles, others of which add organic matter to these rock particles to begin to form the complex substance called soil. The fertility of the soil depends on its origin—the mix of rock and organic matter.

        Tense: _____ Reason for it: _____
        _____ Nature of the argument (cause, effect,
        neither cause nor effect, real, hypothetical): _____
        _____

    3. Why does a block of iron sink and a steel ship float? The explanation is that a ship is not solid but a block of iron is. The ship contains hollow space so its density is reduced. A solid denser than the liquid it displaces will sink; one less dense than the liquid it replaces will float. For this reason an ocean-going vessel sailing up the Hudson River will sink deeper into the river water than it did into the sea, because fresh water is less dense than sea water.

        Tense: _____ Reason for it: _____
        _____ Nature of the argument (cause, effect,
        neither cause nor effect, real, hypothetical): _____
        _____

    4. Certain parts of animals are remarkably similar to human inventions. The heart, with its valves, pipes, and contracting chambers, is a living pump. The poison sac and hollow fang [tooth] of a rattlesnake are a living hypodermic syringe. Any four-footed animal is a walking suspension bridge; its long axis (backbone) is supported by pillars (legs) by means of numerous slanting muscles and tendons. Mechanical principles are involved in every stage of an organism's development, whether egg, embryo, or adult. This does not imply, however, that an animal is merely a machine, for machines neither build themselves nor produce others of their kind.

        —Theodore H. Eaton, Jr., "Living Mechanisms," in *The Book of Popular Science*

Tense: _____ Reason for it: _____

_____ Nature of the argument (cause, effect,

neither cause nor effect, real, hypothetical): _____

_____

5. If a hurricane came straight up the Mississippi River, the effects on the city of New Orleans could be devastating. With most of the city below sea level, imagine river and lake water rising high enough to sweep over the protective levees! Only a few suburban areas on the Metairie Ridge would be high enough to perhaps keep water out of the first floor. Many newer, lower homes would simply be swept away. The electricity would go out city-wide and the city water would be undrinkable for weeks to come. Transportation would shut down totally since most of the city's cars and buses would be under water. The city, in effect, would return to the swamp from which it grew. What further destruction the wind would bring would be too horrible to imagine, but can be projected scientifically from the effects of Hurricane Andrew near Miami in 1992.

Tense: _____ Reason for it: _____

_____ Nature of the argument (cause, effect,

neither cause nor effect, real, hypothetical): _____

_____

B. A friend writes that she might be coming to your city to take intensive English at your school in January. You respond by giving advice about the trip. Your friend fails to follow your advice and, as a result, makes many mistakes in her travel plans. Scold her about what she did wrong, and give advice about what she should have done. Use the hypothetical past unreal form (*If you had brought* or *Had you brought....*, or the past tense modal form, *You should have....*) to create a sense of cause–effect relationships.

Example: If you had followed my advice, you would have been better prepared. You should have brought your warmest clothes from home, but instead you brought warm-weather clothes. If you had brought a warm coat, as I told you to, or enough money to buy one here, you would not be so cold now.... [Continue with at least five more sentences of advice.]

Unifying through Transitions

The following are among the most common phrases used to connect cause–effect arguments and to clarify cause–effect relationships.

Prepositions that are followed by a noun:

As a result of that choice [cause], his life will never be the same [effect].

As a consequence of his sacrifice [cause], numerous lives were saved [effect].

Because of his exhaustion [cause], he decided to stay home [effect].

As an effect of that letter [cause], they are now happily married [effect].

She went to the library *for* a book [purpose].

She went to the hospital [*in order*] to see her sick friend [purposes].

Coordinating conjunctions, separating two main clauses within a compound sentence:

He felt tired [cause], *so* he rejected their invitation [effect].

Adverbials, separating a subordinate clause from a main one within a complex or compound-complex sentence.

Clauses of cause or reason:

Because he felt tired [cause], he rejected their invitation [effect].

Since he felt tired [cause], he rejected her invitation [effect].

(*On account of the fact that, due to the fact that, in view of the fact that, because of the fact that,* and *owing to the fact that* are used in the same way as *because* and *since*.)

She turned down his kind invitation [effect], *for* she was too tired to cope [cause].

Whereas they have committed a misdemeanor [cause], they will be punished [effect]. (*Whereas* is used for legal documents).

Inasmuch as no one was injured in the car wreck [cause], the judge gave him only a light sentence for negligence [effect].

It was *so* hot [cause] *that* they decided to stay home [effect].

It had been *such* a bad storm [cause]*that* the damage was very extensive [effect].

Clauses of purpose:

Her teacher sent her to the library [action] *so that* she could find some research materials [purpose].

He carefully added footnotes and a bibliography [action] *in order that* his readers might be able to find and review his source materials [purpose].

Conjunctive Adverbs between two separate sentences or between two main clauses connected by a semicolon.

He loved music but was not good enough to be a concert pianist [cause]. *Therefore,* he decided to teach music instead [effect].

(*Thus, as a result,* and *consequently* are used the same way.)

- **EXERCISE 15.5: TRANSITIONS**

  A. Combine the following sentences using the different connective patterns seen above to make a single sentence. Notice that the connections between separate sentences differ from the connections within a sentence. Try several different combinations.

  Example: He was tired. Therefore, he decided to go home early.
  becomes
  He was so tired that he decided to go home early.
  He was tired, so he decided to go home early.
  He was such a tired worker that he decided to go home early.
  Because he was tired, he decided to go home early.
  Due to (or on account of) his tiredness, he decided to go home early.
  Tired, he decided to go home early in order to rest.
  The reason that he went home early was that he was tired.

  Are there other possibilities?

  1. His car was getting very old. That is why he decided to trade it in for a new one.
  2. Your company has failed to meet its contractual obligations. Therefore our company has decided to cancel the contract.
  3. It has been raining hard for several days. As a result, all of the fields are muddy, and the children are too.
  4. She went for a walk. That was because she wanted to get some fresh air and exercise.
  5. The young man worked part-time. His purpose was to pay for his college education.
  6. She will complete her business degree this coming May. As a result, she will be looking for a summer job.
  7. It was raining heavily. Thus, the picnic was cancelled.

8. The Mexican earthquake was very strong. The buildings were badly constructed. For these two reasons, many people died.

9. He spent last night drinking with friends instead of studying. Consequently, he failed his examination.

10. Life in urban areas has become dangerous and violent. On account of this, many urbanites are fleeing the city and becoming suburbanites.

B. Carefully consider sentence content and connective words to put the following sentences into a good paragraph order.

1. Since the air is already dangerously overburdened by carbon dioxide from the cars and factories of industrial nations, burning down large portions of the Amazon forests could magnify the greenhouse effect—the trapping of heat by atmospheric CO^2.

2. Because of the huge volume of clouds it generates, the Amazon system plays a major role in the way the sun's heat is distributed around the globe.

3. Moreover, the Amazon region stores at least 75 billion tons of carbon in its trees, which, when burned, send carbon dioxide into the atmosphere.

4. Ultimately, scientists fear that the destruction of the Amazon could lead to climatic chaos.

5. No one knows just what impact the buildup of CO^2 will have, but some scientists fear that the globe will begin to warm up, bringing on disastrous climatic changes.

6. Any disturbance of this process could produce far-reaching, unpredictable effects.

C. Cause–Effect Sentence Patterns:

____x____ causes ___y____ .

_____y___ is caused by _____x_____ (passive).

_____x____ is one of the causes of _____y____.

The main cause of ____y____ is _____x____.

A contributing cause of _____y____ is _____x_____.

The short-term effect of _____x___ is _____y_____.

The long-term effect of _____x____ is _____y____.

_____y_____ is due to _____x____.

___x_____ is true. As a result, _____y___ will happen.

Imitate these patterns to connect the following sets of words in cause–effect sentences.

1. hurricane…flooding, property damage, and loss

2. teenage pregnancy…guilt, economic burdens, loss of personal opportunities

3. war…destruction of property, death of many young men and women

4. gasoline engines…air pollution, dependence on foreign petroleum suppliers

5. overpopulation…overcrowding, discomfort, pollution (short term); destruction of the environment, famine, wars for territory, numerous deaths (long term)

6. poor diet…unhealthy skin, dull hair (short term); ill health (long term)

7. education…self-confidence, greater sophistication, more employment opportunities

8. lack of education…limited opportunities, ignorance about one's world

9. travel abroad…greater sophistication, education, greater tolerance

10. learning a second language…better understanding of first language; knowledge of a new culture, new perspectives, new strategies; improved job opportunities

•• Writing Assignment

Use the following information on the "Black Death" (Bubonic Plague) in the U.S.A. as the basis for a well-organized paragraph, one with unity of structure as well as unity from connective words of time (*then*, *next*, *later*, etc.) and of cause (*as a result*, *consequently*, etc.). Conclude about the unexpected consequences of events.

Pre-1906	San Francisco plague epidemic; 118 deaths
1906	San Francisco earthquake and fire drive rats eastward out of city
Post-1906	Ground squirrels infected
1907-1940	Infected squirrels spread plague north, south, east; infect 200 species of rodents plus rabbits and wild desert camels (camels escaped from U.S. Army experiment to supplement horses)
1924	Los Angeles plague victims total 36
1940	Plague reaches Plains States by means of infected cats and birds as well as rodents
1940-1965	Plague persists, particularly in rural areas, carried from animal to animal by fleas
1965	Western states report six cases of human plague
Today	Wild-rodent plague still found in certain rural enclaves

–Adapted from "Rats, Bats and Human Diseases," *The Sciences*, The New York Academy of Sciences

---

Avoiding Common Pitfalls

As the two case studies on pages 321–322 indicate, the most common mistake made in cause–effect arguments is a tendency to <u>oversimplify</u>, to find a single cause where there may in fact be multiple, interlocking causes of varying degrees of importance, some major, some minor. At other times, however, the mistake may be the reverse: <u>attributing the effect to several causes, when in fact only one cause is responsible</u>. This error may result from the existence of a number of possible causes, all sufficient to produce the effect, and insufficient information to decide among them.

Another common error might be <u>mistaking a cause for an effect,</u> as in the statement, *My teacher gave me a low grade because she dislikes me.* The reality may well be the reverse: *I earned a low grade; my teacher knows I didn't try and didn't work hard; as a result she dislikes me as a student.* The "tailgater" (a person who drives too close to the car in front of him) who blames the driver in front for stopping too quickly to explain why he ran into the rear of that car is also reversing blame. Still another error might be <u>mistaking a contributory cause for a main cause.</u> For example, the person who drinks a six-pack of beer, then helps his friend drink a full bottle of wine, and finally eats a pizza would be mistaken to say, "The pizza made me sick." Obviously the mixture of beer and whiskey had much more to do with his illness than the pizza.

Sometimes the error results from <u>connecting in a cause–effect relationship two events that in reality are totally unconnected</u>. This is the case in most superstitions: *A black cat crossed my path, I broke a mirror,* or *I walked under a ladder so I will have bad luck.* Having a "lucky" ornament or piece of clothing is a perfect example of what is known as a *post hoc* cause–effect fallacy: if someone wears a piece of jewelry or clothing and then has good luck on that day, he may forever after expect to be lucky whenever he wears the same item. The item doesn't "cause" the luck, at least not in any rational or scientific sense, but the human wish for control, to be able to relate causes and effects, makes people behave in this superstitious way to a greater or lesser extent. If the implied connection is based on a person's origins (*He must be a disciplined worker; he is German.*) the error is called a <u>genetic fallacy.</u>

Considering the warnings given throughout this chapter, evaluate the cause–effect arguments below.

Example: When she left for school, she left two windows open. When she came home, her television and stereo were missing. She blamed the police for not patrolling the area more frequently. *Problem?* Failure to recognize that personal carelessness (leaving the door and windows open) was sufficient cause for the robbery and the inadequate police patrols simply contributed to the problem.

1. Wearing my lucky rabbit's foot on a chain, I won a thousand dollars on the lottery.

2. He's from Ireland, so he should be a wonderful conversationalist. That's what the Irish are famous for.

3. The number of young people wearing torn and split blue jeans has increased 75%; at the same time, the number of young people scoring poorly on national exams has increased 68%. If we regulate the wearing of blue jeans, we will surely improve test scores.

4. Let's go to the flea market early—the first customer of the day gets the best prices.

5. He's flunking out of college; he just watches too much television.

6. You must stop eating red meat and high-fat foods; don't you want to live a long life?

7. People who wear expensive jewelry and clothing in high crime areas invite robberies.

8. He's rude and insensitive to other people. He must have been brought up badly by his parents.

9. The economy of that country is failing. I blame the president for not doing his job.

10. Since she was unlucky at cards on New Year's Day, she had bad luck the rest of the year.

Models to Learn From

Model #1: The following paper explores and enumerates the effects of study abroad on students. The writer relies heavily on examples to develop the argument about effects, and, in order to organize these examples and to make discussion of them easier, sets up unifying categories: the positive effects in contrast to the negative.

What is the thesis or central argument? Is the argument complex or simple? Is the argument convincing? Why or why not? Can you suggest any other effects to strengthen and expand this discussion?

Going Abroad to Study

When a student goes abroad to study, the effects are both <u>positive and negative</u>. In other words, there are both advantages and disadvantages, and a would-be student traveler must consider both in order to make a wise decision about studying overseas.

First are the <u>advantages</u>. One advantage is that going abroad to study takes us to a different culture, environment, and language. In a different culture, we can meet people who think very differently from the way we do and who don't always agree with our ideas about life or politics or family or even friendship. When we study in such an environment, we are exposed to different and sometimes disturbing views, and this experience tests our own values and makes us evaluate why we think the way we do. In class discussions at home, most students share certain basic ideas and never argue about them, but abroad we hear very different opinions from what we have heard before and have an opportunity to ask questions about these very different perceptions from the people who live there. As a result, we are exposed to and have to think about very different points of view. Another advantage is that going abroad to study a certain subject means that we have a different experience in our field from other people. For example, when we want to study another language, it is very effective for us to go to the country in which the language is spoken. In the country, we are surrounded by the language that we are learning, and we are forced to use it whether or not we feel like it so we learn more rapidly and more easily.

However, these positives also have a <u>negative side</u>: there are also some <u>disadvantages</u> to studying abroad. At first, when we go abroad, we have trouble knowing what to do and how to do it. We don't know where to go to shop or how to deal with a new banking system or how to use public transportation. If we have an accident, how do we deal with it? If we get into trouble, to whom do we turn? Furthermore, some rules of courtesy and of business are different, so that we might be insulting without realizing it. To whom can we turn for advice or security or reassurance? Also, we are surrounded by people who have such a different culture that we feel very lonely sometimes. Our isolation may cause us to feel very sad. In fact, some students suffer such bad culture shock that they are unable to study or learn or even face the world from day to day. I know of one person who suffered such culture shock that he stayed in his room for a week without leaving, just staring at a picture of home on his wall until dormmates finally forced him to face the world again.

Despite such <u>negative</u> possibilities, the <u>positive effects of study abroad</u> are so valuable that it is important for our future that we <u>overcome the disadvantages</u>. Ultimately, if we overcome our fears and culture shock, overall, going abroad to study is very <u>beneficial</u> to discipline our will, improve our minds, and promote our cultural understanding.

Model #2: The next model relies heavily on specific details, statistics, and personal testimony to strengthen and support its cause-effect argument. Notice that it begins with effects but then seeks explanations or causes. The section on explanations or causes is the most significant part of the argument.

Drowsy America

The U.S. Department of Transportation reports that up to 2,000,000 traffic accidents each year may be sleep-related and that 20% of all drivers have dozed off at least once while behind the wheel. Truckers are particularly vulnerable. A long-haul driver covering up to 4,000 miles in seven to ten days often averages only two to four hours of sleep a night. "I've followed trucks that were weaving all over the road," says Corky Woodward, a driver out of Wausau, Wisconsin. "You yell, blow your air horn and try to raise them on the CB radio. But sometimes they go in the ditch. You ask what happened, and they can't remember because they're so tired."

- ## EXERCISE 15.7: IMITATION OF A MODEL

With Model #1 in mind, brainstorm about the positive and negative effects (advantages and disadvantages) of studying a foreign language, of getting a private apartment instead of a dorm room, of buying a car instead of relying on public transportation to get to work or school, of completing the general college requirements before deciding on a major or of deciding on a major as soon as you begin university work.

Make two prewriting lists: one of the positive effects of your action, the other of the negative effects of that action.

Today, new cultural and economic forces are combining to turn the U.S. into a 24-hour society. Many TV stations, restaurants, and supermarkets operate through the day and night. Business is increasingly plugged in to international markets that require around-the-clock monitoring and frequent travel across time zones. As CEO of Intellicorp, a software company, Tom Kehler, 43, regularly works 12-hour days in his Mountain View, Calif. office and hopscotches [jumps around] the globe. This fall he spent 13 days in Europe, followed by a few days back in California and ten days in the Orient. Then he flew home and went directly from plane to office. He subsists on four to five hours of sleep a night and occasional 15-minute catnaps during the day—and unlike most people, he likes it. "Sleep always felt like an interference with life," he says.

—Anastasia Toufexis, *Time*

Draw a line through the concrete details in the above passage. What is left? Would what is left persuade you to agree with the writer? How do the statistics, quotes, and details strengthen the argument? Do they make you trust the writer more? Do they make the argument seem more credible? Details that clarify, explain, or support improve the quality of writing and make cause–effect analyses sound more convincing.

Model #3: The following paragraph explains the interlocking reasons for the fall of Rome. Such a <u>causal chain</u> is difficult to write well, but it can be an effective, convincing argument. As you read the passage, ask yourself if the progression of events seems logical and if the argument is convincing.

The Fall of Rome

The phrase "the fall of Rome" makes most hearers think immediately of a sudden terrible event, one that occurred within a short period of time for a single, immediately recognizable reason. In reality, however, the fall of Rome was not such a sudden event, but <u>a slow, gradual process of decay, corruption, and disintegration which resulted from multiple, interlocking causes</u>, some so very slow and subtle that they were not at all clear at the time. For example, the combination of high taxes with harsh laws that forbade workmen to change occupations and specialties slowly, but surely, forced urban workers out into the countryside where they more and more frequently found work on the rural estates and the great country villas; there the work was more readily available and the taxes lower. This population movement and the resultant lowering of Rome's tax base, with time, left the imperial treasury bankrupt. Too much was going out and not enough coming in. Fewer funds in the treasury meant that it became harder and harder to man and pay the legions. Fewer soldiers and unhappiness among those remaining in the ranks produced a military weakness that eventually led generals from the outlying country areas, who were normally too afraid of Rome's military might to seriously consider attacking the capital, to crown themselves Caesar; as a result, a series of attempted military coups occurred, one after the other. Thus, slowly but inevitably the government grew weaker and weaker. At last it could no longer function. The final blow was the invasion of the Germanic hordes. These northern barbarians, who in the past would have been unable to face the disciplined strength of the Roman legions with all the weight of a strong urban government behind them, found no organized power to resist them. They raced southward, spreading fear and terror and destroying all in their path. As a consequence of this chain of events, Rome, the once mighty capital of a mighty empire, the leader of the ancient world, fell.

Does this writer's reasoning seem doubtful, or plausible and reliable? Why? What does this paragraph do well? How do the causes interlock? Would it be easy to summarize the argument in a single sentence? Why or why not? The topic sentence prepares you to expect each sentence to comment on causes and on the speed of the fall. Do they? If speed is not mentioned, does the sentence structure and the pace of the explanation add the idea of speed?

- ## EXERCISE 15.8: ADDING CONCRETE SUPPORT

  Continue the brainstorming begun in Exercise 15.7 on page 332. Now develop your positive and negative lists into a paper with specific details that clarify, explain, or support. Underline the specifics that make your ideas sound convincing. Build in a section, either at the beginning or end, that establishes the cause or causes that led to such effects. The references to cause or causes might serve to warn about problems.

- **EXERCISE 15.9: DIAGRAMMING CAUSAL CHAINS**

  A. Look back at the cause–effect analysis of the fall of Rome. Then diagram the causal chain. The chain would begin as follows.

  high taxes combined with harsh laws

  ↓

  forced urban workers out into the countryside

  ↓

  B. Diagram the causal chain in "Vanishing Architect of the Savanna" (page 309).

  C. Create your own diagram of a causal chain which you could then develop into a good, solid paragraph. It might be based on a series of interlocking, historical events, a biological chain like the food chain (*small fish are eaten by larger fish which are then eaten ...*), a series of interlocking causes that lead to social disaster (*bankruptcy, divorce, drug abuse, job loss,* and so forth), an economic or marketing pattern, or even a series of events with personal consequences.

     Example: a wet, rainy spring

     ↓

     increase in insect population and plant diseases

     ↓

     lettuce and tomato plants get eaten by insects or infected by disease

     ↓

     farmers have a poor crop of lettuce and tomatoes

     ↓

     lettuce and tomato prices go up

     ↓

     people eat fewer salads

     ↓

     people eat more meat and potatoes

Final Checklist

☐ Remember that there are not always simple causes for even a single effect. Instead, there may be a series of interlocking causes with different degrees of importance in producing the final effect. Have you considered all of the possibilities?

☐ Have you confused the effect with the cause or the cause with the effect? Does your cause really make your effect happen? Or does the "effect" simply follow the "cause" in time, with no causal relationship?

☐ Have you made clear the logical connectives between ideas? Transition words will help you achieve the clarity; the logic is up to you.

☐ A cause–effect argument can be very persuasive because it is based on the logic of science. Does your argument sound logical and persuasive?

Passages for Discussion and Analysis

Too Many People (1960's)

Americans are beginning to realize that the underdeveloped countries of the world face an inevitable population crisis. Each year food production in undeveloped countries falls a bit further behind burgeoning [increasing] population growth, and people go to bed a little bit hungrier. While there are temporary or local reversals of this trend, it now seems inevitable that it will continue to its logical conclusion: mass starvation. The rich are going to get richer, but the more numerous poor are going to get poorer. Of these poor, a minimum of three and one-half million will starve to death this year, mostly children. But this is a mere handful compared to the numbers that will be starving in a decade or so. And it is now too late to take action to save many of those people…. It has been estimated that the human population of 6000 B.C. was about five million people, taking perhaps one million years to get there from two and a half million…. The doubling time at present, however, seems to be about 37 years. If growth continued at this rate for about 900 years, there would be some 60,000,000,000,000,000 people on the face of the earth. Sixty million billion people! This is about 100 persons for each square yard of the Earth's surface, land and sea….

The world's population will continue to grow as long as the birth rate exceeds the death rate; it's as simple as that. When it stops growing or starts to shrink, it will mean that either the birth rate has gone down or the death rate has gone up or a combination of the two. Basically, then, there are only two kinds of solutions to the population problem. One is a "birth rate solution," in which we find ways to lower the birth rate. The other is a "death rate solution," in which ways to raise the death rate—war, famine, pestilence [disease]— find us. The problems could be avoided by population control in which mankind could consciously adjust the birth rate so that a "death rate solution" does not have to occur.

—**Paul Ehrlich,** *The Population Bomb*

• Questions for Discussion

1. What do Ehrlich's book title and his selection title reveal about his concerns and goals?

2. What modern worry does he try to connect with population growth? Why?

3. What kind of statistics does Ehrlich use? How do they contribute to his argument? Do you trust his statistics? Why or why not?

4. Notice also his hypothetical forms. Where does he use the "unreal" forms? Where does he use "real" forms? Why?

5. What is the effect of giving readers an either/or choice, with one of the choices certainly highly undesirable?

6. Which line tells us Ehrlich's central goal in this passage?

7. What are his tactics to achieve that goal?

8. How specific is his support?

How to Defuse the Population Bomb (1980's)

Except for thermonuclear war, population growth is the gravest issue the world faces over the decades immediately ahead. In many ways it is an even more dangerous and subtle threat than war, for it is less subject to rational safeguards, and less amenable to organized control. It is not in the exclusive control of a few governments, but rather in the hands of hundreds of millions of individual parents. The population threat must be faced—like the nuclear threat—for what it inevitably is: a central determinant of mankind's future, one requiring far more attention than it is presently receiving.

Last year the world's population passed 4 billion. Barring a holocaust brought on by man or nature, the world's population right now is the smallest it will ever be again. How did it reach 4 billion? For the first 99% of man's existence, surprisingly slowly. For the last 1% of history, in a great rush. By 1750 the total had reached only about 800 million. Then, as the Industrial Revolution gathered momentum, population growth began rapidly to accelerate. By 1900 it had doubled to 1.6 billion; by 1964 it had doubled again to 3.2 billion; and by the end of the century it is projected to double again to about 6.3 billion. Given today's level of complacency in some quarters and discouragement in others, the likely scenario is for a world stabilized at about 11 billion.

The sudden population surge has been a function of two opposite trends: the gradual slowing down of the growth rate in the developed nations, and the rapid acceleration of the rate in the developing countries. The experience of the developed countries gave rise to the theory of the demographic transition. It holds that societies tend to move through three distinct demographic stages: 1) high birth rates and high death rates, resulting in near stationary populations, 2) high birth rates but declining death rates, producing growing populations, and finally 3) low birth rates and low death rates, reestablishing near stationary populations.

The fundamental question is: what, if anything, can rationally and humanely be done to accelerate the demographic transition in the developing world? Is that acceleration realistically possible? It is.

With the help of modern mass communications, which are both more pervasive [widespread] and more influential than ever, an increasing number of governments in the developing world are committed to lowering fertility, and an even larger number to supporting family-planning programs. Family-planning services are essential, but can succeed only to the extent that a demand for lower fertility exists. That demand apparently does not now exist in sufficient strength in most of the developing countries. There are a number of policy actions that governments can take to help stimulate the demand. None of them is easy to implement [carry out]. All of them require some reallocation [rearrangement] of scarce resources. Some of them are politically sensitive. But governments must measure these costs against the immeasurably greater costs in store for societies that procrastinate [delay] while dangerous population pressures mount.

What, then are those specific social and economic actions most likely to promote the desire for reduced fertility? The importance of enhancing [improving] the status of women is critical. The number of illiterate females is growing faster than the number of illiterate males.

Of all the aspects of social development, the <u>educational level</u> appears most consistently associated with lower fertility. And an increase in the education of women tends to lower fertility to a greater extent than a similar increase in the education of men. In Latin America, for example, studies indicate that women who have completed primary school average about two children fewer than those who have not. Schooling tends to delay the age of marriage for girls and this reduces their total possible number of childbearing years. Further, education enables both men and women to learn about modern contraceptives and their use. It broadens their view of the opportunities and potential of life, inclines them to think more for themselves, and reduces their suspicion of social change.

Infant and child mortality rates can be brought down relatively simply and inexpensively if national health policies are carefully designed. The return in lowered fertility and healthier children and more equitably served families is clearly worth the effort. Malnourished mothers give birth to weak and unhealthy infants and have problems nursing them. Such infants often die, and this leads to frequent pregnancies, which in turn diminish their occupational and economic status....

—**Robert McNamara, former World Bank President**

• Questions for Discussion

1. What does McNamara's title reveal about his attitude toward population growth and about his purpose in writing this essay?

2. What two ideas does it make us expect the body of the paper to explore? Does McNamara's essay meet these expectations?

3. Why does he compare population growth and nuclear proliferation?

4. Why does McNamara call the population threat "the central determinant of the world's future"? What does he mean by that phrase?

5. What, according to McNamara, are the three demographic states of nations?

6. What does McNamara believe is the dangerous pattern in third-world nations that needs changing?

7. Whose statistics seem more reliable—Erhlich's or McNamara's? Why?

8. What practical advice does McNamara offer?

9. What is the effect of beginning new topic areas with questions?

Pyramid Growth: Coming Catastrophe (1990's)

You can begin to personalize the population problem facing our world and the world of our children when you realize that ten thousand years ago the total world population was about the present population of the city of Paris, 5 million people. In the late 1960's that population had reached 3.4 billion, while today it is over 5.3 billion and climbing steadily. Predictions are that by the year 2100 there will be between 10 and 12 billion people on earth. In other words, as most population demographers [population experts] confirm, the time between doubling is getting shorter and shorter.

Despite optimistic speculation that our planet can support 30 billion people, we only have to see films like *Soylent Green* and *Blade Runner* (nightmares of urban blight, with cannibalism in the first and a world of highrises in the second) or read books like John Christopher's *No Blade of Grass* (drought, destruction of plant life, a return to feudalism) or John Brunning's *Stand on Zanzibar* (a beehive society with myriad cells) to understand what a strain such a population could be on life resources, how destructive it could be, and how effectively any idea of quality of life could be lost. In fact, controversial anthropologist Warren Hern of the University of Colorado goes so far as to call humans an "exotumor" or "planetary malignancy" devouring Earth. Given even present-day declines in quality of life, it is clear that the Biblical injunction, "Be fruitful and multiply," has been all too often taken to heart, even by those of other faiths or little faith.

Yet warnings about how dangerous this policy of freewheeling procreation is began to be taken seriously by educated thinkers as far back as the early 1800's when British economist Reverend Thomas Robert Malthus argued, "The power of population is indefinitely greater than the power in the earth to produce subsistence for man." Malthus believed that even charitable attempts to save the world's starving only perpetuated the problem by keeping more people alive long enough to reproduce more. Writing a century later, Julian Huxley, in his essay, "The Crowded World," used the image of the compound interest rate to agree with Malthus about the rapidity of population doubling; however, Huxley argued that "the real explosion is a twentieth-century phenomenon, due primarily to the spectacular developments in medicine and hygiene, which...drastically cut down death-rates without any corresponding reduction in birth-rate"—a pattern whose dire consequences he feared. More recently, David Chandler, in "He Sought to Solve the World's Population Problem. They Call Him an Enemy of the People," described wars in El Salvador, Biafra, and Bangladesh as "population wars" and feared what such trends might mean, especially with India having the bomb and with China's population exploding despite such rigid legal limitations on child production as enforced sterilization. He pointed out that in 1974 alone, the world increased by another 80 million people—"equivalent to the entire population of Brazil"—with the biggest rates of increase in the densely populated underdeveloped world.

Despite such dire warnings, those who view the future optimistically point out that the Industrial Revolution brought new means of improving farming, and that more recent experiments with agricultural technologies have so improved grain and other crops, in terms of hardiness and yield, that the developed nations have not yet felt the expected food crush. As a consequence of this "Green Revolution," they dismiss as inefficient those third-world countries, like Bangladesh and such African nations as Ethiopa and Somalia, that have experienced harsh famines, and blame their situations on an outgrowth of civil war, internal disorder, bad planning, or unusual weather conditions instead of on population concerns for industrialized nations to worry about. However, Lester R. Brown, the president of the World-Watch Institute, Washington, D.C., warns that farmers in agriculturally advanced nations have increased yields just about as far as they can and that, "we're going to be in trouble on the food front before this decade is out." Another American, Republican Senator Howard Metzenbaum of Ohio warns, "The margin of safety in the race against world famine grows narrower day by day," and, "a single crop failure in even one major food producing area could require the wealthy countries to accept food rationing to avert mass starvation in the poorer countries." Paul Portney, a researcher at Resources for the Future, adds that simply allowing every Chinese family to have a refrigerator and a television will swamp painful efforts in the West to limit global warming.

Japan makes the problem even clearer. About the size of Montana with little arable land and few natural resources, Japan has a population of 123.5 million, with a population density of 860 people per square mile. If Japan had to rely simply on its own land for survival, its people would starve. Yet Japan has been able to maintain this unnaturally large population through trade and commerce, through exploiting the natural resources of less populated and less developed countries, through importing its foods, even rice. By contrast, the United States seems in good condition. The Census Bureau noted a U.S. population of 256.88 million as of December 1, 1992, but it reports the U.S. is adding almost 3 million people a year to its population, with more than 800,000 legal immigrants yearly. Edgar Poe of the Washington Bureau, in turn, warns, "The U.S. now absorbs, through immigration, 1 out of every 100 people added to the world population." The Census Bureau projections suggest that by 2030 there will be 345 million Americans, 96 million more than at present, and that a large number of these will choose to live mainly in California, Texas, and Florida. And what kind of new planning will that take? New housing, new roads, new water sources, new plans for waste disposal, new schools, and so forth? Furthermore, Charles C. Mann in "How Many is Too Many?" (*Atlantic Monthly*) predicts, based on Census Bureau projections, that many of these new citizens will be poor, that in fact, "in the twenty-first century a bigger percentage of the U.S. population will be below the poverty level than is now," and that "one out of five Americans will be 65 or older." Furthermore, he worries about the bureaucratic overload that produces the "disamenities of overpopulation in rich societies": "the waiting, the ugly [city] walls, the blaring horns, the inability to get away from it all"—a greyer, grimier, more frustrating world of shortages, crime, and disillusionment. David Bloom, a Columbia University economist, finds population-driven poverty self-perpetuating: the more mouths to feed, the less families can set aside for savings; the more babies in need of education and medical care, the lower the proportion of savings available for productivity-enhancing investment.

The question of population growth is not an easy one to answer. Experts often disagree about to what degree predicted growth will impact on our future and that of the generations to come. However, it is certainly clear that overgrazing, deforestation, soil erosion, and pollution of waters and atmosphere are inescapable modern realities. It is also clear that the doubling time of world population has increased radically from 1,500 years in 8000 B.C. to 200 years in A.D. 1630 to 80 years in 1850 to 45 years in 1925 to 40 years in 1986 to a predicted 15 years or less in 2100. This progression must reach a ceiling quite soon. How long can this accelerating growth rate continue before mankind realizes that action must be taken to prevent our species from self-destructing?

—V.L. Macdonald

• Questions for Discussion

1. What does the title reveal about Macdonald's attitude and argument?

2. What is Macdonald's goal? How do you know?

3. What is the effect of including so many references to the arguments of other writers and of providing sources for statistics?

4. What arguments does Macdonald raise that the other two writers ignore?

5. What is the effect of ending with a question?

6. All three authors worry about world population growth and consider it more dangerous than war. What do they think can be done about the problem? How do you know? List their advice.

7. Which of the writers is the most pessimistic? The most optimistic? Explain.

8. Check on present world population figures in the *World Almanac*. Are the predictions made in these essays coming true? If not, can you suggest some reasons why not? Have there been "birth rate solutions"? Have there been "death rate solutions"? Where?

9. What about in your own country? Which of the patterns described in the three essays apply?

10. If these writers are correct, what future effects can you predict for your country?

Trends in the Well-Being of American Youth (1990's to 2000)

Youth Indicators, 1993. Office of Educational Research and improvements. U.S. Department of Education, July 1993. Thomas D. Snyder, Project Director.

Population Projections of Young People

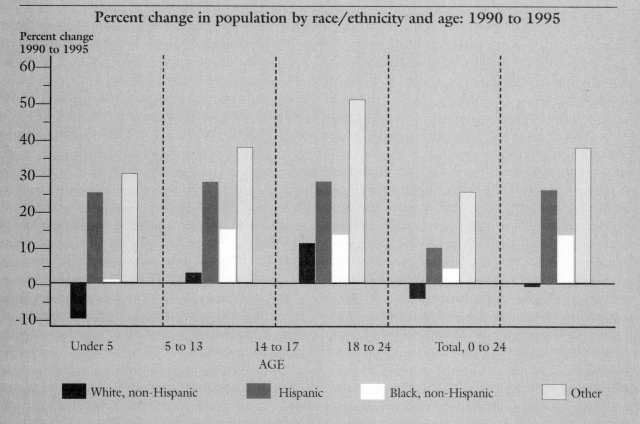

Percent change in population by race/ethnicity and age: 1990 to 1995

Source: U.S. Department of Commerce, Bureau of the Census, Current Population Reports, Series P-25, Projections of the Population of the United States: 1992 to 2050.

•• Writing Assignments

A. List at least three different types of effects for each cause or causes for each effect. Be specific.

   1. The effects of studying in the United States

      a.

      b.

      c.

   2. The causes of war

      a.

      b.

      c.

3 The results of war

    a.

    b.

    c.

4. The effects of a bad diet

    a.

    b.

    c.

5. The causes of water pollution

    a.

    b.

    c.

6. The effects of water pollution

    a.

    b.

    c.

After making your lists, write them as short paragraphs, adding supportive examples and details.

Example: 1) Effects of divorce on children

    a) torn between parents

    b) separated from healthy family environment

    c) feel insecure

    d) feel guilty

1) The psychological effects of divorce on children are highly negative. a) First of all, the children are psychologically torn between the two parents. For example, in the case of _____,...b) Furthermore, they are physically separated from a healthy, unified family environment. That is, they no longer have... and miss... c) As a result of these two, they begin to feel insecure. Such insecurity, in turn, may cause stuttering or bed wetting. It may...or...d) Moreover, sometimes they feel guilty, as if they were to blame. In particular, they blame themselves for...and... 1) The overall end result is unhappiness and emotional trauma. (Conclusion repeats idea of opening in a different way.)

B. Plan and briefly outline one of the following topics in order to produce a well-developed paragraph. Underline your topic sentence and circle your transition words. Although the main pattern of development will be cause–effect, you might need to classify, divide into parts, use process, give examples, or describe to develop your idea. Proofread carefully!

1. Consider the causes of low grades in composition (or some other class) class.

2. Consider the effects of having a month break between university semesters.

3. Consider the physical and psychological effects of having to speak mainly in a new language.

4. Consider the reasons that led you to study in the U.S.A.

5. Pick a successful politician and explain (give the main reasons) why you think he or she was elected or why he or she has been successful.

6. Enumerate or analyze the difficulties of adjusting to a change in physical environment, such as moving from the tropics to a cold, northern area or vice versa.

You might find that you have enough information to expand what begins as a paragraph into a full-length paper.

C. Read the following paragraph on one problem that English-as-a-second-language students have while taking college classes.

Taking notes in a college classroom is a major problem for most non-native English speakers. This may be because of the student's own limited language skills: a small vocabulary or ESL type difficulties with listening comprehension. The lecturer may use unfamiliar idioms or new patterns of syntax or may speak with an unusual accent (Southern, Bostonian, Texan). However, the problem might derive even more directly from the speaker rather than from the listener. The lecturer might speak too softly or even mumble, stutter, or slur words. He might include distracting fillers like "uh" or "er". He may speak too rapidly or fail to finish his thoughts. Even worse, he may not have a clear sense of organization for his ideas and, consequently, may digress in random ways. Students can practice to overcome personal limits of unfamiliar vocabulary, idioms, and accents, but will simply have to rely more heavily on their textbook or seek help from comparing notes with other students to solve notetaking problems resulting from poor lecturing techniques.

1. Where is the topic sentence? What problem does it prepare you for? How does the writer develop the topic idea? Why does the writer keep using the words *may* and *might*? What does this grammatical form suggest about the ideas?

2. Write down two or three other problems that you think English–as–a–second–language students have taking regular university classes. Write two or three topic sentences, each expressing one of these problems.

3. List details you could use to develop these topic sentences, focusing on causes of the problems and possible solutions.
   Topic sentence #1—Problem:
     Reasons for problem:
       Possible solutions:
   Topic sentence #2—Problem:
     Reasons for problem:
       Possible solutions:
   Topic sentence #3—Problem:
     Reasons for problem:
       Possible solutions:

4. Now combine each unit—the statement of the problem, the reasons, and the possible solutions (if any)—into a paragraph, so that you will end up with two or three body paragraphs in addition to the sample.

5. Write a thesis statement or introduction for the problems.

6. Combine the thesis statement and body paragraphs into a unified paper. Add a conclusion (if the solutions are overlapping they might be saved for the conclusion) and include connective words.

7. When you finish, underline the thesis statement and concluding statement once, and the topic sentences twice; circle the transition or connective words.

Applications

A. A Population Exercise
   1. Read the information on population growth which appears in the Passages for Discussion on pages 335–340. Then write a short paragraph summarizing in your own words the key arguments of the Erlich, McNamara, and Macdonald articles, using phrases like the following: *The three agree that…Both Erlich and McNamara offer*

_____ *but Macdonald instead* _____, *Erlich does* _____, *while McNamara and Macdonald do* _____.

2. Based on information from encyclopedias, yearbooks, almanacs, and other sources of population statistics, discuss whether or not these three writers sum up the present realities of world population.

3. Apply their theories and arguments to your own country/region. How do people in your country feel about population growth? Do they consider it a problem or a virtue? What is being done about population growth in your country? Predict the results of population growth in your country by the year 2030. Will there be a birth rate or a death rate solution? Why? Be specific. Wherever possible, support your response with facts.

   You might want to check the *World Almanac*, *The World Population Data Sheet*, *The World Fact Book*, *World Population Profile*, *Area Handbook Series* (by name of country; a Federal Research Division publication), *Statistical Abstracts of the United States*, or even an encyclopedia yearbook for up-to-date population statistics; you might also want to look at the student sample on Peruvian population problems on page 419.

B. Argumentative Topics to Choose From:

1. The death penalty does/does not serve as a deterrent to crime.

2. AIDS testing should/should not be required for university admission. (Focus on the effects of such a requirement.)

3. Ghandi-style non-violent protests are more effective/less effective than violent confrontation.

4. Protecting the environment should/should not take precedence over creating jobs.

5. Prohibiting the manufacture and sale of cigarettes would/would not end cigarette smoking.

C. POPULATION DEBATE: Boom versus Gloom & Doom
Prepare materials for a debate on the population issue. Form two debate teams. The debate should have the following format (flip a coin to decide who goes first; then speakers alternate, with everyone taking a turn):

Boom Leader	Gloom Leader
Introduction Defining Position	Introduction Defining Position
(2 minute minimum)	(2 minute minimum)
Position statement by another member	Position statement by another member
(2 minute minimum)	(2 minute minimum)
Statistics, information about population	Statistics, information about population
in group's countries by <u>other</u> members	in group's countries by <u>other</u> members
Summary/Answer	Summary/Answer
(one minute minimum)	(one minute minimum)
by <u>another</u> group member	by <u>another</u> group member
Questions to group members who	Questions to group members who
have not spoken	have not spoken

An objective judge should decide who wins the debate.

Note: The "Boom" side will argue that population growth is not a problem, at least not a serious international problem. The "Gloom" side can draw on mathematical logic and the readings about population to show growth cannot continue forever.

Information about your position can come from the Passages for Discussion or from your library research. The Charles C. Mann article, "How Many Is Too Many?", *The Atlantic Monthly* (February 1993) might be a good place to begin. The following statistics might also help you. You should write out the presentations or "speeches" and then practice reading them to classmates or friends. After the debate is over, summarize the key arguments of both sides of the issue: boom and gloom.

POPULATION GROWTH WOLDWIDE

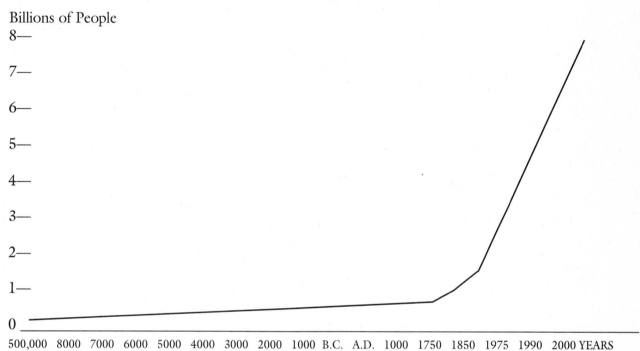

Present Predictions: 10 billion by 2060, with nearly all growth occurring in developing countries:

North America:	1990: 276 million 2025: 332 million (20% change)
Latin America:	1990: 448 million 2025: 767 million (69% change)
Europe:	1990: 498 million 2025: 515 million (3% change)
Africa:	1990: 642 million 2025 1.6 billion (149% change)
Former Soviet Union:	1990: 289 million 2025: 352 million (22% change)
Asia:	1990: 3.1 billion 2025: 4.9 billion (58% change)

Australia, New Zealand
(Plus New Guinea, Papua, Melanesia): 1990: 27 million 2025: 38 million (44% change)

These figures are based on projections from the United Nations Population Fund and take into considerations the effects of an AIDS epidemic in Africa and deaths from disease, starvation, and exposure.

Japan had the world's lowest birthrate in 1989: 10.9 babies per 1,000 people; Japanese women attributed their unwillingness to have babies to overcrowded apartment conditions.

Chapter 16: USING ANALOGY AND METAPHOR

Writing is Building. — Roger H. Garrison

Read everything—trash, classics, good and bad, and see how they do it. Just like a carpenter who works as an apprentice and studies the master. — William Faulkner

Language is fossil poetry which is constantly being worked over for the uses of speech. Our commonest words are worn-out metaphors. — James B. Greenough and George Lyman Kittredge

Understanding metaphorical language and analogy is an absolute necessity for all students, but most particularly for the student of English as a second language. Though most languages make some use of the technique, English is highly metaphorical in both simple, everyday speech and in the complex language used in scholarship and in the professions. It may take some mental adjustment to get used to the way in which English depends so heavily on metaphor and imagery. This chapter provides numerous exercises to help you learn the "feel" of metaphor in English, to master the use of simple metaphors in speech, and to begin to use complex metaphors in writing as well as to understand their use by other writers. Native English speakers, by instinct, frequently use metaphors to present ideas in a brief, visual manner, to explain the obscure and the difficult, and to serve as a kind of "shorthand" (another metaphor!) to save time in communicating. Therefore, the student of English must acquire an

understanding of this mental strategy if she or he hopes to communicate comfortably with native speakers at a sophisticated level. Basically, *imagery* and *metaphorical language* are all-encompassing terms to refer to simile, metaphor, and analogy, methods for comparing unlike things. *Simile* calls attention to the comparison with connective words such as *like* and *as: He dances like a swan—gracefully* or *He danced as gracefully as a swan. Metaphor* states the compared items as equivalents: *He is a swan on the dance floor. Analogy* sets up a four-part pattern: *He is to the dance floor as a swan is to water.*

What specific purposes do metaphorical language and imagery serve in English? They are useful tools, basic to vocabulary building and keys to English-speaking patterns of thought; they provide standard forms for description and creative ways to organize ideas.

Metaphors create concrete pictures in the mind that help others visualize what you mean. If you say that a large corporation is like a whale stuck on a beach, you have drawn a vivid image of the degree of trouble the company is in, as well as how big and helpless it is. Metaphors communicate very efficiently and persuasively. A person who says, "Los Angeles is like an alcoholic, but addicted to gasoline, not alcohol," is trying to express the implications of dependence on the automobile. The dependence is so strong that it creates a destructive lifestyle. The person who argues, "we may inhabit the Indian summer of human history, with nothing to look forward to but the 'nuclear winter' that closes the account" (Gwynne Dyer, *War*), means to provide a very serious warning about the future of the world. Metaphors make language more interesting and even witty, as in the saying, "Old men and comets have been honored for the same reason: their long beards, and their pretenses of foretelling events."

Metaphors also help you to crowd the maximum number of ideas into every word and phrase—as the nineteenth-century British writer George Meredith said "to avoid the long winded." Ultimately, they may help you express ideas for which you do not have ordinary words, so they are vital for extending the language, particularly in science, which must depict often invisible phenomena in clear, explicit

---

• EXERCISE 16.1: RECOGNIZING AND USING METAPHORICAL LANGUAGE

Identify whether the italicized metaphorical language takes the form of <u>adjectives</u> or <u>verbs</u>. Then use a dictionary to explain their meaning: what their pictures tell us about.

Example: She had to *weather* her *stormy* emotions before she would be ready to give her full attention to her job.

Answer: To weather=<u>verb</u>, to pass through a hard time safely; stormy= <u>adjective</u>, unhappy, angry, strong. The metaphorical language emphasizes the strength and uncontrollable nature of her emotions.

1. The *dog-eared* pages of the book revealed its popularity.

2. The teacher wanted a *polished* final version of the paper, not a *rough* draft.

3. He is *bogged down* in studies: too many tests to take and too many papers to write.

4. The president worried about the *snowballing* effect of the oil crisis.

5. His critics pointed to the *roller coaster* economy and *skyrocketing* prices, but he blamed the *fossilized* system.

6. This new program has many possibilities; it can *spin off* in many directions.

7. Father and son *bridged* the communication gap.

8. He began work as a children's doctor, but then he *branched off* into treating adults.

9. The runner suddenly felt a *stabbing* pain.

10. He keeps his emotions *bottled up.*

ways (*food chain, black hole, Milky Way, light waves*), and in economics, which must trace the abstractions involved in the movement of money and wealth (*price freeze, skyrocketing prices, rollercoaster economy, bear and bull stock markets*).

Often, a metaphorical image can have great power. A witness described a suicide from a high building: "About thirty or forty feet before he hit the ground, I heard him scream very, very loudly, and then I heard an incredible noise… like a sledgehammer on a tin roof" (*The Daily Texan*). The witness's comparison forces listeners to imagine the sound of the body hitting the ground. When you try to describe an idea through an image, you are doing exactly what the witness did. You are trying to make someone else "see" what you see, feel what you feel,

or think what you think. When you say, "That travel agency is an octopus, with arms extending almost everywhere," or when you say, "That university is a factory; I wouldn't want to go there," you are using simple examples of a technique with great power to convince and to persuade.

Overall, then, imagery and metaphor are central to thinking and very important to concrete writing. Concrete word pictures explain abstract ideas when it would be difficult or impossible to do so otherwise. For these reasons, you should not only be aware of other people's use of metaphors and images, but should try out some of your own, both in speech and in writing. Metaphor is the cornerstone of vocabulary, description, and thought, and the gateway to literature and science.

Key Concerns in Using Analogies

DECIDING ON FUNCTION

Some people assume only poets use metaphors and analogies since metaphorical language is one of the characteristics of a literary style. However, these techniques are also used effectively by scientists who wish to explain a new and unfamiliar process in common terms; by politicians and statesmen who try to put abstract political and economic theories into concrete and understandable words; and by anyone else who must explain something difficult and complicated or who must relate something new and unfamiliar to known and accepted things.

To Create Concrete Images

In the study of language, image means any word or group of words which creates a picture in the mind. The most common words which create these pictures are proper nouns (the names of particular people, places, and things: Abraham Lincoln, the White House, Washington, D.C.), concrete nouns, concrete adjectives, and concrete adverbs: *The big, gray dog with long, sharp teeth bit deeply into Abraham Lincoln's long, vulnerable leg as he stood in the front door of the White House in Washington, D.C.* The concrete words in this sentence create an image of an event or happening; notice the difference in the sentence, *A dog bit a president in the capital city.* Of

course, you could argue that the second sentence creates an image also, but the image is very vague and imprecise (What kind of dog? Which president? What capital city?). An image becomes a true image, then, when the words provide enough details for a concrete picture, a picture that would mean roughly the same thing to different people.

Science uses many metaphors to create concrete images. It is common to speak of light "waves" in physics to refer to the up and down motion of light. In biology, "food chain" refers to the interconnected way in which small fish are eaten by bigger fish which are eaten by bigger fish, etc. Albert Einstein created one of the best known scientific comparisons when he said: "It is hard to split atoms because it is like shooting birds in the dark, in a country where there are few birds." What does this image help you understand about splitting atoms? Paul Ehrlich uses the metaphor "population bomb" to describe the sudden increase in world population.

Food Chain

Why has the writer used the analytical language underlined in the following passages: to entertain, persuade, criticize, clarify, create a visual picture, or achieve another purpose? Explain briefly.

Example: Anthropologist Bronislaw Malinowski, whose ideas are out-of-date and erroneous, considered human beings as basically passive; he depicted them as molded by a culturally patterned, 'cookie-cutter' world view. [cookie-cutter—a kitchen tool for making standardized cookies]

Answer: The person being quoted, <u>Malinowski</u>, tries <u>to clarify his view</u> through a very simple image but <u>the writer</u> criticizes that view and chooses Malinowski's image <u>to suggest that Malinowski oversimplifies</u>.

1. Writer and political commentator William Buckley praises the change from the typewriter to the word processor as a change <u>from swimming laps with a wall stopping you every few meters</u> (the typewriter) to <u>swimming continually forward with no restraining walls to block progress</u>: a free, unimpeded, continually forward motion that allows for the unrestrained exercise of thought (the word processor).

2. <u>Flattery is like chewing gum</u>; enjoy it, but don't swallow it.—Hank Ketcham in the comic strip *Dennis the Menace* .

3. Former Soviet Prime Minister Mikhail Gorbachev, talking about Western responses to Soviet problems, said, "We are <u>standing knee deep in an ocean of gasoline</u>, and you [Western commentators] <u>throw in lighted matches</u>." — "Dear Editor: You're Fired. Signed, Mikhail Gorbachev"

4. During an earthquake, certainties vanish. <u>The earth liquifies. It becomes as wild as surf. The solid is abruptly fluid.</u> Normally, earth is the refuge, the stability, the foundation of things. The earth should be alive only to grow vegetables and flowers. Now <u>the earth itself becomes a beast, all teeth and gashes and sudden topplings</u>. Reality has turned <u>molten and violent</u>.—Lance Morrow, "When the Earth Cracks Open"

5. Philosopher and novelist Loren Eisley describes <u>man's body as a cosmic prison</u> which limits his intellectual and spiritual potential.

6. Weighed down with its heavy load, the <u>plane felt clumsy, like a duck with clipped wings</u>.—Anne Morrow Lindbergh, *North to the Orient*

The image is very concrete and forceful, since everyone knows of the danger and destructiveness of a bomb explosion. Such an image is certainly a more effective argument than a long list of figures and facts.

To Produce Predictable Reactions

Most analogies or metaphorical language create little trouble for students of English since they use images which are concrete and simple. Once you learn what images are shared by an English-speaking culture, you also learn which predictable reactions they produce. *He works like a horse; He eats like a pig; He's as strong as a bull; I am as weak as a kitten*, all

use commonly accepted characteristics of animals to explain what a particular human being is like—commonly accepted, that is, by English speakers. Notice that, to be truly metaphorical, the two things compared must be <u>unlike</u> in some important way. If you say, "He eats like a pig," and the pronoun *He* refers to a real pig, then you are not really comparing; you are saying that "a pig eats like a pig," which is what you would expect. Also, a simple comparison is not necessarily metaphorical. *Detroit is as dirty as Chicago,* is clearly a comparison between two <u>like</u> things, two cities. To make this comparison truly metaphorical, you must introduce a concrete image to describe the abstract quality of dirtiness: *Detroit is as dirty as a pigpen.*

• EXERCISE 16.3: METAPHORS ABOUT WRITING

Because it is difficult to explain to others what the writing process involves, many writers and teachers use metaphor to make the abstract concrete and visual. What do the following metaphors help you understand about writing and how do they do so?

> *Example:* Just as a sculptor removes the excess clay to reveal the sculpture the artistic vision sees, so the good writer removes the excess words to reveal the heart of the argument.

> *Answer:* This metaphor captures the way good writers have an image of what they want to say in their mind, but must cut out unnecessary words and structures to focus just on words that create the same image in their readers' minds. The picture of a sculptor cutting away clay to create a statue helps suggest how too many words can hide meaning.

1. Writing is [like] making a table. With both you are working with reality, a material just as hard as wood. Both are full of tricks and techniques. Basically, very little magic and a lot of hard work are involved…. What is a privilege, however, is to do a job to your own satisfaction. —Gabriel Garcia Marquez, author of *One Hundred Years of Solitude*

2. Think of your whole subject as a large, delicious pie, but then cut only one narrow slice of it. That way you can stay trim but enjoy the flavor.

3. Writing is like movie-making. A director "mixes" prepared shots and scenes, arranging them to tell a story, while a writer revises sentences and paragraphs to find the best narrative directions. It's easy to shoot scenes and write sentences, but finding the best meaning and order is excruciating for both director and writer.

4. There are stages in bread-making quite similar to the stages of writing. You begin with something shapeless which sticks to your fingers. A kind of paste. Gradually that paste becomes more and more firm. Then there comes a point when it turns rubbery, a point when you feel it's time to stop kneading [squeezing bread dough before completing the final cooking] You sense that the yeast has begun to do its work: the is alive. dough Then all you have to do is let it rest.—Marguerite Yourcenar, author of *Memoirs of Hadrian*

5. Language is a net in which we catch glimpses of reality.—Paul Hermann

6. It is no sign of weakness or defeat that your manuscript ends up in need of major surgery. This is a common occurrence in all writing, and among the best writers.—Strunk and White

7. Just imagine a sentence-producing computer capable of printing out sentences day after day, year after year, without ever producing the same sentence twice. The language area of your brain is like that [capable of far more production than you might think]. —Martha Kolln

8. A definition is the enclosing of a wilderness of ideas within a wall of words.—Samuel Butler

9. [Revisions] are mainly matters of carpentry: fixing the structure and the flow…. Most rewriting is a process of juggling elements that already exist.—William Zinsser

10. Writing is like laying bricks. First you conceive a plan, then you execute it with care and precision, one brick at a time. The building process looks messy and uncontrolled. However, a bricklayer who has planned well and worked carefully ends up with a neat and ordered final pattern, both beautiful and functional.

The following metaphors about the writing process do not work particularly well. How does the picture they create fail to correspond to the writing process? What weaknesses or limitations are there in the metaphors?

1. Writing is a faucet of communication: sometimes the water just goes drip, drip, drip; sometimes it pours out.

2. Writing is like climbing a mountain. You need to be sure of all your steps before you take the next one. Once you are at the top you can look down at all the work you have done. Then as you go down, you should check the work you have done going up, to find a better way to climb up the next time. Once at the bottom, you climb back up and repeat all the steps until you get it right.

To Clarify

As the sentences on the writing process in Exercise 16.3 make clear, metaphorical language may serve to clarify, enlighten, or entertain.

Scientific discussions for laymen, for example, must employ numerous metaphors to clarify and to make visual. Michael Crichton, in his science fiction thriller *The Andromeda Strain*, for example, calls amino acids "the building blocks of proteins," and then goes on to describe these building blocks of carbon, hydrogen, oxygen, and nitrogen using train imagery:

> Proteins were made by stringing these amino acids together in a line, like a freight train. The order of stringing determined the nature of the protein—whether it was insulin, hemoglobin, or growth hormone. All proteins were composed of the same freight cars, the same units. Some proteins had more of one kind of car than another, or in a different order. But that was the only difference. The same amino acids, the same freight cars, existed in human proteins and flea proteins.
>
> ...DNA, the genetic-coding substance,... acted like a switching manager in a freight-yard....once the amino acids were strung together, they began to twist and coil upon themselves; the analogy became closer to a snake than a train.

Crichton goes on to argue that a machine which would give the order of amino acids would be like "a shot in the dark" when dealing with alien substances. What qualities does this image suggest?

A recently created metaphor builds on an image most Americans are very familiar with: the limited access highway or freeway with no traffic lights, stop signs, or crossroads. This highway, compared with a proposed network of telephone lines, computers, and other information devices, becomes the "information superhighway." The term has stimulated a series of half-joking additional terms, including "traffic cops" (control devices) for the superhighway, "collisions" (information interference), and "bad pavement" (poor phone connections). Can you think of other metaphorical terms to describe problems and advantages of the "information superhighway"? What would old-fashioned computers be called? People who get confused by this new technology?

• EXERCISE 16.4: USING METAPHORICAL LANGUAGE

A. Complete the ideas below with appropriate metaphorical images. First, write what you traditionally say in your language and then, if possible, what you have heard in English.

Example: It is as cold as ice, or she is as cool as a cucumber.
The large corporation is like a giant octopus, with tentacles everywhere.

1. She is as pretty as a _____ .
2. The old man is as weak as a _____ .
3. He is as slow as _____ .
4. The bed in my apartment is as hard as _____ or as soft as _____ .
5. She has been sick, so she looks as pale as _____ .
6. He is as fat as _____ while she is as skinny as _____ .
7. The meat served in our cafeteria is as tough as _____ .
8. Parts of the American Midwest are as flat as _____ .
9. The runner is as fast as _____ .
10. The weight lifter is as strong as _____ .

Compare your answers with those of your fellow students. What do you learn from their responses? Are most images universal and shared worldwide, or culturally conditioned and accepted only in limited geographical areas?

B. Use the *as if* pattern to complete the following sentences. Remember that if the relationship is unreal, you must use the hypothetical unreal form, the subjunctive (past tense plural). For example, *He treated her <u>as if she were crazy</u>* means that she was <u>not really crazy</u>, despite the way he treated her.

1. She's too proud. She acts as if _____ .
2. He's too shy. He talks as if _____ .
3. He slept as if _____ .
4. He treated her as if _____ .
5. She bossed him around as if _____ .

Write some sentences like these of your own. Remember that, to be metaphorical, they must compare different, not similar, things.

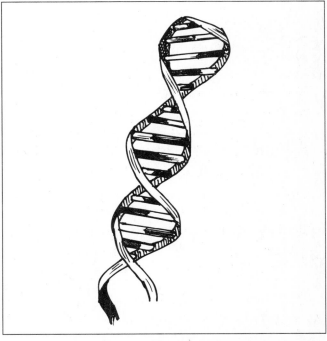

The following examples are typical of the type of metaphorical language you will encounter in college science courses or in scientific journals. Underline the metaphorical language and explain what it contributes to the idea.

Example: The atmospheric <u>envelope</u> moves with the earth but does not rest quietly upon it.

Answer: Comparing the atmosphere to an <u>envelope</u> gives the idea of something that surrounds or contains the earth. In addition, <u>just as a letter slides around loosely inside an envelope</u>, so the earth moves around loosely inside its covering of air.

1. The brain makes all animals unimaginably efficient, like a small-size computer. There are times when computers seem to operate like mechanical "brains", but their achievements are not very spectacular when compared to what the minds of men can do.

2. Nature has operated a vast laboratory for two billion years.

3. The seas blanket more than 71 percent of our planet's surface.

4. Microorganisms are necessary links in the endless chain which binds life to matter and matter to life.

5. Oceanographers are trying to raise food for the world's exploding populations through sea farms on the continental shelves.

6. Assume... that you have a road, with a sharp corner. Now assume that you have two automobiles, a sports car, and a large truck. When the truck tries to go around the corner, it slips off the road; but the sports car manages it easily. Why? The sports car is lighter, and smaller, and faster; it is better suited to tight, sharp curves. On large, gentle curves, the automobiles will perform equally well, but on sharp curves, the sports car will do better.

   In the same way, an electron microscope will "hold the road" better than a light microscope. All objects are made of corners, and edges. The electron wavelength is smaller than the quantum of light. It cuts the corners closer, follows the road better, and outlines it more precisely. With a light microscope—like a truck—you can follow only a large road. In microscopic terms this means only a large object, with large edges and gentle curves; cells, and nuclei. But an electron microscope can follow all the minor routes, the byroads, and can outline very small structures within the cell—microchondria, ribosomes, membranes, reticula.

   —Michael Crichton, *Andromeda Strain*

To Embody a World View or Philosophy

Metaphors or analogies in philosophy, theology, politics, and government often help capture the essence of theories, values, or ideals and aim at understanding, enlightenment, or persuasion. They may embody a world view or a way of life. For example, one important metaphor which shaped American behavior was the concept of the "melting pot." A melting pot is a container whose ingredients are heated to a very high temperature; the substances and materials in the pot melt together as heat is applied and time passes, forming a new material. Thus, America was often described as the "melting pot" of the world, especially at the turn of the nineteenth century. The idea was that people from different countries, races, and cultures would be mixed together in America, warmed by the spirit of freedom and liberty, and, over time, would become a new compound, "American," distinctly different from the original ingredients.

However, much separation of races, nationalities, and cultures still occurs in the U.S. The discrimination against ethnic minorities in the United States probably was encouraged by the melting pot metaphor because of its emphasis on new Americans conforming to the majority culture. The metaphor suggested that the "melting" took place automatically, and therefore no action to remedy problems caused by cultural differences would be necessary in the long run. Now people talk of the United States as more of a "checkerboard" or "patchwork quilt" made up of many distinct elements; some even call the U.S. a "salad bowl." The point is that a political metaphor can shape the way people think and behave, even though it is only a comparison, not a fact.

Note that the melting pot metaphor goes much further than a simple comparison: it is an extended metaphor and involves complex attitudes and complex situations.

To Entertain

Metaphorical language can enliven, entertain, and bring an idea to life in interesting, challenging, and unique ways. It enhances description and makes it interesting and "literary," as in the following portrait of Paris:

> Paris is a woman with too much alcohol in her veins. She talks a little too loud and thinks she is young and gay. But she has smiled too often at strange men and the words 'I love you' trip too easily from her tongue. The ensemble is chic and the paint is generously applied but look closely and you'll see the cracks showing through.
> —Len Deighton, *An Expensive Place to Die*

Such imagery makes a description more visual and more interesting, and it provides insights that simple descriptive adjectives cannot. A good descriptive metaphor should help readers better visualize what is being described. Picture the following passages. What makes them effective visually?

> The dock supports had crumbled away and were "sticking up like broken teeth"
> —Frederick Forsyth, *Dogs of War*

> The dead man's face reminded Miller of "the shrunken… [head]… from the Amazon basin he had once seen, whose lips had been sewn together by the natives."
> —Frederick Forsyth, *Odessa File*

• EXERCISE 16.6: METAPHORS AND ANALOGIES TO EMBODY A WORLD VIEW

Underline the metaphorical language and explain what the picture is. Then explain the idea or basic meaning or world view it reflects. Use the explanation of "melting pot" as a model.

1. Karl Marx said, "Religion is the opiate of the people," but a modern writer claims that television is the true opiate of the people.

2. Thomas Paine says that the "summer soldier" and the "sunshine patriot" will run away from trouble in times of bad weather.

3. John Stuart Mill, in his essay On Liberty, argues, "Human nature is not a machine to be built after a model, and set to do exactly the work prescribed for it." Instead, he calls it a tree, which must be able to grow and develop in all directions, "according to the tendency of the inward forces that make it a living thing."

4. "A State which dwarfs its men" to make them more "docile" will find, according to John Stuart Mill, "that with small men no great thing can really be accomplished."

5. "No man is an island, entire of itself; every man is a piece of the continent, a part of the main[land]…"—John Donne, "Meditation XVII"

6. Garrett Hardin warns that the population explosion will necessitate "lifeboat ethics," for our land, like a lifeboat, has a limited capacity: limited food, limited water, limited space. He says that, if the boat is swamped, everyone drowns, so harsh measures must be taken to protect the overall group.

7. J. Y. Cousteau writes in *The Silent World* that the sea "is a silent jungle."

The commissioner snorted "like a hippopotamus."
—Elspeth Huxley, *Death of an Aryan*

A nasty character withdraws his face from a safe "like a lizard pulling back its scaly head after darting at a fly."
—Elspeth Huxley, *Murder at Government House*

"The train sped through the dark German night … like a giant, one-eyed serpent [snake], stopping frequently to feed on the occasional passenger who waited to board."
—Charles Robertson, *The Elijah Conspiracy*

Notice that each of the above images comes from popular fiction, either murder mysteries or spy stories, and helps add to the atmosphere or intrigue of the adventure.

CHOOSING AN APPROPRIATE FORM

Simile

The word <u>simile</u> (resembling the word *similar*) is used for comparisons which use *like* or *as* to connect the two unlike things being compared. For example, you might say, "My love is like a rose." This simile stresses that the beloved person has the characteristics of a rose: beautiful, fresh, delicate, sweet-smelling, colorful. These connections between the two terms are called <u>correspondences</u>. You would compare your love to a rose because you expect that most people know what a rose looks like and think of good things when they hear "rose." Notice that you wouldn't think of all the bad things about rose: Roses may be bright red and green; they are rooted in the mud; they are all wet in the morning; they have insects crawling over them.

• EXERCISE 16.7: ENTERTAINING IMAGES

The following are famous insults based on metaphor. Explain what is insulting about them.

Example: A common insult is to say someone has his head screwed on <u>backward</u>.

Answer: The insult involves the idea of mechanical assembly. A mistake has been made in putting together the machine so a malfunction is inevitable. A person with *a head screwed on backwards* cannot think normally or at all.

1. British statesman David Lloyd George once said that British Prime Minister Winston Churchill would "make a drum out of the skin of his own mother in order to sound his own praises."

2. Lloyd George also said that World War I's Field Marshal Haig was "brilliant to the top of his army boots."

3. He said that Lord Derby was "like a cushion who always bore the impress of the last man who sat on him."

4. Lyndon Johnson once attacked a rival as someone who was unable "to chew gum and walk at the same time."

• EXERCISE 16.8: SIMILES

Create similes with *like*. Remember that there must be a logical and natural connection between the two terms being compared for the comparison to make sense.

Example: She gave orders like an army sergeant.

1. My apartment is like _____ .
2. That girl is like _____ .
3. This school is like _____ .
4. My first week in the U.S. was like _____ .
5. Her lips are like _____ .
6. They both drove like _____ .
7. He ran like _____ .
8. His eyes are like _____ .

Metaphor

Perhaps even more important than simile is *metaphor*. Usage is confusing, for the word is often used generally, as in the phrase *metaphorical* language, which includes simile, metaphor, and analogy. However, the specific meaning of <u>metaphor</u> is a comparison between two unlike things, one a concrete image, the other an abstraction. It is the same as a simile, except that a metaphor does not use *like* or *as*.

	Idea		Image
Simile:	My love	is	like a rose.
Metaphor:	My love	is	a rose.

• EXERCISE 16.9: METAPHORS

The italicized nouns are metaphorical. Explain how, using a dictionary to help.

Example: His military success was a <u>springboard</u> for his civilian career.

Answer: The image *springboard* literally means a board or a piece of wood with a spring under it, used by athletes or by circus performers to help them jump into the air. However, it is used here to mean the <u>idea</u> of a help or an aid, especially in a job or career, which pushes someone up quickly: *His military success helped him succeed in his civilian career.*

1. A *chain* of events led to his being fired.
2. They encountered a traffic *bottleneck* in the heart of the city.
3. Her life was *a tangled web* of men and parties.
4. New Orleans is a *mecca* for jazz.
5. Human *chemistry* can produce strange *bedfellows*.
6. There needs to be a price *ceiling* to control inflation.
7. "Keep off of my *turf*," said one gangster to another.
8. His father is helping him *launch* a new career.
9. The Pacific northwest coast is a *jumping-off* point for visitors to Alaska.
10. A *window* of opportunity has opened for entrepreneurs.

Simile stresses that different things are <u>alike</u>; metaphor implies that they are exactly the <u>same</u>. For this reason, it is easy to understand when a simile is being used, but sometimes hard to identify a metaphor if you are unfamiliar with its idiomatic use, or if you are unfamiliar with the image.

Analogy

One way to identify, analyze, and understand metaphors is to express them as analogies. An analogy is a comparison having four parts:

A	is to	B
	as	
C	is to	D.

Analogies are really representations or diagrams of the way we think and reason about the relationship of old and new information; they express relationships between different things:

(A) horse	is to	(B) wagon
	as	
(C) engine	is to	(D) car
	*****	
sound	is to	air
	as	
waves	are to	water
	*****	
words	are to	language
	as	
numbers	are to	mathematics.

In the metaphor "I will meet you <u>at the foot</u> of <u>the stairs</u>" you are really using a brief form of an analogy:

Image   (A) the foot is to (B) an animal (or person)
            as
Idea   (C) the bottom is to (D) the stairs.

You could easily say <u>bottom of the stairs</u>, just as you could say, *She makes the best grades in the class,*

instead of *She is at the <u>head</u> of the class* or *She is at the top of the class,* but the metaphorical idiom is very common. The business expression *cash cow*—as in *Joe's insurance business is his cash cow*—analogizes the steady, predictable, and profitable production of milk with the similarly reliable profits provided by a company or investment. In like manner, if an instructor praises your paper as "seamless," the analogy compares a piece of cloth which is all one piece, with no seams or joined-together sections, with the similar strength of your writing and organization.

Sometimes metaphorical/analogical language is the only practical way to express an idea: the <u>eye</u> of the needle (the little hole in the thick part of the needle); the <u>tooth</u> of the saw (the sharp cutting edges of a saw); the <u>leg</u> of the chair; to <u>tune-up</u> a car (tune=sound; tune-up=to make several musical instruments sound good by adjusting them; therefore, to adjust the parts of a car's engine so they work well together and the engine "hums" or "sings" harmoniously). Compare the analogical expression of these metaphors:

eye	is to	animal
	as	
hole	is to	needle
	*****	
teeth	are to	animal
	as	
jagged edge	is to	saw
	*****	
leg	is to	animal
	as	
support	is to	chair
	*****	
tune-up	is to	orchestra
	as	
adjustment of parts	is to	car engine

• EXERCISE 16.10: ANALOGIES

Explain the analogical relationships in the following images.

Example: eye of the needle = hole is to needle

as

eye is to a person

or a world of trouble = large size is to world

as

large amount is to trouble

1. a sea of faces
2. a pool of information
3. a mountain of work
4. a nightmare of problems
5. the face of the clock
6. an explosion of anger
7. the head of state
8. a beehive of activity
9. a swamp of despair
10. a beacon of hope

Now make some analogies of your own that use the _____ of _____ pattern.

Avoiding Common Pitfalls

Confusing Simple Comparisons with Metaphors

Although both a comparison and a metaphor involve finding similarities, a comparison is between like things while a metaphor is between basically unlike things. For example, the sentence *New York is very much like Los Angeles: large, dirty, overcrowded, and exciting* compares two similar cities: New York and Los Angeles. However, the sentence *New York is a madhouse, full of anxious, neurotic people, pushing and shoving their way through life, with no sense of purpose and no understanding of why they do what they do* is a metaphor which compares two different things ("New York" and "a madhouse") so that what you know about "a madhouse" will help you understand more about "New York."

Using Unclear Referents

Unclear referents are sometimes a problem with metaphors, because metaphors lack such verbal indicators as *like, as if, is to ...as... is to* and so forth, and may at times be taken literally instead of metaphorically. For example, if you say, "Joe is like a rat," most readers will assume you are comparing Joe with an undesirable animal and concluding that Joe is not much better. However, if you say that, "Joe <u>is</u> a rat," there are two possibilities:

1. You know of a rat which you call "Joe"
2. Joe, the person, is very like an undesirable animal.

Since few of us keep rats, this example will probably give no trouble, but supposing you use the phrase, "There was a <u>rat race</u> in my last company."

Identify which of the following are simple comparisons and which are metaphorical.

Example: Los Angeles is like New York. (comparison)
New York is a madhouse. (metaphor)

1. A mango, a tropical fruit, is sugar-sweet and pear-shaped. _____

2. Our classroom is a hothouse environment, where ideas are carefully nurtured and allowed to grow under protected conditions. _____

3. He reminded me very much of his father, for both were tall and thin, both stooped slightly, and both had a kindly smile that was infectious. _____

4. She looked as if she had been hit by a car: her hat was twisted sideways, her clothes were rumpled and torn, her knee was skinned, and her eyes were dazed. However, she had only been playing in the park with her six-year-old nephew. _____

5. Racism is a contagious disease that can cause pain and injury. _____

6. Being an international student is like being a duck in a chicken yard; one feels totally out of place. _____

7. Our classroom is like a three-ring circus, with multiple activities in different sections of the room. _____

8. William Shakespeare called England a garden and her good kings gardeners who took care of the land, cut the bushes so they would grow better, and worked for the healthy growth of the kingdom. _____

Here, you can mean:

1. There was a <u>literal</u> race between animals

2. There was a competition between people who were cruel, amoral, backbiting, dishonest, and murderous, just as a race between rats (for food or survival) is cruel, amoral, backbiting, dishonest, and murderous.

The phrase *rat race* will mean an unpleasant competition between people almost every time you hear it, unless you live in a particularly bad part of town where real rats race. However, there is absolutely no way of telling the difference between 1. and 2. on the basis of vocabulary, grammar, or syntax, so it is important to learn to identify such idiomatic uses and the contexts in which they occur.

Taking Too Long To Express Your Idea

Since a key function of metaphorical language is to compress ideas, using too many words and too much detail to develop a metaphor can negate its purpose. The expression, *My love is a rose*, is self-suf-

ficient. It does not need great elaboration, though sometimes the image can be extended to add wit and humor or to direct the reader toward the positive or the negative qualities of a rose. Sometimes, the language itself needs compressing. For example, the sentence *The clouds covered the sea like a blanket* could be strengthened by using the noun/image to replace the dull verb: *The clouds blanketed the sea.*

Using Culturally-Determined Images

Where do the images in our metaphors come from? Some come from universal human experience, but many others derive from the world around us, which means different environments supply different images. People may misunderstand each other because their images don't match up. Most students of metaphor are surprised to discover just how much variation there is, even in apparently "universal" metaphors, such as those based on the human face. Why, for example, does English share "nose" of the airplane with French, but not "eye" of a needle? Many languages use "tooth" as an image (*teeth of the*

Explain the literal versus the metaphorical possibilities in the following, just as was done above for *Joe is a rat* and *There was a rat race*.

1. He is a party animal.

   Literal_____

   Metaphorical _____

2. He barked out orders.

   Literal_____

   Metaphorical _____

3. Roscoe is a team player.

   Literal_____

   Metaphorical _____

4. She cooked her goose.

   Literal_____

   Metaphorical _____

5. He had a brainstorm.

   Literal_____

   Metaphorical _____

6. Victoria was a queen to her supporters.

   Literal_____

   Metaphorical _____

7. Now he was really in hot water.

   Literal_____

   Metaphorical _____

8. They had come to the end of the line.

   Literal_____

   Metaphorical _____

9. He's stuck in a rut.

   Literal_____

   Metaphorical _____

10. They washed all their dirty linen in public.

    Literal_____

    Metaphorical _____

- **EXERCISE 16.13: REDUCING WORDINESS**

    Compress the underlined metaphorical language to reduce wordiness by changing the noun/image to a <u>verb or adjective form</u>.

    Example: The whale <u>that was stuck on the beach</u> was dying slowly.
    Answer: The beached whale was dying slowly.

    1. The grass <u>covered</u> the lawn <u>like a carpet</u>.
    2. The grand piano was <u>as huge as an elephant</u>.
    3. The pattern of organization was <u>like that of an ant colony</u>.
    4. He ate his food <u>rapidly, like a wolf does</u>.
    5. News reports about the conference <u>filled</u> the media <u>with floods of information</u>.
    6. The two opposing sides of the debate <u>attacked</u> each other <u>with the anger and violence of armies in a real battle</u>.
    7. One must carefully develop friendship <u>as one cultivates a garden</u>.
    8. The politician felt he had the right to <u>take</u> his reward, <u>as one reaps a field</u>.
    9. His senses <u>were made sharp</u> by fear.
    10. The pain <u>went</u> through his side <u>like a knife cuts through a body</u>.

---

saw, of a mechanical gear) but not "brow" (Can you say the *brow of a hill* in your language?). Eyes have many metaphorical meanings, for obvious reasons, but their particular use is unpredictable. Can you say in your language, as you can in German and English, for example, *I'll have it finished very quickly, in the blink (or wink) of an eye*?

A further complication is that metaphors change over time. The horse, as the most common Western work-animal, supplied comparisons for many years, the most common in use today probably being *horsepower*. The steam engine replaced the horse and for a while was the most impressive machine of its time, generating images of power and dangerous explosiveness (*He boxes to <u>let off steam</u>; otherwise, he would <u>blow up!</u>*). Now, computers have a central place in our thoughts, so much so that researchers even talk about the human brain as being "like a computer" and use computer terminology for discussions of mental problems and treatment (*Her career <u>crashed</u>; she was <u>programmed</u> for failure.*). Metaphor, without our realizing it, reflects what a culture thinks is important and powerful.

- ## EXERCISE 16.14: QUESTIONS FOR DISCUSSION

Ideas about beauty most definitely differ from culture to culture. What is considered beautiful in your culture? What kind of eyes? forehead? skin? Would any of the ladies in the following pictures be considered beautiful in your culture? Why or why not?

English poetry in the past described female beauty in terms of nature: roses in a woman's cheeks, cherry lips, hair black as night, eyes like the sun or the stars, teeth like pearls, and so forth. What are some traditional images for describing female beauty in your culture?

Using Analogy and Metaphor   361

•• Writing Assignment: Cultural Determination of Metaphor

To test the hypothesis that culture determines reactions to metaphorical language, choose four or five common metaphors or similes from your own language. Translate them into English. Then discuss what is being compared in the metaphor or simile (what image is compared to what idea and why this comparison makes sense in your culture/language). Don't choose limited metaphors like leg of a chair. Instead, choose interesting, living metaphors.

Your paper should clarify which metaphors are often used in which culture, should describe and explain the metaphors, and should consider whether the metaphors translate easily into English, why or why not, and which assumptions are similar and which are different.

Examples for discussion:

The Chinese talk about a life as long as *the South Mountain*, riches like those *of the East Sea*, boys like *dragons*, girls like *phoenixes* (beautiful birds which are supposed to be reborn repeatedly), and the *roads* of life. Peruvians talk about a daydreamer being *on the moon of Paiva*, and describe a good friend as *a foot* and an embarrassed person as *roasted*. In France, something useless is called *the stem of a cherry* and a long, boring novel is called *a river novel*. Iranians talk about a man being as fast as *a bullet* and a woman being as beautiful as *the full moon*. Arabs say, *his knife doesn't cut yogurt, he's afraid of his own shadow*, and *you can't carry two watermelons with one hand*. Can you guess what these expressions might mean? Are any impossible to understand? Koreans might describe a person as like the *center piece of Buddha* or *a licorice root of a Chinese medicine dispensary*. Japanese describe a woman's *skin like snow*, a life like *a burning light before blowing wind*, and a long married couple as *a couple of fleas*. Do these give you some ideas for your own selection of metaphors?

Using Dead Metaphors

Dead metaphor (or simile, for similes can also be "dead") means that the metaphor has been used for so long that no one realizes it is a metaphor; few people hearing or reading the metaphor think of a concrete image, such as an eye of a needle, a leg of a chair, and instead regard it as simply the name of the thing described. Notice that "dead" in itself is also a metaphor. Much of our language is made up of dead metaphors, because comparisons become used so often they are no longer thought of as comparisons.

Identifying dead metaphors can be a problem, particularly for the non-native English speaker; the best procedure is to ask yourself if the literal meaning makes any sense (can a needle really have an eye or a saw teeth?). If there is no literal sense possible, try to identify the concrete image. Once it is identified, try to figure out what idea it represents, that is, what the abstract or "unknown" part of the metaphorical equation is.

Sometimes understanding the literal sense can be tricky. The sentence *A sea of clouds could be seen from the airplane* (so many clouds it looked like the sea) looks very much like *Sea clouds could be seen from the airplane* (clouds which hang over the sea). The preposition *of* is the only sign that the "sea" is made up of clouds, not water. At other times the context will make the meaning clear: *There was a sea of people watching the game.* Here there is less confusion simply because we understand that seas can not really be made up of people, but only of water, so we translate the meaning as "large numbers, as extensive as the sea."

- **EXERCISE 16.15: DEAD METAPHORS**

The following sentences contain dead metaphors or clichés, expressions so overused they are as if dead. Many idiomatic sayings are dead metaphors, for example *he jumped out of the frying pan into the fire, he put all his eggs in one basket, he's pulling your leg, my foot went to sleep, don't count your chickens before they hatch,* and *a bird in the hand is worth two in the bush.* The expression, *pulling the fat from the fire,* for example, means "solving a problem at the last minute and preventing a disaster." Can you explain the other sayings?

Underline the dead metaphors in the list below and explain the original picture. What does the picture help us understand about meaning?

1. He had a mountain of work to complete.
2. The husband was in the doghouse because he forgot his wife's birthday.
3. A wage and price freeze makes life difficult in a time of inflation; we prefer a price ceiling.
4. Some think life is a game of chance; others call it a bowl of cherries.
5. The company was planning its economic game plan.
6. The student worried about carrying such a heavy academic course load, especially when he experienced a crushing defeat on his first major exam.
7. Fearful that his parents would see his grades, hit the ceiling, and make a mountain out of a molehill, he decided to stop sowing his wild oats and to shoulder his responsibility.
8. After wasting half the semester playing instead of studying, he finally turned over a new leaf and worked like a dog day and night until the final exam.

Models to Learn From

An <u>extended metaphor</u> or an <u>extended analogy</u> is a useful way of organizing a complex series of ideas. How do the images in the following models relate the central ideas of the author? <u>Could you use such analogies to explain a complex economic or social idea in your own writing?</u>

Model #1: The following example is typical of the type of extended imagery found in good writing everywhere. What is the extended image it sets up? Explain what the author is trying to say. Why does he use imagery rather than direct language? What does such metaphorical language add to his writing?

A Traveller's Guide to the Kingdoms of Arthur

...Say the words "King Arthur" ... and you conjure up a vision of knights and maidens, quests and adventures, good and evil....

It is tempting to begin a search for a "real" King Arthur by <u>peeling away</u> this romantic <u>veneer</u> [surface covering], but the truth does not lie immediately beneath the sur-

face. Indeed, the task of <u>stripping away</u> the myths and legends about Arthur is <u>like unwrapping the huge "present" that consists merely of one gaily wrapped box inside another</u>. In our search for the gift we believe to be within, we run the risk of <u>ending up with a tiny empty box</u>. Arthur has <u>as many faces as this practical joke has cartons</u>. Somewhere there is a real man, but there is also a giant, a tyrant, a huntsman, an emperor—even a god. The purist who wishes to remove all those <u>colorful layers</u> is left peering at a figure so tiny that all detail is lost. Arthur may have been a sixth-century chieftain, but his importance to European culture lies not in what the was but in what he became. <u>The wrapping is worth far more than the gift.</u>

—Neil Fairbairn

The final line of the above selection, *The wrapping is worth far more than the gift,* is the summary sentence and the essence of the metaphorical argument. It suggests that finding out the truth about the historical King Arthur is irrelevant, that what is

Using Analogy and Metaphor 363

truly important about him is not who he really was or where he really was or what he really did, but what legend ("wrapping") claims for him: all the stories of adventures and exploits, all the fantasies and fantasizing which tell you about the values and the spirit, the longings and the changes of a nation. You might be sadly disappointed by the real, historical Arthur, a primitive sixth-century chieftain, but the chivalric Arthur of legend will continue to inspire and challenge generation after generation.

Think of a famous legendary figure in your culture: does the "gift wrapping" metaphor apply to him or her? If so, how?

Model #2: The following student writer uses analogy to create a vivid picture of a process. What picture does he use to explain what idea? How does his analogy add to his argument or idea?

The Growth of a Business

The small business or shop is like a ship in a big ocean. The shop owner and his employees begin with a sailing boat but hope to progress to a yacht and then to an ocean-going ship  in order to survive the vast ocean of business. The first period, the sailboat, though involving only limited outlay, may tax the owner's small budget; in addition, it has limited space and limited potential, and can easily founder and sink. Only a small crew can ride in it, and they have to control it very carefully and busily, even if the ocean is quiet. Thus the

beginning stages of owning a shop require hard work, diligence, and teamwork, and can still end in disaster.

 The second period is like that of a yacht, which can sail a calm ocean steadily, but in case the conditions change, it has to be very carefully controlled; the yacht is more luxurious than the sailboat and stronger, but it still has to sail carefully and to estimate difficulties before they come. Thus the intermediate stage of small shop ownership is one of increased wealth and expansion, but one is still open to the dangers of a competitive market.

The third and final period is that of an ocean-going ship, which can travel in any weather conditions and survive most difficulties.  However, the ship owner is no longer on board with his own crew, but is a more distant office manager worried about details of high finance. In like manner, the small shop owner who gradually expands his business and markets his ideas may end up with a national or international franchise....

—Kotaro To, Japan

Here again the comparison of the familiar with the unfamiliar is what helps readers visualize the issues and understand the problems. What analogical role does the small shop owner play when his business becomes a "big ocean-going ship"? How does this analogical role define for the reader the new set of problems involved?

- ## EXERCISE 16.16: EXTENDED ANALOGY

In the following paragraph underline all of the words that help create the extended analogy or overall picture. Then explain this very common analogy for describing computer problems. Since this analogy is almost dead, be careful not to take the picture literally!

If you are a computer user, you need to be very careful about computer viruses. Just as you can catch a virus from classmates and friends and get ill, so your computer can catch a virus from contact with disks used in other machines. In fact, a Pakistani student created a computer "virus" that damaged computer programs at three universities in the United States and that required changes in procedures at microcomputer centers across the nation. That incident has recurred with greater frequency ever since, and has resulted in numerous anti-virus programs being installed as regular procedure on new computers.

An electronic virus damages programs or destroys data by erasing three of the 354 data clusters on a standard disk. When you use a computer in a campus lab, the virus can be passed from disk to disk and machine to machine without the users even knowing that their disks have been infected until the damage has already been done. Just as the disease microbes passed from body to body remain invisible until their effects (fever, chills, vomiting) appear, so the computer virus is passed from user to user but remains invisible until its effects (a crashed program, an intrusion of computer language into your text, unusual computer behavior like a failure to save or a sudden, unexplained shut down) are all too visible.

A computer virus is like any other disease in that, during the equivalent of the incubation period when people don't know their disk is infected, they pass it on to others, until pretty soon half the computers on campus have the symptoms. Then a computer "doctor" must come in and play around with programs until a cure is found and the computers can be inoculated against that virus. However, a new strain of the virus will require a new cure and more inoculations.

Final Checklist

Metaphorical language can be a useful tool if handled with imagination and a sympathetic understanding of the other person's experience, as is clear from Kotaro To's comparison of boats and business. When you invent or use metaphor, remember the following:

☐ In practical terms, simple images, similes, metaphors, extended metaphors, and analogies fall into two main classes: those that translate from language to language easily and well, and those that translate badly or don't translate at all. Images and concrete explanations that are based on personal experience and the experience of a certain culture usually translate badly or not at all. Images and experiences based on familiar human perceptions, nature, and happenings usually translate quite well.

☐ When you are trying to understand someone else's imagery, compare their experience with your own.

☐ When you create your own imagery to explain something to someone else, think of pictures and experiences that will mean something to them.

☐ Use your imagination to avoid abstractions and to base your ideas on concrete experiences.

☐ Keep your eyes open for dead metaphors, which can confuse meaning, and for metaphorical language without connective signals (*like, as*), which can cause you to assume a literal meaning when a figurative one is intended.

☐ Remember that a comparison relates similar things but that metaphorical imagery relates unlike things.

Passages for Discussion and Analysis

A. In 1854 the Commissioner of Indian Affairs for the Washington Territory offered the Indians a treaty for the sale of two million acres of their land to the federal government. Chief Seattle of the Duwampo tribe, a famous Indian leader for whom the city of Seattle was named, answered the Commissioner on behalf of his tribesmen. He is said to have worn his blanket "like the toga of a Roman senator"; he spoke in a series of images taken from nature. His speech opened as follows:

> Yonder [That] sky that has wept tears of compassion upon my people for centuries untold, and which to us appears changeless and eternal, may change. Today is fair. Tomorrow may be overcast with clouds. My words are like the stars that never change. Whatever Seattle says the great chief at Washington can rely upon with as much certainty as he can upon the return of the sun or the seasons. The White Chief says that Big Chief at Washington sends us greetings of friendship and goodwill. That is kind of him for we know he has little need of our friendship in return. His people are many. They are like the grass that covers vast prairies. My people are few. They resemble the scattered trees of a storm-swept plain.

Chief Seattle goes on to talk about the cultural and religious differences between the Red Man and the White Man and concludes that "Day and night cannot dwell together" and so "The Red Man has ever fled the approach of the White Man, as the morning mist flees before the morning sun." He agrees to think about the treaty, but pessimistically concludes that the coming of White power means the end not only of Indian power, but of Indians: "Tribe follows tribe, and nation follows nation, like the waves of the sea. It is the order of nature, and regret is useless." However, he concludes, "We may be brothers after all," if time proves him right and if someday the White Man shares the Red Man's fate. In the meantime, the Indian dead will haunt the White living so that, "The White Man will never be alone."

Discuss Chief Seattle's statements and the images which give them strength. What do they reveal about Indian culture? Are the images clear? Effective? Why? How?

B. Before the feminist movement forced meteorologists to name hurricanes after both men and women, it was traditional to give those giant storms female names like "Camille," the name of one that struck the Mississippi Coast and caused great destruction. There is an old English saying, "Hell has no fury like that of an angry woman." What relationship between hurricanes and women were the meteorologists thinking of? Ships and cars are also often given female names in our culture, and, even if they aren't, many people refer to a ship or a car as *she* as in *she's a beauty* or *her* as in *her engine needs work*, though concern with sexist language is beginning to change this practice in some areas. Is this true in your language too? Speculate about why! (The general technique is called personification, giving human characteristics to non-human things or forces, as when we speak of "Mother Nature.")

C. The authors of the following discussion of historical methods are writing to high school students who know very little about the profession of "historian."

How is History Written?

Writing history is in many ways like being a detective, for it involves the search for clues and information that will help form an accurate description and explanation of a past situation or event. After choosing a subject, as a detective would on a case, the historian begins to build from what is known. He searches for other information which will make his story as complete and accurate as possible. He will often meet a dead end in his search, for the records of the past are not complete. But a fact found here and another found there will go together, and a deeper and more exact tale will begin to emerge from the information he has gathered. When the detective, or the historian, has looked in all the places where information on his subject might be found, he evaluates the evidence and files his report—which is the historian's book or article.

Although the physical remains of the past—buildings, tools, roads, and the like—offer some clues, the historian draws on many other sources of information. He may use wills, birth certificates, land titles, court proceedings and other government records. He will use the writings of *eyewitnesses*—letters, diaries, and memoirs. If those who were eyewitnesses are still alive, he will talk to them. He will read newspapers of the time of the event. In these and other sources he will find the facts relating to his subject.

Having found sources of information, the historian is left with three important jobs. First, if there is disagreement, he must decide which of his sources is most nearly correct. Is sworn testimony given at the time of the event or a book written fifty years afterward more likely to tell exactly what happened? Such decisions are an everyday part of the historian's [and the detective's] craft. Second, having decided which of his sources gives the more nearly accurate story, he must organize and present the story in a way which will interest and inform others. Finally, to support his version, the historian [like the detective] must show where he got his information. This is usually done through the use of footnotes, which are the scholar's way of identifying his source of information.

This may all sound very strange and mysterious, but perhaps will be clearer after you do a little historical research.

—James Rease and Lorrin Kennamer, *Texas: Land of Contrast*

• Questions for Discussion

1. Why do the authors compare being an historian with being a detective?

2. If the historian is like a detective, what kinds of skills are necessary to study history?

3. What does this comparison suggest about the authors' attitude toward history? History is usually considered fixed and settled; do these authors think it is?

4. Could a doctor be compared to a detective? an archaeologist? an anthropologist? What about an architect or a dentist? Imitate the above model and write your own description comparing some profession to detective work.

•• Writing Assignments

A. Paragraphs may explain and expand a simile, metaphor, or analogy. The first or topic sentence should establish the key relationship. The sentences thereafter should explain or elaborate. For example, you might write the following:

  1. Being in school is like being in prison. (topic idea)

      2. There are lots of rules to follow in both, rules made and enforced by someone else.

      2. One cannot leave either place without permission or else punishment.

      2. A teacher in class, like a guard in prison, watches the students, gives them orders, and corrects them for bad behavior.

  1. In sum, in the classroom the student, like a prisoner, is not free to do as he pleases, but instead is subject to the rules and regulations of a stern authority. (repeats topic idea in more concrete form)

Written together as a single unit, these coordinated sentences could form the base structure for a short paragraph developed by analogy. Adding subordinated examples and explanations to fill in that base structure would complete the paragraph.

Develop your own paragraph following this system. You may create your own metaphor/simile or choose one of the following.

1. Living in a dormitory is like attending a round-the-clock party.
2. Driving in city traffic is like playing a fast-moving computer game. / Driving on an interstate highway is like driving in the exhausting Daytona 500 or the 24-hour LeMans race.
3. A vacation period is like a time-out period in a sports competition.
4. Visiting _____ is like attending a carnival/a museum/a cemetery.
5. My English class is like a three-ring circus.
6. After his final examinations, my friend always looks like a zombie [a dead person risen from the grave].
7. Ever since I came to _____, I have felt like a fish out of water because _____. / In my _____ class I am like a duck in a chicken yard because _____.
8. Doing research into a new topic is like being an explorer in a new territory.
9. _____ is a good example of the ugly duckling who turned into a beautiful swan.
10. Learning a new language is like opening a gate into a previously hidden, but lovely garden/ or like searching for a rose in a desert/ or like returning to infancy with an adult mind trapped in an infant's abilities/ or like _____.

B A good way to clarify an idea, a process, or a pattern unfamiliar to your readers is to explain it in more familiar terms, through analogy. Sometimes this explanation may be hypothetical as in, *If we were to…*. Such analogical explanations might be introduced with terms like: *Imagine…, Let's imagine…, Take…,* or *Let's take… as an example. If…*. After the analogy has been clearly expressed, then a transition phrase such as *in like manner, similarly, in the same way,* and so forth returns the reader to the topic which the analogy has hopefully helped clarify. For example, Americans often describe military tactics with sports analogies. A military officer might make his discussion of tactics clearer by saying, *Take baseball as a metaphor for war. The three bases are comparable to the cities in dispute. The pitcher is the attacking general, and the batter is the defending one. If the batter shows uncertainty, then the pitcher will become even more confident, and the batter, in turn, will become even more intimidated and will more easily strike out. When the bases are full of players, both sides will be stalemated or equally balanced against each other, so this must be prevented. Just as in baseball, our military campaign must begin aggressively ....* The last phrase introduces the explanation of how the metaphor applies to military tactics.

Choose an idea, process, pattern or concept and help clarify it by using an analogy introduced with at least one of the above transition phrases.

C. Norman H. Tolman, in *Discover Japan: Words, Customs and Concepts*, finds the bending capacity of bamboo reminiscent of "many traits of the Japanese people" because bamboo is both strong and flexible and can be "bent, stretched, and pushed into all sorts of shapes, but when... released..., snaps back into its original form and continues to grow tall and strong," just as the Japanese, after a disastrous war, forged ahead "to become a strong and powerful nation." He also finds the Japanese and their culture often regarded as "exotic in the same way as bamboo," because little is really known about them or their culture in other parts of the world, but he finds them, "just like the plant,... understandable and not inscrutable at all."

Think of a metaphor/analogy that will help describe you, your family, or people from your country to your classmates in the same way that bamboo helps you understand more about the Japanese. Develop this analogy in an explanatory paragraph.

D. Write a paragraph describing something inanimate (a car, a city) as if it were human. How does the personification contribute to the reader's ability to visualize what you describe?

E. Write a well-organized paragraph about the problems foreign students face in a new country. Use a metaphor or metaphors to make these problems visual.

F. Create a metaphor which explains how hard it is to learn a foreign language. Be sure that the image of your metaphor suggests the particular difficulties of learning a foreign language.

G. Choose three of the ten metaphors about writing in the Exercise 16.3 on page 351 and do the following:

1. Explain what the three metaphors reveal about effective writing or a successful writing process.

2. Discuss their limitations. That is, what important steps in the writing process do they ignore? Or where do the metaphors not fit the writing process?

3. Offer a better or more informative metaphor in their place. Your handling of these three requirements should be presented in a paper format with a thesis and a conclusion.

H. University of Iowa foreign student adviser Gary Althen, in an essay on "Metaphors for Foreign Students" in the *NAFSA Newsletter*, notes a number of different metaphors Americans use to describe students from abroad. He writes to American educators, but what he says is of interest to those whom they educate as well. Some of these metaphors are listed below. What do they imply? Which one(s) describes your impression of American/foreign student relationships? Why?

1. "Foreign students are our guests. According to this metaphor, American citizens are in the role of hosts vis-a-vis students from other countries." What does this metaphor imply about the relationship between Americans and foreign students and the proper behavior for that relationship?

2. "Foreign students are valuable educational resources. People who see foreign students as educational assets are likely to support programs that give natives the opportunity to learn from the foreign students' experiences and viewpoints." Give some examples of the type of programs and interaction you would expect from this image. From international festivals? Foreign student involvement in class discussions? What else?

3. "Foreign students are commodities. . . . educating foreign students is a business venture."

4. "Foreign students are potential political capital [resources]."

5. "Foreign students are potential customers."

6. "Foreign students are a threat to national security."

Althen concludes that none of these metaphors is completely right or wrong, that some are incompatible with others, or overlap, but he believes it is important to consider the attitudes that produce university policies and that govern the personal behavior of Americans toward foreign students.

What metaphors best describe your view of your own role as a student studying abroad? Do you think of yourself as a guest? an ambassador? a teacher? a customer seeking a product? a tourist? an investor? Write a paper explaining your image of yourself and its implications. If you think of yourself as a guest, how does this image affect the way you expect to be treated? How would that treatment differ, if, for example, you thought of yourself as an ambassador or as an investor? Explain.

Application: Traditional Romantic Metaphors

Abul-Quasim Al-Bakharai, who died in the year 1075, wrote a compliment to a woman in a poem. It is, at first reading, hard to understand, even translated into English, because of the traditional comparisons used. Can you make sense of it?

Night black as pitch she bids bright day bestride	tar; asks to; ride
Two sugar-plums stars two-and-thirty hide;	reddish-purple fruit
Over the red rose a musky scorpion strays,	perfumed; poisonous desert insect
For which she keeps two antidotes well-tried.	cure for poison

A translation into more common language might read as follows:

Very black hair surrounds her very light, bright face.
Her rich, tasty, dark-purple lips cover thirty-two shining teeth;
A lock of dark hair curls over her red cheek,
While her lips are a well-tested treatment for the pain her beauty causes.

Notice that the "translation" doesn't quite capture all the meaning of the original: calling dark hair a scorpion and lips antidotes to the scorpion's poison implies much about this girl: danger as well as beauty in her looks.

In a famous poem, Shakespeare makes fun of the conventional English Renaissance images used to praise women, arguing that his lover doesn't have eyes as big and bright as the sun, nor hair like golden wires, nor roses in her cheeks; nor does she walk lightly on air like an angel or smell like perfume or sound like music when she talks. Shakespeare's point is that his lover is a real, down-to-earth woman, not a fantasy made up of conventional comparisons. Is Shakespeare's approach an insult or is it real praise? How bound should we be by conventional comparisons when we praise somebody? Is honesty an issue?

What are some of the traditional ways of describing the beauty of women in your country? What types of metaphors do your writers and your young lovers use? Make a list to explain and to compare with those of your classmates. Once you have completed the prewriting activity, write a paper which compares the metaphors of romance in your country/language with those in other countries/languages. Do any metaphors seem to be universal? Do some seem to be bound to a culture or language?

Chapter 17: PERSUADING EFFECTIVELY

Raw emotion cannot win the day against opponents who demand factual evidence, yet the dull recitation of statistical facts may be meaningless unless you motivate readers and get them involved. —James D. Lester

Facts do not speak for themselves, nor do figures add up on their own. Even the most vividly detailed printout requires someone to make sense of the information it contains. — Nancy R. Comley

Your argument is logical when you can demonstrate that anyone using the same reasoning process and the same evidence must inevitably come to the same conclusion. —Winkler & McCuen

---

Cultural Differences in Attitudes toward Persuasion and Argumentation

Universal Characteristics of Persuasion
    Rhetorical Stance
    Universal Appeals
    Universal Types of Logic
    Fallacies

Evidence
    Credibility
    Validity

Assumptions and Premises

Argumentation

Rhetorical Analysis

Models to Learn From

Avoiding Common Pitfalls

Final Checklists for Augmentation and Analysis

Passages for Discussion and Analysis

Writing Assignments

All of the chapters in this text have to a greater or lesser degree stressed persuasion, or what language scholars call *rhetoric*, the use of persuasive language to influence readers or listeners. For example, asking readers to accept your interpretation of a description or your idea about how two things compare or contrast involves a mild form of persuasion even if the discussion is largely factual and objective. So too does having someone accept your definition of an important idea or term or of what you think is comparable or analogous to that term. The point is that almost every form of writing except the listing of purely factual information tries to persuade the reader to some degree. Furthermore, even a completely objective list may try to be persuasive if those facts have been carefully selected with the ultimate goal of changing the reader's mind. Imagine a list of "top restaurants in town" published by the local restaurant owners association: Would the eateries of non-members be included? Some less reputable newspapers and magazines do favorable feature stories on establishments and products that (as if by accident) are advertised in their pages. Persuasion, even in seemingly objective forms, is all around us.

Persuasion of the type required in many college courses is similar to these forms of persuasion, but is more forceful, more argumentative. Tailored definitions, example and classification categories, and carefully chosen cause/effect relationships are common developmental methods used in persuasive arguments.

When describing serious writing, the word *argument* does <u>not</u> mean "verbal disagreement" but rather the logical steps or reasons given in support of a position or a series of statements or ideas in an essay or a discussion. In formal writing and in oral presentations in law courts, in scientific and medical seminars, and in formal business meetings, a special discipline is imposed on discussions. This discipline is the discipline of argument or *argumentation*, and its purpose is to discover the truth or at least the closest possible approximation to the truth.

In Western cultures, argumentation has been heavily influenced by the classical rhetorical tradition of ancient Greece and Rome. Thus, even today freshman English students may study the logic of the Greek philosopher Aristotle, who lived over 2,000 years ago. However, whether an argument follows the strict classical rules or whether it is more modern and casual, its goal is to use language to persuade readers to a particular point of view.

Cultural Differences in Attitudes toward Persuasion and Argumentation

You may find the concept of argument-to-discover-the-truth very similar to what is practiced in your culture, or you may think it alien and peculiar. If your reaction is the latter, it will help to put some effort into understanding this Western tradition which underlies the legal, scientific, political, and social systems of a great number of European-influenced countries, and especially the U.S. The idea goes back, in part, to "trial by combat," the practice of allowing medieval knights to literally fight in defense of their positions, with God and fate determining the winner. Argument-to-discover-truth also reflects the capitalist notion of the "marketplace of ideas," where competing theories and philosophies are tested in an open "market" to see which will be "bought" and which will be left "bankrupt" and failed. Presumably, this testing by a wide variety of "consumers" allows the strongest and most promising ideas to survive and succeed, although whether this is always true is a good question. What is certain is that the practice is highly culture-bound, determined by Western tradition and history.

From the point of view of the individual student writer, the importance of understanding "argument-to-discover-truth" lies in accepting the role of advocate and forceful defender of a position. In many cultures, especially those influenced by Confucian and other Asian traditions, the role of aggressive advocate may seem rude and egotistical, the placing of individual interests before those of the group. The acceptance of such a role is sometimes psychologically painful for students from cultures that stress cooperation and group satisfaction. In fact, even Americans sometimes become upset with lawyers who defend unpopular positions; therefore, it is worth repeating the rules of the game. A person presenting an argumentative position, whether that position is freely chosen or assigned, is supposed to argue as forcefully and as energetically as possible.

Universal Characteristics of Persuasion

RHETORICAL STANCE

All writing involves a persona, the image of the writer created through the writing. In rhetoric or "the art of persuasion," this persona involves a choice of rhetorical stance. Most writers adopt some combination of three stances, that of the scholar or objective investigator, that of the salesperson or promoter, or that of the entertainer.

The first stance, that of the scholar, has truth as its goal. The argument is objective and factual, though, as a result, it is perhaps overly formal and not very exciting. The writer cares less for audience involvement than for a search for truth, and avoids taking a strongly biased position in an effort to be completely balanced. The second stance, that of the salesperson or promoter, is highly subjective and focused on audience. Since the goal is to sell an idea or ideology, the writing is heavily slanted and leaves out evidence and arguments that do not advance the writer's position. In other words, truth is secondary and heavy promoting dominates. The third stance, that of the entertainer, also focuses on audience and subordinates strict fact to audience pleasure. The goal is to give readers what they want. Extreme versions of any one of these stances are to be avoided.

The effective writer chooses a stance that balances the best of all three: a scholarly respect for truth and fact, a salesperson's skill at promoting an idea, and an entertainer's sense of keeping an audience involved. The concept is like that of an acrobat balancing a board with three points on a ball; only if the acrobat/writer stays firmly in the middle of the board or leans only slightly toward a point can balance be maintained; moving too far toward any of the three points means a slip and a fall. However, no matter how you might try, one of the three stances will dominate: you will investigate objectively, or promote, or entertain, or perhaps lean toward two at once, but you can't do all three equally at the same time. Consider a U.S. president adopting a different stance at different times for different purposes: he may be a salesperson, attempting to persuade the public about a policy or program he favors; he may be a scholar, describing a problem or situation as objectively as possible without taking a position about what should be done; he may be an entertainer at a social occasion or celebration. Most likely, a president will combine these stances, moving from one role to another.

Another way to understand the concept of rhetorical stances is to consider effective teachers you have had: Were they pure scholars? Salespeople for ideas or ideologies? Entertaining public speakers? One stance or a combination of any two usually dominates.

- EXERCISE 17.1: RHETORICAL STANCE

Is the rhetorical stance of the following that of the scholar, the salesperson, the entertainer or some combination of the two? If some combination, which stance dominates?

1. Attempts to define alcoholism have been marked by uncertainty, conflict, and ambiguity. Definitions have evolved from classical-historical times to the present, reflecting the prevalent cultural, religious, and scientific biases....

   In 1849, a Swedish physician, Dr. Magnus Huss, coined the term *alcoholism* to describe a diseased condition resulting from excessive alcohol consumption. In 1866, a French doctoral candidate, M. Gabriel, first used the term in its modern sense, as a disease manifested by a loss of control over alcohol intake, leading to excessive alcohol consumption—what we would now refer to as an addiction. He also insightfully designated alcoholism a public health problem. The use of "alcoholism" to designate a disease identified by the symptom of excessive alcohol intake promptly caught on and was adopted into most modern languages.

   —Mark Keller and John Doria, "On Defining Alcoholism," Alcohol World Health and Research, Public Health Service

2. Throughout history, humans have adapted their surroundings to better suit their needs. Glen Canyon National Recreation Area provides a dramatic example of the combination of one of nature's most inspiring and one of man's most ambitious projects. Impounded behind the Bureau of Reclaimation's Glen Canyon Dam, waters of the Colorado River and its tributaries are backed up almost 200 miles, forming Lake Powell. The lake and nearly one million acres of desert and canyon country offer memorable leisure-time activities for American and international visitors. Fishing and water sports are the dominant activities. Exploring on foot can provide intimate contact with the natural and cultural features preserved here for the enjoyment of present and future generations. Earth forces shaped this topography that now appears as talus lopes, buttes, and mesas, canyons and cliffs. Prehistoric human inhabitants occupied the area and left scattered indications of their presence.

   —"Glen Canyon," National Park Service brochure, U.S. Department of the Interior

3. The U.S. Mint's [the agency which makes coins] outlay for models' fees has been practically nil [nothing]. Legend has it that when the eagle was selected as our national emblem the Philadelphia Mint adopted a live specimen named Peter, who posed for several early coins before he got tangled up in the Mint's machinery. Peter died as a result of his injuries, but he retained his Civil Service status through the thoughtfulness of fellow employees who had the bald bird stuffed.

   Though the Mint was not on a first-name basis with the bison who posed for the buffalo nickel, the Indian was long thought to be a chap named Two Guns Whitecalf. According to designer James Earle Fraser, however, the portrait was a composite of three other braves—Irontail, Two Moons, and a taciturn type with long braids who never did give his name.

   The Indian on the old penny was a pale-faced squaw named Sarah Longacre, daughter of a Mint official, while the Lincoln, Washington, Jefferson, Franklin, Roosevelt, and Kennedy coins were all done from portraits. When designer John Sinnock added his initials to the Roosevelt dime in 1946, word spread among the benighted that the tiny

"J.S." stood for Joseph Stalin and was the work of subversives boring from within the Mint.

—"William Iversen's 10 Best Oddities," *People's Almanac*

4. There are many reasons, some purely practical, for preventing the extinction of species. They may have important scientific, medical, agricultural, or industrial uses, known or as yet unknown. They each play an ecological role, and we do not know what the consequences may be if they are lost: other species dependent on them might be lost as well. Endangered species, like all species, are unique genetic combinations, never to be created again. If they are lost, the genetic resources of Earth are diminished. Furthermore, they may be sensitive to environmental change and can warn us of threats to the environment. The decline of peregrine falcons, bald eagles, and other species alerted us to the dangerous effects of DDT. Endangered species have symbolic importance—they tell us that all species may become threatened, including ourselves, if we do not preserve a healthy environment. And we may simply enjoy them as interesting or beautiful living things that share the planet with us. Finally, since many species are endangered because of human action, we must consider a moral question: Is it just plain wrong to cause the extinction of another form of life?

—"Endangered Species in the National Parks," U.S. Department of the Interior, National Park Service

UNIVERSAL APPEALS

There are three key appeals common in persuasion: 1) emotional appeals, 2) ethical appeals, and 3) logical appeals.

Emotional appeals are made to change opinions or motivate action by stimulating strong feelings. Although often looked down upon as a lesser form of argument, there is nothing inherently wrong with using emotion to persuade, as long as the emotions are honest and the final purposes legitimate. Many human passions—love (of country, of children, of the natural environment) or hate (of injustice, of disease, of inefficiency)—can be used to promote important causes. Of course, problems arise with emotions such as guilt, jealousy, fear, and the like, which often are used to appeal to lower instincts and dishonorable political or commercial ends. Even in these cases, though, emotion is just a tool to be used or misused. Famine relief agencies, for example, often use pictures of starving children to move us to contribute, and this use of the emotions of pity and guilt can hardly be called wrong. Advertisements for some products suggest the product will make you more attractive and more popular, and while this emotional appeal to pride and egotism may be a bit foolish, it is not necessarily morally wrong.

Arguments based on ethics appeal to the religious or moral values of readers: *You should do it because it is right, because it has the blessing of your faith, because it is unthinkable to do otherwise.* The problem with ethical appeals is that they may be very much culture based, so that an appeal to the religious ethics of a Moslem might not work on a Confucian, Shinto, or Buddhist, and an appeal to the cultural ethics of Japanese might not work on Belgians, Kenyans, or Chileans. In other words, while people of all cultures use ethical appeals for persuasion, these appeals are sometimes culture bound unless based on broad ethical values acceptable to most people of decency: for example, it is wrong to shoot helpless women and children in war. However, some groups may well reject even these principles. Debates about universal ethics are unending. Ethical appeals often overlap with appeals to emotion.

Appeals to logic are appeals to unemotional statements, usually arranged in an order that others find "true" or "reliable" (see the discussion of validity on page 388). Such appeals are often based on credible statistics, surveys, and studies from trustworthy sources, the opinions of recognized experts, concrete factual information, and predictable cause/effect patterns: *Drunken driving leads to accidents; Depletion of the ozone layer produces higher rates of skin cancer.* They are also based on inductive and deductive reasoning, as will be discussed.

In sum, all three types of appeals are used universally; however, the emotional and ethical appeals that work in one culture do not necessarily work in another. Only logical appeals consistently transcend cultural differences (though sometimes even these may be influenced by cultural perspectives). Furthermore, it is logical appeals that are most significant for college writing.

UNIVERSAL TYPES OF LOGIC

There are two basic types of logic used in all cultures: *inductive* and *deductive*. Scientific persuasion tends to be inductive, while reasoning based on accepted principles is deductive.

Because of its movement from particular observations to general conclusion, induction is often called the scientific method. For example, Sir Isaac Newton is reported to have formulated his theory of gravity from observing apples falling from a tree and the behavior of balls and arrows and other projectiles sent skyward. A key problem with inductive logic,

---

• EXERCISE 17.2: RECOGNIZING APPEALS

A. Bring a magazine advertisement to class. Be prepared to explain the appeal or appeals the ad depends on: emotional, logical, ethical.

B. Decide whether the following writers rely on emotional, ethical, or logical appeals, or some mixture of these. If emotional appeals, identify the type of emotion, for example, the desire to be part of a group; the desire to be unique and individual; patriotism; personal pride; distrust of outsiders; trust of authorities, experts, or famous personalities; sympathy for the homeless, the injured, the weak, the abused, or some other. If ethical appeals, identify whether the ethics are based on religious values, general social/moral values, or universal ethics. If logical, try to explain what kind of logic: cause/effect relationships, statistical evidence, scientific fact, or other.

1. Buy our new, improved Product X. It is quick and easy to use, no fuss, no mess. Nine out of ten doctors use it; so should you.

Goal?_____

Type of appeal? _____

Particular focus or method of the appeal? _____

2. It is wrong of doctors, even with parental consent, to go to extreme measures to preserve the lives of prematurely born infants with only four months development inside the mother. No infant born this early has survived, despite the extreme efforts of the medical community, and during the attempt to save a life that is not yet fully formed, the infant suffers terribly. Hooked up to a machine that reads off its internal data and breathes for it, and bruised by hypodermics, its bones gradually disintegrate from lack of proper nutrition. This disintegration is irreversible and results in great pain. Doctors may learn a great deal about prenatal development from such live experimentation, but it is cruel and unnatural to prolong the terrible suffering of a very premature infant when death is inevitable.

Goal?_____

Type of appeal? _____

Particular focus or method of the appeal? _____

3. Americans have an obligation to support preschool programs throughout the nation, to allow the children of the very poor a chance at education. Children from impoverished homes have not had the experience with books or with parents taking time to begin

their education before they begin school. Many do not know standard English. Their often single parents may not have had time to teach them the alphabet. They almost certainly have never been inside a museum; in fact, they may never have been outside their family's neighborhood. As a result, when they begin classes, they are already behind the other children in knowledge of the world around them. This initial defeat sets the pattern for the rest of their lives. If this nation is to live up to its obligations, both as a Christian nation and as a democracy, it must provide such children a head start on life. Funding headstart preschool programs is not only charitable, it is vital to preserving democratic principles of fairness, equality, and education.

Goal? _____

Type of appeal? _____

Particular focus or method of the appeal? _____

4. Noted journalist Norman Cousins, in "How to Make People Smaller Than They Are," argues that the modern focus on vocational education rather than on general education is dangerous in a democracy because it ignores history, language, literature, and philosophy—the liberal arts in general—and opts instead for "practical" business and computer courses. Cousins agrees with our Founding Fathers that a free society is absolutely dependent on a thinking citizenry. Universities that simply provide job training are failing in their duty to teach the underlying philosophy of our government, to expose students to debates about the principles and ethics that determine a free society, in other words, to prepare them for democracy. Cousins points out that Thomas Jefferson was "prouder of having been the founder of the University of Virginia than of having been President of the United States," because he understood that a system based on the "informed consent of the governed" can only work when the governed are educated, their minds developed, their values tested. In other words, an educational system which provides citizens with a broad general education is necessary for the survival of democracy.

Goal? _____

Type of appeal? _____

Particular focus or method of the appeal? _____

5. Man's use of chemicals to control his environment is dangerous and even lethal. For example, some insecticides sprayed on gardens and crops have a long life. They enter whatever crop is grown and move through the food chain from plant to animal to human being, where they settle in the bones—permanently. Others, like DDT, produce immediately observable effects: beneficial insects killed off, birds laying eggs with soft shells, humans suffering from nervous disorders and brain damage. Still others, carried by rains, pass into underground streams and combine into new, more deadly forms that kill plant and animal life. Noted environmentalist Rachel Carson points out in her essay "The Obligation to Endure" that over 200 basic chemicals have been created since the mid-1940's, chemicals sold under thousands of different brand names, all toxic to our world.

Goal? _____

Type of appeal? _____

Particular focus or method of the appeal? _____

however, is that a larger sampling of observations might require modification of inductively drawn conclusions. For instance, a larger sampling of projectiles, including rocketships, sent skyward, has meant that Sir Isaac Newton's conclusion, "What goes up must come down!" had to be modified to, "What goes up must come down unless it goes beyond the gravitational pull of earth!"

Another problem is that your sampling may not be representative. A conclusion about U.S. colleges based on one or even two or three colleges might not be accurate if it does not consider representatives from both private and public schools, religious and non-religious ones, state universities and community colleges, those located in the East, the South, the West, the Midwest and so forth. Furthermore, just one exception to the pattern undercuts and may negate an inductive conclusion, especially one that begins "all" or "no." For example, an early anthropologist concluded on the basis of a handful of Eskimos he had met that "All Eskimos are depressed and morose." However, just one happy Eskimo would be sufficient to disprove his inductively drawn generalization. In addition to the questions of sufficient and representative evidence, inductive arguments might be judged on the basis of whether the evidence has been randomly selected, whether the observer drawing the conclusions began with preconceptions, and whether the evidence and conclusions are presented in non-biased language. If an inductive argument fails in any of these criteria, it fails as an argument.

Inductive arguments in writing begin with evidence and move toward a concluding, unifying generalization. The inductive pattern is the best one to use with an audience that you predict will disagree with your position. The logic is that, if you state the general argument first, the readers will react according to their prejudices and not pay attention to the evidence; however, if you first provide the evidence, the readers will absorb it and understand your position, so that when they finally hear the conclusion, even if they disagree with it, they will at least be forced to recognize why someone would believe it.

Deduction, in contrast, begins with a general principle that is accepted as truth and concludes about a particular case on the basis of it. For instance, Charles Darwin formulated his theory of evolution based on inductive reasoning: observation over years of study that led to Darwin's conclusion that evolution produced humankind. Today, scientists accept evolution as a scientific truth and can reason deductively on the basis of it: If all creatures have evolved, then the horse, which is a modern creature, has evolved from some ancient creature. Such a conclusion has led to the search for and discovery of the predecessors of the modern horse.

A writer who begins with the generalization that "practice makes perfect" can use this principle to argue deductively that would-be drivers would benefit from driver's training programs. In like manner, a writer attacking plagiarism might start with the general principle that "theft is wrong", demonstrate that plagiarism is a form of theft, and conclude that plagiarism is therefore wrong.

• EXERCISE 17.3: LOGICAL REASONING

Identify the type of logic used in the following paragraphs as either deductive or inductive. Where possible, also identify the problems with the argument. Where does the logic break down? Problems might include an insufficient sample, a non-representative sample, biased wording, mistaking a cause for an effect or an effect for a cause, using information from a biased source, circular reasoning, drawing a conclusion based on a questionable generalization, or a conclusion that does not follow logically from an acceptable generalization. If there are no problems with the logic, write "good argument."

Example: In the space of one hundred and seventy-six years the Lower Mississippi has shortened itself two hundred and forty-two miles. That is an average of a trifle over one mile and a third per year. Therefore, any calm person, who is not blind or idiotic, can see that in the old Oolitic Silurian Period,

just a million years ago next November, the Lower Mississippi River was upward of one million three hundred thousand miles long…. seven hundred and forty-two years from now the Lower Mississippi will be only a mile and three-quarters long…. There is something fascinating about science. One gets such wholesale returns of conjecture out of such trifling investment of fact.
—Mark Twain, *Life on the Mississippi*, 1883.

Answer <u>Type of logic?</u> Induction; reliance on statistics to predict the future and speculate about the past. <u>Problem/Problems with the logic?</u> Twain is purposely and humorously misusing statistics to show us how they can be abused. A change that occurs over a set period of time cannot reasonably be expected to have also occurred historically and to continue to occur at the same rate into the future, or children who grow several inches a year would be twelve feet tall at age forty. Twain ignores cause/effect realities. He relies on intimidation (implying the reader is hysterical, blind, or idiotic if she or he disagrees) to reinforce this bad logic.

1. Although police departments nationwide want stricter gun control laws so, as they put it, "only the criminals have guns," the statistics put out by the United States Rifle Assembly and the American League for the Right to Defend One's Home indicate that stricter gun control laws will increase the crime rates and make the home less safe. It is a God-given right to own a gun, so every American has the right to buy a gun anytime, anywhere, without government restrictions. Moreover, we Americans have the constitutional right to own submachine guns if we so desire. Therefore, the courts have no legal right to deny us our constitutional privileges. Besides, if only the criminals have guns, every citizen will be in danger. Protect your home by voting against the socialist-inspired bill to require a two-day delay in the purchase and registration of a gun.

    Type of logic? _____

    Problem/Problems with the logic? _____

    _____

2. Last night at midnight, when I first arrived here by plane, I couldn't find anyone who would rent me a car. A policeman said, "Lady, why don't you try tomorrow? Everyone's gone home." When I insisted that transportation should be available around the clock at a respectable airport, he told me to take a cab. When I caught a taxi, the driver kept asking me where I was going, even after I had told him twice. Then he took me to the wrong address and claimed it was the address I had said. Clearly then, the people in this city are much ruder than people from my hometown.

    Type of logic? _____

    Problem/Problems with the logic? _____

    _____

3. A survey of my international friends at the university indicates that most American food is very dull and starchy. We have eaten at five different university cafeterias, at a downtown cafeteria in a typical mid-Western town and at a small fast-food diner near campus. The meat is usually overcooked and always served with potatoes. The vegetables are also overcooked and bland. The desserts are too sweet and certainly far too fattening.

   Type of logic? _____

   Problem/Problems with the logic? _____

   _____

4. Noted scientists in a number of government reports and scientific studies on the effects of nuclear explosions and nuclear radiation fear the worst. Gwynne Dyer in his book *War* warns of a possible nuclear war that could end springtime and summer forever, and popular author and scientist Carl Sagan in an essay entitled "Nuclear Winter" describes the horrifyingly destructive effects of a 2-megaton explosive over a fairly large city: "Buildings would be vaporized, people reduced to atoms and shadows, outlying structures blown down like matchsticks, and raging fires ignited." Sagan goes on to add that the effects of such a bomb exploded on the ground would be "an enormous crater, like those that can be seen through a telescope on the surface of the moon." The more than 50,000 nuclear weapons in the U.S. and Russian arsenals would, he argues, be "enough to obliterate a million Hiroshimas." Nobel Laureate Sune K. Bergstrom of The World Health Organization concludes that 1.1 billion people would suffer serious injuries and radiation sickness, and that no medical help would be available. Experts speculate that the immediate aftermath of global thermonuclear war could be the deaths of more than 2 billion people. In such a case, civilization as we know it would cease to exist. In other words, we could possibly bomb the world back to the Dark Ages, before modern science and technology existed.

   Type of logic? _____

   Problem/Problems with the logic? _____

   _____

5. Observing students entering and exiting the student center of my university for a period of two hours on Wednesday from 3 to 5 P.M. has produced the following results. Over 80 percent of the students opened the doors for themselves, both on entering and exiting. All of the men opened the doors for themselves, and 30 percent of those men opened the doors for others as well. The ones who had the doors opened for them were 1) blind, 2) paraplegic, or 3) female. Only ten percent of those for whom the doors were opened went through the open door; the other 20 percent either 1) went through the door next to the open one, 2) took hold of the door and pushed it for themselves, or 3) stopped and stared and waited. From this, one can conclude that 30 percent of the men at this school think women have something wrong with them and are as helpless as the handicapped, and we also learn that the handicapped don't feel as handicapped as they are treated.

   Type of logic? _____

   Problem/Problems with the logic? _____

   _____

FALLACIES

Fallacies are mistakes of logic and argument so common they have been named. The following are some common fallacies. Even if you never use these terms you will see them used in serious critiques of arguments and will sometimes even hear them in newscasts.

1. <u>Consensus</u> or <u>Bandwagon</u>: An emotional argument that "Everybody is doing it so we should too." This is the argument used in many soft drink ads: "The whole world drinks cola," and, by implication, we should too or we will be left out.

2. <u>Red Herring</u>: Misleading an audience through misdirection. The writer begins with one topic but then provides a distraction or an irrelevant question or assertion to focus the audience's attention on some other topic, to direct attention in a different direction. This is a favorite legal defense: "My client is accused of beating up a little old lady and stealing her savings, but isn't the violent television he was exposed to really to blame? Something should be done about the violence and crime on television…". Sometimes the red herring takes the form of an argument which answers an accusation with a counter-accusation: "You're a bad person, too." The red herring in such an argument is to turn an attack against the attacker. The youngster who tries drugs might accuse his parents of drinking too much; the politician accused of taking money might claim that all his colleagues take money too.

3. <u>Either/Or or Black/White Fallacy</u>: The writer sets up limited options to force the reader to make a choice. However, there might be other choices or the options might overlap. The well-known expression, "Either you are for us or you are against us," is typical of this mistake, for a person might belong in a third category and be totally neutral, or might approve of some ideas on one side and some ideas on the other side but not agree with either side totally. In other words, this is a form of oversimplification.

4. <u>Complex Question</u>: This fallacy is a language game. It involves a question set up in such a way that any direct answer (yes or no) will make the respondent look guilty. The most famous example is the question, "Have you stopped beating your wife?" If a person says "no", he is clearly guilty, but if he says "yes", then he admits that he has been guilty in the past. This technique really asks two questions as one.

5. <u>Begging the Question</u>: This is an error of logic related to the complex question. A begged question is treated as if the answer is already clear: "Do you really support building more of those terribly dangerous nuclear power plants?" In this example the real question is not whether you support nuclear power plants but whether or not nuclear power plants are really dangerous. The words "terribly dangerous", however, assume the reader has already agreed with the speaker's answer to the second question. Since the question is often begged by a single adjective or two, this trick is hard to spot: "As your mother, I'm always concerned when you go out with your no-good friends."

6 <u>Argument ad Hominem (to the man)</u>: This is an emotional argument directed against a person, his character, and his personal life instead of against his logic or his argument. Sometimes it takes the form of <u>namecalling</u>, choosing negative adjectives and nouns to defame a person; sometimes it focuses on religious beliefs, military record, marital status, race, or other emotional issues when these characteristics are not relevant to the situation. Sometimes, however, personal qualities might be truly significant, as in evidence of dishonesty in a person running for treasurer. The <u>Genetic Fallacy</u> is a type of *ad hominem* argument which argues that we can predict a person's character, behavior, or nature if we know his origins or the group to which he belongs: "He's a doctor so he must be rich." "He's a respected scientist so I'm sure we can trust him." Most racist statements fit in this category.

7. <u>Argument ad Populum (to the people)</u>: This is an emotional argument aimed at the preconceptions and prejudices of a group, their deep-seated fears and hopes. It is the type of argument Hitler used so effectively with the German people: an appeal to their desire for space, their need for a scapegoat for their economic troubles, their distrust of Jews and Gypsies.

8. <u>Circular Reasoning</u>: This is a logical error which consists of saying something is true because it is true: "She must be right because she speaks with authority,"; "My client can't be guilty because he is an honest man."

9. <u>False Generalization</u>: A logical error in which a conclusion is false because the generalization on which it is based is false. The false generalization often begins with *all* or *none* or includes the words *always* or *never*, as in, "Blondes always have more fun." The conclusion that Jean always has more fun than other people because she is a blonde is bad logic because the initial premise is false. Such statements are stereotypes. Absolutes (claims that 100 percent of a population behaves in a certain way) tend to be false except in science: "All living things die." However, some generalizations including *all, none, always,* or *never* may be asserted as statements of principles, as in the premise, "All men are created equal and endowed by their Creator with certain inalienable rights."

10. <u>Intimidation</u>: An emotional tactic intended to make the listener uncomfortable or even afraid to answer back. *No intelligent person could believe...* suggests the reader lacks intelligence if she believes whatever is discussed, while *All right-minded people agree...* suggests the reader who disagrees has misplaced values. Intimidation often sets *we* in opposition to *they*: "We who agree on this issue think clearly; those who disagree with us don't think clearly. Are you with them or with us?"

Evidence

At least in theory, arguments should avoid the personal and the emotional. An argument may try to move the feelings of its listeners or hearers—pictures of burned forests to persuade campers to be careful about smoking and putting out campfires would be an example—but it should use evidence to do so. The evidence could be of many kinds: statistics, examples, illustrations, the testimony of experts, the results of experiments, quotes from documents, and so on. The nature of the evidence used in arguments is probably less important than its sources, which are supposed to be objective and fair, and its appropriateness to the subject. For example, U.S. supermarkets sell many tabloid newspapers filled with fantastic stories and revelations: *Men from Mars have a cure for cancer* might be a typical headline. However, few people take this "news" seriously because the tabloid newspapers themselves have little credibility, and the evidence used to back up their claims is inadequate or nonexistent. One of the most important ways we evaluate the truth of a statement is by considering its source.

Arguments need not be based on factual evidence; they may instead use a series of generally accepted statements to move the reader toward a conclusion. For example, to convince students that the tuition they pay for classes should be raised, a college might compile statistics about rising costs and examples of comparable costs at other institutions; or the argument could consist of a series of assertions which students might be likely to accept as true: This college has always charged the minimum possible for its classes; the college's costs go up at the same rate as everyone else's; we will have to raise tuition.

The effectiveness of such arguments—whether they are persuasive or not—depends on two main factors, <u>the credibility of the evidence</u> and the <u>validity of the argument</u> itself, with "validity" meaning how well the argument is put together. Let us look at each of these two elements of argument in turn.

CREDIBILITY

The <u>credibility</u> of an argument means whether or not others believe it is true. Credibility is obviously an important value in everyday life as well as in writing, and it is worth considering what makes us believe or disbelieve the statements of our friends, of salespeople, of teachers, and other authority figures. Obviously, some people evoke more trust than others, but that is a circular argument, for it suggests that some people have credibility because they create trust and that we trust some people because they have credibility. It is more helpful to ask what causes these trusting feelings in the first place.

Belief is usually created when what people claim to be true is confirmed later on, when it is <u>verified</u> by later events or by other people. These verifications by other people also affect our initial belief; we tend to go along with the majority, placing a great deal of trust in respected sources such as *The New York Times* or a university or government agency and very little in the supermarket tabloids mentioned above. This is because it is impossible for average individuals to verify facts themselves; we must trust authorities for most of our information, and we learn which authorities have credibility from the opinions of other people. For instance, consider an example like, "There are over four billion people in the world today." This statement is impossible to verify directly: no one could count the world's population alone. Yet it is clearly "factual" since the various agencies which keep track of such figures, such as the United Nations, confirm this figure. It would also be possible to decide that some sources—say a poetry journal or a sports magazine—might not have much credibility in

---

• EXERCISE 17. 4: FALLACIES

Identify what is wrong with the logic of the following sentences. What fallacy is being committed?

Example: She's French; she must cook very well.

Genetic fallacy: assumption about an individual on the basis of belonging to a group

1. Mr. Jones should not be elected to public office for a number of reasons. First of all, he is not a native-born American and therefore cannot understand democratic principles the way <u>we</u> do.

2. In addition, Jones has been divorced, not just once but twice.

3. Furthermore, would you vote for someone who has neglected his parental duties by not being in town for his son's graduation? Anyone who can not be relied on in his private life can not be relied on in public life.

4. Besides, he ate dinner with his secretary three times last week; they must be having an illicit affair.

5. Mr. Jones has read the works of Karl Marx, so he must be a secret Communist.

6. When he was a state representative, he missed meetings three times in a row; he must be very lazy.

7. Vote against Mr. Jones in this next election: either you stand for true family values or you are unAmerican. Your vote will tell your neighbors which you are. If you are not for us, you are against us.

8. Only a woman would drive a car that badly.

9. She's fair-skinned with blue eyes; she can't be a native Spanish speaker.

10. U.S. winters are always very cold, rainy, and gray.

11. He must be a Californian: blond hair, blue eyes, a beach-boy tan.

12. This vacation spot is not for every Tom, Dick, or Harry. It is secluded, private, and very exclusive.

estimating the world's population, were they to do so, although, of course, they might have great credibility in their own field. Thus, careful writers are also careful readers of sources of information and ask themselves whether their sources are considered credible by others, whether these "others" themselves are credible, and whether the sources are operating within their fields of expertise.

VALIDITY

If many of the statements people make are not "facts" but are nevertheless potentially true, what should such statements be called? In argumentation, such statements as *Putting more police on the streets would reduce crime* are called underlines(assertions) or underlines(claims). An assertion may become a fact if enough people begin to consider it true, as in the assertion *The world is round*, or if it can be verified by later experience or scientific experiment, as also happened with the statement about the world's roundness, but most assertions, especially about politics and social questions, remain unproven and "unfactual."

Nevertheless, they are the heart of arguments, since people rarely argue about established, agreed-upon facts, but rather about their relevance to claims and assertions. *Reducing cholesterol will prevent heart disease; Women are discriminated against in the typical mixed-sex office; Poverty is caused by a capitalist economic system.* All such claims may involve factual data for support but are likely to be argued on the basis of assumptions and premises.

Assumptions and Premises

In their classical formulations, deductive arguments take the following pattern:

Major Premise: All men are mortal (they die).
Minor premise: Socrates is a man
Conclusion: Therefore Socrates is mortal (he will die someday).

This formal pattern seems artificial but in fact many of the everyday statements we make follow the same order:

Major premise: All women enjoy flowers.
Minor premise: Jane is a woman
Conclusion: Therefore, Jane would like flowers for her birthday.

It should be very obvious that the weak link in this argument lies in the major premise, *All women enjoy flowers.* Not all women do, and some are even allergic to them. Like most major premises people make, this one is a useful generalization which works much of the time, but which might fail miserably at other

---

•EXERCISE 17.5: IDENTIFYING FACTUAL STATEMENTS

Which of the following statements are verifiable as facts and how could they be verified?

1. Cigarette smoking causes cancer.
2. Water freezes at 0° C.
3. People from outer space have visited earth.
4. Some people believe that people from outer space have visited earth.
5. The folk medicine practiced by traditional healers is sometimes superior to western technological medicine practiced by doctors.
6. Chocolate is my favorite flavor of ice cream.
7. The British are the most disciplined automobile drivers in the world.
8. French cooking is superior to most other western cuisines.
9. French cooking is healthier than most western cooking.
10. A free market economy is the best economic system.

If some of the above are not facts, what changes in the statements would make them verifiable (whether true or false)?

times. The difficulty is that most of the time people don't bother to state their major premises very clearly, assuming them to be unquestionably true: *Jane's a woman; she'll like flowers.*

Of course, some premises on which arguments are based turn out to be completely false, with disastrous results:

Major premise: Disease is caused by bad blood.
Minor premise: Reducing the bad blood reduces the cause of a disease.
Conclusion: Sick people should have as much of their blood withdrawn as possible.

Until this century, Western physicians regularly "bled" their patients, sometimes killing them in the process. It is interesting to note that there was nothing wrong with this logic, which was the standard medical wisdom for many centuries; what was wrong was the major premise, that disease is caused by bad blood, which has only a germ of truth to it.

Examining the premises of an argument is therefore absolutely necessary in order to understand its origin and validity. In practice, this simply means asking common sense questions about our own and other people's arguments.

A good place to begin any analysis is with a question about *assumptions*. In fact, whenever you read anything written by someone else, it is important to ask what assumptions that writer holds. Assumptions are those beliefs and values which lie behind statements and are the reasons for those statements. ("To assume" means to believe or to accept as true without proof.) For example, teachers often make assumptions about students on the basis of where they sit in the classroom. Is the student who chooses a front-row seat more eager to learn than his classmates or just hard of hearing or nearsighted? Is the student who chooses a back-row seat hoping to avoid classroom questions and sleep through lectures, or just shy? Is the student who sits up straight at her desk a more reliable worker than the one who slouches? What other details of appearance might lead a teacher to initial assumptions? Are they always justified?

• EXERCISE 17.6: RECOGNIZING ASSUMPTIONS

A. Write out the assumption each of the following sentences makes.

> *Example:* She is presently studying aerospace engineering, but, as a woman, she can't last long in that field.
>
> *Assumption:* Women cannot succeed in aerospace engineering (It's a man's field).

1. He is from New York so he must be aggressive.
2. He must be good at mathematics, for he's an engineer.
3. The bank reports I'm overdrawn even though my calculations show enough money; I guess I'd better pay the penalty.
4. He must be a millionaire; he's from an oil country.
5. This brand must be reliable, it's the most widely advertised.
6. His name is O'Brien; he can't be from South America.
7. Bijan writes in Arabic script, so he must be an Arab.
8. He is driving badly; he must be drunk.
9. Frank's bad behavior shows he was never punished as a child for behaving badly.
10. I always buy the largest box of any product; it's cheaper in the long run.

B. What erroneous assumptions did you hold about Americans or the United States before you came to this country? Why did you think they were true? What made you change your mind? What erroneous assumptions do Americans make about people from your country? If you have always lived in this country, what assumptions did you hold about going to college that have proven true or false?

C. List some assumptions you disagree with. Who believes these assumptions? Why do they think they are true? Why are they not true and what is wrong with the reasoning of the people who believe them?

D. What assumptions do people in your country or region make about American Indians? What do they think American Indians are like? Where do they get their ideas from?

E. People who have never been to Texas (or Montana or New York or Los Angeles or whatever place you wish to write about) often have ideas about the state (or city or country) which are stereotypes (false generalizations). Imagine that a friend of yours who has never visited the U.S. says, for example, "Ah, you studied in Texas. Did you enjoy meeting all the cowboys and Indians? Is it true all Texans eat barbecue and carry guns on their hips?" (Or makes a similar statement about people from some other area) Correct your friend's impression by contrasting the stereotype with the reality. Focus on one main idea, such as food, clothing, transportation, lifestyle, etc.

Argumentation

The argumentative essay (sometimes called the position paper) is designed to focus on controversial issues, particularly ones frequently and recently in the public eye. It is a common type of assignment for college placement exams in English, but may be required in other classroom situations as well since Western culture considers resolving controversy as vital to intellectual development. The issue may be a college issue (*Should all freshmen be tested for AIDS before they are allowed to register at the university?*), a local issue (*The city should tax automobiles much more heavily to reduce traffic and to lower air pollution: argue yes or no*), or a national or international one (*The military draft or national service should be required for all 18 year-olds*).

There are really no "right" or "wrong" positions on these issues, which are simply meant to "prompt" or stimulate a forceful response. Nonetheless, it is important to recognize that this approach to finding the truth is "trial by combat" between opposing ideas, with the "winner" being the argument with the greatest force. Don't be afraid to take a distinct and clear position, and to argue vigorously. While in other cultures such aggression might be considered rude and self-defeating, in the English-speaking environment this verbal combativeness is admired.

Since argumentative or position questions appear frequently on exams, the following discussion assumes your planning and writing time will be limited. The same general rules apply, however, to out-of-class argumentative essays.

1. Settle on an Argumentative Position and Stick to It

Think of your paper as an energetic defense of your position and therefore be sure your response is truly forceful. Do not "sit on the fence," saying that each side seems to make a lot of sense. Take a position, any position you can argue for, since that is the whole point of the exercise. You should find that choosing one side or the other forces you to come up with more and better arguments. Don't worry about what your reader thinks; you can't know this anyhow, and few teachers care. What they care about is a strongly argued case, a confident paper that takes a definite position and defends it with good logic.

2. Think Carefully About Exactly What is Being Asked

Once you have decided on a position, examine the question or prompt carefully. What does it ask you to do, underlined exactly? Circle the key words, and then be sure to use them in your opening sentences. Your first paragraph should have at least three sentences, and should include one sentence which uses *because* or a synonym (*I support the AIDS test/higher taxes/military draft because of A, B, and C.*) This opening paragraph should give the main points of your argument, but in a general way (*to protect the health of the student body... to inform any AIDS sufferers about their condition... to reduce fear about the disease...*). Many writers fear that they will "give away" their argument in the opening paragraph if they go beyond one sentence; this is a realistic fear but is avoided by staying very general. The trick, of course, is to find good reasons to support your argument.

3. Identify the Issue

One way to find good material to write about is to identify the issue that lies behind the question. Most good questions imply or suggest philosophical, moral, or social issues. For example, the AIDS question mentioned above suggests balancing safety or health against privacy: which is more important, the right of the university to protect itself and its students, or the right of the individual to maintain his privacy? Does a city government have the right to encourage or discourage the use of automobiles by higher taxes, even for a good reason? What do private citizens owe their government? Why should 18 year-olds (but not 30 year-olds or 50 year-olds) give up two years of their lives to their society? All of these questions can be argued endlessly, with good arguments possible on either side. They are questions any thoughtful person should consider, and they are specific cases or examples of general social issues which concern us all. Often, the best course is to identify the larger issue and then discuss that, not just the question itself. As a person from another culture, you may find that some questions, such as the one about the military draft, are unfamiliar to you. Don't complain about this or apologize for your lack of information in your opening paragraph; instead, identify the general issue and then talk about that: in this case, what obligations citizens owe their government.

4. Plan your Argument Carefully

Once you have finished your opening paragraph you should plan and write your body paragraph(s). If the length requirement is short, you may need just one body paragraph. If it is longer, you should plan two or more body paragraphs, each focusing on a single, clear idea, developed with examples, statistics, and concrete details. If you are writing in class, with an hour limit, you probably cannot expect to write more than two body paragraphs. If out of class, you can be more thorough. You should sketch out a brief plan or informal outline, with your general arguments listed and a few specific ways you can support or develop those arguments. Taking a few minutes to make such a plan in class (and longer out of class) will ultimately save you time and possibly help avoid major errors. If the assignment includes a required number of words, you can make a rough estimate of the length you need by multiplying the average number of words per sentence times the number of sentences, or by estimating the average number of words per line in your handwriting and multiplying by the number of lines. Remember, the rule for paragraphs is always the same: one idea per paragraph, with a good body paragraph consisting of about six sentences. (Therefore, at 15 to 25 words per sentence, each of your body paragraphs will be between 90 and 150 words; get in the habit of making these quick estimates.)

5. Develop your Ideas with Details

At this point you might feel, "I can never find enough to say, even writing out of class—how can I write six sentences about one idea?" This isn't easy, admittedly, but it can be done, and again, the best course is to be conscious of the movement of your writing. Introductions are general; body paragraphs are specific. In the body paragraph you begin with one issue but then you present your evidence, proof, details, facts, figures, statistics, names, dates… all the specific facts you know. Supposing you don't have such facts at your fingertips, facts about AIDS, air pollution, or the military draft? It is always better to have such information, of course, but if you don't, and you can't refer to parallel situations in your homeland ("Japanese universities never require students to prove they are healthy…"), simply invent some. This doesn't mean "lie," but rather to rely on the hypothetical example, a time-honored way of arguing a case. The hypothetical example is introduced with the word *Suppose* or *Supposing* (*Supposing a student had AIDS and another student caught it from him…*) and ends with *then* to introduce the conclusion (*then the university might be considered responsible, medically, legally, and morally …*). If the first sentence of your body paragraph explains the philosophical or moral issue to be discussed in that paragraph, and the next sentence or two connect that issue to the original, assigned question, you should have two or three sentences before you even get to the hypothetical example. The pattern looks like this:

> **The university has an obligation to protect everyone against AIDS.**
>
> - It should test everyone before they enter.
> - Suppose, for example, that a student…then…
> - The student's parents would blame the university…
> - Other students might catch…
> - The reputation of the school in the community…

To close the paragraph, add a general sentence which brings the reader back to the topic: *An AIDS test is justified to protect the health of the larger group.*

6. Conclude Well

Once you have your body paragraphs finished, you need a closing paragraph. Like the opening paragraph, it should have a <u>minimum</u> of three sentences and should be general. This is the place to apologize, if you want to, for your unfamiliarity with the topic, and to remind the reader that you are writing in a second language or culture: *Although, of course, I am not familiar with the U.S. military draft....* You might also mention the other side of the issue, just to show you have considered it fairly: *The university should make every attempt to protect the privacy of its students, and should not let anyone but the student know the results of AIDS tests. However, the rights of the majority to be free from disease are more powerful than the right to privacy ....*

7. Proofread Before Submitting your Paper

Professors are generally aware of how difficult it is to write quickly and under pressure even in a first language, so they will not be surprised if you make some spelling and grammar mistakes in in-class work. However, if at all possible, give yourself five minutes at the end to read over your essay quickly, checking for the errors you <u>know</u> you always make.

On out-of-class papers you must proofread carefully because professors are far less forgiving of mistakes when you have time enough to find them and correct them.

The following is a sample argumentative question that might appear on a placement exam.

> The U.S. military draft was ended in the mid 1970's. Some people have suggested, however, that the government reinstitute a draft, with young people serving two years in the military or in a public service program like a domestic Peace Corps. The advantage of such a reinstatement is that it would encourage democratic participation in the army and require young people to contribute to others and their society. People who oppose this idea believe that the government has no authority to interfere in the private lives of its citizens simply because they are young.

Respond to this proposal, taking either a "pro" (favorable) or "con" (against) position. Discuss the issue, using examples to support your generalizations. You may use a dictionary. You have 40 minutes.

SAMPLE POSSIBLE ARGUMENTS

<u>Restatement of question:</u> Whether the draft should be reinstituted, especially to form a domestic services program similar to that of the Peace Corps, is a controversial one for today's young people.

PRO:

KEY ARGUMENTS=PUBLIC GOOD, SOCIAL OBLIGATION, DEMOCRATIC PARTICIPATION

Will allow young people to contribute to their society and to repay an obligation to a government which aids and protects them

Will teach democratic participation, good citizenship, interdependence, teamwork, discipline, and the importance of effort

Will promote education

Will train young people in technical skills that will make them more employable

Will expose young people to new places, new people, new ways of doing things so they learn nationalism and tolerance instead of regionalism and intolerance

Will make the valuable resources of youth work for their country

CON:

KEY ARGUMENTS=INDIVIDUAL LOSS, GOVERNMENT INTERFERENCE FOR QUESTIONABLE BENEFIT

Will interfere with individual's freedom of choice

Will disrupt private lives

Will have a negative impact on young minds

Will train young people to be killers and will teach skills usable later only in criminal pursuits

Will interfere with advanced academic education

Will inevitably lead to other types of government interference in private lives

Might easily be misused by leaders to expand military might and to seek a war (Armies are often used if available)

PRO:

Will toughen young people's bodies and minds and moral fiber

Will make for a strong defense

CON:

Will require tax-dollar spending to set up draft and to maintain a peace-time Army—money better spent elsewhere

Notice that the "pro" arguments are self-explanatory in their detail but that the "con" arguments are more general and abstract. The latter, then, would need more development and discussion: explanations of how the draft will interfere with personal freedom, how it will disrupt private lives, how it will waste the valuable resources of youth, and how power-seeking leaders might misuse it. It might cite some of the negative effects the draft would have on young minds and explain what kind of skills it would teach, skills usable later only in criminal pursuits.

• EXERCISE 17.7: RECOGNIZING GENERAL ISSUES

Find the general issue or issues in the following statements.

Example: All students should be tested for AIDS.

Issue: The protection of healthy students is more important than the right to privacy.

1. Every young man should serve at least a year in his country's military or social service program.
   Issue:_____

2. Every young man and young woman should serve in his or her country's military or social service program.
   Issue:_____

3. Cities should prohibit drivers from using their cars to go into polluted downtowns if other means of transit are available.
   Issue:_____

4. Cigarette smoking should be prohibited on airplanes and in all enclosed public places.
   Issue:_____

5. People who cheat on their taxes should be punished severely.
   Issue:_____

6. No guilty person should be executed no matter how serious the crime they committed.
   Issue:_____

7. Alcoholic drinks should be prohibited to people under age 21.
   Issue:_____

8. Pregnant women who drink too much alcohol or use drugs should be punished by the law.
   Issue:_____

9. People who use offensive racial, religious, or ethnic words in public should be punished by law.
   Issue:_____

10. The police should do blood tests on drivers they think are driving drunk.
    Issue:_____

•• Writing Assignments

A. Write an argumentative paper about <u>one</u> of the above statements. Compare your results with those of your classmates. If your argument seems weak, select another controversy from the above list and try again.

B. Other Argumentative Topics.

1. Is euthanasia [doctor assisted suicide] ethical? Should it be allowed?

2. Is the death penalty immoral? Does it deter murder?

3. Does the good accomplished by animal experimentation justify the pain and suffering involved? Should animals be used in scientific research?

4. Would gun control reduce crime?

5. What amount of AIDS testing is proper?

6. Should there be limits to free speech? Should the news media be regulated? Should pornography be censored?

7. Should immigration be restricted?

8. What should be done about nuclear power?

C. First explain what one of the statements below means. Then attack or defend the assertion with clear and specific supportive evidence.

1. The best kind of education is one in which the student follows rather than questions authority.

2. Philosopher Mortimer Adler proposes a "mandatory nonschooling" period of four years during which young adults aged 18-22 are encouraged to do anything but go to college. This nonschooling period should provide real-life challenges and experiences that will make eventual college study richer and more meaningful.

3. The best learning comes from first-hand experience, not second-hand experience.

4. In a democracy, elected representatives should always act according to the wishes of the people who elected them, not according to their consciences.

5. A doctor's duty is always to save life, no matter the cost.

Sample Argumentative Essay

Study the pattern established in the following model and then imitate it in dealing with an argumentative topic. Italics indicate the skeletal organization of the essay.

Private Charities: The Best Means of Reducing Homelessness in America

Although the government can use tax dollars to create new jobs to reduce unemployment (a key cause of homelessness), can provide job training corps, and can promote free or low-cost education, ultimately private charities provide the best means of dealing *directly (1), efficiently (2), and humanely (3)* with the needs of the homeless, whose large numbers are a national disgrace.

First of all, private charities are *better suited for dealing directly* with the problem than the national government because they have already been doing so successfully for a long time. For example, the Salvation Army, Catholic Charities, the Red Cross, and other such national charitable organizations have already in place the organization and the means for providing food, clothes, emergency shelter, and even some low-pay employment for the homeless. Because these national organizations have local chapters spread throughout the poor sections of all major cities, their volunteer workers know the neighbors and the people intimately and are in a good position to judge just how to spend the money, on whom, for what length of time....

Secondly, such charities are *far more efficient* in getting help to those who need it than are government bureaucrats. In fact, the federal government is only able to get 50 percent of funds designated to the homeless to those people and end up wasting the other 50 percent on administrators and middle-men who have little understanding of who the homeless are and how to deal with them. In contrast, 95% of money donated to the Salvation Army reaches the homeless and 90% of money donated to Catholic Charities reaches the homeless, because such organizations, with time and with local volunteer help, have learned how to make funds stretch and how to make sure they get in the hands of the needy. The Puerto Rican system, for example, demonstrates the types of difficulties federal programs run into in trying to deal with assistance to the poor. There, manipulation of the system by....

Finally, private charities deal with the homeless in a more personal, more humane way than do government bureaucrats. Instead of being simply a number in a welfare worker's book, the homeless person is an individual with a name, known to the priest, minister, or volunteer worker....

In conclusion, because private charities deal with the needs of the homeless more *directly, efficiently, and humanely* than does the national government, they should be the ones in charge of any programs to help the homeless, even if government money is donated to assist.

Title

Thesis
the arguments of the opposition

key arguments

(1)

more discussion

(2)

more discussion

(3)

more discussion of personal

(1), (2), (3)

returns
to thesis idea

Rhetorical Analysis

An important writing assignment given in some classes and in many English composition classes requires the *rhetorical analysis* of a passage or essay. A rhetorical analysis is an evaluation of a writer's persuasive power, with particular attention to how the narrator uses language and logic to persuade. Thus, a typical rhetorical analysis might decide whether a writer uses an entertainer's, salesperson's, or scholar's stance, whether she uses deductive or inductive logic, and which of the three appeals (logical, emotional, or ethical) predominate. Fallacies may be identified, and their role in creating a persuasive argument explained. The persuasive effects of methods such as comparison-contrast, definition, and metaphor may also be examined in a rhetorical analysis.

There are no set rules about how this kind of analysis is written; the only central requirement is that you decide how effective the writer you are analyzing is in persuading his or her audience, and what methods the writer employs. You cannot, of course, know whether all readers, past, present, and future, find a writer's work persuasive; this is a question of fact that could only be decided by surveying all readers, an impossible task. The idea is for you to act as a typical reader, and to evaluate from that "average" perspective.

One other point may help you write analyses of persuasive writing. From a modern critical perspective, most writing is persuasive, even writing that seems basically factual. Thus you should not be bothered if called upon to evaluate a piece of writing that appears to be "true" and "factual"—keep thinking about persuasive intent and alternative ways the writer might have presented the material. In the section that follows you can gain some experience with rhetorical analysis by comparing the different forms of persuasion typified in the models.

Models to Learn From

Model #1: The following persuasive passage is taken from *Out of Africa*, by Isak Dinesen. We say, "Seeing is believing." What does Isak Dinesen help us see? The best place to look for the answer to that question is at the beginning or the end of the essay because this is where most writers place their thesis idea.

In the Reserve [the game reserve in Kenya, Africa], I have sometimes come upon the Iguana, the big lizards, as they were sunning themselves, upon a flat stone in a riverbed. They are not pretty in shape, but nothing can be imagined more beautiful than their coloring. They shine like a heap of precious stones or like pane [piece of glass] cut out of an old church window. When, as you approach, they swish away, there is a flash of azure [blue], green, and purple over the stones, the color seems to be standing behind them in the air, like a comet's luminous tail.

a living Iguana: beauty

Once I shot an iguana. I thought that I should be able to make some pretty things from his skin. A strange thing happened then, that I have never afterwards forgotten. As I went up to him, where he was lying dead upon his stone, and actually while I was walking the few steps, he faded and grew pale, all color died out of him as in one long sigh, and by the time that I touched him he was grey and dull like a lump of concrete. It was the live impetuous blood pulsating within the animal, which had radiated out all that glow and splendor. Now that the flame was put out, and the soul had flown, the Iguana was as dead as a sandbag.

DON'T SHOOT!

a dead Iguana and what is lost

Often since I have, in some sort, shot an Iguana, and I have remembered the one of the Reserve. Up at Meru [an African town] I saw a young Native girl with a bracelet on, a leather strap two inches wide, and embroidered all over with very small turquoise-colored beads which varied a little in color and played in green, light blue, and ultramarine. It was an extraordinarily live thing; it seemed to draw breath on her arm, so that I wanted it for myself, and made Farah [the author's Somali servant] buy it from her. No sooner had it come upon my own arm than it gave up the ghost. It was nothing now, a small, cheap, purchased article of finery. It had been the play of colors, the duet between the turquoise and the "negre",—that quick, sweet, brownish black, like peat and black pottery, of the Native's skin, —that had created the life of the bracelet.

a bracelet on a dark-skinned girl

the same bracelet out of its setting, no longer beautiful

In the Zoological Museum of Pietermaritzburg, I have seen, in a stuffed deep-water fish in a showcase, the same combination of coloring, which there had survived death; it made me wonder what life can well be like, on the bottom of the sea, to send up something so live and airy. I stood in Meru and looked at my pale hand and at the dead bracelet, it was as if an injustice had been done to a noble thing, as if truth had been suppressed. So sad did it seem that I remembered the saying of the hero in a book that I had read as a child: "I have conquered them all, but I am standing amongst graves."

a stuffed fish

the potential beauty of a live fish

negative effects

In a foreign country and with foreign species of life one should take measures to find out whether things will be keeping their value when dead. To the settlers of East Africa I give the advice: "For the sake of your own eyes and heart, shoot not the Iguana."

audience final plea

If you can understand the ideas and methods of this essay, you are on your way to dealing with the persuasive essay.

Model #2: The following rhetorical analysis explains what the writer believes Isak Dinesen does in her essay and how she does it. It refers to particular details from the essay itself as concrete support.

In *Out of Africa*, Isak Dinesen, a famous South African writer, clearly and vividly describes an exotic African lizard, a lovely, brightly colored native bracelet, and a deep-water fish in order to argue that beauty, no matter how alien, exists in its own setting, and that, if that setting is destroyed or the beautiful item is removed from its natural setting, that beauty is lost. Hers is an aesthetic, an environmental, and a humanistic argument. The language is difficult because she assumes a literate, educated audience and tries to create as precise a word picture as possible for them. Her methods to unify, strengthen, and give meaning to her description are contrast and metaphor.

Dinesen's essay depends on a contrast between living and dead, between placement in a natural and appropriate environment and placement in an unnatural, inappropriate environment. The first paragraph describes the beautiful coloring of a living iguana, both with specific descriptive details ("a flash of azure, green and purple") and with metaphorical images. The metaphors emphasize not only light and color, but also the value of the iguana ("like a heap of precious stones") and its exotic yet fleeting natural beauty ("like a comet's luminous tail"), and associate it with reverence and respect ("like pane cut out of an old church window"). The second paragraph contrasts that beauty with a shot iguana, whose blood pouring out puts out a "flame" and reduces what had "radiated out... that glow and splendor" to the "grey" and "dull." Again the images are metaphorical, but this time ugly: the dead iguana is "like a lump of concrete" and "as dead as a sandbag." The third paragraph introduces the next contrast: a leather bracelet embroidered with brightly colored green and blue beads. On the native girl with her "sweet, brownish black" skin the bracelet seems like "an extraordinarily live thing," so alive that Dinesen describes it as seeming "to draw breath on her arm." However, when placed on Dinesen's own pale arm, the bracelet, like the iguana, loses its beauty. The "play of colors," "the duet between the turquoise and the "negre" is lost, reduced to a "small, cheap, purchased article of finery." Dinesen says that the bracelet out of its natural setting "gave up the ghost," meaning that it died, at least metaphorically. Even though the bracelet is a man-made product, the images emphasize life versus death. The final contrast occurs in the fourth paragraph: a light and airy, deep-colored fish stuffed in the Zoological Museum of Pietermaritzburg. The remaining signs of its lost beauty make Dinesen wonder about how beautiful it must have been before reduced to this unnatural display item. The movement of the essay is from colorful to dull, from extraordinary to ordinary, from living to dead. It is also a movement of discovery, one that Dinesen hopes the reader will share in. It is only because of her experience with the iguana that Dinesen can be attuned to the change in the bracelet, and it is only because of these two experiences that she can see through the beauty of the dead fish to wonder about its lost beauty....

alive versus dead

lost beauty

structure

a summary and analysis of method and argument

Dinesen relies on the final paragraph to make clear her central idea; it contains the lesson she wishes readers to understand and accept. She wants to capture the enchantment and beauty of lizard, bracelet, and fish in their natural setting not for the sake of description alone, but instead to persuade others to leave them alone, to not change nature, because changing nature destroys beauty. To make this point she contrasts the living with the dead and beauty in place with the loss of beauty in an alien setting. The pattern depends very much on a sincere, honest, and personally disturbed persona, recording her own progression in understanding, as she recognizes and confesses her own acquisitiveness and senseless destructiveness and her growing understanding of the waste and the loss. She clearly hopes her intended audience—the "settlers of East Africa"—will make the same journey and understand as she has come to understand that the stuffed fish in the museum may be beautiful but that beauty is only a glimmer of its true beauty when alive and in its natural setting. Her goal is to preserve; her description is meant to make others see the natural truths she sees and to undergo the change she has undergone. Her recollection of a childhood hero's sense of loss after conquering all and finding himself "standing amongst graves" sums up her fear that the greed, acquisitiveness, and indifference of the European settlers of East Africa, and their blindness to a beauty not their own may in fact lead them to permanently destroy local life and culture. Her final warning, "shoot not the iguana," departs from the more common grammatical pattern, "do not shoot the iguana," to make it sound more serious, a principle of life, not just one person's private advice. Her warning is not about just one endangered species but an endangered culture: beautiful and alien, intangible and fragile.

author's purpose

persona

intended audience

goals

warnings

author's thesis

This analysis calls attention to the tailoring of the argument and persona to fit audience and purpose. Furthermore, as you can see from this example, the rhetorical analysis grows out of the passage or essay to be analyzed and will differ according to topic and approach. Since the Dinesen passage depends on description, contrast, and metaphor, the analysis highlights these techniques. On page 403, the essay called "Could You Literally 'Run Your Life'?" depends on a hypothetical situation and a cause-effect relationship; therefore, any analysis of it must highlight these very different techniques. The Final Checklists provide the types of questions to ask as you write any analysis. These questions will not apply to every essay, but are a good way to begin thinking analytically.

Avoiding Common Pitfalls

A. A persuasive or analytical paper may summarize but it should not be all summary.

B. Distinguish clearly between your ideas and those of your sources. Be sure to give your sources credit for their ideas. Write *Dinesen observes that...* instead of simply providing her observations as if they were your own.

C. Don't let your sources dominate your paper. Instead, assert your own thesis rather than following the thesis of your sources.

D. Rely on specific textual support from the essay or work being analyzed.

E. Assume an antagonistic audience instead of an agreeable one so that you are forced to defend your ideas rather than merely report them.

Final Checklists

ARGUMENTATION:

☐ Have you clearly stated the issue?

☐ Have you chosen one side or the other and limited your discussion to that side?

☐ Have you provided two or three reasons for supporting the chosen side, and dismissed the opposition's reasons, showing their weakness?

☐ Have you developed your arguments with examples, statistics, quotations and so forth?

☐ Have you maintained a balance between the scholar's, entertainer's and promoter's stance?

☐ Have you relied on logical appeals more consistently than emotional or ethical appeals?

☐ Is your inductive reasoning based on a random or representative sample? Is the sample sufficient? Have you avoided the fallacies?

☐ Have you concluded that the chosen side is the correct side?

ANALYSIS

☐ Have you applied to your passage for analysis the same checklist you would apply to your own writing?

☐ What do you know about the author that might help readers better understand this essay? background? previous works? values? interests? obsessions?

☐ What is the author's purpose or goal? How do you know?

☐ Who is the intended audience? How do you know?

☐ What image does the author create of him or herself? Reliable? Enthusiastic? Concerned? How does the writer establish personal authority or expertise?

☐ Does the date of the essay add to our understanding of the situation or environment that produced it?

☐ What is the significance of the title or of any initial quotations? What do they reveal about the focus or concerns of the essay?

☐ What is the significance of any initial quotes? of striking first lines? of striking concluding lines?

☐ What is the author's writing strategy? Does the writer describe in familiar terms, use vivid details, provide statistics, raise questions, provide authoritative support (expert witnesses), use recognizable patterns of argumentation like cause-effect, comparison, contrast, definition, and so forth?

☐ Does the author provide a clear statement of a problem, a warning, a hope, a call to action?

• EXERCISE 17.8: PRACTICING ANALYSIS

Apply the above Checklist for Analysis to the following paragraphs. Not all categories will apply because these are paragraphs, not essays. Identify the persuasive approach used and, if it is convincing, explain why.

1. Judith Martin ("Miss Manners"—whose column appears regularly in newspapers nationwide) puts on the persona of a rather superior, distant, older relative who is an authority about all things concerning etiquette. She affects an overwhelming confidence about what can and cannot be done, in contrast to the timid apologists for good manners of the last twenty years or so. Miss Manners' persona serves to confront readers who believe manners are only relative; she intimidates and bullies such people by using sarcasm, name-calling, and a not-so-subtle snobbishness. The final effect of these techniques is to reverse the usual situation in which rude and boorish people get their way by being rude and boorish; Miss Manners is even more rude when necessary, but all in a good cause, of course: politeness and etiquette.

2. The ExecPlus corporation uses a bold, black-and-white photograph of its TU-150 cassette-recorder atop its opponent, a stack of scribbled notes, to vividly compare both forms of note-taking and to stress the advantages of its product over the "outdated" method. The prominent caption, in large white print on a black background, identifies the section of society to which the advertisement is directed—the executive businessman, an urban resident in the medium to high income bracket. The writers have carefully assessed his wants and needs and have appealed to them specifically.... The projected persona is that of one executive talking with another,—establishing rapport— seeming to share problems such as sitting "through those meetings scribbling notes furiously," or complaining about the lack of space at the conference table.... Apart from emphasizing the recorder as functional, the advertisement appeals to the practical aspect of the executive's image. Despite the rush that surrounds him, he must look well-dressed, confident, and relaxed. He does not need something big or clumsy to carry around. The ExecPlus product's small, "paperback" size allows it to fit conveniently in an attache case and its trimness makes it a pleasure to show off.

3. The fact that eight out of ten ads in this magazine are for very expensive ($1,000 and up) luxury items suggests that the intended audience is rich and worries more about beauty, class, and quality than economy and practicality. Most of the ads are for expensive cars (53%), vacations abroad (20%), designer clothing (12%), jewelry (10%), and accessories (5%). They center around photos of elegant surroundings (plush country homes, private clubs, elegant hotels, European resorts). Many build on name brands associated with good taste and high quality, names such as Neiman-Marcus, House of Ricci and Countessa. Others rely on snob appeal, as in the phrases "only the very few can afford...", "not for every Tom, Dick, and Harry", and "for those who know how to appreciate..." Still others emphasize how much more expensive their product is than that of their inferior competitor and argue that people of quality are willing to spend a little extra for quality products. "Unique," "one of a kind," and "very special" are repeated over and over again. Such insistence suggests that the advertisers assume their viewers want to think of themselves as unique, special, and extraordinary. Together, the ads' photos and blurbs try to appeal to the wealthy and the would-be sophisticates who want their purchases to reflect social status.

4. Exclusive designs from exclusive shops and famous fashion designers, sexy, skimpy, lace lingerie, European and Caribbean resorts with elaborate bridal suites—these are the typical products advertised in *Bride-to-Be* magazine. Why? Even though the editors and advertisers realize that many of the young brides-to-be may have limited incomes, they also realize that fashion-conscious young people are anxious to make their wedding and honeymoon a unique experience, even if they must go into debt to do so. For this reason 40 percent of the ads are for beautiful, feminine wedding dresses of elegant, ivory satin or white chiffon decorated with fancy laces and pearls, designed by America's leading bridal fashion designers and found only at expensive, exclusive, bridal shops, 30 percent are for honeymoons abroad and honeymoon resorts in Europe, Bermuda, the Bahamas, and Jamaica, 10 percent are for bridesmaid gowns designed to appeal to the young and fashion-conscious, and the remaining 20 percent are for all sorts of accessories, including diamonds, lingerie, and loungewear.

Passages for Discussion and Analysis

Historical Mississippi... Echoes of the Past, Marvels of the Future

Rhythmic Indian names as ancient as the lands they describe... the towering white columns and lush gardens of majestic antebellum mansions... the tremendous roar and brilliant flames of a space shuttle engine test—reflections from the past and glimpses of the future meet in Mississippi, where a colorful heritage combines with history in the making.

For centuries, the region now known as Mississippi was the secluded domain of the Choctaw, Chickasaw, and Natchez Indian nations, and dozens of smaller tribes whose names are forever forgotten. The first European settlement in the Mississippi region was established by the French in 1699. The flags of France, Spain, and England all flew overhead before the Mississippi Territory became the twentieth state in 1817. Historic homes and structures sprinkled throughout Mississippi reflect the architectural styles of the French, Spanish, and English eras.

Reminders of the Old Southern culture and the Civil War are found throughout Mississippi, from the opulent antebellum mansions of Natchez to the cannons of the Vicksburg National Military Park, from the original state capital building where the Ordinance of Secession was passed to the last home of Jefferson Davis, President of the Confederacy. Almost every area of Mississippi boasts a battle site or antebellum home—timeless testimonies to the elegance and majesty of the Old South, and the tragedy and sorrow of the American Civil War.

Mississippi was readmitted to the Union in 1870, and gradually recovered from the War's devastation. New crops were developed, lessening the dependence upon cotton. Railroads were constructed, the timber industry boomed, and colleges were revived or established. Mississippi shifted its economic focus from predominantly agricultural interests to industrial development, a move aided by the manufacturing activity brought on by World Wars I and II.

Wartime prosperity expanded opportunities in other states as well, and record numbers of black Mississippians left the South to work in northern factories. Those who remained in Mississippi participated in the most dramatic phase of the state's history since the Civil War, the Civil Rights Movement of the 1960s. A permanent exhibit in the Mississippi State

Historical Museum in Jackson features photographs and artifacts reflecting the turbulence of the civil rights era.

The same land once prowled by Indians and explorers, cultivated by planters, and shaped by contemporary heroes now yields new legends that the spirits of those adventurers would label even more exciting. NASA's John C. Stennis Space Center on the Mississippi Gulf Coast tests the powerful engines that propel men to the moon. The Waterways Experiment Station in Vicksburg is the United States Army Corps of Engineers' principal consulting and laboratory research complex, and the Grand Gulf Nuclear Power Station explores the awesome capabilities of this futuristic power source.

Preserving a rich heritage while building a dynamic future, Mississippi represents the best of yesterday and the promise of tomorrow. Mississippi is history—a remembered history of legend and myth and a living history of adventures yet to come.

—*Picture It* (Jackson, Mississippi: Mississippi Department of Economic and Community Development, 1990): 1-4

• Questions to Consider

1. Who is the intended audience of this piece? What assumptions does the writer make about his readers?

2. What is his purpose in writing? How do you know?

3. What is the thesis idea? Where can you find it? If you had to summarize this essay, where should you look to find the key ideas? Which sentences in the text summarize the main argument?

4. Explain what patterns of development the writer uses and why. How do these patterns serve his purpose?

5. Underline the parallelism used in this essay. How much parallelism does the author use and why? What does it help him do?

6. What kind of image of Mississippi is this writer trying to create?

7. What negative images from Mississippi's past does the author ignore or try to make positive? Ask some American students about the civil rights troubles in Mississippi during the 1960's. What do they think about the state's history? How do their views differ from this writer's views?

8. You may have seen the films *Mississippi Burning*, *Murder in Mississippi*, or *The Autobiography of Miss. Jane Pitman* about civil rights conflicts as Southern blacks tried to use the right to vote to change their world. These films give a very different view of Mississippi from that of this article. What section in this essay refers to the events from those films? What does the writer do to make even these negative parts of Mississippi history acceptable?

Could you Literally "Run for Your Life"?

Could you literally "run for your life" if a one megaton (1 Mt) warhead was launched in a surprise attack against your town?

Though more warning time is generally assumed, the distance you can run from the explosion point, called "ground zero," in the thirty minutes it takes for a Soviet warhead to reach the United States, helps illustrate the destructive potential of a single nuclear warhead (See Table 1).

Without transportation available, imagine you start running at the first sound of alarm. If you can sprint a 6-minute mile, by the time the weapon explodes you will be 5 miles from ground zero. At this point, the heat is so intense that exposed skin is charred and clothing ignites; winds blowing 130 miles per hour spray the landscape with debris and broken glass; the roof on a nearby hospital flies off and windows shatter. The immediate radiation dose will eventually kill over one-half of those in the area (who do not die from the other effects).

For slower runners, those averaging a ten-minute mile, the surroundings are far more dangerous. At 3 miles from ground zero, typical concrete office buildings are collapsing all around; people and objects in buildings not crushed are blown out of windows by 250-mile winds. Those not killed by the direct effects would receive lethal radiation doses and die in six weeks' time.

These scenes illustrate the local primary effects of nuclear weapons; initial nuclear radiation, thermal radiation pulse, and blast. (Note that conventional weapons have only one destructive effect, which is the blast or shock wave.)

Initial nuclear radiation comes from invisible, highly-penetrating gamma rays which are emitted in the first minute of the explosion when atoms undergo fission [fly apart] and fusion [join together] in a typical nuclear reaction. This radiation alters or destroys human cells. It is so penetrating that people surrounded by 24 inches of concrete one mile from a 1 Mt blast would perish. This radiation effect is a significant difference from the conventional weapons which is generally not appreciated.

The second primary effect, thermal radiation, is more familiar. It is the tremendous energy release in the form of heat and light during the nuclear explosion. Unlike a conventional weapon, which releases energy from a chemical reaction, the punch from nuclear weapons comes from the forces which bind all matter together in atoms. These forces are so powerful that, when released, their energy is millions of times greater than conventional weapons per pound of explosive material. Consequently, temperatures reach tens of millions of degrees, or superstellar level, in the nuclear fireball, as opposed to a few thousand degrees in a conventional bomb. The thermal pulse will cause third-degree burns on persons eight miles from ground zero in a 1 Mt explosion, or over an area of 250 square miles. (See Table 2.)

The hot gaseous materials created by the nuclear burst expand rapidly and form the final primary effect: a pressure wave, known as blast or shock. The shock front races like a wall of compressed air outward from the fireball (which, at a distance of 50 miles from a 1 Mt. burst, appears many times more brilliant than the sun at noon). High winds, still 70 mph even six miles from ground zero, will accompany the blast wave. In addition, great pressures are created, enough to crush frame houses several miles out.

These primary effects by no means tell the whole story. Residual radiation and fallout, which is radioactive debris, remain after the explosion, and can carry great distances depending on the wind. (The Office of Technology Assessment believes survivors should remain indoors for two weeks to a month after an attack to assure safety from fallout.) Also, massive fires would result from the tremendous winds and heat.

In addition, there is an electromagnetic pulse (EMP) effect, something crudely like radio transmissions, which was only recognized in 1960 as a serious nuclear effect. EMP from a single burst high over the United States could damage computer solid-state components, electrical and communications equipment over the entire country.

These primary and residual effects of nuclear weapons are well documented from U.S. Government tests, but also from the two atomic bombs the U.S. dropped on Hiroshima and Nagasaki in 1945. In an instant, a teeming Hiroshima of 340,000 people turned into rubble, swallowing a third of the population. Survivors of the blast depict a nightmare more vivid than mere statistics can express.

How would this nightmare take shape in the U.S.? Because there are so many uncertainties about nuclear war, predictions on exact conditions are hard to gauge [predict with accuracy]. But deaths from a "limited" attack on U.S. land missiles could range up to 20 million. Even this "small" civilian loss would bring tremendous economic, psychological, and long-term genetic effects. For a full-scale attack, the disaster would increase immeasurably. Some 160 million could perish, and those who survive would have little if any medical attention, food, and the means to support life.

Finally, what would be the effect if all nuclear weapons, more powerful than a million Hiroshimas, exploded in a world war? Would it mean the end of the earth? Though the planet would not expire in a strict sense, the earth's ecology could be irrevocably altered. In the words of one writer, the U.S. would become "a republic of insects and grass."

—from *The Effects of Nuclear Weapons*. The Office of Technology Assessment. The U.S. Government.

TABLE 1 Biological Effects of Thermal Radiation	
Type of Burn	Distance from Ground Zero
Third degree: pain experienced only in region surrounding burn as nerve damage occurs in area directly burned; all layers of skin affected, hence long heal time and slow scab formation.	0-5 miles
Second degree: intense and persistent pain, blisters, and scabs form; danger of infection, outer layers of skin affected.	5-7 miles
First degree: mild pain and redness of afflicted area; only superficial layers of skin affected.	7-12 miles
Source: *The Effects of Nuclear War*. The Office of Technology Assessment.	

Table 2 Blast Effects of a 1-Mt Explosion 8000 ft Above the Earth's Surface			
Distance From Ground Zero (ml)	Peak Overpressure	Peak Wind Velocity mph)	Typical Blast Effects
0.8	20 psi	470	Reinforced concrete structures leveled.
3.0	10 psi	290	Most factories and commercial buildings collapsed. Small wood-frame and brick residences destroyed.
4.4	5 psi	160	Lightly constructed commercial buildings and typical residences destroyed; heavier construction severely damaged.
5.9	3 psi	95	Walls of typical steel-frame buildings blown away; severe damage to residences. Winds sufficient to kill people in the open.
11.6	1 psi	35	Damage to structures; people endangered by flying glass debris.

Source: *The Effects of Nuclear War.* The Office of Technology Assessment.

• Questions for Discussion

1. "Could You Literally 'Run for Your Life'?" describes what would happen if a 1-megaton bomb exploded over a city. What type of details make it effective?

2. What is the main, overall purpose of this essay? What do the writers want readers to understand?

3. What is the purpose of the numerous specific details, the statistics and charts? What effect does the writer hope to have on the readers?

4. What major method of development does the writer rely on? Why?

5. Notice the hypothetical example in the second paragraph. How does it personalize the horrors of a nuclear attack?

6. Why does the writer draw comparisons with conventional weapons? What point is he trying to make?

GRANT LEE

After introducing the end of the American Civil War with the surrender of Lee to Grant at Appomattox as the close of one "great chapter in American life" and the beginning of "a great new chapter," Catton contrasts the "old aristocratic concept" that Lee represented with the new "Western frontier" view that Grant represented. If you attempt an outline of the two units, A and B, you will find that Catton follows the same pattern in both sections. First he talks about the attributes and characteristics of each man, then about their values (with a two-part division for each), and finally about their significance to their community or age. Only at the end of the essay, when he is trying to break new ground by arguing that, despite their differences, these men were very much alike, does he switch to the alternating style. In so doing, this essay gives us a sense of the value and use of both forms.

Grant and Lee: A Study in Contrasts

When Ulysses S. Grant and Robert E. Lee met in the parlor of a modest house at Appomattox Court House, Virginia, on April 9, 1865, to work out the terms for the surrender of Lee's Army of Northern Virginia, <u>a great chapter in American life came to a close and a great new chapter began</u>. a significant historical moment

These men were bringing the Civil War to its virtual finish. To be sure, other armies had yet to surrender, and for a few days the fugitive Confederate government would struggle desperately and vainly, trying to find some way to go on living now that its chief support was gone. But in effect, it was all over when Grant and Lee signed the papers. And the little room where they wrote out the terms was the scene of one of the poignant, dramatic contrasts in American history.

They were two strong men, these oddly different generals, and <u>they represented the strengths of two conflicting currents that, through them, had come into final collision</u>. Thesis

Back of Robert E. Lee was the notion that the old aristocratic concept might somehow survive and be dominant in American life. Lee was tidewater Virginia, and in his background were <u>family, culture, and tradition</u>… the <u>age of chivalry</u> transplanted to a New World which was making its own legends and its own myths. He embodied a way of life that had come down through the age of knighthood and the English country squire. America was a land that was beginning all over again, dedicated to nothing much more complicated than the rather hazy belief that all men had equal rights and should have an equal chance in the world. In such a land Lee stood for the feeling that it was somehow of advantage to human society to have a pronounced <u>inequality in the social structure</u>. There should be a leisure class, backed by ownership of land; in turn, society itself should be keyed to the land as the chief source of wealth and influence. Block A
Lee: the aristocratic
South

It would bring forth (according to this ideal) a class of men with a <u>strong sense of obligation to the community</u>; men who lived not to gain advantage for themselves, but to meet the solemn obligations which had been laid on them by the very fact that they were privileged. From them the country would get its leadership; to them it could look for the higher values—of thought, of conduct, of personal deportment—to give it strength and virtue.

Lee embodied the noblest elements of his <u>aristocratic ideal</u>. Through him, the landed nobility justified itself. For four years, the Southern states had fought a desperate war to uphold the ideals for which Lee stood. In the end, it almost seemed as if the Confederacy fought for Lee; as if he himself was the Confederacy, the best thing that the way of life for which the Confederacy stood could ever have to offer. He had passed into legend before Appomattox. Thousands of tired, underfed, poorly clothed Confederate soldiers, long since past the simple enthusiasm of the early days of the struggle, somehow considered <u>Lee the symbol of everything for which they had been willing to die</u>. But they could not quite put this feeling into words. If the Lost Cause, sanctified by so much heroism and so many deaths, had a living justification, its justification was General Lee. End of Block A on Lee

Grant, the son of a tanner on the <u>Western frontier</u>, was <u>everything Lee was not</u>. He had come up the hard way and embodied nothing in particular except Block B
Grant: the Western
frontiersman the eternal toughness and sinewy fiber of the men who grew up beyond the mountains. He was one of a body of men who owed reverence and obeisance to no one, who were <u>self-reliant</u> to a fault, who cared hardly anything for the past but who had <u>a sharp eye for the future</u>.

These <u>frontier men</u> were the precise opposites of the tidewater aristocrats. Back of them, in the great surge that had taken people over the Alleghenies and into the opening Western country, there was a deep, implicit dissatisfaction with a past that had settled into grooves. They stood for <u>democracy</u>, not from any reasoned conclusion about the proper ordering of human society, but simply because they had grown up in the middle of democracy and knew how it worked. Their society might have privileges, but they would be privileges each man had won for himself. Forms and patterns meant nothing. No man was born to anything, except perhaps to a chance to show how far he could rise. <u>Life was competition</u>.

Yet along with this feeling had come a deep sense of belonging to a <u>national community</u>. The Westerner who developed a farm, opened a shop, or set up in business as a trader, could hope to prosper only as his own community prospered—and his community ran from the Atlantic to the Pacific and from Canada down to Mexico. If the land was settled, with towns and highways and accessible markets, he could better himself. He saw his fate in terms of the nation's own destiny. As its horizons expanded, so did his. He had, in other words, an acute dollars-and-cents stake in the continued growth and development of his country. End of major block section B

And that, perhaps, is where the <u>contrast between Grant and Lee</u> becomes most striking. The Virginia aristocrat inevitably saw himself <u>in relation to his own region</u>. He lived in a <u>static society</u> which could endure almost anything except change. Instinctively, his first loyalty would go to the locality in which that society existed. He would fight to the limit of endurance to defend it because in defending it he was defending everything that gave his own life its deepest meaning. changes to minor block style for key contrast
Lee

The <u>Westerner</u>, on the other hand, would fight with an equal tenacity for the broader concept of society. He fought so because everything he lived by was tied to <u>growth, expansion, and a constantly widening horizon</u>. What he lived by would survive or fall with the nation itself. He could not possibly stand by unmoved in the face of an attempt to destroy the Union. He would combat it with everything he had, because he could only see it as an effort to cut the ground out from under his feet. Grant

So Grant and Lee were in complete contrast, <u>representing two diametrically opposed elements in American life</u>. Grant was the modern man emerging; beyond him, ready to come on the stage, was the great age of steel and machinery, of crowded cities and a restless burgeoning vitality. Lee might have ridden down from the old age of chivalry, lance in hand, silken banner fluttering over his head. Each man was the perfect champion of his cause, drawing both his strengths and his weaknesses from the people he led. Summary contrasts in alternating form: Grant/Lee

Yet it was not all contrast, after all. Different as they were—in background, in personality, in underlying aspiration—these two great soldiers had <u>much in common</u>. Under everything else, they were <u>marvelous fighters</u>. Furthermore, their fighting qualities were really very much alike. summary of contrast section
transition to comparison section

Each man had, to begin with, the great virtue of utter <u>tenacity and fidelity</u>. Grant fought his way down the Mississippi Valley in spite of acute personal discouragement and profound military handicaps. Lee hung on in the trenches at Petersburg after hope itself had died. In each man there was an indomitable quality…. the born fighter's refusal to give up as long as he can still remain on his feet and lift his two fists.

<u>Daring and resourcefulness</u> they had, too; the ability to think faster and move faster than the enemy. These were the qualities which gave Lee the dazzling campaigns of Second Manassas and Chancellorsville and won Vicksburg for Grant. Lastly, and perhaps greatest of all, there was the ability, at the end, to run quickly from war to peace once the fighting was over. Out of the way these two men behaved at Appomattox came the possibility of a peace of reconciliation. It was a possibility not wholly realized, in the years to come, but which did, in the end, help the two sections to become one nation again… after a war whose bitterness might have seemed to make such a reunion wholly impossible. No part of either man's life became him more than the part he played in their brief meeting in the McLean house at Appomattox. Their behavior there put all succeeding generations of Americans in their debt. Two great Americans, Grant and Lee—<u>very different, yet under everything very much alike</u>. Their encounter at Appomattox was <u>one of the great moments of American history.</u>

Conclusion: common ground; national unity

—**Bruce Catton** from *The American Story*, edited by **Earl Schenck Miers,** the **United States Capitol Historical Society.**

• Questions to Consider

1. Bruce Catton assumes that most Americans think that Grant and Lee were very different. This is because they were the leaders of the two opposing forces during the American Civil War. Grant led the Union or Northern forces and Lee led the Confederate or Southern (or Rebel) forces. What values does Catton try to associate with each man to demonstrate the differences in values and attitudes and background between the North/West and the South? In other words, according to Catton, how do these men represent their region?

2. Catton assumes that most Americans are so aware of the differences between these men that they ignore the similarities. What does he think they had in common? What does he think made both men great leaders?

3. The Civil War began with differences and disagreement, with a conflict over individual or States' Rights. However, it ended with a dominant Federal Government, one that emphasized a union of North and South as one unit with similarities of purpose. How does the structure of Catton's essay help readers understand these two aspects of the Civil War? Explain.

4. What does Catton imply is the significance of the meeting at Appomattox? In other words, what is his overall underlying argument?

5. Has your country experienced a similar conflict between regions or groups? Has the conflict resulted in war or just tension?

6. From your knowledge of U.S. popular culture, American history, and individuals, is Catton correct about the differences between Southerners and Westerners? If you know about American presidents, were Bill Clinton (Southerner) and Ronald Reagan (Westerner) alike in their cultural personalities? What about people you have met? Does regional culture affect personality in your culture or country?

7. Think of two great leaders from your country or culture who were completely opposed in philosophy, belief, and personal style. Were they alike in any ways?

••Writing Assignment

A. Apply the Final Checklist for Analysis from page 392 to the following passages. Write a short persuasive analysis which considers audience, purpose, strategy and technique, logic, and appeals.

1. …Women have served all these centuries as looking glasses possessing the magic and delicious power of reflecting the figure of man at twice its natural size. Without that power probably the earth would still be swamp and jungle. The glories of all our wars would be unknown. We should still be scratching the outlines of deer on the remains of mutton bones and bartering flints for sheepskins or whatever simple ornament took our unsophisticated taste. Supermen and Fingers of Destiny would never have existed. The Czar and the Kaiser would never have worn their crowns or lost them. Whatever may be their use in civilized societies, mirrors are essential to all violent and heroic action. That is why Napoleon and Mussolini both insist so emphatically upon the inferiority of women, for if they were not inferior they would cease to enlarge.

—Virginia Woolf, *A Room of One's Own*

2. It is a miracle that New York works at all. The whole thing is implausible. Every time the residents brush their teeth, millions of gallons of water must be drawn from the Catskills and the hills of Westchester. When a young man in Manhattan writes a letter to his girl in Brooklyn, the love message gets blown to her through a pneumatic tube—pfft—just like that. The subterranean system of telephone cables, power lines, steam pipes, gas mains, and sewer pipes is reason enough to abandon the island to the gods and the weevils. Every time an incision is made in the pavement, the noisy surgeons expose ganglia that is tangled beyond belief. By rights New York should have experienced an insoluble snarl at some impossible bottleneck. It should have perished of hunger when food lines failed for a few days. It should have been wiped out by a plague starting in its slums or carried in by ships' rats. It should have been overwhelmed by the sea that licks at it on every side. The workers in its myriad cells should have succumbed to nerves, from the fearful pall of smoke—fog that drifts over every few days from Jersey, blotting out all light at noon and leaving the high offices suspended, men groping and depressed, and the sense of world's end.

—E.B. White, *Here is New York*

B. Writing Assignments Based on the Passages for Discussion and Analysis

1. Drawing on the information provided in "Could You Literally 'Run for Your Life'?" and your own imagination, detail the effects on your hometown of a nuclear explosion nearby. How exactly would civilization break down? Make your essay as persuasive and convincing as possible.

2. Write a short, imaginative description of what life in your hometown would be like after a nuclear winter. Your goal should be to awaken your fellow citizens to the possibilities projected in the "Could You?" essay.

3. Describe a region or area you know well in order to downplay its negative stereotype and to emphasize those qualities which would attract and please visitors. Use "Historical Mississippi" as a model to imitate.

4. Compare and contrast the two essays, "Historical Mississippi" and "Could You Literally 'Run for Your Life'?" with regard to how each tries to persuade the audience of the correctness of its claim. How do they differ in approach and method because of their differences in topic and purpose?

5. Using Catton's essay as a model, write a paper comparing and contrasting two leaders, or two important men or women, from your country, culture, or region.

Chapter 18: Taking Essay Examinations

Good Writing imposes… human order on chaos. — Frank D'Angelo

An honest writer makes every word pull its weight. — Ken Macrorie

---

Key Characteristics of Essay Examinations

Preparation and Execution

Helpful Terms for Analyzing Questions

Final Checklist

Passages for Discussion and Analysis

Key Characteristics of Essay Examinations

During the course of the semester, many classes in American colleges and universities require some form of essay examination; some even base the entire semester's grade on such an examination. Many others require two or more essay examinations. In fact, recent studies suggest that as much as 40 percent of the writing done by an undergraduate student consists of answering essay examination questions. This means that knowing how to take essay examinations is essential to college success.

If written in class, the essay examination is characterized by high pressure and high anxiety; if out of class, it requires that students write a paper demonstrating their knowledge of the material studied as well as their ability to organize, explain, illustrate, and analyze the material in a coherent, mechanically competent form. The in-class essay may involve some memorization, but the out-of-class essay will not; it is more likely to involve interpretation, evaluation, or reconsideration of covered materials from a new perspective. In-class writing tends to test particular

knowledge and the ability to grasp concepts and overviews; the out-of-class goal is to test your ability to analyze and synthesize and to go into depth on an original (or at least specialized) topic. Whether the exam is in class or out of class, the fact that a teacher assigns an essay exam instead of the shorter, more easily graded objective test is a strong indication of interest, not just in facts acquired by the students or in their reading comprehension, but in thought processes: the ability to think through the important concerns of the course in their own words, to reorganize, regroup, and reconsider information in the light of principles and concepts that unite facts.

The chapters in Unit One and Two have provided a solid basis for writing a good out-of-class essay, whether for an examination or not; therefore, this chapter will focus on the in-class essay examination itself, an examination form whose rules and methods require strategies somewhat different from out-of-class writing.

409

Even though you have not read the materials asked about, criticize the following student answers and identify problems.

Question: Explain how the families in the two stories "The Lottery" and "The Secret Life of Walter Mitty" are unconventional. Be specific. Give examples.

Answer: The families in the two stories "The Lottery" and "The Secret Life of Walter Mitty" are actually quite unconventional. They both have very strange and unique families. They are not like your average family. The things they do and just the life they live is quite different from other families. They both have this unique flavor to them. A flavor that is not seen in most other families. Living with either one of these families would be quite an experience. It would be very interesting. Basically, the only thing these two families have in common is that they are different from the mainstream family. Not many families such as these two exist. They are relatively hard to find.

Question: Explain how the conflict between Galileo and his critics reflected a shift in scientific thinking from an older, human-centered view of the universe to a modern, observation-based view.

Answer: Italian astronomer and physicist Galileo Galilei was born in 1564 and died in 1642. His study of stars through a telescope made him disagree with the Ptolemaic view of the universe and agree instead with the Copernican view of the universe. His refusal to say that the sun and stars and planets all moved around the earth was considered irreligious. Despite his letters of appeal to important people like the Grand Duchess Christina and his scientific demonstrations, he was found guilty of heresy by the leaders of the Inquisition. He was forced to publicly deny his theory, and he lived the last nine years of his life under house arrest.

Question: Provide a biological explanation of why a visitor to the Andes mountains is breathless and exhausted while the local inhabitants are able to do heavy work and even play soccer without any respiratory distress.

Answer: A visitor to the Andes is breathless and tired while the local inhabitants are able to do heavy work and even play soccer without any respiratory distress. There are many reasons for this difference. Adjustment takes time but after six months the count of the number of circulating red blood cells may be as high as ten million cells per cubic millimeter, which is just about what it is in local inhabitants of the Andes. A few weeks after arrival, the blood shows some increase in the number of circulating red cells. What happens is that the extra hemoglobin circulating through the lungs increases the effective use of the small amount of oxygen available. More oxygen in the blood helps reduce the burden on the respiratory center. When a newcomer first arrives, the shortage of atmospheric oxygen raises the red cell count. It also makes people automatically breathe deeper to try to make up for the smaller amount of oxygen taken in a normal breath. Therefore, newcomers breathe harder and less effectively than natives. This physical change doesn't help much. Newcomers are usually so upset by their difficulty breathing that their extra muscular effort consumes more and more oxygen. That defeats its purpose of increasing oxygen availability. After a few days or more in such a thin atmosphere, the newcomer's body acclimatizes in another way. The red blood cell count goes up. That's why adjustment eventually occurs.

An in-class essay examination answer demands a more direct approach than any out-of-class essay. In fact, the process writing techniques of prewriting and rewriting commonly taught in most composition courses (and in Unit One of this text) are of almost no use at all. Yes, it is helpful to write a sketchy plan of a longer essay question before writing an answer, and it is vital to start with a clear-cut thesis statement, but there is little time to worry about expansion, improvement, correction, or revision. In effect, your study preparation was your prewriting. Limited time forces writers to settle on essentials quickly, jot down what is most important, and move on.

Preparation and Execution

In-class essay exams clearly involve most of the rules for good writing, but with the added problem of a very short thinking and writing time, though the teacher assumes that much of the thinking has already occurred in class and in study for the exam. Be sure to determine ahead of time if dictionaries are permitted during the exam. Arrive early with all necessary materials, and try to be as relaxed and confident as possible. Writing, like all language skills, is inhibited by anxiety. Be calm and rested; you write with your mind, after all, not with your fingers and pen. Most graders dislike pencil (it is hard to read), so pens will be best. Lapses of memory and panic are normal; the important thing is not to let them overwhelm and discourage you. Don't waste time with emotional reactions to the test ("My goodness, it's long! How could she ask us to do this?"); just get down to business as fast as possible. The following steps are vital to success.

1. **SURVEY:** Quickly survey the examination, read the directions, check the number of points per question, and, on that basis, decide how much time to spend on each question. Carefully follow a time schedule, focusing on the questions that count a for more points instead of on minor questions that count less. Some tests reward students who read the directions and survey the materials with care. For example, some of the hardest questions may come early in the examination and some of the easier ones later: yet students might gain more confidence and do better by warming up on the easier questions before tackling the harder ones. Surveying allows you to identify these and to develop a quick time budget and strategy for answering.

If possible, start with what you know—to reduce anxiety and to help you "get your motor running" by thinking out your ideas.

2. **QUESTION:** Think before you write; don't just start scribbling. Thinking first allows you to plan ahead, decide on the most effective approach, recall important details, and provide some basic organization for your answer so that it is more coherent, more focused, and more unified than it would be if you simply plunged in writing. Think by asking questions, just as if you were questioning your instructor: How long? What proof? What points should I make? Make sure you understand exactly what is being asked before you start considering how best to answer.

Quickly jot down notes and maybe even a brief outline or list of points to clarify your thinking before you commit yourself to writing a final answer. This allows you to plan the order and logic of discussion first. If you can't finish, your outline shows the grader your intended direction.

3. **WRITE:** Begin with a good thesis or topic sentence so you can score points for organization and a clear sense of direction. Many successful answers repeat key words from the assignment or from the teacher's question, or rephrase the exam question as a statement. For example, if the assignment is to discuss the key differences between the pre-Civil War economies of the North and the South, you might begin,

The key differences between the Northern pre-Civil War economy and the Southern are..." or "The Northern pre-Civil War economy differed from the Southern in its reliance on _____ instead of _____, in its _____ instead of _____, and its _____ instead of _____..

Remember that a thesis statement is like an answer in miniature. It conveys your understanding of the question, your basic grasp of the key answer, and your plan to explore the answer more fully. Sometimes, in short essay questions, a good thesis sentence is sufficient to earn a minimum number of points for a passing grade, especially when time is tight. Saving the thesis for the end might mean no time to write it and no clear organizing idea to help your teacher decide that you really know what you are talking about. After your thesis, your body paragraphs should include as many concrete examples, illustrations, and other specifics as you can think of and have time for. This specificity is second only to a clear thesis in making a good grade.

Wherever possible, <u>write complete answers</u>. However, if you run out of time <u>diagram, outline, or list</u> the rest of your answer in short sentences and phrases. Sometimes the teacher will count such effort as equal to writing out the essay and give you credit accordingly.

<u>Finally, make sure you do not erroneously omit a question</u>.

4. **REVIEW:** Quickly proofread before turning in your test. Spending a few moments correcting spelling, grammar, and punctuation, checking numbering, and rewriting illegible sections might improve your final grade. Most importantly, remember that, if a teacher cannot read what you have written, all of your effort has been wasted.

Helpful Terms for Analyzing Questions

As suggested above, you should always read the question analytically to determine exactly what it asks you to do. Teachers carefully select their vocabulary to guide students as to what must be done and how. If you answer a question not asked or give the answer the wrong emphasis or choose an approach different from that indicated by the question, your teacher will usually assume that is because you do not know the right answer. Therefore, knowledge of commonly used terms is vital for following instructions correctly.

What can you expect when you are faced with an essay exam? Apart from content, a good answer responds to key words in the directions. You will need to identify such words immediately and perhaps even underline or circle them to help direct your focus.

The most commonly used instruction terms refer to the patterns of development discussed in Unit Two (*compare, contrast, illustrate, describe, define*) but also include *discuss, explain, criticize*, and *evaluate*.

1. <u>Discuss/explain</u> type essay questions. These simply invite you to do what the key words indicate. *Discuss* means "talk about," and *explain* is self-explanatory. Either one might require you to make an idea understandable or to demonstrate logical relationships. To do so, you might illustrate, that is, develop an idea by giving examples, or <u>describe</u>, record observations and paint a picture with words. If you are given this kind of question, you simply have to stick to the topic, think of specifics, and follow the rules of good writing.

2. <u>Compare/contrast</u> questions. Answers to this type of question can also be straightforward. Remembering the discussion in the *Comparison-Contrast* chapter (pages 287-318), you must decide whether you should compare (show similarities) or contrast (show differences) or both. The compare or contrast decision will depend on the nature of the material (Napoleon and Hitler probably share more characteristics than Napoleon and Ghandi), and any guidelines you have received in class. You must also decide whether to use a <u>block pattern</u> (talk about A from start to finish; then talk about B) or an <u>alternating pattern</u> (talk about a characteristic of A, then a characteristic of B; and so on). Make sure to choose your pattern and stick to it; confusing the two can lead to distorted essays that ignore one subject or the other.

3. <u>Analyze</u> questions. Analysis requires you to do several kinds of linguistic and intellectual activities one after the other: <u>classification</u> or <u>categorization</u>, <u>division into parts</u>, <u>process analysis</u> or <u>identification of function, purpose, or methodology</u>. For example, think of an analysis of a sandwich. First, you would name the different parts (*bread, cheese, butter, lettuce, tomato*); then you might indicate at least some of the stages of assembly, how it fits together (*butter the bread, slice the cheese, cut the tomato*); finally, you would probably mention function and purpose (convenience in eating, contrasting tastes and textures, ease of preparation). An analysis of a machine, like a car engine, will be much the same (if much more complex), so

the best advice is to keep the stages of analysis clearly in mind: discuss the parts, their combination, and their function or use.

4. <u>Define/List/Classify/Apply</u> questions. Definition calls on you to explain the meaning of key words or terms. Formal definitions put words into a <u>general class</u> and then add <u>differentiating characteristics</u>: A pencil is a writing instrument made of graphite or pencil lead, wood, paint, and a rubber eraser in a metal holder. This pattern has some of the same characteristics as analysis, since it lists parts, but unlike analysis, it continues, if extended to some length, to show how the term defined is different from others in its class. (If you think there is some similarity to comparison-contrast, you are right, but definition makes no point-for-point connections.) For example, a definition of a bicycle might begin with a simple descriptive statement, *a vehicle powered by its rider and usually with two wheels…*, but then go on to differentiate motorized bicycles, three-wheeled tricycles, bicycles built for two (or three or four), and so on.

You may be asked to <u>list</u> a series of terms or words, following each with a simple definition (*List the qualities of an effective manager, defining each briefly.*), or you may have to <u>classify</u> your list as well. A classification is a list of defined terms arranged according to a principle: all the members of a category, listed best to worst, least difficult to most difficult, cheap to expensive. The question could read, *Classify the psychological strengths of a good manager*, for example, perhaps adding *from most important to least important.*

Finally, you may be asked to <u>apply</u> your definition to a particular situation supplied to you or to one you have to invent yourself. American business schools are particularly fond of such case study approaches, as are other academic departments, so be prepared to apply your defined terms when you study. How would different kinds of taxes affect a small business, how would different advertising approaches sell soap or soft drinks, how would different accounting systems provide differing data in a real or hypothetical case?

5. <u>Argue/Defend</u> questions. This last category of essay questions calls on you to play the role of advocate/lawyer, to make the best arguments you can for a position. As with the argumentative essays discussed in Chapter 17, don't be afraid to take a strong, clear position, and defend it vigorously. To do so is neither rude nor aggressive; it is simply a way of arriving at a sharp and distinct position on an issue. Note that you may discuss, explain, compare, contrast, define, list, and classify when you argue and defend, but you must do so in support of a position. Arguing often involves <u>criticism</u>, a focus on faults, difficulties, problems, and demerits, or <u>evaluation</u>, a more moderate and more balanced approach than criticism, but still requiring the close examination of something (an idea, an approach, an article) in order to judge its value, importance, or truth.

Final Checklist

☐ The most important part of any essay assignment is deciding precisely what the instructor wants you to do. Have you determined exactly what the assignment calls for in terms of length, development, methodology, approach, support, and effort? Are you really answering the question asked?

☐ Once you understand the assignment, employing what you have learned about writing skills and developing an answer that is focused, unified, and thorough will decide your success or failure. Have you done a preliminary sketch of your plan of attack? Have you thought over the best order in which to provide your evidence, examples, or other support?

☐ Does your answer initially repeat the key words of the assignment? Does it provide a thesis statement that is the answer in miniature?

☐ Does your answer develop that thesis statement with concrete supportive details?

☐ Does your concluding statement confirm your answer to the question asked?

• EXERCISE 18.2: THINKING ABOUT TEACHER EXPECTATIONS

Identify the <u>key words</u> in the following assignments. Explain what the instructors expect in terms of content and pattern of development.

Example: Evaluate the long-term genetic effects of the nuclear power plant disaster at Chernobyl, Belorussia.

Key words: evaluate, long-term, genetic, effects

Explanation: The content should be focused only on genetic effects and only on long-term, not short-term, genetic effects. Since evaluation calls for a balanced look at the possibilities, the teacher probably expects an enumeration of genetic effects, perhaps in terms of those with possible solutions or aids and those with no hope for solution. The pattern might be one of degree from the solvable to the manageable to the impossible—those effects beyond control.

1. Illustrate the effects of an earthquake of .9 or higher on the Richter Scale.
2. Compare and contrast the early French and English settlements in what is now the United States.
3. Describe the nature of light waves, their movement and vibrations.
4. Enumerate the positive effects of language study.
5. Define the term *cross-pollination*. What exactly does it involve?
6. Contrast Zen Buddhism with Confucianism.
7. Compare Zen Buddhism with Confucianism.
8. List the key characteristics of Zen Buddhism.
9. Describe a typical Zen garden.
10. Explain the function of a Zen garden.
11. Discuss the <u>structure</u> of at least three of the stories you read this semester. How does the way the author organizes his story relate to the theme of the story?
12. Explain the idea of checks and balances and then show how it works in the U.S. government system.
13. *Fortune Magazine* claims, "America is losing markets and selling off pieces of its economy to pay for its big import binge." What are some of the reasons? What can be done to help reverse that trend?
14. You were recently hired as the Operations Manager of a nationwide accounting firm. One of your jobs is to find a location for a new regional head office in the Southwest region of the U.S. What criteria would you use to evaluate and choose the most appropriate one?

Passages for Discussion and Analysis

A. The following are short essays answering the question, *Identify the <u>following historical and literary figures and explain why they remain</u> important today.* Of the three which identify the same figure (3, 4, and 5), which is the best answer and which the weakest? Explain. How could the weaker answers be improved?

1. **LaSalle:** Sieur de La Salle (1643–1687), a French explorer, led an expedition in 1682 to trace the Mississippi River and to see if it emptied into the Gulf of Mexico. In April 1682 LaSalle reached the river and claimed it for France. He put up the French coat of arms near the Mississippi River. La Salle named the place Louisiana after King Louis XIV, France's King.

    Strength: _____

    Weakness: _____

2. **Columbus:** Christopher Columbus, in the year of 1492, provided Spain a vast land to be colonized. However, his story began years before. In those days, trade with the Orient was very important and long before Columbus' voyage, the Portuguese were the best navigators. Columbus traveled with them and from them learned the techniques of navigating and the routes that they discovered. This travel made him understand that the world was round instead of flat, and he therefore developed new ideas and routes to the Indies instead of the usual way, which was around Africa. His revolutionary idea was to get to the Indies by going west, but Henry "The Navigator" King of Portugal already had contracts with the Indies so they weren't interested in him, but he was strongly convinced that he was right and he refused to quit and he had a new opportunity in the Spanish kingdom and the Spanish King Ferdinand and Queen Isabela supported his project with royal money. On October 12th, after three months of travel in despair, Columbus thought he had arrived in the Indies and died with this belief. This discovery was the final step that got the medieval "intelligentsia" out of the "dark ages." It brought gold and silver to Spain. It left behind the Spanish heritage of today's Latin America.

    Strength: _____

    Weakness: _____

3. **Cervantes:** Miguel de Cervantes Saavedra, having been a soldier and one of the best writers, is a very historical figure in Spanish literature. Cervantes was the author of the famous book *Don Quijote de La Mancha,* considered by many to be the greatest Spanish literary work. During his military career Cervantes fought in the Battle of Lepanto where the Spanish fought the Turks. In this battle Cervantes lost his left arm and since then was known as *El manco de Lepanto.* He is represented as the man who hid his arm under his cloak. Although he hid his injured arm, during his lifetime he carried his wounds with pride and proclaimed his left arm "for the greater glory of the right."

    Strength: _____

    Weakness: _____

4. **Cervantes**: Miguel de Cervantes Saavedra (1547-1616), descended from a family of lesser nobility in Alcala de Menares (Madrid), wrote not only the most remarkable book in Spanish literature, but probably one of the best books in the world. This book started a new literary species, the picaresque. The hero of the romances of chivalry is replaced by an anti-hero, a rogue or a vagabond. Cervantes wrote his masterpiece in this

literary genre, creating a model for and surpassing all the picaresque books written. The anti-hero is Don Quijote, a tall, thin, old and crazy man belonging to the poor nobility with title but no money. His squire, Sancho Panza, is naive, fat, and short, with a better view of reality. The lady, Dulcinea, is the daughter of a local farmer and descended from Muslims but a princess in Quixote's view. To obtain her love, Don Quijote goes over the roads to save the poor people or ladies in trouble, as true heroes used to do. The genius of Cervantes is to use this funny, ridiculous story to criticize the political system in Spain, the expulsion of Jews and Muslims and the wealthy Spanish nobility. A master of irony, his book was read by the high classes. Today this book has been translated into more than a hundred languages and is only surpassed by the Bible.

Strength: _____

Weakness: _____

5. **Cervantes:** In his very famous and still widely read novel, *Don Quijote*, Miguel de Cervantes Saavedra (1547-1616), the most remarkable Spanish writer, deeply analyzed the typical Spanish character. His writing continues to be read because his perceptions of this character are still true today. His main character, Don Quijote, represents the prototype of the Spanish man, an idealistic person with difficulty distinguishing between dream and reality. This character has such big and unrealizable projects that he will never be able to make real and practical advances. Like the Spanish man of today, Don Quijote represents the victory of the heart over the head and of idealism over rationalism that has made it difficult for Spain to advance and to face reality. Cervantes also goes deeply into a problem still at the heart of Spanish society, jealousy. Don Quijote shows the Spaniard as a person who always envies his neighbor's property but will never do anything except dream to obtain the same himself. After four centuries, these two qualities of the Spanish character remain, so much so that Spain is called a "land of Quijotes" or dreamers, and envy is described as the "national sport." Cervantes' vision of the future makes this book still useful to understand the present Spanish character and is why it is read more than any other book except the Bible.   —Altamira Perez

Strength: _____

Weakness: _____

B. Examine the structure and organization of the following essays. What makes them effective or ineffective? Explain.

1. *Question:* Apply Paul Ehrlich's warnings about the "population bomb" to your own country. In which direction do you think your country will move, toward a birth rate solution or a death rate solution? Why? Be specific.

Answer:

Paul Ehrlich warns about the detrimental effects of uncontrolled population growth and warns that, if people do not move toward a birth rate solution, a death rate solution will find them. His warnings apply to Peru, an underdeveloped South American country, which for some time has depended on a death rate solution to solve its population problems and which shows no signs of changing.

Although Peru has extensive territory, only a small percentage of its land is arable. The rest is a strip of desert broken by small river valleys; the highlands are so steep that there is insufficient cultivatable area; and the jungle, despite its lush vegetation, is not fertile enough for sustained agriculture. This means food is basically in short supply.

The lack of educational opportunity and impoverished conditions causes migration, which in turn leads to overcrowding in mushrooming cities: rural families who come to Lima filled with hopes do not have enough education to find a job so they establish their houses in areas around Lima called "barriadas." Promiscuity and the lack of sex education permit uncontrolled reproduction among the poor, who cannot escape from their poverty cycle, their poor health. In other words, social conditions add to the population problem.

Religious authorities discourage birth control through propaganda, government policy, and social pressure. There is no sex education in the schools, no free public clinics to disperse information and medical care, no legal abortions. The poor uneducated people believe that they should have as many children as God sends them. The educated middle or upper class do not follow religious birth control rules, so they use various birth control methods and can afford medical care. In sum, religion worsens the problem.

The economic problems and inefficiency of some governmental reforms, such as the Agrarian Reform, have caused a food shortage and an unequal distribution between rich and poor. The rich get richer, the poor poorer. The rich eat well, the poor eat at a subsistence level or starve. Government reforms do little or nothing for the poor. The social dichotomy and the economic troubles have given the leftist "Shining Path" great power and have resulted in even more deaths from civil war.

In conclusion, the Peruvian population is not conscious of the population-food crisis but the crisis nonetheless exists. This ignorance makes the country's physical and social problems worse so that a death-rate solution is inevitable.

What makes this an effective answer? If the writer were told to revise this paper outside of class, what additions, subtractions, and changes should be made?

2. *Question:* California recently passed an "English Language Amendment" making English the official language of the state and discouraging the official and formal use of other languages. What would Noah Webster, the originator of Webster's dictionaries and a nationalistic supporter of American English, say about this? What do you say given the record of historical attempts to regulate language?

Answer:

Noah Webster wanted standardization and in particular standardization based on American rather than British forms. He created spelling books which he instituted in public schools in an attempt to instill this standard early. He was very upset when Americanisms were attacked by Anglophiles. Given this information, it seems likely that Webster would be happy about this amendment because it fits his concept of an American standard. Throughout linguistic history efforts have been made to proscribe language, to prohibit certain ways of speaking and vocabulary. These have been unsuccessful because, as the doctrine of usage states, language is determined by speech. California can make all of the laws it wants, but neither it nor Noah Webster can make people speak any way except the way they want to.

3. *Question:* The critics in your text argue that change is the most important characteristic of the English language. Explain what has changed and why, giving specific examples.

Answer A:

As our authors point out, the most important characteristic of the history of the English language is change. Change is important because when a language ceases to grow it dies. Growth of a language comes about through changes in word meanings or pronunciation and addition of new words. The overall changes in English can be characterized in two central tendencies: growth of vocabulary and simplification of grammar.

English has changed because of its history of invasions. As groups came together and lived side by side the English language adapted in order for the two groups to communicate. For example, after the Danish Viking invasions many Danish words pertaining to the give and take of everyday life were introduced to English. Also, many of the inflectional endings which stood in the way of mutual understanding were dropped. English also went through a significant period of change after Normandy was lost. It was because of the influence of French (the mixing of the two languages as English came back to power) that English sounds so different from most of the other Germanic languages. French vocabulary and sounds were adopted into English.

Change in a language is often slow and subtle. In English, changes are easier to trace because they often stem from outside invasions or influences (such as Christianity). It is important for us as Americans to study the history of changes in English because it gives us a sense of cultural identity and makes us realize that things happen for a reason. It is also important to keep in mind that change is the source of growth in a language. Learning what changed English in the past may indicate what changes could occur in the future.

What are the strengths of this essay?

Answer B: (opening paragraph):

Humans, whether familiar or strangers, can easily be recognized as living or dead because of definite characteristics. They move, breathe, grow, and communicate. The same is true of languages, which we can recognize as living or dead because of key characteristics. We know that our language is alive because it changes constantly. This essay will identify how a language lives, in this case English, what has changed it over the years, and how these changes can be seen today.

How is this opening paragraph different from that of Answer A? How has this writer decided to extend and interpret the question? Has she made a good decision?

4. *Question:* Social class seems to have a major influence on the language of many cultures. While the U.S. has certainly "democratized" English to some extent, linguistic class divisions are obvious and pervasive. Focus on a particular town or area you are familiar with and explain, as if to a stranger from another country, how the linguistic class divisions can be recognized. What are the features of the different class usages?

Answer:

Hawaii is very much like a spaceship isolated in the middle of a large mass of water. Its people are literally stranded together in a small area to live together and hopefully get along. Yet the element of diversity is great, and not only do the people dress differently, eat differently, and work differently, they speak differently also. A stranger could be blindfolded, and led around the island, and hear many groups with very different things to say, and very different ways to say them.

Our stranger arrives in Honolulu airport, overpowered by the fragrance of plumerias and besieged by a plethora of languages as people greet each other and as hawkers try to sell their wares. Because he is blindfolded, he can't see the people around him, but he can hear them. Those with any kind of continental United States accent are either tourists or newly arrived military personnel. Such visitors make up a large language division on Oahu; their inflections and vocabulary make them conspicuous and, no matter how "General American" their speech may seem on the mainland, they are still regarded as *haoles* (white people who get lost easily, turn red quickly in the local sun, and move at a disturbing pace) by the locals.

Our stranger might also hear a friendly *Mahalo* and a "Welcome to Hawaii" in which *Hawaii* is pronounced *ha-va'-ee*. These are local young people greeting friends or tourists. Their vocabulary is infused with Hawaiian terms; their pace is slow and pleasant. The same type of language can be heard at local community colleges. The young men whistle at *wahinis* or lounge on a *lanai* sipping papaya, guava, or mango juice. While they pronounce their words, especially Hawaiian ones, with a heavy local accent, they also speak General American diction.

After a short cab ride to Honolulu's King Street in the middle of the downtown, a stranger will hear business people discussing finances, accounts, and luncheon. These local, upper-middle class whites and Japanese/Chinese/Portuguese mixes speak a standard mainland dialect in order to do business with mainland and international firms where only "proper" English is accepted. However, when conversing casually with fellow locals they will throw in such words as *pau, poi, luau, lanai, hapai,* will use such local directions as *windward, over the Pali, Kanaoe way,* and so forth, and might discuss Chinese joss or the latest Japanese samurai film.

A trip to the North Shore to sit on the beach and enjoy the fresh Kona breeze will bring exposure to local youngsters talking in local patterns, sometimes with a mixture of Chinese or Japanese terms thrown in, depending on the group mix. They will say things like "Hey, Mishi, like go movies la'dat?" "Ah, no like." "Yeah, da Tyla (Tyler), where he stay?" "He stay down Waimea." "Dat's more betta dan 'ere." All of these sentences overlap in a staccato pattern. Our stranger can hardly understand the grammatical structure of the sentences with their reversals of standard patterns or the reliance on local vocabulary like *bombai* and *da'kine*. An older person who joins the youngsters will continue the conversation in the same manner. Our stranger is hearing local people conversing with other locals. Even educated locals who can and do speak General English at school and business, lapse into this pidgin English, which relies on double negatives, *d*s in place of *th*s (for example, *da* for *the*, dropped *h*s, *wat?* for *what?*), and a patois of Japanese, Chinese, Hawaiian, Samoan and Portuguese. Others are raised to speak pidgin, have parents who speak pidgin, and will always speak it. Although they attend local schools, they are not forced to change.

Thus, our stranger will have heard tourist English (haole), locals speaking General American English, and locals speaking pidgin or linguistic mixes; if he had traveled farther, he may have heard English sprinkled even more heavily with Japanese, Chinese, Samoan, old Hawaiian or Portuguese. Although there is little class prejudice among those living on the islands, except maybe for anti-military feelings, to deal with strangers, Islanders will speak or try to speak standard American English, but will lapse into local terms like *aloha* and Hawaiian pronunciations to remind strangers that Hawaii is a land apart; among themselves pidgin is so common that long-term *haoles* begin to merge with the local populace by lapsing into *mo' betta*s, crossing the *Pali*, taking drinks on the *lanai*, and reversing standard word order.

    5. *Take-home Examination Assignment:* Modern feminism has called for a reevaluation of the gender-related nature of much of our discourse. Choose one area of language or one linguistic focus in which to explore this idea. Is this specialized diction you are focusing on gender related? If so, how? If not, provide evidence.

Introductory Paragraph:

    Nurtured by journalism, radio, and television, American sports have experienced a large growth in popularity. Previously, sporting events such as baseball, football, and basketball have been considered predominantly male spectator sports. However, the medium of television has allowed these games to be viewed in homes and the audience now includes many avid female viewers. In addition to large-scale, professional sporting events, Americans flock to contests at the college, high school, and playground level. Due to the importance we have placed on athletics, Americans have become obsessed with sports and, as a result, "sports-talk" can frequently be heard in discourse on all levels of society. In addition to daily conversation, sports analogies and metaphors strongly permeate the realms of business and politics. The most obvious connection between professional sports, corporate business, and politics is the fact that they are male-dominated fields. <u>Although sports metaphors are widely used among Americans in all spheres of conversation, sports-talk remains gender associated and is predominantly used in the speech of males.</u>   [Thesis idea which paper will try to prove]

C. The following is a take-home examination question for an *Introduction to Religion* course. What are the key words that tell us what the student should do? Does the student answer the question asked? The answer sounds sophisticated, but remember that the student is using both class notes and textbook to support the answer with facts, the appropriate vocabulary, and expert discussion. The specialized terms and definitions are not something this student knew about until taking this course. This question calls for a synthesis of notes and readings.

    1. *Question:* What are the key characteristics of what religious experts call "The Basic Religion"? How do Hindus and Taoists fit these characteristics?

Answer:

What our text calls "Basic Religion" is characterized by Animism, Magic, Divination, Taboo, Totems, Sacrifice, Rites of Passage, and Ancestor Worship.

Primitive people believed the world was alive with souls or spirit forces, either personal or impersonal, and, as a result, worshiped things in nature. Hindus are animists because they bathe in the sacred river Ganges, revere cows, and believe in many major and minor gods, while Taoists have animistic gods of heaven, earth, soil, and harvest, and see man and nature deriving from the same source (Yin and Yang). [Pattern? Characteristics of Basic Religion cited, followed by related characteristics in Hindu and Taoist faiths.]

Primitive people also believe in magic in the sense of attempts to use rituals, formulae, dances, or incantations to control nature: to make rain, improve crops, or kill enemies. Hindus, for example, value the Atharva Veda, a collection of magic spells, chants, and special mantras which they repeat to protect them and to promote their welfare. The Taoists, in turn, are interested in alchemy to promote long life or immortality. One famous Taoist worked with cinnabar (mercuric sulfide) and was said to have been "transformed" so totally that years later, only "his cap and clothing" were found in his tomb.

In basic societies, the prediction of the future through divination is a very important function. While there is no record of Hindu divination, in ancient China, a tortoise shell was heated until it cracked, and patterns were interpreted in a book called *I Ching*. The Chinese also cast coins or stalks of a plant and tried to interpret the patterns which emerged based on the number sixty-four in the *I Ching* to make a prediction.

Basic societies also believe certain actions must be avoided lest the spirit world release harmful effects upon the person or group. The Hindus have taboos about food; many are vegetarians and will never eat meat. They believe the cow is sacred and should be left to roam freely, unharmed and untouched. Taoists don't have taboos per se but they do disapprove of things like "fame, pomp, and glory," which they think are very harmful.

Totemism is apparently based upon the feeling of kinship that exists between humans and other creatures or objects in nature. The Hindus and Taoists don't have specific totems.

The act of sacrifice is sometimes considered a means of feeding the residents of the spirit world. Hindus, for example, believe the person who participates in a horse sacrifice will atone for a great sin or will receive great religious power. The horse sacrifice was also considered helpful to rulers who wished to expand their territory. The Hindus also believe in sacrificing a wife when her husband dies. She is placed on the funeral pyre and burns up with her dead husband's body.

What else should this student discuss? How should this answer end?

D. The next examination question is followed by three student answers. What are the key words in the question? What does it call for the student to do? Which of the three answers best responds to the question? Why? Of the remaining two, which is better? Why? If you were the professor, what grades (A, B, C, D, F) would you give for the three answers? Justify your grade by writing a couple of sentences which explain your decision. Your decision should be based, of course, on how carefully and thoroughly the answer responds to the question, rather than on content and length alone.

The Examination Question: What effects did Darwinism have on nineteenth-century social and economic attitudes?

Student Answer # 1:

The famous book entitled *On the Origin of Species* was written by Mr. Charles Darwin. He did this before his death in 1882. This book really bothered all the other scientists and got a lot of people mad about maybe men coming from monkeys a long time ago. Religious people especially did not like this idea and fundamentalists still don't. No one likes to think of himself as a monkey! Christians didn't like being made monkeys. Some schools are still having fights about whether their science classes will teach Darwin's theories or the Bible's version of creation. A teacher in west Texas almost got fired because of this.

Many people didn't like the monkey-man ideas, and they didn't like people who agreed with Darwin. This caused a lot of trouble socially. Each side of the argument felt that it was the fittest to survive. Sometimes the fight was economic. The rich said that if the poor were more fit, they would be rich too. If they were poor, it was their own fault. Some politicians think like this today.

Student Answer #2:

Darwinism had a very great influence on scientific, social, political, and economic attitudes in spite of the fact that Darwin only intended for his theories to affect science.

With time, several different schools of thought grew up. Wealthy aristocrats quite approved of and supported the ideas called <u>Social Darwinism</u>. They used the argument of survival of the fittest to prove that they were rich because they were better than other people. Their basis for judging superiority was business success. Of course they had only studied or heard about the surface-level ideas of Darwin's theories and had not carefully studied Darwin's works.

The Reform Darwinists disagreed. They were more humanistic and humanitarian and did not feel that change was only in the remote past and future. They hoped that they could improve society right away by making immediate and humanitarian changes for the better. People who carried Darwin's views to an extreme included racists and eugenicists. The racists used the argument of survival of the fittest to prove that their own race was superior to other races, in other words, to support their prejudiced attitudes about blacks and gypsies and anyone else who was racially different from them. Eugenicists believed man should be bred for good genes and people with bad genes should be prevented from having children. Hitler was a eugenicist; so were some of the Serbs who attacked Bosnians.

On the economic level, Darwinism was used to defend imperialism, saying that imperialistic nations like England and France were strongest, best able to survive, and therefore superior to the smaller nations. Also, this was used as an argument for a *laissez-faire* policy. The idea behind this economic approach was that controlling business would interfere with survival of the fittest companies.

Student Answer #3

Although Darwin only meant for his theories to affect science, in actual practice Darwinism greatly affected nineteenth-century social and economic attitudes.

First of all, Darwin's theories influenced and produced several schools of social thought. The most widely accepted of these was called <u>Social Darwinism</u>, an argument adopted by many of the wealthy to prove that they were rich because they were superior. The Social Darwinists argued that Darwin's term "survival of the fittest" applied to business as well as to jungle life and that a key criterion for judging superiority was success in business. Of course their ideas were the result of only surface study of Darwin's theories. Another branch of social thought, also based on Darwin's theories, was <u>Reform Darwinism.</u> The Reform Darwinists were more humanitarian than the Social Darwinists and did not feel that change was only in the remote past and future. They hoped that by making changes for the better in a humanitarian way, they could improve society now. Instead of trying to justify cut-throat practices, they focused on man taking control of his own evolution and choosing to become more humanistic. The <u>Racists</u> and <u>Eugenicists</u> carried this idea of man controlling his own evolution a step further. The former used the argument of survival of the fittest to support their prejudiced attitude toward other races, even to the point of arguing for extermination of the weaker genetic strains. Eugenicists, on the other hand, believed man should be bred, that gene pools should be carefully controlled to perpetuate the best in man, and that the genetically diseased, the weak, and the less intelligent should be sterilized or at least have their reproduction limited.

Inevitably, Darwinism also influenced economic practices. Darwinism was used as a key argument for <u>imperialism</u>. That is, advocates argued that imperialistic nations were the strongest and the best able to survive, and therefore superior to the smaller nations. Such an argument justified exploitation of the weak by the strong, and was an underlying principle in the concept of <u>colonization</u>. In other words, nineteenth-century France and England and the United States felt they had the right to exploit weaker nations (particularly ones with raw materials available in the homeland) as long as they provided protection in return. Darwinism was also used as an argument for a policy of <u>laissez-faire</u> in business practices. The idea behind this was that controlling business would interfere with survival of the fittest companies. The government should not control monopolies and should instead allow corporate take-overs and monolithic expansion as evidence of economic strength and health.

In other words, many of the ideas about a "pure" or "superior" race and about "might makes right" that dominated World War II grew directly out of Darwin's influence on nineteenth-century social and economic thought.

Chapter 19: Summarizing and Documenting

Brevity is the soul of wit. — Shakespeare's *Hamlet*

College students spend much of their time summarizing: recording their reading comprehension in abbreviated form, reducing fifty-minute lectures to a page of notes, condensing an evening's library research down to a handful of notecards. College homework assignments involve reading very large quantities of material quickly and remembering the essential points. Class discussions require you to remember and repeat the key points of your readings.

Written assignments and especially research papers, in turn, involve incorporating those key ideas into arguments on assigned topics and selecting the most significant information. Students are frequently assigned an article or a book to summarize in preparation for a report. Thus, for writing, for test taking, and for good class participation, you must be able to summarize well.

What a Summary Is

A summary is a brief, concise statement of the key idea or key information of a paragraph or essay in the summarizer's own words. A summary states the author's <u>guiding idea or thesis or position on an issue and gives an explanatory statement of each element of that idea or a list of reasons for that position</u>. It translates the difficult into the simple, the odd structure into the more common structure, the writer's statement into the summarizer's own words. In other words, a key characteristic of a good summary is clarity. The length of the summary depends on the amount of important material in a selection, but a rule of thumb is that you use a sentence to summarize a paragraph, a paragraph to summarize an essay, and a page or two to summarize a book. A summary is abstract or general rather than concrete; it does not include specific details (statistics, quotations, names, etc.) unless they are a vital and inescapable part of the main idea. However, a summary must not be so general that the basic argument is lost. In the following paragraph, for example, the statistical details are irrelevant to summary. Only the underlined words are vital.

> <u>A rise in levels of education in the United States of the 1950's meant a rising appreciation of culture</u>. During that period, more dollars were spent on concerts and on recordings of classical music than on baseball. Sales of books doubled from 1940 to 1950. The mid-Fifties boasted a thousand symphony orchestras, and several hundred museums; institutes and colleges began purchasing art and more students began to major in the humanities. Various other indexes can be cited to show the <u>growth of a large middle-brow</u> society during that period, and steadily increasing productivity and leisure helped the United States become an even more active <u>consumer of culture in the Sixties and Seventies</u>.
>
> —V.L. Macdonald, "Consumer Culture"

A rearrangement of these key words might produce a summary like the following:

> A rise in levels of education in the United States of the 1950's meant a rising appreciation of culture, a huge middlebrow society of consumers of culture that would continue to grow in the Sixties and Seventies.

However, these words still sound too close to the original. A good summary should be, as much as possible, in your own words. If a word or phrase from the original must be used to summarize, then it is best to put quotation marks around it. Why is the following better?

> Because more Americans went on to higher levels of education in the Fifties than in the Forties, they began a trend toward being "consumers of culture" that changed Fifties' society and that continued into the Sixties and Seventies.

If a summary is to be used in a report, you must build in information about your source:

> According to V. L. Macdonald in "Consumer Culture," as more Americans went on to higher levels of education in the Fifties than in the past, they began a trend toward being "consumers of culture" that changed Fifties' society and that continued into the Sixties and Seventies.

How to Read for Key Ideas

As you have learned, most good writers sum up the main points of their essay in their introduction (particularly the thesis sentence) and conclusion, and the main point of each paragraph in the topic sentence and concluding sentence. While topic sentences do not always come in the first line of a new paragraph, they do with such frequency that that is the first place to look for a summary idea. For example, in the following paragraph, the first sentence (the topic sentence) gives the general argument and the last sentence (the conclusion) sums up the further idea discussed in detail in the body of the paragraph. A good summary need include only the information from these two sentences.

> <u>The chain of missions established along the San Antonio River in the 18th century is a reminder of one of Spain's most successful attempts to extend its New World dominion northward from Mexico</u>. They were the greatest concentration of Catholic missions in North America. While tales of riches, such as those of the fabled region of Gran Quivira, spurred the conquistadors' advance across the Rio

Grande, encounters with the Tejas Indians, for whom Texas was named, provided even greater impetus for Spain's colonization of its northern borderlands. As dreams of wealth faded, giving way to the more practical goal of propagating the Catholic faith among the frontier Indians, the missions served to introduce native inhabitants into Spanish society. Catholicism, the very fiber of Spanish culture, was an assertive, nationalistic religion controlled and subsidized by the Crown. As an arm of the church, the missions was the vanguard for the spiritual conversion of New Spain's native inhabitants. As an agent of the state, the mission helped advance the empire northward. <u>Contrasted with the military might of the presidio, or the often self-serving policies of civil government, the mission acted as a tempering frontier influence, offering the Indians a less traumatic transition into European culture.</u>

> —"San Antonio Missions: Official Map and
> Guide," National Park Service, U.S.
> Department of the Interior

You might combine the underlined sentences into one sentence through antithesis.

> The line of 18th century missions along the San Antonio River were part of Spain's attempt "to extend its New World dominion northward from Mexico," not through military strength or self-serving civil government, but through a tempering religious influence that offered the Indians "a less traumatic transition into European culture."

Since the middle and last phrases are in the exact words of the original, they must be in quotation marks. Since the vocabulary of this summary is still close to the original, it might be better to rephrase the sentence in simpler terms:

> In the 18th century, Spain used San Antonio River missions to introduce Indians to European ways through religion rather than through the military or civil government.

Because this time the language is the writer's own, no quotation marks are necessary. However, if this summary is incorporated into an essay, a footnote, endnote, or internal reference would be required as well as a bibliographical reference since the material is still the original writer's property.

Often the task of summarizing is not this easy, because not all writers put their key ideas in the topic and concluding sentences. If you underline the topic sentence and concluding sentence of each paragraph, you may still not have enough to summarize thor-

oughly because many of the key ideas may appear in the body of the paragraphs.

However, when you are summarizing for study purposes, marking or highlighting the headings of a textbook is still a good way to make sure you have discovered the most important ideas. Remember, though, that marking more than about one-quarter of a text is simply delaying the inevitable, for sooner or later you will have to reduce the material to focus just on important concepts.

The following headings from the introductory chapter to a composition text suggest the scope of the chapter and the overall ideas to be explored.

> <u>English: an International Language</u>
> <u>Problems Learning English</u>
> <u>Language Reflects Culture</u>
> <u>Grammar vs. a Language "Personality"</u>
> <u>Text Divisions</u>
> <u>The Challenge</u>

Such headings provide a good basis for confirming that you are covering all of the important areas. Look at the following summary of the introduction just mentioned. Do the headings indicate whether or not all the information has been covered?

> English is the most widely spoken world language except for Mandarin Chinese, so knowing English will be very important for you (especially in science or technology), no matter the home country or occupation. However, it presents special problems for the learner: its rapid change, its large vocabulary, and the fact that it reflects many cultures. Understanding grammar and memorizing vocabulary is never enough. Instead, one must experience the language to learn its "personality." This book tries to teach the "soul" of English in order to acculturate; it is difficult due to vocabulary and sophisticated ideas, but as long as you can grasp the overall ideas you should do well.

first heading / *second and third headings* / *fourth heading* / *final heading*

Notice that sentence #1 establishes English as an international language, sentence #2 enumerates the key problems learning English, including the problem of language reflecting culture, sentences #3 and #4 discuss grammar versus a language "personality," and the final sentence presents the challenge. From this you can see that the one section the above summary leaves out is the section on "book divisions."

At this point the writer should go back to the original to include one more sentence:

> This text will teach vocabulary, organization, logic, and argumentation.

At the same time, the writer could try to condense even more, using parallelism and subordination. What makes the following summary even better?

> Since English is an international language, studying it will be very important for the traveler or the professional (especially in science or technology), no matter what the home country or occupation. However, English's large and rapidly changing vocabulary and its cultural dimensions make it difficult to learn. Instead of merely understanding grammar and memorizing vocabulary, students must experience the language to learn its "personality." This book tries to acculturate through sections on organization, logic, and argumentation; it has difficult vocabulary and sophisticated ideas, but as long as students can grasp the overall ideas they will succeed.

This new version is shorter and more compact; it has fewer sentences. It includes information on <u>all</u> of the sections indicated by the headings. It changes the sentence structure to be more in the summarizer's own words. It is also consistent about pronoun reference. The first version sometimes uses *you*, sometimes *one*. This version relies just on *students...they*. However, will future readers know which book the phrase *this book* refers to? If not, the title of the book and the author's name should be included in the summary.

In many textbooks, the last paragraph of a chapter summarizes the key information. Sometimes, in fact, it introduces such information with a heading *Summary* followed by a numbered list; at other times the summary is introduced with such words or phrases as *In sum, To sum up, In summary, To summarize, Overall, then,* or even *In conclusion.* Always look for such signaling phrases as you read. In this textbook, where could you find a summary of the chapters? Where is the summary of this chapter?

How to Suggest the Scope of the Original

A good summary should provide enough information to allow the reader to grasp the essence of the original article. A good way to make sure your summary does this is to reread it and ask questions raised by the summary which might be answered by important information in the original essay. For example, the following summary of an essay on market targeting could suggest questions that you expect the essay to answer:

> According to Philip Kolter, in his chapter on "Market Targeting" in *Marketing Essentials*, undifferentiated marketing, which focuses on common consumer needs, goes after the whole market through mass distribution and mass advertising. It is economical, but intensely competitive and hence perhaps less profitable. Differentiated marketing, which operates in several market segments with separate offers to each, aims for higher sales, a stronger position in each segment, and repeat purchasing, while concentrated marketing, which goes after a large share of one or a few submarkets, is best for limited company resources. It requires specialized knowledge and specialized approaches, and hence may involve higher risks.

Questions you might ask are:

> How does undifferentiated marketing appeal to the whole market? What makes it economical? competitive? less profitable? What kind of market segments does differentiated marketing operate in? Why are higher sales and repeat

---

- ### EXERCISE 19.1: SUMMARIZING TEXTS

  Now that you understand the method, select a section of any textbook and summarize the information under the heading. Doing so is a good way to make sure you have really understood your readings; it is also a good way to prepare for pop quizzes or for major examinations. By translating such material into your own words, you make it a part of your own thinking and therefore will remember it more easily.

purchasing so important to its success? Why is concentrated marketing best for limited company resources? What specialized knowledge and specialized approaches does it involve? What higher risks might it involve?

These questions could lead to an expansion and improvement of the initial summary. They are also a good way to prepare for an examination on the materials. First summarize; then turn the summary into potential examination questions.

How to Avoid Plagiarism

Writing summaries can easily lead to *plagiarism* if you are not careful, and plagiarism is a major concern in American colleges and universities. Many students think plagiarism means copying the exact words of someone else's paper, lab report, homework, or printed ideas, without giving credit. However, the most common form of plagiarism is using some of the words or ideas of an author without giving credit. <u>Even if everything you say is in your own words, but you have gotten the idea from a writer, you must give credit or be guilty of plagiarism.</u> Plagiarism means the appropriation of written materials, either word for word or in substance (<u>even if in your own words</u>), from the writings of another, and the incorporation of those passages as your own in written work offered for credit or for publication.

Written work offered for credit must consist of your own ideas in your own words; if not, you must give careful and proper credit to the original author by the use of internal citations, quotation marks, foot- or endnotes, or other explanatory inserts. Otherwise, American academic and legal custom imposes serious penalties, even if the plagiarism occurs through carelessness or ignorance. Plagiarism can result in an *F* or a *zero* on a paper, an *F* in a course, or even expulsion from your university. In publishing and business it can be punished by large fines and the ruin of a professional reputation.

Following the simple general rules listed below will help you avoid any form of plagiarism.

1. **Direct Quotation**: When you use the exact words of an author, every quoted word must be placed within quotation marks ("in this manner"), and each quoted passage must have attached to it an endnote or footnote reference number or a parenthetical citation within your essay with the author's last name and the page number used, like this (Nesmith: 32), or simply the page number (32) if the author's name appears in your sentence. Endnotes and footnotes are described in #4 below.

2. **Indirect Quotation:** When summarizing or paraphrasing the words of an author consulted, give an exact endnote or footnote reference to each sentence which includes summarized material. Introduce all summaries with internal citation: phrases such as *According to Jones, As Black says, Dr. Smith, Professor of English at Georgetown University, notes that....*

3. **General Acknowledgment of Indebtedness:** When general use is made of the thoughts, ideas, or information in another person's work, always attach an endnote or footnote number to the place in your paper where indebtedness occurs. If indebtedness occurs in several successive paragraphs, state that fact in your foot- or endnotes. For example, an endnote might read, *This entire paragraph and the two which follow are based in general on Nesmith's work.*

4. **Footnote, Endnote or Internal Citation Form:** Every footnote, endnote, or internal citation must identify the source used and

---

• **EXERCISE 19.2: TURNING SUMMARIES INTO QUESTIONS**

Turn your summary written for the Exercise 19.1 into a series of questions that you might use to study for an exam on that section of the text.

give the page on which the borrowed material may be found. Footnote or endnote references include the author's name, the title of the book or article, the name of the magazine or journal, the place of publication and publisher of a book, the date of publication of the book or magazine, and the page used (not the total pages of the book or article). The footnote does so at the bottom of the page where the reference occurs; the endnote does so in a unit at the end of the paper; the internal citation appears in the text in parentheses after the borrowed material.

5. **Bibliography:** Append to each piece of written work you submit a complete list of all authorities which have been consulted, alphabetized by last names, and with the last name first, <u>even if no specific reference is made to them in the body of your paper</u>. This list should include works read as background material. It may also include books, periodicals, encyclopedias, government documents, teacher's handouts, interviews, etc. Sometimes it may be subdivided into Primary Sources (original works like novels, autobiographies or letters; for example, Shakespeare's *Macbeth*) and Secondary Sources (works about original works; for example, *Essays in Shakespearean Criticism*), or, at the direction of your instructor, Works Quoted and Works Consulted.

Use a Bibliography

The form used in a bibliography varies from field to field, so you must always ask your professors for advice about the proper format. However, if you follow the one suggested here, you will rarely get into trouble about sources. If you cite a book, the following arrangement is best:

Cawelti, John L. and Bruce Rosenberg. <u>The Spy Story</u>. New York: Houghton Mifflin, 1987. [This book has two authors so the first one has last name and first name reversed while the second one is in normal order of first name (Bruce) followed by last name (Rosenberg).]

McDuggan, Ray. "Composition Regulations," *Essays for Analysis*. Ed. T. J. Su. Boston: Allyn and Bacon, 1995. 53-56. [This is an essay in a collection of essays compiled by editor T.J. Su.]

The form for a journal or newspaper article differs from that of books and is as follows:

Banks, R. Jeff, and Harvey D. Dawson. "The Quiller Report." *The Mystery Fancier* 4 (Jan/Feb. 1980):8-11. [journal entry: issue number 4, pages 8 through 11]

Martin, Debi. "Tapping New Talents." A*ustin American-Statesman* (December 31, 1989): E1 & E12. [newspaper entry: section E, pages 1 and 12]

The form for recording an interview varies, but the following gives all the basic information.

Jones, James. Author and novelist. Interviewed in New York City on December 1, 1959.

Sample Bibliography

Gabriella, Tina. Reference librarian at Tennessee State University. Interviewed October 10, 1989.

Harragan, Betty L. "Dear Betty Harragan". <u>Working Woman</u>, 14, April, 1989:12-17.

Hopke, William E. Ed. <u>The Encyclopedia of Careers and Vocational Guidance</u>, II. Chicago, Illinois: J. G. Ferguson Publishing Company, 1987.

Martin, Murry S. <u>Issues in Personnel Management in Academic Libraries</u>. Greenwich, England: JAI Press:, 1981.

<u>Occupational Outlook Handbook</u>. Washington, D.C.: U.S. Department of Labor, Bureau of Labor Statistics, 1989. [When no author is listed, alphabetize by first letter of the title]

Sullivan, Peggy. <u>Opportunities in Library and Information Science</u>. Louisville: Vocational Guidance Manuals, 1977.

Use Footnotes or Endnotes

Whereas the bibliography entry begins with the author's last name at the far left-hand margin, followed by a comma, the author's first name, middle name or middle initial, and a period, the foot- or endnote entry begins with the author's first name or first initial followed by middle and last name, indented from the left-hand margin. Where the bibliography uses periods, the endnotes use commas. Where the bibliography uses parentheses for articles only, the endnotes use them to contain the publication information for books as well. Bibliography entries are listed alphabetically, but endnotes are listed consecutively, with the first designated number [1] and the rest in the numerical order that follows. After the complete bibliographical information has been given once, only a short version is needed thereafter. Use Ibid. if one entry is immediately repeated; use a last name and page number if the new entry differs from the previous source. There may be many more endnotes than bibliographic entries because the bibliography has only one entry for each source, while the endnotes repeat entries every time borrowed information appears in the text. Where the bibliography indents the second line, the endnote indents the first and returns to margin on the second, as in the following examples. Note that footnotes follow the same form but appear at the bottom of the page where the reference occurs.

Sample Endnotes

[1]William E. Hopke, ed., The Encyclopedia of Careers and Vocational Guidance, II (Chicago, Illinois: J. G. Ferguson Publishing Company, 1987): 198. [Notice that this is volume 2 and that Hopke is the editor, not the author.]

[2]Ibid. [from Ibidem which means "the same", so this is from Hopke; if the page number were different, the number would need to be added: "Ibid.: 6."]

[3]Occupational Outlook Handbook (Washington, D.C.: U.S. Department of Labor, Bureau of Labor Statistics:, 1989): 120. [There is no author listed in this book]

[4]Murry S. Martin, Issues in Personnel Management in Academic Libraries (Greenwich, England: JAI Press:, 1981): 185.

[5]Peggy Sullivan, Opportunities in Library and Information Science (Louisville: Vocational Guidance Manuals, 1977): 24.

[6]Martin: 183-185. [This entry refers back to the information in endnote #4]

[7]Occupational Outlook Handbook: 123. [This entry refers back to the information in endnote #3]

Use Internal Citation

To save time and space, many academic fields allow students to use a shorthand version of endnote documentation. Instead of endnotes, you put in parentheses at the end of the sentence in which source information is incorporated: the author's last name, a colon, and the page number (Martin: 183). If there is no author, then a short version of the title is used (*Occupational*: 123). Also use a short version of the title if you refer to a second book by the same author: (Martin, *Recent Management Issues*: 422). If the author or title is mentioned in a sentence in the text, then only a page number is placed in parentheses (23).

Compare the following example with the above endnotes. Notice how much simpler and easier this approach is. Notice too the other internal strategies for crediting the source.

In his essay "Graceland," Arthur Goldman, a famous journalist, attacks Elvis as behaving "like so many boy-men": dining informally at a coffee table, watching football games on TV with "the Guys", and lounging in oversized furniture (a "huge sofa" and "oversized armchairs"). (52) Such furnishings, he notes, have an adolescent flavor, particularly an interest in childhood toys: chairs with "huge pawlike armrests," a

Identification information: title, author, appositive, topic idea.

Quoted supportive information; source: page citation

reminder of topic idea followed by

suite like "the Three Bears watching TV," an "animalistic sofa." (53) Goldman's phrase "the Guys," used throughout his text for Elvis's companions in such activities, further suggests the adolescent male gangs of the teenage years.

supportive information; citation;

reminder of source

reminder of topic idea

Use Direct Quotations

Incorporating quotations into your text is a skill that can only be acquired by practice. Nevertheless, it is a skill necessary for all writers. It is very important to learn how to put information into your own words, to digest it, and to use it to build the muscles of your paper. Too often a student is tempted to think, "It sounds much better as it is," and as a consequence to use the language of a source in his own work. The result is teacher comments like the following: "I cannot give you credit for this paper; this does not sound like your writing. What is your source?" The following examples give the source materials, followed by a good way to use these borrowed materials in a paper. The method of giving credit is by internal citation.

1. **Source:** "Probably the most important personal trait necessary for success in the hotel industry is the ability to get along with all kinds of people under all situations." (p. 11)

   "But it does mean that you must be broadminded, tolerant, understanding and humane." (p. 11)

   "The interviewer is looking for a level-headed, self-controlled, pliable personality. He or she is looking for a person who can adapt to changing situations and get along with different kinds of people." (p. 34)

   Text of Paper: In *Opportunities in Hotel and Motel Management*, Shepard Henkin argues that being able to get along "with all kinds of people under all situations" is probably the key trait requisite for success in the field. (11) He adds that this means being "broadminded, tolerant, understanding and humane." In a later section on interviews he adds that being "level-headed" and "self-controlled" helps one to "adapt to changing situations and get along with different kinds of people." (34)

2. **Source:** "This latter requirement is not a catch-all phrase but embodies the ability to listen attentively, have a ready smile, and maintain a reserved manner." (p. 18)

   "A good general educational background will

shape you into a well-rounded person and give you the ability to meet people from all walks of life confidently and intelligently." (p. 18)

   Text of Paper: Among the social traits Henkin lists as important are an "ability to listen attentively," "a ready smile," and "a reserved manner." (18) These, he believes, help one communicate a willingness to be of service but also a cool competence. Later he suggests that a good education helps prepare one socially, making one well-rounded and therefore able to meet diverse people "confidently and intelligently."(18)

3. **Source:** "I would list attention to detail. Very often I find that the most vehement complaints from patrons are due to seemingly insignificant omissions on the part of staff members." (p. 29)

   Text of Paper: Preston Tisch, president of Loews Hotels, believes that "attention to detail" is vital to success in the hotel business, because it is the "seemingly insignificant" omission that disturbs patrons most. (29)

4. **Source:** "As the operating head of the hotel, the resident manager also participates in final negotiations with labor unions or employee groups after initial discussions and agreements have been prepared by the employee relations department of the hotel…. the overall responsibility of the resident manager is to see to it that the guests are satisfied and that the hotel is operated as cleanly and as profitably as possible." (p. 89)

   Text of Paper: A good manager also needs an ability to talk easily with and to get along with people from all social levels, because, says Tisch, he is the one who participates in negotiations with labor unions or employee groups; he has to deal with department heads; and he has to make sure "the guests are satisfied" and the hotel workers are organized, neat, and courteous. In other words, according to Tisch, whether or not a hotel is profitable depends very much on the social skills of the manager. (89)

The Goldman paragraph is also a good model for using direct and indirect quotations because it has a careful mix of both.

Notice the mixture of indirect and direct quotation in this passage.

The pattern is to identify who says what and with what authority, to quote only the most striking phrases and to put the rest into your own words, to follow a quote with an explanation, and to end with a summary in your own words: This last point is important. Never leave a quote hanging at the end of a paragraph or discussion.

Use Indirect Quotations

When writing a paper, particularly a longer paper or one involving persuasion or analysis, it is some-times necessary to summarize the key ideas or arguments of an article or a book in the body of your paper. If you do so, it is very important to make absolutely clear the difference between what you are saying and what the authors whose ideas you are summarizing have said.

Words and phrases like the following introduce borrowed material in a paper and indicate a need to credit a source:

- ## EXERCISE 19.3: ADDING QUOTATION MARKS

Decide whether the following statements require quotation marks, and, if they do, add them. If necessary, capitalize.

Example: 1. Benjamin Franklin, the famous eighteenth-century American diplomat, patriot and wit, once remarked: in this world nothing is certain but death and taxes.

Answer: Benjamin Franklin, the famous eighteenth-century American diplomat, patriot and wit, once remarked: "In this world nothing is certain but death and taxes." (capitalization + quotation marks)

Example: 2. Benjamin Franklin, the famous eighteenth-century American diplomat, patriot and wit, once remarked that life's only certainties are death and taxes.

Answer: Benjamin Franklin, the famous eighteenth-century American diplomat, patriot and wit, once remarked that life's only certainties are "death and taxes." (only three quoted words, the rest is indirect)

1. Winston Churchill, England's famous wartime prime minister, told the British people: I have nothing to offer but blood, toil, tears, and sweat.

2. Churchill, on another occasion, remarked, Russia is a riddle wrapped in a mystery inside of an enigma.

3. Churchill is famous for having called Russia a riddle, a mystery, and an enigma.

4. Alexander Pope warned that a little learning could be very dangerous.

5. Blaise Pascal is famous for having said, if the nose of Cleopatra had been shorter, the whole face of the earth would have been changed.

6. Aristotle remarked, poverty is the parent of revolution and crime.

7. Aristotle, the famous Greek philosopher and student of Plato, noted, poverty is the parent of revolution and crime.

8. Aristotle, the famous Greek philosopher and student of Plato, believed that poverty was the parent of revolution and crime.

9. Aristotle, the famous Greek philosopher and student of Plato, felt that poverty led to revolution and crime.

10. Aristotle, the famous Greek philosopher and student of Plato, called poverty the parent of revolution and crime, by which he meant that poverty produced rebels and criminals.

text: believes, comments, notes, observes, points out, says, states, tells us, remarks, reports

Terms calling into question an author's argument: alleges, asserts, claims, contends, maintains

Terms indicating an interpretation of a statement: contends, implies, suggests

Terms indicating agreement with author's argument: affirms, attests, confirms, reminds us, reveals, stresses

Follow-up terms for further statements: adds, continues, develops, elaborates, expands, goes on to say

Terms indicating different authorial activities: advises, articulates, captures, commands, conveys, credits, delineates, describes, details, discloses, divulges, encourages, enumerates, examines, expresses, explores, is concerned with, indicates, itemizes, lists, narrates, portrays, promotes, records, recounts, relates, requires, retells, shares with us, specifies, speaks to, summarizes, urges, views, voices

The following paragraph uses a summary of a book to support its key idea. The words that make clear who says what are in italics. What does the summary add to the paragraph? How would the paragraph be different without it? In turn, how would this summary be different without the underlined sections?

A law school graduate might find that studying law and practicing law are very different. Upon graduating, he might not be able to pass the bar examination, and even if he does, he might find that it is impossible to start his own practice and that getting into a good firm might be difficult. Even if he gets into a good firm he might have to do all the work no one else wants to do. In their introduction to _Nonlegal Careers for Lawyers in the Private Sector,_ authors Francis Uthy and Gary Munneke inform us that many law students

graduate feeling that traditional law practice isn't what they really want but aren't familiar with available alternatives—from corporation president to sportscasters' advisor. The authors illustrate the magic of a legal education and note three basic skills they believe are acquired only in law school, skills fundamental to obtaining an entry into the business world: 1) ease in dealing with legal terminology and legal concepts, 2) ability to analyze facts, 3) ability to persuade others to one's conclusions. They conclude that law students considering alternative careers have a number of choices open to them. In other words, studying law does not limit a law student to being a lawyer.

Notice that the first three sentences contain the ideas of the writer and that the summary of the Uthy/Munneke book is meant to lend strength and authoritative support to those ideas. Ideas from the book are expressed in the writers' own words, but the writer is careful to give credit to the source through such phrases as: _In their introduction to Nonlegal Careers for Lawyers in the Private Sector, authors Francis Uthy and Gary Munneke inform us, the authors illustrate... and note, they believe,_ and _they conclude...._" Notice too that the selection ends with Uthy and Munneke's own summation followed by a personal conclusion, not one from the source.

It is a good idea to always look back at an original after summarizing it to make sure you have used quotation marks whenever you have used the exact words of the summarized passage. As previously noted, careful writers will usually include a bibliographical list of sources at the end of their paper and some sort of internal reference within the paper so that they are not guilty of plagiarism.

- ## EXERCISE 19.4: INDIRECT QUOTATIONS

Directions:

A. Put the following quotations into a single sentence format with an introductory statement that identifies who is being quoted; add a direct quotation with quotation marks and final citation.

B. Then change it to an indirect quotation that moves away from the original words of the writers and communicates the key idea as clearly and as briefly as possible in your own words.

C. Write a bibliographical entry to accompany this set of quotations.

> *Note:* You might wish to refer to the list of introductory terms given on page 434.

> *Example:* Julia Chang Bloch/Shanghai-born U.S. diplomat/ "Hawaii is already on its way to becoming the intellectual capital of the Pacific for business, politics, research, education and training."/ *Vis a´ Vis* / March 1990/ "Hawaii the Pacific Link" by Bill Wood/ page 127.

> ### *is changed to*

> *Direct:* Shanghai-born U.S. diplomat Julia Chang Bloch asserts proudly, "Hawaii is already on its way to becoming the intellectual capital of the Pacific for business, politics, research, education, and training." (Wood:127)

> *Indirect:* Shanghai-born U.S. diplomat Julia Chang Bloch argues that Hawaii is fast becoming the Pacific's intellectual and business capital. (Wood:127)

Bibliographical Entry:

Wood, Bill. "Hawaii the Pacific Link." *Vis a´ Vis* (March 1990):137.

1. Norman Pearlstine/a lawyer/a journalist/managing editor of the *Wall Street Journal* /"America now has more than 750,000 lawyers and some 65 percent of them make more than $50,000 a year."/*Vis a´ Vis*/March 1990/"Wall Street Journalist: Norman Pearlstine" by Dan Carlinsky/page 74.

2. Jessica Tandy/famous actress who played Miss Daisy in *Driving Miss Daisy*/"Acting is not a creative process, it's an interpretive one. You're not making it up; the author has made it up, and it's your duty to find everything that's in that script and interpret it." /*Vis a´ Vis* / March 1990/"Triumphant Miss Daisy: Jessica Tandy" by Wilbur Mann/ page 72.

3. Thomas Krens/described as the Clint Eastwood of museum directors/head of the Guggenheim Foundation/"The Great Guggenheim shows of the past, such as the Kandinsky and Beuys, defined the way the work of a given artist is understood in the world. That's what I'd like to do."/*Vis a´ Vis*/March 1990/"Innovator at the Guggenheim" by Thomas Connors/ page 76.

4. "Kren speaks of museums as 'industry' and of art itself as 'product'."/*Vis a´ Vis*/March 1990/"Innovator at the Guggenheim" by Thomas Connors/ page 76.

5. James Michener/Pulitzer prize-winning author of numerous books, particularly about the South Pacific/author of *Hawaii*/"I could plot three good novels on this cruise if I wanted to. By the time writers are 70 or 80, we have a wealth of material to draw on. Ideas boom up. There are about 30 books I'd like to write. It takes me three years to

write one, so I figure I'll be 173 when I'm finished."/*Vis a' Vis*/ March 1990/ "Worldly Writer: James Michener" by Nan Birmingham/page 80.

6. Ben Spiegel/professional photographer specialized in music and musicians/"You can't photograph the music but you can show its intensity."/*Vis a' Vis*/March 1990/"Ben Spiegel: Putting Music on Film"/by Margo Hammond/page 82.

7. B. J. Williams/director of the Fitness & Sports Medicine Institute at the Aspen Club in Aspen, Colorado/"Cross-country skiing is one of the most aerobic forms of exercise, combining the fitness benefits of running and biking."/*Vis a' Vis*/ March 1990/ "Fitness on the Run: Cross-country Skiing in Colorado's Backcountry" by Robert Wurmstedt/page 91.

8. Austin Fitts/the first woman partner at the firm of Dillon, Read/ "It won't be long now before being a woman is completely a nonissue.... Because all these men in their fifties who've been running things for years... almost every one of them has a young, ambitious daughter, maybe in college, maybe already in business school."/*Vis a' Vis*/ March 1990/"Working Women: Two Views" by Kate Jennings/page 102.

9. Michael Caine/British actor/appeared in some 70 motion pictures/recognized worldwide for his versatility and for the consistency of his excellence/author of *Acting in Film: An Actor's Take on Movie Making*/"The greatest advice I can give to someone who wants to act in movies is listen and react. Movie actors earn their living and learn their craft through listening and reacting. I notice that American actors always try to cut down on their dialogue.... less is more." John Wayne advised Caine: "talk low, talk slow and don't say much."/"Michael Caine on Acting" by Lloyd Shearer/*Parade Magazine* /August 12, 1990/page 21.

10. Susan Butcher/four-time winner of the 1,200-mile Sled Dog race from Anchorage to Nome, Alaska—she once described it as "the ultimate experience" of wilderness life/ "The greater reward, the real goal for me is the northern magic that lights up my life even on the loneliest trail.... A lot of little things make Alaska come alive: When your sled rounds a curve, for example, and you see a mother moose guarding its young. Or you pause at night on a nameless lake 100 miles from nowhere and gaze at the stars and drink in the silence. Or you sit on a hill and look as far as you can forward and backward and all you see is a ribbon of trail, and then you look to one side and realize no one has ever been there before."/*Vis a' Vis*/March 1990/"Adventurous Alaska" by Susan Butcher/pages 109/112.

Turning Summary into Analysis

While summary is clearly essential in much academic work, it may sometimes be seen as slavishly "parroting" a source with no critical understanding or evaluation being applied. In such cases the student receives comments such as "Go beyond summary!" or "What do you think?", the point being that simply quoting a source does little to show independent thought or judgment. In college classes it is often more effective to be on the attack, to find the weaknesses or loopholes in the arguments of your sources rather than merely summarizing them (unless of course the assignment is merely to summarize). The underlined sections call attention to the fact that this paper mainly summarizes an article by Marcia Peoples Halio about the effects of word processing on the quality of writing, without the necessary skeptical evaluation of its argument.

Marcia Peoples Halio, in her essay, "Student Writing: Can the Machine Maim the Message?", claims that some computer philosophies (specifically that of the Macintosh) are intrinsically destructive to writing maturity.

For many years now the basic medium for composition writing has been the handwritten or typed form, both media requiring a relative amount of both time and energy. Halio argues that this expenditure of time and energy has always, to some degree, produced frustration and what she calls "deep blues," but she also argues that these blues have also given writers a chance to rethink and reorganize their ideas in an intellectual and creative manner. She believes that the basic structure and form have remained constant, but that word processors have brought what some educators call a disturbing change in the overall clarity and level of written work. In fact, she points out that a number of articles indicate that students using the Macintosh word processing program [a program widely adopted by universities because of its "friendliness"] are more inclined to use simpler writing structures than students using the IBM. According to her, the only point where Macintosh writers score high is in "gilding" [making the text look good], because the Mac WP program, with all its fun graphics and format options, allows students to gloss their writings with flashy-looking features of the sort previously to be found only in magazines. Halio claims that too often this "flashy look" is all there is to their writing: form and flash without substance. Teachers who don't read carefully or who are accustomed to judging superficially may take this "flash" to indicate content that is not really there. According to Halio, writing software alone cannot improve writing skills, and it may at times distract the student from his real goal: to write clearly and effectively.

Marcia Halio is sad to find that even with statistics against it, the trend is towards the Macintosh style of word processing, so much so that IBM will begin marketing its OS/2 line operating system that mimics the Mac menu-driven software. She believes an IBM word processing program ultimately leads to more mature, better organized papers simply because the system itself requires the user to think out actions step by step and to treat writing assignments with attention and care. In other words, she argues that a simple tool will produce a simple product and a more complicated tool will produce a more complicated product.

In conclusion, Ms. Halio hopes that, in the future, educators will consider the power of the medium to affect results and will choose a system that requires students to apply the scrutiny and the effort that any serious writer must give to produce a good final paper. I personally have written better papers on the IBM system than I did on the Mac system, but whether this is because of maturity, improved language skills, or the system itself is not provable.

Only the last sentence of the paper provides the writer's view, and it is highly tentative; the rest of the paper is summary. However, adding a few sentences to the above will transform it from simple summary to a persuasive critique that questions Halio's argument. For example, to the opening paragraph you might add a thesis qualifier:

However, she fails to consider the practical classroom fact that students write more and revise more on any type of computer than they do on handwritten or even typed papers.

Such a beginning tells readers that you will not just repeat the ideas of your source. Then, to the sentence *In other words, she argues that a more complicated tool will produce a more complicated product*, you might add the criticism,

—surely a questionable assertion since it is the craftsman, not the tool, that ultimately determines the end product.

Later, just before the conclusion, you might add:

What she ignores in all this is the important role of the teacher in judging the product and in guiding students to use it well. Machines are tools, not magic. Tools must be properly used to produce results. It is true that a good craftsman can overcome difficulties to create; but it is also true that a good craftsman will still create well if he has good tools and a good situation for creativity.

Such criticism would allow you to modify the original's concluding praise for Ms. Halio's call for serious thought in writing, arguing instead that,

rather than preventing serious thought, the extras on the Mac WP free the writer's mind from worries about format and appearance so she can concentrate instead on turning out a good composition

and that

"User-friendly" means that people who would never normally use computers might be tempted to take advantage of the ease of Mac WP and, as a result, through cutting and pasting and spelling checks, will learn to struggle with drafts to produce better final products rather than spending their time copying and recopying first drafts.

Such additions reflect analysis rather than simple summary, so that you both report Halio's argument and make your own.

• EXERCISE 19.5: USING AUTHORITY EFFECTIVELY

Imitate the following two sentence patterns for incorporating authorities into your discussion: the one for disagreeing with authority, the other for agreeing. Vary your vocabulary by referring to the list in "Indirect Quotations" on page 434.

> *Source:* Jones calls *Scarface* a "failed and limited depiction of a second-rate character." (*Magill's Survey of Cinema*)
>
> *Agreement:* As Jones in *Magill's Survey of Cinema* confirms, *Scarface* is a "failed and limited depiction of a second-rate character."
>
> *Disagreement:* Although Jones in *Magill's Survey of Cinema* claims *Scarface* is a "failed and limited depiction of a second-rate character," the film has strengths which are obvious to the careful viewer. First, Al Pacino's performance is not "failed," but in fact is a carefully conceived, realistic depiction of an overreacher.

Notice the slight changes in verbs, with "claims" suggesting disagreement with the quoted authority and "confirms" suggesting agreement. Note too that the pattern is more effective if the writer's view takes the main clause and the authority, the subordinate clause.

1. *Source:* "We must… see drug abuse as a medical and social problem, with medical and social solutions, rather than as a target for 'an all-out war…'."—Eric Scigliano, "Drugs: Could Legalization Work?"

Agreement: _____

_____

Disagreement: _____

_____

2. *Source:* In "What a Cigarette Packs in Radiation," Mark S. Boguski says, "more emphasis should be placed on the real and present dangers of cigarette smoking, which, according to the U.S. Surgeon General, will kill 129,000 Americans in 1982 and cause significant disability in many times this number."

Agreement: _____

_____

Disagreement: _____

_____

3. *Source:* "I think that the great majority of professors agree that grading hinders teaching and creates a bad spirit, going as far as cheating and plagiarizing." —Paul Goodman, "A Proposal to Abolish Grading"

Agreement: _____

_____

Disagreement: _____

_____

4. *Source:* "…for crimes involving the deliberate and inexcusable taking of human life, by men openly defiant of all civilized order—for such crimes it [capital punishment] seems, to nine men out of ten, a just and proper punishment."—H.L. Mencken, "The Penalty of Death"

Agreement: _____

_____

Disagreement: _____

_____

Final Checklist

☐ Is your summary in your own words as much as possible? Have you used the vocabulary of the original only if there is no other way to express the idea (as in scientific words with no synonyms)?

☐ Have you broken long quotations up into indirect quotations and short quoted phrases?

☐ Have you cited the author and title somewhere at the head of the summary?

☐ Does your summary capture the tone and point of view, the "spirit" of the original? The order and arrangement of ideas may vary as long as the essential points are included.

☐ Have you taken advantage of subordination and parallelism as important tools to help compact, emphasize and interrelate ideas?

☐ Have you left out examples and details except those vital to the idea?

☐ Have you summarized a paragraph in a sentence (the topic sentence of the original), and an article in as many sentences as there are original paragraphs (original thesis sentence followed by supportive topic sentences)? Have you used sentence combining to reduce the summary even more?

☐ Have you thoroughly documented your sources through internal citations, foot- or endnotes, and bibliography to avoid plagiarism?

☐ Since different academic fields use different forms, have you found out what pattern of documentation your professors or your discipline prefers?

•• Writing Assignments

A. An important part of any writing, and of summarizing in particular, is cutting out words unnecessary to meaning. Often we are blind to filler words, but learning to recognize and eliminate them through changes in sentence patterns is vital to improving writing and to summarizing more effectively. In the following exercise, reduce the words in the passages to the recommended number—without losing vital ideas or information.

Example:

The article on "Buying a Bike" says that it seems necessary for us to have a car in American society. I keenly realize how much I need a bike to spend time comfortably. The article says that whenever we go to the department store, beauty salon, hospital and so on, we feel that if we have a car, it will be better. But a car is not only expensive, but it also means that we need a driver's license, parking area, and expenses to keep it, says the writer. This is why he believes that a bicycle is a better choice of transportation. **103 words**

Reduced to:

"Buying a Bike" argues that, although a car might seem necessary in America for business and for pleasure, it is not only expensive, but also necessitates a driver's license, a parking space, and maintenance expenses. A bicycle does not. **39 words**

1. The brutal killing or assassination of one of the most kindly presidents that America had ever or has ever had took place on April 14, 1865. The name of the president who was killed was Abraham Lincoln. He was a very humane president. His murder was most probably the result of a good many of his qualities and of acts that are too many to list. Some of the qualities that had made him enemies included his fame and intelligence. His sensitivity to human rights in general was another important factor in his having enemies. Some people were probably really bothered by the idea that a person who was only a hick, backwoods country farmer had become the president of the United States; they were prejudiced toward the idea that class and sophistication and money were important to political success and a success story that demonstrated the chance for someone to go from rags to riches disturbed them. However, it was probably most particularly his stand on the issue of the rights of the black slaves who were used on plantations in the South that made his killer decide to kill him. In fact, what the assassin John Wilkes Booth let people know that he found so irritating was the fact that the Emancipation Proclamation delivered by Lincoln in order to officially and legally free the slaves all over the country in both the North and the South had proclaimed their humanity and said that they were officially human so that not one of them could any longer be called "animal stock" or "possessions." It was this stand on human rights in regards to the slave issue in particular that led to his death.

Reduce to about 120 words.

2. A number of factors are responsible for explaining the success of the first nonstop flight across the Atlantic. This initial and historic flight was made by Charles Lindbergh. Charles Lindbergh's experience was partly responsible for his success. The care that he took certainly was a major factor in his success but one can never forget the important role played by luck even though it seems like it is something no one has control over. In the very first place, the famous pilot Charles Lindbergh had had lots of experience with flying and with planes. He had worked as an airplane mechanic. He had also done some designs of airplanes. He had done aerial navigating and he had also flown as a pilot for many years. Therefore, there is not any doubt that he had wide experience in the field of aircraft. He had even flown the particular plane he would use for his historic

flight. As a result, he knew his plane and its capacity, both from the inside and from the outside. Furthermore, it was this type of plane that he had flown on runs to deliver the mail. Also, it was this type of plane that he had used when he had done acrobatics in the air. Such acrobatics included the action of flying through the doors of a barn. In other words, it is clear that he had invaluable experience and that this experience was in flying in difficult circumstances. More importantly for the purposes of his oceanic flight, it is recorded that he himself had selected his basic plane with great care and then he had redesigned that plane. The aspects of the designing included the fact that he added a wingspan that was longer, landing gear that was stronger, and a fuel capacity that was larger. He did all of these things because he knew that the flight that he would be making across the ocean would not only be long but it would also be difficult. Finally, he had something that others before him had not had and that was, nonetheless, very important to success in a transatlantic voyage and that was good luck with both the wind conditions and with the conditions of the weather. It was all of these reasons together that explain why the man who was called "Lucky Lindy" after his lucky flight succeeded where all the other pilots who had tried before him had not.

Reduce to about 130 words.

3. One can find an interesting sight in the Black Hills of the state of South Dakota. It is there on the granite face of Mount Rushmore, which is 6000 feet high, that one can find carved the faces of four American Presidents. The four American Presidents are carved in dimensions that were meant by the artists who did the work to be symbolic of the greatness that these men achieved during their presidencies. It is because these presidents upheld the rights and dignities of the common man that they are made immortal and are memorialized in this way. It is typically and boldly American to have such a size and and such a scope (though Russians do this too). Mount Rushmore uses its portraits of these likenesses of these heroes to portray the beginnings and trials of the Nation. Its focus is on the actions and men and events during its first century and a quarter. There is first of all George Washington. He is famous for being a revolutionary soldier and also for being the first president that his nation had. Because he led the battles against the British and was our first president, it is his role in the carving to represent the fight that was fought for liberty and to also represent the birth of the Republic. There is Thomas Jefferson, who was known then and is remembered today as an innovative thinker. It is he who was so concerned with justice, humanity, and God-given rights. Therefore, on the mountain carving, it is he who is the expression of the political philosophy of this country. There is Abraham Lincoln, who , as we all know, was the president during the Civil War. He is the one who sought to heal the nation's wounds. He did this by trying to reunite the opposing factions which were represented by the North and by the South and also by the black people and by the white race. It is for these attempts that in the carving he embodies the preservation of the Union of the American States. There is Theodore Roosevelt, who is famous for being tough and for being an imperialist. He was one of those hardy rough riders. He has been used by the artists to depict some qualities of the nation as it is today. These qualities are the nation's expansion and also its conservation.

Reduce to about 120 words.

B. Write the movie critique explained in the writing assignment section at the end of Chapter 3. Then use the *New York Times Film Index*, *Magill's Survey of Cinema*, the *Reader's Guide to Periodicals*, or your library's computer system to find three or four reviews of your chosen film. If the reviews support your claims, use them to provide authoritative support; if you disagree with the reviews, criticize their comments through your own analysis. Be sure to include internal citations and a bibliography.

C. Select any one of the argumentative topics from Chapter 17 (euthanasia, capital punishment, etc.) and find two articles on each side of the issue. Use these to strengthen your own paper on the subject.

D. Take any of the papers written this semester and find authoritative support that will help you expand a paper in revision and lend greater authority or interest to your topic. For example, even a review of a local restaurant could be supported by local newspaper articles or by quotations from people who have eaten there.

Passages to Summarize

Summarize the following passages. Remember: the shorter, the better, as long as you do not lose any key ideas. Vary your vocabulary and find the precise word which summarizes what the author is doing. Include proper citation.

Communication for Business and the Professions

Your success in your career… will depend… upon your ability to communicate, perhaps more… than upon any other ability. You will spend far more time communicating than performing all other aspects of your job. As you move up the ladder of responsibility, communication will become even more important. Your lack of skill in communicating can keep your employment responsibilities at a lower level than they would be otherwise.

In addition to… vocational and professional benefits… from excellent written and oral communication, your personal and social life is vitally affected, for better or for worse, by your relationships with other persons,… relationships… built by communication.

Effective management is effective communication. The business manager must read, listen, speak, write, and think, as well as send and receive messages through various forms of nonverbal communication. Can you think of any business management duties that do not include communication?

Consider the planning responsibilities of managers at any level. Planning consists of the communication process of thinking. In addition to thinking, other aspects of communication enter into planning: jotting down ideas and outlines; discussing our thinking with other persons, reading in business journals or from company records of the experiences of other persons with similar problems; reading the reports… prepared… to provide information on which to base decisions, making such reports for others to read; listening to the ideas and opinions of others; putting our completed plans into written form for the approval or the direction of others, and orally presenting the plans.

—Marla Treece

The Play of Words

In the English language, the heart is often used to denote the seat of passion, compassion, courage, and intelligence. Of all the parts of the body, the heart is the one that throbs most pervasively through our daily conversation. If, for example, we are deeply saddened, we might say that we are *heartsick, heartbroken, downhearted, heavy-hearted* or *discouraged*. At the heart of *discouraged* beats the Latin *cor*, "heart," giving the word the literal meaning of "disheartened." Or if we wish to emphasize our sincerity, we might say *heartfelt, with all my heart, from the bottom of my heart,* or *in my heart of hearts*.

If something pleases us greatly, we might drag out *heart's delight* or *it warms the cockles of my heart*. The latter is a somewhat redundant statement; a cockle is a bivalve mollusk [like an oyster or clam] of the genus *cardium* (Latin "heart") that takes its name from its shape, which resembles that of a human heart.

It was once the custom for a young man to attach to his sleeve a gift for his sweetheart or to wear her name embroidered on his sleeve, thus displaying his feelings for the world to see. Seizing on this practice, Shakespeare gave the world the expression *to wear one's heart on one's sleeve*, meaning "to show one's emotions."

—Richard Lederer

Small Wonder: The Amazing Story of the Volkswagen

The fact that...VWs [1950-1970's Volkswagen sedans known as "Bugs" or "Beetles"]... float... comes... as no surprise to those who know the reasons for the car's seaworthiness: a flat, one-piece steel sheet completely seals and encloses the car's bottom and, as any owner knows, the car is so airtight that one is best advised to roll down a window before trying to shut the door. To prove the truth of an article's title ("The Beetle Does Float"), *Sports Illustrated* lowered a VW gingerly onto the water of Homosassa Springs, Florida, by crane; it remained on the surface for 29 minutes and 12 seconds. In far-off Sidney, Australia, a VW dealer did better than that; he launched a standard VW beetle into Kogarah Bay on the final day of speedboat championships being held there. The driver encountered little traffic as he plowed the car along at a steady five knots, for the race had been delayed because of the rough weather. Yachtsmen admitted the car showed good stability despite the heavy swell [waves], and it even made sharp turns (with the driver archly offering hand signals). On subsequent occasions, the same "Boatswagen" was sent across the half-mile Middle Harbour stretch four times, with the car in water for more than 40 minutes on each occasion. A few modifications needed to be made: a 10- by 8-inch propeller had been fitted behind the rear bumper, driven by the generator drive pulley at the rear of the crankshaft, a snorkel had been fitted to the exhaust, and some grease had been smeared onto standard dust seals. No rudder was required, as the front wheels steered satisfactorily.

—Walter Henry Nelson

California Dreaming

The Horseless Cowboys

Americans are addicted to Westerns; we read Western novels, we watch Western TV shows, we see Western movies. The Western is the great American fantasy. The examination of a patient's fantasy—its repetitions, eliminations, exaggerations, the kinds of people in it—has for years been one of the psychotherapist's most useful tools. If the Western is a kind of mass American fantasy, then we ought to be able to find out quite a bit about what we Americans are like by examining this shared, repetitious, but apparently endlessly satisfying canned fantasy. Americans use their Western fantasy in three ways:

1. *The vicarious experience.* Many people are content for the space of a TV show or a movie, just to watch, to sympathize with the characters, to live in the world of the Western for an hour or so.
2. *The participant fantasy.* For others, vicarious experience is not enough. These are men who join fast-draw clubs or vacation on dude ranches.
3. *The exoskeletal defense.* These are... the men who identify themselves entirely with the Western hero by the simple expedient of wearing his clothes. The clothes form an external skeleton, a kind of armor against the world. They transform the average domesticated American into the prototypical Western hero—a tough, hard-riding, gun-toting figure exuding sex appeal.

—John A. Popplestone, *Trans Action*

The Assassination Revisited

At 12:30 P.M. President John F. Kennedy was shot to death while riding in an open Lincoln Continental limousine (without bubble-top) as part of a motorcade parade in Dallas, Texas. That tragedy shook the nation and the world. The Zapruder film (made on the spot during the assassination) raised questions about responsibility, and the Warren Commission's failure to provide convincing answers added to the public doubt. The fact that fifty-one government files on Lee Harvey Oswald are, by a decision of the Supreme Court, buried in the National Archives and unavailable to the public has spurred the public belief in a conspiracy. The Oliver Stone film *J.F.K.* reflects the continued public concern with how and why a young and popular American president was shot in the prime of his life and the height of his career. Paul Sheatsky and Jacob Feldman argue, in the *Public Opinion Quarterly*, that the assassination of J.F. Kennedy continues to attract much public attention and controversy because it was unique in the American political experience. They cite two key reasons for this uniqueness: the sudden and unexpected nature of the assassination and the special nature of the man killed. Other recent modern events lack this telling combination. Despite attempts on the lives of Presidents Roosevelt, Truman, and Reagan, no American President has actually been assassinated for more than eighty years, and, although President Franklin Roosevelt did die in office during his fourth term of office, he was advanced in age and his death was due to natural causes, not murder. Kennedy, in contrast, was in his first term, he was still in his forties, and, despite the fact that he had bad back problems and suffered from a debilitating disease, in the public eye, he seemed youthful, vigorous, and full of energy. For such a president to have been cut down so suddenly and so shockingly and under such a cloud of suspicion at a time when his best years and his best public contribution still lay ahead was then and remains today unbelievable.

—V.L. Macdonald

Marriage is not a Personal Matter

Perhaps the newest wrinkle in the old game of courtship is matchmaking by computer. It goes something like this: a young man lists in a "data bank" what he most desires in a prospective female companion, along with information on his own characteristics. The computer compares the qualities and interests desired against those of a (presumably vast) inventory of candidates who have likewise put themselves on file. After some adjustment and compromise, our young man is presented with the name, address, and telephone number of a "Miss Just-Right-and-very-nice-too." Since electronic matchmaking is not quite yet an exact science, he may also be informed of a few alternates (who are also very nice), just in case something goes wrong and he doesn't quite hit it off with Miss Just-Right…. [However,] any programmer will tell you that a computer is no better than the information put into it and the program whereby it is analyzed. In many respects, the verbal professions [statements] of persons facing marriage are the last thing on which to base predictions about the future condition of the families thus formed…. [Besides,] successful computer matching—unlikely anyway—would only spoil the fun [and the mystery of dating].

—John Finley Scott, *New York Times Magazine*

The Silent Language

Of late, psychologists have been preoccupied with learning theory, and one anthropologist, John Gillin, has worked learning theory into his text on anthropology. What complicates matters, however, is that people reared in different cultures *learn to learn* differently. Some do so by memory and rote without reference to "logic" as we think of it, while some learn by demonstration but without the teacher requiring the student to do anything himself, while "learning." Some cultures, like the American, stress doing as a principle of learning, while others have very little of the pragmatic. The Japanese even guide the hand of the pupil, while our teachers usually aren't permitted to touch the other person. Education and educational systems are about as laden with emotion and as characteristic of a given culture as its language. It should not come as a surprise that we encounter real opposition to our educational system when we make attempts to transfer it overseas.

Learning to learn differently is something that has to be faced every day by people who go overseas and try to train local personnel. It seems inconceivable to the average person brought up in one culture that something as basic as this could be done any differently from the way they themselves were taught. The fact is, however, that once people have learned to learn in a given way it is extremely hard for them to learn in any other way.

—Edward T. Hall

The Carbon Chemistry of the Moon

It seems increasingly likely that we are not alone in the universe. There may be millions of inhabited planets like our own. It is a prime goal of science to search for life or its remnants elsewhere in the solar system or the universe. We want to know how unique the earth's life forms may be and how they originated. We want to test, if we can, the hypothesis of chemical compounds from simple precursors, leading to the spontaneous generation of life wherever conditions are favorable. We cannot, however, dismiss an alternate hypothesis: that the emergence of life is extremely rare but that living forms can seed themselves in some fashion across the vast reaches of space.

The samples returned from the moon have provided the first opportunity to test our life-detection methods on samples that have been carefully collected and protected from terrestrial contamination, thereby avoiding the bitter controversy surrounding the analysis of meteorites. This first search has now been completed. No life-forms, living or dead, have been found in the lunar samples after intensive studies with sophisticated techniques capable of revealing any bio-chemicals or their derived products in amounts exceeding a few parts in a thousand million (10^9).

The samples have revealed much, however, about the carbon chemistry of the moon. It is entirely different from the carbon chemistry of the earth and is more closely related to cosmic physics than to conventional organic chemistry....

There may or may not be life on Mars, but its carbon chemistry should provide a fascinating contrast with the carbon chemistry of the earth and with what we now know about the carbon chemistry of the moon.

—Geoffrey Eglinton, James Maxwell, and Colin Phillinger,
The Scientific American

The City as a Biological Community

The social unit for man is the family. It is unlikely that a child reared in a non-family circumstance would ever behave as a human in human society, and this is probably true for other animals when they are removed from their natural surroundings. The experience of Elsa in *Born Free*, demonstrated the difficulty of "teaching" a lion how to become wild again after being raised in captivity. Without the patient and persistent efforts of the individuals involved, it is almost certain that Elsa would not have readapted to the wild state. Jokingly we sometimes refer to our dogs as though they were people, and a dog raised from puppyhood as a member of a human family often acquires behavioral responses similar to those of the human members of the group. This is not to argue that the dog really becomes human, for obviously it cannot since its genetic makeup is that of a dog. Nevertheless, it has learned social behavior that is acceptable in a human family, behavior quite different from that acceptable to a pack of dogs. The habitat of the orangutan in New Guinea is being destroyed by logging and agricultural development. An organization established to save the orangutan is finding that because the orangutan so quickly became socialized to man, their future is uncertain when they are released to the wild. Orangutans, of course, are by nature highly social animals and man's efforts to save them must allow for this social behavior.

Contrary to popular belief, the principal difference in the socialization of a human child and the socialization of an animal is not the language component. With or without language man's offspring must be socialized by him in order to function in the human community. The rearing of an elephant is much the same as the rearing of a human child and just as rigidly controlled biologically. For the first six months of its life the infant elephant remains at its mother's side and is not allowed to wander outside the circle of the herd. It is closely watched by the mother for about two years, and does not join the herd as a full-fledged member for about eleven years. The elephant's life span is about sixty years, so this development process roughly corresponds to the upbringing of a human in a similar life span. It should be noted that before the advent of sanitary engineering and public health, the life span of elephants was much longer than that of man. If behavior learned in a social grouping is necessary to function in the group, then it follows that an individual reared outside the group and deprived of the proper learning experience will not fit into the group.

Families can form in any number of ways. In modern Western society the typical family is the nuclear family consisting of the mother, the father, and the children. In other parts of the world polygamous marriages (both polyandrous and polygynous), matriarchies, and patriarchies can be found, and in some of the "hippie" communes of the United States group marriage is practiced. The particular arrangement of the family does not seem to be very important as long as each member of the family understands his or her status within the family and responds behaviorally in ways that stabilize the social group.

—Theodre W. Sudia, *The Urban Ecosystem*, Urban Ecology Series No. 5.
U.S. Department of Interior, National Park System.

Body Language: Nonverbal Communication

According to sociologists like Elizabeth McGough, author of "Body Language, It Can Tell on You" and anthropologists like Desmond Morris, author of *Manwatching*, humans can communicate non-verbally through kinesics, a form of body language that sends messages faster, and sometimes more effectively, than words, because it conveys what you really think or feel, not what you say to be polite. Such messages are conveyed through eye movement and eye contact, eyebrow position, crinkling of brow, position and movement of lips, and other key facial actions, as well as through body position, leg, arm, or hand movement, hair twisting or grooming actions—all of which flash a loud, clear message to those who can read the signs. Kinesics experts claim eyebrows can assume more than 20 positions, each to rapidly qualify spoken words, and that men "talk" with their eyebrows more than women do. According to McGough, a raised eyebrow might indicate doubt, or a question, or a request to repeat a message, while a pause, along with a rather long glance by the speaker, might signal a listener's turn to talk. Compressed lips and furrowed eyebrows suggest doubt or disbelief, while raised eyebrows, open eyes and slightly opened mouth express wonder or amazement. In American culture, polite or acknowledging glances, open body posture, and little smiles communicate friendliness while a stare into space, closed body posture and a frozen expression communicate hostility.

For international students, the problem is that body language differs from culture to culture. The acceptable physical distance between people differs so that someone moving away to a more acceptable distance might communicate coolness or dislike or someone coming too close to those accustomed to a greater socially-accepted distance might seem too pushy or even threatening. Mid-eastern students moving close in a group to communicate interest and concern to a male American teacher might really be communicating a threat through body language and wonder why the teacher is behaving so nervously and moving backwards away from them. The Japanese student who relies on the facial language of her culture might find that other students respond to her as cool and distant and unfriendly; in fact, a major change in Asian students learning English is a change in facial expressions to fit a new system of nonverbal communication. Meeting eyes openly might be rude in one culture and expected in another. Some mid-Eastern women are never supposed to look directly into a man's eyes (unless a husband or close relative), and yet American male teachers will expect eye contact as confirmation of interest and understanding. For an American, the way you meet someone's eyes and look away tells many things. It may be romantic or threatening, depending on the situation. Most Americans are careful about how, and for how long eyes meet, with normal eye contact lasting only about a second before someone looks away. Holding a gaze for longer than usual might suggest the relationship is a close one or might be a threat or a challenge. On the other hand, avoiding direct eye contact may also indicate that a person has something to hide. The eye signals and their interpretation depends on the situation.

Dr. Sue-Ellen Jacobs, anthropologist at Sacramento State College, points out that psychologists consider the formula for communication to be 7 percent verbal (choice of words), 38 percent vocal (tone), and 55 percent body language. If these figures are true, maybe we should all make an effort to discover what body language communicates to help us better understand not only others, but ourselves.

—G. Whitten Macdonald